THE PEACEMAKERS

The Great Powers and American Independence

THE
PEACEMAKERS

THE GREAT POWERS

AND AMERICAN INDEPENDENCE

by Richard B. Morris

A Classics Edition
NORTHEASTERN UNIVERSITY PRESS
Boston   1983

TO BERENICE

Northeastern University Press edition 1983

Copyright © 1965 by Richard B. Morris

Library of Congress Cataloging in Publication Data

Morris, Richard Brandon, 1904–
The peacemakers.
Reprint. Originally published : New York : Harper & Row, 1965.
Includes bibliographical references and index.
1. Treaty of Paris (1783). 2. United States—Foreign relations—Revolution, 1775–1783. 3. Europe—Politics and government—18th century. I. Title.
[E249.M68 1983]   973.3'17   82-23271
ISBN 0-930350-35-9
ISBN 0-930350-36-7 (pbk.)

Manufactured in the United States of America
87 86 85 84 83   5 4 3 2 1

CONTENTS

PREFACE TO
THE BICENTENNIAL EDITION

This book tells the story of the men who negotiated and signed the Treaty of Paris between Great Britain and the United States in Paris on the morning of September 3, 1783. By any standard, their accomplishments were extraordinary when measured by such criteria as the treaty's durable character, the almost insuperable obstacles strewn in the course of the American negotiators, and the revolutionary objectives they sought, ends that invest the 1783 treaty with a special relevance to our time.

Where today are the treaties of Utrecht of 1713, of Paris and of Hubertusburg of 1763, or of Kuchuk Kainarji of 1774? They are all ghosts of a vanished past, along with the empires of the Spaniards, the Dutch, the French, the Turkish, and the British: a past associated with the departed, if not mourned, Bourbons, Hapsburgs, Hohenzollerns, Romanovs, and Ottoman Sultans.

Not so the British-American treaty of 1783. The map of Europe has been altered beyond recognition since the American and French revolutions, and the old treaties have been consumed in new wars and new annexations. But the present bounds of the continental United States seem in retrospect to have been an inevitable outcome of the territorial gains achieved by the American peacemakers at Paris in their negotiations of 1782–83—concessions made, it may be added, without help from the Spanish Court but with the fortuitous assistance of an amiable Scot negotiating for Great Britain and his conciliatory prime minister.

Having secured generous boundaries that exceed by far those of any republic since the days of Rome, the United States, spurred by the initiatives of continental-minded statesmen, quickly entered into a period of unparalleled creativity, establishing new rules for the admission of these newly acquired territories as states of the union on an equal footing with the original thirteen—not as dependent colonies. Thus was created a republic, not an empire. So spacious a republic needed a unique kind of federalism to infuse the central authority with energy and operative powers, while conceding to the States and the people rights not explicitly granted the national government. These two creative pieces of statescraft—the Northwest Ordinance and the Federal Constitution—were invented and put into operation within four years of the Definitive Treaty's ratification. Without that treaty their adoption would have had no meaning.

The peace negotiations of the American Revolution suggest all sorts of tantalizing analogies to the recent past and the troubled present. The secret agents and double agents that crowd the following pages seem to come out of one of today's international spy thrillers. But on a more serious level, we may, if we choose, find striking parallels between the negotiations of 1782–83 involving the Great Powers and the American insurgents, and the long, protracted parleys some decades back between the French government and the Algerian rebels. The American commissioners, it must be remembered, sought not only independence but territorial integrity, defined by Congress as the lands lying between the Appalachians and the Mississippi. The Algerians demanded the French Sahara as well as Algeria to its north be governed as part of France. Moreover, in both cases, the negotiations tried to resolve the thorny problem posed by a substantial segment of a population loyal to its mother country. In neither case were the Loyalists effectively protected, and the conclusion of such negotiations witnessed mass Loyalist emigration.

Even more tantalizing is the analogy between King George III's obstinate stand in refusing to recognize the insurgent Americans who held part but not all of the thirteen states and the refusal of the United States for long years to deal directly with the Viet Cong while they were holding part, but by no means all, of South Vietnam. More recently, one might cite the role of the United States as a concerned third party in having to make choices between established governments and insurgent groups in Central America and the Caribbean, not to mention Israel and the P.L.O. and the plethora of Middle Eastern issues revolving in no small part around the matter of recognition.

The American peacemakers capitalized on the factors of time and distance to keep the initiative and even to ignore humiliating instructions that they felt were contrary to the national interest. In these days of TV and Jet Age diplomacy, negotiators, as even Henry Kissinger learned, are no longer given plenipotentiary and binding powers; the heads of state reserve the right to repudiate them. When the final settlement nears, one can be certain that a president will make the formal appearance before TV cameras to wrap up and sign the diplomatic package. Obviously, diplomatic decision making would profit from careful reflection and sober judgment, but neither is readily bestowed in this age of instantaneous communication.

The peacemakers of 1783, fortunately for America, were men of independent judgment, skilled in diplomatic maneuvering and endowed with stiff backbones. Above all, these extraordinarily interesting and contrasting personalities were dedicated to the national interest. What they did shaped the American future, and how they did it is the theme of the book.

Columbia University
November 1982

RICHARD B. MORRIS

FOREWORD

John Adams, who was not given to understatement, particularly as regards his own role in great affairs, hailed the negotiations which brought independence to thirteen rebellious states as "one of the most important political events that ever happened on this globe," and one that "has had, and will have, the most important consequences." Few if any would presume to challenge that judgment in retrospect. A few days after the Preliminary Peace had been signed, Adams confided to his Diary the hope that he himself, "or some other who can do it better," would some day collect and publish the record of these negotiations abroad. Having weathered the buffetings of "angry nations and more angry factions," he contended that he had a singularly interesting and instructive tale to tell. He was even prepared to resume his seat in Congress and "rise up now and then and tell stories of our peregrinations, and of the robbers we have met with in the highway."[1]

Fate and the service of his country conspired to keep Adams from telling his story to Congress, to which he never returned. Although his pen was never idle, Adams recognized that he was not in a position to tell the full story any more than his distinguished associates in the peacemaking at Paris. Clashing national interests, wide-ranging revolutionary pressures, secret agreements secretly arrived at, tactics of deception, factional strife in all the European centers of power and in the halls of the American Congress—these were some of the threads that would have to be disentangled from the larger tapestry and evaluated piece by piece. Before the historian could write a balanced account, Adams quite correctly insisted, "everything" that the four American peacemakers possessed which shed light on these transactions would have to be disclosed, and the secret files of the French, Spanish, and Dutch diplomats made available. Adams urged the British

---

[1] *Diary*, III, 89 (Dec. 4, 1782); Adams to Richard Dana, May 1, 1783. *RDC*, VI, 399.

ministers and plenipotentiaries, their secretaries, agents, and confidential clerks, together with the Tories and refugees, to open up their papers. He perceived, too, the relevance of the unpublished dispatches, private letters, and journals of the diplomats representing the mediators and the neutral powers. "Let posterity have all means of judging and let them judge," he declared solemnly.[2]

Posterity proved impatient, and proceeded to form judgments on the great peace negotiations of 1782-83 too often on the basis of a fragmented and even partisan review of the evidence. Scholars in the early nineteenth century with access to documents picked those that suited their purposes, used the blue pencil without conscience, and produced a partisan record that bore little resemblance to reality. Most indefatigable of that generation of historians, Jared Sparks, the first to edit on an extensive scale the diplomatic correspondence of the American Revolution, set himself up as a prosecutor and judge of the actors whose documents he edited and published in garbled versions. Quite rightly did John Quincy Adams, who as a youth was in Europe during the peacemaking, discount the credibility of Sparks's notes by which, he remarked, the record was "impoverished from the hand of the editor."[3] Francis Wharton, a later and far more objective editor of the American diplomatic documents, could not refrain from passing judgments on incomplete evidence. Unable to locate Barbé-Marbois' notorious dispatch critical of the American claims to the fisheries, he branded it as a forgery, while protesting against the innuendoes that the sinister Dr. Edward Bancroft was a traitor and a spy. He was proved wrong on both counts. The Barbé-Marbois letter innocently reposes in its proper file in the Quai d'Orsay, and the Auckland Manuscripts have uncovered Bancroft's extraordinary career as a double agent.

Such deficiencies in the publishing and editing of diplomatic papers for the period are by no means confined to the United States, but also taint the archival publications of the other powers involved in the War of the American Revolution. The dispatches of the Comte de Vergennes, France's magisterial foreign minister, were copiously but imperfectly published by Henri Doniol. That French scholar's *Histoire de la participation de la France à l'établissement des États-Unis d'Amérique* (Paris, 1892) is a massive but subjectively selected collection. Even where Doniol published

[2] *Boston Patriot*, July 24, 1811. For the view that the nonmilitary story of the Revolution would be "most liable to misrepresentation, and future relations of it will probably be replete with intentional and accidental errors," see John Jay to Charles Thomson, July 19, 1783. N.Y. Hist. Soc., *Coll.* (1878), pp. 174, 175.

[3] John Quincy Adams to William Jay, Aug. 23, 1832. J. Q. Adams Letterbook, Microfilm No. 150, AP.

a document in full, he accepted the Comte's professions at their face value. As Samuel Flagg Bemis has elsewhere remarked, the Comte put into his dispatches what he wanted his diplomats to say. Like other diplomats he selected, colored, and even invented facts and arguments which he wished to instill. This caution about the Comte's dispatches may fairly be applied to diplomatic dispatches in general for this period. In the first place, they served two levels of government—the responsible officialdom charged with conducting foreign affairs and the secret operatives of the invisible governments. Secondly, while such dispatches can and often do contain extremely frank revelations, they are quite as likely to constitute pieces of special pleading to mask a diplomat's indiscretion or poor judgment.

One can now venture to tell the story of the peacemaking in the assurance that the records in totality (save for accident or deliberate destruction) are more fully available to the investigator than at any time since 1783. The prodigies of editorial labors which are currently being expended to assemble the papers of the Founding Fathers and to edit and publish them according to impeccable standards of historical scholarship should provide a fillip to studies of the Revolutionary and early national periods of American history. Projects are well under way for collecting and publishing the papers of the four American peace commissioners, Benjamin Franklin, John Adams, John Jay, and Henry Laurens. Modern low-cost methods of photo reproduction have greatly facilitated the task of assembling and studying the huge masses of relevant documents that have been gathering dust in distant chancelleries.

My own involvement in the pursuit of the peacemakers came by way of my responsibility for searching, assembling, and editing the papers of John Jay, which in original or photocopy are now housed in Columbia University Libraries' Special Collections. The collecting and editing of these papers, with a view to publishing the items hitherto unpublished, along with a complete calendar, has been made possible by a series of grants from the Avalon Foundation. Mr. Jay's notable public career had numerous facets, but the documentation covering his important, if controversial, role in the making of the Peace of Paris of 1782-83 proved particularly intriguing. Any judicial appraisal of that role, however, involved an analysis as well of the parts played by Jay's three colleagues, along with their counterparts among the Great Powers who were charged with responsibility for seeking a peaceful ending of what had turned out to be a world war.

The quest consumed some five years and necessitated travel to places far removed from that battle site of the Revolution on Morningside Heights wherein my teaching and research activities are centered. Ann Arbor and Washington furnished documents of the first importance. The British story had to be pieced together at London and Wiltshire, and at Sheffield and Oxford. The voluminous and systematically organized records of the Quai d'Orsay exacted a prolonged stay in Paris during the era of the *plastiquage*. Madrid, Salamanca, and Seville, along with the invaluable collection of photocopies in the Library of Congress, provided the main sources for the Spanish side of the negotiations, and The Hague, of the Dutch involvement. For the special role of mediators and nonbelligerents essential items were unearthed among the diplomatic archives at Vienna, Copenhagen, Stockholm, Venice, Florence, Turin, the Vatican Archives, and Lisbon.

This account of the peacemakers does not pretend to be a diplomatic history of the American Revolution in the traditional sense. True, the central thread that runs through the story is the winning of independence, but cognizance is taken of the rival stakes of empire of the various belligerents caught up in a world war, of war aims that jeopardized the attainment of a durable peace and kept the issue of American independence in suspense until almost the very end. Meaningful diplomatic history transcends the sententious tolling of dispatches. In addition to giving due account to geopolitical factors, along with underlying economic and social forces, the historian of diplomatic negotiations may not ignore the human factors involved or fail to consider the inner drives of the prime and secondary movers whose handiwork changed the face of the globe. Hence, if I have scrutinized the measures, I have not neglected the men. Above all, this is a book about the peacemakers, an extraordinary band of vibrant, subtle, prideful, and complex human beings, who tried to bend, or shape, or stretch, but, most of all, to dominate their world according to the set of national interests to which they were devoted.

The statesmen of the Old World provided their American counterparts with a liberal education in diplomacy as it was conducted in the *ancien régime*. A façade of exquisite refinement only partially concealed the operations in back alleys, the corruptors, secret agents, and flamboyant adventurers who were the special trademarks of Great Power diplomacy. "It seems to me impossible that even Arnold should have been a traitor, if he had ever made the journey from Ferrol to Amsterdam," John Adams remarked meaningfully long before the peacemaking was finished.[4]

This investigation has been the beneficiary of generous assistance from a number of hands. The Rockefeller Foundation, by a special grant to the

---

[4] Adams to Mercy Warren, Dec. 9, 1780. AP.

John Jay Papers, underwrote the cost of calendaring the massive Xerox print collection of diplomatic sources which constitutes a supplement to the Jay archives proper. The Foundation's Villa Serbelloni at Bellagio offered hospitality and seclusion during the summer of 1961, when I sketched the detail plan of the book and drafted some of the early chapters. Grants from the American Council of Learned Societies and the American Philosophical Society underwrote certain expenses involved in travel, photocopy, and calendaring. My stay abroad in 1961-62 was made possible by a Guggenheim Fellowship and a Fulbright Research Fellowship.

The author benefited from the unstinted cooperation he received from a considerable company of scholars, archivists, and librarians in this country and abroad. He must, first of all, acknowledge the assistance from the small revolving staff of younger scholars serving the Jay project, including Professors Herbert A. Johnson and Rebecca Gruver of Hunter College, Miss Norma de Candido of the City University, Dr. David B. Ralston, Misses Harriet Shorr, Roberta Tansman, and Mary-Jo Kline of Columbia University, and Mrs. Karen Humphrey and Dr. Catherine Crary of Finch College. Mrs. Jantien Brinkhorst of Leyden and Mrs. Marjolijn Werman proved indispensable in the translation of Dutch and Scandinavian documents; Mr. David Griffiths, Cornell University, was helpful in dealing with the Russian language sources; and Professor John J. Waters, Jr. of the University of Rochester lent his skills in the translation of Portuguese items. Mr. David Syrett has been indefatigable in pursuing leads in England. Painstaking typing chores were performed unflinchingly by Misses Antoinette Fleur Empringham and Pamela Damman and by Mrs. Barbara Greenwald. Miss Kline's scholarship and resourcefulness were heavily drawn upon in collating and proofreading. The responsibility for the index was assumed by Miss Barbara Bennett.

Indispensable to this investigation were the Shelburne Papers and other British documents related to the peacemaking assembled at the William L. Clements Library of the University of Michigan. For kindness in permitting copious microfilming and many other courtesies I am indebted to its Director, Dr. Howard H. Peckham, and its Curator of Manuscripts, Mr. William S. Ewing. The notes on the diplomatic negotiations of the period under review gathered by the late Randolph G. Adams at that repository provided a number of helpful leads. This study is a beneficiary of the full cooperation of the National Historical Publications Commission and its successive directors, Drs. Philip M. Hamer (now editor of the forthcoming Laurens Papers) and O. W. Holmes, Jr. From time to time I have drawn upon the valued counsel of Miss F. Helen Beach, Archivist of the

Commission. The staff of the Library of Congress, including Dr. David C. Mearns, Chief of its Manuscript Division, and Mrs. Dorothy S. Eaton, Manuscript Historian, were ever gracious. I have repeatedly called upon Dr. Lyman H. Butterfield, editor of the Adams Papers, and Dr. Leonard W. Labaree, editor of the Franklin Papers, and they have patiently clarified numerous points upon which their collections shed light. Others to whom acknowledgment is due for their courtesies include Dr. James J. Heslin, Librarian, New York Historical Society; Mr. Robert W. Hill, Chief, Manuscripts Division, New York Public Library; Mr. William A. Jackson, Librarian, Houghton Library, Harvard University; Mr. Stephen T. Riley, Director, Massachusetts Historical Society; Mr. Thomas Amelia, Head, Bureau of Archives and History, State Library, Trenton; Dr. Francis S. Ronalds, Superintendent, Morristown National Historical Park; Dr. Richard H. Shyrock, American Philosophical Society; Mr. R. Norris Williams, Historical Society of Pennsylvania; Drs. John E. Pomfret and Allan Nevins, Huntington Library and Art Gallery, San Marino; and Mrs. Granville T. Prior, South Carolina Historical Society.

My Columbia colleagues have been courteous, patient, and ever helpful during what must have been a trying period for them, and the staff of the Columbia Libraries, including Dr. Richard H. Logsdon, Director, and Mr. Roland O. Baughman, Head, Special Collections, have cooperated beyond the line of duty. My friend and long-time associate, Professor Henry Steele Commager of Amherst College, encouraged me to embark upon this enterprise and uttered cheering sounds along the way. I am additionally indebted to that dean of American diplomatic historians, Professor Samuel Flagg Bemis, for illuminating leads at several crucial phases in the research, and to Dr. Frank Monaghan, Washington, D.C., and my good neighbors in Butler Library, Dean and Mrs. Harold C. Syrett of the Hamilton Papers.

My researches in private collections in Great Britain were invariably facilitated by Mr. Roger Ellis, Secretary, Historical Manuscripts Commission. In tracking down privately held items I have also drawn heavily upon the great store of information possessed by Miss W. D. Coates, Registrar, National Register of Archives. For special courtesies I am indebted to the Secretary, Public Record Office, the Keeper of Manuscripts, British Museum, and the Librarian, Merton College, Oxford. I am under special obligation to the Marquess of Lansdowne for permission to consult the Shelburne Papers at Bowood, and to Mr. J. H. Hickish for his cooperation in using that collection, to George Fortescue, Esq., Boconnoc, Lostwithiel, Cornwall, for an opportunity to examine the Grenville Papers, and to the

Marquess of Bute and the Earl of Harrowby, as well as Miss Catherine Arnett of Edinburgh for aid in locating Bute and Mountstuart Papers. Professor Thomas W. Copeland and Mrs. Valerie Jobling graciously facilitated my hunt through the Wentworth Woodhouse Manuscripts and the Burke Papers at Sheffield City Libraries, and Professor I. R. Christie, University College London, generously made available to me photocopies of Grantham Papers in the Bedford County Record Office. Mr. David Holland, Assistant Librarian, the House of Commons, graciously turned over pertinent letters among his Thomas Walpole Papers, and Dr. J. H. Plumb, Master of Christ's College, Cambridge, conducted on my behalf a search of his own extensive collection of Walpole items.

In Paris M. Jean Baillou, Directeur du Services des Diplomatiques et de la Documentations, Archives, Ministères des Affaires Étrangères, secured permission for extensive microcopying of the French diplomatic archives. For courtesies extended during my stay in Paris I am also indebted to the Directors of the Bibliothèque Nationale, the Archives Nationales, the Bibliothèque de l'Arsenal, the Bibliothèque de l'Institut de France, and the Archives, Ministère de la Guerre, Château de Vincennes. Acknowledgment must also be made to Comte René de Chambrun and the late Comte Odon Gravier de Vergennes. I have also benefited from the critical insights of two Vergennes specialists, Professor Orville T. Murphy, State University of New York, Buffalo, and Miss Svetlana Kluge, Barnard College, and from suggestions made by my former student, Miss Darline Shapiro, an expert on Simon Linguet, one of Vergennes' severer critics.

In Spain I leaned heavily on the counsel of Professor Juan Pérez de Tudela, Instituto Oviedo, Madrid. Señor Tomás Pérez Sáenz was freely consulted on the records of the Archivo Histórico Nacional in Madrid and the Archivo General de Simancas, and I am indebted to Señor Otto Pikaza for assistance in culling relevant items from the Archivo General de Indias at Seville. Senhorinha Rosalinha Cunha, Secretário Geral do Gabinete, Gabinete de Historia et Leitura Paleográfica, was indefatigable in pursuing and uncovering pertinent documents in the Portuguese Ministry of Foreign Affairs, Torre do Tombo, Lisbon. Other archivists to whom acknowledgment must be made include Messrs. N. M. Gapikae, Algemeen Rijksarchief, The Hague; Svend Aakjaer, Rigsarkivet, Copenhagen; the Reverend Monsignor Martino Giusti, Prefetto, Archivio Segreto, the Vatican; and Professor Alberto Monticone of the University of Rome and Richard Webster, University of California, for assistance in selecting relevant documents from the Vatican diplomatic letterbooks. In addition, the Chief Archivists of the Haus-Hof-u. Staatsarchiv, Vienna, of the Archivio di

Stato, Venice, the Archivio di Stato, Florence, and the Riksarkivet, Stockholm, demonstrated their traditional hospitality to visiting scholars.

At every stage of this protracted enterprise my family has shown patience, understanding, and sympathy. My wife Berenice accepted with fortitude the strenuous itinerary exacted by this project and shared the drudgery of note-taking in country estates and foreign libraries, and my sons Jeffrey and Donald have participated to an extent they themselves have not realized. Lastly, my editors, Cass Canfield and Margaret Butterfield, provided sage counsel throughout this undertaking, and I am handsomely in their debt.

To tell the story of the peacemakers of 1782-83 necessitated searching, sifting, and evaluating a mass of evidence both ponderous and discrete drawn from instructions, dispatches, letterbooks, diaries, journals, and other sources in substantial part unpublished and to some extent never utilized before. This evidence may not be concealed from the reader. Whether or not he shares the opinions of the author, and some of those opinions are decidedly revisionist, he has a right to insist on the full disclosure of the sources on which such judgments were founded. Accordingly, the annotations, for which tables of abbreviations to both characters and sources provide a key, are fully set forth at the end of the book.

RICHARD B. MORRIS

Columbia University
May 15, 1965

I

THREE VOYAGERS IN SEARCH
OF PEACE

IN LATE OCTOBER OF 1779, the Continental frigate *Confederacy* weighed anchor and stood out into the Delaware Bay for the long voyage across the North Atlantic. Crowded on and below her decks was a complement of three hundred, mostly sailing and fighting men, but including a dozen passengers. Two of the latter were men of special distinction, and the captain of the thirty-six-gun warship, a Connecticut Yankee named Seth Harding, had been entrusted by the American Congress with the responsibility of ensuring their safe passage to Europe. They were Conrad Alexandre Gérard, the retiring French minister plenipotentiary to the United States, and John Jay, the newly appointed American minister plenipotentiary to Spain.

Over the past months Jay and Gérard had worked in close association. Though the latter was crowding fifty and sixteen years the American's senior, the careers of the ship companions ran somewhat parallel courses. Both came from upper-middle-class French backgrounds, Gérard from a family of Alsatian public servants and Jay was the son of a wealthy New York merchant of Huguenot descent. Both had been trained for the law and turned to diplomacy; Gérard had behind him a quarter of a century of experience as a career diplomat, while Jay stood at the threshold of a new career. One epitomized the diplomacy of the *ancien régime;* the other the untutored approach of a revolutionary government. To accept his assignment to Spain, John Jay had resigned both the Presidency of the Continental Congress and the Chief Justiceship of the State of New York.[1]*
The persuasive and conscientious New York lawyer headed the first of three

* Superior numbers refer to Notes, beginning on page 469.

missions dispatched in the course of the fall and winter of 1779-80 to win friends and support for the cause of American independence and bring to a victorious conclusion the lengthening War of the Revolution. Gérard was returning home for reasons of health, and the achievements of his mission were still to be evaluated.

On departure John Jay and his vivacious young wife Sarah were showered with farewell gifts and the cordial good wishes of a host of friends. Robert Morris, the Patriot merchant prince, had promised a box of "seegars," if needed. From West Point General Washington sent Sally a lock of his hair enclosed in a note expressing the wish that "prosperous gales, unruffled seas, and everything pleasing and desirable, may sooth the path she is about to walk in." Unfortunately the General did not possess the kind of magic that could make this wish come true. Jay's boyhood friend, classmate, and former law partner, Robert R. Livingston, New York's Chancellor, delegate-designate to Congress replacing Jay, and an upstate feudal lord, wrote him a note admonishing the voyager to "omit no occasion of lessening the pain I feel in your absence by writing to me by every conveyance." Little did either man realize how distance and a divergent view of the way peace should be made were to bring about the first rift between the man who signed himself "Dear John, your friend," and the minister plenipotentiary, a rift which would widen with the passing years.

Sally would be missed, too. In a poignant letter her father, William Livingston, the Patriot Governor of New Jersey, a man pre-eminent among the Whig intellectual leadership, confessed the pain at parting with his daughter "across a wide ocean and to a foreign land." Considering his age and "the mortality of man," Livingston thought it probable that he would never see her again. Invoking God's protection for his "dear child," he enjoined her not to suffer "the gaieties and amusements of the world, and the particular avocations of what is called *high life*" and not to banish from her life a sense of religious obligation. In lighter vein, Sally's brother, William James, spoofed that neither the mountains nor the fleas of Spain should "terrify the mind of an American" and admonished his sister not to fail to report "every piece of knight errantry" she would experience on reaching "the land of the renowned Don Quixote." That "fine sensible woman," as Richard Bache described Sally Jay in a letter to his father-in-law, Benjamin Franklin, was destined to see little chivalric behavior and even less of that hospitality for which Spain was proverbial.[2]

Smothered by the attention of friends and armored with the cautions and prayers of relatives, the Jays, along with the motley ship's party, embarked for France en route to Madrid. Five days later Jay's private secretary and brother-in-law, Henry Brockholst Livingston, wrote his own mother that the ship was still becalmed in Delaware Bay and had covered a mere forty miles, with seventy more to go before reaching the Capes. The sea air proved a tonic for Sally's appetite, and seasickness had not yet struck. Jay took advantage of the motionless trip to send Robert Livingston a simple numerical cipher to be used in their personal correspondence.[3]

On the sixth day out from Chester the becalmed ship underwent a dramatic change of fortune. Gale winds now pounded the *Confederacy*. "Who saith," Sally asked her mother, "unto the wave thus far shall thou go. And to the winds, peace, be still?" If most passengers henceforth were to suffer intermittent bouts of *mal de mer*, the American minister plenipotentiary seemed to be especially signaled out by Neptune. "My dear Mr. Jay suffered exceedingly at least five weeks and was surprizingly reduced," Sally wrote home. One consolation was that in the turbulent sea the *Confederacy* had managed to elude the British frigates *Roebuck* and *Romulus* believed to be standing off the coast to intercept her.[4]

Other and severer trials were in store. "About 4 o'clock[5] in the morning of the 7th November," Sally Jay wrote her mother, "we were alarmed by an unusual noise upon deck, and what particularly surprised me was the lamentations of persons in distress." Her brother Brockholst tried to calm her, but he had little reason for composure. When the passengers scrambled on deck they grasped the situation at once. A freak accident had befallen the frigate. As the *Confederacy* had moved out of the chill gray waters of the North Atlantic coast into the great indigo mass of the Gulf Stream the warm air had caused the taut rigging to slacken. The master ordered the watch into the shrouds, but before steps could be taken to fend off disaster, the mainmast crashed to the decks, followed almost immediately by mizzenmast, foremast, and even bowsprit. The groans of the injured heightened the terror of those first moments. Among those struck by the falling timber was a sailor whose hand was broken and a gunner whose injured leg required amputation. A few days later the amputee was buried at sea.

The ship was now rolling heavily in a high wind and rough sea. While all hands cleared away the wreckage, Captain Harding took a shot to get his bearings. The *Confederacy* lay like a log in the water south-southeast of Newfoundland, some eleven hundred miles from the Capes of the Delaware and under nine hundred from the Azores. A small mast with improvised sail was erected, but a south-southeast wind of gale proportions combined with a turbulent sea wrenched and split the shank of the rudder, which now began banging against the stern. To steady the ship into the wind a floating anchor was thrown off the bow. By heroic efforts the rudder was temporarily bolted in place and made to function after a fashion. More than two weeks of strong winds and heavy seas elapsed, however, before the jury masts were securely rigged. Still the rudder demanded daily attention, as the steering ropes would snap and the rudder's uncontrolled banging against the stern sent the ship's company into a constant state of alarm. To prevent further damage bags filled with oakum were hung on each side, but not before considerable water had leaked in through the stern and ruined the bread supply. By now the improvised sails were little more than rags. Splits had to be sewn every day, and the ship was virtually out of twine.

By November 23rd the weather had moderated and the frigate was in fair condition to proceed. But how far and where to were the big questions. A council of commissioned officers advised Captain Harding that the most prudent course now would be to head south for the first safe port in the West Indies.[6] Harding concurred, and reported accordingly to Jay and Gérard, whose orders, by the instructions of Congress' Marine Committee, were to govern. Jay saw no other prudent course but to follow the captain's advice. The alternatives would have placed both ship and crew in jeopardy. Frigates, in the current state of the Continental Navy, were hardly expendable, and crews, as Harding himself had too recently found out, were hard to come by.

Notwithstanding hazards which made a winter crossing of the North Atlantic almost certain suicide, the Chevalier Gérard, impatient to return to France for reasons that were entirely personal, lost both his head and his temper. If France had to be ruled out, why not the Azores? he expostulated. The Portuguese islands were five hundred miles nearer than Martinique, and there the diplomats should have no difficulty in getting passage to the Continent on another ship. Harding patiently explained that an open roadstead, which was the best that the Azores could offer, would not provide safe anchorage for a ship in the condition of the *Confederacy*, nor the opportunity to repair and refit the vessel. Again Jay concurred. Furious that the American diplomat did not override the captain, Gérard now sulked apart. To add fuel to the flame, the secretary of Jay's mission, William Carmichael, appointed to that post by Congress in an ill-advised moment, openly took Gérard's part and began his systematic intrigues to undermine the authority which the American minister plenipotentiary jealously guarded. It was perhaps a small chink, but the dispute over the ship's course was the first of those differences with European diplomats which were in time to persuade John Jay, then one of America's foremost Francophiles, that the best course for America was to go it alone.

Jay was too much the responsible diplomat to let a private argument hamper his mission. To thaw the diplomatic ice the Jays arranged a birthday party for Madame Gérard. Despite the "intolerable" roll of the ship even in the smooth southerly sea, elaborate day-long festivities took place. Following a formal breakfast, the participants spent the day under a huge awning stretched out across the deck, playing chess, cards, and drafts, and ended with what was, considering the circumstances, described as an elegant dinner, culminating with numerous toasts, punctuated with the discharge of cannon. That same day the sailors insisted on shaving and ducking all voyagers who had never crossed the Tropic of Cancer before, not forgetting the Jays' twelve-year-old nephew, Peter Jay Munro, who did not entirely relish the initiation rites.

Any thought that the festivities would have mollified Gérard was quickly dissipated. As the *Confederacy* approached Martinique, Gérard suddenly resumed his belligerent posture. He insisted on making for St. Pierre on the north side of the island on the ground that if the ship went to the south side it would be in danger of running to leeward of the island, then be unable to get up to Fort Royal, and very likely fall to the British squadron operating out of St. Lucia. Astonished that Gérard should presume to direct the navigation of the ship, Jay again left the decision to the captain, who reserved judgment until they were in sight of the islands. On the fourteenth of December Sally wrote: "A land bird! a land bird! Oh! the pleasure of being near land." On the eighteenth she reported seeing "the most verdant, romantic country I ever beheld." This was the volcanic island of Martinique, and as its lush green Mount Pelée loomed on the horizon the ship's company distinctly heard the sound of cannon fire to the south. The decision had been made for them by Rear Admiral Parker, whose squadron from St. Lucia had slipped across and chosen that moment to attack a convoy heading for Fort Royal. For the *Confederacy* there was no choice but the northern port of St. Pierre, and the fact that Gérard was shown to be in the right only made him more unbearable. Had the southerly course been chosen, the *Confederacy* would almost surely have become a prize of the Royal Navy, and Mr. Jay's mission would have ended for him in the Tower of London.

The ten days spent at Martinique provided welcome diversion for the Jays. At gay, crowded St. Pierre, glistening white in the tropic sun at the foot of slumbering Mount Pelée, the Jays were the guests of William

Bingham, Robert Morris' trading partner and one of the numerous tribe of international war profiteers. Bingham, then acting as agent of Congress in the French West Indies, was concerned with the procurement of supplies for the Continental Army. Accorded every politeness by the Marquis de Bouillé, the island's Governor, including a military review in their honor, the Jays combined official business with pleasure. Mrs. Jay shopped, observed beekeeping techniques, visited sugar mills, saw the wild *bal doudou*, and was fed every bit of gossip about the duel fought between an officer of the *Confederacy* and a lieutenant of a French frigate over a quarrel arising in a bagnio, with no harm to either participant. Mrs. Jay's husband, whose aversion to slavery was one day to culminate in his affixing his signature as Governor of New York to an emancipation act, saw at firsthand that system in its most degrading aspect. He saw slaves going about their duties, with iron collars around their necks and dragging fifty-pound chains. He saw canoes laden with hogsheads of sugar rowed by slaves chained by one leg to the boat and bearing on their backs the marks of the lash. These sights he would not soon forget.

With Gérard, Jay visited Fort Royal to have Admiral La Motte Piquet expedite the refitting of the *Confederacy* and arrange their own passage to Europe. Jay advised Harding that, once his ship was outfitted—and the French officials seemed to give that operation a rather low priority—he should proceed to an American port for supplies.[7] On Christmas Day Jay drew against the meager funds alloted for his own salary and divided a hundred guineas among the officers of the *Confederacy* so that they would not be "obliged to sneak, as they phrase it, from the company of French officers for fear of running in debt with them for a bottle of wine, or a bowl of punch, because not able to pay for their share of the reckoning." Such a situation Jay considered "too humiliating to be tolerated, and too destructive to that pride and opinion of independent equality which I wish to see influence all our officers. . . . Indeed," he added, "it would have given me pleasure to have done something towards covering the nakedness of the crew, but the expence I have been put to by coming here, and the preparations for another voyage would not admit of it." Prideful of his position, Jay himself was soon to share the humiliating experiences of these ship's officers, when Congress, with its accustomed financial irresponsibility, overdrew against his accounts abroad and left him without resources until the Spanish government in a most grudging fashion came to his rescue.

Three days later the Jay and Gérard parties set sail from Martinique on the French frigate *Aurora*. How unlike the first phase of the journey was the "short passage" to Europe. "Sailing sweetly before the wind," was the way Sally headed a letter to Jay's father, dated January 9th, in which she reported that her spouse was enjoying perfect health, something that Jay seldom confessed to throughout a very long life. The *Aurora* may have seemed to Sally Jay to be a "dull sailor" after her previous adventure, but it did offer some excitement. A few days before coming in sight of land the *Aurora* was chased by a British man-of-war, and cleared for action, but managed to outsail her pursuer and reach the safe harborage of Cádiz on January 22nd. There it was learned that the naval superiority of the enemy in the Mediterranean rendered it unsafe to proceed to Toulon, the frigate's destination. "Admiral Rodney had saved us the necessity of going that round about way to Madrid," was the way Sally put it, little realizing how long the distance from Cádiz to the court of Spain would prove to be.[8]

Before Jay left Philadelphia Virginia's elder statesman, Edmund Pendleton, volunteered advice which in retrospect was to take on an ironic note. "I cordially wish you may be able to heal the new-made breach between Spain and Britain," he wrote Jay, "since France appears disposed to peace, and I am mistaken if the Court of London are not ready to make up with us, if nothing respecting our allies hinder it. Indeed we want an honourable peace; but I hope there lives not a wretch who wishes it upon terms of dishonor to our noble allies."[9] It was a piece of wishful thinking to suppose that Jay would be able to step into the role of peacemaker between France's ally and America's enemy and that he could secure a peace which would both satisfy Spain's honor and meet the necessities of the Thirteen United States. The American minister was too much of a realist to take so exalted a view of the role he was expected to play. It had taken the Jays three months to negotiate the waters between the Delaware and Cádiz, and they were still months away from Madrid.

Jay's selection by the Continental Congress had come as a climax to a great debate over foreign policy which almost completely monopolized the business of Congress for virtually the whole of the year 1779 preceding his appointment. What touched off the debates was the arrival early in 1779 of the Chevalier Gérard, designated by His Most Christian Majesty as minister to the United States, and charged with taking measures to implement the alliance between France and America. On reaching Philadelphia Gérard lost no time letting Congress know how urgent it was for that body to spell out its terms for peace. To make sure that the members of Congress could have the benefit of his expert knowledge, he took a residence within a stone's throw of Congress' meeting place, the State House at the eastern end of the town. There he wined and dined

Congressmen nightly, and made his presence felt at Congressional committee meetings. A born meddler, Gérard never learned to let well enough alone.

The French minister proved an acute observer of the American scene. Though insensitive to the broader implications of the American Revolution, he quickly demonstrated a range of knowledge of the Thirteen United States and their delegates in Congress which would have gratified the omniscient French Encyclopedists had they been privileged to read his confidential reports. In weekly dispatches to the Comte de Vergennes, Gérard reported the intense factional struggle that was shaping up, and reassured his chief that he was throwing all his weight as well as his not insubstantial pecuniary resources on the side which he considered, if not openly pro-French, at least the more amenable to the wishes of Louis XVI.[10]

Over the issues of peace an outsider like Gérard might have anticipated that there would be a rather clear-cut division in Congress along North-South lines, since the South was concerned about the West, to which its states had territorial claims under their old charters, and was equally concerned with having the Mississippi open to American shipping. In both these areas the vital interests of the North were not involved. Contrariwise, the New Englanders could be expected to insist on regaining the rights of fishing off the Grand Bank of Newfoundland which they had lost by Parliamentary reprisal for their contumacy, and the fisheries were a matter of indifference to Southerners.

This was not what Gérard found when he came to Philadelphia. For a very curious and special reason the evolving parties did not divide on strict geographic lines. Congress, and with it the country, was torn apart by an intense and savage personal feud between two of the three American commissioners to France, Silas Deane, Connecticut merchant and onetime schoolteacher, and Arthur Lee, scion of the aristocratic Virginia planter family. Prosecuted with a degree of acrimony that makes the later breach between Jefferson and Hamilton seem like a decorous spat at a vicarage garden party, the Deane-Lee dispute was to have a profound impact on both the conduct of the war and the objectives of the peace. The Deane faction, heartened by French support, believed in trimming peace demands to the realities of the sober military situation; the supporters of Lee, known as the anti-Gallican party, were outright expansionists.

Like its predecessors of ancient Rome, Congress' triumvirate of Deane, Lee, and Franklin, named back in 1776 as commissioners to France, was destined to founder on the rock of mutual distrust. Arthur Lee, albeit a man of considerable abilities, knowledgeable about conditions abroad, and fluent in a number of foreign tongues, was bitten by ambition and envy, and these not uncommon traits were compounded by a frightening paranoidal streak. Lee begrudged Franklin his enormous popularity in France and ready access to the court at Versailles, and never forgave him for having outsmarted him in some big land deals. He suspected Deane of lining his own pockets by complex, secret, and highly irregular financial operations. As the first commissioner to come to Paris, Deane had originally performed yeoman feats in acquiring arms and supplies for the American cause, but he soon betrayed a lack of sound judgment in the associations he formed and the decisions he made, and showed himself utterly devoid of that sense of the proprieties that we have now come to expect of public characters.

The fact is that in the days of the Revolution the concept of conflict of interest had by no means crystallized. Men like Robert Morris and Nathanael Greene found no inconsistency in representing the government and private business interests simultaneously and in the same transactions. Government officials engaged in procurement, commissary, and quarter-master matters, intermingled the government's business with their own, bought goods for themselves or their partners and employed their own ships in the public service or public ships for private business. Robert Morris, who became the virtual manager of foreign procurement, once remarked to his protégé, "I shall continue to discharge my duty faithfully to the public and pursue my private fortune by all such honorable and fair means as the times will admit of, and I dare say you will do the same."[11]

Benjamin Franklin, prince of pragmatists, chose to be ignorant or tolerant about the nature and extent of Deane's private speculations. If Franklin was associated with Deane in a great Western land speculation known as the Vandalia enterprise, which involved correspondence with British subjects in wartime,[12] and if he allowed his own grandnephew Jonathan Williams to be set up by Deane as a shipping agent at Nantes, the third commissioner in Paris did not share the philosopher-statesman's complacency. Lee quickly became Deane's implacable enemy. Convinced that the original supplies France furnished America through the fictitious business house set up by that talented adventurer and past master of blackmail, Caron de Beaumarchais, were a gift from the French court, Lee denounced Deane's agreement to reimburse Beaumarchais as improper if not fraudulent. Since Lee had initiated the negotiations with Beaumarchais in London, much weight must be given to this accusation. Other accusations were not so well substantiated. Lee passed along to his friends in Congress every rumor, regardless of how slender, so long as it was discreditable to Silas Deane. In fact, he made so many charges that some of them could not have failed to have hit their mark.

One charge that Lee could not prove then, but was later substantiated, was the accusation that Deane, in association with Samuel Wharton, Philadelphia merchant and land speculator, and Dr. Edward Bancroft, had leaked news of the signing of the treaty of alliance with France in order to promote their speculations on the London Stock Exchange.[13] The true character of Bancroft was unknown at the time, except to a select few. Of New England birth and once a student of schoolteacher Silas Deane, Bancroft had studied medicine in England and came to Franklin's attention during the latter's prewar residence in England. When war broke out he acted as a spy on Franklin's behalf, subsequently joined the doctor in France, and continued to make cross-Channel journeys from time to time. It did not take long before Bancroft, an amoral opportunist, became a double agent, furnishing secret and confidential data to the British under the name of Dr. Edward Edwards. In retrospect, Bancroft's close working relationship with Silas Deane, with whom he engaged in various dubious speculations, carries sinister overtones, and lends credence to, if it does not confirm, some of Arthur Lee's worst suspicions.[14]

Lee found ready ears in Congress, including those of his influential brother, Richard Henry, and the New England contingent headed by Samuel Adams. Soon shrill voices were raised in the halls of Congress against Deane. Summoned home to give an accounting, Deane returned in July, 1778. Although he demanded a prompt hearing, he was kept waiting for months while his accusers held the floor. Finally, he blew the lid off the case himself, with a published account in the *Pennsylvania Packet* of December 5, 1778, in which he defended his own conduct and made countercharges against Lee. In quick rejoinder Tom Paine, secretary of the Committee of Foreign Affairs, entered the lists against Deane with an indiscreet letter to a newspaper exposing the nature of Louis XVI's secret aid to America prior to the alliance. Paine's admissions made mockery out of Vergennes' endless protestations of innocent neutrality, protestations which Britain's last minister to Paris, Lord Stormont, knew from British intelligence sources had to be taken with more than the proverbial grain of salt. With the battle transferred momentarily from Congress to the newspapers, Gérard stepped in, remonstrating that the honor of France was involved. In its first of many acts of obeisance to the French minister, Congress dismissed Paine from his post.[15] Notwithstanding, the Lees and their New England allies pressed the attack against Deane, and secured a recruit in the person of Henry Laurens, the South Carolina merchant Patriot, whom age had not mellowed, but rather made increasingly quarrelsome, petulant, and, perhaps in some part because of his Huguenot father, critical of France. In protest against the Deane faction, Laurens resigned the Presidency of Congress on December 9th,[16] and John Jay, a strong champion of Silas Deane, was elected in his place the very next morning.[17] Congress, which had heard all Deane's accusers, permitted its Paris commissioner only to submit written answers to the charges. Enough was heard, however, to prove one or two irregularities, and to suggest countless others.[18]

In assuming the mantle of virtue the Lee faction might have had a stronger case if its own operations had been aboveboard. But the Lees did not come into court with clean hands. On his return to America in the fall of '79 Dr. Lee shipped a cargo of his own merchandise on the Continental frigate *Alliance*, thereby providing his enemies with ground for court-martialing Pierre Landais, the eccentric French captain of that naval vessel.[19] Arthur's merchant brother, William, the only American to hold the post of alderman of London, was not above trying to capitalize on his inside knowledge of the approaching alliance with France. Employed by Congress on missions abroad, he charged Congress excessive commissions in his dual capacity of commercial agent and commissioner to Berlin.[20] The older brother, Richard Henry Lee, who carried the gauntlet for his family in Congress until, worn down in body and spirit, he resigned his seat in May of '79, had only recently been involved in an ugly scandal. To protect himself from currency inflation he had changed the rents due from his tenants under leases from money to payments in wheat or tobacco, thereby bringing down upon his head the wrath of the tenantry and the condemnation of holier-than-thou Patriots.[21]

It is only fair to observe that, if there was a conspicuous lack of self-restraint in high places, Congress and the states could not escape their share of the blame. The unchecked flow of printing-press money and the unwillingness of the states to invest Congress with adequate taxing power had fanned the flames of speculation. "The inundation of money appears to have overflowed virtue, and I fear will bury the liberty of America in the same grave," Richard Henry Lee confessed in June of '79, adding, "The demon of avarice, extortion, and fortune-making seizes all ranks."[22]

The Deane-Lee imbroglio, despite its divisive impact, had two constructive effects on the peacemaking to come. The quarrel convinced Congress that it was now necessary to be represented abroad by ministers who could be counted on to put the public good above private gain or personal rancor, and it impelled Congress to spell out its peace aims. A committee consisting of one delegate from each state, appointed on January 20, 1779, to investigate the Deane affair, brought in its report on March 24th.[23] It reinforced its revelations of imprudent conduct of public affairs abroad with the recommendation that, as a result of "suspicions and animosities . . . highly prejudicial to the honor and interests of the United States," the commissioners be removed and "but one plenipotentiary minister or commissioner" be appointed for each foreign court.[24]

If Deane was sacked, Lee failed to escape the shake-up. One of the chief complaints against the latter was that, aside from his quarrelsome disposition, he had been unrestrained in his expressions of "contempt for the French nation."[25] His supporters, chief among them Sam Adams, vainly sought to elicit from Gérard a statement to the effect that Lee enjoyed the confidence of the French court. Instead, the French minister showed Congressmen William Paca and William Henry Drayton a letter from Vergennes in which the foreign minister confessed: "*Je crains M. Lée et ses entours.*"[26] This was enough to bring about the downfall of that self-righteous troublemaker and to make Gérard forever *persona non grata* with the Lee faction. Franklin was now left in sole command of Congress' business in Paris.

Even after Lee's recall was voted, his partisans were determined to have him named minister to Spain to secure an alliance with that nation, and to have John Adams, an acknowledged friend of the cause of Lee, designated peace commissioner to treat with Great Britain once negotiations started. On September 25th Adams was put up for the latter post by Henry Laurens. Meriwether Smith of Virginia countered for the Deane faction by proposing John Jay. On the first ballot Adams failed to win an absolute majority. On the second he shaded Jay by a vote of six states to five, but, with South Carolina still divided, he again failed of nomination.

To break the deadlock the Deane partisans now proposed that a minister plenipotentiary be appointed to the Spanish court in lieu of a commissioner, a post to which Arthur Lee had earlier been named. The negotiation of a treaty of alliance, they argued, involved duties quite different from those which Lee had been performing. Laurens promptly nominated Lee, but the anti-Lee forces, pursuing what Laurens recognized as the rule of "divide and conquer,"[27] put up the name of John Adams. Then, having split the Lee faction, the Gallican party put up a third name, the man they really wanted, John Jay, Congress' President. "Mr. Jay," as Laurens ungenerously put it, "squeezed in," helped by his own vote as a member of the New York delegation.[28] Desperate to have Adams in Paris conducting the peace negotiations, the New Englanders were ready to strike a compromise, one which sent the President of Congress to Madrid, resulted in Adams being unanimously chosen for the post of peace commissioner, and made Arthur Lee the sacrificial goat.[29]

The die-hard supporters of Lee took it hard. James Lovell denounced Jay's election "to take the post of a man murdered on purpose to make room" as "the crowning act of all Deane's base arts,"[30] and Henry Laurens wrote hopefully, "Our friend Arthur Lee will rise again."[31] But after a little time for reflection most New Englanders put the best face on the results that they could. "Away with sackcloth and ashes when evitables become inevitables," Lovell wrote in more sensible vein in his very next letter to John Adams.[32] As might have been expected, Gérard plumed himself on what he considered a victory for the pro-French party. "The choice of Jay leaves nothing to be desired," he wrote to Vergennes. "To much intelligence and the best intentions he joins an amiable and conciliatory temper."[33] If by "conciliatory" he really meant pliable, he was soon to find out that he had misjudged his man. The Spanish observer in America, Juan de Miralles, was equally exultant. Jay, with whom he had been on cordial relations, possessed in his eyes the background and temperament of the true aristocrat. In addition to his impeccable social standing, Jay had shown a sympathetic attitude toward Spain, which would make him, Miralles felt, most acceptable in Madrid.[34]

In the long tedious months before Jay took up his duties at Madrid he could not have helped reflecting on the heated battle which had been fought over his selection, and, more to the point, on what Congress expected him to accomplish in Spain. The instructions binding Jay and Adams had been adopted only after extended debate, to which the Deane-Lee controversy had served as curtain raiser. The Congress had to consider the effect on America's peace objectives of two alliances, the one with France, which had been cemented in 1778, and the other between France and Spain, in which the United States was not even a junior partner. It was clear to Congress that America's peace objectives would have to be reconciled with those of their ally, His Most Christian Majesty, and their ally's ally, His Most Catholic Majesty. Should they for one moment forget it, the Chevalier Gérard, considered the representative of Spanish interests in America, was there to remind them of their duty.[35]

So far as France was concerned, that nation had virtually renounced large territorial aspirations in America. Specifically, she had abandoned the idea of recovering Canada lost in the previous war, even secretly resolved that it remain in British hands.[36] France was determined nonetheless to gain trade advantages from the war, advantages which England had commanded when the Thirteen Colonies were a part of her vast mercantile empire. France was immensely concerned about recovering the fishing rights she had once exercised, since the Seven Years' War, while allowing her to retain her right to fish the banks of Newfoundland and to retain the two tiny fishing islands of St. Pierre and Miquelon, deprived her of the right of fishing along the edge of the coasts and of curing fish except in specifically allotted places. To enhance her fishing opportunities France hoped to acquire Newfoundland and her old possessions around the Gulf of St. Lawrence. It must be borne in mind that eighteenth-century states-men looked upon the fisheries as the nursery of seamen and as holding one of the keys to a powerful maritime and naval establishment. In the light of this traditional point of view the French national interest in the North Atlantic fisheries seems perfectly comprehensible.[37] The issue had come up on two occasions, at the time of the treaty of alliance with America in 1778 and the following year, in the Franco-Spanish negotiations. Franklin and Arthur Lee failed to persuade France to insert a clause in her treaty with America renouncing the right of conquests "in the islands of Newfoundland, Cape Breton, St. John's Anticosti, and the Bermudas."[38] Herein lay a potential source of trouble. The New England fishing fleet had enjoyed immemorial privileges of fishing and curing on the coasts of Newfoundland and Nova Scotia. Though Parliament, as a punitive measure, had canceled these privileges, the New Englanders had never conceded Parliament's authority to enact that repressive measure.

If the potential rivalry with France was in a fringe area, the brewing controversy with Spain struck at the heart of America's territorial aspirations as a nation. Until the spring of '79 Spain was a bystander, courted by France to enter the war on her side and by England to remain neutral. The Spanish court found itself in an excellent position to blackmail both sides, and it made the best of its opportunities. Spain had put pressure upon England to accept her mediation, but at a very high figure. Her price for compelling France to quit the war was the fortress of Gibraltar, facetiously described by her Principal Minister, the Conde de Floridablanca, as "that pile of stones," which was "only a matter of expense and trouble to them, disturbing to us, and an impediment to permanent friendship."[39] The British government was unwilling to pay this kind of blackmail, and remained unbudgeable on the question of referring to outside mediation her private quarrel with the Thirteen Colonies.

On April 3, 1779, Spain issued an ultimatum to Great Britain, calling for an indefinite suspension of arms in England's wars with France and the United States and a peace congress at Madrid to settle boundaries. Significantly, the ultimatum suggested that the territorial limits be fixed on the basis of the ground held by each side at the time the truce went into effect (the *uti possidetis,* as it was called in the language of diplomacy).

The proposal for a truce came up again and again. Suspicious delegates in the American Congress recognized that it would "let the wolf into the sheep-fold,"[40] for it would have left America a badly truncated collection of states, hardly a viable nation.[41] At the time of the Spanish ultimatum, it should be borne in mind, Great Britain held New York City as well as Long Island, Rhode Island, a substantial part of Georgia, and vast if indeterminate parts of the Northwest.[42] The issue of the recognition of the United States was evaded in the ultimatum; at best Spain proposed *de facto* recognition during the negotiations.[43] France, when notified of the ultimatum, bitterly protested the terms as humiliating and "fatal to the dignity of the King,"[44] but Great Britain prevented a breach between the two members of the Family Compact by flatly turning them down.[45]

The ultimatum was in fact a brazen piece of deception, for, without waiting for England to reject it, Spain went ahead and signed a secret treaty with France at Aranjuez on April 12th, committing Spain to war. By its terms an invasion of the British Isles was to be undertaken.[46] Every effort was to be made to recover for Spain Minorca, Pensacola, and Mobile, lost in the previous war, to expel the British from the Bay of Honduras, and revoke the privilege of British subjects to cut wood in the Bay of Campeche. For France the parties agreed to expel the British from Newfoundland, to recover Dominica, to secure liberty of trade with the East Indies, to get back Senegal, along with the liberty to trade on the coasts of Africa not pre-empted by English factories. Significantly, in the light of Spain's later concern about America's claim to fishing privileges off the Grand Bank, it was agreed that, were France to regain Newfoundland, she would admit Spanish subjects to the fisheries there, presumably no one else;[47] and, reciprocally, French subjects were to be allowed a share in the woodcutting on the Campeche coast should the British be expelled from that area. The two courts bound themselves to make no peace or enter into any truce until Gibraltar should be restored to Spain and France's control over the port of Dunkirk fully achieved.

Vergennes had sought to win from Spain a pledge not to put down arms until the independence of the United States was recognized by England, since American independence was the ostensible cause of France's original entry into the war. The most he could secure by the secret treaty was a Spanish promise not to attempt to interfere in this matter or to conclude any understanding either with the United States or with another party regarding American independence without consulting France.[48] The ostensible reason given for Spain's declination was that she had as yet not concluded any treaty with the United States, but Charles III of Spain let it be understood in the chancelleries of Europe that France's alliance with the insurgents had no bearing on Spain's decision to enter the conflict, that she had little interest in the new United States, and regarded a successful rebellion as a bad example to her own colonies.[49]

The secret pact of Aranjuez seemed on its face to be a triumph for the combined diplomatic efforts of the Comte de Vergennes, France's respected Foreign Minister, and Spain's ambassador to Versailles, the Conde de Aranda, the prowar leader of the Aragonese faction critical of Florida-blanca. All along Vergennes and Aranda had been pressing the Spanish court to join France in the war and thus fulfill the obligations of the Family Compact existing between the two branches of the Bourbon House.[50] The fact is that cooperation between the two nations had virtually come to a dead end before the American Revolution had gotten under way, and at most there had persisted an outward show of intimate union. The cooling-off process began at least as far back as 1770, when Spain tried to force England to quit the Falkland Islands. Instead of rushing to Spain's support, Louis XV dismissed the Duc de Choiseul, his anti-British Foreign Minister, and informed a shocked Spanish court that it could not count upon military assistance from France. Forced to yield the Falklands, Spain suffered a public humiliation so proud a nation was unlikely to forget quickly. Deprived of French support, Spain was also obliged to take a more conciliatory stand toward Portugal, with whom she had been having a running feud.[51]

What the insurgent Americans could not have known at the time Congress dispatched Jay to Europe, because of the secrecy with which the Franco-Spanish understanding was cloaked, was that France, by agreeing not to make peace without Spain and to continue the war until Gibraltar was obtained, had in effect modified her alliance with America and changed and enlarged the purposes of the war without America's consent and even without her knowledge.[52] With America about to send a minister plenipotentiary to the court of Charles III it would not be long before Spain's objectives would be revealed as in fact incompatible with those of the Thirteen States.[53] France's Minister to Spain was among the first to recognize that incompatibility of peace aims between an absolutist Catholic monarchy and a revolutionary republican and secular state. "Let us not conceal from ourselves," Montmorin warned Vergennes, "how little interest Spain takes in the United States of America. We shall certainly have evidence of this not only in the course of the war but more especially when the question comes up of concluding peace."[54]

In view of her vast holdings on the North American Continent, Spain could hardly be expected to view with equanimity either the dangerous example which the Thirteen rebellious Colonies offered to her own restless possessions in the Americas or the threat that American expansionism posed to her interests in the Mississippi region. Vergennes sought to dispel Spain's suspicions and to reassure her that she had nothing to fear from the United States, since the new nation was bound by that "inertia that is characteristic of all constitutional democracies."[55] Floridablanca, perhaps the greater realist of the two, quickly recognized the challenge to Spanish possessions that an independent America posed.

By the Convention of Aranjuez, France was obliged to watch over Spain's interests in her negotiations with the United States. Gérard had, even before the Convention went into effect, anticipated its mandate. Concerned about rumors of impending peace talks between the United States and Great Britain apart from France,[56] he elicited from Congress the declaration "that as neither France or these United States may of right, so these United States will not consider either truce or peace with the common enemy, without the formal consent of their ally first obtained."[57] In a communication to Congress on February 9th and in a private audience before that body the next week, Gérard declared that Spain had made her final offer of mediation to George III. Were it to prove fruitless, she would honor her commitments under the Family Compact. It was imperative, therefore, for the United States to prepare to take part in the impending peace negotiations planned for Madrid, to designate "a proper person" to participate, to furnish him with "ample powers," and allow him that discretion which the remoteness of the negotiations from America dictated. The United States, Gérard told Congress, should draw up instructions and decide upon its ultimata. Should these be moderate, there was a good chance that Britain would accept them, Gérard advised. The French Minister counseled that in drafting these peace objectives the states should consider "the peace in relation to Spain," and bear in mind that Spain wished some terminal limits placed on the territorial claims of the United States, and that she intended to close the navigation of the Mississippi to other powers, and to recover the Floridas.[58] The diplomatic archives reveal that Spain was determined to control the entire Mississippi Valley,[59] a claim which Vergennes considered "*gigantesque*," and viewed

American expansionist activities in the West with grave concern. At first the French Foreign Minister saw no reason why Spain should not share the navigation of the Mississippi with the United States.[60] That he was later to adopt a more inflexible and even unsympathetic position toward America's claims in that area seems in no small part to have been the result of Gérard's influence.

The committee to whom had been assigned the task of putting the several issues of the peace into form suitable for discussion brought in its report on February 23rd. In the handwriting of Gouverneur Morris of New York, a moderate who wished to put a brake on expansionist fever,[61] the report recommended that, first of all, independence, absolute and unlimited, as well "in matters of government as of commerce,"[62] must be granted as a precondition to opening negotiations. Then followed six stipulations to be considered in the nature of ultimata—namely, securing minimum boundaries from Canada to the Floridas and west to the Mississippi, the evacuation of the country by the British forces, fishing rights on the banks and coast of Newfoundland, the navigation of the Mississippi River to the southern boundary of the United States, free commerce with some port or ports on the Mississippi below that boundary, and, lastly, the cession to the United States of Nova Scotia or the latter's independence, this last subject to the willingness of the Allies to support the claim.[63]

Over these peace objectives debate waxed furious and unabated for the next six months despite constant prodding by Gérard. The French Minister took every occasion to warn Congress that the King of Spain would be alienated by delays and to oppose pressing claims to land west of the Appalachians, or to the fisheries.[64] The Lee faction's response to Gérard's ill-concealed pressures and his readiness to exploit factional difference for France's ends was to bristle like a porcupine. "I am afraid," James Lovell wrote to General Horatio Gates, "of the arts [they] are using to hurry us into a rash ultimatum."[65]

Of the six stipulations, three provoked sharp controversy. These were the boundaries, the fisheries, and the navigation of the Mississippi. Oddly enough, the first and the most important was in essence settled on March 19th, with a permissible modification of the northwest boundary if the ultimatum could not be obtained without continuing the war for that purpose (but not south of 45° NL), and a similar provision was later inserted in the instructions with respect to the northeast boundary.[66]

While Congress was quickly united in setting national boundaries which would include what was later known as the Northwest Territory, assigned by Parliament to Canada under the Quebec Act, and the lands claimed

THREE VOYAGERS IN SEARCH OF PEACE

by colonial charters from the Appalachians to the Mississippi, it was sharply divided over two issues which were to prove far less consequential to America's future. Over the fisheries and the free navigation of the Mississippi Congressmen split along Deane-Lee lines, with the Deaneites, mostly from the Middle States and the South, adopting the more moderate position on both demands that Conrad Gérard was nightly preaching.

The "long struggle about cod and haddock,"[67] as James Lovell, a manager of the Lee cause, described it, began early in February and continued virtually nonstop until the middle of August. On the twenty-second of March a resolution was adopted demanding the acknowledgment of the right of the fisheries provided that the Allies were so circumstanced as to be able to back the United States in continuing the war to obtain this concession. In no event, however, were the fishery rights to be abandoned in any treaty of peace.[68] This was too weak an instruction to satisfy the cod-minded New England delegation. Two days later the Lee faction obtained a reconsideration of the question and the adoption of a substitute moved by Richard Henry Lee and designed to counter the French argument that the colonies by rebelling had forfeited their ancient rights to the fisheries which they had exercised as British subjects.[69] Now, Gérard was not prepared to accept the fishing rights as an ultimatum, nor even to tie the King to a commitment as to specific boundaries for the United States.[70] Working through his pro-Gallican supporters in Congress, he maneuvered to have the demand for the fisheries reduced to the negative assertion, "that in no case, by any treaty of peace, the common right of fishery be given up."[71] Notwithstanding the Frenchman's best efforts, the New Englanders persisted in what one participant in the affray called their "pertinacious" efforts to put teeth into the fisheries articles.[72] On June 3rd and again on the 19th Elbridge Gerry, speaking for his Marblehead fishing constituency, touched off a renewed debate on the question.[73] Again Gérard came before Congress to press for moderation.[74] Finally, on July 29th a resolution was adopted to the effect that, if after the treaty of peace Great Britain were to molest the inhabitants in taking fish on the banks, Congress would deem it a breach of the peace.[75] Every state from New Hampshire to Delaware voted for this resolution; every state to the southward against it. The outcome was that the New Englanders were not able to insert into the instructions an affirmative acknowledgment of the fishery rights, but had to content themselves with the negative stipulation that the fishery rights be not yielded at the peace. Congress went even further in soft-pedaling the issue. Two weeks later, in preparing instructions for the minister who was to be charged with negotiating the peace, it inserted the sentence: "Yet a desire of terminating the war hath induced us not to make the acquisition of these objects an ultimatum on the present occasion."[76]

The free navigation of the Mississippi, so consequential to states having territorial claims west of the Appalachians, was argued at great length, but with perhaps less vehemence than the right to catch cod. Gérard took it on himself to warn Congress that any attempt to treat directly with Great Britain for the navigation of the Mississippi might mean war with Spain.[77] His lobbying paid dividends. Congress on March 24th overwhelmingly defeated an attempt to make the navigation of the Mississippi an ultimatum.[78] The issue was not closed, for in midsummer an effort was made to have the minister to Spain instructed to secure cession of Canada, Nova Scotia, Bermuda, and the Floridas, along with the free navigation of the Mississippi.[79] Again Gérard intervened. If Congress expected aid from Spain, Gérard advised, it would be prudent not to ask that power to yield two such cherished objects as the Floridas and Mississippi navigation. John Dickinson moved to make these demands conditional and to propose a number of *quid pro quo*'s.[80] There was even a proposal by Samuel Huntington that the United States should assist Spain in the conquest of the Floridas, but it gained few backers.[81] Gérard found that he could not sit on the lid indefinitely. On September 17th, the very day that the retiring French Minister took his formal leave of Congress, that body resolved that, if Spain should join hands with France and the United States, Congress would make no objection to her acquiring the Floridas, provided "always, that the United States shall enjoy the free navigation of the river Mississippi into and from the sea."[82] Although some members feared that even this was demanding too much of Spain, and it was proposed that the American minister to Spain be privately instructed to recede from the claim to navigate the river on condition that Spain grant America a free port, the majority stood by the proposition as adopted. In addition to this instruction to Jay to insist on the free navigation of the Mississippi, which was to prove the stumbling block to all negotiations, Jay was instructed to obtain a free port on the lower Mississippi for American commerce and to secure a loan of five million dollars "upon the best terms in your power not exceeding six per centum per annum, but before borrowing to try to get a subsidy in consideration of America's guaranteeing the Floridas to Spain if they were reconquered."[83]

All this Jay had closely observed as presiding officer of the sessions of Congress. Now he was responsible in part for carrying out the instructions which Congress, despite the constant meddling of Gérard, had wrung from its steamy debates. Little wonder that Jay had remarked to Washington, "There is as much intrigue in this State House as in the Vatican but as little secrecy as in a boarding school."[84] But when he wrote these words he had not enjoyed the privilege of witnessing at firsthand the operations of the court of Madrid.

Since the Lee-Deane feud had placed all of America's commissioners abroad under a cloud, John Adams took his appointment as peace commissioner to Great Britain as a vindication of his record. "There is no character in which I could act with so much pleasure as that of a peacemaker," he wrote the Chevalier de La Luzerne from his Braintree home on October 17th, but added this caution: "Alas! When I reflect upon the importance, delicacy, intricacy and danger of the service, I feel a great deal of diffidence in myself." Nevertheless, since he was technically the unanimous choice of Congress for the peace mission as a result of a compromise between the contending factions, Adams expressed the view that, considering how divided Congress had been "about most other characters," this was an honor he could not decline.[85]

The clear-headed and forthright New Englander foresaw the pitfalls ahead. "Peace is an object of such vast importance," Adams wrote Samuel Huntington, who succeeded Jay in the Presidency of Congress, "the interests to be adjusted in the negotiations to obtain it are so complicated and so delicate, and the difficulty of giving even general satisfaction is so great, that I feel myself more distressed at the prospect of executing the trust, than at the thoughts of leaving my family and country; and again encountering the dangers of the seas and of enemies."[86]

Adams' party of seven embarked at Boston on the French frigate *Sensible*. His companions included his two sons, the precocious John Quincy, then twelve years of age and destined to carry on notable missions abroad on his own, and Charles, nine, along with Francis Dana, a Boston lawyer who was serving as Adams' secretary and chargé d'affaires, and two servants. If in retrospect Adams dramatized the circumstances of his parting, events proved him a sound prophet. "On the thirteenth of November 1779," he later recorded, "I had again the melancholly tryal of taking leave of my family, with the dangers of the seas and the terrors of British men of war before my eyes, with this additional aggravation that I now knew by experience how serious they were, much better than I had when I embarked in Nantasket Road in 1778."[87]

Adams' party had not been out to sea a full two days before the *Sensible*, hardly justifying its name, sprang a leak. Soon all hands were at the pumps, and a large stream of water was constantly flowing over the sides. The planks and timber were so decayed that another strong gust would have torn the old frigate to pieces. In the unhappy event of pursuit by a superior British foe she would have been forced to spread all sails. If that had occurred the leak would have become a deluge and the ship would have foundered. So critical was the situation when they passed the Grand Bank that the captain determined to head for one of "the Western Islands." Missing all of them, the exhausted ship's company found themselves by the beginning of December within a hundred leagues of Corunna, off the coast of Spain. Adams and Company got into Ferrol on December 8th. Within an hour after coming to anchor the *Sensible* was found to have seven feet of water in her hold.

To render the frigate seaworthy would be a matter of weeks. Adams realized that it would be best for him to continue on to Paris overland. Traveling over mountainous Galicia through January frost, snow, and ice, Adams and his party observed the poverty and economic sluggishness of the Spanish countryside. He saw men, women, and children "with naked legs and feet, standing on the cold stones in the mud, by the hour together." Although the Inquisition had had some of its fangs removed by now, he found that the huge numbers of regular clergy encountered everywhere were "drones enough to devour all the honey of the hive." Journeying over mountainous roads where neither horse nor mule could be trusted, where carriage axles were frequent casualties, the Adams party spent their nights at filthy accommodations, windowless houses without chimneys. "Smoke, soot and dirt, everywhere, and in everything," John observed of the evil-looking taverns in which he was put up. Ragged and dirty people, fleas and lice, a land where nobody "appeared rich but the churches, nobody fat but the Clergy." Taking a southeasterly course over rugged mountains from Galicia to Leon, Adams found at the walled town of Astorga "clean beds and no fleas for the first time since we had been in Spain." At Leon's cathedral the Braintree Puritan drew the "eagle eye of the Bishop" when he failed to fall to his knees to receive the apostolic benediction. As he journeyed across the plain to Paredes de Nava he saw villagers dance the fandango. He also noted crumbling villages of mud and straw, an impoverished countryside exploited by "Church, State and Nobility." By the time he reached Burgos, a town "held by an army of ecclesiasticks," he had caught something of the spirit of Spain that he was unlikely soon to forget.

"I had never experienced anything like this journey," Adams confessed many years later. For the travelers, devoid of any knowledge of Spanish, there was no relief from rain, snow, sleet, fatigue, poor food, and want of sleep. Small wonder that everybody in the company was soon down with violent colds. Where to now? Should the party proceed to Madrid? The idea was quickly dismissed. Not only was Madrid the long way around to Paris, Adams' destination, but a visit at this time might well prove embarrassing to John Jay, who had not yet reached the Spanish court. Quitting Spain saved Adams some embarrassments, too, and the Comte de Vergennes some sleepless nights,[88] for the New Englander's information about the attitude of the Spanish court toward America was derived almost entirely from conversations with naval officials and Irishmen resident in Spain. These friendly discussions fortified his "very sanguine hopes that a solid treaty will soon be concluded with Spain." He could not have been worse informed.

Having made the decision not to go on to Madrid, Adams set his course northeast toward Bilbao. The party accomplished the serpentine descent to the village of Orduna, set in the midst of a fertile valley crowded by monasteries and convents. Reaching Sugar Loaf, the pyramidal-shaped mountain before Bilbao, called by its denizens "a republic," the Yankee Patriot was impressed by a sense of liberty pervading the autonomous community. Thence across the border to St. Jean-de-Luz. "Never was a captive escaped from prison more delighted than I was, for everything here was clean, sweet and more comfortable in comparison of anything we had found in any part of Spain." On to Bordeaux and at long last the arrival in Paris on February 9th, almost three months since their embarkation at Boston. "We were more than twice as long in making the journey by land, as we had been in crossing the Atlantic Ocean," Adams observed.[89]

Like Jay, Adams had plenty of time to ponder his instructions before getting down to work. In rereading the ultimata adopted by Congress after prolonged debate, the American peace commissioner could not help but be struck by a concluding caution. "You are to govern yourself by the Alliance between his Christian Majesty and these States; by the advice of our Allies, by your knowledge of our interests; and by your own discretion, in which we repose the fullest confidence."[90] Those who knew their man would expect him to give at least as much weight to his own knowledge and discretion as he would to the advice of the French government.

Adams had few illusions about the difficult task ahead. A quick face-to-face confrontation with a peace emissary of the British government seemed unlikely to take place so long as "the English continue in their old ill humour and insolent language, notwithstanding their impotence grows every day more apparent," he reported to President Huntington.[91] It should certainly have been clear to him, from his previous mission abroad, that Louis XVI was most reluctant to have the uninhibited American commissioner press peace talks with England, and, more serious, was unwilling to support American peace objectives which clashed head on with the avowed interests of France's own ally, Spain. If he had forgotten this, France's Foreign Minister, the Comte de Vergennes, was soon to give him a curt reminder.[92] As the war continued its seesaw course, diplomatic intrigues burgeoned. To John Adams, who soon recognized that the American republic had the most to lose by outside mediation efforts, it appeared that the most perilous portion of his peace mission lay before him.

Still a third diplomatic mission was dispatched to Europe in the fall of '79. For the post of commissioner to the United Provinces Congress chose an ex-President, Henry Laurens, the Charleston merchant-Patriot, who along with the Virginia Lees had given a slight Southern coloration to the anti-Gallican faction. Laurens was instructed to secure a loan of ten million dollars from the Dutch and to negotiate a treaty of commerce and amity. The short, swarthy, cocksure Laurens, who had renounced slave trading after it had yielded him a fortune, was by temperament perhaps better suited for an executive role than a diplomatic assignment, although even in the former he had betrayed a spirit of intense partisanship hardly in keeping with his role as Congress' presiding officer.

Laurens was on the point of sailing from Charleston on the frigate *Ranger* in February, 1780, when news of the arrival of British transports and landings close by, within sixteen miles of South Carolina's capital, caused him to postpone his departure. "Were I to study my own private interests and desire, I should remain here and stand or fall with my country," Laurens declared, but he was persuaded by public duty to proceed to North Carolina to seek another passage.[93] Abandoning his vast business interests and landed properties to the enemy converging on Charleston, Laurens did not find the opportunity to sail for Europe until August 13th, when he embarked at Philadelphia on the swift-sailing brigantine *Mercury*, commanded by Captain William Pickles. The *Mercury* was to be convoyed by the sloop-of-war *Saratoga*. However, at the Capes of the Delaware they encountered two frigates commanded by the celebrated Nicholson brothers. The Nicholsons promised to return to convoy them as soon as they had run up the bay to replenish their water supply. For four or five days

Laurens and his party waited aboard the *Mercury* anchored off Port Penn. Hearing nothing further from the Nicholsons, Laurens ordered the *Mercury* to set sail without escort. Laurens justified his decision on the ground that in the Continental Navy "little regard was paid to orders inconsistent with the captain's own convenience." Furthermore a favorable wind and the advancing equinox suggested that it was perhaps now or never. For six days the *Saratoga* struggled to keep up with the *Mercury*, but the brigantine was obliged each night to shorten sail so as not to outdistance her escort. Laurens then made his second fateful decision. He advised Captain Young of the *Saratoga* to break off her escort duty and return to the Delaware.

On September 3rd, as dawn broke off Newfoundland, a sail was sighted far to leeward. Captain Pickles put the *Mercury* close upon the wind, and then, for reasons that are still not clear, he changed his mind and put her before the wind, her worst sailing, especially since she was badly ballasted with sand. The distant vessel obligingly altered her course, too, and about nine o'clock came within gun range. Two hours later a shot went over the *Mercury* and two more were fired between her masts. Captain Pickles hauled down the American flag.

All papers thought to be of importance were thrown overboard or burned, save a trunkful of Laurens' own papers, which, at his order, remained untouched. This was his third fateful decision. When he realized that there were confidential papers among them, he yielded to urgings to have them thrown overboard. The papers were put in a long bag and some twenty pounds of shot upon them. Unfortunately for both Laurens and his mission, the air inside buoyed up the bag, and the seamen of the British frigate proceeded to hook it up. Among the papers was discovered a draft of a proposed treaty drawn up the year before by William Lee, as roving American agent abroad, with Engelbert Van Berckel, an agent of the burgomasters of Amsterdam.[94] The treaty draft was never considered binding by anybody. Lee had no power to treat, and the burgomasters no authority to make treaties with foreign powers. It now served two purposes quite different from its original design. The British pounced upon the discovery and made it a convenient pretext to declare war upon the Netherlands and a ground for confining Henry Laurens in the Tower of London. There he remained from October 6, 1780, until New Year's Eve of the following year. His claims to diplomatic immunity were ignored, and his status as a state prisoner held on suspicion of high treason prevented his exchange as a military prisoner. Laurens' mission had ended in ignominious failure before it really got under way, and if blame was to be allotted, the South Carolinian, who had made a series of luckless decisions, deserved the lion's share of it.[95]

Fortunately for the American cause, there was able John Adams ready and willing to take over. However much he may have commiserated with the South Carolinian in the latter's suffering and humiliation, the New Englander must have recognized that Laurens' capture was a providential stroke for him, if not for the country. Peace, as Adams would soon find out, seemed far removed when he arrived in France in early 1780. One could hardly expect so dynamic a personality to sit patiently offstage waiting for his cue, a call that might never come. Now he had a part to play, and he assumed his role with his accustomed zeal.

destructive raid on Plymouth, also proposed, came with the passing of the days to loom large among the war planners. Portsmouth, however, was finally picked as the prime target, but diversionary raids, including an assault on Ireland, were still a part of the master plan.[6]

In so daring a project time was of the essence. Notwithstanding, the invasion of '79 slowed down to the stately pace set by the superannuated leaders entrusted with its execution. To start with, the chief of the French Cabinet, the Comte de Maurepas, of the renowned Phélypeaux dynasty, had been born in the first year of the eighteenth century. Described by an unfriendly critic as "a man who winnows with every wind, and has not the strength of mind enough to be steady to the truth,"[7] Maurepas was unfitted by age and temperament to infuse vigor and consistency into so enormous an undertaking. But the Comte was only the first among the ancients. At the last moment the Maréchal de Broglie, brother of the invasion planner and originally slated to command the invasion forces, was supplanted by reason of court politics. For the role which the Duke of Parma had filled in a parallel situation two centuries earlier the French government chose the seventy-four-year-old Noël Jourda, the Comte de Vaux, a general whose laurels were still fresh from his victory over the Corsicans. Suffering from hernia, the aged de Vaux was physically much below par.[8] Placing an additional premium on experience rather than vigor, the Ministry named the seventy-one-year-old Comte d'Orvilliers to command the combined fleets of the Allies. His immediate Spanish subordinate, Admiral Luis de Córdoba, was two years the Frenchman's senior, and lacking in battle experience.

From the start the combined operation was hobbled not alone by senescent leadership but by inept civilian direction as well. Gabriel de Sartine, who headed the French Ministry of Marine, was a former lieutenant general of police, who knew nothing about naval affairs, and proved wavering and incompetent under wartime stresses. France's War Minister, the Prince de Montbarrey, was a protégé of the Comte and Comtesse de Maurepas, and better suited to the boudoir intrigues of the palace than to bold martial exercises. He had little stomach for an enterprise which resulted from the diplomatic initiative taken by his colleague, the Comte de Vergennes. The latter had been the chief advocate of the American alliance, whereas Montbarrey was the most outspoken anti-American in the Cabinet. Not only had he opposed the sending of aid to the rebellious colonies, but he had disapproved of the fateful step that France took in 1778 in involving herself openly in the war with England. As Montbarrey saw it, any success which came to the "rebels in Boston" would be a dangerous precedent for all colonial empires. Vergennes had nothing but contempt for the Prince, and the latter viewed the Foreign Minister as a queer bird, or, as he put it, "an exotic plant."[9]

If the division in the French Cabinet could not fail to have a braking effect on the momentum of the armada, the long-standing feud between the Conde de Floridablanca, Spain's formidable Prime Minister and Foreign Secretary, and the Conde de Aranda, Spanish ambassador to Versailles and liaison with the French war ministry, jeopardized the smoothness and efficiency of a delicate operation. Floridablanca had pointedly kept Aranda in the dark about his diplomatic moves that spring and summer, and the correspondence between the two Spaniards carried the chilliest overtones.[10]

To meet the threat of invasion the armed forces of England, riddled by patronage and rent by faction, looked to the King and Ministry for direction. George III could be counted upon to be a conscientious meddler, but he did not determine grand strategy, and Lord North, however affable in manner and adroit in political management, was too evasive and irresolute to assume the mantle of war leader. The direction of the war was a fragmented responsibility. The fighting in America was the charge of the Colonial Secretary, the unpopular Lord George Germain. The war on the sea fell to the Earl of Sandwich, First Lord of the Admiralty, and the European military theater presumably fell within the jurisdiction of Charles Jenkinson, the humorless Secretary at War, a rigid civil servant close to the King but lacking in spark. Between Germain and Sandwich constant friction prevailed, and the absence of harmony among the chief defense planners made for a cautious and disjointed strategy. Commanding the home forces was the taciturn Jeffrey Amherst, now sixtyish, and wearing with little grace the slightly faded laurels gained in America in the French and Indian War. The home fleet, entrusted with the island's defense, was now commanded by Sir Charles Hardy, aged sixty-three and dragged out of semi-retirement for this assignment.

Early in June the lumbering armada was under way. On June 3rd, the French fleet, anticipating a probable move by the British Channel fleet to bottle it up, slipped quietly out to sea from its station at Brest. Delayed by shortage of men and provisions, Hardy put to sea a fortnight later, seemingly too late to prevent a junction of the French and Spanish fleets. By June 10th the French armada came in sight of the Isles of Sisargas, some twenty miles west of Corunna, and the point of rendezvous with the Spanish fleet. Still, not a single ship of war of their new comrades in arms was to be sighted for many weeks. Córdoba took unaccountably long to get under way. On April 12th the joint operation had been agreed upon, but it was not until June 23rd that the Spanish fleet weighed anchor at Cádiz. Seasonal northerlies, which obliged the fleet to head westward first before turning up the coast of Portugal, combined with inexpert navigation, were blamed for the four full weeks that the Spanish squadron took to sail the six hundred or so miles from Cádiz to Corunna. Not until July 23rd did the main Spanish fleet join the French naval armada,[11] although a small squadron from Corunna had managed the much shorter distance earlier that month. By that date Vergennes realized that a "wonderful opportunity" was "slipping from our grasp without anyone to blame."[12]

Fifty precious days of good sailing weather had elapsed when, in the first part of July, smallpox struck the French fleet, its ravages spreading with fatal celerity. D'Orvilliers' own son died in the Admiral's arms, a victim of the dread epidemic,[13] and casualties among crews closely confined below decks mounted as the summer advanced. Some ships were not left with enough healthy hands to execute their maneuvers.[14] Days were wasted while the Spanish fleet was furnished with the French signals, and the two squadrons were regrouped. To Córdoba, with a Spanish squadron of sixteen ships, was assigned the vaguely defined task of reconnaissance. The remaining naval armada comprising forty-five capital ships and sixteen frigates was divided into three squadrons, more French than Spanish in numbers, with the forward group under the Comte de Guichen, the center commanded by d'Orvilliers, and Lieutenant General Don Miguel Gaston bringing up the rear. Finally, a mixed light squadron was placed under the orders of Lieutenant General de Latouche de Tréville.

At long last even the most laggard ship in the rear squadron had placed the sea between its stern and the Torre de Hércules, Corunna's ancient lighthouse. Whether or not it was a fateful coincidence, no one on the expedition could have failed to recall that it was from this very point three hundred years earlier that the Duke of Medina Sidonia had headed his leaden-footed armada toward the Channel.

"Is it pleasant to know that the fate of one's country may be decided in a few weeks?" Horace Walpole asked[15] as England was flooded with rumors of imminent invasion. Alarm, if not panic, spread up and down the Channel coast. To secure prompt compliance with emergency orders the government needed the cooperation of the great landowners and local officials of the southern counties, but some of the most affluent estate owners, men of the stature of the Duke of Richmond and the Earl of Shelburne, were most vocal in their criticism of the government and looked with jaundiced eye on the defense efforts. In fact, the frantic summer of '79 underscored dramatically the lack of political unity in England which existed through-out the years of the War of the American Revolution.

On July 9th a royal proclamation had commanded that in the event of invasion all horses and cattle be driven from the coast and other provisions be removed or destroyed. As lord lieutenant of Sussex, entrusted with the defenses of that exposed county, Charles Lennox, the third Duke of Rich-mond, responded by summoning a county meeting, where a resolution was adopted not to aid in carrying out the King's order. Infuriated, George III, who threw himself into the defense effort with his customary industry and painstaking attention to detail, wanted Richmond removed forthwith regardless of the political risks, so as not to give him the chance "to clogg the wheels of government, and if he see the opportunity, to encourage insurrection."[16] Contrariwise, Richmond's offer to raise personally twenty-four companies was viewed by the King as a highly suspect proposal that would give the lord lieutenant the chance "to bring forward his own creatures."[17] During these feverish months the King and his ministers were quite prepared to attribute the worst motives to their opponents, to assume that they were even capable of treason if they had not already had treason-able intercourse with the enemy. The aggregation of Whigs who opposed the North Ministry in Lords and Commons took an equally vehement view of the government in power. "They have hurried us, and then blundered us, into a civil war, a French war, and a Spanish war," Horace Walpole expostulated,[18] and other Whig critics felt that the incredible errors of the government hardly entitled it to the confidence, not to speak of the support, of the people.

The gathering storm over the defense posture of the government broke during the closing sittings of Parliament in late June. At that date there were hardly twenty thousand effective regulars in Britain to oppose an in-vasion force three times that number, and while the militia constituted on paper a somewhat more numerous force, few persons held delusions about its worth.[19] In its desperate urgency the government had sought to recruit the convicts lodged in Reading Gaol. That was a stopgap measure, of course, and even then half the convicts preferred the security of their jail cells to the risk of battle in their country's defense.[20] On June 21st Lord North proposed in Commons a bill to double the militia, and two days later Attorney General Wedderburn moved to facilitate the impressment of seamen by taking away existing exemptions and suspending the right to sue out a writ of habeas corpus for a breach thereof.[21] On their face such pro-posals seemed innocent enough and not nearly so drastic as the situation would seem to warrant. Jeffrey Amherst confessed that recent efforts to recruit men for the army had bogged down.[22] With its regular army heavily committed overseas, the government was understandably reluctant to bring down to the South coast the unreliable Scottish troops already engaged that year in a series of mutinies in their home bases, and continuing their mutinous behavior well on into the fall.[23] In addition, during June and throughout the summer troops badly needed for defense had to be diverted to Nottingham and Derby to put down riots among the North Country stocking weavers.[24] As regards naval reinforcements, Wedderburn pointed out that if men were available six or eight more ships could be put to sea to reinforce Hardy's fleet.

Despite the imminent threat of invasion, the Opposition pounced upon the proposed bills and proceeded to attack both the war and its mishandling by the government. Charles James Fox delivered a withering attack on the Cabinet, whose members he charged with treachery and corruption, demanding that Lord North, as the latter put it with his customary good humor, "retire with the plunder" he had amassed.[25] Then David Hartley, a member from Hull, who was both a long-time friend of Franklin and a leading advocate of conciliation with America, picked that moment to move that hostilities with the rebellious colonies be suspended for ten years and that the British troops be withdrawn from America.[26] Hartley's peace proposals had not the slightest chance. The confident ministers remained silent, while the Earl of Shelburne, one of the government's severest critics but, as a protégé of the elder Pitt, one still unreconciled to the loss of the American empire, pointed out that the Franco-American treaty of the previous year prevented the rebellious colonies from making a separate peace.[27] Hartley's proposal was quickly voted down.[28]

The Opposition's hostility to the defense effort stemmed from no lack of martial ardor or patriotism. Many in its ranks, as the Duke of Richmond put it, regarded the American War as "worse than lost"[29] or shared Horace Walpole's feeling that there was "as little chance of recovering America as of reconquering the Holy Land."[30] Such critics wanted to cut their losses and turn all their guns upon their ancient foes. At the same time they considered it more important to bring about "a total change of the system" which had involved England in her present difficulties than to enact war measures piecemeal.[31]

The militia bill was batted around by the Commons[32] and torn to shreds in the Lords. The excitable, driving, and dependably tactless Duke of Richmond reminded Parliament of the rioting that had accompanied the raising of the militia the previous year.[33] Disemboweled of all its original substance, the bill went back to the Commons with a solitary supplemental clause authorizing the raising of volunteer companies, which the lower house accepted. New volunteer companies sprang up throughout the country, including such ill-assorted units as the workmen employed by the Board of Works and the tradesmen employees of the London theaters recruited by the playwright-politician, Richard Brinsley Sheridan.[34] Lord North condescendingly referred to these improvised home forces as "the new armed peasants,"[35] and, from Strawberry Hill, his Gothic-style country estate, Horace Walpole caustically observed that "even this little quaint Village is grown a camp. Servants are learning to fire all day long, and, I suppose, soon will demand their wages *le pistolet à la main*."[36] But whether the aristocrats liked it or not, these local volunteer units were all that stood between the approaching invader and the main army encamped at Cox Heath near Maidstone.

The impressment bill did not escape unscathed either. The Duke of Richmond with disarming frankness pointed out that his personal fortune would be adversely affected if the exemption for workers in the coal trade was not continued, and that industry throughout England would feel its cramping effect. On his motion sympathetic peers omitted the coal trade from the categories whose exemption from impressment was temporarily taken away by the bill, and in this form it passed both houses.[37]

In the spirited attacks over the impressment bill the Opposition's chief fire was directed against John Montagu, Earl of Sandwich and First Lord of the Admiralty. Bearing the blame for the limping naval effort which stemmed in no small part from the penny-pinching and shortsighted policies of North and the King, Sandwich stood before his peers the naked symbol of profligacy, corruption, and administrative ineptitude.[38] For poor Sandwich this had been a bad year indeed. At the start of the year Augustus Keppel, one of Britain's most trusted naval officers, whose refusal to serve "in the line of America" had redounded to his popularity in the Royal Navy, was court-martialed for his direction of the British fleet in an inconclusive encounter with the French off Ushant the preceding summer. The Whigs rallied to Keppel's support, and his acquittal touched off riotous demonstrations in London and Westminister, with the Admiralty buildings a prime target.[39] At the height of the storm another blow descended upon Sandwich. The actress Martha Ray, his mistress for sixteen years and mother of two of his offspring, was murdered outside Drury Lane Theatre by an unbalanced clergyman. Out of deference to his grief a vote of censure of Sandwich was deferred, and Lord North managed to ward it off,[40] but once again, in the June debates, the assault was renewed. Shelburne denounced Sandwich as "the man, who by his neglect and incapacity had invited an attack from France," and the Marquess of Rockingham was equally critical.[41]

To what lengths might the Opposition go in this time of crisis? The pro-American Parliamentarian Colonel Isaac Barré, a protégé of Shelburne, discounted the King's stubbornness and courage when he suggested that in the event of a landing by the enemy George III would not put up a "well-judged and obstinate defense." Convinced that an "underhand armistice" would "steal upon us," and that "the real business" would be taken out of military hands and entrusted to some intimate of the King, Barré warned Shelburne of the possibility that the French could make a peace, "sword in hand and upon English grounds." In such an event, what course should the Opposition take? "We cannot stand aside and permit the country to take a cowardly course," Barré argued, with his flair for the melodramatic. Instead, the Opposition should unite by entering into immediate correspondence and alert the public to the danger, and "by some bold and daring measure stun the Court, awake the people, and then take the reins of government into their hands."[42] Whether this cryptic allusion to a "bold and daring measure" might reach so far as a forced abdication of the monarch is by no means clear, but it speaks eloquently of the decline of public confidence in the government.

As though invasion threats and internal discord were not enough, the government recognized its especially vulnerable position in Ireland, long in a state of uneasy dependency upon the British Crown, and sympathetic with the American cause. Unfortunately for England, these pro-American sympathies seemed to flourish as vigorously among the Presbyterians in the North, embittered by oppressive trade conditions, as among the Catholics of southern Ireland, still nursing ancient hatreds against their religious oppressors.

On the basis of cautiously optimistic forecasts the invasion of Ireland was at this time projected by the Bourbon Houses,[43] and elicited the enthusiastic sponsorship of the Marquis de Lafayette, who gave it a high priority among the half dozen large ventures that he was then pushing. To find out whether the time was opportune, Franklin picked Dr. Edward Bancroft to go on a mission to Ireland and report back to Lafayette. "No American in Paris, save M. Bancroft, merits sufficient confidence to be credited with such a mission," Lafayette told Vergennes,[44] little knowing that Bancroft was a double agent.

Bancroft crossed to Dover at the beginning of June, then journeyed across England to embark for Dublin. He toured northern Ireland, and what he saw he professed not to like. On his return to France Bancroft met

Lafayette at Le Havre on July 1st and told him that "the fruit is not ripe," and that the military associations then springing up in Ireland could be expected to resist the invaders.[45] But all was not black, he informed the Marquis. Continued mistreatment of Ireland by the British and a prolongation of the war might justify an invasion in the spring of 1780. Lafayette proposed to send to Ireland a few loyal Americans to foment the discord to which Franklin's adroit propaganda had significantly contributed,[46] and was encouraged by Bancroft in the view that two thousand men could take and destroy Cork, where the antiwar spirit was at that time perhaps most pervasive.[47]

Bancroft could have been expected to have reported all this to the British government, which had in fact penetrated the sievelike security of Franklin's establishment at Passy and been forewarned of a probable Irish descent as well as of an invasion of England proper.[48] George III distrusted that "stock jobber," as he called Bancroft, and considered him unfriendly to England. "All Bancroft's news," he told North, he had discounted "for a considerable time" as being "calculated to intimidate."[49] Despite Bancroft's divided loyalties, his advice to Lafayette seemed both accurate and objective. There is no evidence that a secondary attack upon Ireland, something transcending a raid, could have been successfully mounted.[50]

While England in one of her darkest hours faced the invaders without friend or ally, unable to count upon the true neutrality of the nonbelligerent powers who continued to supply America and the Allies with the sinews of war,[51] the combined fleets headed north to do battle. On August 11th they sighted the isles of Ushant off the tip of Brittany, and on the fourteenth d'Orvilliers' ships were off the Lizard, Britain's extreme southerly point. Two days later the Franco-Spanish armada cast anchor in sight of Plymouth, riding out the current at ebb tide, sails flattened to the masts in dead calm. Its first victory was achieved within twenty-four hours, when the sixty-five-gun *Ardent*, mistaking the hostile formation for Hardy's squadron, was captured by the armada.

While the King was strangely optimistic,[52] his mood was not shared by Plymouth's defenders, who were uncertain whether d'Orvilliers planned to burn and sack the town and then withdraw or was awaiting transports to mount a full-scale invasion.[53] Had the attack on Plymouth been pressed, the Allies, in the opinion of the military commander on the spot, could have taken the dockyard in six hours, so laggard was the government in defending this great port, so insistent was Amherst, despite intelligence reports disclosing Portsmouth and Plymouth as invasion objectives, that the main forces be concentrated near London.[54] The defenders could not make up their minds whether to place a boom across the Channel or to sink vessels to block the approach to the harbor.[55] As a result, neither was done. Neither were handspikes available to work the guns and give them the necessary direction, nor wadding, rammers, sponges, or other essential apparatus. The balls did not fit the guns nor the guns the balls. To man the two hundred guns, requiring six men to a gun, less than forty aged or infirm men were assigned.[56] "It would be impossible for us to fire ten shots at an enemy if it came," declared Lieutenant General Lindsay, commanding the defenses. The reinforcements which he had received, including heavy allocations from the press gang, were so mutinous that he was obliged to assign other troops to guard them.[57] Had a landing been made by the enemy some ten miles west of Plymouth where the coast is low, Richmond later brought out, either Mount Tor or Mount Pleasant, commanding Plymouth Harbor, might well have been taken from the rear, and the other inevitably fallen, and along with them the prize of Plymouth itself.

For d'Orvilliers this was his great moment. French intelligence had also penetrated the vulnerability of Plymouth.[58] The French Admiral's ships, now nearly double the number in the Grand Fleet, were between the Royal Navy and the exposed Channel ports. To prevent the French from sending over their transports and making their embarkation while the British fleet was far to the westward and an easterly wind would prevent their quick return, Vice Admiral Sir Hugh Palliser proposed that a detachment of frigates be sent off Le Havre and other French Channel ports to intercept the invading forces. "For God's sake and your own," Palliser pleaded with Sandwich, "take the opinion of as many sea officers on the spot as may be confided in upon this and other important points!"[59] But this sound proposal, like too many others, was not acted upon, and the Channel lay momentarily open to the Comte de Vaux's transports. Only momentarily, for the indecisive d'Orvilliers' brief hour was quickly dissipated. The calm before Plymouth was soon succeeded by an easterly gale which struck with sudden fury and drove the armada out of the Channel.

While d'Orvilliers was playing out his minuet in the waters of the Channel, his superiors at home were rapidly cooling off toward the enterprise. Vergennes voiced this changing climate of official opinion when somewhat earlier he wrote France's ambassador to Spain, the Comte de Montmorin, that unless the mission could come off that year the project should be dropped, although it might be useful to keep up the pretext of an invasion. "Perhaps it will be decided that the great blows should be struck in America rather than in Europe," he added.[60] Aranda strove desperately to counter Vergennes' defeatism, but with each passing day the French Minister became more deeply convinced that the invasion was becoming less feasible, particularly in view of the fact that the English were strengthening their fortifications on the Isle of Wight and the military camp at Salisbury was close enough to the sea to repel invaders.[61]

Lacking in neither resourcefulness nor presumption, the impatient and expostulating Spanish ambassador proposed, as an alternative plan, an attack on the coast of Cornwall.[62] For this project he won over the Queen, who invariably meddled in affairs she did not understand and had been known at court to be against the whole cross-Channel invasion venture. The Conde also persuaded her royal spouse, who managed to take time off from his endless rounds of hunting and his absorption in his clock-repairing to throw his weight behind the proposition for the more limited Cornish operation. With some misgivings the Spanish government gave its blessing, but on condition that the project was not credited to Aranda.[63]

The new plan had serious weaknesses, as d'Orvilliers was quick to point out. Under the original proposal to seize the Isle of Wight and secure Spithead as anchorage for the fleet, the armada would contain the enemy on one side, while Córdoba, with a sufficient number of ships of the line and frigates, would protect the convoy crossing from Le Havre from possible attacks on the eastern flank. However, the new orders to d'Orvilliers, substituting Falmouth for Portsmouth as the point of landing, would offer no comparable shelter for the armada. Thus, by switching from the safe and accessible roadstead at Portsmouth to a fourth-rate and exposed harbor, the strategic planners renounced the only opportunity they might have had of securing a base of operations during the fall and winter months. A sheltered Channel anchorage was essential to the armada, for at that time France had no adequate port on the Channel, and the violent westerlies which prevail in the fall and winter would have driven the combined fleet into the North Sea.

Why so remote a corner of the country as Cornwall, which posed no threat to interior communications and could be readily pinched off by the defenders, should have been preferred to the Portsmouth area was something d'Orvilliers could not fathom. True, if the Allies were seeking a relatively cheap if hollow victory for purposes of prestige or face-saving or for harassing British commerce and even sealing off an entry to the Channel, Falmouth seemed a soft spot. Intelligence reports showed it to be weakly defended, short on powder, slim on regulars and militia, and heavily dependent on its unruly Cornish miners armed with nothing more lethal than sticks.[64] D'Orvilliers, believing the safety of his fleet was paramount, protested his new order, but before he could receive an answer to his remonstrance, an easterly gale blew up for several days and once more drove the Allies out of the Channel.

During all these weeks the Grand Fleet, which had gone to sea on June 16th, had managed to elude or evade the Franco-Spanish armada, depending on how one interprets the ambiguous orders Sir Charles had been given. At the start he stationed his ships ten to twenty leagues southwest of the Scilly Isles off Land's End, conforming to orders to keep far enough out not to be forced into the Channel by a westerly wind.[65] Even after he failed to prevent the French from approaching Plymouth, the King had sublime confidence in the mulish British admiral. "The eyes of all the world are upon you," he wrote Sir Charles on September 2nd.[66] Meantime, his subordinate officers were beginning to feel that Hardy had lost his grip on the situation. Rear Admiral Richard Kempenfelt wrote a confidant that "the confused conduct here is such that I tremble for the event." He found an absence of over-all planning, a total neglect of essential details, with Sir Charles' staff plagued by minutiae and trivia from dawn to dusk. "My God, what have your great people done with such an appointment!" Kempenfelt cried out in despair.[67] Events, on the other hand, seemed to be working in Hardy's favor. The West Indies merchant fleet, with a cargo believed worth four million pounds, managed to make port safely, and the rich India fleet found refuge in Shannon.[68] The British high command was heartened by the hesitancy of the armada when it stood before Plymouth, by reports that the ravaging epidemic and the gale winds of the Channel were conspiring to take their toll of men and ships, and that the enemy was low on water and provisions.[69] Sir Charles was now ordered "to give the enemy battle" and prevent the armada's return to Brest,[70] but Hardy seemed no more anxious than did d'Orvilliers for a head-on encounter. On August 29th the Channel fleet was sighted by the armada on its return up the Channel, but Hardy, holding the windward position, bore away to the eastward, and the Allies were unable to force the issue. Then a fog gave him cover to make for the safety of the English coast and the anchorage of Spithead. On Admiral Ross's ship the sailors wrapped their clothes around the bust of George II so that he "should not see an English fleet chased up their own Channel."[71]

On September 3rd, to the nation's astonishment and chagrin, Sir Charles slipped quietly into Portsmouth to replenish his stocks of water and beer.[72] Considering the relatively good condition of ships and men,[73] Hardy left himself wide-open to criticism for his "retreat," as it was generally called. Horace Walpole summed it up succinctly, when he commented on September 5th: "Last week the enemies were between our coast and our fleet, and that was bad. Now our fleet is at Portsmouth, and the enemies' nobody knows where, and this is bad." All of which, as he put it with his customary malice, came from entrusting the defenses of the nation to "two dotards,"

Amherst and Hardy.[74] Palliser also thought that the situation could hardly be worse, fearing that for the fleet now to be attacked at anchor "would be the most disadvantageous mode on our side in which the battle could be fought."[75] "I wish to God you would come down," Captain Constantine Mulgrave pleaded with Sandwich, "as I think your presence here would be of the utmost service."[76] With the imminent reopening of Parliament, even North and the King felt that Sir Charles would have to assume the aggressive.[77] "We must be ruined if every idea of offensive war is to lye dormant untill this island is thought in a situation to defy attacks," the King reminded the First Lord of the Admiralty.[78]

Once again the indecision of her enemies and the capricious weather of the Channel had saved England. Commenting on England's narrow escape, the acidulous Frederick the Great remarked, "There is a special Providence for fools."[79] But if Hardy had brought back his fleet intact, he had scarcely covered himself with glory. "Sir Charles Hardy is crowing upon what may very properly be called his own dunghill," Walpole inelegantly put it.[80] Critics at home like Walpole asked why the Channel fleet had not blockaded Brest months before and prevented the French naval squadron from slipping out and joining up with the Spaniards. They wanted to know why, when d'Orvilliers managed to elude the Royal Navy, he was not followed up and attacked off the coast of Spain during that six-week period when he awaited the arrival of Córdoba's ships, a period when the home fleet enjoyed a numerical superiority. Sandwich was understandably more concerned about fending off attacks on the over-all direction of the fleet from Whitehall than in putting up a vigorous defense of the squadron commander. By the spring of 1780 Sir Charles had died, a victim of anxiety, overwork, and malicious attacks.[81]

If the British defense effort was more faltering than one might have expected, the Allies had exhibited singular ineptitude in failing to exploit their great opportunity. Unaccountably, the vacillating French Ministry neglected to fill the pressing deficiencies of its fleet, although it had ample time to do so. The unfortunate d'Orvilliers never recovered from the shock of his son's death.[82] After retiring to Brest, he threw up his command in disgust and retired to a monastery. Irresolute and dispirited he may well have been, as his severest critic, the Conde de Aranda, insisted, but the basic mismanagement lay at the doors of the incompetent Marine and War ministers.[83]

Having entered the war with suspicion and misgivings, Spain now found them abundantly confirmed when her French ally failed to press that initiative which the temporary naval superiority of the combined fleets seemed fully to justify. As Aranda was careful to point out to his superiors in Madrid, Spain seemed more anxious to take the fight onto British soil than did France.[84] More dispassionate than his envoy, Floridablanca felt that the Spaniards could not escape censure for permitting Hardy's squadron to slip through their net. Spanish officers, he complained, still looked on the English Channel with a sense of horror and lacked the daring and freedom with which the English and French navigated those misty waters. True, a commander should be prudent and cautious, but he believed that Gaston and Córdoba had made a vice of these virtues.[85] If Floridablanca was just in his appraisal of British seamanship, he was overgenerous to his French ally, a luxury that he seldom spared himself. It seems unaccountable that d'Orvilliers lacked navigational charts of the coasts and currents on the English side of the Channel, but the fact is, according to his own admission, he felt insecure in any close approach to the shores of the enemy and had to sail by guess and by God in waters that washed the coasts of Normandy and Brittany.[86] For their part, the French were hypercritical of the Spanish performance. When it was deemed essential to replace the vacillating d'Orvilliers, Montmorin wrote Vergennes to name a French general at once. "I fear," he confided, "that a Spanish general might be proposed. Profit from the moment. We would be lost if we were obliged to accept a Spanish general."[87]

Following the retirement of the combined fleet to Brest the French government continued to cover its indecision with a heavy cloak of mystery. "We are here in limbo," wrote Prince Montbarrey's sister-in-law, the Comtesse de Coislin. "Nothing concerning the truth penetrates there," she intimated to the Duc d'Harcourt, who commanded the Normandy division.[88] But the officers in the field were as much in the dark as the court circle. Montbarrey failed to brief the army commanders on the means to carry out the invasion if one were ever mounted. "This is incredible," complained the Duc du Châtelet, commander of the King's division, "but then everything that has come out of Versailles for some time is incredible."[89]

All along the coasts of Normandy and Brittany morale was crumbling.[90] The five hundred vessels assembled in or near the invasion ports stood idle. By mid-September eight thousand seamen had been invalided by the epidemic, with a death toll too heavy to be tallied up, and dysentery ravaged the army camps. Spanish sailors from Cádiz, dressed for the milder climate of their own country, were facing the penetrating cold of Brest for the most part ill-clad and barefoot. It was necessary to remind the War Ministry that, were the campaign to drag out through the winter months, blankets and winter clothing would have to be provided for the soldiers as well. Otherwise the army would be decimated before spring.[91]

As the September days passed without activity and the Allies had long since sacrificed the advantage of surprise,[92] serious doubts were widely voiced about the high command's intention to mount an offensive that fall. "The ministry appears to want it, the ambassador from Spain preaches it from the rooftops, but sensible men will not believe it," was a typical comment.[93] The replacement on September 24th of d'Orvilliers by the Comte du Chaffault suggested that the invasion plan was shelved along with the naval commander.[94] With the coming of October everybody realized that the Channel storms of the late fall and winter, and the impenetrable fog, would make a cross-Channel invasion a perilous affair.[95] "It is a lost campaign," Marie Antoinette exclaimed, when by the middle of that month the high command scrapped the invasion project at least for the remainder of the year.[96] Shortly thereafter the Spanish fleet was dispatched to Gibraltar to head off a convoy protected by Rodney's squadron,[97] and, to no one's surprise, the camps at St. Malo and Le Havre were shut down in November. Their closing and the departure of the Spanish fleet were admissions that the Franco-Spanish effort, so prodigious in contemplation, so ineffectual in operation, was now in fact dissolved.[98]

The dismal motions in the Channel waters were matched elsewhere that year. France's naval collaboration with her American ally had proven up to now as fruitless as had been her joint effort with Spain. On the very day that Hardy entered Plymouth the French Admiral d'Estaing began his siege of Savannah, only to falter again, as he had the previous year at Newport. While Lafayette and the little American colony in Paris grieved in silence over the failure of the invasion, they were heartened by word of Anthony Wayne's bayonet charge at Stony Point and Paul Jones's dramatic victory over the *Serapis*.[99] That fall Jones's little flotilla spread panic throughout Britain's east coast,[100] and retrieved some measure of assurance for the friends of American independence.

If the failure of the armada made clear to the French just what they might expect from Aranjuez, the Spaniards, in turn, became increasingly pessimistic about France's ability and intention to prosecute the war. With the year 1779 ending in a deadly stalemate on both the military and diplomatic fronts, peace held more appeal to the Bourbon partners than it had back in the spring. Henceforth Floridablanca bent his mind to ways of quitting the war with both honor and profit for Spain,[101] and in France disillusionment and division encouraged the appeasers. The year to come was to prove a fateful one for American independence.

III

PRIEST AND PLAYWRIGHT
AT THE PARDO

N O REGIMENTAL BANDS greeted the Jays and the Gérards upon their
arrival at Cádiz. No invitations awaited them to make their formal
appearance at court. Though long the center for the Spanish trade with
America, Cádiz opened up to the Jays an entirely different world from
the one they had left some months back. It was the sort of place, Jay quickly
discovered, where a man could be hanged for murder after being imprisoned for that crime for some twenty-three years.[1] It was the sort of
place where you could be certain that your mail was being tampered with,
and where you had to resort to a private cipher even when writing to
friends.[2] While Cádiz was only the threshold of Spain, Jay found its
inhabitants disillusioned about the war, and, save for the officers of the
Irish brigade quartered in the town who were hot for American liberty,
nobody showed the least enthusiasm for the rebel cause. These tentative
impressions were unfortunately reinforced by a few months' stay on Spanish
soil. Jay soon discovered most Spaniards to be "in total darkness" about
America and gripped by anti-Protestant prejudice. Whether the officials set
the tone or mirrored public opinion, it seemed patent to the American visitor
that "the bulk of the nation" was "cold" to America. "They appear to me
to like the English, hate the French, and to have prejudices against us,"
he reported back to Congress.[3]

Bred to the law and taught the virtues of caution, Jay had learned not
to press a suit when the circumstances appeared unpropitious. Having in
mind the awkward fate of his predecessor, Arthur Lee, who, though dispatched on a mission to Spain, was never permitted by Charles III to come
closer to the court at Madrid than the Basque town of Vitoria,[4] Jay sent

on William Carmichael, secretary of the American mission to Spain, to ascertain the lay of the land at Madrid. This may have been sound strategy, but it proved poor tactics. Carmichael had some knowledge of the Spanish language which Jay unfortunately lacked,[5] but his charm of manner was matched by his capacity for intrigue and an unduly inflated sense of his own authority. In any event the pair slipped while taking the first cautious step. On the advice of the Chevalier Gérard, presumably steeped in diplomatic protocol, Jay had addressed a letter to Don José de Gálvez, Minister of the Indies, who handled American affairs and was considered sympathetic to the rebels against George III. The American was embarrassed to learn that he had unintentionally circumvented the Conde de Floridablanca, who was to assume full command of the negotiations with the Americans. One did not presume to snub the austere Foreign Minister and principal adviser of Charles III. Fortunately the Comte de Montmorin, France's young and able ambassador at the Spanish court, who was cordially disposed to the Americans, straightened out this contretemps and arranged a meeting between Carmichael and Floridablanca.[6]

Jay was prepared to find that in matters of state, as in all else in Spain, the adage *"Festina lente"* was held in almost religious veneration, but how slowly his own suit would proceed even he could scarcely have anticipated. Had he glimpsed the contents of the diplomatic dispatches neutral observers in Madrid were sending back to their own chancelleries or had he known as much about the real attitude of the court and its calculated tactics as did the French ambassador, it is not unlikely that Jay would have taken the first ship back to Philadelphia. From his remote vantage point the omniscient Frederick the Great assumed that the belligerents had no alternative but to give financial help to America, since without it the rebels could not carry on.[7] That the Spanish court would see it that way appeared highly dubious to other neutral observers, realizing as they did that deep down the Spanish court was hostile to the notion of American independence.[8]

Even later on, when Jay and Montmorin were on terms of intimacy, the latter was in no position to reveal to the American that a fortnight before Jay reached Cádiz Floridablanca had declared that "the day we can be certain of dictating the law to England, the King his master would recognize the independence of America." This was the only prudent course, the Spanish Minister argued, and it might prove "very useful" to France in the event that an unfortunate war forced her "to retrace her steps on recognition." After so frank, if disheartening, an exchange with Spain's

Foreign Minister, Montmorin felt certain that Jay would not be permitted to have any official character in Madrid.[9]

What Floridablanca really wanted, so far as America was concerned, he revealed in another talk with Montmorin a few weeks later. Here he expanded on his favorite notion that the American states should be feudal dependencies of England, holding a relationship to George III very much like the states of the Empire did to the court at Vienna. Such a scheme would reduce the American states "to a sort of anarchy which would render them absolutely nothing," the Spaniard conceded. In short, the only kind of "independence" Floridablanca was prepared to accept was a precarious independence calculated to cause "ceaseless quarrels" between England and America, quarrels which France and Spain could exploit to their own advantage. This was stark balance-of-power realism devoid of ethical or moral considerations. In Montmorin's less shortsighted view Floridablanca's notion of a dependency status for America would be "a source of perpetual war."[10] The harassed French Foreign Minister urged Montmorin to get the best deal he could from Floridablanca. If he would not recognize the United States, at least try to keep him from rejecting the idea out of hand. Keep pounding away on the need for attacking England on all fronts. Bring home to Floridablanca the value of supporting the United States, Vergennes grimly reminded his ambassador.[11]

Before Floridablanca's wily game would be fully disclosed to Jay months would elapse. Meantime there were some straws in the wind. Charles III let it be known that he would not receive the Chevalier Gérard in his capacity of retiring French Minister to the United States, scarcely a gracious return for that diplomat's valiant advocacy before the Congress of Spanish interests. But this was hardly a time for *politesse*. To receive Gérard would signify an implied recognition of the United States. Such an implication would be entirely unfounded. As Floridablanca put it, "It would be like a marriage which would not exist without the agreement of the two parties." Rather than accept the Spanish concession that Gérard might appear as a "distinguished foreigner," Montmorin told the Spanish court that the returning minister lacked a suitable wardrobe for a court appearance.

The Spanish affront to Gérard came as a tremendous shock both to the French Foreign Minister and his ambassador at Madrid. Vergennes bitterly resented this "inconceivable" snub to France and was fearful of what it portended for Jay's mission. Nobody would be so foolish as to imagine for a moment, he pointed out, that a French diplomat who was in Madrid for a whole week could not manage to acquire a decent suit of clothes. Henceforth, let us keep vigilant watch, he counseled Montmorin.[12] To the junior French diplomat the incident spelled trouble and protracted negotiations. "All goes badly here and will continue to go even worse," he reported. In pessimistic vein he even feared that Jay might return to America and thereby precipitate an international scandal. Gérard warned Montmorin that although Jay was well intentioned and strongly attached to the French alliance, he could be persuaded to treat with Spain without confiding in the French.[13] For the short run Gérard was wrong, but for the longer term he proved prophetic.

Still Jay was waiting at Cádiz, and one could not crouch concealed in cloak and sombrero for an indefinite time. The man had to be faced. Toward the end of February Floridablanca sent word to the American minister that "there is no obstacle" to his coming to the Spanish court to explain his and Congress' "intentions." Nevertheless, the King hoped that, until "the manner, the forms, and the mutual correspondence" are settled "upon which that Union must be founded, which the United States of America desire to establish with this monarch," Jay would not "assume a formal character." That must depend on "a public acknowledgment and future treaty."[14]

With cautious optimism[15] the Jays now set out on the road to Madrid. From Cádiz they were rowed by barge to Puerto de Santa María where they enjoyed the warm hospitality of Count O'Reilly, the Governor of Andalusia. Then came the tedious journey over dusty, flea-plagued roads, doubly a chore for Sally Jay, who was with child. They were outrageously overcharged to ride in mule-drawn coaches, and bilked by extortionate inn-keepers, who made them pay for all the beds in the chambers they occupied (fourteen beds in one instance!) despite the few persons in their party and the fact that they brought along their own folding Catalonian beds. Before turning in for the night Sally had her two servants wield a savage broom to clear the room of the filthy beds, the carpeting of dirt, and the astounding hordes of fleas and lice that infested such lodgings. Sleep for the exhausted party proved out of the question. In the adjoining room their mules were quartered, and, as the animals paced the floor, the incessant tinkling of the bells garlanded around their necks provided them with an unwelcome and continuous serenade. Although unappreciative of the rustic disorder that a Goya would have perpetuated on canvas, Sally would have liked to have lingered at Jerez and Cordova, to have explored pleasant Andalusia, but her husband was insistent that business came first. When they passed through La Mancha they scoured the landscape in vain for the great trees that afforded a safe retreat to the "affrighted squire" attached to "the renowned knight of the rueful countenance." But the rest of their trip was less circuitous and certainly more sober than that of Don Quixote. Pushing across the arid plains of central Spain, they reached Madrid on April 4th. Its spacious layout and design, largely the result of the imaginative efforts of the monarch to whom John Jay was paying suit, was, after the cramped Moorish towns, a breath-taking surprise.[16]

The Jays located a house formerly occupied by the Saxon minister and situated in San Mateo Street. In this residence Jay was destined to spend only a limited amount of time while in Spain, for he was to learn almost at once that, in addition to Madrid, the court alternated its perambulations at four *sitios* or country seats, all of which provided Charles III with a chance to carry on his fixed routine of hunting, which he deemed so essential both to his physical well-being and his mental stability.[17] These alternate capitals were El Pardo, just nine miles from Madrid, favorite winter home of Charles III; Aranjuez, some twenty-six miles to the southeast of the capital, where Charles had enlarged upon the summer palace started by Philip II; and to the north the two sitios of El Escorial, that austere and massive monument to Philip II seated at the knees of the Guadarramas, and San Ildefonso, set in the cool fastnesses of the same mountain range, but on the outskirts of Segovia. These perambulations of the court made Spain the most expensive of all diplomatic assignments on the European Continent.

Such information the American diplomat quickly acquired, but he also learned something about the great personages whose acts might well settle the issue of American independence and decide the peace of the world. Although on first impression a staunch Protestant hailing from Revolutionary America might find Spain to be a land lacking in political freedom and gripped by intense religiosity, Jay soon realized that here, as most everywhere in Europe, the spirit of reform was in the air. Even in Madrid, whose Plaza Mayor had been the scene both of many a *corrida* as well as of many an auto-da-fé, and where the steel vise of the Inquisition had not yet been loosened, big changes were taking place. Most of these changes centered on the enhancement of royal authority at the expense of the Catholic Church, but the liberation of colonial trade was not overlooked nor were efforts lacking to improve the lot of the landless peasantry. Chief targets of the Spanish reformers were the Jesuits, long active in the Inquisition.

None of these reforms could have been carried out had it not been for the support of a short, stooped, elderly man, whose distinguishing characteristic was a nose of more than Roman protuberance, bad teeth, and a complexion sunburnt from daily rounds of hunting. Frugal and devout, the most intelligent and persistent of the Bourbon rulers of Spain, Charles III set an unusual standard for his court by his austere devotion to the memory of his prim, bigoted, and ill-tempered Saxon wife, Marie Amélie, deceased some twenty years. So uxorious a monarch was horrified at the licentious court over which his son Ferdinand presided at Naples. Scornfully he warned Ferdinand of rampant rumors that his power-thirsty wife, Maria Carolina, daughter of Maria Theresa, was conducting an amorous intrigue with the dashing John Acton, the Minister of War and the Queen's chief collaborator. "Open your eyes," he was to write his son a few years later. "Having transformed you into a pasteboard king, they have now made you lose your honor, the welfare of your children, and your soul."[18]

Nobody could accuse Charles III of being a pasteboard king. He had ascended the Spanish throne in 1759 after ruling the newly independent Kingdom of the Two Sicilies for a quarter century. There he had early shown his talents as an art collector and student of antiquities and as a beneficent administrator. In Madrid he quickly acquired a reputation as one of the enlightened despots of that age. His outward simplicity of manner belied his capacity for dissimulation. He proved more than a match for the Jesuits. He brought about their downfall and achieved the subordination of the Church to the state in temporal matters, because he appreciated the intense religiosity of his subjects. In religious matters he moved with greater caution than did the impetuous Austrian Joseph II, and his changes were more durable. Charles could move ahead cautiously knowing that nobody in Spain was prepared to challenge the monarchy and that republican notions were regarded with odium by grandee and peasant alike. When he became King, Charles had brought with him from Italy a number of Italian advisers, but in 1766 a so-called popular revolt, known as the "Mutiny of Esquilache," because its target was the detested Secretary of State for War and Finances, the Italian-born Marqués de Esquilache, led to the Jesuits being singled out as scapegoats.

The man who executed Charles III's decree expelling the Jesuits from his realm was an astute Aragonese politician, Don Pedro Pablo Abarco de Bolea, known to the world as the Conde de Aranda. The Conde became president of the Consejo de Castilla, the supreme governing body for all Spain. Charles III was not content to have the Jesuits settled on papal lands. To secure the abolition of the Jesuit Order everywhere, he dispatched to Rome a man of middle-class background named Don José de Moñino y Redondo, trained to the law. The mission was a brilliant success, the Pope was persuaded, and for his achievement Moñino was given the title of Conde de Floridablanca. In 1776 he replaced the pro-French Secretary of State for Foreign Affairs, the Marqués de Grimaldi, Charles' last prominent foreign adviser. Henceforth the government was Spanish-controlled and Spanish-centered.[19] Floridablanca saw to it that his chief rivals were removed far from the scene of power. Grimaldi was dispatched to Rome, Aranda to Paris. There the latter was to play a far greater role in shaping the destiny of Spain than Floridablanca could have possibly imagined.

Floridablanca, the vain forty-nine-year-old statesman who put Spain's interests ahead of her obligations under the Family Compact, was notorious for his temper tantrums, and his unwillingness to brook contradiction. Montmorin and Aranda seemed especially adept at provoking passionate outbursts from Spain's Foreign Minister.[20] Floridablanca had come far since his early years as a provincial attorney, but Vergennes felt that he never lost "the spirit of the pettifogger." Master of finesse and duplicity, he was a match for his chief rivals in the other chancelleries of Europe in the great diplomatic contest which the American Revolution inaugurated. In Spain Floridablanca had something of a reputation as a liberal, largely because of his support of royal absolutism and because both he and Aranda were denounced to the Inquisition as readers of prohibited books authored by the intellectual exponents of the Enlightenment in France,[21] but the Inquisition could not risk moving formally against such powerful officials, especially since the authority of the Sancto Oficio had been curtailed on orders of the King. Of the two, however, Aranda was much more sympathetic to the advanced currents of his day, and may well have deserved the title of the "vanquisher of the Inquisition."[22] Floridablanca was prepared to follow his royal master in his cautious steps of reform, but he was intellectually as conventional a mind as Charles III, if far more egotistical, and was in almost complete disagreement with Aranda as regards the waging of the war and the goals of peace. By turns contemptuous or suspicious of France, he shared his monarch's aversion to the presumptuous American rebels. For him the alliance with France was but a means to an end, and if he could achieve the end by mediation or even by private negotiations with the British he would not hesitate for a moment to scuttle the alliance. He had long disagreed with Aranda about the desirability of recognizing the United States and allying with the rebels, and for some time had been toying with the notion of obtaining some kind of de facto independence for America through a long-term truce which would put the new nation under the joint protection of France and Spain.[23]

Jay had picked up some, but by no means all, of this information about the internal politics of Spain and the views of its leaders before paying his first visit to Floridablanca the very next morning after his arrival at

Madrid. Both the Foreign Minister and the Minister to the Indies treated the American with civility if not cordiality. But it was clear from a communication from Floridablanca that Carmichael had already turned over to Jay that the Foreign Minister, as a preliminary to negotiating, would have to have detailed information about the United States. Floridablanca asked so many questions that it took Jay three weeks to complete his reply, in which he made the point of stressing the determination of the Americans to win their independence and of showing how France and Spain could best help America achieve this goal. For a start, ammunition, clothing, and money would be welcome.[24]

Money above all else was the desperate need. On April 27th Jay received letters from America informing him that Congress had by resolves of November 23rd and 29th drawn bills upon him to the amount of £100,000 sterling payable at sight in six months. "You will find," the Committee of Foreign Affairs frankly confessed to him, "that we are become more dependent upon your vigorous exertions for the amelioration of our currency, than you perhaps expected when you left Philadelphia."[25] Since payments were due in less than a month and no serious negotiations had yet begun with Floridablanca, Congress' observation was one of the master understatements of the war.

No money was to be had in Madrid, as the court had already moved on to Aranjuez, where all serious business would have to be undertaken. To that flower-scented royal residence Jay and Carmichael promptly betook themselves, arriving in May when that perfumed land is at its most seductive. In a letter written following a later visit Jay described that summer *sitio* as

a charming place, containing a tract of several miles in circumference, and divided into gardens, meadows, parks, cultivated grounds, and wilds, full of fine trees, fine roads, and watered by a slow winding river, which, if more clear, would be very beautiful. But still, my friend, it is not America. A genius of a different character from that which presides at your hills and gardens reigns over these. Soldiers, with fixed bayonets, present themselves at various stations in these peaceful retreats; and though none but inoffensive citizens are near, yet horsemen with drawn swords, guarding one or other of the royal family in their little excursions to take the air daily, renew and impress ideas of subjection.

To republican Jay "power unlimited" prompted "uneasy reflections" and took the edge off the pleasing scenery.[26]

Jay's own relaxation took the form of solitary walks in the woods around Aranjuez. Even bullfighting, described by Sally Jay as "that darling spectacle of the Spaniards," was temporarily suspended by order of the King, who substituted in its place "directions for fasting, as a means of deprecating the calamity that is feared from a drought."[27] When, in midsummer, the ban was lifted and Jay attended his first *corrida*, he found it, according to his brother-in-law, Brockholst Livingston, a "cruel" and "inhuman" diversion, and he was shocked quite as much by "the pleasure the Spanish ladies received" from the injuries inflicted upon the tormented bulls and the disemboweled horses.[28] Indeed, all this pageantry and display quickly disenchanted the American visitor.

Burdened with financial worries which the court's studied aloofness scarcely lightened, Jay had a still greater shock awaiting him at Aranjuez. At the same inn at which Carmichael stopped there happened to be another lodger, a mysterious Irishman named Thomas Hussey, garbed in clerical robes. Carmichael described him to Jay as an intriguing and enterprising priest, "with a conscience as pliant as a lady's kid skin glove."[29] A giant of a man, then nearing forty, Father Hussey knew his way around Spain. He had received a degree in theology at the University of Seville, then became a Trappist monk, but at the Pope's request he left the monastery and took Holy Orders. So far as one can judge from the record, the eloquent Irishman was never silent thereafter. During the early years of the Revolution he was in London as chaplain to Prince Masserano, the Spanish ambassador, and continued to serve Masserano's successor, the Marqués de Almodóvar. An intimate of Edmund Burke, he was also a paid secret agent of the Spanish government, a member of the spy ring that supplied Spain with a steady stream of reports on ship movements and supplies as well as such diplomatic secrets as could be uncovered by the best cloak-and-dagger methods of that day. When Spain entered the war Hussey used the good offices of the Neapolitan ambassador to London, Count Pignatelli, to transmit his secret reports to Paris.[30]

Visiting Paris in 1779, Hussey made contact with an Englishman named William Wardlaw, whom he thought to be a spy in Spanish pay but who was in reality a secret agent of Lord George Germain. After obtaining a dossier of documents from Wardlaw about the state of the British Navy and the defenses of Gibraltar,[31] Hussey returned to London. Posing as a purchaser of mathematical instruments, a pretense which fooled nobody, Hussey enlarged his acquaintances in Lord Germain's intimate circle. His most important contact was a prolific playwright named Richard Cumberland, a man of industry without inspiration, with a fund of anecdotes drawn from the theater. Then holding down a minor post on the Board of Trade, Cumberland had been kept on the government's payroll largely through the good offices of George Germain. Among his other talents Cumberland, a great social climber, knew how to toady to men in power. His peculiar powers of perception are evidenced by his estimate of the controversial and violently anti-American Colonial Secretary as both a great man and a great minister.[32] The feeling was mutual. Germain considered Cumberland the very man to serve as intermediary, along with the crafty Irish priest, and to join with him on what proved to be one of the strangest diplomatic missions in all history.

Cumberland told the Ministry what he had learned from Hussey about Spain's disposition toward an accommodation with England. At the prompting of the Ministry he urged Hussey to go to Madrid "to secure testimonials to Spain's desire for peace." Whether or not the peace mission originated in Hussey's fertile brain,[33] the energetic Irishman was ready and eager to go. Cumberland extracted a promise from the priest not to return with a demand from Spain for the cession of Gibraltar without an offer of sizable equivalents, such as a strong footing on the Mosquito Shore and the Barbary Coast, although Hussey warned him that Charles III's obstinacy over Gibraltar "might throw His Majesty into a convent for life or end in his resignation."[34] It is perfectly clear from the evidence that Cumberland did not act on his own, but that the Ministry knew all about the mission and heartily endorsed it.[35]

Hussey reached Vitoria on Christmas Day of 1779, and in a message to Floridablanca suggested that George III would be prepared to yield Gibraltar.[36] This propensity of the former Trappist monk to tell each side what would be most pleasing for them to hear rather than what the other side was really prepared to pay for peace was to prove the undoing of the mission. When Floridablanca and Hussey finally got together, the former provided the priest with a memorandum pointing out that, while Spain was agreeable to making peace with England, such a settlement would have to be reached quickly as John Jay would shortly arrive at the Spanish court to negotiate a treaty with the United States. Warning Hussey that the invasion plans of the previous fall would be put into operation that coming summer, Floridablanca spelled out Spain's terms. In essence they boiled down to *Gibraltar*, along with the Floridas, Campeche, and Honduras. Floridablanca drew an attractive picture of the advantages to England of such a settlement. Once the Rock was yielded, Britain could deploy her troops either in defense of the homeland or in America, confident that she would not be invaded and that the King of Spain would not become an ally of the rebellious colonies. While the King would not falter in his obligations to France, he would back some compromise whereby the colonies would remain as vague feudal dependencies of the mother country, very much like the relation of the cities in the Holy Roman Empire. Peace, Floridablanca made clear, "did not include the point of independence."[37]

Pledged to secrecy by both parties, Hussey made a quick turnabout. In London again at the end of January, he told Germain that Floridablanca had given his pledge not to recognize the United States until an answer was received from England, provided it came before the end of February.[38] He passed on to the Ministry what he claimed to be Floridablanca's willingness to reach "a *separate* and honorable accommodation with Great Britain," again illustrating his propensity to stretch the point to please his listeners. Since Gibraltar was the crucial demand among those Floridablanca listed, Hussey pressed Germain to give assurances that the fortress would be yielded up, even before the matter was fully discussed in the Cabinet.[39]

If Charles III was immovable over Gibraltar, George III was almost pathologically obstinate about not permitting any third parties to arrange matters between himself and his rebellious subjects. Every time independence in any form, *de facto* or *de jure*, was to be raised, he bristled like a porcupine. Here was, perhaps, his great chance to end the war, but he missed it by temporizing. Britain's reply, rushed to Spain in a cipher dispatch by one of Hussey's personal servants, brought no cheering news to Floridablanca. England would not agree to the evacuation of Gibraltar as a first and indispensable article of the negotiation, but, once negotiations had begun in good faith, would consider exchanges of territory. If Spain were prepared to negotiate, England would appoint a secret agent. Hussey, who saw himself as a central figure in these talks, offered it as his own opinion that Gibraltar would enter into them, but he admitted that his view lacked any authorization.[40] Whether it was wishful thinking or an unusual capacity for self-deception, Hussey saw to it that neither side would abandon the game.

Hussey's cipher dispatch prompted Floridablanca to summon a meeting of the Council of Ministers at the Pardo for the night of February 28th. The Foreign Minister put three questions to the Council: (1) Should Spain enter into peace negotiations with the British government? (2) If such negotiations were begun, should France be informed? (3) If not, when should Spain's ally be told? By all means, let us begin negotiations, but in strict secrecy, urged González de Castejon, who held the navy portfolio, for we are always free to break them off. That Minister had all along insisted that his government be "the last country in Europe to recognize *any* sovereign and independent state in North America,"[41] and was soon to play, according to repute, a backstage role in the Cumberland-Hussey negotiations. José de Gálvez, the pro-French Minister of the Indies, and reputed to have been in the pay of France,[42] and Conde de Ricla, Minister of War, both agreed that the time to tell France was when the negotiations had been successfully concluded.[43] Backed by the Council, Floridablanca notified Hussey of the King's willingness to negotiate, but again inserted the caution that speed was of the essence. "I shall not be able to detain the course of the negotiations of Señor Jay, who is even now on the road to Madrid," he added, implying that Jay's arrival would set in motion a whole new set of projects involving collaboration with the insurgents.[44]

Floridablanca now cleared the way for Hussey to treat and conclude the negotiations either at Lisbon, The Hague, or London,[45] and as a basis for such negotiations proposed a treaty made up of two parts. The public part provided for the restoration of the *status quo ante bellum* except for West Florida, and for the imposition of restrictions on British establishments on Campeche and Honduras. The secret part provided for the cession to Spain of Gibraltar and Minorca, with Oran and Mers-el-Kebir on the Barbary Coast offered to Britain as equivalents for the former. Another provision obliged George III "to concert with the colonies in terms which can leave them no just grounds for claiming or complaining against France on the score of the stipulations of the said alliance." From a marginal note to this crucial article in Floridablanca's own hand it would appear that he interpreted such a "concert" between Britain and her insurgent colonists as releasing the Franco-Spanish alliance from any "claim" upon it as regards recognition.

From Floridablanca's note to Hussey of March 5th it is clear that the Spaniard had in mind for the Americans the terms offered by the British commissioners in 1778, and disdainfully rejected by Congress. These terms amounted to a dominion status for America, but fell considerably short of independence. Perhaps such terms would have been satisfactory to the rebels in 1775, but three years later they offered too little and came too late. Again the Spanish Minister reminded the British that Mr. Jay was on his way to Madrid. Hurry before it is too late![46]

The English draft of the preliminary articles with Spain drawn up around this time shows that there never was a meeting of the minds on equivalents for ending the war. The British would have required the King of Spain to agree not to furnish men or supplies to the United States, to receive no agent from the rebels, nor engage in any trade with them. Spain might well have been willing to accept this, but in return all that England was prepared to yield was West Florida, and even that territory she proffered as an exchange for Puerto Rico. Nothing about Gibraltar.[47]

Had Hussey held the field all to himself, his task would have been sufficiently arduous, but there were other well-meaning meddlers who went back and forth across the Iberian peninsula and offered the Irish priest some healthy competition. Most voluble among these self-appointed emissaries was Commodore George Johnstone, who was conducting his own negotiations in Lisbon, where he commanded a British naval squadron on the Portuguese station. Only the previous year he had been one of the three Carlisle peace commissioners dispatched by Parliament to America, and had demonstrated little tact and worse judgment. On his return to England he was "violent against Congress."[48] Undaunted by his egregious failure as a peacemaker in America, he made a contact with Floridablanca in Lisbon through a Portuguese trader named Luis Cantofer. The former royal governor of West Florida, more recently a member of Parliament, confided to Cantofer that he had only lately conferred with Lord North, and that George III and the Prime Minister were prepared to come to a secret understanding with Spain. He made several sets of proposals, but they boiled down to two: for the neutrality of Spain, England was prepared to yield Gibraltar; for Spanish help in putting down the rebels, England was ready to cede Florida and the right to fish on the Grand Bank.[49]

Hussey sought frantically to have all the eggs put in the basket he was carrying, but his competitor was already offering bigger ones that the customer was prepared to buy. Unless North would promptly repudiate the big-talking Commodore, Hussey would be shoved off the stage.[50] Floridablanca jumped at Johnstone's bait, while managing to avoid the hook. In a counterproposal he suggested that Spain, in lieu of the fisheries, would be satisfied with West Florida, allow East Florida to be retained by England, while insisting that Spain's sovereignty over the Honduras be explicitly acknowledged.[51] Now, Floridablanca knew full well that Johnstone carried no official powers, even though he may have been prompted by Lord North to feel out the Spaniards. Hence, he made a profession of his good faith to his ally by passing on the proposals to the French, while preserving silence about his dealings with Hussey.[52] The King of Spain would not sell his neutrality and his obligations to his friends for "a pound of pears," Floridablanca grandiloquently proclaimed to the Spanish ambassador at Lisbon. Contrariwise, he was careful not to let the French court know that the conversations between Johnstone and his intermediaries were continued, off and on, until May,[53] giving one the distinct impression that he would not have hesitated to make the sale if the offer had been more substantial. In fact, Floridablanca chose to continue these talks despite a semiofficial disavowal of Johnstone by the British government through the Abbé Hussey as intermediary.[54]

The Commodore was not the last intruder into the Abbé Hussey's private preserve. In the middle of April, before the Irish priest returned from London, a Scotsman named Sir John Dalrymple paid a visit to Spain. He had already brought himself to the attention of the British Ministry by his naïve proposal to end the war with the American Patriots by offering Washington a dukedom.[55] A confidant of men in high places, Dalrymple represented himself as an intimate of Lord North, and carried a letter of introduction from Madame Necker, wife of France's Director General of Finances, but he was probably acting on his own initiative. In a long memorandum to Floridablanca he set forth his own proposals for a peace settlement. This would have involved a guarantee of the colonial territorial integrity of all parties and the common participation in colonial trade of all the four Atlantic powers—Great Britain, France, Portugal, and Spain. Dalrymple's document also spoke vaguely of a "Magna Carta to the liberties of America," an expression sufficiently vague to mask some kind of dependency status for the United States. This must be assumed, since Dalrymple was at great pains to point out the disadvantages to Spain were America to secure her independence. "Europe, wishing for the independence of America," Dalrymple's memorandum observed, "resembles a man asleep on ice and not sensible that ice thaws." Perhaps as a token of his naïveté, Dalrymple told Floridablanca that he was also sending a copy of his paper to the French as well as to Benjamin Franklin, whom he esteemed as "the first genius of the age." Again, since Floridablanca was extremely dubious of Dalrymple's powers, he made a point of sending a copy of the memorandum both to Jay and to Montmorin to show his good faith.[56] On its face Dalrymple's propositions were those of just another well-meaning meddler, and Montmorin reassured Jay that he had nothing to fear from that "garrulous scatterbrain." The Comte de Vergennes remained uneasy. To him there was something fishy about the whole business. Why should Dalrymple have been permitted to enter Spain in the first place? he asked.[57] Henceforth his suspicions of his Spanish ally were to mount rapidly.

As the curtain rises on act two Richard Cumberland is found holding the center of the stage. Although the playwright's only qualifications to assume so crucial a mission was his mental outlook, which was that of a Spanish grandee, and his self-evident need to earn the esteem of his superiors, he persuaded the plodding Secretary of the Southern Department, the Earl of Hillsborough, to give the mission his offical blessing. Hillsborough entrusted him with a letter to Floridablanca recommending the bearer and expressing George III's ardent longing for peace.[58] Along with the letter went very specific instructions. He was ordered to accompany the Abbé Hussey to Lisbon. This in itself was significant. Since Cumberland lacked any training as a diplomat and could not read Spanish, he was bound to be largely dependent on the services of the multilingual double agent. Cumberland was to wait at Lisbon while Hussey went ahead to Spain. If Hussey informed him that the Spaniards were prepared to negotiate without insisting on Gibraltar or Minorca, he could then enter the enemy nation and propose as a basis of reconciliation the Treaty of 1763 which terminated the last war. If Floridablanca seemed favorably disposed, Cumberland could get down to terms. The kind of terms Hillsborough had in mind involved the restoration of conquests on both sides in return for pledges from Spain that she would give neither money nor supplies to the rebellious colonists, have no correspondence with any agent of the insurgents, conduct no trade with the Americans, and be strictly neutral toward powers at war with England. This meant, of course, that Spain was invited to break with France.

Hillsborough expected a great deal of Spain, but the King's Minister was not prepared to pay too high a price in return. Specifically, Cumberland was instructed *not* to negotiate any terms of reconciliation between the mother country and the colonies or between England and France. Hillsborough was explicit that he was *not* authorized to negotiate the cession of Gibraltar or Minorca. After depriving Cumberland of virtually all the larger and juicier pears that Floridablanca might care to munch, Hillsborough also told him that he had no authority to agree to anything without first transmitting the proposition to London and that he was to keep his mission secret and discuss it with no one except His Majesty's Secretary for the Southern Department.[59]

Perhaps Cumberland felt that his black-robed companion could benefit by some indoctrination. He made a point of taking Hussey through the dockyard at Portsmouth before sailing and of showing him the vast supplies of stores which were hoarded there.[60] Regardless of which side Hussey might be on, he could not fail to be impressed by Britain's display of naval might. The voyage of Cumberland, his wife, two daughters, and the Abbé, aboard the British frigate *Milford* was marked by the customary delays due to adverse winds, by an encounter with a French privateer which became a British prize, and by eluding a Spanish squadron. The party reached Lisbon on May 18th. While Hussey, in accord with instructions, left at once for Aranjuez, the playwright utilized his time in Lisbon to be briefed by Johnstone on the progress of his negotiations, to escape the city's heat, first by catching some of the Atlantic breezes at the romantic resort of Cintra, whose Moorish palaces fascinated him, and then by moving himself and his family back aboard the *Milford,* at anchor in the Tagus off the ancient fortress of Belem.[61]

Hussey's report to Cumberland was as enigmatic as one would expect considering the fact that it was couched in language suggested by Florida-blanca. The priest advised the playwright to come to the Spanish court to give the negotiations a fair trial, as the Spanish Minister was "very desirous of finding means to bring things to a happy conclusion." By his servant Daly, who took the dispatches from Aranda to Lisbon, the Abbé sent an oral message: "All is well."[62] Not a word about Gibraltar.

If Cumberland had been searching for reasons to sail for home, he did not have to look very far. He had been expressly instructed not to enter Spain unless he had assurances in advance that the issue of Gibraltar would not be raised. He had been forewarned a fortnight before by a conversation Father Hussey had had with Fernán–Núñez, the Spanish ambassador to Lisbon, when he was arranging for his passport to enter Spain. The Spaniard asked the priest whether Floridablanca had proposed any equivalent for Gibraltar. When he answered none, the Conde, in Cumberland's words, "withdrew from the question with that sort of gesture, which seems to in-dicate a conviction of having touched a wrong string."[63] The playwright was perfectly aware that Hussey's failure to mention Gibraltar could be ominous. "Silence with you," he wrote the Irishman, "is never the result of inattention or forgetfulness; it is the silence of premeditation."[64] Fur-thermore, he was advised point-blank by Robert Walpole, the British Minister in Lisbon, not to continue his journey to Spain. But he was hardly the man to walk off stage before he had a chance to speak even his opening lines. He rationalized his impatience to go ahead by arguing that to decline Hussey's invitation would be to offend the Spanish court and ruin the priest's influence. Then, to reassure Hillsborough, he reminded the British Minister that he need not deliver his letter to Floridablanca until he was quite certain that Gibraltar would not be mentioned.[65]

Some rather disagreeable medicine awaited Cumberland at Aranjuez. Now that Jay was also at hand ready and eager to negotiate, Floridablanca told Hussey that he was becoming increasingly distrustful of Britain's delaying tactics. How could Cumberland expect Spain to abandon France and make a separate peace, he asked, especially since the Englishman's visit had been publicized both at Lisbon and Paris? But the Spaniard left the door ajar. He intimated that Spain was prepared to make a settlement with England without including the American colonies. Since France was adamant on this question, it would be necessary to find some "middle ground," some formula which would cut the ground from beneath the Thirteen States if they sought to hold France to her treaty obligation. Following the Spanish Minister's subtle reasoning, a settlement worked out between England and her colonies, by which the latter would remain dependent, would release France from her obligations to the Americans, since they had in fact discharged her of that obligation by their own action.

So far so good, but the tenacious Foreign Minister clung desperately to the Rock of Gibraltar. If that fortress could not be mentioned in the peace treaty, then it could be dealt with in a separate treaty covering reciprocal territorial guarantees by the two crowns in Europe and America. With all his deviousness Floridablanca managed to convey his message quite bluntly. If Spain got Gibraltar she would be willing to guarantee Britain's colonial possessions in America; without the Rock, she could "never become a true friend of England." Whether the Abbé Hussey gave Cumberland orally a doctored version of what Floridablanca had written down or whether the neophyte in the ways of diplomacy chose to grasp at straws, it was purest casuistry for him to write Hillsborough that Gibraltar would not be mentioned "either in the preliminaries or final treaty."[66] He omitted mentioning the vital fact that Floridablanca intended to settle that issue by a separate secret treaty. There was really no excuse for Cumberland to stay on any longer, but the fact that he was not more promptly repudiated suggests that his presence in Spain served some oblique purpose of the British Ministry.

With wife and two coquettish daughters Cumberland settled down in a spacious house in Madrid and fortified himself for protracted negotiations aimed at effecting a separate peace with Spain and at convincing Floridablanca that England's proposals for reunion with America were both fair and temperate.[67] But Spain's Foreign Minister was in no mood for haste, particularly when word came to Madrid late in June that dangerous rioting had broken out in London.[68] Not alone in Madrid, but in every European capital, diplomats wondered whether the North Ministry could survive the storm, and if the Opposition seized the helm, whether it would favor a quick end to the war. This might be an opportune moment, thought Charles III, to remind the British that the King of Spain would not be found wanting in his engagements to his nephew, Louis XVI.[69] Even before learning that the London riots had been put down,[70] news that Floridablanca had not been in any hurry to convey to the Englishman, Cumberland insisted to his superiors back in London that the moment for detaching Spain from her alliance with France was as propitious as ever. Charles III, he reported, was being badgered by his son, the slow-witted Ferdinand of Naples, and by the Queen of Portugal to make peace. He passed on the gossip that the King's own confessor had threatened to leave the court when he learned of the plan for attacking Gibraltar proposed by the Duc de Crillon, the French commander of a combined operation being readied to storm that fortress.[71] Now was the time to make a prompt overture to the colonies, which would impale France on the horns of a dilemma. The Spaniards had been frigid to Jay, Cumberland wrote home. The rebel diplomat had been kept at arm's length, and all the bills Congress had drawn on Spain had been sent back unpaid.[72]

The overt intimacy of the royal court with the British emissary and his family, in stark contrast to the distance the court kept between itself and Mr. Jay, was calculated to impress neutral diplomats that Spain was on the verge of making a deal with England.[73] This deception fitted Floridablanca's purposes, but it could not be pursued indefinitely. Floridablanca's delaying tactics made Cumberland more reckless. He now put down on paper some specific proposals, including an offer to let Floridablanca have his personal opinion on the possibility of an exchange of possessions, excepting, of course, Gibraltar and Minorca.[74] Both Germain and Hillsborough promptly reproved Cumberland for his presumption in submitting what the playwright had pompously styled "British overtures."[75] But the Ministry still did not order him home.

When it was clear to the Spanish Foreign Minister that Cumberland had no authority to yield Gibraltar, he used the playwright very much as he had used Jay. Each was encouraged to stay as long as possible. Cumberland's presence might cause Jay to moderate his demands. The threat which Jay posed might finally force the British to yield Gibraltar. Cumberland, a perennial optimist, chose to attribute the delay to what he called "the French junto," headed by José de Gálvez, and even had the presumption to suggest to his superiors that Britain reconsider her adamant stand on the disputed fortress. Gibraltar's value, he claimed, had been discredited by previous negotiators, most recently by Sir John Dalrymple, who had offered the Spaniards Gibraltar in exchange for the Canaries.[76] Cumberland did manage to elicit from Floridablanca a reaffirmation that Spain would never recognize the independence of the United States until England had done so, one promise, incidentally, which the Spaniard did keep; but word that Russia had offered to mediate the conflict disrupted the negotiations again, and gave Floridablanca the excuse to wait upon England's response to the

Czarina's proposals.[77] In point of fact no formal mediation offer was made by Russia until December, 1780, but the Spaniards did not choose to let Cumberland know that and preferred to keep him in a state of jitters. "Stupid Cumberland with his fantastic genius has become uneasy about the Russian business," sneered Bernardo del Campo, Floridablanca's English-speaking secretary, "thinking already his coming negotiation is about to expire."[78]

The playwright's dependence upon the priest became more total when in midsummer he fell off a mule and fractured his arm. The doctors argued for an hour over the proper treatment, but Cumberland had been in Spain long enough to know the reputation of Spanish physicians. Only a few days before his own accident the Conde de Ricla had died "of physicians, a distemper fatal in this country," Cumberland wrote Hillsborough.[79] His own physicians were perhaps less expert, since he survived their treatment.

By the end of August the negotiations had badly bogged down. It seemed transparent to everyone save Cumberland that George III was unbudgeable on both Gibraltar and the American colonies, and that more would be needed than a British willingness to accommodate Charles III in his punctilio respecting France.[80] Floridablanca now frowned upon further interviews which caused too much gossip, and urged Cumberland to put his propositions down on paper, assuring him that they would be considered "as conversations only."[81] But the playwright had been sternly forbidden to take up pen and ink. They had now reached an impasse. Floridablanca wanted to revive the Johnstone offer, but Cumberland had no pears that appealed to the Spanish Minister. Frantically Cumberland summoned Hussey to San Ildefonso to make a last effort to remind Floridablanca of his presumed commitment to refrain from demanding Gibraltar. The meeting was inconclusive, but just as it broke up Floridablanca warned the Abbé that the day Cumberland left Spain without settling matters he would "immediately treat with Mr. Jay and acknowledge him."[82]

It finally dawned on Cumberland that he had been tricked, but he put the blame for the failure of his mission not on his own bullheadedness, but on circumstances over which he had had no control, such as the June riots in London, the junction of the West India fleets, and the presence in Spain around that time of the French Admiral, Comte d'Estaing, who tried every argument to persuade the Spaniards to embark upon another joint naval operation.[83] One day Cumberland, his arm in a sling, encountered d'Estaing in the gardens at San Ildefonso. The Admiral's head was all bandaged up from a recent overturning of his coach. Our politics might differ, d'Estaing politely observed to the enemy agent, but "our persons agree in suffering the same mischance, both being maimed in the service."[84] While it was apparent to all that Cumberland's fall from the mule was easier to remedy than his fall from grace at the British court,[85] Hillsborough advised him to stay on, abiding strictly by instructions. Why he should be kept there after so egregious a blunder is a matter for speculation. John Adams' theories were about as sound as anybody's. Cumberland's "errand" the Yankee diplomat labeled as "a mere finesse of the British Ministry, intended to aid the stockjobbing, to keep up the stocks, aid the loans and canvass for an election, and lull the belligerent powers, while they prepare their measures for future enterprizes and another campaign."[86] Nobody has ever come up with a better explanation.

Meantime, as the plot thickened, Father Hussey was kept busy by his Spanish employers. He was now sent back to London, ostensibly to conclude an exchange of prisoners with England,[87] managing to continue the unusual arrangement of being paid by both sides for his various junkets between Spain, Portugal, and London.[88] He turned over to the British Minister a memorandum written for him once again by Floridablanca, revealing, if there could remain any further doubt, that Gibraltar and the "middle road"—some kind of dependency status for the United States to save France's honor—were the indispensable ingredients of a settlement. It was understood at the time Cumberland left London that both these points would be incorporated in a separate secret treaty, Floridablanca insisted.[89]

Floridablanca's ultimatum caused some kind of Cabinet crisis, if we are to trust French intelligence reports. Hillsborough was reputed to have proposed changing places with Lord Stormont, then Secretary of State for the Northern Department. In his new post Stormont would have the unpleasant duty of yielding Gibraltar. Stormont, so went the account, refused the dubious honor. The man who ceded Gibraltar would be pursued to the block by a vengeful multitude, Hillsborough declared, an eruption would take place, fomented by "our British Catalines," such as would "bury the sovereign, ourselves, and the constitution itself in its ruins."[90] Whatever really happened, it is clear that neither George III nor his Cabinet could, on the eve of the general election, consider so suicidal a step as to yield Gibraltar, and the King himself could not be persuaded to have a third power tell him how to deal with his rebellious subjects. A Cabinet meeting of October 19th decided that no further steps be taken in "this business for some time."[91]

On his return trip Hussey came no nearer to Floridablanca than Lisbon. The Spanish Minister was so dissatisfied with the results of the mission that he refused to allow the Abbé to bring his report to Madrid in person.[92]

Nevertheless, since Hussey had initiated the mission, it was only fitting that he should be the cause of bringing it to a close. Floridablanca made a last plea for Gibraltar through a separate secret treaty, and guaranteed that there would be no difficulty in handling France, since both Spain's ally and the American rebels were disenchanted with their alliance, he insisted.[93] Once more Hussey was sent back by his Spanish masters, but Cumberland, regarding this final trip as "in great part a finesse," washed his hands of the whole business.[94] Hussey's delivery of Floridablanca's ultimatum forced the British government to call a halt. In February, 1781, Hillsborough ordered Cumberland to pack his bags and come home.[95]

In Spain Cumberland may have been a dismal failure as a diplomat, but he and his family achieved a resounding social success. While Mrs. Cumberland and her two stunning daughters enjoyed the highest society, and the girls broke hearts right and left, if we are to believe the playwright's own account,[96] he himself was hobnobbing with royalty, collecting Andalusian marble, and viewing the art treasures of Spain. One day while strolling through the gloomy monastery of El Escorial, he chanced upon the King in his private bedchamber. He noted the humble state in which that absolute monarch chose to live, his starkly furnished apartment, his narrow camp bed covered with faded crimson damask, and no other furnishings but a table holding crucifix and prayer book, and a religious subject by Titian on the wall. Like his person, he found Charles III's dress "plain and homely." For the chase he wore a buff leather waistcoat and breeches and old-fashioned Pall Mall-made boots. His drab coat was covered with snuff and dust, and upon his head was set "a bad wig and worse hat." But this simple king graciously received his visitor, and recognized his consuming interest in the arts. At the Escorial Cumberland was permitted to roam at will through the picture galleries, feasting his eyes on the Raphaels, Titians, Rubenses, and Velásquezes, and he was invited to prepare a catalogue of the paintings at the Royal Palace at Madrid. With royal permission Cumberland later issued this as a two-volume compilation entitled *Anecdotes of Eminent Painters of Spain*.

In cruel contrast to Jay's shabby neglect by the court, Cumberland was taken up by royalty and grandees alike, and was the recipient of princely gifts from Charles III. To "the secret and untitled agent of a court at war with Spain," as Cumberland denominated himself, the King turned over as a gift for George III two horses of the royal stud, which the playwright himself rode until he had them delivered to His Majesty's grooms at the Royal Mews in London. To top it all, on the fourth of June, while the Cumberlands were celebrating the birthday of George III, they were serenaded by a company of regimental musicians, and Cumberland expressed unrestrained pleasure at hearing "those who were in arms against my country unite in celebrating the return of that day which gave this monarch birth."[97]

Cumberland returned to his native land, in his own words, "bankrupt, broken-hearted, and scarce alive." He melodramatized his alleged mistreatment in Spain and even had the effrontery to claim that "the American agent and Carmichael were caressed by the Court."[98] Repudiated by the Ministry for having exceeded his instructions, Cumberland was never reimbursed by the government for the major part of the expenses of his mission.[99] "I wearied the door of Lord North till his very servants drove me from it." The bankrupt playwright was forced to sell the estate jointured on his wife by marriage, and out of the entire experience salvaged a mere £500 from the publication of his *Memoirs*. To crown his humiliation, he lost his sinecure in the Board of Trade when the North Ministry was toppled and Edmund Burke's reform bill was enacted. An embittered man, he put London behind him and took up an establishment at Tunbridge Wells, where for years he entertained the great and near-great.[100]

Despite his deplorable lapses as a diplomat, his poor judgment, and that inordinate vanity which proved his undoing, Cumberland deserved better of his government than he received. He served a purpose, else Hillsborough would have recalled him long before he did. His very presence in Spain had held up aid to America and jeopardized the Family Compact.[101] This was, perhaps, sufficient accomplishment for any man, certainly for one whose outward charm concealed an extreme shallowness of intellect and an inflated self-esteem.

The playwright was bitterly critical of both Floridablanca's duplicity and the inflexibility of his own government over Gibraltar. "They wanted me to talk Gibraltar, and I was not permitted to hear it named; the most nugatory article would have satisfied them."[102] How he felt about the Abbé Hussey will perhaps never be known, but after the war was over Cumberland wrote a comedy called *The Walloons*.[103] One of the principal characters was a treacherous Irish priest named Father Sullivan, in the pay of France and involved in a plot to burn the British shipyards. The father confessor double-crosses both his patroness and his confederate in espionage. In the nick of time the familiar frigate *Milford* arrives with a Spanish prize full of officers, captured off Cádiz. Though Cumberland disavowed any intention of portraying Hussey, the Irish priest recognized himself in the person of Sullivan.[104] And so did many others. Cumberland had paid off an old score through the medium with which he was most familiar.

Cumberland's stay in Portugal and Spain paid other literary dividends. The playwright appears to have made contacts with numerous Marranos, or crypto-Jews, and their tragic experiences left a lasting impression upon him. Henceforth, instead of depicting in his plays the typical stage Jew of that time, the rogue, usurer, and buffoon that we find in the comedies of his more talented contemporary, Richard Brinsley Sheridan, Cumberland chose to portray him in more sympathetic and charitable vein. In *Nicholas Pedrosa*, *The Jew*, and *The Jew of Magadore*, three plays of the postwar period, Cumberland made a plea for religious toleration which placed him abreast of the more advanced currents of his day.[105]

Father Hussey found it difficult to disentangle himself from his offices of double agent. For a time he was back in London resuming his services as a spy for his Spanish masters.[106] Then he disappeared on the Continent. His trail was picked up once more when he acted as a tutor to a wealthy young expatriate Englishman of the Catholic persuasion.[107] Next he turned up in Turin, where he had numerous conversations with Lord Mountstuart, the British ambassador who was to court rebuke trying to end the war singlehandedly.[108] For a time Hussey resumed his post at the Spanish Embassy in London, but he later renounced foreign affairs to assume religious duties, first as rector of the new Catholic College of Maynooth in Ireland, and shortly thereafter as Bishop of Waterford and Lismore.

By its protracted and not-so-secret negotiations with the Abbé and the playwright the Spanish court had committed a calculated affront to the American minister plenipotentiary and placed a severe strain on the Family Compact. The American diplomats abroad made the discovery that traditional diplomatic dealings involved finesse, duplicity, and concealment. Although Congress might continue to express blind trust in France's selfless benevolence toward America, it was patent to clear-headed John Adams that no power, "not even Spain nor France, wishes to see America rise very fast to power." Since that was the case, "we ought, therefore, to be cautious how we magnify our ideas and exaggerate our expressions of the generosity and magnanimity of this power," he cautioned.[109] Interest alone determined foreign policy in Europe, Adams observed to an aide of Vergennes,[110] and he reminded the experienced Franklin that European diplomats seriously attended to no argument save force.[111]

Jay's frigid reception at the Spanish court could not fail to affect him, as it did John Adams, who was having his own difficulties in Paris. "There is something in the European understanding different from those we have been used to," Adams remarked. Men like Floridablanca, "of the greatest abilities, and the most experience, are with great difficulty brought to see, what appears to us, as clear as day. It is habit, it is education, prejudice, what you will, but so it is."[112] A note of realism now strongly tinctured Jay's own thinking. Resolved not to appear at court as a suppliant, he was becoming acutely sensitive to the equivocal position that France was henceforth likely to be forced to play in her dealings with her two allies. Reading between the lines of Jay's letters penned during those black months of the Hussey-Cumberland negotiations, it is not difficult to see how he really felt. In early September, 1780, he told Franklin: "Our affairs here go on heavily." As regards financial aid: "The fact is there is little corn in Egypt, this *entre nous.*" Cumberland is "here still," Jay reminded his Paris correspondent. "I am told we have nothing to fear," he added. "It may be so, but my faith is seldom very extensive. If we have nothing else to fear we have always danger to apprehend from such a spy—so situated, so surrounded by inquisitive, communicative, and some say friendly Irishmen. In short, I wish you could hear me think."[113] His thoughts were not always happy ones. That an unofficial agent of an enemy nation could secure in wartime so many marks of personal attention did not escape the observation of John Jay, to whom both court and grandees had turned the cold shoulder. That fall Jay wrote Franklin of his indebtedness to the "politeness" of the Neapolitan diplomat, Prince Masserano, for "except at his table" he had "eaten no Spanish bread" that he had not paid for since his arrival in Madrid.[114]

The alert but tense Vergennes was enormously provoked by Spain's private peace. By turns he was frightened, infuriated, embittered, but always deeply suspicious.[115] How weak the ties were that bound Spain to France was all too painfully disclosed by the negotiations between Floridablanca and Cumberland.[116] One result of this disclosure was to make Vergennes revamp his diplomacy toward the Thirteen United States. Henceforth, he no longer came forward as a champion of American territorial claims which conflicted with those of Spain, but instead sought for a formula to settle the war on the basis of some kind of quasi or *de facto* independence for America, a formula which would satisfy Spain and preserve the honor of Louis XVI. Henceforth, too, Vergennes never trusted his ally south of the Pyrenees and devoted enormous energy and considerable expense to uncovering the documents which would prove the extent of Floridablanca's double-dealing.

IV

EIGHT DAYS IN JUNE

(June 2-9, 1780)

IT HAD BEEN BREWING for a long time. The closing days of '79 portended
an eruption, although when it came everyone was caught by surprise. A
sense of crisis gripped the nation, and everywhere there was unrest.[1] In
the shires country gentlemen called for a free Parliament. In stately
mansions on Berkeley and Grosvenor Squares noble lords decried the influence of the Closet. The halls of Westminster resounded to shouts of
treason.[2] In filthy courts and alleys off the Strand, in squalid tenements in
Chick Lane and Black Boy Alley, and in countless dramshops in St. Giles's,
journeymen and apprentices, pickpockets and pimps, spread rumors of a
conspiracy among the Popish powers to enslave England and establish an
inquisition in London. Starving Dublin crowds, muttering against trade
restrictions, besieged the Irish Parliament for relief, and throughout Ireland burgeoning companies of armed volunteers, originally formed to
thwart the Franco-Spanish invasion threat, now posed a sinister challenge
to British authority.

One thing was clear. The present Ministry had to go. That Ministry
which had driven America to revolt, treated Ireland with cruel neglect, and
conducted an unpopular war with scandalous incompetence had reached the
end of its rope. With this conclusion no one would have agreed more
heartily than the witty and urbane Frederick North, who as First Lord of
the Treasury headed that Ministry and now seemed neither witty nor
urbane. Nerves frayed, mood despondent, North was gripped by a curious
paralysis which had restricted his decisions during the invasion threat earlier
that summer.[3] Superbly resourceful when confronting his opponents on the
floor of the House of Commons, Lord North felt pitifully inadequate in

dealing with the rising hostility within his own Cabinet. And that Cabinet showed signs of falling apart. Soon Lord Gower quit as President of the Council, shortly to be followed by Lord Weymouth as Foreign Secretary.[4] Attorney General Alexander Wedderburn, a name proverbial for cupidity and meanness, made it clear that he would be only too happy to follow his former colleagues just as soon as North kept his promise to promote him to the Chief Justiceship of Common Pleas and elevate him to the peerage. Meantime, he was not even on speaking terms with his chief.[5]

"I am in a fever with my situation," North wrote early in November. "I have been kept in it by force. If the house falls about my ears, I cannot help it. All I can do is not to quit a falling house and to use every means in my power to sustain it as long as possible."[6] On the eve of the opening of Parliament North, realizing that he could not keep the lid on the incompetence and scandals of his administration which an inquiry would be sure to expose, turned once more in desperation to his friend and sponsor. "I have been miserable for ten years in obedience to Your Majesty's commands," he wrote George III, pointing out that it was "impossible to bear misery and guilt at the same time."[7] Charles Jenkinson, the Secretary at War, described North's tormented condition "as nothing permanent, but as a disease of the mind, which goes and comes; and which, as long as it lasts, is very unpleasant to those who have anything to do with him."[8] The Chancellor was less kind about the First Minister. "Damn him!" Thurlow exploded. "Nothing can goad him forward. He is the very clog that loads everything."[9]

The man who had an unstable prime minister on his hands in a period of national crisis was hardly a model of mental stability himself. George III, had he lived today, would be the perfect sitting duck for the amateur psychoanalyst. A manic depressive, rigid, moralistic, and censorious, he appeared to casual acquaintances to be equable and reserved, whereas his intimates knew him to be hot-tempered, tense, and loquacious, to bear grudges, and to make a virtue of obstinacy. His close attention to his duties was admirable if obsessive, but his minute, almost hourly, instructions to his ministers made him often appear as a downright meddler.

In the early years of his reign George III seemed to rebound from his bitter disappointment at not being permitted to marry the Duke of Richmond's sister, Lady Sarah Lennox, one of the most renowned beauties in England. George had been madly in love with her, but his adviser, Lord Bute, in league with his mother, the dowager Princess Augusta, blocked the match. Dutifully he wed the prim, unattractive Princess Charlotte of Mecklenburg-Strelitz, who, with patient resignation, presented him with nine sons and six daughters, but his severe repressions bubbled to the surface when he went insane in 1788. He used foul and indecent language and had to be kept away by force from the ladies of the court.

George III was a tyrannical parent. His discipline permanently alienated most of his sons. Inspired by the scapegrace Prince of Wales, their careers were noteworthy, chiefly as rebellions against their father. Their scandalous behavior shocked the aging monarch and disgraced the House of Hanover. George was hardly more successful with his daughters. He forbade them to marry before they reached the advanced age of thirty, and one or another was afflicted with hysteria, melancholia, epilepsy, and other illnesses.

Although the rotund and ruddy-faced monarch was always teetering on the brink of a mental breakdown, he functioned smoothly and efficiently enough during the crisis of '79-'80. Indeed, there was something admirable about George III's courage and undaunted optimism, qualities worthy of John Bull himself. Ignoring the timid whiners by whom he was surrounded, the King managed to save Lord North when the latter proved incapable of saving himself.

Now, with the opposition mounting and the Cabinet falling apart, the King turned in desperation to Edward Thurlow, his Lord Chancellor, to try to form some kind of coalition government, if necessary without North.[10] George was prepared to let bygones be bygones provided "it be understood that every means are to be employed to keep the Empire entire, to prosecute the present and unprovoked war in all its branches, no blame to be laid on any past measures."[11] The beetle-browed, bitter-tongued lawyer, who was not on the best of terms with North,[12] made approaches to the Rockinghamites, who insisted on independence for America, and then to Shelburne. The latter, while making it clear that he "did not pretend to be a director of opposition," voiced the view that "the more connection that could be preserved with America the better," but failed to spell out that connection.[13]

From the "cold disdain" with which the King's proffer was treated by the Opposition, it finally dawned upon His Majesty that "nothing less will satisfy them than a total change of measures and men." To abandon all his friends and admit the Opposition "without any terms" constituted bitter medicine that the King was not prepared to swallow.[14] As a result, Thurlow's negotiations collapsed. The King then felt he had no alternative but to retain North and to try to bolster his First Minister's flickering determination to put through the Irish propositions and to rouse him from his despondency by holding out the roseate view that "America is nearer coming into temper to treat than perhaps at any period," and that the timely reinforcement of Gibraltar will make the King of Spain "more willing to end the war."[15]

With Parliament again in session and the Opposition already making political capital of the Irish situation, North simply had to act. Not only the Opposition, but responsible figures within the administration were insisting that Ireland's grievances be redressed. There happened, for a change, to be a lord lieutenant of Ireland who was sympathetic to that nation's needs and acutely sensitive to her rebellious mood. North would have ignored the Earl of Buckinghamshire if he could, but there was John Robinson, Treasury Secretary and one of the most trusted of the King's friends, who was writing: "For God's sake, let something be done [about Ireland] soon or it will be lost, if French money, French emissarys and French supplies of arms and ammunition have time to get there."[16] Goaded into action at long last, the slothful Cabinet, meeting at Lord North's on December 5th, authorized him to propose a trade relief bill for Ireland.[17]

This decision was arrived at only after the heaviest guns of the Opposition had already been turned on the King and his government at the very first session of Parliament on November 25th, within minutes of the King's address. In the House of Lords Richmond, as expected, ripped into the government for its lamentable defense posture the previous summer.[18] Shelburne in the Lords, and Charles James Fox in Commons, demanded a vote of censure over Ireland.[19] Hitting on a different front, Burke gave notice that after the Christmas recess he would present a plan for reducing royal expenditures, and bringing an end to that "enormous prodigality," which was "a force of most positive evil."[20]

"What has become of the American war?" Charles James Fox asked in Commons, a question which was reiterated in the Lords by Townshend and the pro-American Earl of Effingham, who on the eve of the war had resigned his commission in the army rather than draw his sword against the Americans.[21] And David Hartley, who was wont to spell out his advanced notions of imperial relations at intolerable length, charged that North had pulled the rug from under him when he was negotiating some time before with Benjamin Franklin. Edmund Burke then observed that the kind of ministers George III had picked to run and ruin the American War reminded him of a remark of Charles II in regard to Louis XIV. Since he had "to be gratified in that way," Charles pointed out, "the French monarch's ministers selected the oldest and plainest women they could find, in order to correct, if not totally subdue, the lusts of the flesh." As a political simile, the Irish-born Commoner found it perfectly applicable to

George III. The long and short of it was, as Lord Townshend saw it, "America was lost."

That so many things had gone wrong was no accident. As the Marquess of Rockingham put it on the opening day of Parliament, the recent decline of England's fortunes was "owing to a baleful and pernicious system" and "originated in unconstitutional controul and advice." It was this system that "must be done away." Speaker after speaker attacked the "pernicious system." What was needed, said Shelburne, were "new councils and new counsellors," and a return to the system of responsible ministers. The King, he charged, and his words were echoed in the Commons the very same day by Thomas Townshend, was "his own general," "his own secretary," "his own first commissioner of the admiralty," and he proceeded to call the roll of offices that His Majesty pre-empted. To Shelburne the whole idea was "most preposterous," and the very language "totally unknown to the constitution." What the present administration had degenerated into was "a system planned in secret device and supported by corruption."

Shelburne's accusations of unconstitutional usurpation and "corrupt and fatal influence" were reiterated by the Dukes of Grafton and Manchester in the Lords, where Rockingham and Richmond joined in the attack on "the secret influence" which directed the government. Rockingham charged the King with coming into office with "a fixed determination to govern this country under the forms of law through the influence of the Crown." No sooner had he perceived this "than he set his face against it." Expounding what became the classic Whig interpretation of eighteenth-century English history, the Marquess insisted that "this traitorous principle" had caused the American War, while the swollen civil list had augmented that pervasive influence. On the floor of Commons Fox belabored the monarchy with somewhat more than his customary blend of rhetorical extravagance and pointed barbs, attributing to the "enlarged influence" of the Crown "all our misfortunes."[22]

Despite its brilliant pyrotechnics the massive attack sputtered to a temporary halt as each of the motions of censure went down in turn to defeat, and Parliament proceeded to pass Lord North's trade reform bill for Ireland.[23] It is perhaps significant of the bitter temper of the Opposition that its partisans were less than joyous over the passage of this measure, certainly not as complacent about the remedy as were the patriots in Ireland.[24] However, if the movement for change and reform seemed to bog down in Parliament, it was sweeping the countryside.

The apostle of the shires was a dissenting Anglican clergyman named the

Rev. Christopher Wyvill, who was among the leading gentry of York-shire's North Riding. Imbued with reformist zeal, although perhaps not quite so extreme as Dr. John Jebb of Westminster and other London radicals, Wyvill linked the public economy with the reduction of the Crown's influence in Parliament. He also advocated shortening the duration of Parliament, even annual Parliaments. Paying lip service to the universal suffrage which the more extreme radicals were advocating, he really wanted the franchise limited to men of property.

The extensive publicizing of Wyvill's views toward the end of '79 spurred Shelburne and Burke to advance their fiscal and other reforms in the public economy. Even Rockingham, a conventionally minded Whig conservative, with little sympathy for the broad spectrum of reforms that Wyvill supported, was a shrewd enough politician to try to exploit so popular a movement within his own country. With a number of adherents the Marquess attended the Yorkshire freeholders' meeting called by Wyvill for December 30th. A Westminster meeting held under Jebb's auspices, and favored by the presence of Charles James Fox, who from a notorious roué was becoming the darling of the masses, took up the cry of Yorkshire. Jebb's radical group even went so far as to propose a constitutional repre-sentative body superior to Parliament, which might supersede that body should Parliament fail in its trust, and Wyvill was prepared to set up such an extra-Parliamentary organization.[25]

As the new year began, pressure on Parliament mounted. Wyvill arrived in London on February 2nd, and six days later Sir George Savile, a Rock-ingham adherent and friend of America, presented to the Commons the petition that the Yorkshire freeholders had adopted toward the close of '79. Bearing the signatures of upwards of eight thousand freeholders of that county, the petition asserted that sinecures, exorbitant emoluments, and unmerited pensions contributed substantially to the acquisition by the Crown of its "great and unconstitutional influence, which, if not checked, may soon prove fatal to the liberties of this country."[26]

The Yorkshire proposals were but a start. Propositions were now raining down from the counties which anticipated by a half century the Reform Bill of 1832. This was a good deal more than the Whig leaders had bar-gained for, and they were more than ever determined to keep the checkreins in their own hands. Behind the scenes Rockingham worked feverishly.[27] Even Shelburne, who was acutely sensitive to the differences between the various Whig factions over such issues as American independence and Parliamentary reform,[28] and whose intimate contact with leading radical intellectuals had brought him more abreast of the advanced currents of his day than Rockingham, was prepared to keep the pot from boiling over. Along with Richmond and Rockingham, the Earl agreed to a memorandum, dated March 19, 1780, urging that the question of shortening the duration of Parliament and altering its representation be not included by the counties in their articles of association, although hope was held out for shorter Parliamentary terms and for adding more independent members.[29]

It was Fox who set the stage for Burke's formidable campaign by throwing down the challenge: "Come now, let us see whose child Corruption is!"[30] Three days later Burke introduced his Establishment Bill with one of the most scintillating and informed speeches of his career.[31] To the chagrin of Wyvill and his following, the Irish-born orator failed to press for the abolition of sinecures and unmerited pensions. To propitiate the reformers, Savile then moved for a list of all pensions, but that motion was lost, and, when renewed on February 21st, was in substance defeated by an amendment moved by that adroit tactician, Lord North.[32] While not so drastic as the radicals had hoped for, Burke's bill did provide for a "temperate" and "prudent" reform of the civil list, for across-the-board economies, and the payment of salaries in certain key offices whose holders had hitherto been paid by fees and commissions.

The fireworks were set off by Richard Rigby. The bluff and arrogant Paymaster of the Forces, who enjoyed an enormous income as long as the war lasted, and who was reputed to voice the innermost thoughts of the King himself, had the presumption to assert that Parliament had no right to control the King's civil list.[33] Fox, whose revolutionary fervor was crescendoing to a climax, retorted that Rigby's maxim would mean " a dissolution of the government as modelled at the Revolution" and "an end of the liberty of this country." In such event, "a rebellion, and nothing but a rebellion, could possibly save the Constitution."[34]

Again North's tactics triumphed over public opinion. Piece by piece Burke's recommendations were taken up. The proposal to drop the third secretary of state, or the American Secretary, a post filled by the detested Lord Germain, was defeated by a mere seven votes.[35] On the other hand, Burke's witty denunciation of the Board of Trade as "a crow's nest, in which nightingales were kept prisoners," was endorsed by the House by 207 votes to 199. The result was amazing. It was as though the government had accepted the contention of the Opposition that the American colonies were lost beyond recovery, and that there was no further need for a board to administer their affairs. This was to prove Burke's only victory, for his crucial proposal to regulate the King's household in the interest of economy was snowed under by 211 votes to 158. Thoroughly worn down by his exhausting efforts, Burke now declared "his indifference to what became of the rest of the Bill." "It now lies with the nation at large," Burke wrote to one of his Bristol constituents, "whether it is to be received again."[36]

"The nation at large" kept showering Parliament with petitions. On the sixth of April an ugly and ungainly figure rose to address the House of Commons. The witty barrister John Dunning, a Shelburne follower from Wiltshire who now spoke with Rockingham's blessing,[37] called attention to "that pile of parchment now on your table." The last occasion on which so many petitions of this sort had been offered to the House was just 140 years ago, ex-Governor Pownall had pointed out, and the year, ominously, was 1640. In a voice harsh and guttural, but clearly heard throughout the House, Dunning read his first resolution: "That it is the opinion of this committee *that the influence of the Crown has increased, is increasing, and ought to be diminished.*" This resolution epitomized the chief tenor of all the county petitions, beginning with that of Yorkshire. Dunning now charged that "many men" in that very House were "corrupted" and actually paid in "hard, sordid, dirty guineas."

Now at last the attack on the monarchy was out in the open, and the government was stunned. Its spokesman was strangely unconvincing in defense of the throne, even slipping into damaging admissions concerning the Crown's influence. North lost his temper, something that rarely happened to him, and his countercharges that the Opposition planned to ruin the Constitution caused a tumult in the House.[38] With the Ministry in retreat and disorder, the Dunning resolution carried by 233 votes to 215, the margin of victory being attributed to the independent country members who switched to the Opposition side on this question.

"The 6th of April ought forever to be a red-lettered day," Horace Walpole wrote the Rev. William Mason, one of Wyvill's stalwart supporters.[39] While Whigs rejoiced, North felt the end had come. Once more he besought the King for permission to resign. George III, a man not easily stampeded, sought to reassure his Prime Minister that the resolutions were not personal to him. "I wish I did not feel at whom they are personally levelled," the King wryly confessed.[40] George's dogged determination to fight it out staved off a rout, for, save for a few minor resolutions whose adoption Dunning secured, the man who had struck the greatest blow at the influence of the Crown since 1641 failed to win any further victories.[41] When the Contractor's Bill proposed by Shelburne was defeated in the Lords, its sponsor warned that the people without doors were "ripe for any violence" and might be readily led to adopt such measures "as would shake the kingdom to its center." Perhaps Shelburne would rue these very words before long. Despite the bitterness and frustration of the chief advocates of reform, it was clear that the movement had now run its course, not only in Parliament but in the counties as well. Even Wyvill, reacting to the lack of ardor which the Rockinghamites had shown for thoroughgoing reform, felt the need to caution the people to take care not to "disgust and alienate that respectable body which holds the balance between the Crown and the People."[42] Not so the Westminster radicals, however. Spurred on by Fox,[43] they still talked loosely about "recurring to the first principles of our constitution," and urged not only annual parliaments and equal representation, but claimed universal manhood suffrage as a "transcendent right."[44] Country gentlemen and London radicals might make futile efforts to pressure Parliament into doing something about constitutional rights, but it remained for mobs, using the weapon of direct action, to impress the government with the language of ugly force.

Meantime, it was clear that three of the Opposition leaders, had, by the acerbity of their criticisms of the government and their avowed sympathy with Irish protest and county reformers, marked themselves out for especial enmity. Whether it was the result of conspiratorial action or merely a series of isolated and fortuitous cases, Fox, Richmond, and Shelburne were each singled out for destruction, either of their persons or their reputations.

First it was Fox's turn. One of the passing targets of that orator's vitriol was a warm if recent supporter of the Minister named William Adam, nephew of the eminent architect Robert Adam, whose designs had already reshaped to classic lines parts of London, Bath, and Edinburgh. Back in November, 1779, Adam announced his intention to desert the minority and support the Cabinet, and Fox chose now to depict him as a monster of depravity. A duel followed in Hyde Park. A massive target, Fox was slightly wounded. "I should infallibly have been killed," contemporary gossip had Fox remark, "if Mr. Adam had not been using government powder."[45]

Next Richmond, Fox's uncle, was singled out. "If there were two Dukes of Richmond in this country I would not live in it," one of the King's intimates remarked.[46] The Duke, who was considerably to the left of Wyvill,[47] had fanned long-smoldering resentments and suspicions by his uncooperative behavior during the invasion crisis of the previous summer. When the King had tried to remove him from his lieutenancy of Sussex, he could not find a lord in the whole country who would accept the post.[48] Now the pensioned scribes of the Ministry darkly insinuated that Richmond, whose great-grandmother, Louise de Keroualle, Duchess of Portsmouth and Aubigny, had been a paramour of Charles II (giving the Duke a title in French as well as English nobility),[49] was engaged in treasonable relations with the enemy. The author of this venomous attack was the Rev. Henry Bates, editor of London's *Morning Post*, an Anglican clergyman and insufferable bully, who, as Trevelyan once remarked, was a duelist or pugilist according to the social rank of his antagonist. Richmond brought a criminal prosecution against Bates, whom a tough-minded jury found guilty of criminal libel. The offender was committed to prison for a term of twelve months.[50]

Before the Bates case had come to trial, a third leader of the Opposition appears to have been marked down for liquidation. During the debates on the eighth of March Lord Shelburne had disparaged the Ministry's recent innovation of awarding military rank disproportionate to their service to persons of no military experience who had raised battalions from among their own tenantry. He then slurringly referred to William Fullarton, an Ayreshire landed proprietor presently sitting in the House of Commons, whom North had recently made a lieutenant colonel. Fullarton, by denouncing Shelburne in the press, forced the latter to challenge him to a duel. In the Hyde Park encounter two shots were fired, Fullarton's second, fired from the same pistol Adam had used to shoot Fox, wounding Shelburne in the groin, the identical spot where Fox had been shot. "Adam and Fullarton had tried not only to cutt off them, but their posterity," Sir George Savile sallied.[51] The duel made Shelburne a hero to the whole Whig Opposition,[52] and raised serious questions not only as to whether this was part of a plot to shoot down the Opposition leaders one by one, but was also calculated to curtail free debate in Parliament.[53]

Into the simmering political caldron a new and malevolent ingredient was now tossed. It was nothing less than the poisoned entrails of religious bigotry. The brewmaster who brought the pot to a bubble was an eccentric Scottish lord named George Gordon. Whether in debate on the floor of the Commons or in private lectures to which he would from time to time subject George III, Gordon was widely regarded to be as mad as a March hare. And "so all his family have been too," Walpole bitingly observed. Rejoicing that Gordon was a Scot, Walpole asked whether one would "deny them the benefit of the Union and monopolize lunacy to ourselves."[54]

The "Lilburne of the Scottish Presbyterians" came from a family of Scottish nobility celebrated for their eccentricity, and through his blood hot and rebellious liquor coursed. A younger son, born in Upper Grosvenor Street in 1751, Gordon was reared in Scotland on the vast estates of his family. After Eton he served a long stint in the navy, where he made himself something of a nuisance by his insufferable complaints to his superiors, and was kept at the rank of lieutenant for ten years. In the manner of the time he was bought a seat in Parliament, the pocket borough of Luggershall in Wiltshire, and he entered the Commons in 1774. There the lank, humorless figure, clad in somber Puritan black, long hair falling down to his shoulders, quickly attracted attention by his extreme attacks on the "mad, cruel, and accursed American war." While in the navy, he had visited the American colonies and returned infatuated with the country and its people. Gordon soon gained something of a reputation as a lone wolf, claiming to belong to no faction but to the "party of the people." Perhaps to underscore this point, he unaccountably attacked Burke's reform bill and was alone in the division against bringing it in.[55] There were now, according to coffeehouse wits, three parties in Parliament—"the Ministry, the Opposition, and Lord George Gordon." Unfortunately his egotism and preposterous self-confidence, his grotesque sarcasm and downright rudeness, concealed a considerable measure of idealism and a degree of incorruptibility unusual for the day and age. As Shelburne once observed, it seemed regrettable that with all this fine fury and good intentions, Lord George Gordon, from whose mouth poured forth an unchecked cataract of words, should really have nothing to say.

Even before Lord George fanned the conflagration which almost consumed London, people had begun to talk about him. Gordon had quarreled with the Church and had called the Archbishop of Canterbury a whore. This prompted Mrs. Montagu to remark, having in mind Gordon's indiscriminate passion for the opposite sex, that if Lord George had called the Archbishop the Whore of Babylon "then it was very uncivil as it is the only whore his Lordship dislikes."[56]

The events that plummeted Lord Gordon to the center of the arena stemmed from well-intentioned, if hardly disinterested, legislation enacted by Parliament. Back in 1778, the North Ministry proposed to ease the harsh anti-Catholic laws long on the books. These proposals had the double purpose of enlisting English Catholics in the war effort and counteracting an anticipated exodus of farm tenants which was feared might result from the thousands of handbills distributed in Ireland at the instigation of the American Catholic Patriot, Charles Carroll, and containing an offer by the American Congress of land grants and full toleration to such Irishmen as ventured to come to America. Since the important Whig personages in Parliament saw everything to gain by keeping their tenants on their vast holdings in Ireland, North counted on little opposition. In fact, he turned to one of these Whig holders of Irish lands, the liberal-minded Sir George Savile, and had him sponsor the bill in Commons. The Savile Act,[57] which was carried without division in both houses, was a moderate measure relieving Catholics of disability with regard to property, allowing them to worship in their own way, but requiring them to take the oaths of allegiance and supremacy in such manner as would deny the temporal power of the Pope and abjure the Stuart Pretender. The act applied only to England.

Despite its moderation, the new law infuriated Dissenters and Presbyterians alike. John Wesley, towering over all dissenting ministers, exhorted by sermon and tract that "no government, not Roman Catholic, ought to tolerate men of the Roman Catholic persuasion." It was soon intimated that a similar measure applying to Scotland would be introduced in Parliament the following session. Almost immediately Protestant associations sprang up from Berwick to John o' Groat's, and, in January and early February of 1779, riots broke out all over Scotland. At Edinburgh and Glasgow Catholic residences were pillaged, chapels and mass houses burnt down.[58]

At this psychological moment a leader appeared to organize and coalesce this inchoate movement. It was none other than Lord George Gordon. To his revolutionary ardor he brought the crusading zeal of intense, obsessive anti-Catholicism and a copious supply of Scottish national feeling. When the movement spread south of the Tweed, it was only natural that Gordon should be looked to for direction. Soon, as President of the Protestant Association of England, he besieged King and Parliament, while his associates stirred up the fears and passions of the masses by a torrent of lurid and hatemongering broadsides. Gordon saw to it that a petition to Parliament was drawn up, and when Lord North declined to present it, warned that before long he himself would introduce the petition, "which will extend, Sir, from your chair to a window of Whitehall that Kings should often think of." This remark came close to treason. Having gone so far, Lord George could scarcely backtrack. At a meeting held on May 29th at the Coachmakers' Hall, Gordon proposed to the Protestant Association that they assemble in St. George's Fields on Friday, June 2nd, at 10 A.M. to accompany his lordship to the House of Commons to deliver the petition in person. After it was carried unanimously, Gordon warned that if less than twenty thousand of his fellow citizens attended him on that day he would not present their petition. Every true Protestant and friend of the petition was asked to wear a blue cockade in his hat.

What happened in London on June 2nd was not out of character with the city's recent past. Riots and mass demonstrations were nothing new. From time to time the mob had been worked up against Papists, Jews, Scots, and wage-cutting Irish blacklegs. On this hot oppressive Friday in June some sixty thousand persons, three times as many as Gordon called for, assembled at St. George's Fields, an undrained tract on the Surrey side of the Thames. Formed in semimilitary array, waving "No Popery" banners, with Methodists chanting hymns and Scotsmen skirling their bagpipes, a motley throng, led by Lord George himself, crossed the Thames by Westminster Bridge. Two other parties crossed at Blackfriars' and London Bridges respectively. All three then converged on the Palace Yard toward midafternoon. Those who could forced their way into Westminster Hall and laid siege to Parliament. The mob overturned the carriages of lords and commoners approaching Parliament, singling out for personal attack persons suspected of having a hand in the passage of the Catholic Relief Act. Fortunate was the victim who escaped with nothing more than a diswigging, a ripped gown, or a mud pelting. Lord Mansfield, whose direction to a jury in a recent prosecution of a Catholic priest for saying mass led to the priest's acquittal, barely escaped with his life. When he reached the House of Lords, he presided in Lord Thurlow's absence, and, according to an eyewitness, "quivered on the Woolsack like an aspen." Ironically, this was the day the upper house had set to consider the Duke of Richmond's motion for introducing annual elections and manhood suffrage, and nothing deterred the noble lord from having his say.

The Commons found itself under siege as the mob raged unrestrained in the lobby. General James Murray turned to his kinsman Lord George and warned him that, if the first of his "rascally adherents" ventured to enter the House, "I will plunge my sword, not into his, but into your body." The Horse and Foot Guards managed to extricate the imprisoned members from the House around 11 P.M.

Meantime the mob had found two other targets for their malice. One was the chapel of the Sardinian Embassy on Duke Street, the second the Bavarian Chapel on Warwick Street. The former was burned and gutted, and Madame de Cordon, the wife of the Sardinian Minister, was carried to safety barely in time. The Bavarian Chapel was sacked, as well as the house of Count Haslang, the Bavarian ambassador. In the course of their depredations the mob uncovered beneath the chapel a large cache of contraband articles, as the eighty-year-old Haslang had for years lived a double life, and in addition to his diplomatic duties was a notorious receiver of smuggled goods, a "prince of smugglers," Walpole called him. Having done mischief enough for one day, the crowd dispersed.[59]

Saturday started quietly enough. In the Lords, Richmond blamed the riots on the Quebec Act of 1774, virtually establishing the Catholic Church in Canada, and joined inseparably with the "Intolerable Acts" in the minds of American Whigs. Bosh, said Rockingham. True, he had heard the crowd call out "No Popery," but "clapping my hand to my watch to secure it, I felt several hands directed to it." To the Marquess it was pretty obvious "what the mob came for." Shelburne took the occasion to deliver a timely lecture on the need for reorganizing the police force of the metropolis. The inadequacy of that body was alarmingly demonstrated that afternoon when a crowd jeered at and jostled soldiers as they brought thirteen men, arrested at the Sardinian Chapel the previous night, to be committed by Sir John Fielding at his home in Bow Street. Thence the prisoners were taken to Newgate without further trouble. Again the lack of proper security was highlighted that evening at nine o'clock when a mob gathered in Ropemakers' Alley, Moorfields, one of the poorer districts heavily inhabited by Irish laborers who worked for as little as half the wages of ordinary Londoners. Since the Catholic chapels were threatened, a merchant of Irish Catholic extraction named Malo appealed to the Lord Mayor of London, Alderman Brackley Kennett, for protection. That one-time tavern- and brothel-keeper, now a wine merchant, declined to intervene on the ground that "there are very great people at the bottom of the riot." Finally, prodded by Lord Stormont, the Lord Mayor took some halfhearted security measures.

By Sunday, the fourth of June, biting cold fanned by a brisk wind replaced the sultry heat which had hung over the city. All day the mob gathered around the Catholic chapel in Moorfields. After contenting itself with smashing windows, it became emboldened, and in the evening the edifice was burned and gutted. "That's pretty well, gentlemen, for one day," commented the Lord Mayor, an onlooker. "I hope now you will go to your own homes."

Monday, the fourth day of the riots, happened to be the King's birthday. The mob celebrated by parading through the West End to Lord George Gordon's house in Welbeck Street, by destroying a Catholic chapel in Nightingale Street as soldiers stood by doing nothing, by damaging other Catholic properties in Moorfields, and by demolishing a Catholic seminary in Hoxton. That evening Gordon's "blue cockade banditti," having learned from the press the names of the witnesses against the thirteen persons committed at Bow Street, leveled the houses of two of these unfortunates, and pillaged the residence of Sir George Savile in Leicester Square.

By Tuesday, the sixth, the military were at long last being assembled on orders of Baron Amherst. But the events of the previous day had shown that the civil magistrates had not been prepared to read the Riot Act or give orders. Now, it was the position of the Secretary at War Jenkinson that the troops could not intervene unless instructed to do so by the civil magistrate, and only after the Riot Act had been read. Jenkinson's ruling rested on a long-standing opinion which failed to take into account the commission of felonies, which at common law justified intervention on the spot by any citizen. It was only when Attorney General Wedderburn reversed Jenkinson that the army was able to act.[60]

For several days, beginning with Tuesday, an ugly mob laid siege to Lambeth Palace, but a strong detachment of guards held them off. Not so fortunate was Mr. Malo of Moorfields, whose Catholic home was gutted, and whose Popish canary birds were tossed into the bonfire. Once more an ugly armed crowd entered the Palace Yard. This time the Earl of Sandwich barely escaped with his life. When Justice Hyde had the presumption to read the Riot Act and order the mob to disperse, the rioters retaliated by converging on St. Martin's Street and ransacking and burning the justice's house. From Sir Isaac Newton's former observatory, Susan Burney saw not only that blaze, but flames ascending from Newgate, from Justice Fielding's house in Covent Garden, and from Lord Mansfield's town house in Bloomsbury Square.

The conflagration at Newgate was the most spectacular and insurrectionary deed of that lurid night. That prison was a new structure, built of stone and not entirely completed. When the prisonkeeper refused to release the confined rioters, the mob battered the doors down with pickaxes and sledgehammers, scaled the walls on ladders, and hurled firebrands into the keeper's dwelling house. As the flames quickly spread to the prison structure and jailers and turnkeys fled or begged for their lives, some three hundred prisoners were dragged out by the mob. Within a few hours England's strongest prison had been demolished, and nothing remained standing but its bare walls. An infernal orchestration rent the air. Shouts of "No Popery" were countered by the clanking sound of hammers, as irons were knocked off the prisoners at Newgate as well as at Clerkenwell Bridewell.

Events were fast moving toward a climax. Horace Walpole described "Black Wednesday" (June 7th) as "the most horrible night I ever beheld, which for six hours together I expected to end in half the town being reduced to ashes."[61] The day did not start propitiously. By morning's end, gangs of young hoodlums armed with iron bludgeons torn from the railings of Lord Mansfield's house, or wielding crowbars stolen from an ironmonger's in Holborn, extorted money from every shop they passed. Soon all shops were shut down from Whitechapel to Tyburn. The Jews of Houndsditch and Duke's Place followed the general example by scribbling on their shutters, "This house is a true Protestant." Writing from "my garrison in Berkeley Square," the incorrigible Horace Walpole jibed, "I am decking myself with blue ribbons like a May-day garland."[62] Though the military authorities gave notice that the blue cockade would be deemed an "ensign of rebellion" and the King issued a military proclamation, the mob did not seem in the least intimidated. Toward evening they picked as their target a huge distillery on the south side of Holborn. By 9 P.M. the buildings were enveloped in smoke and flames. The mob staved in the casks. As the scorched spirits gushed forth, men and boys, women with infants in arms, poured out of lanes and alleys and stooped in the gutter to drink from the pools, only to be set aflame in blazing rum and gin. Suddenly the vats ignited and columns of flame shot up, to be visible thirty miles around. Finally, troops dispersed the crowd, that is, all but the wretched corpses scorched to a crisp in the fiery draught.

Meantime, on the Surrey side, the King's Bench Prison was soon enveloped in flames, then Fleet Street Prison. Shots, which were fired by troops for the first time the previous evening at Lord Mansfield's, now rang out again at Blackfriars' Bridge, where a mob set fire to the toll-gatherers' houses. Casualties were heavy. A threatening crowd moving along Cheapside once more confronted steel and lead. Again the troops fired, leaving some twenty dead.

Sometime during the evening of the seventh and before dawn the following morning attacks were launched upon the Bank of England, but a strong force within and around the building was ready and waiting. The mob beat off the Horse Guards, but the Foot, by keeping up a deadly fire, dispersed them. Eight were killed, many wounded. This was perhaps the decisive battle, for, as Frederick the Great saw it from his sheltered remoteness, had the rioters seized the bank, the result might well have been a full-scale revolution.[63]

As reinforcements from the countryside began to pour in, London assumed the aspect of a garrison town. Redcoats were quartered in all the churches. Armed guards were placed before the residences of all Cabinet ministers. West End mansions bristled with civilian defenders armed to the teeth. Law students at the Middle Temple and Lincoln's Inn formed their own home guard. Everywhere soldiers were now pulling down the blue flags flown from every house and tearing the blue cockade from every hat. At the Tower of London the drawbridge was kept up and water let into the moat.

With nightfall of the eighth of June, a sudden calm descended upon the terror-stricken city. The Gordon Riots had ground to a halt. Next day Newgate's escapees were beginning to give themselves up. The felons, truly pathetic outcasts, had discovered that they had lost the only place that was home to them. Now the authorities had to house them in impoverished sheds, hastily thrown up. That Friday night people even ventured to the opera. "Our danger is at an end, but our disgrace will be lasting," was the comment of the historian Gibbon.[64] After showing exemplary patience or timidity the government finally acted against Lord George Gordon and James Fisher, the secretary of the Protestant Association. Both were seized and committed to the Tower.[65] Fisher, who had taken the precaution of destroying all his correspondence as soon as he heard of Gordon's arrest, proved an evasive witness at a hearing held before privy councilors, and was dismissed for lack of evidence. Alderman Kennett, the Lord Mayor whose refusal to act had been perhaps the most provocative feature of the riots, came into the presence of the privy councilors reeking of brandy, and whining that he could not act for fear of his life. He was later convicted of neglect of duty, but his death prevented the passing of sentence. Lord George's trial for high treason was not held until the following February, when a pair of gifted barristers, the learned Lloyd Kenyon and the elegant and brilliant Thomas Erskine, secured his quick acquittal. Considering the man and the circumstances, it is difficult to conceive of any other verdict. As Fitzjames Stephen later remarked, Gordon was guilty "of nothing more than hare-brained and criminal folly in heading an unlawful assembly[66] Released from the Tower, Lord George never again threatened the Constitution and the monarchy, but managed to live up to his reputation for enthusiasms and unconventional behavior. He soon astounded his former Protestant associates by his conversion to Judaism, and then ran afoul of the law by publishing a libelous attack on Marie Antoinette, whose private life was ever the subject of derogatory innuendoes. At the instigation of the French government he was prosecuted and found guilty, but went into hiding. Finally located in the Froggery, Birmingham's Jewish quarter, he was sent down to London, and as a bearded Jew, Israel bar Abraham, he entered Newgate Prison in January, 1788, never to leave it alive.[67]

The government did manage to arraign a cluster of minor figures, felons, juvenile delinquents, and prostitutes. What they bagged Walpole called just a pack of boys and ruffians and "a regiment of street walkers."[68] Of the 135 arrested and tried for taking part in the riots, fifty-nine were sentenced to death and twenty-one duly executed. Among the assorted ruffians who paid the extreme penalty was the public executioner, Edward Dennis, the wretched hangman of infamous memory in *Barnaby Rudge*, who participated in the burnings. Otherwise, they were small fry. The official casualty figures neared eight hundred, with property damage running into the hundreds of thousands of pounds.[69]

During the riots and for some time thereafter, it was common gossip that France, Spain, or America was behind the disturbances. After the Blackfriars' Bridge had been attacked, it was said that bodies were found lying in the streets "with *louis d'or* in their pockets." One anonymous scribbler charged that large sums were paid out to the mob by men who to judge from appearances were not worth a sixpence, and that on the second and sixth of June there were seen in the Adelphi and the Palace Yard "men in long blue gowns, disguised like quack doctors' servants, who distributed, from large bags under their gowns, handfuls of halfpence to such of the rioters as chose to take them," and that stands of arms had been secured of either French or Spanish make.[70] Other reports darkly hinted that it was publicly talked of at The Hague, Amsterdam, and Paris that London would be in ashes on the eighth of June, or that an American prisoner of war named Colonel Scott, or a recently arrived British officer, had declared that the American rebels were being "buoyed up by Spanish gold and by French promises of the conflagration of London."[71]

One witness of dubious repute claimed to have seen with his own eyes evidence of enemy participation or antiwar feeling. The Abbé MacDermott, formerly chaplain of the French embassy and long enmeshed in French espionage, had been accorded the liberty of providing religious offices to the French prisoners in England. He reported to Vergennes that on Tuesday evening, the sixth of June, he encountered some twenty thousand rioters on foot and horse, "some with the flags of the thirteen provinces; others with black standards.[72] Perhaps he mistook these flags for the black and red standard hoisted that same evening by James Jackson, a watch-wheel cutter, who, when Justice Hyde started to read the Riot Act, shouted, "Hyde's house a-hoy!"[73] Shortly thereafter the Abbé was attacked by the mob and barely escaped with his life as his lodgings were burned down.[74] Perhaps, too, it was a bit of wishful thinking when the *Gazeta de Madrid* reported, on the basis of Paris information, bearing date of June 12th, that the cry of the mob was not only "No Popery" and "An End to the Influence of the Crown," but that there were loud calls for peace with America and a finish to the war against France and Spain.[75]

True, London was crawling with French and Spanish secret agents and Americans were everywhere. Admittedly, Franklin and Company in Paris were not without resources for stirring up trouble across the Channel. The strange case of John the Painter, allegedly paid by Silas Deane and Dr. Bancroft to set fire to a number of English dockyards, had come to light some years before,[76] and the Ministry still remembered that sensational trial. Now, by order of the Privy Council, an American named James Smith, living abroad and notorious as a propagator of the American cause in England, was apprehended as "the Catiline of the conspiracy and the secret agent of Dr. Franklin to burn the city." But the government did not get its hands on enough evidence to hold him for trial.[77] Other Americans in London were under suspicion as well, among them the artist John Greenwood, proprietor of Greenwood's Great Rooms where the Protestant Association sometimes gathered, along with a few English businessmen reputed to be in correspondence with American Patriots. Again nothing was ever found against them. That Franklin himself had any advance knowledge of a plot is not supported by his correspondence. A letter he wrote to Carmichael in Madrid, dated June 17th, merely passes on information culled from the London dailies. The Sage of Passy, however, was not unhappy about the destruction of Lord Mansfield's residence. "He who approved the burning of American houses has had fire brought to him," Franklin remarked, nor was he exactly crestfallen about the reported death on June 3rd at Croydon of his old archenemy Governor Thomas Hutchinson of Massachusetts, which he attributed to "fright."[78]

Horace Walpole, among others, thought at first that the Americans had exploited the mob for their own ends once the riots started.[79] But within a week Walpole was conceding that "not a Frenchman, not an American, appears to have had a finger in a single outrage."[80] Still the story would not down. Months later the Attorney General, in his opening speech on behalf of the Crown at the trial of Lord George Gordon, attributed the riots to "the execrable designs of our inveterate enemies," but then signally failed to corroborate this reckless assertion.

If the common enemy could not serve as a convenient scapegoat, why not the hated Whig leaders who had taunted and defied the Ministry at every turn? Shelburne seemed the likeliest suspect. Privately convinced that the Catholics were against "a Constitution here or in America," whereas the dissenters were pro-American,[81] he had given halfhearted support to the Savile bill and then chiefly on the ground of military expediency.[82] The case against the Earl was extremely circumstantial. On the riotous evening of June 2nd the Earl was one of the few peers to reach the House of Lords without molestation.[83] He was conspicuous in opposing the calling out of the military. "I ever will resist and prevent such a matter if possible," he declared that same evening.[84] The next day, when it looked for a time as though the tumults had subsided, he defended the assemblages of the people, and felt that their shouts of "No Popery!" and

"No more bonfires in Smithfield!" came from sincere, if misguided, conviction. Instead of rigorous prosecution, his formula was the repeal of the Quebec Act, which, of course, had nothing to do with England, and a reform of the police of Westminster.[85] Shelburne chose this occasion to leave for his Wiltshire home, as his wife, the second Lady Shelburne, was expecting her first child momentarily, but to his enemies it looked very much as though he was quitting his post at a time of extreme peril.[86]

Another target of malicious rumor was the pro-American peer, Lord Effingham, who was seen at the burning of Newgate, recognized by ruffles he never wore, leading a mob on Blackfriars' Bridge. Finally his dead body was identified, disguised as a chimney sweep, in Fleet Market. Frederick Reynolds recounts how as a young boy he rushed home to tell the sad news to his father, Effingham's most intimate friend, only to encounter the peer himself in the drawing room. "This is my *third* death during these riots," Effingham announced.[87] When, some time after the riots, he made his appearance at court, and someone commented on the coat he wore, Burke rejoined, "It is the same in which he was killed at the riots."[88]

While its ends were ignoble, the Gordon Riots were in fact a great upsurge of mass discontent, social, economic, religious, and political, disorganized and fragmented, and flowing into illicit channels when it found no outlet elsewhere. It was not immediately prompted by the failure of the government to achieve peace, nor was it the result of American or foreign intrigue, but the costly and unpopular war was an essential ingredient in the brew that boiled over during the eight days in June.

It was the fashion of the time to attribute all untimely events to deep-laid plots, and it is true that the close relations of some leaders of the political opposition to the Irish and the county reform movements, along with their well-advertised desire to end the war with America, made them the ideal subject for charges of conspiratorial activity. Contrariwise, opposition leaders and foreign diplomats were not above laying the tumults to the Court and the Ministry. In the debates on Burke's bill Charles James Fox had remarked that "he had sometimes heard that a rebellion tended to strengthen the hands of government."[89] Indubitably, the Gordon Riots supported this observation. As far back as March a secret agent of Vergennes was asserting that the Irish "revolution" was "the secret work of the court of Great Britain," who would surely become more powerful thereby.[90] Horace Walpole, who felt that the calling out of troops provided the government with "no very disagreeable opportunity," remarked caustically, "Even Lord Mansfield has risen like a phoenix from the flames,

and vomits martial law, as if all law books were burnt as well as his own;
nay, like *his* plate, almost all party is melted into a mass of bullion
loyalty."[91]

That the government, as Burke observed, managed to augment its power
"from a tumult which appeared to threaten the subversion of all order
and government"[92] was scarcely evidence to support the innuendoes of the
Opposition. If there was a deep-dyed government plot, George III was
certainly not aware of it. "We must get to the bottom of it," he insisted
to North. The King demanded vigorous action by the government, and
attacked "the great supineness of the Civil Magistrates."[93] George III was
hardly so Machiavellian a statesman as to seek to profit by discontent that
he himself had fomented.

Nevertheless it must be conceded that the Gordon Riots proved both
a timely and fortunate happenstance for an administration reeling from
a series of seemingly lethal blows coming from all directions at once.
The government's prestige was immediately enhanced. George III was
fortified in his resolve not to accept Rockingham's terms to join a coalition ministry.[94] The King and North then took a calculated gamble by
dissolving Parliament and calling a general election. This move caught the
Opposition unprepared, and Rockingham hastily denounced it as "a wicked
measure."[95] The smooth if expensive operations of John Robinson, Secretary to the Treasury and government campaign manager, paid ample dividends.[96] The government won a narrow victory, with a working majority
of a mere six votes.[97] It was not much, but it was enough to keep North in
office until some months after Yorktown.

Meantime, buoyed up by news which had reached London on June
15th telling of the fall of Charleston,[98] the government a fortnight later
easily defeated a proposal by Hartley of a new bill for an accommodation
with America and rejected a resolution of Sir George Savile denouncing
the war with America as threatening "the final ruin of the British
Empire."[99] Now, North and the King chose to regard this election as a
mandate to continue the war. By so doing, they sacrificed what indubitably
was the most opportune moment to bring the war to a close under terms
more palatable to the Crown than could have been secured at any time since
France had joined the conflict, or on any later occasion down to Yorktown.

V

JACQUES NECKER'S PRIVATE
PEACE FEELERS

THAT SUMMER OF 1780 all Paris was hotly disputing the rival talents of the revolutionary Gluck and the more tradition-rooted Piccini, and storming the Opéra to hear their current productions.[1] Few Parisians seemed aware that the French government, like the British, had to deal with a crisis of its own. No crowds demonstrated at the Palais Royal. No torch was raised against the Bastille, which still housed a few prominent offenders imprisoned under *lettres de cachet* issued by the King. No troops poured out of the Champs de Mars. Save for the perennial gossips and printers of defamatory tracts, who managed to keep one step ahead of the police, the silence was almost ominous.

For generations now the government had invested its decision-making with a cloak of secrecy. For a hundred years the kings of France had preferred Versailles to the Louvre as a seat of government. For almost a century and three-quarters that government had functioned without recourse to the moribund Estates-General. That the councilors of the King were now split into warring factions over foreign and internal issues could still be concealed from public scrutiny. It was still possible to keep the people in the dark, but not for too long.

To handle this crisis Louis XVI's First Minister seemed scarcely better equipped than his counterpart in the British Cabinet. Jean-Frédéric Phélypeaux de Maurepas, now in his eightieth year and in declining health, still treated affairs of state with a frivolous touch belying his years. Opportunistic rather than profound, age had made the Comte de Maurepas increasingly suspicious of rivals who might seek to displace him. Despite the best intentions, the Comte lacked the bold and firm line needed to head a war Cabinet. At the beginning of Louis XVI's reign some six years before, Maurepas had supported the naming of Turgot as Controller General, but when that renowned physiocrat's proposed reforms aroused a storm of protest from the privileged classes and the *parlements*, he joined the pack against him.

Turgot had bluntly warned that France's involvement in the American War could lead to serious economic troubles,[2] and Maurepas, especially after the Patriot defeat at Long Island, was cold toward active intervention.[3] Pressed by his Foreign Minister, the Comte de Vergennes, Maurepas agreed to the treaties with America and the resulting war with England, not because he favored the Revolutionaries but because he wanted to weaken the British.[4] He had never rid himself of his doubts about France's belligerent role, and now these doubts were becoming increasingly insistent.

Four years before, Silas Deane, the former American commissioner at Paris, had pointed out that Maurepas was far from being that "great and daring genius" which the French needed at their head.[5] Time had scarcely made the venerable First Minister more venturesome, nor was the torrent of distasteful news which had to be digested during the summer of 1780 calculated to prompt an octogenarian courtier to assume a bellicose posture. Not the kind of news Maurepas was hearing. First of all, there were black reports from America. The fall of Charleston to Clinton and Cornwallis seemed to expose the pitiful military weakness of the insurgents. From Spain, Jay informed Congress that the effect of that reverse "was as visible the next day as that of a hard night's frost on young leaves."[6] Not only in France, but all over the Continent friends of America made desperate efforts to dispel the thick fog of pessimism which settled down after news spread of the loss of the largest city of the American South.[7]

If the military reverses in America caused much head-shaking in Europe's chancelleries, the news that Congress had averted bankruptcy by deciding to redeem its Continental paper money at a fortieth of its face value[8] evoked shrieks of anguish from Parisian bankers, war contractors, and speculators.[9] Vergennes, who found John Adams' strictures on the proper conduct of the war quite insufferable,[10] now had a bitter if fruitless interchange with the American. The self-righteous Patriot saw no reason why Congress should distinguish between French and American holders of depreciated paper.[11] Not only did John Adams appear to Vergennes to be lacking in gratitude for French aid, but he threw a fright into the Foreign Minister by avowing his intention of going to England to sound out that government on a separate peace. Vergennes had to tell him very firmly that "the time to communicate your plenipotentiary power to Lord Germain is not yet come."[12] Since Adams had proven far less amenable to suggestions from the court of Versailles than Franklin, neither Vergennes nor Maurepas felt confident that he could be restrained.

Something is going on with the Americans, the Abbé Véri, a close confidant of Maurepas, warned that minister early in September. Franklin had kept his mouth shut for a whole year. "Well, if we are deceived," Maurepas replied, "I won't be too sorry. We will then be able to make the peace that much sooner since the stumbling block [American independence] will no longer exist."[13] Meanwhile, at San Ildefonso Floridablanca continued his discussions with Cumberland, inspiring fears in France that Spain might soon have to be written off as an ally. All Europe was speculating with amused detachment about the possibility that either America or Spain would, as Adams put it, "give France the go-by" and make a separate peace.[14]

If Maurepas was beginning to lose faith in his Foreign Minister's system of military alliances, he now had ample grounds to question the tough line that Vergennes had pursued toward another ally, Austria. In 1778 Vergennes had refused to back Joseph II in his attempted annexation of the greater part of Bavaria, despite the treaty of alliance between France and Austria reposing in the archives since 1756. Backed by a Russian troop mobilization, Vergennes forced the Emperor to pull his armies out of most of the territory they had occupied. The peace of Teschen, as this settlement was called, was still a fresh and galling memory to the young and ambitious son of Maria Theresa. This very summer the unpredictable Joseph II was off in the wilds of Russia for talks with Catherine the Great at Mogilev and Tsarskoye Selo. Desperately Vergennes sought to penetrate the mystery of those talks. Could the two powers be concocting some such formidable project as the joint dismemberment of the Ottoman Empire, a power with whom France cultivated cordial ties? Whether or not the two monarchs were in fact negotiating a secret treaty, the highly publicized meeting boded ill for France's aspirations as the arbiter of Europe.[15]

Closer to home, the young Queen of France had blossomed into a major problem for the government. Long before, that notorious prude, Maria Theresa, was outraged by her daughter's frivolities and extravagances, even by her extreme hair-do, which the mother deemed more suitable to "women of the lower sort and prostitutes." As reports streamed in to Schönbrunn of Marie Antoinette's indiscretions at Versailles, the Austrian Queen had sadly remarked, "She runs headlong to her ruin."[16]

While a jaded court was inured to Marie Antoinette's extravagance and gambling, her increasing propensity for court intrigue aroused special anxiety at this time when she was known to stand unabashedly for appeasement. It hardly seemed possible to remove the Queen from the clutches of the grasping Duchesse de Polignac and her parasitic entourage,[17] but at least, by the quick thinking of Vergennes, the Ministry contrived to snatch the young and handsome Axel Fersen from attendance upon the Queen and ship him posthaste with Rochambeau's army to the American theater of war. This quieted the gossipers for a time. However, Maria Theresa's death late in the year came as a severe personal blow to her daughter and created new difficulties for the French government. Neither the Queen's brother, Joseph II, nor the veteran Austrian envoy in Paris, the Count Mercy d'Argenteau, could hold the Queen in line. More than ever the Trianon became involved in court politics, and, whether correctly or not, the Queen's hand was seen in the impending Cabinet shake-up that seemed to portend the end of the Maurepas-Vergennes regime.[18]

Some of this bad news was fresh, some stale and warmed over, but the most disturbing fell like a bombshell at the feet of the King's ministers. The man who fired it off was the Genevan-born Paris banker, Jacques Necker. Although he had replaced Turgot's successor, Clugny, the compliant tool of the pillagers of the Treasury, and although he was a man of immense fortune, Necker was denied the post of controller general because he was a foreigner and a Protestant. Instead, he was named Director General of the Treasury and then of Finances. A man of magisterial aspect, pompous, vain, and ambitious, he had a talent for expressing platitudes in sepulchral tones. Necker frantically courted the support of the highly placed[19] and sedulously cultivated public opinion as the term was then understood. His reputation was to be enormously enhanced in the salon presided over by his wife Suzanne and through the literary efforts of his talented daughter, Anne Louise Germaine, known to the world as Madame de Staël. Necker had quickly won recognition both at home and abroad as a reformer and an activist on the basis of modest though needed economies,[20] but his popularity rested largely on his ability to finance the war without resorting to heavy taxes that nobody wanted to pay.[21]

Like Turgot, Necker opposed France's going to war to save the United States.[22] One concerned with tidying up accounts could hardly view so costly an enterprise with complacency, certainly not an Anglophile like the Swiss banker. Beaumarchais, who was running an undercover operation to keep America supplied with the sinews of war, found it advisable to mask his moves from Necker.[23] When the Director General could not stop Vergennes from bringing France into the war openly on America's side, he reputedly tipped off his own banking house, enabling that firm to make a big speculative killing.[24] Now that France had been openly involved in the war for almost two years, Necker submitted the Treasury accounts to a fresh audit.[25] During the late summer of 1780 he informed Maurepas that he had discovered a serious discrepancy in those accounts. "A blow of a bomb," he called it, "as unexpected as it is unbelievable."[26] Neither the King nor the members of his Council were spared this serious news.[27] Since estimated tax returns would not make up this deficiency, it was clear that the only way to finance another military campaign would be by floating huge war loans, which would sit perilously atop the vast debt already accumulated.[28] The only sensible course, Necker urged, was to come to terms with the enemy.

On September 26th Maurepas revealed Necker's disclosures to Louis XVI, along with the split in the King's Council over the course to pursue. Maurepas was now ready to desert the war, and the King himself was perilously poised. Vergennes decided to risk a showdown. The following day he dispatched a note to Louis XVI, whose martial ardor he had managed to enkindle at critical moments. Vergennes now confessed that the financial news was "truly alarming," and seemed to leave France no alternative "save peace and peace the most immediate." Spain's needs for peace appeared no less pressing than France's, Vergennes pointed out. Although he was prepared to carry out the King's orders to encourage the Spanish court in its appeasement move, he cautioned that such a step might seriously compromise the prestige of the King. If Louis, after considering the long-range implications of his decision, favored making a *démarche* to Spain, then, his Foreign Minister requested, he should give him the order in writing.[29]

On the surface Vergennes seemed prepared to go along with Maurepas and Necker, but it was not very difficult to read between the lines and see how badly he would have taken a decision to quit the war. Even the King, not the most perspicacious of rulers, saw the point. Louis XVI recoiled from the brink, and decisions were made to continue the war somehow. The very next day, September 28th, Vergennes got off four dispatches to Montmorin to quiet any fears on the part of Spain that France was quitting, and to promote the idea of joint mediation efforts on the part of Russia and Austria as a dignified alternative to self-abasement.[30] The Foreign Minister seems also to have rung from Maurepas his reluctant consent to the fateful third campaign in America, the one that would prove decisive.[31]

So far as Vergennes was concerned the war was still on, but Necker was not easily rebuffed. Taking advantage of Maurepas' poor health, the Director General campaigned to undermine the war party in the Council, while at the same time he seems to have had reason to count on Maurepas himself as an ally. What Vergennes does not seem to have realized was that earlier that summer, doubtless under pressure from Necker, the old Comte had sent out a peace feeler to Lord North, using as an intermediary a dissolute, loose-tongued Englishman named Nathaniel Parker Forth. Known to be an intimate of Lords Mansfield, North, and Stormont, Forth had been employed by the British government intermittently from 1777 to the end of the war. Maurepas had found this notorious madcap an entertaining companion, while Vergennes had labeled him a man "who has been alternately an angel of peace and of war." Since this pseudo-secret agent managed on one pretext or another to journey back and forth across the Channel, it was only natural that Maurepas should have employed him now that he happened again to be in Paris.[32]

Maurepas turned over to Forth a private letter to Lord North, which Britain's First Lord of the Treasury transmitted to the King on July 29th. In North's opinion the letter carried a ring of sincerity "notwithstanding the very deceitful character of the writer." Why all those "oaths and affirmations" if the old Comte was "not at all inclined to peace?" North asked. He advised his King that he thought it advisable to take the letter up with Stormont and Hillsborough, the two Secretaries of State concerned with foreign policy. With his usual punctuality, the King replied the very next day. Labeling Maurepas' communication as "very extraordinary," he declared, "Were I not too well acquainted with the duplicity of his conduct, I should suppose his life almost depended on the success of his proposal." The least we can assume is that Maurepas, at the time of writing the letter, "had some very weighty reason to wish for peace," George added. All of which suggests that Spain is resolved to end the war, and that Maurepas must do the same, or else, by centering the negotiations in Paris, obstruct Spain in her intentions of coming to terms. To the King one circumstance was especially agreeable. "America cannot make part of any proposition Forth might be entrusted to communicate." Provided Stormont agreed, there was no reason, George stated, why Forth could not return to Paris and see Maurepas, but the agent was to be told to do nothing but listen.[33]

Judging from papers later turned over to Lord Shelburne, it appears that Maurepas at this time, and perhaps as early as the late fall of 1779, was prepared to accept an armistice, which would allow the British to keep possession of what they then held in America, and provide for a restoration of any conquests made by France, Spain, or Great Britain since the Treaty of Fontainebleau of 1762.[34] Since the North Ministry had another iron in the fire, the Cumberland-Floridablanca negotiations at San Ildefonso, which from that distance still held some promise, it was disinclined to become too heavily involved with the French at this time. Certainly it would not be rushed. From Turin reports had come of a frank conversation between the Spanish ambassador and the British chargé, in which the former confessed that the Spanish army encamped before Gibraltar was low in morale, that the notion that the Spanish court felt that the capture of Gibraltar was a matter of national honor was perhaps exaggerated, and that "the bulk of the Spanish Nation" looked upon the issue with indifference.[35] Perhaps Floridablanca could still be persuaded to drop his demand for Gibraltar and end the impasse. At St. Petersburg unsubstantiated rumors had the King of Sardinia, at France's behest, proposing a truce on the basis of independence for only a fragment of the American colonies.[36]

By fortuitous circumstances Thomas Walpole, a London banker and close associate of Necker, arrived in Paris at the end of July. His personal affairs under a heavy financial cloud, Walpole was in Paris ostensibly in connection with litigation arising over some properties he held in Granada. Before leaving England he had dropped in at Downing Street to offer his services to Lord North "toward forwarding the good work of peace to which he knew that many of the French Ministry were well inclined." Not deterred by North's polite declination, Walpole committed his proposals to writing. Again North told him that "the moment was not favorable."

Without authorization Walpole moved on his own. Within a week after coming to Paris he sounded out Maurepas on the prospects of peace. On August 8th he wrote North reporting "several conversations" with the Abbé Véri, Maurepas' friend and confidant. When the London banker pointed out that the Americans had broken faith with their ally by pursuing a ruinous paper-currency policy, Véri was reported to have replied that France by herself could not end the war short of American independence and that it would be "better policy to suffer America to be reduced to the necessity of destroying the alliance with France," an event which the Abbé felt might not be far off. On September 5th Walpole had a long talk with his "particular friend" Necker, whom he found "very desirous of peace." How to convince Maurepas that he was misinformed by La Luzerne and Franklin as to the real state of affairs in America was the nub of their conversation, although Necker cautioned against pushing Maurepas too hard.[37]

Walpole was not the only self-appointed peace intermediary. While he was putting out his own peace feelers, the British secret agent Paul Wentworth dispatched a letter to his Ministry from the double spy, Dr. Bancroft, very much to the same purpose. As regards both the Walpole and the Wentworth communications, the King informed North that he could not sanction any negotiation so long as "America is only to be treated with through the medium of France or the strange *unauthorized* propositions of the Commissioners are to be the basis of any agreement with the rebellious colonies." Furthermore, Walpole, a cousin of the caustic opposition critic Horace Walpole, held the wrong politics for the King, who considered him to be neither a "safe" nor an "impartial" intermediary.[38]

A lesser man might have been discouraged by the absence of any official backing for his one-man peace effort. Not so Thomas Walpole. On October 2nd he visited the Abbé Véri, not improbably at Necker's prompting. "Can I ask you," the Abbé recorded Walpole as inquiring, "if M. de Maurepas would accept at present the *truce* that our court refused last year?"

"I do not know its intention," Véri replied. "I only know that we have not spoken about it for a year. I think, moreover, that one could not make the overture without first informing Spain, and that since our court had previously refused the proposition, it is not for France and Spain to propose it anew."

Walpole conceded that it was now up to the British court to make the overture. "I know that the court desires peace," he asserted, adding, "It is not hard to see that my nation needs it. Yours needs it likewise. Neither have had a decisive success which could force the other to yield on the sole quite troublesome issue, that is the independence of the Americans." In Walpole's opinion the truce resolved that difficulty, and he did not foresee any others. "I myself did not believe a year ago that we could accept the truce," he admitted. "Today I think differently." Walpole knew that Véri could not disclose the precise terms that Maurepas would find acceptable, but asked him merely for his personal opinion. "Do you think the overture of a truce on our part can obtain a hearing, and serve as a basis of negotiations?"

"Yes, I think so very much."

"In that case, read the letter that I have thought of sending this evening to M. North. You will see from it that I believe we ought to make the overture, that I offer myself to carry out this mission, and that I hold out the prospect that M. Maurepas and he are not far apart."

"You can send the letter," the Abbé reassured him after he had read it, adding the likelihood that North could suspect from the tone of the letter that "M. Maurepas was behind the curtain without wishing to appear." Walpole reassured his confidant that he had no wish to give that impression, but that he did want the Abbé to report the conversation to the Comte. "Tell him that my idea would be only the first overture made between him alone and M. North without the participation of the other ministers, even of M. de Vergennes." Once the preliminary grounds are acceptable, the parties can pursue serious negotiations.

Several hours later the Abbé Véri reported this conversation to Maurepas, whom fever and gout had confined to bed. "I am ready to receive everything and to listen to everything," the Comte replied, pointing out that certain difficulties could not be ignored. Spain must agree. Vergennes did not like the notion of a truce, and, as for Maurepas himself, while he preferred peace to war, he would rather seek it through Russian mediation. When Véri reminded Maurepas that England was weaker than France, the bed-ridden invalid rejoined sharply, "She has her funds for the next year, and we do not have ours." Maurepas also mentioned the likelihood that Walpole had been put up to this by Necker, reminding the Abbé of the close banking ties between the two financiers and suggesting that Walpole's peace bid disclosed Necker's ambition to run all the departments of the government.[39]

On the basis of such encouragement as Véri had to offer him, and doubtless with the full backing of Necker, Walpole dispatched his letter to North. In this letter of October 2nd he urged that he be authorized "to open a treaty negotiation here upon the ground of a truce," and assured him that such an overture to Maurepas would be "well received and entered upon *immediately*." Walpole followed up a fortnight later with a warning to North that attempts were being made to negotiate "thro' another channel," obviously a reference to the Wentworth-Bancroft feelers, and a reminder of the growing ascendancy of Necker, "my particular friend." North put Walpole's October 2nd letter before the King. The monarch dismissed it as arising purely from France's "difficulties of finance not fully known here." Not wishing to close the door on "all propositions of a pacific nature," the King endorsed North's draft reply to Walpole, stressing both the dangers of private negotiations and the disadvantages to Britain of starting talks from the ground of a truce. Even if Walpole were "not an avowed enemy of the present administration," the King remarked, he should not regard him as possessing "those qualities which are essential in a prudent and able negotiator." Finally, the King hammered home the point, which he had been doing with staccato regularity, that "whilst the House of Bourbon made American independency an article of their propositions no event can make me a sharer in such a negotiation."

It was Necker himself who, in the absence of the Abbé Véri, had the embarrassing task of reading to Maurepas North's rejection of the Walpole overture. The old Comte took the obvious course. He repudiated any peace feelers the Abbé may have put out on his behalf. Disowned by both parties, Walpole, in a surly reply to North, magnanimously offered to step aside in favor of a more acceptable negotiator, while warning that the uncompromising attitude of the British government would play into the hands of the prowar faction in France. Even Véri, aware of Britain's stepped-up military campaign in America, despaired now that peace would come that winter.[40]

Meantime in France the crisis was drawing nearer. With Maurepas laid low by illness, Necker posed more of a threat than ever to the war faction. He and Sartine were now at daggers drawn. Early in October Necker had gone to the King and demanded that Sartine be removed from the Ministry of Marine. It was now Necker or Sartine. There seemed no real choice. Together the King and Maurepas went through the Royal Almanac and came up with no one as a replacement for the Director General, who, in Maurepas' words, was not "a simpleton or a rogue." In contradistinction, the head of naval affairs seemed clearly expendable. Few could deny that Sartine's administration had been both wasteful and incompetent.[41] But insiders felt that Necker's real reason for insisting on Sartine's dismissal was that he and Montbarrey were now marked down as Vergennes' chief supporters. Should they fall, Vergennes could not linger long, and the Swiss banker would be in fact if not in name the master of the government. The King capitulated. Sartine was dismissed in October, to be replaced by the far abler Marquis de Castries. Again the ax fell. At year's end the scatterbrained Montbarrey was dropped, and the war portfolio given to the Marquis de Ségur.[42]

Now Necker's star was in the ascendant. Could Vergennes hold on much longer? The Foreign Minister had been Necker's most severe and consistent critic. He had repulsed move after move on Necker's part to pull out of the war, and made it known that he suspected the banker of having secret intelligence with England to the profit of his bank and for even less pardonable and more sinister reasons.[43]

Not content with weakening the prowar faction in the Ministry, Necker struck a crippling blow at the new war effort of France's two allies, Spain and America. Writing to Congress' Committee on Foreign Affairs on September 9th, Carmichael had pointed out that the failure of the Spaniards so far to honor the bills drawn on Jay was imputed "to the interference of M. Necker and others influenced by that minister." Concerned over the inflationary aspects of Spain's funding operations, Necker was reported to have given prompt orders to the Caisse Royale in France not to receive the bills of exchange of the banking houses named in the Spanish loan proposal. Not only did Necker have Gerardot, Haller & Company, one of the chief banking firms in Europe, which the Genevan once headed and in which his brother still held a partnership, refuse the Spanish bills, but he sent a circular letter throughout Europe discrediting the loan. As a result Spain was deprived of nearly two million pesos to run its war program.[44] Necker's action caused widespread financial embarrassment in Spain and aroused the liveliest resentment of the Spanish Ministry. The French, by Necker's action, have done more to injure Spain than Lord North and the entire British Ministry, Floridablanca shouted at Montmorin, in one of the Spanish Foreign Minister's most splenetic outbursts.[45] Even as late as the end of November the Spanish Ministry, whose current expenditures for 1780 had exceeded revenue by some $25 million, had not yet completed their loan for $9 million "in part owing to the obstacles thrown in its way by M. Necker." "I am afraid," Carmichael acutely observed, "prejudices thereby excited will not soon be eradicated, although common interest may stifle them apparently at present."[46] Through Spain Necker hit at America. More directly he was reputed to have opposed the King's pledging his personal credit for loans Franklin was seeking to procure, and the finance director's proposals for supplying the French Army overseas were denounced by French officials in America as calculated to hamper the combined Franco-American war effort.[47]

If Maurepas at Necker's prompting had not succeeded in ending the war, and if the Director General had not yet managed to supplant Vergennes, there was still no reason why the Swiss banker should not assume some of the Foreign Minister's functions and make peace on his own. Necker possessed just the right combination of important connections and effrontery to pull it off. At least so he thought. In his first moves he prudently hid behind the curtain.

In the fall of 1779 the newly appointed British envoy extraordinary and plenipotentiary to the court of Sardinia chanced to be in Paris. Viscount Mountstuart came from a family that was well known in both France and Sardinia, and he himself had extensive contacts on the Continent. The Viscount was the eldest son of Lord Bute, George III's intimate friend and First Lord of the Treasury in the early years of his reign. It was Bute, who, without the knowledge of his Cabinet, had, through the mediation of the Sardinian ambassador, made overtures of peace to the court of Versailles, and had forced Parliament to accept a less than Carthaginian peace with France in 1763. His reward was to be hounded out of office by malevolent attacks, indubitably inspired in part by Frederick the Great, the ally whom England had let down, and spearheaded by the rabble-rousing John Wilkes, who accused Bute of having a liaison with King George's mother, the Princess Augusta, and of having been bribed by France.[48] One might have expected that the father's experience would have marked out the path of caution for the son, but the latter possessed some of the theatricality that Lord Bute's career had abundantly demonstrated, and was not likely to turn down a big part if chance brought it within his grasp.

Mountstuart had obtained permission from the French government to travel through France en route to his post in Turin,[49] and for a variety of reasons he tarried in the enemy country longer than he had expected. At Paris he made it his business to see informed people, and reported home that "all ranks of people talk loud against the war; the nobility more than any." In the spring of 1780 Mountstuart asked his government for permission to leave Turin and go "for a month or six weeks in the hot part of the summer to the mountains of Piedmont or Savoy or perhaps as far as Geneva." He pleaded the effect of the "immense heats" of Turin on the health of Lady Mountstuart and his children. The leave was promptly granted him.[50]

Sardinia, a neutral power which, like all the rest, had refrained from recognizing the American rebels, initiated various steps to augment its own prestige by attempting to mediate the conflict raging among the great powers. The Queen, according to the British chargé d'affaires, William Deane Poyntz, had opened up a correspondence with Charles III of Spain, in the thought that "this very channel might, perhaps, preferably be made use to detach the King of Spain from the interest of France, or lead him to a separate peace." The chargé who ran the Ministry pending Mountstuart's arrival, thought that the utilization by Britain of the Queen's good offices would require great delicacy, but was worth trying.[51] Pro-British sentiment still ran high at court, despite the Gordon outrages to the Sardinian chapel in London, and especially after Mountstuart had expressed to the King in person his government's deep regret and desire to make amends.[52]

Mountstuart set out for Geneva on July 11th to join Lady Mountstuart, "whom the great heats had already drove away."[53] Before leaving he had taken the precaution of applying for a passport to Baron de Choiseul, the French Minister at Turin, "in case they make some trips to France." Since Mountstuart had explained that the trip was for reasons of health, the French envoy informed Vergennes that he thought the request should be granted and that Mountstuart would not abuse this courtesy. True, it may seem odd that the British diplomat should choose to travel in an enemy country in wartime, but, Choiseul patiently explained to his suspicious superior, "one knows the taste of the English for very extended trips from their home." They are not like Frenchmen, who find everything they need inside their own country. Mountstuart, who had spent some time in his youth at Geneva, had a warm spot for that city. "These motives," Choiseul urged, could well be the "only ones" behind the trip. Approving the issuance of the passport, Vergennes, always cautious and normally skeptical, expressed the hope that the Minister would have the "prudence" not to get mixed up in the factional quarrels which were then tearing Geneva apart and "to repulse the intriguers who may try to involve him."[54]

Apparently Mountstuart at the time managed to avoid involvement in the intrigues of the revolutionary or counterrevolutionary factions which divided the defiantly Protestant city and republic of Geneva, enclosed save for a few miles along Lac Leman by the Catholic kingdoms of France and Sardinia.[55] On the surface his behavior was that of a typical British tourist vacationing in a Swiss summer resort. True, he met acquaintances from previous visits, but this seemed scarcely a ground for suspicion. Mountstuart spent a good deal of time with his former tutor, Paul-Henri Mallet. The Swiss professor and historian had toured Italy with the young Viscount in 1765. James Boswell was a companion on that journey. Mountstuart, the handsome, indolent, twenty-year-old dandy, Boswell, the talented and undisciplined neurotic some years his senior, Mallet, the hypersensitive and melancholy tutor, and Scottish Colonel James Edmonstone, serving as "the discreet governor," made an eccentric foursome on the Grand Tour. Boswell and Mallet did not hit it off very well, but the young Viscount and Boswell, despite their quarrels, pursued together their uninhibited explorations of the customs and talents of the courtesans of Rome and Venice. Mountstuart thought enough of Boswell to hand him over to his former mistress, Porzia Sansedoni, the wife of the Mayor of Siena. Mountstuart was later to marry the homely heiress, Charlotte Jane Windsor, and on her death took for his second wife the daughter of the banker, Thomas Coutts. Boswell, an avid name-dropper, kept his contact with the Viscount in the hope that Bute's son might obtain a pension for him from the King, as his father had managed years before to procure for Samuel Johnson. While mistrusting his "strange incoherency" of temper, Mountstuart thought Boswell had "fine old noble ideas."[56]

Mallet, best known for his history of Denmark, had important connections in royal circles, having been preceptor to the Prince Royal of the Danish court and was at that very time committed to write a history of Brunswick for George III.[57] He knew Paris well, and from childhood had been an intimate of Jacques Necker, a fellow Genevese. Now, Mountstuart, during his long sojourn in Paris the previous year, had doubtless been the object of careful scrutiny by France's Director General of Finances. Necker also realized that the middle-aged tutor was the ideal person to approach Mountstuart without arousing unnecessary suspicions. Certainly he had good ground for hoping that Mountstuart was out of sympathy with the war and had little or no use for the government that was prosecuting it.[58] Perhaps Lord Bute might even have imbued his son with a friendly feeling toward France.

In the spring of 1780 Mallet spent two and a half months in Paris, in good part in Necker's company. On his return to Geneva he made contact with Mountstuart immediately. The tutor talked freely to his former pupil "under solemn oath of secrecy." Were these talks to be disclosed, he cautioned, they might "greatly prejudice M. Necker," who was now winning the support of the King against a powerful faction headed by the Queen, Sartine, and Montbarrey. Necker had been frank with the Swiss historian, according to the latter's own account. To introduce fiscal reforms, the court of France had to have peace; otherwise, with resources exhausted, taxes would have to grow more burdensome and the country's credit might be dealt "a mortal blow." It would be a pity if the kingdom were to be ruined and Necker himself disgraced because he had been forced to risk his reputation to support "a war he never had nor could approve." The country needed peace desperately, Necker insisted. The only thing that was holding up that peace for a single minute was the American rebellion. As regards the latter, Necker, apparently not yet aware of the fall of Charleston at the time of this talk, was quoted by Mallet as expressing the fervent hope "in God the English would be able to maintain their ground a little better this campaign." Mallet, who had done quite a bit of preliminary cogitating on this problem, then proposed to Necker that "some one province," say New England, be declared independent, "and the others obliged to return to their former allegiance." Necker's response was favorable, but he talked in general terms, avoiding specific details.

In his talks with Mountstuart Mallet kept the light touch. He threw out this proposition for dividing America in a semi-serious way, presumably inviting a counterproposal from Mountstuart. After quite a few such talks had taken place in Geneva, the British envoy-on-leave asked his Swiss friend to ascertain "for my own information" whether the French Ministry really gave serious thought to obtaining peace. Mallet agreed to go to see Necker, and to get him to speak to the King, whose "secrecy and firmness were well known." In fact, he was prepared to set out "instantly" for Paris, but he wanted permission to use Mountstuart's name. Having full confidence in Mallet's discretion, and knowing full well that there was nothing so easy "as to disavow a conversation *entre quatre yeux*," Mountstuart replied that if Mallet went to Paris it was only to satisfy the British envoy's personal curiosity and that he himself would reserve the right to decide what, if anything, should be communicated to the King's ministers.

Although he had replied with customary diplomatic reserve, Mountstuart was in fact thrilled at the prospect of playing an important role in ending the war, and he believed that, with the American reverses in the South, the timing was right to "incline our enemies to think a little more seriously of peace."[59] From Geneva he rushed by a personal servant a report of these conversations to Hillsborough. Mountstuart ventured his own opinion that "we are not in a situation to carry on a war which is destructive in every part, and which each hour preys more and more on our vitals, and if of much longer duration must inevitably terminate in total ruin." The envoy to Turin was fully aware of the risks he ran by seeking peace for his country. "My family know too well what is the lot of those who engage in making peace," he added ruefully.[60] Was Mallet disinterested; if not, what was in it for him? Mountstuart conceded that his old tutor "partakes of the little low selfish ideas so inseparable from the name of Genevoise," but that he was close-mouthed, prudent, and given to an "uncommon turn to negotiation." What Mallet wanted was that the sums advanced him by George III for writing the Brunswick history would be increased and given to him for life. Discounting these selfish interests, Mountstuart felt the man could be "safely trusted."

Before Mountstuart had heard from home Mallet initiated from Geneva a long and detailed correspondence with his British friend, who had returned to Turin on October 8th. Picking up the thread of their conversations, Mallet wrote Mountstuart from Geneva on October 15th that he had "the strongest reason" to believe that Necker was now even better disposed than when he had left him four months ago. The difficulties confronting the Director General in his task of fiscal reform predisposed him to peace, to which he was now increasingly sympathetic. Necker's powers, the tutor wrote his pupil, are increasing, and with them go the means to achieve this goal.

Mountstuart in reply offered to accompany Mallet on his trip to Paris if he could be of the "least use." Because the delicacy of the affair demanded a great deal of circumspection, the envoy begged his Swiss correspondent not to send him by post or ordinary carrier observations on the activities of his *"ami,"* but to use one of the businessmen who operated between Geneva and Turin. That very same day Mountstuart dispatched another "Most Secret" dispatch in cipher to Hillsborough, in which he stated it as his opinion that Mallet "had been desired" to approach Mountstuart on the subject of peace, and, to alleviate any doubt respecting the propriety of employing the Swiss scholar, the envoy declared, "I am willing to go myself, and make use of him." A thousand pretexts could be advanced for joining Mallet—for example, the bad health of his family which necessitated his returning home. He then included an excerpt from Mallet's letter of October 15th reporting Necker's increasing prestige.[61] Up to and including December 19th Mallet sent in all six letters to Mountstuart reporting news about his friend, the *"juge"* in Paris, and the impending Cabinet shake-up.[62]

That the Genevese counterpart of Richard Cumberland failed to prosecute his peace moves beyond this point was no fault of his former pupil, but must be attributed to decisions taken by the stiff, unimaginative British Secretary of State and the obstinate monarch whom he served. On November 21st Hillsborough wrote Mountstuart that he had laid his communications before the King. That monarch had expressed the view that any negotiations with France were out of the question so long as "she continues to abett and support the Rebellion now raging in His Majesty's North American colonies," and certainly no attention could be paid to "proposals made or suggested" in the "unavowed and private manner" of Mountstuart's "Genevan friend." Mountstuart was bluntly told that it would be "very improper" for him to go to Paris "with any such ideas or to encourage your Genevan friend in the prosecution of them." Hillsborough reminded his Sardinian envoy that the King did not object to peace with France on honorable terms, but not so long as her "iniquitous and unjustifiable league with the American rebels remains in force." Accordingly, Mountstuart was to hold out no hope of a treaty with France while she continued "her connection with the Rebells" and to receive no proposals whatsoever from the French "if the Rebell Colonies are in any manner included."[63]

Crushed by the rebuke, Mountstuart replied that he would observe Hillsborough's instructions and would not trouble him with future news he might receive from his Genevan source. The envoy did take the occasion to point out that he had "ever held out the language your Lordship points out respecting America," and assured him that he would "still continue it, as well to my Genevan friend," as to "everyone else." Then came the brash assertion: "No conversation that has passed hitherto betwixt us could possibly tend to make him think otherwise. It was my business to listen, and no more."[64] Since Mountstuart clearly had given Mallet the impression that he had fallen in with the latter's idea of holding out some degree of independence for at least a part of the colonies, the remainder to return to their former dependency upon the Crown, and had even ventured to pass this formula for the independence of New England on to his chief, it is difficult to accept his professions of innocence. Not only the documents, but the envoy's later comments and behavior, prove that a formula for America was indeed the crucial point in these preliminary explorations with Necker's intermediary.

How heavily Necker counted upon the Mallet-Mountstuart conversations will perhaps never be known, but as winter was approaching and the British envoy to Turin failed to appear in Paris, Necker became increasingly restive and made no secret of his desire for peace. Peace, no matter of what kind, was essential if war prospects did not improve, Necker was quoted by Austria's ambassador as having remarked.[65] Thus, in one way or another Necker was prepared to go behind Vergennes' back and effect a peace without satisfying even the minimum goals of France's two allies and without regard to Louis XVI's own honored commitments.

On December 1st Necker, in the full assurance of his growing power, dispatched a secret message to Lord North, "for you alone, my Lord." It was transmitted in a package, along with a pamphlet, by a French trader who was ignorant of its contents. Necker, in his letter, claimed to have been prompted to write as the result of a conversation with Thomas Walpole, who appears to have shown the Director General some extracts from a letter North had written him expressing his desire for peace. Nevertheless, he did not entrust Walpole with the secret of this communication. "You desire peace," Necker wrote. "I wish it also." Why should not the two of us, he asked, attempt what our respective ministers of foreign affairs will some day attempt to initiate? We would not deprive them of the honors of a treaty but merely lay the ground for the first steps and ascertain at the least whether the time has yet arrived. Professing that he had always believed that moderation, good sense, and loyalty were the bases of such negotiations and would provide assurance against their being prolonged, Necker, tongue in cheek, complimented North on possessing the confidence of the King, which he had earned by his "honorable" and "brilliant" administration. While Necker conceded that he himself did not have the same authority, he felt he had every reason to be confident in giving North assurances that "reasonable overtures" could lead to success "quite as well in my hands as in those of anybody else's."

Getting down to specific details, Necker proposed as *"un premier aperçu raisonnable"* a truce "more or less long," during which the belligerent parties in America could hold "in a sovereign manner" the territory they now possess there. To Necker no difficulties should arise in minor adjustments between France and England, such as eliminating the useless and irritating commissioner at Dunkirk, who had been for long a thorn in the side of the French. As to Spain, to whom Necker's King owed fidelity and attachment, Necker would not presume to speak of her claim, but, with ironic overtones, suggested that it was highly likely that they were known to North.

Necker conceded that if his ideas were contrary to the sentiments of George III, North's reply would end the correspondence, but he added the caution that in any case it could scarcely suit the interests of the King to commence a public negotiation before the bases were secretly assured. A public negotiation, Necker reasoned, would redound to Britain's credit and be of little advantage to France, since credit was only a portion of France's resources, which were more significantly derived from good internal administration than the political exigencies of the moment.[66]

North received Necker's letter on the afternoon of December 15th. He showed it to Hillsborough, who in turn let Stormont have a look at it. "With these two exceptions," North told the King he was prepared to honor the secrecy imposed by his correspondent. Stormont hoped that no answer would be sent until he had had a chance to reply to the recent approaches of Catherine the Great to act as a mediator of the conflict. Admitting that it would be "rather difficult to draw a proper answer," North sent it on to the King on Sunday evening of the 17th.[67] George III, who less than a month before had indicated his displeasure with the Necker overtures pursued through Mallet, did not linger long over this letter. His reactions should have been a foregone conclusion even to a neophyte in diplomacy like Necker. Writing from Windsor Castle at twenty-two minutes past 10 A.M. on December 18th, the King replied:

Within these few minutes I have received Lord North's letter accompanying the secret he has received from M. Necker. It shews France is certainly in greater difficulties than we imagined or she would [not] by such various channels seek to court peace. No one has more inclination or interest in wishing so desirable an event as myself provided it can be obtained on honourable and solid terms. With France it [is] easily to be settled if she would desist from encouraging Rebellion and not add to her insults by wanting to affect independency which whether under its apparent name, or a truce is the same in reality; till she gives up that view I do not see how peace can be a safe measure.[68]

The next day North sent off to Necker, "in a feigned Italian hand" and under conditions of secrecy,[69] a note incorporating the substance of the King's response and repulsing the Director General's personal peace move.

One might well speculate on what the subsequent course of world history might have been had George III encouraged Necker's desperate intervention to halt the war. Aside from dodging the issue of American independence, a settlement in the winter of 1780-81 on the basis of territories then effectively controlled by each side would have chopped up the Thirteen United States into little pieces and prevented the establishment of a viable nation. Having first reputedly considered a tiny northeastern federation of quasi-independent states, Necker was now prepared to settle for a nation comprising New England, the Middle States without the port of New York, and a fractured and blighted Southland lacking access to the sea. The Swiss financier had gone behind Vergennes' back because he knew that the Foreign Minister had always rejected these terms as inconsistent with the fidelity and honor of France.

Years later Madame de Staël was to quote her father as having remarked that "Louis XVI was wrong to mix into the war between America and England, although the independence of the United States was desired by all generous spirits,"[70] but this comment scarcely jibed with "Premier" Necker's loud and insistent cries for peace and his operations from behind the arras. Had he succeeded, Necker would most certainly have become First Minister and Vergennes been swept out of office,[71] in the wake of Sartine and Montbarrey. Fate decided otherwise. Neither in the winter of 1780 nor seven years later was Jacques Necker destined to become the savior of France. Vergennes, alerted probably by the secret police to Necker's approach to North, and convinced that the Director General was involved with the British through his bank,[72] made frantic efforts to secure the correspondence which would expose his rival's double-dealing and even treachery and bring down upon him and his supporters lasting disgrace. In the Ministry he met Necker's peace cries head on. "Peace is a fine thing," Vergennes retorted, "only you should propose the means of attaining it in an honorable manner." Count Mercy reported the Foreign Minister as declaring, "I will express no opinion on Necker's financial operations, but in all other parts of the administration he is shortsighted and ignorant."[73] Even the King, who had been cautioned by Maurepas not to talk public business with Marie Antoinette, let his wife know that he was tired of the war and wanted to make peace before the end of 1781. With her customary indiscretion, Marie Antoinette, now partly preoccupied with another pregnancy, relayed the tidings to the Austrian envoy. Maurepas was reported as expressing an identical sentiment in a conversation with the Duc de Polignac.[74]

Just when everyone seemed to have turned against Vergennes and the whole country feared imminent bankruptcy, Necker astonished the world by the publication in January, 1781, of his *Compte rendu*.[75] That historic report, extravagantly praised and savagely denounced, revealed that, despite the enormous subventions to the court entourage, despite the deficit which Necker had inherited from his predecessors, despite the immense expenses of the war and the heavy interest payments on loans, current revenues apparently exceeded expenditures by 10,200,000 livres. A successor, Calonne, was to charge the Franco-Swiss financier with legerdemain and to expose the grave deficit which Necker's report had in fact concealed.[76] If, for reasons of ambition and political expediency or to maintain the credit of the government, Necker lied now, there is no reason to believe that he had not deliberately provoked the financial crisis of the previous summer by grossly exaggerating France's difficulties at that time. Certainly these embarrassments had not prevented Necker from floating a war loan in the fall of 1780, and at a high rate of interest.

Aside from demonstrating to the world that France had sufficient funds at hand to run the war for the current year—figures which contradicted everything Necker had been preaching for months—the *Compte rendu* betrayed an unrestrained streak of admiration for the adversary across the Channel. It attributed the immense credit of England to the publicity given its finances, an encomium which Shelburne and Burke might find hard to digest, and by implication praised England's war efforts as out of all proportion to her cash resources and population. Furthermore, the favorite maxim of the Swiss financial wizard that expenditures should be adjusted to revenues held out a veiled threat to the war party.[77]

The *Compte rendu* proved to be the climax of Necker's first administration as Finance Minister. He had shot his bolt. His enemies, now including the temporizing Maurepas, along with Vergennes and the Queen's confidante, the Duchesse de Polignac, marshaled their forces to smash the power-hungry Director General and the formidable peace party he headed, a faction allegedly composed of Protestants, bankers, and intellectuals. It was Necker himself, however, who forced the showdown by demanding that the King give him a seat in the Council. Taken aback by Louis XVI's prompt and curt refusal, the Director General had left himself no way out but to resign, which he did on May 19, 1781.[78]

This time the news was not confined to the small court circle at Versailles. All Paris seethed with unrest. Stocks dropped sharply on the Bourse. A run started on the Caisse d'Escompte. At the Théâtre Français, Collé's *La partie de chasse de Henry IV* was presented. Referring to the calumnies invented against his minister Sully, Henry IV declared: "Oh! How the wretches have deceived me!" A voice from the parterre rang out, "Yes! Yes!" and the whole theater took up the cry. Extra guards had to be called in to prevent a riot.[79] No Desmoulins was on hand, however, to incite the mob, as there was on an oddly similar occasion eight years later. The protests sputtered to a halt. The war went forward. Nonetheless, the Comte de Vergennes, though master of the Ministry henceforth, was visibly shaken by the struggle. The massive dosage of appeasement administered through the separate efforts of Floridablanca and Necker had prepared him to consider a truce on terms not too far removed from his adversaries'. The only difference was that the Foreign Minister would not accept so unpalatable a prescription from any physicians other than outside mediators. Vergennes' approach to a truce had a subtle difference from Necker's, to be sure, but the consequences could have been equally ruinous to the young republic across the Atlantic.

Despite the stern rebuke from Hillsborough, Lord Mountstuart merely licked his wounds and bided his time for another foray into the diplomatic jungle. In the spring of 1782 the moment seemed propitious. Hillsborough, along with the whole North Ministry, was out of office, and Charles James Fox, the only person in the new Rockingham Cabinet with whom Bute's son was on personal terms, was the new Foreign Minister. Mountstuart opened up his correspondence with Fox in a letter of April 17th,[80] in which he made the point that he was totally unconnected with any party, "without clog, fetter, or engagement whatever," and called Fox's attention to his secret dispatch from Geneva of September 18, 1780, and his subsequent communications on the same theme from Turin. The envoy told the Foreign Secretary that "it conveys a kind of proposal which, could it be now made, would not I think meet the same ill fate." Mallet was still available—

in fact Mountstuart had seen him as recently as November, 1781—and still on intimate terms with Mountstuart, and this intimacy, Fox's correspondent ventured to suggest, "might perhaps be of use." "You can imagine how mortifying it must have been to me," he confessed to Fox, "to find all my endeavours neglected, I may add, censured and ill received."

Anxious to get the jump on his equally ambitious rival, Lord Shelburne, who as Colonial Secretary considered relations with America his private province, Fox not only assured Mountstuart that he would be treated on his merits as regards a new assignment but encouraged him to explore the Genevan situation afresh. As a result, Mountstuart made contact with Mallet, who had been pressing his former pupil to get his pension from George III increased and awarded for life, in return for which the historian was prepared to send on to England confidential information from Paris. Mallet replied sadly that he now rarely heard from Necker, and that his former hopes were dashed as "everything changes ceaselessly and those who were on top yesterday are often not so today." Mallet's reply was a bitter disappointment to Mountstuart,[81] who now had the embarrassing duty of telling the Foreign Minister that his hopes had been stirred up in vain. In a letter of June 26th he reported that the result of pursuing the inquiries which Fox had authorized confirmed "strongly the opinion I submitted in September, 1780, and one can regret that so favorable an opportunity was then thrown away, for my friend seems to think there is now little chance of his being able to render those services his former connections might have afforded him the means of doing." Nevertheless, if Fox could use a person of "uncommon quick parts and perspicuity joined to a wonderful turn for political intrigue," Mallet was just the man for him. Since Fox was out of office before he received Mountstuart's letter, it can safely be presumed that no action was taken on the latter suggestion.[82]

Mountstuart still seethed with a sense of frustration. To the notorious double spy, the Abbé Hussey, then at Vienna, the British envoy at Turin indiscreetly wrote: "Had a late correspondent of mine [Fox] continued, I am certain he would have received, with eagerness and satisfaction certain offers I threw in his way and with which you are not unacquainted." Mountstuart ventured the prediction that the change would not be so favorable.[83] He was so right. Lord Shelburne was too farsighted a statesman to press a solution which, by dividing America into hostile camps, offered no prospect of lasting peace between the two English-speaking nations.

Even with Fox out, however, the new administration, whether inadvertently or not, did find a role for Mountstuart to play in the peacemaking, and at a strategic moment. Granted leave to return home,[84] he reached

Paris on December 16th, after the Americans had signed a preliminary peace, but before France and Spain had completed their own preliminary negotiations. "I have made good use of my stay," he modestly reported to Robert Liston, in charge of affairs at Turin on his departure.[85] On December 22nd Mountstuart dined with Richard Oswald, Britain's negotiator with the Americans. That same evening John Jay made a social call upon the British peace commissioner. Oswald, as Jay recorded in his diary, told him that Lord Mountstuart, who "execrated the American War," had brought along his letterbooks, "which he did not chuse to leave with his chargé d'affairs." Oswald was permitted to read the correspondence with Hillsborough, beginning in September, 1780, dealing with the overtures made by Necker through Mallet as intermediary "about putting an end to the war by dividing America between Britain and France, the latter to have the eastern part." To pound the point home, Mountstuart read Oswald from his letterbook of French letters the Mallet correspondence, revealing, as Jay summarized it, Necker's concern that the expenses of the war would disarray his financing and perhaps bring about his disgrace. Jay was also informed "that the overtures about America were conducted with a variety of precautions for secrecy, and with a stipulation or condition that both parties, in case they did not agree, should be at liberty to deny all that passed." Mountstuart conceded that Hillsborough had told him that "the subject was out of his line." Of course, the genuine letterbooks never suggested such a division between France and England, although the formula proposed was left purposely vague, and much else might have been suggested in the Mallet-Mountstuart talks that was never recorded.

By coincidence the identical terms were allegedly proposed by Vergennes to a British visitor, provided one accepted the word of Sir William Pulteney. Franklin, who had received a secret peace proposal from Pulteney several years before, had found that his visitor could not be trusted then.[86] Nevertheless, during the preliminary peace negotiations Oswald relayed to Jay and Adams Pulteney's completely undocumented assertion that Vergennes had offered to end the war by dividing America with Britain, "and in case the latter agreed to the partition, that the force of France and Britain should be used to reduce it to the obedience of the respective sovereigns." Pulteney's story was somebody's baseless concoction—"whispers which should not be credited to us," Adams put it[87]—but the Turin letterbooks of Mountstuart provided Oswald with just enough corroboration to hammer home the point that America's ally was prepared to sell her out at any time. Jay passed the "extraordinary story" on to Adams, and whether or not the former was taken in, his liveliest suspicions had already been aroused, not only by his long exposure to double-dealing in Spain, but more recently by the secret peace mission that Vergennes' undersecretary, Rayneval, undertook to England in the fall of '82.[88] True, Jay did not learn of the Mountstuart-Necker negotiations until after the peace preliminaries had been concluded, but the information was scarcely calculated to instill in the breast of the suspicious American diplomat a more trusting attitude toward France's Foreign Minister. For all his clumsy and indiscreet efforts, Mountstuart had failed to bring a world war to a close through a face-to-face meeting with Jacques Necker, but he did have his moment of revenge in Paris in December of '82, and it must have tasted like fresh honey in his mouth.

Years later Edmond Genêt took it upon himself to deny that the Necker-Mallet-Mountstuart negotiations had ever taken place. He managed to do this by mistaking the time of the negotiations for 1782, when Necker was out of office, instead of 1780, when the banker was at the height of his power, and by blandly asserting that Necker had never interfered in the concerns of the department of foreign affairs. His error was compounded, for at the time in question Genêt's father, Edmé Jacques Genêt, served as *premier commis* of the Bureau of Interpretation and passed on to Vergennes intelligence received from England and America. The elder Genêt held that post until September, 1781, when, on his death, his precocious son, then a minor functionary, succeeded him. By that date Necker had been out of office for months. Since Edmond Genêt had never heard of Mallet's activities, directly or through his father, and was in Vienna not Versailles in 1780, serving as an attaché to the French ambassador, Baron de Breteuil, he assumed that the report of them was baseless.[89] And diplomatic historians have invariably made the same assumption. Needless to say, Necker had seen to it that his negotiations looking toward peace were carefully concealed from Vergennes and his subordinates. We know now what really transpired, despite the weak disclaimer of a petty functionary, long removed in time and place from the feverish events he was describing.

The summer of 1780, like all other summers, had come and gone, and with its passing George III had lost the last serious opportunity to capitalize on his adversaries' desperate problems, divided counsels, and low morale. A settlement short of full independence for all the thirteen rebellious colonies was no longer in the cards, thanks less perhaps to America's ally, France, and her cobelligerent, Spain, than to the myopia and tenacity of the monarch whose rule she had long since repudiated.

VI

---~---

THE LION, THE FOX, AND THE ASS

IN THE SUMMER OF 1780 Charles Gravier, the Comte de Vergennes, was in his sixty-first year, and universally respected as a cautious man, whose prudence and moderation were matched by his indefatigable industry. The legendary stream of dispatches which issued from his pen, or from those of talented undersecretaries working under his close scrutiny, helped fashion the portrait of a foreign minister chained to his desk, of one who acted only after studying all the available information, and certainly never on impulse. This difference between the man and the myth had been carefully cultivated by Vergennes himself. His characteristic reticence, even icy reserve, more often than not masked a quality of indecisiveness when confronted with perplexing problems, and his patronizing and didactic manner covered a basic insecurity.

For a reputedly cautious man, however, the Comte had managed to make some pretty rash decisions. Twenty years before, when ambassador to the Sublime Porte, Charles Gravier had a secret liaison with a Madame Anne Testa, the attractive thirty-year-old widow of a physician of Constantinople, herself of a Franco-Greek family several notches beneath Vergennes' in social standing. Knowing that Louis XV, despite the notoriously loose moral standards the monarch set for himself, would most certainly have refused permission for him to marry Madame Testa, and that approval in advance was required of diplomats in the French foreign service, Gravier kept silent about his relations with her. By the time he did formally marry her in 1767 Madame Testa had already borne him two children, the eldest being six years old. For two years thereafter the ex-ambassador and his family lived in virtual retirement at Gravier's château of Toulongeon in Burgundy. When, in 1771, Gravier was named ambassador to Sweden, it was stipulated that he proceed on his mission without his wife. To sweeten the pill, Louis XV conferred upon his ambassador the title of the Comte de Vergennes. Nonetheless, the separation of several years did not weaken Vergennes' devotion to Madame la Comtesse, and theirs was considered to be one of the outstandingly happy marriages of the *ancien régime*.[1]

A truly cautious diplomat would not have put love ahead of his career, and have jeopardized his future by a *mésalliance* so distasteful to his king. True, Vergennes' delay in making the public avowal perhaps evidenced an understandable desire to enjoy the best of two worlds. A more cautious foreign minister, cognizant of the enormous fiscal problems besetting the monarchy, might have hesitated before pressing the kings of France and Spain to provide quasi-secret aid to the American insurgents, and certainly could have been expected to abstain from plunging into open alliance and full-scale war, steps of such enormous consequence for the United States, France, and in fact the whole world. Not so Vergennes. On the brink of that fateful decision he wrote to Montmorin, his energetic and perceptive young ambassador at Madrid, "Take for your motto, M. le Comte, and have it adopted where you are: *Aut nunc aut nunquam.*"*[2]

For a seasoned diplomat, Vergennes ran a curiously informal and unsystematic intelligence operation. Aside from the information gathered for the Foreign Office by accredited French envoys to foreign capitals, the Comte seemed to set great store by the services of persons of checkered and unsavory backgrounds, whose contacts a far less austere personage might have found distasteful. In the summer and fall of 1780, and even for some time thereafter, the Foreign Minister's intense suspicions of Floridablanca and Necker led him to cast ordinary prudence to the winds. Chance seemed to throw in his path a man who claimed to be able to reveal the inside story of the Spanish Minister's peace negotiations with the priest and the playwright.

Less than a week after the Gordon Riots had subsided across the Channel a stranger presented himself at the embassies of Spain and France at The Hague. The Conde de la Herreria and the Duc de La Vauguyon in turn heard their caller's tale. An Englishman going by the name of Montagu Fox, he claimed to be related to the family of Sir Joseph Yorke, at that very moment the British ambassador at the Dutch capital. Fox told a fantastic story. He had only just escaped from the Tower of London, where he had been confined for his activities in the Gordon Riots. He had been personally involved in the physical assault on Lord Sandwich, and with a party of some dozen others raided both Sandwich's private residence and the Admiralty, where he snatched certain secret naval plans and papers. An opponent both

* Now or never.

of the North Ministry and the American War, Fox put a number of intriguing propositions to both diplomats that were not likely to be dismissed
out of hand.

Most pressing of these was a request for four thousand guns, which
were needed to start an uprising in Cornwall. Fox claimed to have close
contacts with the traditionally restless miners, and was prepared to go
back to England to expedite this project. Of course the visitor realized
that his auditors could take no action without consulting their respective
governments, and he had the ambassadors arrange appointments for him
with the Conde de Aranda in Paris and the Comte de Vergennes at Versailles. In addition, he requested a letter of introduction to Franklin at
Passy, which the French ambassador obligingly provided.[3]

The principal intermediary between Montagu Fox and the Allied powers
was Paul François de Quelen de Stuer de Caussade, the Duc de La Vauguyon. From a family of high nobility, son of a military hero of the War
of the Austrian Succession, and a childhood companion of the young prince
who became Louis XVI, La Vauguyon had had no previous diplomatic experience before entering upon his duties at The Hague, although he had
done some writing in politics and philosophy. When he was dispatched to
the Netherlands four years earlier, the post had not appeared to demand
a veteran diplomat and might safely be awarded to a young man whose only
service had been in the army. The expanding American War and the deep
cleavage between the followers of the House of Orange, the pro-English
faction, and their opponents, the Patriot party, put an entirely different complexion on the status of this ambassadorial post. Only thirty-four years old
in 1780, and far from being a ripened diplomat, La Vauguyon had the
responsibility of swinging the Netherlands into the French orbit.

Whether or not the French ambassador was prepared to swallow Fox's
story, he dutifully passed it on to Vergennes. With his proverbial caution,
the Foreign Minister put a few questions to his envoy in the Netherlands.
Is it likely, he asked, that a man who had only just escaped from the Tower
of London would be consumed with eagerness to return to London and possibly put himself on the gibbet he had just so narrowly missed? Would it
be appropriate for Catholic France to arm the miners of Cornwall for what
the London riots had revealed to be an anti-Catholic cause? Let us bear
in mind, Vergennes declared didactically to his envoy, before we start
providing Fox with the arms he requests, just how much the English really
hate us and whether they would not prefer to use these guns against Frenchmen than against each other.[4]

Meantime La Vauguyon had already provided Montagu Fox with a

French passport. Armed with this document, the secret agent crossed the border, and reached Paris on June 22nd, when he went directly to the residence of the Conde de Aranda. At the latter's advice that he stay close by, Fox took lodgings at the Hôtel de Malthe on rue St. Niçoise, using the common French name of "M. Dumont." Aranda heard him out, looked over his papers, and passed him on to Vergennes, with the cryptic comment: "It appears to me that our man has need of money." To avoid arousing suspicion, Aranda advised Fox to call on Vergennes at the crowded court of Versailles rather than at the Foreign Minister's more isolated country home.[5]

That same evening Vergennes, after receiving his caller, dashed off a note for Aranda's courier. He warned the Spanish envoy that Fox's visit might well tie in with the highly publicized efforts of the British government to incriminate the Allies in the Gordon Riots. "I incline to believe that Montagu Fox is a ministerial emissary charged with setting a trap for us," he warned, once more raising doubts about Fox's credibility that had been in his mind the instant he had heard about him from The Hague.[6]

The very next day Fox truthfully admitted to Aranda that Vergennes was cold to the idea of arming the Cornish miners. Aranda then asked to see the papers that Fox claimed to have filched from the Admiralty. Fox informed him that he had left them behind in England, but was prepared to go back at once to retrieve them. Without receiving any further credentials, Aranda advanced "M. Dumont" some small sums, and the agent went off to see Franklin. At the next meeting with the Spanish ambassador Fox told him that the American was enthusiastically in favor of stirring up a rebellion among the Cornish miners. In fact, however, the old doctor had given him little encouragement. He pointed out to Fox the difficulty of landing four thousand stand of arms in England without being observed and the chances that government troops could put down the insurgents before they were properly trained. When pressed by Fox for his opinion of the feasibility of the project, the Sage of Passy, according to his own account to Joseph-Matthias de Rayneval, Vergennes' able undersecretary, "told him I could form none without knowing more particulars of it than he had communicated, and also the persons who were to conduct it." Franklin promised to let Vergennes know if he heard anything further of substance from Fox,[7] but presumably the latter was discouraged by his lukewarm reception from pursuing the matter further with the American envoy.

Aranda never checked with Franklin but did speak to Vergennes. If Fox convinced them of his credentials and of the soundness of his project, Vergennes said, he would be given funds to purchase arms at Liège. These were perhaps two big "ifs," but the impulsive Spanish envoy, acting on the assumption that he had the cautious blessing of the French Foreign Minister, sent Fox back to The Hague to secure from the Spanish and French ambassadors in Holland such assistance as he needed for his project.[8]

Not only Franklin's reaction but the observations of his own undersecretary should have made Vergennes pause for second thoughts about Montagu Fox. Rayneval, at Vergennes' request, had cross-examined Fox pretty rigorously regarding his plan for a Cornish uprising. Fox told him that the Opposition would be prepared to aid a Franco-Spanish invasion if the combined fleet entered the Channel. He advised bringing the armada as far west as Plymouth, whose defenses were still depicted as shaky, while making a simultaneous diversion on the Thames, moves which could be prepared in part from Dunkirk and in part from Holland. In Fox's judgment, one or two fifty-gun ships, a couple of frigates, and some fire ships would suffice for the latter project, and he promised to procure a detailed plan of the estuary of the Thames and to provide pilots both for this operation and the Plymouth sortie.[9]

Montagu Fox by no means settled all of Rayneval's doubts any more than he did Franklin's. Granted the widespread discontent in England, to which the Association movement abundantly attested, Rayneval warned his superior that Parliament had managed to ignore the bombardment of petitions with no serious consequences to the government. The anti-Catholic manifestations, on the other hand, Rayneval downgraded as purely "ephemeral," lacking support from the principal Opposition leaders. Shrewdly appraising the discontent in England as unlikely to cause a real blow-up, he advised that it would be folly to count on the success of a rising which lacked the backing of the Whig grandees. Even conceding the possibility of such a move, was Montagu Fox the sort of man who would be mixed up in it? Who was he? What were his credentials? What backing did he have? Who were his fellow conspirators? Unless Fox could give satisfactory answers to all these questions he would have to be put down for a fool or an imposter, Rayneval concluded.[10]

On the basis of his own impressions and those of his undersecretary, Vergennes told Fox that he would have to produce some very solid evidence of his relation to the Opposition groups in England before the Foreign Minister would commit himself further. "I have neither accepted nor rejected, his propositions," Vergennes wrote La Vauguyon, pluming himself on his circumspection. Despite his handsome offer, Montagu Fox, in Vergennes' opinion, lacked by himself the credit to build even a sloop.[11] Nevertheless, even discounting his wild story, Fox had made out a plausible case, and Vergennes felt he could not afford to shut the door in his visitor's face. He paid for Fox's trip and promised to reward him were he to turn over any "interesting" papers taken from the Admiralty. While putting La Vauguyon on guard, he authorized his envoy to continue the contact.[12]

At the end of June Fox reputedly made a visit to England, entering by way of Scotland.[13] On his return to The Hague in July he turned over to either the French or the Spanish ambassador a miscellaneous batch of naval and military documents, including data on the defenses of Gibraltar,[14] followed shortly by the plan of a British naval operation by which a junction of the Franco-Spanish fleet would be prevented.[15] This plan seems to have been based upon secret instructions sent on May 27th to Admiral Geary, commander of the Channel fleet, which in fact had been scrapped as a result of the Gordon riots, necessitating the posting of the fleet in the Channel to guard against a possible French invasion, especially from the Dunkirk area. A few weeks later Fox turned over a register of the Admiralty and a plan to break the blockade of Gibraltar by attacking the Spanish coast, striking hardest at Vigo. So far as can now be determined, the Admiralty register was a work of fiction. Among the ships listed was the *Lynx*, reported as carrying forty cannon and 288 men, whereas she was just a modest sloop. Three other boats noted in the "register" were dreamed up by its author.[16] Fox continued to turn over additional naval data to England's enemies down through the spring of 1781. He passed on Admiral Hughes's plan of March 1, 1781, and the instructions to General William Medows of April 21, 1781, both outlining operations against the Dutch possessions in the East Indies, along with the instructions to Commodore Johnstone for an attack to relieve Gibraltar (March 8, 1781). All these projects had either been scrapped or drastically modified when Fox turned the reports over, or were ingenious counterfeits devised to confound Franco-Spanish naval strategy.

In addition to the naval data, Montagu Fox purported to have brought back from England documents of a political or diplomatic character bearing on the prospects of peace, which he handed over a bit at a time. In August La Vauguyon sent on to Vergennes a copy of a manifesto allegedly written in July, and reading as follows:

Since in the present situation it would appear prudent to place ourselves on guard against the misfortune which cannot fail to follow a state of despotism resulting from the anti-constitutional or tyrannical measures of the administration, repugnant to every reasonable idea and subversive of all liberty, and since foreign aid is indispensably necessary, we the undersigned have designated William Montagu Esqr to negotiate and transact overseas and to do whatever is possible for the well-being of the English people and the establishment of the Constitution in its original foundations with such restrictions only that he will make no specific proposals and will agree to nothing with any state, prince, or political body without a new authorization.

London   the   (21)   July   1780
[Signed]   SHELBURNE, FOX, WYVYL,
Is. BARRÉ, JOS. MILLES.[17]

Here on its face was a treasonable proposition. The Conde de Aranda felt that the Opposition faction should be encouraged to promote confusion in England.[18] The less volatile French Foreign Minister, considering the distinguished personages involved, names all carefully chosen to represent the wide spectrum of reform and opposition, was inclined to tread warily, and to put some checkrein upon the Duc de La Vauguyon. Commenting on the alleged manifesto of the British Opposition leaders, Vergennes admitted to Montmorin that the French and Spanish envoys at The Hague took it seriously enough to rush copies by courier to Madrid and Versailles. As for himself, Vergennes insisted that he was still unconvinced. If only he had in his hands the original Shelburne autograph to compare with authentic Shelburne signatures readily available! Nevertheless, despite doubts that would not down, France's Foreign Minister authorized La Vauguyon to advance Fox anywhere from 1,200 to 1,500 livres monthly, with an understanding that his pay would be increased should he turn over information of real value. Let us keep this to ourselves, Vergennes cautioned his envoy to Spain. If the man turns out to be a fraud, we should appear ridiculous were it to get around that we have swallowed his bait.[19] Montmorin fully shared his chief's doubts about Fox. "Would Shelburne, who professed to be a follower of Lord Chatham, be led to make a démarche to the House of Bourbon?" he asked. The whole business made no sense. On the other hand, Montmorin conceded that so far as the rest of the Opposition was concerned, they were so hostile to the government that "we can believe anything" about them.[20]

On Vergennes' orders, La Vauguyon informed Montagu Fox that the King of France wished for an equitable peace, one that did not encompass the destruction of England. While His Majesty hoped that the patriotic efforts of the Opposition would halt the progress of royal despotism and re-establish the original Constitution, he could not venture to assist them without information "in the most precise manner" as to the plans of the Opposition leaders. In turn, Fox promised to ask his "friends" to confer upon him "more power abroad" and also agreed to write to England to obtain a signed copy of the Ministry's instructions to Cumberland.[21]

Fox continued to feed La Vauguyon with scraps of information on the status of the Cumberland negotiations in Spain, and other documents, among them a memorial of Lord Stormont of August 3rd, disclosing England's intention to use force against the neutral Dutch.[22] He again asked to be sent back to England to secure more data on the British fleet and to make contacts with the Rockingham Whigs, in addition to Shelburne's faction.[23] Clearly the English agent had been given some encouragement, for only a few days after his meeting with La Vauguyon he was complaining to La Herreria's successor at The Hague, the Conde de Sanafé, that the French had turned over to him the wrong kind of guns, lacking standardization and not suitable for use in England.[24]

If in fact the guns were turned over, the transfer only whetted Montagu Fox's appetite. Around this time he presented his clients with a copy of a communication signed by the Rev. Christopher Wyvill (spelled "Weyvil" in this document), allegedly written at Westminster September 4, 1780. Therein the delegates of the County Association, while careful to disavow any specific propositions to "any state or foreign political body," declared that in the event that "pacific measures to attain their ends are inefficacious," they would be put "in a state to make a respectable showing to sustain their demands" were France to turn over to them twenty thousand arms and four thousand barrels of powder.[25] Since this was a time when Wyvill was most optimistic about the results to be obtained from the fall Parliamentary elections,[26] it seems preposterous on its face that he should have ventured everything on a treasonable intrigue.

With that consummate talent for duplicity which he had already abundantly demonstrated in his dealing with the British, Floridablanca was understandably suspicious of double-dealing on the part of others, including the enemy. He took it upon himself to caution Aranda. The King feels that we must not compromise ourselves with Fox, he warned his more enthusiastic ambassador in Paris, lest he be a counterspy or an agent of the very Ministry he is ostensibly opposing. But he advised against shutting the door in his face. Indeed, it is truly astonishing, Floridablanca confessed, that a personage of the caliber of Barré would sign such a document. "Verily, only in a country like England can such things happen," he concluded.[27]

However suspicious Fox's sensational disclosures might seem on their face —and Vergennes had backed up Floridablanca in impressing Aranda with the need for caution in dealing with the secret agent[28]—France's Foreign Minister was no more inclined than was his Spanish counterpart to break off all contact with a person who might provide him with the inside story of what Floridablanca was really up to in his current meetings with Cumberland, information which Montmorin was unable to obtain. Presumably with La Vauguyon's approval, Fox made still another trip to England to satisfy Vergennes' demand that he produce dispatches between Richard Cumberland and the British Ministry as proof of his good faith.[29] Now Fox began to deliver the merchandise. On his return to The Hague he turned over to the French ambassador what he professed to be Hillsborough's report to the Cabinet on the progress of the Hussey-Cumberland negotiations, several dispatches of the British playwright-diplomat, and several more covering Hillsborough's replies to that emissary. All these documents showed the extrordinary efforts being put forward in London and indicated that the British might even settle for peace with Spain by ceding Gibraltar.[30] Conceding that these efforts had not succeeded, Fox held out hopes that the Ministry would consider broad peace proposals in the coming winter, and viewed the British government's embarrassments as stemming from a shortage of funds and seamen, and from its fear that civil war was imminent. Fox further reported that while in London recently he had talked privately with Shelburne. The Earl had sharply criticized the government. Fox also quoted the Duke of Richmond as being prepared to address a private letter to the Duc de La Vauguyon, which would leave no doubt as to where the British peer stood. If he could go to Brussels next month, Fox told the French envoy, he would have a chance to confer with Richmond along with other notables. Fox promised to secure additional secret information through the channel of the Duke of Richmond, and left La Vauguyon the distinct impression that the documents would relate to the Cumberland mission, Vergennes' big obsession at the moment. To top it all, the self-confessed British refugee promised to forward a letter from Shelburne in his own hand spelling out the details of the Opposition program.[31]

The Cumberland documents, the first batch of which had been shown to the Spaniards, were proving as much of a sensation in Spain as in France. These papers purported to show that González de Castejon, Charles III's Minister of Marine, was privately working to make a deal with England. Little wonder that Floridablanca, by the end of October, was promising to turn over to the French the papers that "adventurer" had given to Sanafé, and was denouncing the Cumberland revelations as "absolutely false."[32]

With his right hand Fox was demonstrating that the Opposition was desperately seeking peace; with his left he was documenting the intention of the British government to fight an all-out war. Believing that Fox's alleged relative, Sir Charles Yorke, had put the agent up to passing on the Stormont revelations with an idea of intimidating the Dutch, Aranda was becoming increasingly suspicious of the peace emissary, whom he now denominated a weathercock, blown most easily by the winds from his court.[33] Still the game went on.

At long last, after infinite prodding, Montagu Fox on his return from yet another trip to London in the winter of 1781[34] turned over to the Duc de La Vauguyon the "original" signed paper from the archconspirators that he had promised to produce months before. The document read as follows:

> London, January 16th, 1781
>
> The underwritten being excluded by the constitutions of the associations formed by their Fellow Citizens for the preservation of their rights from interfering in the executive department, address themselves in their individual capacities, to His Most Christian Majesty's Secretary of State for foreign affairs and to His Ambassador at the Hague to engage Their Excellencies to interest themselves with the King their Master, to afford them, the underwritten, at a future date such assistance, as circumstances may render necessary, and may tend to the mutual interest of His Most Christian Majesty, and of their Country.
>
> [signed]   RICHMOND
>   SHELBURNE[35]

Without taking the pains to make even a cursory check on the authenticity of this amazing *démarche*, La Vauguyon, now completely taken in by Montagu Fox, passed it along to Vergennes, with the observation that the signatures of Richmond and Shelburne left no doubt of the "actual part" that the two Opposition leaders were playing in forwarding the project of the County Committees. Along with this document, La Vauguyon forwarded what he claimed was an original letter of Cumberland, together with a copy of one of the other dispatches from that envoy in Spain, which, as Vergennes' envoy reported it, had brought down upon the head of Cumberland the "bitterest reproaches" of his government. La Vauguyon further revealed to Vergennes that Fox had also shown the Cumberland documents to Sanafé and had pledged to procure the original letter sent by Castejon to Hillsborough, mentioned in one of the dispatches from Cumberland included in this batch.[36]

Those startling papers, Vergennes conceded, necessitated the "ripest reflection." As to the authenticity of the documents, they depended on the degree of confidence that the person who transmitted them merited. So far as Fox was concerned, the French Foreign Minister still had not made up his mind. Meantime, "far from stopping" M. Montagu (generally referred to in this correspondence as "M.M."), we ought to "aid his activities and propose objects which could be of real utility," including the procurement of data on naval projects, finance, Cabinet decisions, and any news regarding the peace. "We will receive with equal pleasure the original letter of M. de Castejon to Lord Hillsborough, and the plan proposed by the British Ministry to serve as a base for a private peace between England and Spain." If Fox satisfies us in all these objects, Vergennes added, please assure him that we will not be lacking in gratitude of a tangible character. It was indeed too bad that Fox had disclosed the Cumberland papers to Sanafé. True, there was nothing to be done about it now, but precautions should be taken against such a disclosure in the future. Vergennes himself assumed full responsibility for passing on to Spain what he thought would be useful for their ministers to know.[37]

In his desperate eagerness to get the inside story of Floridablanca's proposals to Cumberland and of Castejon's alleged treachery, Vergennes seemed to scorn the ordinary lessons of caution. The fact is that Fox had taken an enormous risk in turning over the Shelburne-Richmond document. Had Vergennes acted with his usual circumspection he could easily have checked the authenticity of those signatures, for Richmond and Shelburne letters were abundantly available in France. The Abbé Morellet, an acquaintance of Vergennes and an intimate friend of Shelburne's, had many of the Earl's letters in his possession. A comparison would have shown that this was a labored forgery or a traced signature, and not from Shelburne's own hand.[38] Richmond likewise had numerous correspondents in France, and his signature had only recently been affixed to papers in connection with his application for the title of Duc d'Aubigny. The real Richmond signature bears not the slightest resemblance to the flowery one affixed to this document.[39] Whether or not the French authorities took the trouble to match these signatures with originals at hand, they should have been forewarned by the sensational text itself. Would two of the most respected leaders of the Opposition, regardless of how desperate they conceived their situation, have entrusted their reputations to so slippery an agent as M. Montagu Fox? Suffice to say, nothing in the Shelburne correspondence suggests that the Earl was ever for a moment contemplating a treasonable course. Richmond, by his more fiery temper, had made himself perhaps a more exposed target. Not long before, he had ventured the opinion that, if the British government continued its ruinous course, he might have to seek refuge on his estates in France.[40] While privately he had condemned the Gordon Riots as "unjust," "extravagant," and "weak," he seemed most concerned because the disorders tended "to discredit any attempts of the People to do justice on any future occasion when the cause may warrant it."[41] Just what Richmond had in mind he did not spell out. Certainly he was about as unpopular with the King and the Ministry as any member of the Opposition. George III had commented adversely on the Duke's readiness to give up his military commission and quit his country for France,[42] and Charles Jenkinson, one of the closest of the King's friends, was currently denouncing the Duke as "that plaguing fellow." "If hard words will enable me to get rid of the Duke of Richmond I will lose no opportunity of using them."[43]

It should have been obvious to Vergennes that some individual or group was desperately anxious to bring disgrace upon Shelburne, Richmond, and other outspoken leaders of the Opposition. When the duels and the libels failed of their purpose, the enemies of Shelburne and Richmond were still not discouraged. In the fall of 1780 the news of Major André's execution caused a sensation in London. John Trumbull, the young American artist who was studying in the British capital under another American, Benjamin West, was arrested as a spy and imprisoned in Tothill Fields Bridewell in reprisal. It was alleged that letters discovered on his person proved conclusively that leaders of the Opposition like Richmond and Shelburne were traitors. Actually, no such incriminating letters were found.[44]

It is perhaps no coincidence that around this time a satirical tract appeared in London, obviously written by one of the army of expatriate French libel writers plying their trade in the British capital, containing similar allegations of contact between Shelburne and Richmond on the one hand, and Vergennes on the other, to set up a new government in England.[45] Thus far there had been nothing but innuendoes and allegations. Now "evidence" was manufactured, and Montagu Fox was to be the instrumentality for setting the trap for the Opposition peers.

Whether or not the Shelburne-Richmond forgery was spotted, the document did nothing to allay suspicions in Paris and Versailles. Commenting on a report from Fox that the English squadron had sailed for Gibraltar, Aranda wrote in March of '81 that he had little confidence in the man, "who seems to me very English at heart" and sells to both us and the French. Let us wait and see if the British fleet movement corresponds with Fox's report, he counseled Floridablanca.[46] By this time these strange counterintelligence efforts, calculated either to discredit the Whig Opposition or ruin the Cumberland-Hussey negotions, were no secret to neutral diplomats in Paris.[47]

Fox deserved good marks for effort if not for integrity. After another trip to England in the spring of '81 he promised to turn up "new original" Cumberland items, provided that those he had already handed over were turned back so that they could be restored to those from whom he had procured them. What Fox wanted to know specifically was the impression which "the original writing signed 'Shelburne and Richmond'" had made. La Vauguyon parried this question by asking one of his own regarding the concrete views of the Opposition leaders. Fox explained that they wished to put the British Constitution back on its original base, and would only have recourse to force after they had employed all peaceful means to obtain their objects.

Now that Holland was a reluctant belligerent, "M.M.," speaking on behalf of his confederates, indicated their readiness to provide the Dutch with some armed ships of war to raid the coasts of Britain. Fox asked La Vauguyon to address the proposal on his behalf to the officials of Amsterdam, and the gullible diplomat felt that so long as he put nothing in writing his chief could scarcely disapprove his role as an intermediary. In fact, without even waiting for Vergennes' authorization, and in defiance of a warning from the Foreign Minister against acting in the dark, the French envoy went ahead and put the proposition to the Dutch officials. Montagu Fox was prepared to provide ten English frigates mounting twenty-four to thirty-six guns for a price of £80,000 payable on delivery.

The burgomasters of Amsterdam referred the proffer to The Hague. Pensionary Visscher served as intermediary, and a purchase agreement was actually signed. A merchant named Fizeaux was authorized to post bond for delivery of the first ship, a thirty-six-gun frigate named *Dorset*. The ships were to be brought to the Dutch island of Texel, leaving one by one from different ports of England to avoid suspicion. With the deal on paper and signatures affixed, Fox then left presumably for London, promising to procure the ships "in a very few days."

The Dutch impatiently awaited the signals arranged to announce the armada's arrival. The frigates were to fly an English pendant under a Dutch tack and to fire off two guns to larboard. Although by mid-April the Dutch had drastically trimmed their expectations, and looked forward to two or three ships at most, they had not yet abandoned hope. One evening toward the end of that month the Pensionary, seated at supper and hearing cannon shots apparently fired according to the signals agreed upon, announced "There are the English ships." He was overly optimistic.[48]

As the negotiations dragged out, despite La Vauguyon's intense activity, neither side seemed content. Once more Fox asked, with mounting impatience and ostensibly on behalf of the Opposition leaders, whether the

Shelburne-Richmond writing was sufficient proof of their intentions. The resourceful agent, whose head was full of wonderful projects, now came up with still another scheme. This time he proposed a Franco-Dutch descent upon England, either along the coast north of the Tyne or at the Thames estuary, a modest variation of the lamented Franco-Spanish enterprise of '79. For this venture he was prepared to furnish tested pilots with perfect knowledge of the coast and inland waters and authentic documents on the state of naval and military defenses in the area in question. He even agreed to go himself on one of the invading ships, presumably as a hostage. La Vauguyon, not sensing a trap, was convinced that such an expedition could "strike a fatal blow at our enemies." So important did he consider the project that he asked permission to go to Paris to take it up with Vergennes and Castries in person.[49]

Meantime no turncoat British ships appeared at Texel, nor was the long-promised letter from Castejon produced. The hard-trading Dutch were becoming understandably agitated, and Vergennes did not conceal his exasperation. The Comte told La Vauguyon to his face that he had been duped. Badly shaken by his interview, La Vauguyon returned to The Hague, only to confront the angry burghers clamoring ever more loudly for their warships. Through it all Montagu Fox remained imperturbable. Confronting La Vauguyon on July 6th, the British agent reported that he now had the Castejon letter, but that he could not permit the ambassador to forward it to either Madrid or Versailles. Instead, Fox asked La Vauguyon to have Vergennes send on to The Hague some specimens of handwriting of Spain's Minister of Marine to enable the French envoy to make the comparison himself with the dispatch Fox was prepared to show him. Fox explained that he was now obliged to return the letter within three or four days' time to those who had procured it for him. To mollify the now thoroughly aroused La Vauguyon, Fox promised that a twenty-eight-gun ship would arrive at Texel in the course of the coming week.[50] Within a few days La Vauguyon was informed by Vergennes that there was something fishy about Fox's naval data, that his naval signals and reports of squadron size seemed false or erroneous.[51] How about the Castejon letter? Vergennes asked impatiently.[52]

The denouement could hardly be postponed longer. On July 24th the French ambassador reported that Fox had presented to the Dutch Admiralty the three pilots reputedly brought from England to help the armada in navigating the English coast, while at the same time he renewed his hoary promise to bring the warships to Texel. Finally realizing that they had been completely taken in, the Dutch officials would have nothing to do with the pilots. Coincidentally, some sailors reputedly from the English ships off Texel, who had been roving the streets of Amsterdam, "were told they had better find themselves a good hiding place."[53] In righteous indignation Fox rejoined that he now washed his hands of the whole warship deal. If they wished to pursue it further they could contact his compatriot in Rotterdam, a man named Browning. Even La Vauguyon's confidence in the agent was fast waning.[54]

Whether Fox or those behind him were now prepared to break off further contacts with the Allied governments after sufficient mischief had been done is by no means clear, but his next act amounted to a severing of relations. Fox allowed La Vauguyon to look at an alleged letter from Castejon dealing in vague terms with an expedition to Gibraltar which was called off. However, instead of the letter bearing the signature of "Castejon" it was signed "De Castegonde." Unfortunately for Fox, La Vauguyon knew the Spanish naval minister personally and was acquainted with his signature. At last the revelation dawned that he had been dealing with a forger and a double-dealer, and had been completely taken in. He had been dull-witted about the business, but now his wrath knew no bounds.

It just happened that at this time a former member of the Paris police force named Receveur, a protégé of La Vauguyon, who had performed services on and off for Vergennes,[55] was in Holland. Utilizing Receveur, La Vauguyon conceived the notion of luring Fox across the French border to Givet, where the double-dealer would be arrested and sent to the Bastille by *lettres de cachet* to be issued from Versailles.[56] The trap was set. Fox was flitting between Brussels and Liège, where Receveur, armed with a *lettre de cachet* from Vergennes, was waiting to pick him up.[57] Whether because Fox still furnished crumbs of information of use to France[58] or out of fear that his arrest and incarceration at the very moment when England was making direct peace overtures to the Dutch might provoke a scandal in Holland, Vergennes' nerve failed him at the last moment. He suddenly countermanded the order to his police agent to seize Montagu Fox,[59] and the trap was never sprung. On August 17th the French ambassador reported that Fox told him that the Duke of Richmond was at Spa for some days. Since he was constantly astonished by the strange mixture of truth and falsity in Fox's reports, La Vauguyon ventured the opinion that this one sounded authentic. Would it not be profitable, he asked Vergennes at this late date, to sound out Richmond in a circumspect manner as to his relations with Montagu Fox? Receveur would be the perfect man for this assignment. No, Vergennes replied sternly. Leave Richmond alone. If the Duke has a communication or a request to make of us, there is reason to believe he will find means of doing so. As regards Fox, so long as he needs money, it is doubtful whether we have seen the end of him.[60]

This time Vergennes was wrong. Montagu Fox knew that the game was up. Reacting with the instincts of a hunted animal, he, along with four thousand florins he had only recently wangled from the Allies, vanished. Some half year later a "M. Montagu," posing as an officer of the Royal Navy, turned up at Stade in Hanover. Claiming to have recently been in Russia, he made contact with the French legation and offered his services for intelligence and propaganda. Vergennes prudently declined them.[61] That is all that was heard from Montagu Fox, whose disappearance from the stage of history was quite as mysterious as his entry upon it.

Whoever "Montagu Fox" really was, France's counterespionage service failed to penetrate his secret. He curiously combined two names of families famous in England. There were many distinguished Montagus, including the onetime Prime Minister, the Earl of Halifax, the witty Lady Mary Wortley Montagu, whose daughter married Lord Bute, and perhaps by coincidence John Montagu just happened to be Lord Sandwich, the head of the Admiralty. Fox was a name borne by the grasping Lord Holland and his eloquent son, Charles James, a thorn in the side of the North Ministry. But we have no reason to believe that the agent was either a Montagu or a Fox. Like everything else about Montagu Fox, the name was counterfeit.

That audacious secret agent may have been operating in Holland as a lone wolf, but, if so, he was only one of a corps of British spies who used Holland as a center for their operations. From a little bookshop in Rotterdam Frouw Marguerite Wolters, an innocuous-looking burgher's widow, had for years been feeding Philip Stephens, the permanent undersecretary of the Admiralty, with reports, political, diplomatic, military, naval, and financial, gleaned from her agents in every European nerve center, including Paris and Madrid. When at the end of 1780 England declared war against the Dutch, her espionage center was merely moved to Ostend in the Austrian Low Countries, where it was headed by Frouw Wolters' trusted chief clerk, L. C. Hake.[62] In addition, Sir Joseph Yorke, who removed himself from The Hague when the British went to war against Holland, merely shifted the intelligence operations that he himself had supervised from the Dutch capital to Antwerp.

While Montagu Fox might have availed himself of the services of both Frouw Wolters and Sir Joseph, several clues in his strange case point directly to Whitehall, specifically to the British Admiralty's secret service which Stephens headed. Someone had to have steady access to naval papers and plans, however obsolete, and that was easiest done with the assistance of the Admiralty. It is highly unlikely that Stephens would have ventured to carry on so extended and critical an operation without the knowledge and implicit approval of his chief, the Earl of Sandwich. Nor is it probable that the diplomatic materials involving the Cumberland mission could have been fed out over a period of time without the help and even the connivance of either or both of the two Secretaries of State, Hillsborough and Stormont. We know from other operations that Philip Stephens did not work in isolation, and cooperated fully with the departments handling foreign affairs. In this case, Stormont, who as the former ambassador to Paris had for years run a vast espionage machine, and whose department was responsible for conducting relations with Holland, seems a likely party to the plot. An implacable opponent of America, a die-hard supporter of the government, Stormont, the nephew of Lord Mansfield, fits the role as well as any man. In the spring of 1780 his former secretary, Fullarton, believed by Vergennes to be behind the old project to stir up revolts in Spanish America,[63] had managed to lodge a bullet in the Earl of Shelburne, and almost at the very moment when Montagu Fox was setting foot on the soil of the Low Countries Stormont was denouncing Shelburne in the House of Lords for treasonable correspondence with the enemy, a charge which he could not at that time substantiate.[64]

Still another source cannot be ruled out. Lord George Germain's department had managed to procure naval secrets for the spy Wardlaw, who had been in contact with Thomas Hussey, and Germain himself was Richard Cumberland's sponsor. Germain's department had been known to be leaking secrets, and the finger of suspicion pointed to Benjamin Thompson. The Tory Thompson, afterward to achieve world renown as Count Rumford, the scientist, was Lord George's undersecretary, and gossips imputed an improper relationship between the two. A flagrant opportunist, Thompson was allegedly involved in a treacherous act against the Patriots at the start of the war, and the Earl of Sandwich was convinced that he was a double agent. Thompson was dropped from his post in October, 1781, thereafter serving with the British Army in America. Thus he had access to confidential papers during the crucial months of the Montagu Fox affair.[65]

What was gained by this prolonged deception? In the first place, the Admiralty papers which were turned over seem carefully timed and calculated to sow the seeds of distrust between the naval chiefs of France and Spain. In the summer of 1780, when Fox began his deliveries of documents, the French Admiral d'Estaing was at San Ildefonso on a mission to re-establish between the two powers effective naval cooperation, which had broken down after the fiasco of the armada of '79. While he tried to bolster the Spanish effort, d'Estaing made it painfully clear to Charles III that France considered Spain's naval effort up to that point to have been something of a joke.[66] Now, the insinuations, coinciding with the d'Estaing visit, that Spain's naval minister was anti-French and pro-English were hardly calculated to make the French more trustful of their allies or increase a frank exchange of plans and projects. Indeed, the misleading naval data served to throw a smoke screen over Britain's actual naval plans, and could very well have led the Allies into a trap.

More important than the naval "leaks," the diplomatic documents bearing on the Hussey-Cumberland mission, beginning with the first one dated August 19, 1780, were doctored in such a manner as to indicate that both courts were more willing to make concessions to achieve peace than the facts warranted. Instead of the real Hillsborough instructions dated August 4th, Fox turned over false instructions under date of August 25th, which suggested that the British Secretary of State, while not committing himself to yielding Gibraltar, did not in fact refuse. We know that the Ministry instead had flatly refused even to discuss the Rock. Most disturbing to the Allies were the "revelations" that Castejon, backed by the Marqués de Almodóvar, Spain's former ambassador to England, was a third party in the Cumberland negotiations, pulling every wire behind Floridablanca's back to secure peace with England. Not a single authentic document supports these insinuations, but both Floridablanca and Vergennes were deeply shaken by them. That after many months Vergennes had still failed to unmask the impostor and was taking Fox's Cumberland dispatches quite seriously is suggested by his comments to his ambassador to Spain. Writing on March 15, 1781, Vergennes observed that "the role that M. de Castejon appears to have played in the intrigues of Cumberland confirms the opinion I have always had of the Anglophilism of that minister. I am curious to see whether the King of Spain will see the proof of this with indifference."[67] In turn, Montmorin, after calling the attention of Floridablanca to the "proofs" France had of the liaison of Castejon with Cumberland and the British Ministry, warned Spain's Principal Minister that the various maneuvers of several persons would be unmasked should the English publish everything that had transpired in the Cumberland negotiations. Floridablanca angrily retorted that one of his spies in London had reported an observation of Vergennes to a French envoy on the lack of help France had had from Spain. "Yes, if Spain refuses to unite her force with ours in Europe," Vergennes was reputed to have remarked, "we must consider making our peace by one means or another." Admitting that such a feeling ran deep in France, Montmorin pointed out that, so far from inducing France to consider a separate peace, his country would never be reduced to that extremity unless she concluded that it was impossible to continue the war. Thus, while the French feared that Spain was seeking a separate peace, the Spaniards in their turn were led to believe that France was ready to break with her ally. Floridablanca was badly served by his spy, Vergennes caustically rejoined to Montmorin.[68]

Fox's mission had still a third purpose. He was used, prior to England's declaration of war against the Dutch in December, 1780, to convey through the French a warning to Holland to act as a true neutral. Thus the Stormont memorial of September 7, 1780, coupled a denunciation of the anti-English spirit prevailing in the United Provinces with a threat to seize the vulnerable but rich Dutch East Indies if Holland did not behave. The revelation of this memorial was calculated to curb the patriotic ardor of towns like Amsterdam, and thus obviate England's need to declare war upon the Dutch in order to shut a vital supply line to Britain's enemies. Whether or not this memorial is authentic, it is certainly not out of line with what Stormont was writing to Sir Joseph Yorke at The Hague or telling the Dutch ambassador in London.[69] If the memorial failed of its purpose, it was not because the Dutch could not be bullied but because the little nation was too divided to take a stand one way or another. In the end Stormont forced the issue by having England on the flimsiest pretext declare war against Holland on December 18, 1780.

Lastly, a consistent thread runs through the Montagu Fox political papers. Here was a diabolically clever move to compromise the opposition leaders, Shelburne, Richmond, Charles James Fox, Wyvill, et al. Had France been enticed into making even one direct approach, or, worse still, had Vergennes been so rash at to have entrusted Fox with a direct communication to his alleged backers, the political foes of the North Ministry would have been severely, perhaps fatally, compromised. Fortunately, Vergennes' instincts about the probity of the British Opposition proved sound. In other respects, however, the bizarre episode of Montagu Fox suggests that France's notoriously cautious Foreign Minister acted with less than his customary circumspection, while his ambassador to the Netherlands displayed a gullible streak which strains the limits of credibility.

Before he left Paris for The Hague in the summer of 1780 John Adams purchased for his sons, John Quincy and Charles, thirteen and ten years of age respectively, copies of La Fontaine's *Fables*.[70] The American boys, like generations of French children before them, were now able to read a number of charming renditions of Aesop. How they must have enjoyed the tale of the Lion and the Fox who went off hunting together! The Ass was enticed into joining them, and the Lion, after pouncing upon his caller, ordered the Fox to guard his prey for him. When the Lion went away, the Fox ventured to take out the brains of the Ass and eat them up. When the Lion returned he demanded of the Fox in a terrible voice, "What have you done with the brains?"

"Brains, Your Majesty! It had none, or it would never have fallen into your trap."

The father of John Quincy and Charles had been baiting the Lion for a good many years. Although it is probable that he never laid eyes on the Fox, he had to hurdle a whole series of obstacles thrown in his course in the spring of '81 by the polite but tenacious French envoy at The Hague in his frantic effort to head off the American's one-man campaign to get Dutch recognition for his country.[71] Adams should have had no difficulty in identifying the third principal in the fable in case his sons did not see its present relevance.

VII

ON THE TRAIL OF THE APPEASERS

PEACE was the special province of the Comte de Vergennes, and he never accepted with equanimity the raids upon his territory launched by interlopers like Floridablanca or Necker. If either was prepared to come to terms with England at the sacrifice of France's interest or honor, as the Comte construed them, the French Foreign Minister wanted to be forearmed. Whether out of sheer vindictiveness or just plain caution against another turn of the wheel, he pressed his search for evidence of their backstairs operations long after Richard Cumberland had said his last farewells in Spain and Necker had been forced out of his post.

When Montagu Fox proved to be a spurious source of intelligence Vergennes found himself obliged to establish new undercover contacts. This task suddenly assumed immense difficulty because, at the beginning of January, 1781, secret intelligence filtering into Versailles from Britain's capital and chief ports suddenly dried up. For some time a series of dispatches had been relayed from England to the French Foreign Ministry from "Mr. Soyez," "B," or "D." Coincident with the ending of all such communications was the sensational arrest by the British in the first week of January, 1781, of a former French colonel, going by the name of Henry Francis de La Motte, or La Mothe. Of distinguished bearing, the middle-aged La Motte, who claimed the title of Baron Deckham, had inadvertently dropped some papers on the staircase as he was leaving Lord Hillsborough's office. These papers were confidential British documents which gave his game away. La Motte was committed a close prisoner to the Tower and charged with high treason. Additional papers found on the prisoner's person led to a roundup of French agents in England. The most talkative of these was a scapegrace German named Lutterloh, who was apprehended near Portsmouth. Lutterloh implicated a clerk in the Admiralty named

Ryder, who was alleged to have furnished naval signals and data relating to the dockyards of Plymouth, as well as a Frenchman named Rougier and a woman named Dobrey with whom he lived in Soho's Greek Street. The couple were charged with conveying various packets of intelligence to France by way of Margate and Ostend.

The La Motte affair came to a climax in July, when the courteous and debonair prisoner stood trial for high treason. Lutterloh, the Crown's star witness, tore the veil from French espionage activities in England. He admitted that his arrangements with La Motte to furnish the French court with naval intelligence went back to the year 1778, and that he had even held a conference with Sartine, the former French Minister of Marine. It appeared from the evidence that La Motte, who had been a colonel in the regiment of the Maréchal de Soubise in the Seven Years' War, had dissipated an inheritance and turned to espionage for a livelihood. A procession of Crown witnesses revealed how espionage data were passed across the Channel. A British counterintelligence agent took the stand to disclose how copies of many of these reports had been passed on to Lord Hillsborough's office, while the originals were allowed to proceed on their way to their illicit destination in France. Despite the avowals of the defense that the prisoner was merely an innocent trader, victimized by Lutterloh, the jury wasted little time in bringing in a guilty verdict. The court sentenced the prisoner "to be hanged by the neck, but not till dead; then to be cut down, and his bowels taken out and burnt before his face, his head to be taken off, his body cut into four quarters, and to be at his Majesty's disposal." The prisoner accepted his fate with the composure of one who had carefully weighed in advance the risks of his ancient profession. Later that month La Motte was put to torture and executed, and with his death the literary careers of "Mr. Soyez," "B," and "D" likewise came to an end.[1]

After La Motte's arrest and considerably before the macabre penalty was meted out to him, Rayneval called on M. Baudouin, coordinator of intelligence for the Foreign Office, to rebuild the espionage network in England. Baudouin settled on a man known to us as James Baxon or Belsson, a Frenchman then resident in London's Soho district.[2] During the winter of '81 Baxon journeyed to Versailles, bringing with him William Wardlaw, the double agent working out of Lord George Germain's office. Wardlaw, who had sold information to Father Hussey during the latter's visit to Paris in 1779, now claimed to be the man through whose hands passed the correspondence between Richard Cumberland and his sponsor, Lord George. Vergennes was sufficiently impressed by the plausible agent to authorize Baxon to work with him. Not to be outshone by his new associate, Baxon in turn told Vergennes that he could put his hands on a recent body of correspondence between Necker and Lord Stormont, now British Secretary of State. Both agents had dangled bait best calculated to hook their fish. Accordingly, Baxon and "George Smith," the alias that Wardlaw was soon given, returned to London, gratified with the results of their visit, each perhaps for quite a different reason.

The first objective of the pair was to penetrate the Hussey-Cumberland negotiations. Through Wardlaw, Baxon claimed to have made contact with Father Hussey, and the latter, as an earnest of what was to come, transcribed in his own hand and turned over to him a letter Floridablanca had written the priest. What is more, Father Hussey professed himself to be so well disposed toward France that he was prepared to go to Versailles in person to discuss with Vergennes terms for entering his service. To the bag Wardlaw contributed several private letters. Some time in May Baxon crossed over to the Continent and turned the documents over to Baudouin in the Flemish town of Courtrai.

Vergennes insisted on obtaining more directly incriminating evidence, and, toward the end of May of '81, pressed Baxon for the Necker letter. That will cost £3,000 to be paid to an intermediary, Baxon informed him, and a like sum as indemnity and damages in the event that the intermediary were to suffer loss of his post if discovered. "It is worth the price," the agent assured the Foreign Minister. The correspondence of Necker and Stormont "is not by any means innocent; on the contrary, *it is criminal.*" "Were this correspondence brought to light," he assured Vergennes, Necker, despite his influence at the court of Versailles, which Baxon did not realize was about to vanish, "would have nothing left but exile. In America a communication of this nature would be put on a par with the Arnold-André relationship."

At the time Baxon made his proposals Montagu Fox had been stringing along both the French and the Dutch for many months. His guard up, Vergennes refused to pay a sou in advance either for the Necker-Stormont or the Cumberland-Floridablanca correspondence, for which the asking price was much steeper.[3] Instead, subject to verification of handwriting, he agreed to pay Baxon £3,000 sterling on delivery of the Necker letters, and an equal amount as damages should the procurer of the letters be discovered. Because the affair in which Baxon was acting was "of a nature so delicate," Vergennes told Baudouin, "I could not appear to act out of personal motive, which would seem to be the case were I to move in advance of the proof."[4]

Still at Courtrai in midsummer, Baxon stalled on delivering the promised letters, threatening to let Necker know of the negotiations if he were not paid for services already rendered. Father Hussey and Wardlaw, Baxon warned, could be counted upon to view his return to them empty-handed as a discouraging omen.[5] Under threat of blackmail Baudouin did not think it prudent to sever the connection with this slippery agent. Instead of dismissing Baxon out of hand, he diverted him to a less risky enterprise involving the good name of the royal family. Baxon was instructed to take such steps as necessary to prevent the publication in London of certain scurrilous tracts defaming the King, the Queen, and the Comte d'Artois. Baxon, responding on a surly note, pointed out that he had not as yet discovered the secret of doing anything without money.[6] Thenceforward he was reduced to writing with grim politeness, now to Baudouin, now to Vergennes himself, begging that his precious documents be returned to him, with nagging reminders of the "criminal" character of the Necker correspondence they had been too niggardly to buy.

Toward the end of September, by which time Vergennes was aware of Montagu Fox's long series of deceptions and was becoming equally disenchanted with Baxon, "George Smith" arrived in Paris and informed Baudouin that Baxon had never so much as laid eyes on Hussey, that by his maladroit tactics he had antagonized everyone who might have helped him, that he had padded his bills, and distorted his role. "Smith" was careful to reassure Baudouin that he himself was prepared to maintain his contacts and deliver the incriminating papers into more reliable hands. He talked freely about Hussey, who was then in Ostend, reportedly en route to Madrid, a trip which suggested that the Cumberland negotiations were about to be renewed. He now professed to have the inside story of the Hussey-Cumberland negotiations from an intimate friend, the Hanoverian General Budé, governor of the royal princes and a favorite of George III. The King was quoted as remarking that his government might have to give up Gibraltar if that was the only way to disrupt the coalition against England. This, then, Wardlaw added, was the reason behind Hussey's present secret journey to Madrid.[7]

By his mission to Paris the British counterintelligence agent had accomplished two objectives. He had destroyed the usefulness of Baxon as a French secret agent, and he had planted on French soil a few more seeds of suspicion about their Spanish ally. Although within a year George III seemed reconciled to yielding Gibraltar, there is no direct evidence, save for gossip, that either the King or the North Ministry was prepared for so drastic a sacrifice in the fall of '81. It is perhaps hardly coincidental that

Wardlaw should have been reporting the same misleading intelligence as had Montagu Fox.

With Baxon on the way out, Vergennes sought a replacement. While the Foreign Minister still picked up snatches of gossip about Necker and his English ties,[8] he seemed to have been reconciled to abandoning the quest for the Necker letters and to have concentrated on obtaining the secret Anglo-Spanish correspondence. The new and unconventional secret agent who was picked for this mission was originally known as Louis-Valentin Goëzmann, but he added "de Thurne," and used such aliases as Lerchenberg, Klebsattel, and John Williams. Of Alsatian birth, he spoke both German and French with facility, traced his lineage to a family of imperial nobility, and presented himself as inheritor of certain claims of the house of Ensisheim on the Upper Rhine. In his fifty-one years he had had a busy career as a lawyer, jurist, and publicist on feudal and constitutional law, and had been involved in the most notorious litigation of the century.[9]

Like La Motte and Baxon before him, Goëzmann had turned to the dangerous game of spying out of desperation. The precipitate decline of his fortune could be put down to two causes—his own avarice and the tenacity of his redoubtable antagonist, Caron de Beaumarchais. The playwright's celebrity in no small part stemmed from the wrongs he had suffered at the hands of Goëzmann. The latter, who had once served as a judge of the superior court of Alsace, became a judge of the new and unpopular Parlement Maupeou, which had been set up in Paris in the closing years of Louis XV's reign. The feud started when the Comte de la Blanche appealed a lawsuit founded in debt arising out of a partnership, an action brought originally by him as a legatee against Beaumarchais. Goëzmann, as was his practice, kept his door shut to Beaumarchais. To gain a private audience with his judge Beaumarchais turned over to Goëzmann's wife a hundred louis and a watch set with diamonds, and complied with her further demand for fifteen louis for the judge's secretary. Despite the bribe Goëzmann handed down a decision crushingly adverse to Beaumarchais. In turn, the Goëzmanns scrupulously returned the watch and the hundred louis.

Gabrielle-Julie Goëzmann, the judge's young and coquettish second wife, boasted that she and her husband knew "how to pluck the chicken without making it cry out." Exercising her woman's prerogative to be inconsistent, she refused to give back the fifteen-louis *pourboire*, which seems never to have found its way into the pockets of the judge's secretary. Aroused by this trivial treachery, Beaumarchais, taking pen in hand, furiously composed in staccato style five historic pamphlets attacking the

Goëzmanns for corrupting the judicial process. "That brilliant, hare-brained fellow is in the right against the whole world," the great Voltaire reluctantly conceded. Despite the labored literary efforts of the *famille* Goëzmann in refutation, Beaumarchais had succeeded in making the couple ridiculous and the Maupeou *parlement* monstrous. The parties to the new controversy were now brought before the bar of justice. In February 1774, the court, with Solomonic wisdom, censured both Madame Goëzmann and Beaumarchais for their behavior, and removed Goëzmann from his judicial position. When, a few months later, Louis XV died, his successor supplanted the *parlement* of Maupeou upon which so much scorn had been heaped. "Louis XV founded the *parlement* which fifteen louis destroyed" became the slogan of a new era which the Beaumarchais-Goëzmann episode appeared to have inaugurated.[10]

The ignominy of the judicial decision seemed to spell finis to the public careers of both Beaumarchais and Goëzmann, but in the *ancien régime* persons and events took a more devious, if less logical course. In this notorious affair both playwright and judge had amply demonstrated exceptional qualities of audacity, impudence, and amorality which would make them useful instruments in the secret service of His Majesty in foreign parts. Each party had his chance in turn. Early in 1774 Beaumarchais was dispatched to London under an assumed name to prevent the threatened publication of an alleged exposé of Madame du Barry, and upon the accession of Louis XVI he performed a like service for Louis XVI, whose Austrian wife was threatened with libel. In both cases he paid off the blackmailers, but the cynical Prince von Kaunitz, the Austrian Chancellor, surmised that Beaumarchais, in pursuing the blackmailers, had himself become a master of the art.[11] On a mission the following year to procure certain politically incriminating papers from a former secret agent of Louis XV,[12] Beaumarchais became convinced of the desirability of France's supporting the American Patriots, a conviction that was to have enormous consequences for the course of the War of the Revolution.[13]

Not long thereafter, Beaumarchais' archfoe, Goëzmann, entered the secret service of the Ministry of Marine, and his activities brought him to the attention of Maurepas and the King.[14] In the summer of 1781 he was sent to London to pay blackmail to suppress libels against the French court manufactured by expatriate Frenchmen holed up in London's foreign quarter. With a dispatch comparable to Beaumarchais' and in striking contrast to the foot-dragging of Baxon, Goëzmann acquired from a French bookseller in London named Vendeur the plates as well as printed copies of the latest libelous tract, *Les Amours de Charlot et Toinette*, defaming the royal household. Making light of the usual difficulties in dealing with blackmailers, Goëzmann loaded his superheated cargo on a fishing boat, brought it to Ostend, and turned it over to the purchaser. For his special services Maurepas gave him fifty louis, and commended him to Vergennes to serve the Ministry of Foreign Affairs along with the department of marine.[15]

Goëzmann de Thurne, as he now called himself, had no wish to share the spy La Motte's fate. In fact, he remained on the Continent until Christmas of 1781, some five months after his predecessor's execution, before venturing back to London. Meantime he had made himself useful to Vergennes by engaging an agent to shadow John Adams in Holland. For him there was to be no cloak-and-dagger operation, no purloining of papers from desk drawers and rifling of wastebaskets. His plan was to win the confidence of influential persons in the government by posing as a German gentleman who had come to London to place bank funds that he had withdrawn from Holland and to seek land in America under the protection of the British government. Styling himself a financial expert, Thurne hoped to win the confidence of the British Ministry, and in exchange for such crumbs of economic information about affairs in France as he would drop to obtain whole loaves of important intelligence.[16] The new secret agent conceived of himself more as an adviser on foreign policy and a reporter of news and views than an espionage operative in the classic mold. He also saw the propaganda possibilities of his role and sought the support of Vergennes in setting up in Ostend an opposition paper to the *Courier de l'Europe*, published both in London and at Boulogne-sur-Mer in the French language by a secret agent of the British Admiralty—Samuel Swinton.

It did not take Thurne long to establish rapport with a least one anonymous well-born official who was an irreconcilable enemy of the North Ministry and its measures, an advocate of the view that peace alone could save the country. To correspond with his contact Thurne devised a special cipher, and during his stay on the Continent he also worked out code words for correspondence with Baudouïn and Vergennes. His code, with later amplifications, ran as follows:

le pauvre philosophe	The King of England
les sophistes	His ministers
le panthéon	Parliament
le procès	The war
les bons fermiers	The Americans
Prométhée	Franklin

mauvais fermier	The British government
le bon père	John Adams
Annibal	France
Hannon	The Stadholder
Louvelstein	The opposition faction in Holland
Cromwell's tea-garden	The patriotic party in England
l'émétique	The petitions of the counties
mon avocat	Vergennes[17]

Through all Goëzmann de Thurne's confidential reports on the diplomacy of the peace runs an unconcealed vein of distrust of the Americans, if not an open and avowed opposition to their objectives. At the very start of his espionage mission in London he cautioned his principals to render the ties between France and the United States so indissoluble that one party could not possibly treat of peace without consulting the other.[18] He rang the alarm bell a few days later when he reported an alleged conference between an English emissary and Franklin, and suggested that there was nothing left for the parties to do but to negotiate the manner of independence.[19] In May of 1782 Thurne reported the existence of "secret intelligence" between the English and the Americans to promote uprisings in South America,[20] and in the course of his many dispatches revealed that the kind of United States he hoped to see after the war was over was a weak power, one not able to achieve its territorial ambitions at the expense of either Spain or Canada, one forced to make terms with the Loyalists, with whose fate the French agent seemed strangely preoccupied.

Whether Vergennes and his staff should have been alerted by the outrageous advice of their paid agent at a rather early date, they continued to send him his monthly stipend despite a stream of reports and counsel from him that were more appropriate from the pen of a British counterintelligence agent than a French spy. The Foreign Minister made no effort to stop the flow of advice and conjecture so heavily spiced with an anti-American flavor. This seemed scarcely the right time to change secret agents. In the spring of '82 word came to Baudouin that the British Ministry's suspicions were becoming aroused about Thurne, and the three known agents who worked with him by the names of Harris, Merkel, and Sheridan. The high style in which Thurne's mistress was living was becoming a matter of comment.[21] That summer the man from whom Thurne secured his information about Parliamentary debates was arrested, tried, and convicted at Winchester of high treason for holding correspondence with the enemy. The trial of David Tyrie proved another La Motte affair. Crown witnesses testified that Tyrie, who held a post in the naval office at Portsmouth, was regularly sending over naval intelligence to France. To facilitate his easy access to Parliamentary debates, which were then not reported publicly, Tyrie had had the effrontery to run for Parliament from Hindon.[22] Now Thurne would have to establish another contact to cover Parliament. Meantime, despite the obvious risks of continuing his services, he was the established contact with "Mr. Smith," who still was counted upon to live up to his agreement to deliver the Cumberland-Floridablanca correspondence.

Thurne claimed to have kept in contact with Wardlaw by letter during his sojourn on the Continent from August to December, 1781. "Mr. Smith" was then using the cover name of "Baron d'Issola." From London he was tincturing his assurances to Thurne that he would get the papers with complaints of difficulties encountered in his negotiations.[23] Toward the end of November Baudouin reported that "Smith," recovering from a long illness, had left England on the tenth of the month, and that arrangements had been made for him to pass through Brussels to see his friend, Father Hussey. But the negotiations for the letters were still tortuous and "aggravating."[24] Soon word was forthcoming from London that the prospects looked bright for securing "the pair of horses" (the Cumberland letters) at the offering price. We will pay in full, Baudouin replied, only if the horses are up to the "required quality."[25]

Thenceforward the delivery of the "horses" was a story of constant postponement and frustration. "The horses are still unsold," Smith wrote from London at the beginning of 1782. "You will have a pair, but my friend tells me that you cannot have them till the middle of this month," when he will explain in person the reason for the delay. "Our friend Patterson" (Father Hussey), Smith also reported, "has quitted his masters and has gone to Italy." In addition, some other documents, described as "the telescope and case," but not identified further, were assured for the coming week.[26] In forwarding this letter to his chief, Baudouin stated that he proposed to write by courier that "there is no point in bringing the horses unless they are of the required quality."[27] I would hold "exactly" to the conditions stipulated, Vergennes insisted.[28]

Still no news of the horse merchant in February and March, leading to speculation that he was indisposed.[29] And so it went down to Christmas Eve of '82, when Mr. Smith reported from London that the horses had been ready and waiting for a long time, but that he could not accompany them because of some litigation that confined him. Baudouin replied to Smith on January 8, 1783, to the effect that he had reported this information to the King, who directed him to conclude the negotiation for the horses and if necessary send over a man to procure them, one in whom Smith could safely confide. It is of the first importance that the horses have the "strength," "weight," and "color" of the specimen we already have. On that condition we will pay the price agreed upon, Baudouin assured Wardlaw.[30] The day before, he had asked Vergennes' permission to instruct "our man" at Ostend to verify, not the existence of the horses, which was established by La Motte and confirmed by Smith, but the reason for the latter's long silence.[31]

You will get the horses in two or three months, Smith promised toward the end of January of 1783. However, the litigation would keep him from crossing over with them, and he needed someone in whom he could confide. He had no one in mind except his "daughter who, although young, is very prudent." He was forced to hedge a little, too, conceding that when the horses were delivered the purchasers might find the tails "rather short."[32] Although Vergennes and his chief of intelligence shared misgivings about entrusting the delivery of the letters to a girl, they sent Wardlaw the letter of exchange he requested to cover "the cost of shipping the horses," but coupled the payment with a warning that, despite some disappointment over the shortness of the tails, they would insist that the horses be "strong" and clearly identified.[33]

Nothing further was heard from the horse dealer until April 16th, on which date Wardlaw wrote complaining cryptically that the "very disagreeable affair into which he had been brought by Baxon prevented the conclusion of the mortgage," and though the horses were still unsold, he sent assurances that the deal would soon be consummated.[34] All along, Baudouin now reminded Vergennes, he had feared that Baxon's return to London would block the transaction. A secret agent scorned posed perhaps more of a threat to his home country than one who was exposed, he implied. Vergennes was still itching to get his hands on the incriminating papers, even though both Spain and France had long since signed a preliminary peace, Minorca was now in Spanish hands, and the siege of Gibraltar had been abandoned. Baudouin accordingly sent Smith fifty louis to buy "two field glasses" and "two mathematical instrument cases," and to defray the shipment of the horses. Even if Smith were to send us nothing, he consoled Vergennes, that in itself would seem to be "the only way to put our man at the bottom of the wall and finally discover what sort of person he really is."[35]

As the horses, either regular or short-tailed, never showed up on the French side of the Channel, Vergennes and Baudouin must reluctantly have come to the realization that in the game of fishing in each other's waters the British were quite as skilled as the French, and that the Florida-blanca correspondence was a tin minnow of the same species as Thurne's fictitious reports on French finance generously made available to the British Ministry.

With the negotiations over the short-tailed horses dragging out to a dead end, the French Foreign Office became increasingly discontented with Thurne, who in this case seems pretty quickly to have lost the confidence if not the trail of Wardlaw. His gossip and summaries of Parliamentary speeches were scarcely top secret intelligence and his correspondence was remarkably indiscreet. "Thurne's news are of the kind of which the news-papers are full," Vergennes complained to Baudouin back in March, 1782. "Moreover he has added some reasoning which could bring about his exposure."[36]

British suspicions of Thurne, dating from the spring of 1782, forced him to move more circumspectly; agreement on preliminary peace terms by the major belligerents made his intelligence operations expendable to France.[37] Anticipating a recall, Thurne proved equal to the emergency. Bearing in mind the libel-suppressing operation he successfully undertook back in the summer of '81, Thurne realized how rich a vein remained untapped. He now conveyed to Baudouin a warning of new libelous matter, produced in London's French refugee circle and about to be introduced into France. The new piece was entitled *La Naissance du D . . . a Dévoilée*, and it cast aspersions on the legitimacy of the heir to the French throne and vilified his mother. The French officials reacted by dispatching Receveur, the confidential police agent employed in the Montagu Fox affair, to London to investigate, and took precautions that Thurne should not be forewarned of his mission. Coincidentally, a new warning was received—this time from a former associate of La Motte—that British officials were going around asking questions in an effort to establish a relationship between the executed spy and a man by the name of Thurne or Goëzmann. Thurne's troubled but ever generous masters, while ordering him home, sent him a letter of exchange to discharge his debts and defray his return trip to Paris.[38] Even as the pack began to close in from both sides, Thurne insisted on being assigned the recovery of the libel, and had the effrontery to demand, as the price of his return to France, that pensions be granted both for himself and the wife he left behind in France while living ostentatiously in London with a mistress.[39]

For Receveur to by-pass Thurne and deal directly with the libelers proved about as difficult as it did for Beaumarchais' Rosine to get a message to the Comte Almaviva without having Dr. Bartolo intercept it.

In the first place, the kind of talents Receveur possessed were not shown to best advantage in England, a land where *lettres de cachet* and strong-arm methods were frowned upon by the populace. The Marquis de Moustier, who headed France's diplomatic mission to England after the preliminaries had been signed, suggested that they use Thevenande de Morande, a specialist in blackmail whose cooperation in the past had been procured for a price. Morande agreed to help, and even provided a list of all French fugitives resident in London and their occupations. With many misgivings, Vergennes promised to ask the King to be indulgent to the reformed blackmailer.[40]

Receveur and Moustier were soon to discover the obstacles in the way of suppressing libels in England, where, as the envoy saw it, libelers operated with impunity, venturing so far in the recent past as to suggest a liaison between King George's mother and Lord Bute. Legal counsel advised Moustier that the truth might be pleaded in defense to a civil action for libel, and, worse, that nonresidents of England were not entitled to redress under the common law. Moustier went so far as to lobby for the passage of a special Parliamentary act to cover libels of this nature.[41]

Morande had as many different reasons as Receveur to exclude Thurne from these profitable negotiations. To discredit his rival, he now reported that Thurne had recently quarreled with a cleric named Landis, to whom he had been introduced at Lord Shelburne's, and who apparently believed that Thurne had supplanted him in the Earl's confidence.[42] The vengeful cleric in the presence of both Receveur and Morande accused Thurne of being in Shelburne's employ, and of offering to disclose to the Earl "the secret French correspondence here."[43] In view of the fact that Thurne's dispatches disclosed a consistently hostile attitude to Shelburne and considerable sympathy for the Earl's rival, Charles James Fox, it is more probable that he was in the pay of the latter than the former.

Goëzmann de Thurne, British counterintelligence agent or dedicated French spy, or both, was a hard man to ignore. Moustier suspected that he was involved with an expatriate named Boissière in the publication of a series of libelous pamphlets again involving Marie Antoinette. By his bullying tactics Receveur only sowed suspicion broadcast and alerted Thurne to his new danger.[44] The latter evaded the trap and countered by having Boissière issue a warning broadside denouncing Receveur as the master of a plot to kidnap the authors of the libelous pamphlets.[45] Vergennes, who wanted the libels at all cost, yielded to Thurne's demands for another hundred louis to pay off his debts before he left England.[46] Mortified that a price should be put upon his zeal, Thurne uttered shrill cries about a still more dangerous libel overhanging the market while his confederate, Boissière, took an even more obstinate stand.[47] Back in Paris the avaricious Madame Goëzmann pressed further demands on Vergennes to relieve her husband's financial embarrassment.[48]

A grain of common sense was injected into the *opéra bouffe* by the arrival in London of the new French ambassador, the Comte d'Adhémar, a favorite of the Polignacs. Adhémar took a cool look at the antics of his court and its clumsy agents in dealing with the blackmailing libelers. His first move was to order Receveur home. The latter's stay in London, Adhémar felt, was one long comedy. It is time to revise these conventional cloak-and-dagger operations in foreign countries, he instructed Vergennes, and to abandon the notion that libels could be suppressed by bribery or threats. The prudent course was to ignore the libels, to treat them with the scorn they merited. He even intended to write the King and tell him the whole story. That would be fatal, Vergennes excitedly warned. "It is a very delicate matter to tell a husband that one dares suspect and accuse his wife, regardless of how little foundation there is for one or the other.[49]

With Receveur removed, Thurne tried to squeeze a few more sous out of the sordid business of the libels. Adhémar summoned him. Trembling like a leaf, the double-dealer was forced by the wrathful ambassador to turn over what was presumably the only extant copy of the libel, *Les Amours de Charlot et Toinette*, whose purchase he had triumphantly negotiated back in the summer of '81, when the edition was ostensibly destroyed in exchange for the handsome sum of 14,500 livres. This incident convinced Adhémar that the payment of blackmail only served as a fillip to the manufacture of still more outrageous libels, particularly since the war had severed all ties between Frenchmen in England and their homeland. The ambassador realized, too, what little trust could be placed in French spies in London, who ever since the torture and execution of La Motte had lived in mortal fear, disposed to turn informers to escape complicity with the master spy who had paid the extreme penalty. Finally, Adhémar recognized that the whole tone of French espionage threw ridicule on the French presence in London.[50]

Having transparently implicated himself in the blackmail plot,[51] Thurne pleaded for mercy. "I cry, I lament, I solicit," he besought Vergennes. "All is in vain." Threatened with imprisonment, broken in health, Thurne still managed to wangle his allowance from the government he had served so badly.[52] After giving him an extra fifty louis for the "odious obscenity," *Les Amours de Charlot et Toinette*, for which he had been so well paid several years before, and despite the grave doubts of French officials that he would ever dare show his face at Versailles again, Thurne left for Ostend at the end of July, and when he arrived at the Flemish seaport, he had his wife solicit another ten louis to pay his expenses on to Paris.[53]

Goëzmann de Thurne did not come to Paris with his tail between his legs. Triumphantly, with a histrionic gesture so typical of the man, he turned over some solid evidence of his espionage contacts in England, along with a further request for two hundred louis to defray his debts. The letter he entrusted to the officials of the Ministry of Foreign Affairs presumably bore the signature of John Kent, Auditor of Impost in Lord Mountstuart's office, and a first cousin of Lady Mountstuart. Addressed to Thurne at No. 34 Grand Rue du Faubourg Saint Denis, Paris, it was in substance a report setting forth Fox's desire for favorable commercial arrangements with the United States at the expense of England's trade ties with Europe, and pointing out that the Bedford faction stood for commerce for all countries on an equal basis. On this issue, Thurne's informant indicated, the Bedfordites held the majority. Bedford's faction, Kent's information ran, were about to demand that all the documents dealing with the definitive peace treaty be opened to the House of Commons to disclose whether the delays had stemmed from wrongful conduct on the part of the present administration. Naturally the Ministry would refuse to produce the documents on the pretext that they would reveal too much to foreign powers disposed to renew the war. Here, too, Kent ventured to prophesy that the Bedfordites would succeed. Kent concluded by requesting Thurne "for good reasons" never to address him at Gray's Inn, but always to "James Kent Esqr Auditor of Imposts, Lord Mountstuart's Office, Scotland Yard, London." In a gloss on the text Thurne advised Vergennes to hold off signing the definitive treaty until the return of Parliament in order to give the Bedfordites a chance to bring the documents of the peacemaking out into the open.[54]

With supreme audacity Thurne, by enticing Kent into continuing to send intelligence reports to him, even after he left England, had risked disclosure for himself, disgrace for his contact, and embarrassment for his government presumably engaged in negotiating in good faith the final details of the peacemaking. However the Foreign Minister might have felt about the value of the concluding advice of his extraordinary spy, it seemed much too late to act upon it. This was fortunate for all the war-weary nations concerned, including the new republic across the Atlantic. Six days later the final treaties were signed at Paris and Versailles, and the espionage of the peacemaking, with all its queer involvements, its wheels within wheels, ground to a halt.

Drawing upon his long-drawn-out legal duel with Goëzmann de Thurne, Caron de Beaumarchais was inspired to write *Le Barbier de Séville*. Out of his rich experience in undercover diplomacy during the American War for Independence came the satirical comment on diplomats in his tour de force, *Le Mariage de Figaro*, with its revolutionary overtones. What a picture of diplomacy *Figaro* paints!

Pretend to be ignorant of what everyone knows, and to know what others do not know. Seem to understand what nobody comprehends, not to hear what all hear, and most of all appear able to do the impossible. Seem profound when one is only empty. Spread spies, pension traitors, loosen seals, and intercept letters. Magnify the poverty of the methods by the importance of the object.—That's politics, or I'm a dead man.

It was not many months after peace had come that the *Comédie Française* gave the first public performance of this enjoyable satire, and even the diplomats in the audience could not withhold from the author the credit that was due for the acute analysis of their craft.[55] If further corroboration were needed, one might well cite the cases of Goëzmann de Thurne, "Mr. Smith," and the elusive horses.

VIII

THE GORDIAN KNOT

B ACK IN JULY OF '76, upon reading the newly proclaimed Declaration of Independence, Ezra Stiles, the Puritan clergyman soon to become president of Yale College, observed that "for the first time" he "realized Independency." "Thus, the Congress," he acutely prophesied, "have tied a Gordian knot, which the Parliament will find they can neither cut nor untie." As Stiles saw it, "the *thirteen united Colonies*" now emerged "into an *Independent Republic* among the kingdoms, states and empires on earth."[1] That knot binding the colonies in common rebellion withstood the clumsy strokes of King and Parliament. As the War of the American Revolution spread from North America to other continents, the Gordian knot of American independence, a metaphor likewise favored by the Comte de Vergennes, continued to defy the efforts of the ablest magicians in the diplomatic corps both in the belligerent and in the neutral camps. It was worthy of the talents of Count Cagliostro, whose legerdemain was then entrancing European courts. Here was indeed something more complicated to unravel than the legendary fastening by which a Phrygian peasant had once fixed the ox yoke to his cart.

"Independence" was a new word in the lexicon of European diplomacy, for the great powers were unaccustomed to treating rebels as equals. When France intervened in Corsica's war of liberation from the Genoese and took over that island in 1768, the patriot Paoli was forced to flee for his life. Catherine the Great used arguments armed with cannon and bayonets to convince the reform-minded Polish Diet of the error of its ways. In 1773 she crushed the Pugachev rebellion and decapitated its principal ring-leaders. George III had his troops fire on the Gordon Rioters as well as on the Minute Men on Lexington Common, and, some years after the American Revolution, Joseph II, the very model of the Enlightened

Despot, resorted to force to suppress an uprising in the Austrian Netherlands.

Almost all the evasive tactics used by England in her various conciliatory moves with the Thirteen Colonies were employed at one time or
another by the other belligerents or the neutrals in their anxiety to end
the War of the American Revolution short of independence. England's
supreme peace effort along these lines had been made in 1778, when
Parliament authorized the North Ministry to dispatch the Carlisle Commission to America to effect a reconciliation with the rebellious colonies.
The Commission had been instructed to treat with Congress "as if it were
a legal body." Should the Americans insist, Congress could be retained
as a permanent institution so long as it did not infringe upon the sovereignty
of Parliament. In effect, what was proposed was home rule.

How well intentioned the North Ministry was in its proffer of conciliation is perhaps impossible to determine at this distance from the events.
It is perhaps significant, however, that Emperor Joseph II, in a conversation
with the Spanish chargé at Vienna in 1781, revealed that he had been reliably informed that "the Court of London was determined not to keep
their word" if the proposition of accommodation made in 1778 "had been
accepted" by the Americans "and followed by their submission."[2] Even
granting the sincerity of the North Ministry's conciliation efforts in '78,
one must bear in mind that its other diplomatic operations were almost
uniformly tainted with duplicity.

Honest or no, the peace offer of 1778 could scarcely have been timed
more ineptly. The overture of the British commissioners coincided with
the evacuation from Philadelphia of the British Army, along with the
Loyalist leaders, upon news of the imminent arrival of the French fleet
in American waters. Speaking for the Congress, President Laurens coldly
informed the commissioners that as soon as the King had demonstrated his
good faith either by an acknowledgment of independence or by the withdrawal of his fleet and army, Congress would be prepared to discuss a
treaty of peace and commerce. Since the commissioners were not authorized
to order an evacuation of British forces and took the casuistical position that
they had in fact recognized independence, the negotiations broke down
before they ever got under way. Compounding the embarrassments of the
Carlisle Commission, one of its members, ex-Governor Johnstone, was involved in a clumsy attempt to bribe some of the Patriot leaders and, when
exposed, sailed for England in righteous indignation. The two remaining
commissioners, the Earl of Carlisle and William Eden, entertained the
notion of making one last appeal to Congress for a truce on the basis of the

uti possidetis, leaving the question of reciprocal rights to lie dormant during that time. Finding Congress impervious to their blandishments, bribery, or threats, the commissioners then made the same offer to the Revolutionary state legislatures that Congress had spurned. After this last futile gesture, they sailed for home.[3]

A tragic fiasco signalizing the end of the first British Empire, the Carlisle Mission had nonetheless set up the guideposts for subsequent conciliators. From time to time various formulas were to be devised short of outright separation of the colonies from the Empire and complete independence. First, an armistice would be sought, during which, while the parties held their ground, the details of a settlement would be worked out. Should Congress prove adamant or should England refuse to deal with the commissioners of Congress, then the individual states would be approached. As reports spread that both Governor Johnstone and Lord George Germain now favored making separate peace offers to the states, one American diplomatic agent abroad pointed out that this was adhering to that "old maxim, *divide et impera,*" long Britain's "sheet anchor."[4] In the months and years ahead, however, the notion of dealing with the separate states demonstrated remarkable vitality.[5]

As the war cast its lengthening shadow over the globe, the formula for peace with America continued to divide parties and factions in England and to remain a bone of contention between France and Spain. One proposed solution was the partition or fragmentizing of America. In essence the Mallet-Necker plan, it was seriously advanced by such diverse figures as Charles Jenkinson, of the inner circle of King's friends,[6] and Josiah Tucker, the anti-imperialist dean of Gloucester. Both men by 1780 favored the renunciation of New England, but the Dean was even prepared to yield the area running from Pennsylvania down through North Carolina, with Britain retaining New York, New Jersey, South Carolina, and Georgia. Tucker would also turn back West Florida to Spain, along with the "totally useless" fortress of Gibraltar, with England getting Puerto Rico in compensation. Indeed, rumors had it that partition was the basis of a peace offer allegedly made by England to France in 1780.[7] "Absurd and idle" talk like this convinced sensible John Adams that "we shall have no peace for some time."[8]

Aside from notions of home rule, separate negotiations with each of the Thirteen States, and various ideas for partition, the truce was an essential ingredient in every peace formula advanced in this period. Short of independence, almost everyone, it would seem, sought an armistice, including, as John Adams described them, "some well-intentioned, though visionary,

Americans." From Brussels, Adams' correspondent, William Lee, the American agent to Berlin and Vienna, had already pointed out how a truce would play into the hands of America's enemies by enabling England, once her hands were free of European involvements, to employ her full strength in a resumed war against her rebellious subjects.[9]

A long-term armistice comparable with the truce between Spain and Holland in 1609 was proposed by Spain as far back as 1778. So long as American territory would be evacuated under such a truce, Vergennes found the notion congenial and passed it on to Franklin under seal of secrecy. Franklin, according to Vergennes, acquiesced because he believed that independence existed in fact and was irrevocable, and formal recognition by Great Britain was not crucial. True, Franklin lacked the powers to treat, Vergennes admitted to Gérard, but the doctor had taken the position that he could sign treaties and conventions subject to ratification.[10] A few months later Franklin told a British intermediary, David Hartley, that he was prepared to accept a long-term truce which would involve a tacit cession of independence to America. He soon backed away, however, apparently at Vergennes' insistence.[11] Tenacious in his quest for peace, Hartley then submitted to Parliament a proposal for a ten-year suspension of hostilities, with British troop withdrawals tied to a stipulation providing for the security of the Tories in America. The proposal was defeated without debate, as the Parliamentary account reports it, "the ministers not saying a word."[12]

The idea of a truce joined to a compromise over American independence died hard in Madrid. Prompted as much by her desire to contain the rebellion in America as by her own national aspirations, Spain in her ultimatum to England which preceded her entry into the war proposed an armistice during which the British, under Spain's good offices, would treat with the plenipotentiaries of the American Congress. During these negotiations the "American Colonies" were to be regarded as independent *de facto*. In the long-term truce which would pave the way for final peace both parties were to remain in possession of the ground their respective forces held in North America at the cessation of hostilities. But, fortunately, as Vergennes saw it, the British found even the tacit grant of independence as inadmissible as the proposal for troop withdrawal.[13] The French government clearly saw that such a truce would give England precious time without corresponding benefits to France or America, and control over the principal ports of America as well as a great part of the North Atlantic coastline.[14] Although Spain withdrew its proffer of mediation and joined the war, she was soon prepared to make even greater concessions at America's expense, to settle matters on the basis of the actual war map in America and what amounted to home rule for the Americans within the British Empire. America's acceptance of these conditions would release France from her pledge to fight until independence was obtained. Very ingenious of Floridablanca, but British intransigence foiled one of the most artful plots against American independence of the entire war.

England and Spain had both failed in turn to untie the Gordian knot, and now the initiative in the peacemaking shifted to the great neutral powers, Austria and Russia. The Thirteen States could hardly have viewed a mediation by Austria with anything but mixed emotions. Only the previous year William Lee, whose captious brothers, Arthur and Richard Henry, had contributed their full share to creating discord over America's peace aims, and who himself had time after time exceeded both his instructions and his powers, had spent some lonesome months in Vienna seeking recognition for the United States. Lee's efforts constituted a phase of that "militia diplomacy" which the Adamses and the Lees had persuaded Congress to endorse in 1777. Congress in its wisdom arranged to mobilize and dispatch militiamen of diplomacy to the various courts of Europe to secure recognition without knowing in advance whether these missions had any likelihood of success. Franklin had warned Arthur Lee that, "while we are asking aid, it is necessary to gratify the desires and in some sort comply with the humors of those we apply to," and reminded his hypercritical colleague "that a virgin state should preserve its virgin character, and not go about suitoring for alliances, but wait with decent dignity for the application of others."[15] Sensible as were Franklin's arguments, there was certainly ground for the opinions of the Lees and John Adams that the only way to prevent peace from being settled between France, Spain, and England without reference to America's interest was for Congress to require consultation not by *one*, but by *all* the commissioners abroad.[16]

William Lee, who had previously spent considerable time in London attending to his mercantile affairs and who still held the office of alderman of that city, had been named by Congress to the courts of both Berlin and Vienna. Virgin or no, he could not wait for an invitation. Like his brother Arthur his temperament was better suited to the role of prosecuting attorney than peacemaker. Lee had to learn some elementary lessons about the Hapsburg Empire. He had first to instruct Congress that the commission authorizing him to treat with Joseph II, the Emperor of Germany, overlooked the fact that Joseph's mother, Maria Theresa, was the reigning sovereign and coregent with her son, and that negotiations had to be carried on in Vienna in two courts rather than one.[17]

Even before Lee left for Vienna he had been aware of the long-standing cordiality between Vienna and London, a cordiality interrupted only by the Seven Years' War.[18] He realized too, as he wrote Ralph Izard, the unacknowledged American envoy to the court of Tuscany, how much the success of his mission depended upon the French court, where Franklin's was the paramount American influence. "Unless he has some private end to answer," Lee stated, he could expect nothing from the Sage of Passy.[19] Knowing how Franklin felt about militia diplomacy, Alderman Lee's pessimism seemed well grounded. In fairness to Franklin, however, it should be pointed out that even had he pulled every string at Versailles to promote the mission to Vienna of which he cordially disapproved, the times were out of joint for such a visitation. Austria, finding herself with a war on her hands against Prussia over Bavaria, was not likely to take a precipitate stand on recognition of the United States for fear, as Lee saw it, of "throwing the weight of Great Britain into the scale of Prussia." Hence Lee never assumed a public character at Vienna, but continued the posture of "an American traveller."

Backstage Sir Robert Murray Keith, the forthright and vigorous British ambassador at Vienna, pulled every wire to see that this "gentleman traveller" was not given an audience by the Empress. Sir Robert, who had earlier expressed the view that the ungrateful Americans might well be left "to their own tottering independence," was determined, too, that for her presumption the French be paid back in a way "they will remember for half a century to come." Now he was able to rejoice that the audience was denied Lee, for had it been granted, Britain's enemies would then "have built a thousand false stories upon that single circumstance." Instead, this "decisive rebuff" proved "a great mortification to France."[20] Despite the good offices on his behalf by the Baron de Breteuil, the French ambassador at Vienna, Lee, save for informal meetings with Austrian officials, including several icy interviews with Prince Kaunitz, the Chancellor, met a variety of diplomatic and social rebuffs.[21] For Lee there was perhaps some consolation in the knowledge that the conduct of Vienna, the haughtiest court in Europe, was "infinitely more insulting to *France* than America, because the thick heads look on the business as a matter entirely between *England* and *France,* leaving the other totally out of the question."[22]

In refusing recognition to the United States the Austrian government gave expression both to its ill-concealed desire to placate England and to its dislike of the American rebels. Not only did Maria Theresa refuse to receive Lee, but she issued a proclamation prohibiting all commerce between her subjects in the Low Countries and the rebellious colonies.

"The cause in which England is engaged," Joseph II pointed out to Keith, "is the cause of all sovereigns, who have a joint interest in the maintenance of due subordination and obedience to law in all the surrounding monarchies. I observe with pleasure," he added, "the vigorous exertions of the national strength which the King is employing to bring his rebellious subjects to submission, and I sincerely wish success to the measures."[23]

Rebuffed at Vienna, Lee was scarcely more successful at the Prussian court. Unable to persuade Frederick to recognize the United States, since that monarch was unwilling to take a step which would antagonize England,[24] Lee, without authorization, tried to induce the Prussian ruler to act as a mediator.[25] However jealous Frederick might have been of the glamorous role that Austria was seeking to carve out for herself, he was shrewd enough to see that any foreign mediation would be detrimental to the cause of France, and that he could scarcely pose as an impartial mediator since he was at that very time seeking to substitute an alliance between Prussia, Russia, and France for the existing Austro-French tie.[26]

One year after Lee's frustrating stay in Vienna Austria's rulers decided to project themselves into what had become something more than a private quarrel. For a time it seemed as though the fate of America and of the peace might be determined by four personages most closely identified with Austria's mediation efforts. Such an offer of mediation, allegedly made in return for France's good offices at Teschen, was submitted on May 15, 1779, in the name of Maria Theresa, whose venerable reign was fast drawing to a close.[27]

A domineering wife, Maria Theresa still conspicuously mourned her long deceased husband, that good-natured mediocrity, Duke Francis of Lorraine. Her tears and timidity notwithstanding, she possessed a certain horse sense, mixed with an almost pathological suspicion, traits not shared by her illustrious children. Her piety, conventional morality, and deep conservatism were as much offended by the reckless tactics and advanced notions of her brilliant son Joseph as by the empty-headed frivolities of her daughter, the Queen of France. Obsessed by the horrors of war, Maria Theresa was convinced that her own monarchy needed peace, and that her ally, France, could not sustain a long war against England. Yet, despite her pessimism, she was regarded by the French themselves as the only person in the monarchy attached to the King of France.[28]

Only a few yards distant from the Burg stood the Chancellery presided over by Prince Wenzel Anton von Kaunitz-Rietberg, who for twenty-seven years had been Maria Theresa's alter ego and managed the fast-aging Queen with matchless craft. A master diplomat in the tradition of

Machiavelli, his worship of order was surpassed only by his notorious vanity. Proverbial for his unshakable poise and steel-blue eyes which chilled the beholder, the septuagenarian Chancellor fancied himself the "coachman of Europe." With the aid of Madame de Pompadour he had long before effected a diplomatic revolution by allying traditional enemies, the Houses of Hapsburg and Bourbon, thereby touching off the Seven Years' War. This coup was by no means unprofitable to the Chancellor, as documents which the French revolutionary government published in 1793 disclose that Kaunitz, aside from presents, received a French subsidy in 1759 in the amount of 100,000 livres. It was Kaunitz who dedicated so large a portion of his career to curbing Frederick of Prussia. That lean, gnarled, sharp-tongued flute player, versifier, and correspondent of Voltaire had for a whole generation been the *bête noire* of the Austrian Chancellor. To the Austrian the King of Prussia was a wild enthusiast, and "the greatest driveller and liar on the whole surface of the earth."[29] A believer in absolute monarchy, Kaunitz would have no truck whatsoever with revolutions or revolutionaries. While he worked harmoniously with the cautious Maria Theresa, her impulsive son could drive him to distraction. "All in good time," he would remind Joseph with exasperating froideur. Long disillusioned by the French alliance he had engineered, Kaunitz was by now less than lukewarm toward the court of Versailles, for whose military and naval capacity he had scarcely concealed contempt.[30]

Perhaps even more outspoken in his antipathy to France and the French alliance was the brilliant if egocentric and domineering Joseph II. The hook-nosed Emperor never recovered from the shock of losing his young wife, Isabel of Parma. He loathed his second wife, the repulsive Josepha of Bavaria. Upon her death he never married again and acted the confirmed misogynist. Joseph's initial prejudices against the French court were reinforced by a private visit to Versailles in 1777. He found Louis XVI "a little weak, but not an imbecile," possessing but "apathetic" body and mind. Of Marie Antoinette's husband he observed, "The *fiat lux* has not yet been spoken, the matter is still in a lump." "Despite our alliance with France we prefer roast beef to '*boeuf à la mode*,'" his secretary was reputed to have written a friend in The Hague,[31] and the rumored remark faithfully reflected the Emperor's mood. Arrogant and opinionated, yet disdainful of pomp and pretense, Joseph managed to combine a sympathy for liberal and even democratic notions with a distaste for rebels and rebellions.

For many years the link between the Hofburg and Versailles, between Schönbrunn and the Trianon, had been the veteran diplomat Comte Mercy d'Argenteau. Born at Liège of an old seigneurial family, he served for thirty years in the Austrian diplomatic service and for half that time as Kaunitz's ambassador at Versailles. An immense landowner with huge estates and well-stocked wine cellars in several countries, Mercy had obtained letters of naturalization in France in 1766 to inherit properties in Lorraine, but this did not make him any the less acceptable to the Emperor of Germany and the Queen of Hungary, in whose service he remained. Epicure and host par excellence, Mercy preferred the company of financiers, men of affairs and littérateurs to that of the court. He lived in Paris in elegant style, first at the Palace of the Petit-Luxembourg and then in a magnificent home on the right bank where he maintained a beautiful mistress, Rosalie Levasseur, twenty-two years his junior and one of the celebrated operatic stars of her day. It was Mercy who, whether through direct approaches to Vergennes or his backstairs influence with Marie Antoinette, pressed the cause of France's ally and the arguments for mediating the war under Austrian auspices.[32]

It was no accident that Maria Theresa's proffer of mediation should have come just two days after the Treaty of Teschen had been signed. Her move represented a desperate effort to retrieve some measure of prestige which that pact had tarnished and to retaliate against France for having thwarted Austrian ambitions. To understand Austria's impaired position one must go back to the death of the Elector Maximilian Joseph at the close of 1777. Then the ambitious Joseph dispatched troops to occupy Lower Bavaria. Fearing that Prussia might be drawn into the war and ultimately shift to England's side in the larger struggle then going on, France refused to back Joseph. That "intolerable pedant," as Vergennes was called in Vienna, had little difficulty in persuading Louis XVI that the treaty of 1756 between France and Austria was purely defensive, and that it was vital to France to maintain Prussia's influence in equilibrium with Austria's. In the summer of 1778 Frederick the Great, the poacher now turned gamekeeper, intervened. A series of skirmishes and rear-guard engagements between Austria and Prussia ensued. Finally, yielding to a combination of French diplomatic pressure and a threat of military intervention on the part of Catherine the Great, Kaunitz accepted the proffers of comediation made by France and Russia.[33] Teschen provided for the evacuation by Austria of most of the Bavarian territory she had occupied. Jointly guaranteed by Catherine and Louis, the treaty left a bitter taste in Austrian mouths and served to intensify anti-French feeling. While Kaunitz and Joseph wished to maintain the French alliance, they hoped to see France humbled sufficiently to redress the balance and permit Austria to dominate the alliance. As Vergennes reminded his envoys, the plans and ends of the two nations were quite different; France needed to be incessantly on guard against every diplomatic move by her ally[34]

Maria Theresa's overture of mediation was sprung at an unpropitious moment, for only a month before Spain had secretly agreed to enter the war against Britain. With brightening prospects, France was in no mood in the spring of '79 to consider outside meddling. In a polite declination Louis XVI pointed out that Spain's previous proffer of mediation had been rejected by George III.[35] That was France's ostensible reason for saying "No, thank you," but her real reason was her fear that Austria might use this operation to let herself be wooed away from France and wedded by alliance with England. To "draw all to herself without making any return to others," was Vienna's way, Vergennes advised his ambassador at Vienna. Such deception might well throw France into the arms of Russia or Prussia, Vergennes declared, coupling his warning with a reminder that the Empress, though a friend of peace, was aging rapidly, while the Emperor and Kaunitz were already in the camp of the enemy.[36]

The French rejection of Maria Theresa's proffer served only to exacerbate anti-French feeling in Vienna. "I have not received from four persons even a tiny compliment on the successful mediation of King Louis XVI" in the recent dispute between Austria and Prussia, Breteuil reported to his Foreign Minister. French diplomats met a chilly reception everywhere in Vienna, while the British Minister was conspicuously and cordially entertained. On the stage at Vienna aspersions were cast on French character, vigor, and masculinity, and it took arduous months of diplomatic protests to elicit a grudging reprimand.[37]

With the launching of the Franco-Spanish armada against England Maria Theresa bombarded her daughter at Versailles with a barrage of missives skillfully mingling expressions of hope for peace with manifestations of concern over the naval prospects of France and Spain.[38] Marie Antoinette was under unremitting crossfire, for Kaunitz kept the pressure on Mercy to play his part at Versailles. That astute ambassador recognized that the fall of '79 was hardly a propitious time to launch the mediation. What he advocated was a policy of watchful waiting to see which of the belligerents would be the soonest exhausted, confident that France would first qualify. He stood in the wings ready to step forth and advance the cause of mediation as soon as prospects seemed more favorable. As Mercy saw it, the only beneficiary of the war would be the Americans. They were likely to secure either their independence or a more or less modified status of dependency. Kaunitz, on the other hand, never considered America for a moment. The other belligerents, he felt, would lose more than they could expect to gain from a prolongation of the war, which might well, in his judgment, now take a favorable turning for England.[39]

Any hope Austria might have nurtured of driving a wedge between the Allies was quickly dispelled. Having intercepted a dispatch from Vergennes to Montmorin, in an era when the diplomatic correspondence of even one's own allies was not respected, Spain was well aware of France's distaste for a mediation at the hands of so suspect and biased a power as Austria, and hastened to inform Kaunitz that the interests of His Christian Majesty were inseparable from those of Charles III.[40]

There was still one more blow to come. Despite the optimism of Sir Robert Keith which had inspired Kaunitz's proffer of mediation and despite that transparent concern for England's fate which in no small part prompted Austria's proposal, the British were still not ready to submit their case to outside mediation. So long as the French insisted on including America in any negotiations, England would not be prepared to talk peace. That was the substance of Lord Hillsborough's response to Count von Belgiojoso, Austria's ambassador at the Court of Saint James's.[41] The fiery Sir Joseph Yorke put it less diplomatically when he remarked to a colleague that "unless any of our mediators offers to disavow the Independancy of America I would send them all packing and fight it out."[42]

Repulsed on all fronts, the Austrians kept their mediation offer alive during the course of 1780 by renewed insinuations at the leading European capitals. In Paris hints were dropped that a nine-year truce, during which everything would remain in statu quo and both sides keep hands off the colonies, would be a useful approach to a general settlement.[43] In Madrid the younger Kaunitz, Austria's ambassador, made informal soundings of the Spanish court.[44] At St. Petersburg Austria's sly envoy, Graf Ludwig von Cobenzl, openly described American independence as "an obstacle difficult to surmount."[45] At the Hofburg Maria Theresa kept prodding Breteuil about peace. "Peace must wait on the campaign of 1781," that envoy replied in oracular vein. Because of the hurdles thrown in the way of a peace settlement by the American War and the moot issues of neutral rights, a solemn Congress was needed to settle outstanding issues, Prince Kaunitz advised Breteuil, and presumably Vienna was the ideal spot.[46] In Spain Graf von Kaunitz and playwright Cumberland were thick as thieves, and as the summer of 1780 drew to a close the Austrian envoy again reminded Floridablanca of his nation's availability as mediator.[47]

How the Emperor felt about American independence was implicit in almost every word of a three-hour talk he had with Breteuil in October.

Joseph reminded the French envoy that the British would never consent to the independence of America unless compelled by adversity to do so, and that there was much resistance in Spain to France's professed intention of continuing the war until that goal was attained. Indeed, should Gibraltar be ceded to Spain, Joseph doubted that the Spaniards would remain in the war for Franco-American objectives. Breteuil demurred. "Each to his lorgnette," was the envoy's laconic comment on this revealing conversation.[48]

So far as Britain was concerned independence for America remained the insurmountable obstacle to peace. Spain and France might talk about independence, but no one at the British Court would listen to them, Austria's London envoy advised Kaunitz in October.[49] Alone, Austria could not entice the belligerents to accept mediation, but at the same time each of the warring parties wanted to keep the door ajar. The voice for which they seemed to be waiting did not come from Vienna, but from the banks of the Neva. It was toward St. Petersburg that France now began to look for mediation as a possible counterweight to the pro-British exertions of the House of Hapsburg, and it was in that Russian capital that London also pressed her suit either for an outright military alliance or an armed mediation on her side to right the balance of power.

Should Russia participate in the peacemaking it was clear to foreign observers that the major roles would be played by a few powerful personalities who shaped that nation's foreign policy.[50] Pre-eminent in decision-making was that dazzling daughter of the Prince of Anhalt-Zerbst, who as a young girl had exchanged the narrow horizon of Stettin for the ampler vistas of the Neva. Underestimated in both Versailles and London, Catherine II was accorded by the intellectuals of Paris the recognition she craved. In a time of lavish and cloying compliments, the philosophes laid their fulsome eulogies of the Empress on with a trowel. Baron Friedrich Melchior Grimm, Catherine's confidant, addressed her from Paris with fawning adulation as "*ma très gracieuse et amabilissississississime Souveraine*" and told her that he wanted to be counted among her dogs.[51] Diplomats who dealt with the Empress at shorter range were inclined to err in the other direction, to downgrade Catherine's capacity for creative statecraft, her shrewdness, independence of judgment, and interest in reform. The disapproving French ambassador, Baron de Breteuil, who had himself transferred from St. Petersburg to Vienna, looked upon the Semiramis of the North[52] as both superficial and unscrupulous, and prophesied that her influence would be temporary and insignificant.[53] Corberon, the chargé d'affaires of the

French legation, reported the scandals, prodigality, and indolence of the court, but often missed the big political stories. The young, energetic, and imperious British ambassador, Sir James Harris, with his stiff and proper British background, considered the Russian court to be depraved and immoral. Sir James could scarcely be expected to approve a woman who openly flaunted every rule of conventional morality and was generally believed to be implicated in the murder of her drunken, besotted husband, Peter III, six months after his accession to the throne.[54] Catherine's vanity, levity, and theatricality were equally offensive to the Briton, and biographers and historians ever since have been divided in their estimates of the Empress. The celebrated quip that advancement at Catherine's court did not depend on the size of one's *brain* testifies to the insatiable sensuality of the German princess and to her extraordinary succession of lovers, twenty-one in all, from Saltykov to Zubov. The fact remains that, save for Potëmkin, and, at the very end of her life, Zubov, the Empress' amours played no significant role in policy-making.

A self-educated enthusiast, convinced of the merits of the police state with benevolent goals, Catherine showed herself to be a pragmatist rather than a theorist, who carefully avoided big issues like emancipation which would have lost her the support of the feudal nobility. During her reign she made Russia a respected participant in European politics and presided over a burgeoning commercial and industrial society. In the War of the American Revolution the Empress, placing Russia's national interest first, was swayed by neither sentiment nor cajolery.[55] Disinclined to see England prostrate and the House of Bourbon in a position to lay down the law for Europe, Catherine throughout the early years of the war managed to walk the tightrope of strict neutrality in thought as well as action. At the very beginning of the American Revolution she had rejected Britain's request for Russian troops to fight in America.[56] Though traditionally pro-British and tied to England by a treaty of commerce, Catherine had little respect for *"Frère George,"* and less for the way in which he was handling his colonies. On the eve of the American Revolution she had predicted that if England refused to negotiate she would lose her colonies and much of her standing as a world power.[57] She followed closely the activities and speeches of the Parliamentary Opposition, which served both to color and confirm her impression of Britain's woeful leadership.[58]

After the Franco-American alliance was announced Catherine felt that England had no alternative but to make peace with her colonies. Accordingly she let Ambassador Harris know just how she felt. What would you do if they were Russia's colonies which were to be given their independence? Harris asked her. *"J'aimerai[s] mieux perdre la tête,"** she admitted.[59] But the American colonies happened not to belong to Catherine and she could afford a liberal posture. Thus, even though she wrote Grimm in February, 1778, that she washed her hands of the American upheaval by interest if not by inclination, she did nothing to discourage her correspondent's outspoken prorebel sentiments. "If she has a grain of wisdom left," Grimm wrote her in September, 1780, "England will say: 'My children, we cannot live together any more.'" Again, the following year: "It is a strange delusion of papa George that he believes he can enter the house of his children after having burned it for six years in succession."[60] Perhaps Catherine did not fully share these sentiments, although she was quoted as both favoring and opposing American independence depending upon her hearer.[61] When the war was over she wrote Grimm: "Do not speak to me about Brother George, because his name is never mentioned to me without making my blood boil."[62]

Publicly Catherine scrupulously avoided any act which could be construed as even leaning toward recognition of the United States. Thus, after Franklin had been given his public audience with Louis XVI as minister plenipotentiary, Catherine's ambassador to France declined to pay a courtesy call upon the American.[63] Elsewhere American emissaries were pointedly ignored by the Russians, and the special envoy dispatched by the Continental Congress to St. Petersburg was fated to find in that cold city nothing but solitude and frustration. Frederick summed up her attitude quite pithily. Catherine did not wish to commit herself, but wanted at the same time "to have a finger in every pie."[64]

One of the very few members of the Russian court who did not stand in awe of the Empress was her Chancellor, Count Nikita I. Panin. The corpulent diplomat was legendary for his devotion to the table, women, and gambling in roughly equal proportions, and for his quite deceptive indolence. A late riser, he concentrated public business in the half hour between 6:30 and 7:00 P.M. and in the few hours before dawn, by which time all the foreign diplomats should have been in bed. His candid appearance belied his craftiness and guile. His notorious aversion to giving a straight "No" answer masked a stubborn opposition once his mind was made up. Skillful in camouflaging his predilections and avoiding commitments, he was regarded both by the American William Lee and the Briton Sir James Harris as inimical to their respective countries.[65] The British regarded him as an instrument of Frederick II, a strong advocate of the

---

* "I would rather lose my head."

Northern System, of the protection of neutral rights, and of a *rapprochement* with France.[66] If anyone surrounding Catherine could devise a formula which would resolve the issue of American independence Count Panin indeed seemed to be the man. However, Panin's star was already declining and that of Catherine's favorite, Prince Grigori Aleksandrovich Potëmkin, was in the ascendant.

Though no longer Catherine's lover, Potëmkin still exercised an authority over her mind. An intellectual like the Empress, Potëmkin was accepted by her as an equal, and it is even believed that the pair had been secretly married back in 1774. A strong man rather than a decorative lover, one whose moods alternated between exuberant activity and gloomy indolence, the one-eyed, bowlegged, unkempt giant played in St. Petersburg much the same role as had Pompadour at Versailles toward the close of Louis XV's reign. Technically in charge of the College of War, Potëmkin devoted himself to relations with Turkey and the development of Russia's southern provinces. His deep commitment to southern expansion did not prevent him from contesting Panin's influence with the Empress in other areas of foreign affairs. Potëmkin made little secret of his dislike of France and his cordiality toward England. The French explained this by insisting that he was on the payroll of Sir James Harris, who intrigued with him for Panin's downfall, but the Russian, with virtually free access to the Privy Purse, had more than enough wealth to satisfy his voracious appetite. The amount of Harris' secret funds was probably exaggerated by his envious rivals,[67] and the Briton scornfully dismissed as a "Potsdam calumny"[68] rumors of having bribed the Empress' favorite. Though Potëmkin seemed proof of the soundness of the British diplomatic maxim, "Never go to the North without the purse strings in your hand," power rather than money prompted Potëmkin's liaison with Harris. In contrast to Catherine and Panin, who were neutral though not unfriendly to the new United States, Potëmkin had no interest whatsoever in America, and could not conceive a nation as large as the United States operating on libertarian principles which ran completely counter to his own absolutist notions.[69]

The fact that Catherine and her advisers had sedulously avoided being involved in the war on Britain's side and were prepared instead to offer Russia's services in mediation attests to the diplomatic revolution which had taken place within just a few years. Traditionally Russia had been opposed by France, whose satellite states of Turkey, Poland, and Sweden served to contain Russian expansion to the north, west, and south. Thus Catherine, with her expansionist proclivities, required a moderately powerful England as a counterpoise to the Bourbon bloc.

Of the French policy of containing Russia, Vergennes in Russian eyes stood as the chief protagonist. As ambassador to Constantinople he had instigated the Turks to declare war on Russia in 1768; then, heading the French legation to Stockholm, he had ended the preponderant influence of the pro-Russian party in Sweden when Gustavus reasserted the monarchical prerogative in 1772, with Vergennes at his right hand.[70] The treaty of Kuchuk Kainarji of 1772 which terminated the Russo-Turkish War compelled Vergennes to reappraise his position. If that treaty, as Frederick II viewed it, changed the whole political structure of Europe,[71] then perhaps a Franco-Russian *rapprochement* was needed. Providing for the free navigation of the Black Sea, on which Russia was now given a port, and guaranteeing Tartar independence, Kuchuk Kainarji constituted a hard blow to France's eastern policy. "France, sad and silent," Catherine then remarked, "walked alone, with arms folded pensively."[72]

Vergennes now decided to woo Russia away from her Prussian ally.[73] Contacts between France and Russia were sharply stepped up, and the coming of the American Revolution increased France's need for Russian naval stores. In a *volte-face*, by no means unusual to diplomacy, Vergennes now accepted Russian influence in Poland as likely to maintain peace and equilibrium in that satellite state[74] and refused in 1777 to renew the subsidy agreement to increase Sweden's military expenditures.[75] Not only did France join with Russia in mediating the War of the Bavarian Succession, but she also endorsed a Russo-Turkish Convention clarifying conflicting interpretations of the peace of Kuchuk Kainarji.

Thus by the year 1779, though old prejudices still lingered in the Russian capital, where pro-British feelings was still evident,[76] the climate of opinion toward France had dramatically changed. A warm welcome awaited the new French ambassador to St. Petersburg, Charles-Olivier de Saint-Georges, the Marquis de Vérac, dispatched to Russia that summer.[77]

Even Catherine the Great could not possibly have satisfied all her suitors, but she readily saw the mediation as an opportunity to acquire prestige with little risk. As early as the winter of 1778-79 Panin had thrown out hints to Harris of Russia's desire to mediate.[78] In May he proposed to Corberon that, in return for France's good offices in promoting the recent agreement with Turkey, Russia be permitted to serve as a mediator; and Russia's ambassador to France, Prince Bariatinski, passed on the word at Versailles of the Empress' availability as an "impartial mediator." Shortly thereafter Panin called upon Harris for Britain's peace terms, assuring the Britisher that he had viewed and treated "the behavior of the Americans with abhorrence" and considered France's association with the rebels as a "shameful" action violating "the reciprocal obligations all Sovereigns owe to each other." Acting entirely on his own authority, the British ambassador, who failed to apprehend either the extent of the Franco-Russian *rapprochement* or Russia's genuine commitment to strict neutrality, called in turn for a Russian ultimatum to France along the lines of Catherine's ultimatum to Austria the previous year at the height of the Bavarian dispute. Panin naturally declined the invitation, explaining to the impetuous Briton that it might "plunge Europe once more into that state of general disorder from which it had so lately and so miraculously escaped" and that it would be a poor return for France's good offices.[79]

In the spring of '79 France was not interested in outside mediation, and Britain took up a position of watchful waiting.[80] In one way or the other, however, the proposal kept on coming up. Once Spain entered the war Panin warned Harris that Britain, gaining new enemies daily, "must have peace at any price and should make substantial concessions to obtain it."[81] On August 11, 1779, the Secret Committee of the College of Foreign Affairs convened at Catherine's request to consider the imminent threat to England posed by the Franco-Spanish armada, and the internal discord which seemed to prevail on that beleaguered island. The Secret Committee reassured the Empress that a decisive turn in the balance of power was not imminent, and urged her at the same time to seize "the enviable role of mediator in the present war which threatens to encompass all parts of the present world." A general peace under Russia's mediation, Catherine was informed, would "exalt the reputation of Her Imperial Majesty to still greater heights."[82]

Soon all Europe was humming with rumors of a move by Russia. From his listening post at Frankfort William Lee reported at the end of August "great movements," a mediation by Russia to be backed by an armed combination of the nations of the North to take an open part in the war if the mediation were rejected. Not long thereafter he warned a British correspondent of "fatal consequences" for Great Britain from a quarter "least expected" should England fail to make peace that coming winter."[83]

The rumors bore only a slight resemblance to the plan being shaped inside the Hermitage. To be acceptable to both sides as a mediatrix Catherine realized that she would have to maintain her posture of strict neutrality. Her ambassador at the Court of St. James's, I. M. Simolin, was instructed to show "not the slightest prejudice against France," but at the same time to work to prevent a breach between England and Holland, since Catherine counted on the combined naval power of the two maritime nations to counter the Bourbon strength on land.[84] Insensitive to Catherine's real mood, Sir James Harris, ever the activist and intriguer, chose this unpropitious moment to press Russia for an alliance with England.

His sustained efforts over a period of many months on behalf of a commitment by Russia to enter the war on Britain's side or at least to come in as
an armed mediator were regularly repulsed.[85] Notwithstanding Prince
Potëmkin's outward show of sympathy for Britain, nobody in court circles
would venture to endorse a measure that would have discredited Catherine
in the less risky but perhaps more glamorous role of mediatrix. The British
tried to entice Catherine into the war by offering a pledge of British assistance in the event of a war with Turkey. Panin stood his ground and prevailed with the Empress against making such a commitment.[86] "You have
given me insomnia," Catherine told Harris at a small supper party that
winter. In return for such a gift she was hardly likely to reward her suitor
with the armed mediation for which he was now prepared to settle.[87]

The fact is that Catherine had several strings to her bow, and mediation
was but one of them. The role of mediatrix might have gratified her vanity,
but more insistent problems arising out of the spreading conflagration now
engrossed her. She became increasingly concerned with protecting neutral
rights on the seas. Like the Scandinavian countries, Russia traded naval
stores to the belligerents, but unlike them her merchant fleet was small,
tinier than her navy, and she was less troubled than her neighbors about
protecting neutral ships but much more determined to assure access to her
ports for foreign ships to take up their cargoes.

However, as ship seizures by privateers of all the belligerents, including
the Americans, mounted, Catherine seized the initiative in the assertion
of neutral rights. Essentially, the issues involving neutral trade were two-
fold. First, neutral powers had traditionally favored the doctrine "free
ships, free goods," a doctrine which also suited France, Spain, and the
United States, belligerents with insufficient shipping of their own. Contrariwise, England, whose navy and merchant fleet were adequate for her
needs, insisted that enemy goods on a neutral ship were good prize.
Secondly, a war of diplomatic words and admiralty court decrees was being
waged between the Allied powers and England over the definition of
contraband, and the neutrals were caught in the crossfire. Generally, provisions were regarded as noncontraband, and, under the Treaty of Utrecht
of 1713, naval stores as well. To keep essential raw materials from getting
into her enemies' hands, Britain sought to enforce on the seas a broad
definition of contraband, which covered ships' timber, masts, sailcloth, pitch,
tar, hemp, and cordage.

These views Britain had spelled out in the fall of 1778. Then she informed the Dutch that, despite a special treaty between the two countries
covering such items, she would purchase cargoes of naval stores on Dutch

ships already seized, whether enemy or neutral property, and, going even further, that she was also prepared to pay for the naval stores on all neutral ships that were intercepted before November 10, 1778. She warned, however, that for the future naval stores would be condemned as contraband, and her admiralty courts would settle the nature of the cargoes.[88] Neither Britain's enemies nor the neutral nations allowed her position to go unchallenged. Count von Bernstorff, Denmark's Foreign Minister, considered pro-British and avowedly anti-American,[89] had already appealed to Russia in September for the use of joint armed squadrons to protect neutral shipping, and upholding free ships, free goods, and the broad definition of contraband found in the Treaty of Utrecht.[90] These views were substantially what the American Congress had enunciated in 1776, drawing upon the provisions of the Treaty of Utrecht of 1713.[91] By November, 1778, Vergennes, who in midsummer had issued a declaration on the subject restating the provisions found in the Franco-American treaty providing for the freedom of enemy cargoes under a neutral flag and limiting contraband to arms and munitions,[92] was urging Russia to assert leadership in the matter of neutral rights.[93] Soon Sweden entered the act with a proposal of her own for a joint arming of the fleets of Sweden and Russia to defend the trade of the North.[94] For a time Russia backed away from the notion of an armed pact and favored a limited coastal patrol. The latter would have in effect protected British trade to Archangel against French and American privateers, a scheme which Vergennes was quick to deplore.[95]

Finally Russia took the plunge. A League of Armed Neutrality was created on paper by Catherine II's declaration of March 10, 1780. Although the basic principles enunciated therein seem to have been borrowed from Bernstorff, with some cheers from Vergennes in the wings, Catherine assumed full responsibility for the Declaration. It was her own brain child even though Panin prepared the text and tried to grab the credit.[96]

Vergennes, who, unlike Harris, had sought Russia's neutrality rather than an alliance, welcomed Catherine's Declaration as a step that might well tip the scales in favor of the Allies, and so did the American Congress.[97] Neutrals viewed it as a move both to protect their commerce and to hasten the coming of peace.[98] However, at the time the League was launched, its motivation appeared to be quite the contrary of Vergennes' expectations. What immediately touched off Catherine's Declaration was the large number of seizures made by the Spanish Navy in January and February of 1780 of ships flying Danish, Dutch, and other neutral flags, including the Russian. "Those Visigoths," as the Queen Mother of Denmark denominated the Spaniards, had no intention of allowing the neutrals to break the blockade of Gibraltar and went beyond the British in their narrow interpretation of neutral rights, confiscating neutral goods in enemy ships as well as cargoes of provisions or materials of war carried by neutral vessels ostensibly bound to Mediterranean ports but suspected of being intended for the besieged port of Gibraltar.[99] No one was more embarrassed than Vergennes, long a champion of neutral rights, by this sudden burst of misplaced zeal on the part of his Spanish ally. As pressures mounted on all sides, Spain was forced to restore the seized Russian ships, and to make public her adherence to all articles of the Russian Declaration saving that regarding enemy cargoes under neutral flags.[100] In fact, however, Catherine was equally irritated by Britain's suspension of her treaty with the Dutch, thereby ousting Holland from the status of a privileged neutral. She was prepared to have her instrument utilized against Spain and Britain alike.

On sober reflection it seemed clear that, if enforced, the League of Armed Neutrality was calculated to hurt Britain much more than her enemies. The principles which the Empress of Russia set forth in her Declaration provided for the free navigation of neutral ships along the coasts of nations at war; for the exemption from seizure of contraband cargoes aboard neutral vessels; for the definition of contraband contained in Russia's treaty with Great Britain which did not list naval stores as among prohibited articles; and for defining a blockaded port to mean one where the vessels of the attacking powers are stationed sufficiently nearby to render access thereto clearly dangerous. These principles were to serve as rules for determining the legality of prizes.[101]

On paper the Armed Neutrality was a formidable instrument which would assure the Allies a guaranteed flow of materials of war. In operation its reluctant members showed slight inclination to risk Britain's displeasure by carrying out the spirit of the Declaration. Bernstorff was taken aback by a proposal which would commit his nation to protecting the trade of her privileged commercial rivals, the Dutch. Using the threat of Danish adherence to the Neutral League, he secured from the British an agreement to permit free trade in salted provisions, the one commodity in which he was vitally interested. Thus, while Denmark formally joined the Armed Neutrality, she in fact agreed privately with Britain to give up the right to carry naval stores in favor of free trade in the foodstuffs which provided the bulk of Danish exports. At the news of Bernstorff's defection a storm broke out. Spain retaliated by declaring salted provisions found aboard Danish ships for the use of the enemy would henceforth be regarded as contraband.[102] Panin made Russia's displeasure patent, and in November, 1780, Bernstorff's enemies succeeded in driving him from office.[103] Thus the nation which, through its control of Norway, was to play the crucial role in patrolling the North Sea, never really was a full-fledged partner of the Empress in the venture. Sweden sought a reward for her adherence by being invited to share the mediation with Russia.[104] She found it expedient to adhere although her bid was turned down, but she was incapable at that time of making any serious effort on the seas.[105] As Sir Joseph Yorke summed it up from his excellent vantage point at The Hague, "The Danes make believe to Russia and promise us to do nothing. Sweden pretty near the same."[106]

Closest of all the neutrals to England, Holland tried desperately to avoid driving Britain into war. Torn between her pro-British and pro-French partisans, she adopted a cautious attitude, postponing her adherence.[107] When the Dutch plenipotentiaries came to St. Petersburg they made it clear that Holland's price for adherence to the Neutral League was a Russian guaranty of Dutch possessions. They, of course, were too widespread and too vulnerable for Catherine ever to consider making a commitment for their defense.[108] Soon Holland had no choice. In a desperate move to prevent Holland from continuing to ship naval stores to France and Spain, England issued a savage ultimatum, using Henry Laurens' seizure on the high seas as a pretext. Britain might profess that her quarrel with the Dutch had nothing to do with their joining the League, but the die was cast, and the Dutch had no choice but to seek friends wherever they could find them and to join Catherine's Armed League. By the time they joined a state of war existed between Holland and England.[109] Since Holland's fleet was quickly smashed by the British, her adherence added little or no muscle to the Armed Neutrality.

Finally, Russia herself was unwilling to court Britain's displeasure by pressing her patrolling operations too intensively. Secret orders were given to Russia's commerce-protecting squadron not to extend their protection to belligerent property in neutral bottoms, but only to Russian vessels and Russian property on neutral vessels. Like most other Russian secrets, this one was soon discovered by Harris and relayed home.[110] Thus, while on paper the League of Armed Neutrality was a substantial net gain for the Allies, there was much to be said for the view that in practice it was the "armed nullity" its critics called it. It did contribute to persuading the British, though, that, if they could not have Catherine on their side, it might be best to bring her in to act as a mediatrix of the peace.[111]

More exigent matters were on the mind of the Empress during the summer of 1780, however. At that time Joseph II journeyed to Mogilev for extensive talks with Catherine while the whole world wondered what the cooks were brewing. The French diplomatic mission thought that the Emperor had accomplished little in his mission; Sir James Harris took the rosy view that Austria would throw herself into Russia's arms and abandon the French alliance.[112] Both sides were misled. Joseph, who made a very favorable impression on the Empress, had no intention of taking so drastic a step. Instead, acting in secrecy, he authorized Cobenzl in November to make an informal proposal to Russia of an alliance, and thereby set in motion another diplomatic revolution.[113]

Aside from the initiation of the Armed Neutrality, several events occurred during the course of the year 1780 which served to revive the notion of Russian mediation. The Hussey-Cumberland negotiations caused Vergennes great perturbation, and he much preferred a Russian mediation to a deal on the part of Spain and England behind his back. Still, he wanted the Russians to know that he was determined upon independence for America.[114] Spain, too, was moving toward mediation by the Empress. The task of mollifying Russia's anger over the ship seizures fell to Don Pedro Normande, the fatuous and self-important Spanish chargé, who bored Panin and irritated his French colleagues. He was instructed to inform the Empress that the King of Spain would be prepared to accept her as a mediator should she formally offer her services.[115] Floridablanca counted on Russia's devising a formula which would technically satisfy France's honor as regards her commitment to America.[116]

While courting the Bourbons, the Russians did not neglect the British. In mid-March Harris received a message indirectly from the Empress urging Britain to renew her conciliation efforts with the Americans and implying that she had reason to believe that such an approach would not be rejected.[117] What Catherine had in mind, judging from what she later told Joseph II, was some kind of partition, by which "a part of the colonies" would obtain their independence.[118] With studied vagueness Panin also counseled Harris to relinquish the colonies, not so much on the ground of necessity, as he had in the past, but "from their insignificancy."[119] Stormont's answer conformed to the classic formula. The King, he told Harris, was invariably disposed to receive "his rebellious subjects into his allegiance, whenever they are disposed to return to their duty and to a constitutional dependance upon this country."[120]

Getting nowhere at all with the British, Panin turned once again to the French and Spaniards. To Corberon he proposed that, in order to counter British rumors that many Americans remained loyal to the Crown, the insurgents issue a declaration of their determination to defend their liberty until the last drop of their blood, and asserting that this resolution was not that of Congress alone but of a united nation speaking with a unanimous voice. For some reason Panin did not consider the Declaration of Independence sufficiently explicit on this score. Vergennes obliged by transmitting to the French embassy at St. Petersburg a copy of such an American declaration, although what document he selected is not known.[121] Corberon was explicit about the French position. "The independence of the Americans is, as you yourself feel, M. le Comte," he told Panin, "the indispensable base from which to move the project toward a definite accommodation."[122]

Next Panin proffered Russia's services as a mediator to Normande. In his tireless search for a formula the Russian Minister wanted to know "the middle ground" that would reconcile France and Spain on America. To Panin, everything else appeared easy to settle.[123] Floridablanca made a point of letting Cumberland know about this offer, while Harris hastily assured Stormont that there was nothing sinister in this approach.[124]

Despite the informal approach to all three parties, none of whom was quite prepared to have the Empress intervene,[125] Panin pressed his peace talks. The Chancellor realized that, of all three belligerents, France considered Catherine the most eligible of the mediators. Vergennes was now moving in this direction. In August he wrote Montmorin about the "Gordian knot" of independence. If only some means could be found which would "fundamentally preserve the integral independence of the United States," then the only remaining difficulty would be the means of spelling it out.[126]

Toward the latter part of the summer, Vérac, who had now taken over the reins from Corberon, had a significant talk with Panin. The latter allowed his mind to wander over various proposals for bringing the war to an end. The independence of the United States, the Foreign Minister declared, was very advantageous for all nations, and in particular for Russia. On the other hand, a general armistice would be favorable to France, as that nation would then be no longer committed to upholding American independence. During such an armistice, the wily Panin proposed, the King of France could then require *each* of the Thirteen States to declare its intention, and would thereafter only be obliged to maintain the independence of those states who wished to keep it. If some, for example the two Carolinas, preferred the path of submission, then the engagement as regards them would be annulled. This may well be the best means of satisfying "the point of honor" of France, Panin suggested.[127] Panin and Catherine could talk about some form of independence because neither was perturbed about the economic impact on Russia of the American Revolution. They were never persuaded by the British arguments that the loss of the American colonies would bring the Americans into direct competition with the Russians in the export of naval stores. The Russians realized that, on the contrary, American independence would spell the end of British bounty payments to the colonists for naval stores, and as a result that hitherto subsidized industry would be less rather than more competitive thereafter.[128]

Doubly disturbed by the peace offensive of Cumberland in Spain and Necker at Versailles, Vergennes was now turning his mind in the very same direction to which Panin was pointing. When apprised of Vérac's interview, he inquired, with his customary caution, whether the Chancellor's formula for independence was inspired from England and whether it reflected the true sentiment of the court or was personal to Panin himself.[129] Panin's approach must have appealed to others in the French government beside Vergennes, for, without awaiting a reply to his questions, he wrote Vérac on October 12th that the King was interested in Panin's ideas on American independence and disposed to expedite the mediation along those lines. Panin's proposal, Vergennes now conceded, tended to resolve the great issue of American independence, truly "the Gordian knot of the present war." If this knot could be cut, there could be no doubt that peace would be the immediate consequence.

Getting down to specifics, Vergennes favored an immediate armistice of at least four or five years along with a mediation of the warring powers. They could hardly refuse to consult "*separately*" with the "united provinces of America" and to secure from each an authentic declaration of its intention to maintain the state of independence which it had claimed for itself. Such a move, Vergennes argued, would not violate good faith, for it would leave the Americans the arbiters and masters of their condition. Should some of the "united provinces" prefer to return under the domination of England, the guaranty of the King of France would no longer hold for them except as regards the preservation of peace. Such an approach would have the advantage of being both agreeable to France and honorable for England. True, France would run the risk of England's seducing her former colonies to make a separate peace and break their connection with their ally, but he implied that the risk was worth taking.

In his comments, which were meant to be read by the Russian court, the French Foreign Minister expressed his conviction that the flame of liberty burned so brightly in America that even in New York, with the refugees sequestered on "that little island," the people would favor independence unless the presence of the enemy there could by force or seduction move them to betray their principles. We know now that Vergennes did not believe his own rhetoric. Only a month before, he had written the Chevalier de La Luzerne that on the basis of so veracious and patriotic an American as Silas Deane (secretly gone over to the enemy camp by this time) he had been given to understand that the disposition of the colonies toward independence was equivocal and that Congress had neither authority nor credit.[130] Again, toward the end of October he wrote La Luzerne that France long had intelligence about the indifferent attitude of the South toward independence, and instructed him to ascertain what the reaction of the other colonies would be to the defection of Georgia and the Carolinas. Keep your inquiries secret, Vergennes enjoined.[131] From these dispatches it is clear that, despite his confident predictions to Vérac of American unanimity, Vergennes anticipated that a separate polling, colony by colony, as Panin advised, would then have resulted in partition. He was prepared, so it would seem, to turn back to the British the whole of the Lower South in accordance with Panin's shrewd formula.

Vergennes now took a favorable view of a Congress in which all the issues of peace could be treated and direct consultation be held with the American deputies. He was even prepared to accept Catherine as a mediator or arbiter, because he felt that one impressive result of her intervention would be the establishment of a maritime code which would give the force of law to the Empress' principles of neutrality.[132]

Vergennes' cordial response to Panin's proposal was turned over by Vérac to the Russian Chancellor for transmission to his Empress and her eyes alone. Vergennes did not want it to fall into Potëmkin's hands, which would assure its reaching Harris, Cobenzl, and Normande in that order. The Empress gave vague assurances in reply. Panin, in a further exploratory talk with Vérac, showed little enthusiasm for a Peace Congress, but, if one were to be held, he considered Leipzig a more suitable site than Vienna. To such a Congress he now proposed that *each* of the "united colonies of America" send delegates who would be accountable to their respective assemblies and not to Congress. That federal body would remain suspended until each province had ruled on its own fate. During the period of the armistice what would happen to America? Vérac asked the Chancellor. Panin replied unhesitatingly that America must have complete liberty to decide her own fate and be free to engage in commerce with all nations. These would be conditions *sine qua non* to an armistice, and, once accepted, the other issues like disarmament should be easy to settle.[133]

Finally, Panin told the Marquis that he had sent a verbal message, an *insinuation verbale*, identical in wording, to all three belligerents exhorting them to make the peace. Panin was not worried about the Allies' response, but was naturally concerned about England's. As relations between the Chancellor and Potëmkin continued to deteriorate, he must have wondered whether he would have a hand in the mediation in any event. That summer he had been ignored when Joseph visited Mogilev,[134] and as a result Harris paid all the more insistent court to the Empress' favorite. It was Potëmkin who suggested to Harris the price of an alliance with Britain: Minorca, Harris had been told.[135] In a private audience with the Empress on December 19th Sir James boldly attacked Panin as "the most dangerous" of England's enemies and criticized the Neutral League for its aid to the Allies. The Empress did not encourage him to pursue either topic. Instead, she pressed Panin's formula upon him. "Make peace," she urged. "Deal with your colonies separately. Try to divide them. Then their alliance will fall of itself. That will provide the loop-hole for them, because one must realize that each power wishes to save his honor." From the gist of her remarks it is clear that Catherine had abandoned the notion that the whole of America could be recovered.[136]

Harris left the audience with the impression that, though adamant about her "Armed Nullity," the Empress, if suitably flattered, would be a mediatrix favorable to England's interests. Before this interview even took place, however, Stormont made it clear to Simolin, in answer to Panin's *insinuation verbale*, that at long last England was agreeable to mediation, but preferred it to be under both imperial courts.[137]

For many reasons those closing weeks of 1780 seemed momentous. On November 29th Maria Theresa died, and, as Vergennes predicted, her passing might well work "a great revolution" at the court of Vienna. One could no longer count on the Emperor's commitment to the pacific policies of his mother.[138] The projection of Joseph into a joint mediation made that prospect even less appealing to the Allies than the earlier proposal of an Austrian mediation by Maria Theresa, whom they regarded as more truly neutral in spirit than her ambitious son.

The day after Christmas the ailing Benjamin Franklin attended memorial services for the Empress Queen at Versailles, joining all the diplomats in deep mourning, with flopped hats and crepe bands, and long black cloaks. There he heard from Vergennes that England had at last declared war against Holland. "Much fatigued by going twice up and down the palace stairs," Franklin noted in his diary, "from the tenderness of my feet and weakness of my knees." He had to forego making the rounds and declined a dinner invitation of the Comte de Vergennes. For the American envoy it was to be the simple life until he had recovered his strength.[139] It had been a hard year for diplomats, a year when America's independence and integrity seemed weighed in the balance.

IX

THE PLOT TO PARTITION AMERICA

WITH THE BEGINNING of the new year, 1781, all Vienna was astir. Public buildings and foreign embassies were still heavily draped in black, but the city prepared to put on more festive colors. Having made obeisance to the departed Empress Queen,[1] diplomats now awaited a new era in which the gay and sophisticated capital on the Danube would, it was expected, assume a role in keeping with her traditions.

Vienna's sudden new prominence came largely as a result of Britain's unexpected reaction to Catherine's oral peace feeler. The North Ministry had now indicated its willingness to accept comediation and to make peace with France as soon as she ceased to be allied to the insurgent Americans.[2] Kaunitz leaped on the word "mediation," which appeared in Stormont's reply to Panin's verbal message. "Lord Stormont has baptized the baby!" the Austrian Chancellor exclaimed.[3] Jubilantly he realized that Stormont had done more than give the baby a name. By insisting on comediation, he had in effect placed the infant in the keeping of Vienna rather than St. Petersburg.

Before the Allied powers could recover from their embarrassment at Britain's counterproposal to bring Austria into the mediation with Russia, Joseph II seized the initiative and suggested his capital for the holding of a peace congress.[4] Capitalizing on their own maneuver, the British accepted Vienna with alacrity.[5] Contrariwise, the French, who had long suspected and even feared such a move by Joseph II, had been counting on the Empress of Russia—the most eligible of mediators in their eyes—to save them from embarrassment,[6] and the Spaniards, equally hostile to the notion,[7] resorted to their customary evasion. Increasingly preoccupied with expansionist goals at Turkey's expense, the Empress accepted Vienna without a struggle and named as her commissioner to the proposed Congress

Prince Mikhailovich Galitzin, her ambassador to the imperial court and an utter mediocrity.[8]

At this turn of events the mortification of the Allies was painful to behold. Far better continue the war, France's ambassador to Vienna advised his Foreign Minister, even with unfavorable consequences, than to allow Kaunitz to dictate the peace. Reminding his court of the Emperor's hatred of France, he protested: Any city but Vienna![9] With Austria a nominal ally of France, Vergennes could not find a formula to decline. Instead, he and Floridablanca managed to qualify their acceptances. The French and Spaniards demanded assurances that both Holland and the United States be included in the mediation.[10] In addition to a long truce, Spain, as might be expected, desired an advance commitment awarding her the Floridas and Gibraltar and barring Englishmen from cutting wood on Campeche.[11]

Kaunitz quickly recognized that American independence stood as the chief obstacle to securing unqualified acceptances of mediation by the belligerents, and talked both to Paris and London of sacrifices which England would be expected to make. At St. Petersburg his ambassador, Graf von Cobenzl, told Vérac that Austria favored both the freedom of the seas and American independence, which seems to have been stretching a point in both cases.[12] France's and Spain's formal consent to the comediation soon followed, Floridablanca being left with no alternative when the British recalled Cumberland.[13] A similar tack was taken by the Empress when in mid-February she finally acknowledged Britain's invitation to act as a comediatrix. In her instructions to Simolin she incorporated Kaunitz's formula that the parties should demand only what was feasible and what they would be willing to accept if in the other's place. The formula annoyed Stormont. What touched off his liveliest indignation was the inclusion of a phrase concerning the necessity of "being considerate of the dignity of France." This was Panin's evil work, Stormont charged. Consistent with his original response to Simolin back in December of 1780, he again made France's discontinuance of aid to the Americans an essential precondition of peace.[14]

"All the world would mediate for us, but nobody helps us!" exclaimed Sir Joseph Yorke, England's watchdog at The Hague on an earlier occasion.[15] Yorke's remarks revealed how little the British government welcomed an objective intercession. Stormont, first of all, laid down impossible preconditions to a peace congress. He insisted that there could be no cessation of hostilities "before the colonies have returned to their allegiance."[16] Secondly, he sought secretly to win the Empress to the British side by offering her the bribe of the island of Minorca and to obtain Austria's partiality to England by promising to support any project for opening the Scheldt, the river which passed through the United Provinces en route from Antwerp to the sea and deemed vital in Joseph's plans for the Austrian Netherlands.[17]

Prince Kaunitz quickly scotched the notion that Austria would be a party to so transparent a bribe.[18] The British then pushed ahead with their scheme of bribing merely one of the mediators, perhaps without calculating the consequences on the other member. The Austrians got wind of it, and so did the Allies.[19] The King, first unalterably opposed to yielding Minorca to Russia, had to be won over, and Sir James Harris' dispatches proved powerful ammunition. It was later asserted by an intimate of Harris that the cession of Minorca was Potëmkin's idea and that he was promised a princely bribe if the deal were consummated.[20] At a Cabinet meeting on January 19, 1781, the Ministry persuaded the King of the advantages of the proposition.[21] With Minorca as his bait, Harris was instructed to ask the Empress to restore peace on the basis of the Treaty of Paris of 1763, as modified by the conquests of the war, with the *uti possidetis* to provide the rule. The French were to evacuate America forthwith, and no agreement should be made as regards the Americans, whom the King could never suffer "to treat through the medium of a foreign power." Once the preliminaries of peace were signed, a treaty of perpetual alliance between Britain and Russia could be concluded, but, more immediately, the arrangement for the eventual transfer of Minorca could be secretly made. In an accompanying memorandum the King agreed to show clemency toward his rebellious colonists, to place them in the same situation they were in before the controversy began, and to concede to them the right to tax themselves. Stormont cautioned Harris that the proffer was for the present to remain "an inviolable secret, trusted only to the Empress, Prince Potemkin, and yourself."[22]

St. Petersburg was frigid to these new approaches, and shocked at the presumption of the British in offering gifts to the Empress with one hand while with the other they appeared to be striking at the Empress' program of neutral rights by warring against the Dutch. Despite the provocation, Catherine had not ventured to come to Holland's military defense, aid to which the Dutch were entitled through membership in the League. Instead, the Empress tried to force the British to accept her as a mediatrix of that nation's new conflict with the United Provinces.[23] Although Harris intrigued long and lustily and even sought the backing of Catherine's erstwhile favorite, Count Alexis Orlov, in addition to Potëmkin, the Empress disdained the bribe. Aroused by a stern warning from Panin, she responded to the British offer of Minorca with the assertion: "It is too much of a good thing. Somebody is trying to pull my leg." Her basic common sense kept her from being party to a hare-brained scheme which would have involved Russia in incessant conflict with the Bourbon powers. The only consolation Sir James Harris managed to salvage from his persistent, if futile, attempts at seduction was provided by the reports passed on to him by both Orlov and Potëmkin, quoting the Empress as "strongly against the independence of America."[24] At the height of these backstairs negotiations Harris privately observed: "We are an odd people, and never are rightly understood but by those who are as odd as ourselves and who possess good intellect."[25]

If the British government ignored longer-range strategic considerations by offering the Russians a base in the western Mediterranean, it should be credited with some degree of caution for failing to act upon a proposal made to the North Ministry at this very time calling for a joint Anglo-Russian attack on Mexico and California. The author of this plan was not merely a slave trader and merchant with extensive American interests, but one who was to be entrusted by the British government with the peace negotiations carried on with the Americans in Paris the following year. Richard Oswald, a Scot but never frugal in his advice on how to run the war,[26] proposed a daring project for an alliance with Russia in February, 1781, which he revised the following April.[27] While but one of numerous plans projected in England for an invasion of the Spanish colonies, Oswald's takes on special significance both because of the large role its author was soon to play in the peacemaking and because of its extraordinary timing.

In his February proposal Oswald had suggested a Russian attack upon Peru for which England was prepared to offer "a perpetual alliance." Once Oswald found out that Russia was "tied up in the character of mediation," he recognized the dubious propriety of his proposal. What he then submitted in April was a plan more far-reaching in conception but more circumstantial in its approach. Now the Russians were to be informed that England was preparing a Nicaraguan expedition to divert a part of the Spanish forces. To release British forces for the Gulf of Mexico the Russians would be asked to provide five or six thousand troops for garrisoning New York and other towns in North America. But behind the screen of furnishing auxiliaries to England, Russia would be seduced into transporting troops from Siberia to conquer "the whole of these Spanish settlements on the South Seas." England would then divide the Pacific conquests with the Empress, showing remarkable self-abnegation by contending herself with conquests in the Gulf and yielding the Pacific acquisitions to Russia, who would now entrench herself in the northern part of Mexico, "in a manner unoccupied by the Spaniards," as well as in California. Oswald viewed with perfect equanimity the presence of the Russians on the Pacific coast and even the ultimate extension of Russian power down the coast to Peru and Chile.

To expedite Russia's intervention England, according to Oswald's proposal, would advance a loan or even a large cash gift as bait to defray the costs of the transport of troops from Siberia to California. Aware of recent discoveries which the Russians had made in the North Pacific, Oswald was quite ready to provide a solid basis for explorations in an area which constituted as yet no more than a fringe interest in Catherine's empire.

If nobody else took Oswald's plan too seriously at the time, the Scotsman did not dismiss it from his own mind. A year later, in May of '82, hardly two weeks after he had been dispatched by the Earl of Shelburne, Secretary of State for the Colonies in the new government, to open conversations with Benjamin Franklin in Paris, Oswald warned the American that an intransigent stand by the Spaniards could jeopardize the peace treaty. Nevertheless, Spain's unreasonableness might yield to proper measures. As Franklin noted, Oswald reminded him that "Russia was a friend to England, had lately made great discoveries on the back of North America, and made establishments there, and might easily transport an army from Kamchatka to the coast of Mexico, and conquer all those countries." "This appeared to me a little visionary at present," Franklin drily observed, "but I did not dispute it."[28]

Then once more, in the summer of 1782, Oswald, gloomily reviewing England's military situation, prepared another memorandum suggesting that even the "bare report" of an expedition from Siberia to the Pacific coast would greatly "facilitate the progress of the treaty now in hand."[29] Accordingly, the British ambassador at St. Petersburg should request leave for British ships to provision at Kamchatka and take the occasion to point out with what ease the Russians could become "masters of the whole of the Spanish settlements on the South Seas." The mere rumor would be sufficient, Oswald insisted, to induce France and Spain "to hush this din of war" and "to close with England more speedily, and on more reasonable terms, than we might have otherwise reason to look for."

Just what the realistic Shelburne thought about this visionary project he failed to put down on paper, but since the British had been unable to lure the Russians into the tempting reaches of the western Mediterranean, no sensible minister could have thought that at that time Russia would be prepared to embark on a vast scheme of overseas conquests in the New World. Oswald would have pushed the clock of Russian expansion years ahead, with what ominous consequences for the new American republic as well as for the Spanish-American colonies soon to launch their own wars of liberation. A Russian army in the streets of New York City and other coastal towns would indubitably have added a bizarre note to Britain's problems of occupation.

In the winter of 1781 no one, not even Vergennes or Floridablanca, was more crestfallen at the turn of events which propelled Joseph and Kaunitz to the center of the world stage than Nikita Panin, whose dismissal was believed about to occur.[30] He could have derived some consolation from the fact that his proposal to consult the American states separately on their independence took firm root in Austrian soil. This ingenious approach to the greatest issue of the war came as a surprise to the Emperor, who was cautious about committing himself,[31] but it was cordially embraced by the Austrian Chancellor. When Breteuil met with Kaunitz in mid-February he pointed out how unrealistic it was for England to bring America back *"as she was!"* Kaunitz pounced on the words "as she was,"[32] and replied, "That is precisely the idea. It is in that phrase 'as she was' that we can perhaps find a means of conciliation between yourself and England. . . . The English cannot flatter themselves," he continued, "of bringing America back under the rule of the Mother Country," and you simply must come up with a formula which will relieve all "the embarrassed parties" as much for their prestige as for their interest. Should England put to the United States a proposition acceptable to the latter, then you will be "free of your greatest shackles," Kaunitz reminded his French listener.[33] Alert to any formula which could get France off the hook, Vergennes, when this conversation was relayed to him, chose to ignore Breteuil's warning that Austria was suspect. Instead, he instructed his ambassador to Vienna that Kaunitz's phrase "as she was" might well provide the means of cutting the Gordian knot by establishing American independence without wounding England's dignity.[34]

If Vergennes agreed that England could not be restored to her position "as she was," he was also moving rapidly to the view that a settlement might be effected on the basis of the ground then possessed by the opposing forces. For America this, of course, meant partition. At the very start of 1781 alarming rumors swept the Southern states to the effect that the British were prepared to end the war by retaining Georgia and possibly South Carolina. Georgia's delegates to the Continental Congress were impelled to issue a pamphlet pointing out the importance of Georgia to the remaining states, warning that no part of America could expect to be free long while England retained "both ends of the continent," and affirming their confidence that the King of France would continue the war until "all the states of the Union to which he is allied shall be established."[35]

Had the Georgian Patriots been privy to the diplomatic conversations and dispatches among the Great Powers they might have been less sanguine about France's intentions. Early in February Kaunitz passed on to Comte Mercy in Paris a proposal then being mooted by which the King of Prussia would transmit through the Danish court a plan of pacification enlarging on the propositions of the Empress of Russia already in the hands of the belligerents. This plan was reported to provide for the division of the North American colonies into three parts. Canada would be returned to France. The Southern provinces would be retained by England, and the remaining American states would be "declared a free republic."[36] Almost simultaneously, but without knowledge of the way the winds were blowing in Europe, La Luzerne, in a dispatch to his chief, weighed the pros and cons of dismembering America and concluded that an American union would be more advantageous to France, partition more favorable to England.[37]

In February, and before La Luzerne's dispatch reached his office, Vergennes, with Rayneval's assistance, drew up a confidential memorandum revealing his attitude toward both the truce and the *uti possidetis* as well as his conviction that a mediation at that time might be of service to France. Since it was impossible to attain everything for the United States and France, the question became: What must be sacrificed? What could the King of France yield with honor and without too much loss of dignity?

Vergennes recognized that the King of England was unwilling to negotiate directly with his former subjects. To do so would constitute recognition. Hence a formula had to be devised to save face all around. A long-term truce, which would constitute *de facto* recognition of the United States, might be advantageously substituted for a definitive treaty. One might take for a model the truce negotiated between Spain and the United Provinces in 1608, by which the Dutch won their liberty. Understandably, the Americans would prefer a definitive peace treaty to a truce, but, Vergennes added significantly, "such considerations are not important enough to influence the Congress to prolong the horrors of the war." Pointing to the war weariness in America and the depreciating credit of Congress in Europe, Vergennes satisfied himself that a continuation of the war would keep America exposed to British intrigues and make Congress susceptible to treason, whereas once the war were ended by truce, all Americans, he predicted, would be patriots "by habit, by sentiment, and by interest."

Having satisfied himself that the war should be halted, Vergennes then grappled with that aspect of the truce which presented "great difficulties." He noted that England then occupied New York, South Carolina, Georgia, and Penobscot, the last-named of crucial importance to England as a source of masts and other timber for the British Royal Navy.[38] He neglected to include the interior posts from which the redcoats dominated what became the Northwest Territory, as well as northern Vermont and northwestern New York. Vergennes had not heard that the Spaniards had recently driven a British garrison from their post at Saint Joseph, Michigan, and now claimed the Illinois Valley for Charles III, but he did know that Spain was already in possession of West Florida and had moved up the east bank of the Mississippi opposite the mouth of the Arkansas.

The only British holding in America that seriously concerned Vergennes was New York. That city, he felt, would have to be evacuated in the interest of America's security. On the other hand, South Carolina and Georgia could with less inconvenience be permitted to remain in British hands, he argued. He was even prepared to yield the American-held portion of South Carolina. Georgia was still not peopled, and the heat of Carolina was destructive to energetic activity, Vergennes rationalized, while the port of Charleston in English hands would facilitate the provisioning of Britain's West Indian possessions. Conceding that every Patriot from Washington down had gone on record against a truce, Vergennes insisted that the fear of prolonging the war might very possibly induce Americans to make the kind of sacrifice that would have been inadmissible two years earlier.

Who would put the proposition to the Americans? Would it be the King or the two mediating courts? For His Majesty to make such a démarche would be a delicate and risky business. He would open himself up to charges of bad faith were he himself to propose that Congress sign a truce leaving to the British what they presently held on the American Continent. "Only the mediators, disengaged from all parties, could appropriately put so painful a proposition to the United States," Vergennes concluded.

Beyond that, the King should not permit the King of England to have the slightest link of sovereignty with his former colonies along the lines proposed by the British in 1778. As Vergennes saw it, the best strategy would be to defer raising the issue of the *status quo* until the plenipotentiaries were assembled, because then it would be the work of the mediators. A condition *sine qua non* to both a truce and the *status quo* should be the restitution of New York to the Americans, Vergennes repeated.

What kind of a truce would be acceptable? One long enough to assure the independence of America, at least twenty years and possibly as long as thirty, Vergennes stated. Of course, France would guarantee the independence of the United States as required by her treaty of 1778 and even furnish guarantees against attack by a new treaty.[39] As is now known, a submission by the Americans to a mediation on that basis would have been a case of lambs led to the slaughter.[40]

That Vergennes should have so misjudged American determination as well as the deteriorating position of the British in America was due as much to the kind of confidential information he was being fed from America as to his own innate skepticism of the durability of the American republic. For example, at the end of March La Luzerne wrote him that should the Confederation suffer great reverses and find it necessary to make peace, he felt that Congress could be persuaded to agree to yielding Georgia, a state of "small importance." Beyond that he was persuaded Congress would not go. Americans would prefer to run the risks of continuing the war rather than losing anything further.[41] Early in April he favored providing aid for each state separately rather than dealing with Congress alone.[42] His reports tell of a dearth of patriotism and spread fears that the Southerners were forming an army to fight against the Middle States and the North.[43] Any pretensions of the American states to the West or Vermont he consistently viewed with alarm.[44]

Small wonder that Vergennes on the eve of an unanticipated but great victory wrote La Luzerne that if a sacrifice by the Americans should be proved necessary, they would have to be resigned to it. Thus the greater part of the Belgian Provinces had been held under the Spanish yoke while the remaining portion preserved their independence, Vergennes remarked. The Americans must be made to realize that the war cannot go on forever, and that, should it become necessary to propose a formula for terminating it, the task should be put to the mediating courts.[45]

While the mediators and America's ally seemed reconciled to the need for partitioning America, they realized that they would have to work out a formula to overcome British resistance to American representation at the congress. Early in March Joseph II held a long private audience with Breteuil.

"Do you think that the Americans will absolutely insist on having their own representatives in the Congress?" the Emperor asked the French ambassador. "Would they not prefer to charge the King of France with the handling of their interests?" Breteuil replied that he was far from persuaded about the former, but that he was convinced that the King himself would want the Americans represented and would decline to treat their affairs without their participation.

"I do not know," the Emperor observed, "just how one could induce England to accept the assumption by the Americans of the character of a power at the Congress." That was the object of the war, Breteuil reminded Joseph, and could not be separated from other primary conditions of peace. Suppose the English and Americans were to treat separately in a congress of their own choosing? the Emperor then asked. Difficult and unlikely, Breteuil answered.

Breteuil came away from this audience with the distinct impression that Joseph II, while not favoring complete independence, had swung around to the notion that England should abandon the idea of recovering complete authority over the Americans and be prepared to allow them at a minimum absolute freedom of trade. Joseph was well aware of the economic role America played in British Empire trade. To others he pointed out that the colonies purchased British goods which could not be sold in the highly competitive European market.[46] "Were America to return under her laws," the Emperor remarked to Breteuil, England might indeed be persuaded to yield Gibraltar. To this Breteuil made no reply, but managed an enigmatic smile.[47] From these remarks it was patent that in the winter of 1781 Joseph was no more prepared than George III to accept the complete independence of the United States.

Vergennes was now giving the most serious thought to the issue of American representation. He reminded Breteuil that the King would not consent to having an American plenipotentiary barred from the congress, and that there was presently in Europe John Adams, a man holding such a character, who could be counted upon to attend the congress on assurances of being suitably admitted thereto. Let the mediators waste no time in giving him such assurances, Vergennes remarked.[48] In the front of the Comte's mind was Panin's ingenious notion of separate consultations with each of the Thirteen States. Should the Emperor propose Panin's idea of having each state polled for its opinion on the peace, let us act surprised, he instructed his ambassador at St. Petersburg in March.[49] Several weeks later he asked Vérac to ascertain from Panin the basis upon which he was proposing to admit the American delegates to the congress.[50]

In mid-April Breteuil urged Kaunitz to settle the issue of American representation forthwith. He pointed to the Teschen settlement, where a positive basis for negotiation was laid down prior to assembling the congress. In a placatory mood, Prince von Kaunitz disclosed to Breteuil that once the deputies of the American Congress were admitted they would carry "de facto recognition of the independence of the Americans, because this word 'deputies of the Congress' signifies deputies of a body of a nation exercising all the rights of sovereignty and independence." Why not just call the American deputy to the congress "the American plenipotentiary?" Breteuil asked. Kaunitz thought for a moment, and then remarked, "You seem to believe that the United States do not wish more than one deputy." When informed that a single delegate seemed to be their intention, Kaunitz pointed out that a representation by one man would cause embarrassment. Would it not be possible, he asked, to have *each* state send a deputy to the congress to treat separately of its affairs with England and in that way secure England's consent to their representation?

Now that Kaunitz had picked up the Panin proposal and thrown it on the agenda, Breteuil, who did not realize how sympathetic Vergennes was to it, raised various objections. A considerable number of American deputies would provide the British with an opportunity to foment disunion and discord among the United States, he pointed out. Kaunitz and Breteuil parted on an inconclusive note, and the French ambassador wrote pessimistically to Vergennes about the future role of the mediation.[51]

As soon as Vergennes learned that Kaunitz had broached the Panin plan of admitting a deputy from each of the United States instead of a single deputy from Congress, he pounced on it. "I would be quite of a mind to follow up this lead," he wrote Breteuil, buttressing his instruction with a number of arguments. Such a plan would be more palatable to England. The deputies might be chosen by their separate assemblies. Finally, the Americans, despite differences between the various states, were committed to independence even in the provinces the English had reconquered.[52] Perhaps bewildered by his new instruction, Breteuil failed to obtain from Kaunitz a clarification of the notion of thirteen American deputies instead of a solitary delegate before the mediators adopted a series of preliminary points to serve as a basis of negotiation.

If Vergennes was cordial to the Panin-Kaunitz plan, the British could be expected to give it a chilly response. To Stormont the inclusion of America in the congress came as a complete and unwelcome surprise.[53] As Britain's Secretary of State saw it, America remained the great object of the war. To him that object admitted of "no *mezzo termine*." The Americans, he insisted, "must be subjects or separate states."[54]

Toward the end of March Kaunitz revealed his approach to American representation in a talk with Sir Robert Keith. He hinted that a way must be found "to be able to learn from the Americans *themselves* as to how far they would be satisfied" with stipulations concerning their "future state." With his customary circumlocution, he implied that some indirect contact should be established between the mediators and "some one confidential person who might be authorized by the Rebel Congress to say that such or such terms would or would not be accepted by America." Thereupon Keith read to him a long-winded dispatch from Stormont, pointing out that England did not now insist upon the severance of ties by France with the rebels as a precondition *sine qua non* to opening the peace negotiations. While ostensibly yielding with one hand, Stormont seemed to be holding tight with the other, for he insisted that "the dependence of the rebel subjects ought to be preestablished" before the congress convened. "One would have to be an Apollo" to make peace on such a basis, Kaunitz remarked to Keith,[55] and to Breteuil: "It is useless to break one's head to find grounds of conciliation." As a result of this new impasse, Sir Joseph Yorke, who was ordered to join Keith as a commissioner at the Congress of Vienna, never set out on his appointed task.[56]

Despite seemingly insuperable obstacles, Kaunitz and Galitzin, possibly with some backstairs advice from Panin, agreed upon a series of preliminary points to serve as a basis of negotiation. These were dispatched to the various belligerent courts on May 21st. Four articles were proposed by the comediators: (1) Without exclusion, all proposals put forward by the belligerents were to be considered at Vienna. Parallel discussions between Great Britain and the American colonies should go forward at the same time in Vienna but without the intervention of the other belligerents or the mediators unless mediation should be formally requested. (2) A separate peace between Britain and the colonies would be signed at the same time as the general peace, both to be guaranteed by the mediators and "by every other neutral power whose guarantee the belligerent powers may think proper to claim." (3) During the negotiations there should be a general armistice for the term of one year during which everything should remain *in statu quo*. (4) Once the preliminary bases were accepted, the negotiations were to proceed at once, the respective plenipotentiaries to be provided with full powers and instructions without delay.[57]

The mediation articles were unfortunately timed, for neither side recognized how close the military conflict was to a termination. Gleefully Frederick the Great, who viewed Joseph II's mediation efforts with his usual rich blend of realism and envy, observed, "In politics, just as in other things, everything has its season." Predicting that the peace congress would most certainly not take place that year, the Prussian monarch remarked at this time, "One does not eat cherries in February which are not ripe until June."[58]

In June a cold wind blew down from the North and chilled the royal summer residents of Tsarskoye Selo outside St. Petersburg, while an equally frigid blast from the British Foreign Office had a similar effect on the diplomats quartered in Vienna. The British made it clear to Graf von Belgiojoso, Austria's envoy to London, that they still refused to negotiate with the rebels and would consider nothing less than their submission. They would most certainly not treat with the Americans at Vienna. Stormont in private dispatches to Harris as well as Keith charged that Kaunitz and the French had double-crossed England behind her back, perhaps motivated by the smell of trade with an independent America. Kaunitz's "*mezzo termine*," he screamed, was nothing but "the identical proposal of France with a trifling alteration in point of form." No longer would he regard Kaunitz as a friend, but rather as an equivocator. Now he hoped the mediation would die still-born.[59] The formal reply of the British government to the mediation articles was naturally more temperate in tone, but equally obdurate in substance. The mediators were reminded of the King's "immutable resolution" not to permit any interference by foreign powers with his rebellious subjects. Such interference obliged him to decline the "different articles relating to the rebellious subjects of His Majesty."[60] Count Belgiojoso was informed that the British Ministry insisted on excluding the American rebellion from the mediation, which should be concerned merely with the restoration of peace "between the belligerent powers," including Holland but not America.[61]

The comediators took the British reply with ill grace. Kaunitz tartly characterized the behavior of the British Ministry as "rash and even desperate." While each of you stand on diametrically opposing grounds, it is vain to strive for reconciliation, the Austrian Chancellor bitterly concluded.[62] "Stop in time and sacrifice a little," he warned Keith.[63] Up at St. Petersburg, where Panin was on the way out, Vice Chancellor Ostermann, a precise and unimaginative functionary of German origin, reputed to have little or nothing to do with policy-making, took a scolding tone with Harris, finding fault with the English for their "backwardness" in the matter of peace.[64]

If the British were chagrined by the proposals of the comediators, France and Spain were equally disgruntled, although more restrained in their declinations. Rayneval pointed out to Vergennes that the one-year armistice the comediators proposed would be "entirely to the advantage of Great Britain who occupies at the moment Penobscott and New York, with posts in Virginia, the two Carolinas and Georgia; and if the Court of London could hold on to these positions she would keep half of America, which would be too exhausted, harassed, and weakened to re-establish itself through an armistice." Throughout the world, Rayneval added, England was in "a state of inferiority," and therefore an armistice held no advantage to France. In India it would serve to reverse the favor-able operations of Hyder Ali Khan, France's ally; in Europe it would allow England to capitalize on long-standing envy of France. Still, while we must reject the proposal of an armistice, and with it, the *status quo,* we should not shut the door completely to mediation, Vergennes' aide counseled. Instead, we should stress the imprecision with which the sub-ject of the American plenipotentiaries was treated, along with the pro-vision for the *status quo,* which the Americans might well oppose.[65] That was exactly what Vergennes did. France, he declared, had no right to stipulate for the United States, and if she did, she would run the risk of disavowal.[66]

The omission of any stipulation for treating the cession of Gibraltar disposed the Spaniards most unfavorably to the propositions of the comedi-ators. Nor were they impressed by Panin's notion that Britain would recognize deputies named by *each* provincial assembly while challenging the naming of deputies by the American Congress. Anticipating British objections, the Spaniards proposed treating with the colonies without specifying the quality of their representation, or as a marginal note in a French hand suggested: "When the article proposed by the mediators is accepted by the Court of London, would it not be deemed to have pro-vided for setting up some new rules for the nomination of the American deputies?"[67]

The answer of the Bourbon courts put Kaunitz "out of spirits and more reserved than usual." He now seized the issue of American independence to drive a wedge between the Allies, sharply warning La Torre, Spain's commissioner to the congress, that the independence of the insurgents could bring disastrous consequences to Spain's own empire. The Chancel-lor could understand Spain's launching another campaign to recover Gi-braltar, but "certainly," he pressed, "the independence of America cannot be agreeable to you. It is too bad an example." France had engagements that her faithful ally must respect, La Torre replied laconically.[68]

The "name of the Americans" did not come readily from the mouth of Prince Kaunitz, as Breteuil observed,[69] but Prince Galitzin, who had in the past displayed utter subservience to Kaunitz as well as exceptional reticence on controversial subjects, now showed more open sympathy to the rebels. In September he told the French chargé at Vienna that England's hopes of subjugating America were indeed vain. On a later visit to Vienna Russia's Grand Duke similarly voiced his admiration for America's "internal force and national virtue."[70] However, at St. Petersburg Russian officials acted as though America did not exist, as Francis Dana, a trusted New England Patriot, dispatched by Congress as a regularly accredited minister to Russia, found out upon his arrival at the Russian capital in August, 1781.[71]

In mid-July Kaunitz shrewdly remarked that England's intransigence stemmed from her hope of decisive victory in the campaign ahead,[72] and not long before Sir Robert Keith, who shared the strange complacency of that Ministry whose fatuous orders he so faithfully executed, observed, "We must lay hold of the Italian proverb, *chi ha tempo ha vita.*"*[73] Both comments served to underscore the wishful thinking which characterized the North Ministry's conduct of the War of the American Revolution from start to finish. Indeed, only a few days before news reached London of the surrender of Cornwallis, Stormont was quoted as having told Simolin that England would not recognize the independence of America until the French took the Tower of London, and that she would exchange Gibraltar only for Madrid.[74]

Vergennes was much more pessimistic about his side's chances of victory than the facts as they were soon revealed would have warranted. As late as July 27th he instructed La Luzerne to ascertain the attitude of the preponderant party in Congress toward the *status quo* and an armistice.[75] By early fall news was reaching the Comte from La Luzerne reporting that the tide of battle had turned, and that Georgia and the Carolinas were in Patriotic hands.[76] In addition, Vergennes had a chance to sound out John Adams on the mediation. Now a change of tone creeps into Vergennes' dispatches. The *status quo* in America does not enter into our system, he wrote La Luzerne on September 7th, a notion we have combated in our replies to the mediators, even though such a formula would be advantageous both to ourselves and Spain.[77]

Although a British army in America was on the brink of catastrophe, the Chevalier de La Luzerne dutifully proceeded to broach to various delegates the notion of the dismemberment of the United States, one part to be free, the other dependent. He informed them that this would be

* He who has time has life.

one of the initial issues that the mediators would consider. "I have sought to render the idea less revolting and more familiar to different delegations, but I cannot flatter myself to have attained the slightest success," La Luzerne ruefully admitted. The idea is rejected with horror, he truthfully reported.[78] Finally, on October 3rd, the Chevalier, in reporting the re-establishment of civil government in Georgia by the Patriots, conceded that dismemberment of the United States was no longer a realistic proposition.[79]

Thus for a time the fate of America rested in the hands of her wavering ally and of two neutral powers far from cordially disposed to revolutionaries. Though Congress seemed the passive and even pliant creature of France's American envoy, the American plenipotentiaries abroad were alert to the peril. They sniffed the mediation from afar and did not like its odor. Any compromise which would have meant the dismemberment of the American Union or a settlement on the basis of the ground possessed was not one they were prepared to accept.

Cornwallis' surrender at Yorktown on the eighteenth of October sealed the fate of the mediation. Upon hearing the news, Frederick II chuckled that England would now have to "get off her high horse. . . . Superb Albion will be forced to put some water in its wine," while, as he correctly forecast, the Houses of Bourbon would now be less inclined than ever to accept mediation.[80] Before the mediation took on the pallor of death more proposals emanated from the two imperial courts; more replies were in turn issued by the belligerents, but the picture never changed in its essentials. The British still insisted on treating with their own rebels themselves; the French continued to protest that their engagement with the Americans was "inviolable." They kept the issue of representation at the head of the mediation agenda. Would the agent of the United States, they asked, be considered a representative of a free people at the congress or a deputy of a people subject to the British Crown? The first would leave nothing to the King's desire; the second would be entirely inadmissible. The Spaniards would make no move toward mediation without consultation with the French, and on this subject the Bourbons presented a united front.[81] Finally, on instructions from his home government, the Spanish delegate to the Congress of Vienna packed his bags and headed for his post at St. Petersburg, making clear by that gesture the futility of waiting around for a congress that would never meet.[82] In desperation both Kaunitz and Ostermann were prepared in one way or another to circumvent American representation at the congress in order to placate the British,[83] but to no avail.

In the last flickering moments of the North Ministry word spread that the British had sent an agent to Paris to make peace directly. Kaunitz made a desperate effort to forestall a separate peace by reviving his plan of a congress at Vienna. The blow was not long delayed. Kaunitz learned with dismay that the Rockingham Ministry which succeeded North was sending an emissary to Paris to treat with the Allies. Although Mercy kept the pressure on Vergennes and the Queen to defer the negotiations to the congress,[84] the farce could hardly be dragged out much longer. Benjamin Franklin now made it clear to the British that he did not think outside mediation either necessary or proper,[85] a position to which the American commissioners at Paris held unwaveringly. Although Kaunitz's hopes were kept alive by vague and flowery statements emanating from the belligerent courts, which refused in fact to budge one inch from their previous positions,[86] he knew in his heart that the belligerent powers were determined to by-pass him. In his wrath he struck out in several directions, but most of his blows were aimed at the Comte de Vergennes, whose reticences had proved so infuriating to the Austrians, and whose behavior in retrospect seemed to the Chancellor both vain and disingenuous. Unable to nudge her Foreign Minister in the direction of mediation, Marie Antoinette attributed Vergennes' direct negotiations with England to personal ambition and his desire to supplant Maurepas, an uncharitable judgment shared alike by Mercy and Kaunitz.[87]

Assuming that all prospects for a mediation congress had vanished, could Austria salvage anything from the wreckage? The Imperial Consul at Dunkirk came up with the interesting proposal that the island of Tobago, which France had conquered from England, could be sold to Austria for a fair price. In fact, it was argued that such a deal would not be incompatible with Austria's role as a mediator. Both the Emperor Joseph and Comte Mercy felt that the proposal should not be lightly dismissed, indeed that Tobago was well worth trying to obtain.[88] In the final peace Tobago, which changed hands more frequently than perhaps any other island in the West Indies, was destined to elude the clutches of the Austrians.

For Kaunitz perhaps the greatest blow of all was the signing of the preliminaries between England and the United States. That news produced in Vienna, according to Baron de Breteuil, "the most painful sensations." The gloom was so thick it could be pared with a knife. Not only did these preliminaries finally deny to Vienna its coveted role of mediator, but it was a stunning surprise to those Austrian diplomats who had taken little pains to disguise their antipathy to the cause of American independence.[89]

X

MYNHEER ADAMS PUTS A SPOKE
IN THE WHEEL

WHILE ALL THESE WHEELS within wheels were furiously turning the cumbersome mechanism of pacification, one American abroad did not choose to remain silent. As might well have been anticipated, that American was John Adams. Minister plenipotentiary appointed by Congress in the fall of '79 to negotiate and conclude a peace with Great Britain, along with a treaty of commerce, Adams had sailed for Europe scarcely three months after he had returned from a former mission to the court of Versailles. For the third time the Braintree lawyer ran the Atlantic gauntlet of storms and enemy men-of-war, putting aside personal considerations to make the trip, because, as he later saw it, "I considered the voice of my country as the command of Heaven." Adams like Martin Luther was "determined to go, though there were as many devils in the way as there were tiles in the houses of London."[1]

Adams' return to France evoked no manifestations of joy from the French government nor on the part of the Foreign Minister, who scarcely veiled his disappointment with Congress' choice for the peace mission. Between the Comte de Vergennes and the New Englander there never had in fact been any degree of rapport. The former was the personification of the old-school diplomat, whose reserved manner suggested both cunning and flexibility.[2] In contrast, the short, stout, middle-aged Puritan from Braintree, Massachusetts, despite his many virtues, had never learned to conceal his inner feelings. He was outspoken to the point of being downright quarrelsome. During the later peace negotiations in Paris David Hartley remarked that he was "the most ungracious man I ever saw," and Adams perpetuated the remark.[3] Adams' habit of letting his tongue get the better of his judgment earned him a reputation for being indiscreet, and his didactic manner and argumentative inclination were never so painfully manifest as in his confrontations with the French Foreign Minister. Determined to rule the peacemaking, Vergennes expected the agents of client states to follow his counsel without "ifs" or "buts." With the suspicious Adams, who could whiff a conspiracy at a thousand leagues, he could always count on an exasperating argument.

If only Congress had entrusted the peacemaking to the more agreeable Benjamin Franklin, how much less tedious would Vergennes' delicate tasks have been! Not that the Sage of Passy was lacking in perception as to America's interests, but he always managed to cloak his sentiments in agreeable deference to the French court. Where Adams was inflexible, Franklin was adaptable, even devious; he was admirably taciturn where the New Englander was maddeningly garrulous. Master of the graceful compliment as well as the homey anecdote, Franklin seemed the courtier born. In contrast, the stiff, awkward Adams, with his labored French, did not shine in mirrored halls.

John Adams had long been aware of the preference of Versailles for Franklin, and it long rankled. Vain and pompous, Adams expected to be recognized for what he was. When he had first come to Paris, Frenchmen mistook him for Sam Adams, the great Patriot, and John did not consider this a compliment. Among Adams' many virtues generosity toward rivals did not appear high on the list. A big streak of envy colored his neurotic personality and led him into a variety of personal feuds. Adams never would have admitted this, because he considered envy to be a terrible distemper. As he wrote his friend James Warren, he would rather be infected with the French pox, "contracted here by an acquaintance with the elegant nymphs of the boulevards," than with envy.[4]

Introduced everywhere in Paris as "*le collègue de Monsieur Franklin,*" Adams was constantly reminded of the Philadelphian's enormous popularity at court, among intellectuals, with the masses, and not least with the ladies. As Adams put it, French ladies had "an unaccountable passion for old age," whereas his own "countrywomen" had "rather a complaisance for youth, if I remember right." Later in life Adams grudgingly conceded, with Jefferson, that Franklin was "an honor to human nature." He freely acknowledged the scientist-statesman's genius, his creative and inventive mind, his vast imagination, and his Rabelaisian-streaked humor. Franklin's fame, Adams granted, was truly universal, and when people spoke of him, they seemed to think "he was to restore the golden age." Yet, though Adams might have preferred to live in amity with the doctor, he was destined to work in steady opposition to him. He found fault with Franklin's morals. He was censorious of his habits of sloth and indolence. He distrusted his associates, from Silas Deane down, men whom he felt put the private interest ahead of the public good. He was infuriated by his reticence, his apparent lack of candor. Above all, he disagreed with him about the wisdom of following the line laid down at Versailles.[5]

It was this very independence of judgment which assured Adams a frosty reception at Versailles. While the American envoy considered himself to be faithful to the alliance, which he held to be "a rock of defense" and "an honor and security" ever near to his heart,[6] the French Ministry had not forgotten that at the outbreak of the Revolution he had opposed making a treaty of alliance with France and favored only a treaty of commerce.[7] Vergennes had made the personal acquaintance of Adams during his earlier mission to France in 1778-79. Finding him pertinacious and unbending, entirely unprepared to leave the management of the diplomacy of war and peace in the hands of the Ministry of Foreign Affairs, as the Comte had in effect suggested, Vergennes tried in vain to get Congress to entrust the peace powers to Franklin.[8] His suspicions of Adams ripened with time and further contacts.

On his return trip to America in '79 Adams had talked freely, perhaps too freely, with his ship companions, the Chevalier de La Luzerne, dispatched to America to replace Gérard, and the new secretary of legation, François Barbé-Marbois. He had made no secret of his disapproval of Franklin, and cautioned the pair that the alliance might be imperiled by any French minister or consul who attempted to meddle in America's internal affairs and to attach himself to a particular party or faction. La Luzerne chose to ignore this sensible advice, and kept Vergennes closely informed about the party alignments in the American Congress, identifying John Adams with the Sam Adams–Lee faction reputedly opposed in principle to the French alliance and eager to enter into separate negotiations with England.[9] The French envoy's reports presented an oversimplified, even distorted, picture of Adams as a potential peacemaker. Adams had always been clear on one point. He would never consider a reconciliation with the mother country short of independence. To do so would be, he declared, acting "a base and perfidious part."[10]

Knowing as much as he did about John Adams and the faction with whom La Luzerne classified him, Vergennes could hardly be expected to welcome the peace commissioner with open arms. What could not have been anticipated from so experienced a diplomat as the Comte was that he would let his animosity get the better of his judgment, and that he would treat the American with a studied rudeness which one far less touchy than Adams would have found offensive. When, on his arrival at Paris in February, 1780, Adams notified Vergennes that he had been designated by Congress to negotiate treaties of peace and commerce with Great Britain, he also assured him of his determination to "take no steps of consequence" in pursuance of his commissions "without consulting his Majesty's Ministers." The precipitate Adams did have some questions, and he begged the favor of His Excellency's advice upon them. Would it be "prudent" for him to notify the British Ministry of his arrival and to publicize the nature of his mission, or should he remain "upon the reserve" as he had already done since his arrival in Europe?

Vergennes' reply took the form of a calculated insult. It informed Adams that it would be "convenient to wait for the arrival of Mr. Gérard, because he is probably the bearer of your *Instructions* and he will certainly have it in his power to give me explanations concerning the nature and extent of your commission." Meantime, it would be the path of prudence for Adams to conceal his "eventual character" and take precautions that the object of his commission "remain unknown to the Court of London."[11] Adams quite rightly felt that the instructions of a sovereign state to its ambassador were a "secret and a confidential communication between them," and that the Comte, a seasoned diplomat, could not be ignorant "of the sacred nature of instructions." With a touch of malice Adams later observed that the Comte "had been so long in the habit of intrigues to obtain the instructions from foreign Courts to their ambassadors, and probably paying for them very dear, that he had forgotten that the practice was not lawfull." Doubtless he had charged Gérard to penetrate into the secrets of Congress and was counting upon Gérard's soon arriving "with the trophies of his success."

More than Adams' *amour propre* was involved. Discontented with the orders he had received from Congress, he was anxious lest the court of France learn about them. He was quite correct in believing that Vergennes would wish him "to go to the utmost extent" of his instructions "in relinquishing the fisheries and in contracting the boundaries of the United States." Contrariwise, Adams was fiercely determined "to insist on the fisheries and on ample extention of our boundaries, as long as my instructions would justify me." Adams was practical enough to realize that should the French at some point reveal these instructions to the British, the American negotiations could be greatly embarrassed on these "very essential points."[12] In addition to the points of independence and necessary boundaries, Adams' instructions, hammered out by Congress in the lengthy debates of '79, contained two other items that would bring him into collision with Vergennes. He was authorized to agree to an armistice with the consent of France, but only on the condition that "all the forces of the enemy shall be immediately withdrawn from the United States," and he was ordered to govern himself "by the Alliance between his Most Christian Majesty and these States, by the advice of our allies, by your knowledge of our Interests, and by your own discretion, in which we repose the fullest confidence."[13] The Comte de Vergennes did not share with Congress that confidence in Adams' discretion to which these instructions bore evidence, and he was determined to have the American minister's powers more rigorously circumscribed.

Despite the provocation contained in Vergennes' acknowledgment, Adams replied politely, sending on copies of his commissions. Five days later Vergennes gratuitously informed the American that the full powers he had forwarded to Versailles were "perfectly conformable" with the "account" that Gérard had written of them, and "they leave us nothing to desire either in form or substance," but he again cautioned Adams to conceal his powers from the British Ministry.[14] Adams made no secret of his impatience with Vergennes' "delicacy." "If I had followed my own judgment," he told Congress, "I should have pursued a bolder plan, by communicating, immediately after my arrival, to Lord George Germain my full powers to treat both peace and commerce."[15] Adams' sense of timing could not have been more inept, and it was indeed fortunate that he was spared entering upon so headstrong a course, one certain to end in humiliation.

Adams' Puritan conscience prevented him from enjoying to the full the delights of Paris which his enforced inactivity now opened up to him. He complained of his situation as "so idle and inactive" and "not agreeable to my genius."[16] "There is everything here," he wrote his congenial wife Abigail, "that can inform understanding or refine the taste, and indeed, one would think, that would purify the heart. Yet it must be remembered there is everything here, too, which can seduce, betray, deceive, deprave, corrupt, and debauch it."[17] On his previous visit to France Adams had proved impervious to seduction. Now, instead of wading knee-deep in debauchery Adams spent his days and a goodly part of his nights at his writing desk at the Hôtel de Valois, jammed on the crowded and dark rue de Richelieu, sending dispatch after dispatch to Congress with up-to-the-minute intelligence of events in Europe. Convinced that France was far behind England in propagating her cause, he set himself to take up the slack by feeding American propaganda to the *Mercure de France*, a journal edited by Edmé Jacques Genêt of the French Foreign Office.

Adams also managed to fill the tedious summer months of waiting by having a full-scale row with Vergennes. It was the Frenchman this time who started the quarrel. Adams had forwarded to him a report from the Treasury Board relating Congress' decision to redeem its depreciated currency at forty to one. The French Foreign Minister was quick to remonstrate that this action, making no distinction between Americans and foreigners, was hardly calculated to advance the credit of the United States abroad.[18] Why he should not have taken the matter up with Franklin, who was Congress' accredited minister in France, instead of with Adams, who bore no responsibility for Franco-American relations, is indeed difficult to fathom. Even a captious mood on the part of Vergennes came as the result of careful calculation.

Now, Adams was long convinced that the French Ministry should be treated with "frankness" and "candor" rather than abject servility.[19] He proceeded to assume a magisterial tone toward Vergennes, to expose him to a lecture in defense of the action of Congress, and gratuitously to assert that "the United States of America are a great and powerful people, whatever European statesmen may think of them." Vergennes found Adams' "long dissertation" even more insufferable than he found Adams, and not pertinent to the claims of the subjects of the King of France. He turned to Franklin to have Congress make an exception for "strangers, and especially Frenchmen." Franklin went out of his way to assure the Comte that the sentiments of America with regard to the alliance "differ widely from those that seem to be expressed by Mr. Adams in his letter to your excellency." Franklin chose to put a strained interpretation upon Adams' defense of Congress' currency measure. He went further, perhaps further than he need have gone. Writing to Congress, Franklin dexterously avoided any personal judgment on the merits of the controversy, but complained that Adams was trespassing on his preserve and insinuated the expediency of not having more than one minister at the French court. Taking issue with Adams' view that America had been too free in expressions of gratitude to France, Franklin insisted that the French court be treated with "decency and delicacy." So long as he remained in France, Franklin assured Congress, he intended "to procure what advantages I can for our country by endeavoring to please this Court."[20]

Adams' course may well have seemed to Franklin that of a mischievous busybody, but neither envoy emerged blameless from the controversy.

Adams was too precipitate and argumentative in his reply. In view of the bad military news from America, he had chosen a maladroit time for strutting. He should have either let Franklin answer Vergennes or consulted Franklin before replying. The latter, in turn, was not above a piece of backbiting that did not augur too well for the smooth operation of the American diplomatic mission abroad.

Adams, without even a hint of encouragement, again pressed on Vergennes his arguments for permission to negotiate directly with London.[21] He could not have picked a worse moment to prod the Comte. In Spain Cumberland and Hussey were in direct negotiation with Floridablanca. From Versailles it looked very much as though one ally might make peace without the other. Certainly Vergennes was not going to allow the Americans to pursue similar, if more candid, tactics, and, with the huge war deficit that Necker was reporting, to tolerate criticism by the insurgents of France's war effort. The summer of 1780 saw the mounting of the Necker peace offensive, and the direct appeasement gesture by the aged Maurepas to the British court. The French Foreign Minister was determined to keep the American negotiations in his own hands. He could afford to reassure Adams that "the King is far from abandoning the cause of America," and was planning to dispatch the Chevalier de Ternay and the Comte de Rochambeau to the United States,[22] for the Comte had decided to get Congress to drop Adams as the American peace commissioner. Meantime he admonished the New Englander that the time had "not yet come" to communicate his plenipotentiary powers to Germain. What Vergennes seemed particularly exercised about was the disclosure to the British of Adams' powers to negotiate a treaty of commerce. Quite rightly, he pointed out that "to be busy about a treaty of commerce before peace is established, is like being busy about the ornament of a house before the foundation is laid." In an attempt to silence the irrepressible envoy he ordered Adams to transmit this letter to Congress and to take no other action until he received specific orders of Congress "with regard to the English Ministry."[23] Vergennes told Adams that he would communicate his own observations to La Luzerne, and when that snub failed to discourage further direct approaches from the New Englander, he informed him curtly, and in a tone reserved for agents of client states, that Franklin was "the sole person who has letters of credence to the King from the United States," and it was with him only that he could treat with regard to the subjects raised in Adams' correspondence. The King, he concluded crushingly, does "not stand in need of your solicitations to direct his attention to the interests of the United States."[24]

Clearly Adams came off second best in this encounter, and it is difficult to understand why he had chosen that moment to press the issue. True, he had no knowledge of the appeasement moves within the French Cabinet, but he completely agreed with the view of William Lee that "a speedy peace" was not in view. The British were "in such a sulky, mulish, suicidal temper," Adams conceded, "that they would not make peace if you took every island they have."[25] He was even more pessimistic in replying to a letter from David Hartley, felicitating him on his appointment as a peace commissioner. "War cannot last forever," Hartley had asserted. Quite true, Adams replied, "but it will probably last long enough to wear you and me out, and to make room for our sons or grandsons to become the blessed peacemakers."[26] At the same time he seized the occasion to deny by implication any sympathy with the notion of a separate peace between England and America which had clearly prompted Hartley's letter. "Peace will never come," he protested, "but in company with faith and honor."

While Adams was acting to discredit himself at Versailles and was needlessly sowing suspicions of America's loyalty to the alliance, the Chevalier de La Luzerne back in Philadelphia was quietly making himself the master of Congress and exercising a sway over the government of the Confederation denied to any other foreign diplomat since that time. Following Vergennes' instructions, he pressed Congress to modify its currency redemption arrangements, to have Adams' commission to negotiate a commercial treaty with Britain revoked, and to neutralize Adams himself by having other ministers added to the commission to negotiate the peace.[27] Despite the sizable block of votes he controlled, La Luzerne failed to budge Congress in the matter of the currency. Instead, that body explicitly endorsed Adams' vigorous defense of their monetary measure. For the moment all that La Luzerne was able to elicit from Congress was a caution directed toward Adams' future tactics as a negotiator.[28]

Mildly rebuked by his own government, frustrated by the French court, Adams determined to quit Paris and go to Holland to ascertain, as Franklin reported to Congress, "whether something might not be done to render us less dependent on France."[29] Although Franklin could not stop him he took a jaundiced view of the mission. "I have long been humiliated with the idea of our running about from court to court begging for money and friendship, which are the more withheld the more eagerly they are solicited, and would perhaps have been offered, if they had not been asked. . . . God helps them that help themselves," Franklin reminded Adams, "and the world, too, in this sense, is very godly."[30] If Franklin was pessimistic the Comte de Vergennes was less than amiable about the mission, manifesting no anxiety to loosen the bonds of dependency between the rebels and the King of France. The Comte stalled Adams for a week, and then permitted him to leave. Totally oblivious of the dissensions within the French Cabinet on the conduct of the war and of the possibility that the French government at that moment might have been prepared to compromise the issue of American independence, Adams left Paris on the twenty-seventh of July. A fortnight in Amsterdam convinced him that the chances of obtaining a loan there were more feasible than proved to be the case. Henry Laurens had been designated by Congress to borrow money from the Dutch, but the South Carolinian had been forced to delay his departure from America, and some time after Adams reached Holland he learned that Congress had added that chore to his variegated tasks until Laurens took over.[31] Meantime he had been acting as a private citizen.

The two years in which Adams largely concerned himself with Dutch affairs kept him from being an idle spectator of the diplomatic jousts. This was doubly fortunate, first, for a New England Puritan who deplored idleness, and, second, for the cause of America in Europe, since the duties of the American peace commissioner were distressingly light during the interval when the European powers were searching for a formula to settle the war without advance consultation with England's rebellious colonies. The politicians in Philadelphia assumed that Holland would be protected by Russia against hostile acts on the part of the British. They confidently expected the Empress to recognize the United States, and took it for granted that the Dutch would follow suit. Adams shared this unfounded optimism.[32] The delegates in Philadelphia authorized Adams to accede to the maritime regulations, if such an invitation were extended.[33] Since such an invitation would have been tantamount to *de jure* recognition of the United States, not to speak of its changing the character of a neutral league by bringing into it one of the belligerents, Congress proved both naïve and overoptimistic.

Faithfully following instructions, Adams communicated this resolution to the States-General and to the envoys of Russia, Sweden, Denmark, and France stationed at The Hague, even though none of them except the last recognized the United States.[34] For long Adams nursed the illusion that the Neutral League would acknowledge American independence, and even that the Northern countries would go to war against England. He was even prepared to treat with these powers, and sought a formal commission to that end from Congress.[35] These were big dreams, however.

More immediate and mundane challenges which the Hollanders posed occupied the larger measure of Adams' time.

Adams might well have agreed with another foreign visitor who spoke of Holland as "a land, where the demon of gold, crowned with tobacco, sat on a throne of cheese."[36] If material values permeated the Netherlands, there was also a stout tradition of independence and republicanism which could not fail to warm the heart of the New Englander. Adams was quick to learn and quick to impart to Congress what he had discovered about the Dutch. When he had leisure he wrote John Jay at Madrid confessing that he was in the "most curious country, among the most incomprehensible people and under the most singular Constitution of Government in the World."[37]

In fact, the Dutch system of government, which bore a striking resemblance to the American Confederation under the Articles, was ill-suited to times of crisis such as the Dutch were now facing. The United Provinces, as the Netherlands of that day was known, comprised a federal union of seven provinces, ruled by a legislative body known as the States-General ("Their High Mightinesses") and by a chief of state or Stadholder. The latter, despite the republican character of the nation, claimed the office by hereditary right as a member of the House of Orange long venerated for its role in winning independence for the Dutch. In actual operation the great municipal oligarchies, like that of Amsterdam, principal city of the rich and powerful province of Holland, held the executive in leading strings.

When Adams came to the United Provinces in the summer of 1780 a power struggle was in fact being waged between the chief of state and the municipalities dominated by the wealthy bourgeoisie. Willem V, the goggle-eyed, bulging-cheeked, petulant, and drunken Stadholder, was notorious for his devotion to all things British as became a grandson on his maternal side of George II of England. "My booby of a nephew," Frederick the Great uncharitably but quite accurately called him. The Stadholder was completely under the domination of "Fat Louis," one of the numerous sobriquets by which Willem's chief adviser, the Duke of Brunswick, was known. Drawing support from the Orangist peasantry, the Stadholder was vociferously opposed by the Patriots, or bourgeois republicans, who claimed political lineage from Barneveldt, Grotius, and the De Witts. The latter faction was anti-British and pro-French. With proper direction, Adams felt, it might be swung over to the American cause. To this end he made contact immediately upon his arrival in Amsterdam with such anti-Orangist leaders as the Van Staphorst brothers, important bankers.[38]

Adams saw that apathy, caution, and deep division gripped the Nether-lands. He learned that the Dutch businessmen who carried on a hugely profitable contraband trade with rebellious America by way of the Dutch West Indian island of St. Eustatius were as conspicuously anxious to avoid an open breach with England as was the Anglophile Stadholder. "With his swarms of agents," Sir Joseph Yorke, Britain's formidable emissary at The Hague, devoted his energies to bolstering the Stadholder, while the French ambassador, the Duc de La Vauguyon, intrigued day and night with the Patriot faction.[39]

For a people who carried on so much trade with both France and America, the Dutch, Adams found out, were astonishingly ill-informed about America and the cause for which it was fighting. Even in Amsterdam they were pessimistic about the chances of a rebellion being successful against so powerful a nation as England, suspicious that America would fall under the control of France and Spain, and unfamiliar with either the government or resources of the United States. "These chimera, and many more," Adams informed Congress shortly after his arrival, "are held up to people here, and influence men's minds and conduct to such a degree that no man dares openly and publicly disregard them."[40]

Ahead of a loan or a treaty Adams placed his battle for the minds of the Hollanders. He soon demonstrated his exceptional talents as a propagandist for the American cause, achieving in the United Provinces results com-parable with Franklin's in France. Convinced that the cause of America had "never suffered from anything more than from the failure of giving and receiving intelligence," Adams perceived the strategic position of the United Provinces as a center to collect and circulate intelligence both from across the Channel and from the rest of the Continent.[41] Adams started out by answering questions about America, by demonstrating how both Europe and America complemented each other's economy, and assuring his listeners that America posed no threat to the peace of the world, since Americans "love peace and hate war" and can hardly keep together an army necessary to defend themselves. "While we have land enough to conquer from the trees and wild beasts," he assured the Dutch, "we shall never go abroad to trouble other nations."[42] Having played the major role in the drafting of the new Massachusetts Constitution, he had that document published in the *Gazette de Leyde*, edited by Jean Luzac, a Leyden lawyer and university professor, destined to be one of Adams' important collaborators.[43] In addition, he composed a group of twenty-six letters addressed to a Dutch jurist named Hendrik Calkoen.[44] Therein Adams stressed America's continued will to resist and support her political leaders, and disclosed America's financial position, and her need for a loan. Nevertheless, he assured his readers that "the Americans will labor through, without a fleet, and without a loan."

Adams' second task was even more difficult than the first. To induce the stolid Hollanders to lend money to a rebel nation at war with the most fearsome power of Europe demanded all the arts of persuasion and advocacy which the New England lawyer happily possessed in abundance. Many years later Adams looked back upon his initial efforts with some degree of humor, relating how he sought to carry on negotiations with "capitalists, brokers and Hebrews, many of whom could speak or understand as little of the French or English language as I could of Dutch." But somehow Adams made himself understood.[45] Adams called in turn upon a long list of Amsterdam bankers with which he was furnished, but the news of the fall of Charleston and of French naval reverses, combined with the threatening posture of Sir Joseph Yorke, threw a chill on financial houses. Only the firm of Jan de Neufville & Zoon ventured to help at a time when American credit had reached its nadir, and the results were disappointingly meager.[46]

Then suddenly panic gripped the banking firms of Amsterdam. The publication by the British of Laurens' papers, notably the draft treaty drawn up by William Lee and van Berckel several years before, was now seized upon by Stormont and Yorke as a pretext to end Holland's neutral posture and with it her contraband trade with America carried on through the Dutch West Indies. From the moment the Laurens papers were published everyone was afraid to see Adams, he wrote to Congress. A loan was out of the question, as the sponsors were fearful of being pointed out to the mob or the soldiers. Pro-Americans slunk out of sight in fear of their lives, and Adams himself was avoided like the plague, and considered himself to be in some physical danger.[47] Sir Joseph threatened, "Pinch the Dutch till they squeak."[48] Their High Mightinesses abjectly denied any knowledge of the alleged treaty, and sharply rebuked the burghers of Amsterdam, whom they threatened with a court prosecution. To no avail. On December 21st England declared war on Holland. The British government had made a calculated decision to declare war against the Dutch before the latter had adhered to the Neutral League, a decision unpalatable to the Whig Opposition.[49] As Horace Walpole put it, "We lose provinces and islands, and are comforted by barrels of pickled herrings!"[50]

For Adams, in more ways than one, the year 1780 ended cold and damp. "I shall cover me with baize, flannels, and furs, like a Dutchman," he wrote one correspondent. To another he confided his longing for "the air of Passy" and "the amusements of Paris," or even the gout, "or anything else" which would be more agreeable to him than "this capital of the reign of Mammon." To still another he called it "the dullest year" that he had ever seen, one that had "completely finished our credit in Europe," and he confessed to Congress that it was "the most anxious and mortifying year" of his whole life.[51]

The New Englander had now seen the Dutch at their most abject, but he was confident that "Sir Joseph will kick and cuff and pinch this republic, until he forces into them a little spunk."[52] The tide turned quickly enough. On New Year's Eve he recorded that patriotic addresses were presented in the theater, popular songs sung in the streets. America's popularity was already evident in Amsterdam, and soon he found anti-British sentiment in Haarlem, Leyden, The Hague, Delft, and Rotterdam as well.[53] He was encouraged by these signs to make himself and his mission known to the Dutch government. Adams spent the last part of March and early April of 1781 in Leyden, where he drafted a memorial stressing the historic ties between America and the United Provinces and indicating the advantages that could be expected to flow from close commercial relations between them. Then he went to The Hague and notified La Vauguyon that the time had come for him to make his move. The French ambassador, acting under firm instructions from Vergennes and privately boasting that he had the American under control, used every argument he could muster to dissuade Adams but failed to convince him.[54] Adams first submitted his memorial to the grand pensionary of the province of Holland, then to the president of the States-General. Neither dignitary would receive the paper officially, but no objections were raised to its publication. In publicizing this memorial both in the Netherlands and elsewhere Adams drew upon the services of Charles William Frederic Dumas, indefatigable man of letters and capable linguist, who from the start of the Revolution had been enlisted in the services of America as agent and correspondent at The Hague.[55] With a peace congress believed imminent, Adams was convinced that the United States should seek to obtain recognition from as many European powers as possible before that congress formally opened. To such an overture Holland, now that it was a belligerent, seemed perhaps the most receptive.[56]

Adams had been long enough in the Low Countries not to expect quick action. He knew that Their High Mightinesses would refer his memorial to the several provinces and cities, that these would "deliberate and deliberate, and deliberate," and that some would be for, and one or two, like Zeeland, would be against it.[57] Although the Stadholder had only recently issued orders against granting formal recognition to "the flag of North America,"[58] Adams' memorial was well received. The popular cry now was "Health to Myn Heer Adams, and success to the brave Americans!" Amsterdammers, long under a cloud for their pro-American sentiments, were heartened by the response to the memorial; in turn the Duke of Brunswick and his pro-British following were in full retreat.[59] Adams' mission in Holland had signalized the triumph of energy over inertia. Despite the gloomy forebodings of Franklin, the obstructions thrown in his path by his French ally, and numerous contretemps springing from unchecked zeal and fierce determination, he managed to write a brilliant chapter in America's diplomatic history.

While standing on the threshold of success in Holland, Adams in the summer of 1781 was summoned back to Paris in his capacity of peace commissioner. Vergennes issued the summons with obvious reluctance. He had been pulling every string in Philadelphia to have Adams recalled, or other commissioners added to the peace mission, and to have the instructions for the peacemaking modified so as to place the Americans under French control. Unaware, owing to the length of time dispatches took to cross the Atlantic, that he had achieved his major objectives with Congress, he felt that he could no longer put off consulting with the New Englander about the comediation then looming on the diplomatic horizon.[60]

Adams had long been awaiting a call to a peace congress, but with some trepidation. When he had first come to Holland he had entertained nothing but "dread" for a congress at St. Petersburg, which was then being proposed. "They understand not the subject," he wrote of the mediators. "It is impossible they should. America is not represented there, and cannot be heard." Furthermore, Adams was properly apprehensive that attempts would be made to salve "the pride" or "dignity" of England. Any such move would be "more dangerous and pernicious to America than a continuance of the war," he believed. In fact, he was not afraid of a continuance of the war. "I should dread a truce ten times more!"[61] Only a month before his summons from Vergennes Adams had informed Congress of the current gossip on the comediation. If any negotiations were being conducted, however, they had been "carefully concealed from me," Adams charged, adding significantly, "Perhaps something has been expected from the United States, which was not expected by me."[62]

Obedient to the invitation, Adams hastened to Versailles in the first week of July. He was told by Rayneval, Vergennes' undersecretary, that the Comte wished to talk with him about the new prospects of peace under the mediation of the Emperor and Empress. Rayneval remarked that, although the English had not made any proposition, it was necessary to consider certain points, and make certain preparatory arrangements. First of all, France needed to know whether the Americans were *British subjects*, or in what light they were to be regarded. Rayneval smiled when he uttered these words, but to Adams it was no laughing matter. "I am not a British subject," he replied. "I renounced that character many years ago, forever. I should rather be a fugitive in China or Malabar than ever re-assume that character."

Five days later Adams met with Rayneval and Vergennes in the Comte's office at Versailles. The French officials then showed the American the text of the bases for mediation proposed by the two imperial courts, not all of it, but only the three articles relating to America. "All the rest," Adams remarked later on, "was carefully covered up with a book."[63]

Back at the Hôtel de Valois Adams rushed off a report to Congress. Only a few weeks before he had predicted that the comediators would propose a short truce, the *uti possidetis*, and other conditions, "which would leave our trade more embarrassed, our union more precarious, and our liberties at a greater hazard, than they can be in a continuance of the war."[64] The clairvoyant Adams had now seen his prophecy come true. He told Congress that nothing was likely to come of this "manoeuvre, at least for a long time," indicating that he had no objection to treating with the British separately "in the manner proposed," but that he could never agree to an armistice. Nor was he prepared to accept the mediation of any powers "however respectable" until they had acknowledged the sovereignty of the United States "so far at least as to admit a Minister Plenipotentiary from the United States as the representative of a free and independent power."[65]

In substance Adams made the same points in a series of letters to Vergennes. He entered "very great" objections to the armistice and the *status quo* of the third article proposed by the comediators. Any truce, in Adams' opinion, would be productive of "another long and bloody war at the termination of it," and a short truce would be especially dangerous, he added. For the United States to entertain the notion of a truce at all, two express conditions would be "indispensable preliminaries," Adams pointed out: first, that the alliance remain in full force during the truce until the final acknowledgment of independence by Great Britain; and, second, that British evacuation of land and sea forces from "every part of the United States" be antecedent to such a truce. He called Vergennes' attention to two further difficulties. There was a constitutional one. The British could not agree to a cessation of war without an act of Parliament repealing or suspending any laws relating to the United States. More consequential, Adams insisted that the United States could not be represented in a congress of European powers, "whether their representative is called ambassador, minister, or agent, without an acknowledgment of their independence, of which the very admission of a representative from them is an avowal." Indeed, the United States, could never consent "that their independence shall be discussed or called in question by any sovereign or sovereigns, however respectable, nor can their interests be made a question in any congress in which their character is not acknowledged and their minister admitted." Adams then proposed that the two imperial courts acknowledge and lay down as a preliminary the sovereignty of the United States and admit their minister to the congress. If that were done, he argued, treaty negotiations could be initiated between Great Britain and America without any express acknowledgment by the former of America's sovereignty until the treaty should be concluded.

Finally, Adams cautioned Vergennes on the motives of the British Ministry in making propositions of reconciliation at this time. Its only purpose, he felt, was to stir up discontent in America, encourage desertions from the American Army, and "many apostacies from the American independence and alliance." The British would then be continuing their pursuit of "their long practised arts of seduction, deception, and division." Adams concluded with the hope that the powers of Europe would see through these transparent artifices.[66]

Since Adams had dashed off his reply at a furious rate, he understandably had second thoughts about the mediation. He now informed Congress that while he did not agree to the bases of mediation proposed by the two imperial courts, he was prepared to go to Vienna, seeing nothing "inconsistent with the character or dignity of the United States" in his journeying there and entering into a treaty with a British minister without prior acknowledgement of independence, excepting, of course, the armistice and *status quo*.[67] The next day he reassured Vergennes similarly. If Vergennes so advised, Adams was prepared to withdraw every objection to the Congress on the part of the United States, rejecting nothing but the *status quo* and the armistice.[68]

Adams could hardly have drawn a more frightening picture for the Comte. If there was one thing that Vergennes did not want, it was for the New Englander to go scurrying off to Vienna. Any day now he was expecting word that Adams had been supplanted or that a plural peace mission in which Adams had but one voice would assume his duties. Vergennes had kept Adams from going to England. He had tried to discourage him about approaching the Dutch. Now he was not going to permit so headstrong a character to meddle in the mediation, which Vergennes considered his very special preserve. "There are preliminaries to be settled and inserted in regard to the United States," Vergennes curtly reminded the American minister. "As long as they shall remain unsettled, you cannot appear, nor by consequence, allow yourself to perform the smallest ministerial act towards the two mediators." To do so would be to expose oneself to compromising the character with which Adams was invested, he warned.[69]

The touchy Adams was infuriated as much by the tone and substance of the reply as by the manner in which it was addressed. The clerk who wrote the letter bearing Vergennes' holograph had addressed it: "*À Monsieur Adams, Agent des États Unis de l'Amérique Septentrionale à l'hôtel de Valois, rue de Richelieu, à Paris.*" Why did he presume to address me as "agent" when "he knew I was a minister plenipotentiary, both for the peace and to the states of Holland?" Adams fumed. Was this action in conformity to the views of the mediating courts, which, in Adams' opinion, "the court of France ought not to have countenanced?"[70]

It was not in Adams' nature to ignore a slight nor to allow time for careful reflection. He dashed off two notes to the Comte in the heat of anger. In the first he assured Vergennes with somewhat ill grace that he never had any thought of appearing on the scene or of taking "any step towards the two mediators" unless "properly called upon." Since the two imperial courts have now proposed that an American representative attend the congress, it would seem proper, Adams argued, that their propositions be communicated to the Congress at Philadelphia. Unless a formal invitation were transmitted to the American Congress, Adams, in another quick turnabout, conceded that he could not presume "with strict propriety" to appear at the Congress of Vienna "at all." Nevertheless, with strange inconsistency, he volunteered to go to Vienna "if your excellency should invite or advise me to go." His justification: "The dignity of North America does not consist in diplomatic ceremonials or any of the subtleties of etiquette; it consists solely in reason, justice, truth, the rights of mankind, and the interests of the nations of Europe; all of which, well understood, are clearly in her favor."[71]

The very next day Adams deemed it necessary to clarify his status in the unlikely event that the Comte thought he should go to Vienna. If he were to appear, he reminded Vergennes, he would assume the title and character of "a minister plenipotentiary," and could enter into no treaty or conference with any minister from Great Britain until they had mutually exchanged copies of their full powers. Such an exchange would amount to an "acknowledgment" both of his character and title and those of the United States as well, Adams pointed out, but such an acknowledgment he held to be "indispensable." As a consequence, Adams informed the Comte, he would expect to enjoy all the prerogatives of a minister plenipotentiary, and "the moment they should be denied him, he must quit the congress, let the consequences be what they might."

After a careful rereading of the three articles, Adams now took exception to the designation "American colonies" appearing in the first article. That title, Adams insisted, implied "a metropolis, a mother country, a superior political governor, ideas which the United States of America have long since renounced forever." Adams would now have to insist on "a more explicit declaration" that he would be considered at the congress as a minister plenipotentiary from the United States of America. Let no power be deceived into believing that the Americans would ever appear at a congress "in the character of repenting subjects," he warned. Remember, Adams again cautioned, the United States can never agree to having her equal station among the nations questioned by other powers.[72]

Having made it abundantly clear that American independence and equality could not be compromised or qualified by other powers, Adams now served notice that the proposal then mooted of carrying on separate consultations with each of the Thirteen States was entirely unacceptable. Somehow Adams had gotten wind of the Panin-Kaunitz scheme, although it was not until many months later that he was to receive confirmation of this proposal through copies of letters which the Marquis de Vérac at St. Petersburg had indiscreetly written to Francis Dana[73] and in which the project of admitting to the congress "deputies of the United States" was mentioned. On July 21st Adams wrote the French Foreign Minister that "an idea" had been "suggested of the several States of America choosing agents separately to attend the congress at Vienna in order to make peace with Great Britain, so that there would be thirteen instead of one." Now the American jurist and authority on constitutions proceeded to deliver a lecture to Vergennes on the Articles of Confederation, ratified and communicated to the courts of Europe and as "universally known as any constitution of government in Europe." The American Constitution expressly delegates to the United States in Congress assembled the power and authority of negotiating with foreign powers, he stated. For any power to apply to the governors or legislatures of the separate states would be "a public disrespect," he reminded Vergennes (a reminder that was badly needed, for at that very time La Luzerne in America was proceeding to make direct contacts with the several states in derogation of Congress' authority). It would be both an error and a misdemeanor for a state official to receive and transmit such a communication to his respective legislature. In short, "there is no method for the courts of Europe to convey anything to the people of America but through the Congress of the United States, nor any way of negotiating with them but by means of that body." With these constitutional obstructions in mind, Adams strongly urged that Vergennes discountenance the notion of "summoning ministers from the Thirteen States."[74]

Overwhelmed by this Niagara of words, concessions, protests, and admonitions, Vergennes, who had tried to keep the Panin-Kaunitz plan secret, maintained an inscrutable silence. Adams waited hour by hour and day by day for some messenger from Versailles with a reply, or for an invitation to a conference at which he might learn Vergennes' own views. "But nothing appeared," he later confessed. "All was total silence and impenetrable mystery."[75]

Reviewing these tortuous negotiations a generation later, Adams asserted that his stand back in July of '81 had "defeated the profound and magnificent project of a Congress at Vienna, for the purpose of chicaning the United States out of their independence," and established the principle that American ministers plenipotentiary were not to appear without their public titles and characters nor to negotiate but with their equals after an exchange of full powers.[76] Of course, Vergennes could bide his time in the confidence that Congress would handcuff Adams and deliver the peacemaking into the hands of the King of France. But the Comte could not afford to ignore Adams' stern warning. In the winter of '81 the French Foreign Minister had seriously considered a partition of America. In the late spring he had revitalized the notion of negotiating a settlement with the deputies from each of the Thirteen States. After Adams' summer interlude in Paris, followed in the early fall by the arrival of favorable military news, Vergennes was less inclined to speak for America, both as regards the terms of an armistice and the question of representation at the congress.

France's reply to the mediators, in which she had insisted on a determination in advance of the character of the "American agent" and had indicated that there were American objections to an armistice on the basis of the *status quo,* incorporated the arguments Adams had advanced in his July letters to Vergennes. This reply represented a less pliable position than the one that Vergennes had recently assumed. "Had his excellency condescended to give me the smallest intimation of the King's approbation or his own, of these principles, he would have spared me many anxious hours and months," Adams later complained with considerable justice. Adams attributed "this midnight silence" to the negotiations then being carried on by the Chevalier de La Luzerne to get Adams' commission revoked. Not having access to Vergennes' correspondence with Breteuil and Vérac, the American envoy was not aware that the French Minister only abandoned his new approach when he realized that it would have been entirely unacceptable to the Americans. Adams' vigorous protest, along with La Luzerne's reports, convinced him of that once and for all. Truly, Mr. Adams had put a spoke in the wheel, and the mediation soon came to a stop.

On a second front Vergennes' war with Adams was pressed relentlessly, and with astonishing results. Waged in Philadelphia rather than at Versailles, its stakes were nothing less than control of America's foreign policy. In command of the battle forces was the big, plump, and ruddy-faced Chevalier de La Luzerne, whose affable demeanor was better calculated to obtain results than the acrid and pedantic manners of his predecessor Gérard. In Barbé-Marbois he had an able lieutenant, whose enthusiasm for the cause sometimes carried him beyond the line of duty. The French Minister to the United States could draw upon a well-stocked arsenal. He had, first of all, abundant documents to show the low standing of John Adams with the court of Versailles. In letter after letter Vergennes harped on Adams' unsuitability to perform the duties of peace commissioner. La Luzerne's chief wanted Adams' instructions redrawn, as he himself brutally phrased it, to render "us masters of his conduct."[77]

The Chevalier had other ammunition. He was liberally furnished with secret funds, which he judiciously paid out to penmen like Tom Paine, Dr. Cooper, and Hugh Henry Brackenridge to propagandize on behalf of the French alliance, and to General John Sullivan, who served as floor manager of the pro-French party in Congress. New Hampshire-born son of Irish redemptioners, Sullivan had had a stormy military career in Washington's army. His role in the battles of New York, Brandywine, and Newport stirred up controversy at the time and still does. He had, however, achieved dramatic results in his campaign to lay waste the Iroquois country in '79. The General, who had served in Congress for a brief time in 1775, reappeared in that body in 1780-81. At that time the British reputedly approached his brother, Daniel, who was fatally ill as a result of an enforced stay aboard one of the notorious British prison hulks. Through Daniel there was conveyed to the Patriot general a peace overture from Sir Henry Clinton, with a promise of suitable rewards to promote the work of conciliation. The enemy knew that Sullivan was in financial straits, and so did La Luzerne. "I have remitted him 68 guineas 4 septième," he reported to Vergennes in May of '81, and to the end of his mission the Chevalier paid Sullivan 2,500 livres every six months.[78] The disbursements of the French legation brought speedy returns. Sullivan broke the solid anti-Gallican front, weakened by the departure of Sam Adams from Congress before the strategic votes were taken, and by the absence of all the Lees save Arthur, who left for the Virginia Assembly before the debates over the revised peace instructions and the election of the new peace commissioners.[79]

Apart from private interest and the temporary absence of strong anti-Gallican leadership, Congress was scarcely in a position to stand up to the Chevalier. The war still seemed to be going badly. In January Washington informed Franklin of the "infinitely critical posture of our affairs."[80] The winter and spring of '81 were punctuated by mutinies of the Pennsylvania and New Jersey lines, and it was still too early to assess the military consequences of Cowpens, where Dan Morgan smashed "Bloody" Tarleton, or of Nathanael Greene's campaign in the Carolinas. At that very time Congress was stepping up its demands for more money, more supplies, more fighting men and ships from its ally, and was in the process of receiving still another subsidy from the King of France.[81]

La Luzerne seldom moved in the dark. If Congress locked away any of its secrets, the French legation managed to get a duplicate key. Barbé-Marbois sent on to Vergennes copies of ciphered dispatches from Congress to its commissioners in Europe, along with a key to the cipher. The French Foreign Minister was furnished with the cipher used by John Adams in confidential correspondence with his intimates in Congress, as well as the cipher covering communications between the Congress and John Jay. This last, so Vergennes was informed, would be used by most of the American ministers in Europe. Finally, La Luzerne managed to get his hands on the cipher that Laurens used.[82]

To secure for the Comte de Vergennes greater control over the peace-making La Luzerne pressed Congress to accept the notion of a truce, to modify its peace pretensions, and to change its peace commission. He was favored by a persuasive if less than candid manner, an aggressive floor leader in the person of General Sullivan, and the luck of the mails. Throughout the winter of '81 he sought to trim America's aspirations down to size and to prepare the delegates for certain unpalatable contingencies. To Congressional delegates he pointed out the exorbitance of their pretensions to Western lands, which conflicted with those of Spain, and sought to dissuade Northerners from pressing for a Canadian expedition. Privately to Vergennes he suggested the possibility of a partition of the American states at the peace, though conceding that in the long run a union of the Thirteen States would be more beneficial to France than a segmentation of the new republic. La Luzerne was kept busy denying rumors spread by the British that the French intended to hold on to Rhode Island after the war,[83] and he was embarrassed by persistent rumors in America that the Lower South would be abandoned under the terms of an impending truce.[84]

La Luzerne's activities reflected the views of his chief. By February of 1781 Vergennes had become reconciled to the notion of an armistice on the basis of territory held by each side, save for New York. Although he did not disclose his full hand even to La Luzerne right away, the Comte decided to have the ground prepared in Congress and to eliminate or undermine John Adams, whose opposition he correctly anticipated. Vergennes' first move took the form of a dispatch to La Luzerne under date of March 9th. It would be difficult for France to avoid the offer of comediation without "grievously wounding" the dignity of the offerers, Vergennes pointed out. France's final acceptance, nonetheless, was contingent upon Congress, and the Foreign Minister had no doubt that its delegates would follow the example of his King and accept the comediation. Advise Congress of the state of the negotiations, La Luzerne was told, and have the American plenipotentiary instructed regarding a truce in the event that peace cannot be effected by the mediators. Vergennes cautioned his envoy to refrain from making known France's views as to the real object of the truce. He was to point out to Congress the urgency of moderating its pretensions to win the goodwill of the mediators, "save in the matter of independence which admits of no modification." Should the comediation take a decided turn, the King of France was prepared to accept the mediation offer conditionally both for himself and the United States.[85] Vergennes apprised his envoy that, though the admission of an American plenipotentiary to a congress at Vienna presented formidable difficulties, it was a point which had to be settled before entering into the mediation.[86]

Two later dispatches by Vergennes, of April 19th and June 30th, touched more directly on the sensitive subject of the *status quo*. Congress should empower the King's minister to curb Adams whenever necessary, he urged, and should be made to realize that, in view of Britain's fixed opposition to outright recognition of independence and in consideration of the military situation, the mediating powers might not improbably propose a truce based on the *status quo*. Such a sacrifice, which the King as much as Congress would regret, lay "in the order of possibilities," the Comte warned, and Congress would be expected to accept the inevitable with as good grace as possible. Ominously, he chose to remind La Luzerne that, though the greater part of the Netherlands had originally thrown off the Spanish yoke, only seven provinces managed to maintain their independence.[87]

Vergennes' instructions of March 9th reached La Luzerne around the middle of May.[88] At the envoy's request Congress appointed a committee to whom he might communicate these instructions. The committee, which included General Sullivan, had a strong pro-French coloration. La Luzerne told the committee on May 28th only what he had learned from Vergennes' earlier dispatch of March 9th, but he did not choose to disclose all of that dispatch. He hinted at the possibility that the mediators might propose the *uti possidetis*[89] but did not reveal that the French government was prepared to accept it.

Lacking all the facts and relying upon the assurances of La Luzerne, the innocent and the corrupted together marched meekly to the slaughter. On June 6th the committee reported the gist of its conference. Thereupon Congress resolved that the minister plenipotentiary be authorized to concur with the King of France in accepting the comediation, but to accede to no treaty which did not "effectually secure the independence and sovereignty of the thirteen states."[90] Then the Rev. John Witherspoon, revered President of the College of New Jersey, and long reputed by the anti-Gallican party to be a tool of the French legation,[91] moved, first, that the peace commissioner of the United States be instructed to use his "own judgment" and "prudence" in securing "disputed boundaries" and "other particulars" spelled out in the earlier instructions, and second, that the commissioner "make the most candid and confidential communication upon all subjects to the ministers of our generous ally, the king of France, to undertake nothing in the negotiations for peace without their knowledge and concurrence."

The next day the committee had the Witherspoon resolution considered again, and proposed additional and secret instructions, all of which were drawn up under La Luzerne's eyes.[92] With respect to the boundaries of the United States the minister plenipotentiary was to be instructed to use his "utmost endeavors" to secure the limits fixed in the former instructions. Were that to prove impossible, then he could make peace without fixing the northern and western limits, but leave them to future discussion. If that, too, proved impractical, he was "to obtain as advantageous a settlement as possible." The first proposition was unanimously agreed to, the second overwhelmingly carried, but the third failed to win support from more than six states. The purpose of the third secret instruction, as La Luzerne saw it, was to allow the plenipotentiary to yield ground as circumstances and the advice of the court of Versailles dictated, leaving the boundaries to be in effect fixed by the peace commissioner, in fact by Vergennes. In connection with the boundary instructions, La Luzerne made a point of cautioning the delegates that extreme demands would make a poor impression with the mediators, especially since two or three states were still in British hands. Notwithstanding, the delegates from Massachusetts and Virginia insisted that the Treaty of 1763 should serve as the basis of their ultimatum. If you continue to assert such pretensions to the Western lands and hold to such a rigid position, La Luzerne rejoined, you might well change a peaceful mediation into an armed mediation.[93]

On the floor of Congress Virginia, ignoring La Luzerne's threats, sought to deny to the peace commissioner the right to yield certain territories in the Northwest, but that state, which traditionally had the greatest pretensions to Western lands, failed to prevent the adoption of the Witherspoon resolution.[94] As finally hammered out in Congress, the instructions authorized the commissioner to concur with France in the mediation, but to accede to no treaty of peace which should not be such as would, "first, effectually secure the independence and sovereignty of the thirteen states according to the form and effect of treaties subsisting between the said States and his most Christian majesty; and, second, in which the said treaties shall not be left in their full force and validity."

As to boundaries and other particulars John Adams was referred to the former instructions of August, '79, and October, '80. Conceding that it was "unsafe at this distance" to tie up their commissioner "by absolute and peremptory directions upon any other subject than the two essential articles above mentioned," Congress instructed Adams to use his "own judgment and prudence in securing the interest of the United States in such manner as circumstances may direct and as the state of the belligerent and disposition of the mediating powers may require."

Lastly, Adams was instructed

to make the most candid and confidential communications upon all subjects to the ministers of our generous ally, the King of France, to undertake nothing in the negotiations for peace or truce without their knowledge and concurrence, and to make them sensible how much we rely upon his majesty's influence for the effectual support in everything that may be necessary to the present security or future prosperity of the United States of America.

The very next day, June 9th, on another motion of the Rev. Mr. Wither-spoon the commissioner was additionally instructed:

If a difficulty should arise in the course of the negotiation for peace from the backwardness of Britain to make a formal acknowledgment of our independence, you are at liberty to agree to a truce, or to make such other concessions as may not affect the substance of what we contend for, and provided that Great Britain be not left in possession of any part of the thirteen United States.

Only Rhode Island voted against this additional instruction, Virginia's delegation dividing.[95]

With a pliable peace commission, these instructions would give the check-reins to Vergennes, but so long as Adams was the sole plenipotentiary, La Luzerne felt, he would be master of the peacemaking. Was Adams the sort of minister to whom they should confide such immense powers? the French envoy asked the delegates of Congress. Over the weekend the com-mittee met at La Luzerne's house and was persuaded by the French Minister to make still further revisions in the instructions, and Congress, except for scattered opposition from New England, to endorse them. Fol-lowing La Luzerne's counsel, Congress, by the bare minimum of seven votes, struck out the words "will therefore use your own judgment and prudence in securing" in the third clause of the instructions and inserted in lieu thereof "are therefore at liberty to secure." The fourth clause was now introduced by the words "for this purpose." Finally, after the word "concurrence and" Congress voted to insert the following words: "ulti-mately to govern yourself by their advice and opinion, endeavouring in your whole conduct."[96]

In its final form the controversial instruction read:

For this purpose you are to make the most candid and confidential com-munications upon all subjects to the ministers of our generous ally, the King of France; to undertake nothing in the negotiations for peace or truce without their knowledge and concurrence; and ultimately to govern yourselves by their advice and opinion, endeavoring in your whole conduct to make them sensible how much we rely upon his majesty's influence for effectual aid in everything that may be necessary to the peace, security, and future prosperity of the United States of America.[97]

Were they to be obeyed, these instructions would completely handcuff the minister plenipotentiary. But a still further triumph was in store for La Luzerne. Congress, heeding his admonitions, added four more members to the peace congress. On June 13th John Jay was elected, and the following day Henry Laurens, Benjamin Franklin, and Thomas Jefferson were also named. These four Patriots were now joined with John Adams in the commission of the peace, whose powers were wisely granted to all five, or the majority of them.[98]

Although Thomas Rodney of Delaware claimed that it was he who had persuaded Congress to add four commissioners instead of three and thus made it possible for Franklin to serve,[99] La Luzerne, indubitably the best informed, gave the lion's share of the credit to General Sullivan both for the plural commission and the revised instructions. Nowhere could one encounter "more zeal for the alliance," he reported with unintended irony.[100]

Not until June 18th, ten days after Congress had shaped its new peace instructions and picked its new commission, did La Luzerne choose to reveal to the committee of Congress the remainder of Vergennes' dispatch of March 9th which he had up to then carefully concealed from the delegates. It was only then that the delegates heard from La Luzerne's lips that the mediators "might propose the *uti possidetis* as the basis of the negotiation." Although he recognized that such a proposition was "inconsistent with the independence of the United States," the Chevalier implied that France, because of possible further involvements on the European Continent, might be obliged to agree.[101] Had Congress known this before the balloting it is inconceivable that enough votes would ever have been mustered to change the peace instructions of 1779, even if the exchequer of the French legation had disbursed its last sou.

Determined to solidify its gains, the Gallican party in Congress beat off an election bid by Arthur Lee for the newly created post of Secretary for Foreign Affairs, but to accomplish this feat the French Minister felt obliged to inform the President of Congress that he did not trust the Virginian and would not deal with him if elected.[102] When the question was reopened in midsummer La Luzerne threw his full weight behind Robert R. Livingston of New York, who was elected on August 10th.[103] A landed aristocrat on terms of intimacy with La Luzerne and Barbé-Marbois and one of the acknowledged leaders of the French party, he could be counted on to heed the advice of the court of Versailles. True, he was lazy and entirely inexperienced in diplomacy, but that did not bother the Chevalier too much.[104] The French legation at Philadelphia was prepared to assume most of his duties.

Vergennes had gagged and handcuffed John Adams, so he thought. He had added to the mission a group presumably more amenable to Versailles. He had bound the commissioners to humiliating instructions and placed at the head of America's Foreign Office a man who could be expected to see that they were carried out. "Blush, blush, America!" cried James Lovell. That anti-Gallican leader, who in the absence of his friend John Adams saw no impropriety in carrying on an artful and seductive correspondence with John's wife Abigail,[105] summed up the recent proceedings in Congress with the prediction, in cipher, that "our allies are to rule the roast [*sic*]," and that the only effect of increasing the peace commission would be to have them share their "insignificance."[106]

In his meddling with Congress the French Foreign Minister had over-reached himself. Never perhaps was so dear a victory bought so cheap. Adams never forgot and never forgave. He believed that Vergennes was behind the frustrations of Jay at Madrid, of Dana at St. Petersburg, and of himself at The Hague.[107] "There is a Vulcan at Versailles whose constant employment has been to forge chains for American ministers," he wrote his friend Dana.[108]

On his next visit to Paris John Adams would be forearmed.

XI

JACOB'S BARGAIN

WHEN CONGRESS DISPATCHED John Jay to Spain no American Patriot could then have foretold how deeply Philadelphia and Madrid were soon to be divided over peace aims, how irreconcilable differences would arise over what are now termed geopolitical issues. In 1779 the Americans no longer thought of the Spaniards as being consumed with a lust for land. Spain, a great name dwelling in the shadow of her former might, seemed to hold more territory already than she could possibly hope to exploit. The last war had richly added to her possessions in North America. Before the final peace of 1763 was written, France had secretly transferred to her Bourbon ally all of Louisiana that lay west of the Mississippi, along with some 2,800 square miles to the east thereof, including the mouth of the Mississippi and the town of New Orleans.

Long recognized by the French as a white elephant, Louisiana was accepted by the Spaniards with rather ill grace as a peace bribe. It compensated them for their loss of the Floridas, as well as for the transfer to the British of all French territory east of the Mississippi. Now that the English controlled strategic ports on the Gulf of Mexico as well as the east bank of the Mississippi, Spain regarded those northern borderlands which comprised her new acquisition primarily as a buffer to insulate Spanish-American power rather than as an area for quick exploitation.[1]

At the time John Jay courted a Spanish alliance for the United States the empire of Charles III, including the recent acquisition of Louisiana, embraced three-fourths of the habitable parts of North and South America, along with the most affluent of the West Indies. Within her grasp were mines as fabulous as the world had ever known, and some of the richest soil. Would an empire already so extended be likely to begrudge living room to the poor embattled Americans? Patrick Henry as Virginia's Governor sought to assuage fears among Spaniards of America's expansionist aspirations. He assured one Spanish territorial official that the Americans had "more land than can be settled for many ages to come."[2] As he quietly smoked his pipe in Conrad Alexandre Gérard's Philadelphia drawing room, John Jay bolstered the French envoy's complacency. "Our empire is already too great to be well governed, and its Constitution is inconsistent with the passion for conquest," Congress' President was reported by Gérard to have remarked.[3]

About the American Revolution the Spaniards were cold-blooded realists. They took up first things first. Recognizing the American insurgency as a club to smash Britain's colonial power and trusting to the proven maxim, *"Divide et impera,"* Charles III at the start of the War for Independence gave the Patriots aid on a limited scale. In 1776 Louis XVI's uncle joined with his nephew in setting up an initial fund for the thinly masked operation by which Caron de Beaumarchais was enabled to ship desperately needed munitions to America. In Louisiana Spain's enterprising young Acting Governor, Bernardo de Gálvez, the favorite nephew of the powerful Minister of the Indies, José de Gálvez, sent arms and powder up the Mississippi and the Ohio to George Rogers Clark and other American border fighters, and even to the Continental Army. In applying prize law at the port of New Orleans Gálvez was indulgent to the Americans, and as late as the autumn of 1778 he proposed a joint attack on British-held Pensacola. In the latter he was backed by Virginia's venturesome agent in New Orleans, the Spanish-speaking Oliver Pollock. Congress was obliged to confess that the undertaking was beyond its powers.[4]

The notion of an Hispano-American expedition against the Floridas was not inconsistent with Floridablanca's own views at that time. As late as October, 1778, he was known to favor peace on the basis of the independence of the American colonies, the retention of Canada and Nova Scotia by England, and the cession to the colonies of all of Florida, save for a part to be turned over to Spain to safeguard her navigation in the Gulf of Mexico.[5] These notions were at least as generous as those entertained by the Comte de Vergennes, who reminded his envoy to Spain that France did not wish to see "the new republic mistress of the entire continent. . . . We insist only on the independence of the thirteen United American states without including therein any other English possessions which have not participated in these insurrections," he declared significantly. On Canada the French Foreign Minister remained consistent to the end. He wished that great territory to be retained by the English, "both to prevent too great an aggregation of power" on the part of the Americans as well as "to subserve the alliance of the new republic with France." As regards the Floridas, he would be happy to have Spain recover so much of them as was necessary for her security and for curbing the expansionist proclivities of her American neighbor.[6]

As the drift toward war with England seemed inevitable the Spanish line toward the Americans hardened. Cordially detesting rebellion, the Spanish Bourbons were even more outgoing in their detestation of a successful one. The probability that American independence would be won was a bitter pill for Spain to swallow. The fact that the aggressive Americans posed a threat to her own borderlands only compounded the medicine. In the second phase of the war's diplomacy the Spaniards, with the pro-American Bernardo de Gálvez perhaps a notable exception, assumed toward the Americans a posture of sullen negation which remained unshaken to the war's end. "It is only too apparent," France's ambassador to Spain, the Comte de Montmorin, confided to his chief, "that Spain looks upon the United States as prospective enemies before very long. In consequence, far from suffering them to approach her possessions, she will omit nothing to keep them away, and specifically from the banks of the Mississippi." In reply, Vergennes expressed the view that the American republic, torn as it was by diversity, was too weak to justify alarm in Spain. "I confess to you that I have only faint confidence in the energy of the United States," he declared.[7]

Between Spain and America the Father of Waters now loomed as the major divisive issue. The mighty Mississippi, whose source as a gurgling little brook 2,500 miles north of the Gulf of Mexico remained to be discovered and whose control unlocked the vast interior of the continent, offered access to world markets for settlers in the trans-Allegheny region. In the days of the flatboat and rugged mountain trails, the Mississippi furnished the only practical avenue from the interior for shipping to market bulky commodities like flour. Spain, long committed to the principle of colonial exclusivism, would hardly be expected to admit the Americans to the trade of the Gulf of Mexico nor to grant them genuine rights of navigation on the Mississippi. To secure that monopoly Spain required control of both banks of that great river.

Spain's new hard line toward America reflected the growing apprehension of Don Juan de Miralles, Spain's unofficial observer. Miralles, who reached Philadelphia in the spring of 1778, soon became convinced that the Americans intended to settle the area of the West they had already conquered from the English and to export their produce from the interior by the Mississippi River. Not only did he alert the Minister of the Indies, but by midsummer he appears to have persuaded Conrad Alexandre Gérard that Spain must reconquer all that the British had acquired by the treaty of 1763 both in Florida and along the Mississippi. The Americans, he kept reminding Gérard, would soon be the enemies of Spain. Together, Miralles and Gérard put the pressure on acknowledged moderates like John Jay and Gouverneur Morris to have them curb the extreme pretentensions of the anti-Gallican leaders, those "Swelled Heads" (*Têtes Exaltées*) of whom the French envoy was contemptuous. The pair even broached to Congress the possibility of selling to Spain America's recent conquests in eastern Louisiana and in the Illinois country.[8]

If Miralles across the Atlantic in Philadelphia sensed more quickly then did Floridablanca in Madrid the danger to Spain which American expansionism posed, it is equally true that the Chevalier Gérard assumed a more intransigent stand against some of America's war aims than was warranted by the original instructions he received from Vergennes. In the fall of '78 Gérard began to lobby in Congress for a guarantee to Spain of the exclusive navigation of the Mississippi.[9] The Gérard-Vergennes dispatches on this topic crossed each other. Six days after Gérard wrote Vergennes reporting his sudden interest in the Mississippi, but months before the Foreign Minister received the communication, Vergennes in turn sent off a dispatch to his envoy in America announcing France's acceptance of Spain's offer of mediation and urging Congress to formulate its peace terms. Vergennes pressed for the renunciation of Canada and Nova Scotia, along with at least part of the Floridas, but he carefully avoided any reference to the pretensions of the United States to lands east of the Mississippi. To the contrary, he indicated that he would be astonished should "anyone" refuse the demand of the Americans for the free navigation of that river. On this subject, Gérard was instructed to confer with Miralles. Should the latter refuse to make this concession, then Gérard was to prepare the Americans for this deprivation "with prudence and management."[10]

Vergennes' dispatch did not reach Philadelphia until February of '79. In the meantime, Gérard, acting on his own initiative and believing he had the backing of President Jay, had warned a committee of Congress that "the King would not prolong the war a single day to procure for them the possessions they coveted."[11] When he finally did receive Vergennes' new instructions the French envoy lost no time in giving them the most liberal interpretation to provide full support for Miralles. In mid-February he addressed Congress as a body on the subject of peace terms. To a group of delegates who gathered around him after his speech he made the point that the possession of Pensacola and the exclusive navigation of the Mississippi were essential to provide security for the Spanish frontier. Not long thereafter he warned the delegates that the King of France could be counted on to stand by Spain in the dispute.[12]

Remote as he was from the American scene, Vergennes had to rely pretty heavily upon Gérard for information about the views of Congress. In this case he accepted without further verification the inaccurate report that the majority of Americans did not care to challenge the rights of Spain in eastern Louisiana. This news came to France's Foreign Minister at a time when he was desperately concerned with reaping the harvest promised by Franco-Spanish military collaboration. Yielding to these double pressures, Vergennes now reversed himself. The Americans, he informed Gérard's successor, La Luzerne, in midsummer of '79, had no right to the navigation of the Mississippi, "since at the time the Revolution began the boundaries of the thirteen United States did not extend as far as that river." It was presumptuous of them to assert the rights of a nation whose authority they themselves had just abjured.[13]

The Franco-Spanish diplomatic team in Philadelphia used threats and blandishments in turn, but Congress, after long and bitter debate, refused to toe the line. John Jay was instructed to insist upon "the free navigation of the Mississippi into and from the Sea," and to seek to secure a free port or ports below 31° NL on that river. In turn, America's newly appointed envoy to Spain was informed that the United States was prepared to guarantee the Floridas to His Catholic Majesty if he succeeded in wresting them from Britain.[14]

Upon Spain's formal entry into the war she more precisely defined her military objectives in America to include the expulsion of the English from the Gulf of Mexico and the banks of the Mississippi, where, as Gálvez put it, "their settlements are so prejudicial to our commerce, as well as to the security of our richest possessions."[15] By capturing Mobile and Pensacola Spain tightened her control of the Mississippi's east bank. Her daring raids upriver and as far north as the Illinois challenged American territorial aspirations. It was not long before Spain recognized that in expelling the English from the Missspipi she had only replaced an old enemy by a new one.[16]

These were the stakes of empire. For this prize a prolonged and inconclusive duel was fought between the tenacious John Jay and the inflexible Conde de Floridablanca. Once in Spain, the American envoy soon discovered that he was to be treated not like a potential ally but more like an enemy agent dispatched by a power which the politics of the Pardo had decided to keep weak and insecure. Jay's mission to Madrid had a dual objective. He sought an alliance and financial aid. He was to find that the dispute over the Mississippi would prove a stumbling block to the attainment of either objective, that it would affect both the waging of the war and the making of the peace.

Jay's pride and fierce independence were not calculated to make him anybody's man. As he relates in his own account of the Spanish mission, of which only a few fragments survive in his papers, Gérard and Miralles had, prior to his appointment to Spain, "entertained higher opinions" of his "docility than were well founded." The American made it an invariable rule not to discuss with them the debates of Congress, presumably secret. When Gérard would hold forth of an evening on the necessity of America's abandoning any pretensions to the Floridas or the Mississippi as "prerequisites to a treaty," being careful at the same time to disclaim any instructions on that head, Jay kept his own counsel. He had first been of the opinion that, provided Spain gave the United States a free port on the Mississippi, recognized her independence, and defended her with arms and money, these concessions were a cheap price to pay. When, however, Spain declared war for objects, as Jay put it, "that did not include ours, and in a manner not very civil to our independence," he became persuaded that the United States "ought not to cede to her any of our rights, and of course that we should retain and insist upon our right to the navigation of the Mississippi."[17]

Presumably Jay had reached these conclusions by the time he was designated minister plenipotentiary to Spain. Certainly his prolonged exposure to his shipboard companion, Conrad Gérard, did nothing to alter them. Upon his arrival at Cádiz in the winter of 1780 Jay sent his secretary of legation, William Carmichael, on ahead to Madrid to feel out the lay of the land. He reminded Carmichael "to do full justice to Virginia and the western country near the Mississippi." He was to call attention to the heroic exploits of the border settlers against the Indians, and to the growth and extensive settlements in the Western territories. Yet at the same time he was to reassure the Spaniards "that ages will be necessary to settle those extensive regions."[18]

Regardless of his private feelings, Jay was quickly made aware that, if America were to gain recognition from Spain, she must trim her territorial aspirations. From the Pardo Floridablanca's very first communication to Jay made that quite clear, "divested of the gloss which its politeness spreads over it," as Jay himself put it. Spain's First Minister had only succeeded in putting Jay's back up. He dashed off a note to Congress declaring that it would be "better for America to have no treaty with Spain than to purchase one on such servile terms. . . . There was a time," he continued, "when it might have been proper to have given that country something for their making common cause with us, but that day is now past. Spain is at war with Britain."[19] In short, from the very start of his mission Jay sensed the antagonism entertained in Spain to its purposes and was disinclined to compromise America's peace aims. Others around the court sensed it too. The Venetian ambassador commented that it was highly problematical that Spain would recognize American independence because to do so would be to throw an obstacle into her peace negotiations with England.[20]

Jay's quest of Spanish dollars was, if anything, more exigent than his suit for an alliance, but here too the Mississippi question frustrated him at every turn. Without even waiting for Laurens to embark for Europe or even pausing to learn the results of Jay's mission Congress, as has been noted, drew on both envoys in the amount of £100,000 sterling apiece, payable at six months' sight. "We are with every wish for your prosperity," wrote the committeeman who broke the news, and with unwonted sincerity. It was not until the end of April that Jay received this communication, and by then the notes had only a month to run.[21] In his embarrassment he rushed off to Aranjuez to draft a personal appeal to Floridablanca, which he requested be laid before the King.[22]

Finally, on May 11th Floridablanca received Jay and Carmichael. In a moment of unusual irritation Vergennes once called Floridablanca "that pettifogger," and it must be conceded that Spain's Principal Minister had not lost the cautious and even legalistic approach of a provincial attorney. He first sought to blunt Jay's resistance to his propositions by painting a sad picture of Spain's finances, which the ill-fated campaign of the previous year had placed in such disorder. Then he proposed that the King, as a private individual, might be prepared to advance a sum running as high as £40,000 sterling over the next dozen months, in the meantime pledging his credit toward the payment of the bills of exchange when they were presented. In return the King was prepared to accept naval vessels, light frigates, cutters, or swift sailing vessels. These Congress could dispatch to ports in Biscay with cargoes of tobacco, timber, or other produce, and, after unloading, they could be turned over to Spain.

When he spoke of money matters, Floridablanca made it clear he did so as a private individual, whose offer would have to be ratified by his government, but when he touched on the larger stakes of diplomacy, he assumed the mantle of First Secretary of State. The principal obstacle to concluding a treaty with America, he made it clear, was the pretension of the insurgents to the navigation of the Mississippi. In defense of American claims, Jay pointed out that many of the states were bounded by the Mississippi, certainly a moot point which Floridablanca did not choose to challenge at that time. While these states were "highly interested" in its navigation, they would be prepared to consider some amicable arrangements to obviate the use of the river for contraband "or other objects, which might excite the uneasiness of Spain."

Since Jay would not back down on the fundamental issue, Floridablanca bluntly warned him that "the King will never relinquish the navigation of the Mississippi." If Don Juan Jay would turn his thoughts to devising some middle way to get around the difficulty, then, he implied, both the agreements and the aids would be quickly forthcoming.[23] Floridablanca's idea of a "middle way," in Carmichael's opinion, was the exclusion by Spain of "every other nation" not only from the navigation of the Mississippi but also from the Gulf of Mexico.[24] Jay, on the other hand, was still optimistic that if Congress stood firm on the Mississippi issue Spain would be content with "equitable regulations." Accordingly, he asked Congress for instructions as to whether they would consider any regulations to prevent contraband inconsistent with their ideas of free navigation.[25]

Jay soon had serious ground for doubting the candor of the Spanish Minister. Father Hussey had now arrived at Aranjuez, and Richard Cumberland was presently expected. To quiet the gossip which this unusual visitation stirred up and to allay the concern of the Americans, Floridablanca summoned Jay and Carmichael to his office the evening of June 2nd. Father Hussey, he explained, only returned because of the death of an uncle, a court chaplain. Richard Cumberland was traveling through Spain en route to Italy. One of his daughters was recovering from a shattered romance with the Duke of Dorset. Perhaps the English traveler would have some proposals to make for an exchange of prisoners "and possibly others of a different nature," but, the Spanish Minister reassured Jay, they would be communicated to him with candor. Floridablanca, whose nervous irritability had mounted with the advance of spring, seemed in a surprisingly genial mood. When Jay told him that he had a couple of bills drawn on him by Congress running somewhere between $600 and $700, the Spanish Minister smiled, and said, "I might accept them."[26]

The procrastination of the Spanish court toward the American business, combined with the transparent duplicity of its dealings with the nation with whom it was presumably at war, soon soured Jay toward Spain. Were Britain to acknowledge American independence ahead of Spain, "would it not be a little extraordinary?" he asked in a letter to John Adams. He went on to point out that if Britain had any wisdom left she would do it.

"She may yet have a lucid interval though she is long out of her senses." Indubitably, Spain must be convinced, Jay asserted, that "the power of the United States added to that of Britain and under her discretion would enable her to give Law to the western world, and that Spanish America and the Islands would be at her mercy." In a passage which he deleted from his final draft Jay declared that America would never purchase such an acknowledgment "of any nation by terms she would not otherwise accede to."[27]

When he deleted this ringing declaration Jay may well have had forebodings that he was summarizing in capsule form the story of his own mission. On June 5th Floridablanca reminded Carmichael that he hoped Jay would find some "middle means" to obviate the difficulty over the navigation of the Mississippi. Two days later Floridablanca submitted to Jay propositions in writing not dissimilar to those he had sketched out in the May conference. The King would be prepared to advance over a two-year period the sum of £100,000 sterling to honor bills outstanding. To reimburse His Catholic Majesty Congress would be expected to turn over to Spain four "handsome" frigates and some other lighter vessels of war, fully equipped.[28]

The flagrant insincerity of the Conde's offer infuriated the American envoy. The city lawyer told the country lawyer that merchants holding bills regarded them as money at hand, "not money lying still," and that they would prefer recovering the face amount thereof, with the usual damages on protests, to a delay of payment for two years with interest. He reminded Floridablanca that such a delay would have an incalculable effect on the credit of the United States and its ability to conduct the war. How could Congress repay Spain at this time by providing frigates when it lacked cash to defray its own war expenses? With disarming candor, Jay stated it would not be in the power of the United States to pay their debts until the coming of peace, but to such eventual repayment with interest the American stood ready to pledge the faith of his country. Jay closed on a warning note. Congress, he told Floridablanca, would view with "painful concern" the news "of the failure of their bills."[29] As if to drive home the urgency of his personal situation, Jay sent on to the Conde only ten days later a bill just presented to him for the trivial amount of $333. "From this his Excellency will perceive the painful situation Mr. Jay is in," the American envoy added laconically. Almost at once came a curt note in reply, accepting this small bill. Floridablanca took the occasion to warn Jay that "it will be impossible to show the same complaisance for other bills without consulting the pleasure of the King." Since Congress had not found the proposals of Spain acceptable, it was up to Jay to initiate some counterpropositions.[30] Jay thought the note "looked dry, and indicated a degree of irritation, though it held up the idea of further means."[31]

Determined to bring the issue to a head, Jay again reminded Floridablanca of the latter's earlier proposal to advance up to £40,000 sterling "at the end of the present year." While Congress could not repay immediately in either ships or money, one would not expect this even of long-established and opulent nations, he pointed out. Even they usually found it expedient to put off settlement of war debts until the war's end. Could more be expected from "a young nation brought forth by oppression, and rising amidst every species of violence and devastation which fire, sword, and malice can furnish for their destruction"?[32]

Pressing his moral advantage, Jay then reported to Floridablanca the Congressional resolution of March 18, 1780, retiring "Continentals" in circulation and accepting them in payments due Congress from the states at one-fortieth of their face value, as well as the concurrent proposal to issue bills, redeemable in specie, with interest, at the expiration of six years. Should His Majesty furnish the credit backing for a certain proportion of the sum to be emitted, the United States would not only give their pledge to indemnify the King, but also furnish him with certain aids, among them the vessels he requested. "Draw out a more clear and precise plan on this subject," Floridablanca replied.[33]

At the very moment when the parties seemed to be drawing closer together news came, early in July, of the American loss of Charleston. The defeat cast a pall over the Madrid conference of July 5th between Jay and Floridablanca,[34] and Jay knew from the start that his request for immediate acceptance of certain bills would fall on deaf ears. Nothing could be done, the Spanish Minister informed him, until the arrival of the person who was to succeed Don Juan de Miralles, news of whose death at Washington's encampment at Morristown had only just reached Spain. "In this conference not a single nail would drive," was Jay's succinct summation.[35]

While Floridablanca continued to procrastinate, Jay's financial predicament became ever more serious. Two Bilbao houses presented bills for payment, and Congress celebrated the news of Jay's safe arrival in Spain by drawing an additional $25,000 in bills against their envoy, payable at sixty days' sight. A horde of American seamen stranded at Cádiz, many of them former captives of the British, clamored for assistance. Time and again Jay had to dip into his own pocket to meet such demands.[36] As the pile of bills mounted steadily higher, Jay scolded Congress for its fiscal irresponsibility.[37] Neither he nor Carmichael received their salaries on time and had to accustom themselves to being poised on the brink of insolvency. At a court whose diplomats were conspicuous for their style of expenditure, the penurious Jay cut a humiliating figure. Although Franklin from time to time came to Jay's rescue with modest advances,[38] Jay was reduced time and again to borrowing money for his own subsistence and that of his household.[39]

To the palace of La Granja at San Ildefonso, whither the court had now removed to escape the summer's heat, Jay addressed a succession of notes on his financial obligations. We await the arrival of Miralles' successor, Floridablanca replied, suggesting that the mysterious diplomat was on the point of setting out on his journey. It was widely believed that the designee was one of the Gardoqui brothers, members of a Bilbao firm long engaged in shipping supplies to America, but when a Gardoqui was reported to have turned up there was no response to Jay's solicitations. Floridablanca continued to stall when further bills were presented,[40] and Jay's letters were becoming more importunate. "I must entreat your Excellency to relieve me and my country from this painful situation," Jay pleaded. For a prideful man he was reduced to a pretty low estate.[41]

To this barrage of solicitations no answer was forthcoming. On the morning of August 26th Jay made a personal call upon the First Secretary of State. On being informed that the Spanish official was indisposed, the American visitor left his card. Floridablanca was not too indisposed, however, to see the French ambassador, among others, that very morning, or to ride out as usual that afternoon. To add to Jay's uneasiness, Carmichael's servant picked up from a barber of his acquaintance a choice morsel of gossip. An English-speaking gentleman was now lodging with Bernardo del Campo, Floridablanca's undersecretary.

In his frustration and anxiety Jay turned to the French ambassador, who all along had served as a go-between for the Americans at the Spanish court. A few months Jay's junior, Armand-Marc, Comte de Montmorin de Saint-Hérem, held the very highest credentials at Versailles. Parisian born, he came of the Auvergne aristocracy. His forbears had distinguished themselves in diplomacy and on the battlefield. Companion to the Dauphin who became Louis XVI, Montmorin, on that monarch's accession to the throne, was dispatched first as minister to the elector of Trèves, and then, in 1777, to Madrid. Solemn but not pompous, dignified without arrogance, and cautious without seeming craven, the French ambassador was a formidable figure to have on one's side.

Although Montmorin agreed to speak to Floridablanca himself, he was visibly annoyed when Jay reminded him how, in reliance upon

Floridablanca's original promise to furnish financial aid by the end of 1780, he had not requested Congress to stop drawing bills on him. As a result, Jay declared, he was left with no alternative but to send Congress a true account of all that had transpired between the Conde and himself. "I cannot answer for the disagreeable effects such intelligence will produce," Jay added. The Comte's behavior seemed to Jay "dry, and not cordial and open as before."

Montmorin promised to speak to Floridablanca on Wednesday, August 30th. That afternoon Jay waited upon the French envoy to learn the results of his talk. Montmorin could scarcely conceal his annoyance at Jay's punctuality. He informed the American that he had had no more than cursory conversation with Floridablanca as the Comte d'Estaing happened to be present at the same time. "Write another letter to the minister requesting a conference," the French ambassador urged.

"While four letters on the subject remain unanswered, I do not see the necessity of writing a fifth," Jay replied. He expatiated at some length on the Spanish Minister's having persisted in allowing him to remain "unanswered and unnoticed." Unless he met with more "tenderness" from the holders of the bills, they would be returned protested, and such an event "would of necessity be an end to the confidence of America in the Court of Spain," Jay declared.

Montmorin replied in a conciliatory vein. "Remember, you are yet only rising states," he reminded Jay, "not firmly established, or generally acknowledged. . . . By all means," he counseled, "write the minister another letter, *praying* an audience."

The idea of getting on one's knees to the Conde de Floridablanca was a little too much for a man of Jay's fierce independence. "The object of my coming to Spain was to make *propositions, not supplications,*" he asserted. He would forbear troubling the Minister with further letters "till he should be more disposed to attend to them," he added. Then Jay went on to inform Montmorin, for the benefit of both the French and Spanish courts, that he "considered America as being, and to continue independent in *fact,* and that her becoming so in *name* was of no further importance than as it concerned the common cause, in the success of which all the parties were interested. . . . I do not imagine," he declared, "Congress would agree to purchase from Spain the acknowledgment of an undeniable fact at the price demanded for it." For Jay there was no recourse but "to abide patiently the fate of the bills," and to transmit to Congress a full account. After dispatching this report, he promised to write Floridablanca one final letter on the subject of the treaty. Should he be treated "with like neglect," or should he be informed that His Catholic Majesty "declined going into that measure," he would then consider his business "at an end," and take the necessary steps to return to America. For his own part, Jay added significantly, he was inclined to think it the interest of America, instead of multiplying treaties with European nations, "to rest content with the treaty with France." "By avoiding alliances with other nations" she might "remain free from the influence of their disputes and politics."

This ultimatum shook up the French ambassador. Montmorin had struggled manfully to advance American interests while at the same time continuing to enkindle the Spanish war spirit. Tactfully, he expressed the hope that Jay's mission would have an agreeable issue.

"Are you content with the conduct of France?" he asked.

"Most certainly," Jay answered, for France, unlike Spain, was spending her blood as well as her treasure for America.

Montmorin would not be put off by this diplomatic answer. He phrased the question in more specific terms. "Are you content with the conduct of France relative to the proposed treaty between America and Spain?"

"So far as it has come to my knowledge, I am," Jay replied. He seized the opportunity to point out that he still remained ignorant of the progress France had made in mediating the issues between Spain and the United States. Montmorin did not see how his intervention could be proper except where points of the treaty were actually being discussed and at issue. Jay retorted that these were only "*secondary*" objects of the expected mediation. The "*primary*" one was to have the King of Spain begin the negotiations. To this Montmorin made no reply.

"My mind is made up," Jay declared. "I shall not write another letter to the Minister," he announced firmly, and coupled this refusal with a promise to show Montmorin the next day the letters he had already written.

"How far the tone of this conversation may be judged to have been prudent," Jay wrote Congress, "I know not. It was not assumed, however, but after previous and mature deliberation. I reflected that we had lost Charleston, that reports ran hard against us, and therefore that this was no time to clothe one's self with humility." Jay hazarded the guess that "these strange delays were not avoidable," and that behind them lay Floridablanca's desire to secure more news of Britain's military operations in America as well as the indecisive stage of his negotiations with Cumberland. The more distressed America became, Jay pictured Floridablanca as reasoning, the more "pliant" she would be and the "less attached to the Mississippi."[42]

Jay's surmise was correct. Floridablanca's delaying tactics were closely tied to his negotiations with Cumberland. Soon after the news of the fall of Charleston the Spanish Minister had reassured the British playwright that Spain would never acknowledge the independence of "the revolted Colonies" until it was conceded by Britain. He went on to express the hope that the recent defeat of the Americans would be followed by their "total submission,"[43] a calculated piece of indiscretion which betrayed the real feelings of his court. This was pretty generous of one enemy to another, and a lot more generous than Floridablanca need have been. Early in August the combined Franco-Spanish fleet under Córdoba intercepted the rich English armada headed for the Indies, inflicting the greatest naval disaster England suffered in the entire war.[44] For the Spaniards peace no longer seemed as exigent as it had in the Spring.

Jay was not privy to the Cumberland negotiations, but his instincts told him that, as regards the Americans, Floridablanca could not afford to sever the tenuous ties that remained. On Montmorin's advice Jay authorized Carmichael to make on his behalf a personal request for a conference with Spain's Principal Minister. On September 2nd Carmichael stopped by Montmorin's on his way to Floridablanca's office. He was told that when the French envoy had relayed Jay's request for an audience, the Spanish Minister replied that he was too busy. Despite this rebuff Carmichael was advised to "go and see."

Carmichael was kept waiting a long time in Floridablanca's antechamber. Finally he was told that the Spanish Minister could not possibly see Jay until Tuesday evening next, and that he should check with him on Tuesday morning to confirm this appointment. He was also told that "the person so long expected" had arrived, that Floridablanca was preparing instructions for him and would try to have him converse with Jay in the meantime.

Between August 30th, when Jay issued his ultimatum, and September 5th, when Floridablanca felt obliged to take some steps to mollify the Americans, the diplomatic outlook had dramatically changed. On August 31st Floridablanca had heard from Hillsborough. The news was bad. The English could not possibly consider yielding Gibraltar.[45] Oddly enough, they too felt no need for a quick peace. With reports of victories in America and of strong appeasement sentiment in the French Cabinet, King George was not disposed to make so great a concession in order to detach Spain from her ally. On September 2nd Floridablanca made it clear to Cumberland that Hillsborough's answer was unacceptable to Spain. Some days later the Spanish Minister bluntly told Father Hussey that the day Richard Cumberland and the Irish priest left Spain "without settling matters he would immediately treat with Mr. Jay, and acknowledge him."[46]

Floridablanca's apparent *volte-face* was merely a feint in the backstairs swordplay at La Granja. On September 3rd "the person so long expected" paid a call on Jay. He was Don Diego de Gardoqui of Bilbao, who bore a letter of introduction from Floridablanca from which his name was carefully omitted. Gardoqui reminded Jay that America "offered no *consideration*" for the money she solicited, and suggested payment in ship timber. Jay pointed out that it could answer no purpose to borrow money with one hand and repay it instantly with the other, and that a repayment in money or in ship timber was the same in effect. Gardoqui returned that evening with a proposal that Jay offer to yield the navigation of the Mississippi as a consideration for the aids he sought.

Gardoqui had come at last to the real point of his visit. "Such an object could hardly come in question in treating for a loan of a mere £100,000," Jay replied sharply. "The Americans, almost to a man, believe that God Almighty had made that river a highway for the people of the upper country to go to the sea by," he declared. The Western areas were being rapidly settled, he pointed out, and men of the stature of George Washington were "deeply interested" in the West. He made it clear that its inhabitants would not readily be persuaded of the justice of being obliged "either to live without foreign commodities, and lose the surplus of their productions, or be obliged to transport both over rugged mountains, and from an immense wilderness, to and from the sea, when they daily saw a fine river flowing before their doors, and offering to save them all that trouble and expense, and that without injury to Spain."

"The present generation would not want this navigation," Gardoqui replied. "Let us leave future ones to manage their own affairs."

September 4th, the day following this conversation, Jay met with Gardoqui at the office of Bernardo del Campo. Dispensing with the customary amenities, Campo launched at once upon a lengthy complaint. It was entirely improper to draw bills without previous notice and consent. If drawn, they could with more propriety have been drawn on France, who was richer than Spain. "Spain has been brought into the war by your quarrel," Campo charged, "but up to now has received no advantage from you."

"You told us you were prepared to assist us in taking Pensacola, but instead of aids, we have heard nothing but demands from you," Campo reminded Jay. "You are scarcely in a position to make demands. Your situation is deplorable. The enemy is even talking of the submission of some of the states, and there are reports of negotiations on foot for that end."

Unruffled by Campo's calculated rudeness, Jay painstakingly went over the ground he had previously covered with Floridablanca and Gardoqui, skillfully parrying each of Campo's thrusts. He pointed out that men in arms against the enemies of Spain were serving her as well as themselves, that he knew nothing of Spain's having been drawn into the war by or for the Americans, nor was this ground to be found among the reasons she had alleged for entering it. American troops could hardly cooperate against Pensacola when they were repelling the enemy's assaults at their very doors. "Do not listen to the tales told of our dependency and submission," Jay advised. Such stories spring from enemy policy, not from fact, he pointed out. "I believe no more of there being private negotiations between America and Britain than I do of there being private negotiations between Spain and Britain for a separate peace, which your Minister assured me was not the case."

Before the meeting broke up, Campo disclosed his hand. "The United States," he remarked to Jay, "did not seem inclined to gratify Spain in the only point in which she was deeply interested," namely, the navigation of the Mississippi. Jay's reasoned arguments failed to move the Spaniard. "There are seasons when men mean not to be convinced," Jay commented philosophically to Vergennes in reporting these talks, "and when argument becomes a mere matter of form."[47] However much the Spaniards might scold the Americans, they were not prepared to break with them completely. Two days after the meeting with Campo Gardoqui authorized Jay to accept bills running to around a thousand dollars.

The Mississippi issue was now out in the open. Carmichael saw it as the "sole" obstacle to an Hispano-American understanding.[48] Jay, lacking further instructions on that question, was completely in the dark about the recent policies of Congress and fearful that the delegates had changed their minds about the Mississippi. Jay's fears seemed justified. All letters addressed to him coming by regular post, whether transmitted via France or directly to Spain, were systematically intercepted, often never even delivered. He found it necessary to send his personal secretary to the Spanish coast to await the arrival of American ships and put into the hands of trusted American sea captains his own dispatches to Congress.[49]

Jay knew for some time that Montmorin was in receipt of a dispatch from La Luzerne dated May 12th, whose contents he had chosen to conceal from the Americans. When pressed, Montmorin admitted that the Chevalier had merely reported that two unnamed members of Congress "thought it would be best not to bring up the question of the navigation until Spain should become possessed of the adjacent country," at which time "it might be ceded with a better grace."

It was obvious to Jay that the Spanish court was stalling until Congress sent him new instructions, but he also understood that Spain was seriously embarrassed in her own quest for funds to finance the war. On September 13th Gardoqui told Jay that "the exigencies of the State" would not permit payment of more of the bills drawn upon the American than had already been accepted, a total amounting to a mere $14,000. From Montmorin and other sources Jay learned that Jacques Necker had in effect vetoed Spain's proposal to float a huge war loan, thereby placing a severe strain upon the Spanish Treasury. "This has irritated the ministers here, and perhaps we may be the innocent victims," Carmichael reported to Congress.[50]

On the very same day that Jay dispatched a note to Floridablanca requesting that he tell him "frankly whether the United States may expect any, and what aids from Spain,"[51] some news of American military victories arrived. "It seemed as if she had risen like a giant refreshed from sleep, and was doing wonders," Jay observed. Whether it was the peremptory tone of Jay's request or the reports that the total submission of the colonies had been unaccountably put off, the Spanish Minister had Gardoqui deliver a paper dictated "in his Excellency's name" by Don Bernardo del Campo. Floridablanca hastened to reassure Jay. Though money was tight "through the undermining of some persons of rank in France," the King had no intention of stopping his assistance of "the States, whenever means can be found to do it." Although His Majesty "might have just cause of disgust" because of the failure of Congress to procure his consent before drawing the bills, he was moved by his feelings of "humanity, friendship, and compassion" to provide for Jay "or his constituents" the sum of $150,000, to be payable over three years. Their generosity was not matched by any equivalents from the States, Campo reminded Jay, and this in the face of rumors that "some understanding" had been reached between the colonies and England, to which the court, of course, would give no credence.[52] With a caution verging on the pathological, the letter had been delivered unsigned, and it was with difficulty that Jay persuaded Gardoqui to affix his own name thereto.

A showdown with Floridablanca could not be postponed, because, as Jay wrote to both Vergennes and Franklin, bills in the amount of $50,000 had become due, and the honor of Congress "now hangs as it were by a hair."[53] The confrontation took place on September 23rd. Floridablanca, heartened by the better news from America, seemed in a more conciliatory mood and apologized for not yet having made available the amount of thirty or forty thousand pounds that he had agreed to provide at the Aranjuez conference in May. Jay, in turn, pointed out that he had never requested a donation from Spain, but rather a loan, for the repayment of which with interest he had offered to pledge the faith of the United States. Jay reported that the Conde appeared "rather uneasy and desirous of waiving the subject." But the American pressed his advantage. He could conceive of "no higher tokens" of goodwill that one nation could give another, he asserted, than their commissioning a person to enter into treaties of amity and alliance, "and that on terms of reciprocity" and "mutual advantage."

With unexpected candor Floridablanca now made it clear to Jay that to raise the treaty between France and America in Spanish court circles was to wave the *muleta* before the bull. "We are not prepared to accede to that treaty," the Conde declared sharply. In a hitherto unpublished cipher portion of Jay's notes on his conference which he forwarded to Congress, Floridablanca was quoted as revealing that the King of Spain had been so provoked at France's concluding the treaty with America without his knowledge that it almost caused a rupture between the two courts. "Consider this a secret," he added, conceding at the same time that Montmorin was well aware of it. "No, do not raise the French treaty," Floridablanca advised. Instead, "let us make a new one," adding, "there seems to be no reason for haste." Since Congress apparently was not disposed to make the cessions without which the King would not consider a treaty, it would perhaps be best to continue the present arrangements of mutual aids, "and not excite animosities and warmth by discussing points which the King would never yield." On the Mississippi, Floridablanca told Jay, the court was unbudgeable. "Unless Spain could exclude all nations from the Gulf of Mexico, they might as well admit all," the Spanish Minister declared with considerable heat. Again he reminded Jay that for Spain this was "the principal object to be obtained by the war," and that obtained, he would be reconciled, whether or not Spain acquired anything else. From the tenor of his remarks it was clear that Spain was now of a mind to defer the issue until a general peace settlement.

John Jay summed up the whole disheartening business in a full report to Congress. "For my own part," he told the delegates, "I shall be disappointed if I find Courts moving on any other principle than political ones, and, indeed, not always on those. Caprice, whim, the interests and passions of individuals, must and will always have greater or less degrees of influence." Certainly that was true of Spain, whose cordiality had been tested, Jay added. "I know of a certainty that it was in her power easily to have made the loan we asked." His experiences at the various Spanish courts had confirmed him in his staunch republicanism. "We shall always be deceived," Jay warned, "if we believe that any nation in the world has, or will have, a disinterested regard for us, especially absolute monarchies, where the temporary views or passions of the Prince, his Ministers, his women, or his favorites, not the voice of the people, direct the helm."

Let us try, Jay concluded, "to be as independent on the charity of our friends, as on the mercy of our enemies." A close reader of the Bible and later President of the American Bible Society, Jay found the lessons of the day clearly presented in the book of Genesis. "Jacob," he pointed out to Congress, "took advantage even of his brother's hunger, and extorted from him a higher price than the value of the Mississippi even for a single dinner. The way not to be in *Esau's* condition is to be prepared to meet with *Jacob's*."[54]

Bills rather than rain descended in torrents[55] to bring the long hot summer to a close, a summer of frustration for John Jay, a summer saddened for both John and Sally by the death on August 4th of an infant daughter only three weeks after birth. "My Susan, she was a lovely babe," Sally Jay wrote to the folks at home. Throughout her ordeal the husband whom she adored was her pillar of strength. She found him "composed in danger, resigned in affliction, and even possessing a cheerful disposition in every circumstance." To Sally he was "virtue's own self."[56]

Aside from Sally, the company on San Mateo Street close by the Royal Glass Manufactory provided Jay with scant relaxation. Jay never did hit it off with William Carmichael, whom Congress had designated as the secretary of the mission, considering Carmichael to be too confiding in Montmorin and too intimate with various personages at the Spanish court.[57] He regarded him as an intriguer who sought to undermine his authority, and eventually to supplant him.[58] At the start of the mission Jay had been obliged to let Carmichael know that he himself had "sole direction" of affairs, and though the private breach never assumed a formal character, Jay continued to distrust his secretary and refused to permit him to copy his confidential reports to Congress. To Carmichael, whose convivial manner contrasted with Jay's standoffishness, the latter seemed a stickler for protocol, vain, touchy, and self-righteous, a view that others in the household took, including Henry Brockholst Livingston, Sally's brother and Jay's private secretary. This twenty-three-year-old Princetonian, one day to sit on the Supreme Court of the United States, acted captious, sulky, and ill-mannered, and constantly baited his brother-in-law by making indiscreet remarks to foreigners hypercritical of the Americans and their government. His provocative rudeness sorely tried the Jays, who breathed a sigh of relief when he took passage for home in the spring of '82.[59] A further note of disharmony in the ill-assorted legation ménage came from a handsome, foppish, eighteen-year-old Virginian named Lewis Littlepage, whom Jay in a generous moment had agreed to place under his tutelage at Madrid. Littlepage, whose ingratitude was surpassed by his colossal insolence, was entirely dependent upon Jay for funds, but his passion for women rather than books and his streak of "military Quixotism" sorely tried his mentor.[60]

The minuscule achievements of his mission provided Jay with little comfort. Although he stayed on at Madrid for another year and a half, he did not raise a single centavo beyond what the Ministry had already promised him. The defeat of Gates at Camden, Laurens' incarceration in the Tower of London, the report of Benedict Aronold's treason—in fact any sort of gloomy news from America—darkened the Spanish skies with clouds that Jay was powerless to dispel. Rescued once again by credits added by Vergennes to Franklin's account,[61] the American envoy was obliged to complain to his old friend, Robert R. Livingston, that Congress' bills had placed him *"in forma pauperis* and inspired a very mortifying idea of the state of our affairs."[62]

Meantime, Jay's request to Congress to clarify his instruction concerning the Mississippi was taken up in Philadelphia. Again the French legation put enormous pressure on the delegates to modify or withdraw the Mississippi instructions, capitalizing on the division over this question between states like Virginia, with claims to the trans-Appalachian areas resting on ancient charters, and others like Maryland, with no pretensions to Western lands. As a condition to ratifying the Articles of Confederation, Maryland insisted that all the states surrender their Western lands to the new government. Competing with Virginia for title to the Western lands were companies like the Illinois and Wabash Land Company, which claimed large tracts of land along the Wabash, the Ohio, and the Mississippi rivers and numbered among its proprietors Conrad Gérard, former Minister to the United States, and John Holker, a French consul and

marine agent in Philadelphia, in addition to many other celebrities.[63]
To the Chevalier de La Luzerne the pro-French delegation from Maryland
proved a pillar of strength. First among his allies was Daniel of St.
Thomas Jenifer, an Illinois-Wabash shareholder, who unabashedly walked
the French line, going so far as to support the right of the Spaniards to
conquer any portion of the Western lands and even such states as Georgia,
should they fall into England's hands.[64]

Congress stood fast in the face of unremitting pressure. On October 4,
1780, that body formally resolved that John Jay should be notified to
adhere to his former instructions and continue to insist upon the free
navigation of the Mississippi.[65] This uncompromising stand came as a
rude shock to the French legation in Philadelphia. For some weeks in the
fall of 1780 Barbé-Marbois acted as chargé d'affaires during La Luzerne's
absence from Philadelphia. A facile penman, perhaps as celebrated for
his diplomatic indiscretions as for his political opportunism, the man who
was one day to sell Louisiana to America worked untiringly at this time
to keep eastern Louisiana from the Americans. In consultation with St.
Thomas Jenifer and Francisco Rendón, the agent of Spain who replaced
Miralles, Barbé-Marbois prepared a memoir, entitled "Observations on
the contested points in the negotiation between Spain and the United
States." On its face a plea to both sides for moderation, the "Observations"
was in fact a brief for the Spanish position. It reviewed the moot questions
raised by charter claims, the effect of the Treaty of 1763, and the necessity
of having a well-defined frontier such as the Mississippi. It advanced the
Spanish position that the lands had been ceded by France eighteen years
earlier to Great Britain, not to the colonies. It incorporated St. Thomas
Jenifer's own view that, should such lands become "the property of any
common enemy," Spain had "a full right to make the conquest" of them.
It insisted that American claims to be legitimate should rest on actual
settlement, not "temporary incursions," and that "an impartial mediator"
might well be asked to draw the line between the contending parties. Do
not risk missing this "present fair opportunity" of obtaining "solid and
lasting advantages by running after a shadow and a chimerical object,"
Barbé-Marbois warned.

Barbé-Marbois showed the "Observations" to young James Madison of
Virginia, named chairman of a committee to draft a letter to Jay "explaining the reasons and principles" underlying the instructions. It is difficult
to say whether or not Madison toned down his draft as a result of these
arguments, as has been contended, for on the main points at issue Madison
was uncompromising, and his reasoning was to be endorsed by John Jay
himself.[66] Madison's report, in substance adopted by Congress on October

16, 1780, rested America's claims to having the Mississippi constitute the boundary line between the United States and the Spanish settlements upon the Treaty of Paris of 1763, upon the claim of the United States to the benefits of the French cession to Britain, and upon recent military conquests in the Northwest. It denominated Spanish pretensions as incompatible with America's treaty of alliance with France. Madison claimed for the United States "an indisputable right to the possession of the East bank of the Mississippi for a very great distance." Hence the navigation of that river was essential for the prosperity of its citizens. It provided a natural route for their articles of trade. Furthermore, international law, notably the authority of the Swiss jurist Vattel, was asserted to deny the right of a nation holding the mouth of a river to bar "innocent passage." Congress was nonetheless prepared to accept equitable regulations to prevent contraband.[67] Madison's appeal to the "rights" and "usages" of nations was hardly calculated to move the Spanish court, where ideas of international law were quite different from Congress'. As Jay took pains to point out, Vattel's *Law of Nations* was "prohibited here."

Jay's difficulties as a negotiator were enormously enhanced by the time lag between Philadelphia and Madrid. Thus Congress took ten days to prepare and dispatch its instructions to Jay. They did not reach him until January 30, 1781, and then not before the French court had been apprised of them.[68] Within a fortnight the instructions were already obsolete, but Jay had no way of knowing that. Congress' *volte-face* on the Mississippi question was the result not so much of Franco-Spanish pressure as of the rapidly deteriorating military situation in the fall of 1780, particularly in the South, and of desperate shortages of both money and supplies. On November 18th the Georgia delegates recommended abandoning the "ultimatum" of the free navigation of the Mississippi.[69] In James Madison's own delegation the initiative seems to have been taken by Theodoreck Bland, who frequently opposed the young Virginian and shared his wife's dislike of that "gloomy stiff creature," clever in Congress but out of it unbearable in manners, "the most unsociable creature in existence."[70] He now persuaded Madison to support a revision of the Mississippi instructions,[71] and together they brought about the capitulation of the Virginia Assembly on that point.[72] With the foremost proponent of free navigation deserting the cause, all but three states fell into line. On February 15, 1781, Congress altered Jay's instructions, permitting him to recede from his demands for the free navigation of the Mississippi in order "to remove every obstacle" to the accession of Spain to the alliance with the United States.[73]

Meantime, during the winter of 1780-81 Jay, still following the earlier instructions from Congress, was not prepared to yield anything to Spain. As a result, his bargaining power was zero. In forwarding the new instructions Congress prayerfully asked Jay to try to get Spain to yield on the point, but it was obvious from as far off as Madrid that they had struck the flag. Knowing that something new was in the air, Montmorin manifested less sympathy for the American position and Floridablanca, if anything, became more obdurate. The French ambassador was unimpressed by Madison's argument supporting the October resolutions to the effect that the Franco-American treaty guaranteed the navigation of the Mississippi, and Jay tactfully decided not to press the point. Floridablanca kept insisting that "the King of Spain must have the Gulf of Mexico to himself" because the maxims of policy adopted in the management of Spanish colonies required it. Late in March he told Jay that Spain could not pay his bills soon due, leaving the American once more on the brink of protest. What was behind this "cruel" behavior? Jay asked Montmorin. The latter intimated that the Spanish court expected some new overture concerning the Mississippi. Jay told him he had no authority to make any others. Montmorin replied bluntly, "The Minister believes you have."

Although the Spaniards were obviously apprised of the revised instructions of Congress, Jay did not learn about the resolution of the fifteenth of February until May 18th, when he heard from James Lovell.[74] Jay could not consider Lovell's note an official communication, and feared that the delay in receiving the resolve of Congress might have resulted from its having been reconsidered, altered, or repealed shortly after passage. Accordingly, he dragged his feet. At a conference with Floridablanca on May 19th, when Jay renewed the subject of the proposed treaty, he was met by a smiling Minister, who remarked that whenever Jay announced he had the authority to yield the point of the Mississippi, he could expect frankness in return. Floridablanca was a man of mercurial moods, however. Four days later he showed much less cordiality to Jay, and went so far as to suggest that the treaty be put off until the general peace.

If Jay could have presumed that the Spaniards did not already know the contents of the new instruction, he should, so he told Congress, "without the least hesitation, have played the game a little further, keeping this instruction in my hand as a trump card, to prevent a separate peace between Spain and Britain, in case such an event should otherwise prove inevitable." Now that Spain was in the war, there was little reason, in Jay's opinion, to assume that the cession of this right of navigation would render her exertions more vigorous or her aid to America more liberal. The Spanish Ministry's actions spoke more eloquently than their words. "The cession of this navigation will, in my opinion," Jay declared, "render a future war with Spain unavoidable, and I shall look upon my subscribing to the one as fixing the certainty of the other."[75]

Taking this realistic view of the prospects of a treaty, Jay did not rush ahead impulsively when word finally came to him from Congress of the adoption of the new instructions. On July 2nd he informed Floridablanca that Congress had authorized him to waive the navigation of the Mississippi, and, with that obstacle removed, he now looked forward to forming an alliance with Spain. The very same day he asked Montmorin for his good offices in these negotiations.[76] A few days later Floridablanca handed Jay a number of letters addressed to him, among them one from Samuel Huntington, President of the Continental Congress, expressing that body's approval of his conduct in Spain.[77] No letter ever gave him "more real pleasure," Jay confessed. He had experienced "one continued series of painful perplexities and embarrassments." He had been engaged in "intricate and difficult negotiations, often at a loss to determine where the line of prudence was to be found." His situation had exposed him "to the danger of either injuring the dignity and interest" of his country, on the one hand, or of "trespassing on the overrated respectability and importance of this Court on the other." It was little wonder, then, that Congress' approbation gave him "most singular and cordial satisfaction."[78]

The long hot summer, which scorched the fields as though by fire, kept Jay in a fever of "suspense and expectation." Floridablanca was ill. Floridablanca was too busy. Master of all the Spanish arts of procrastination, Floridablanca simply would not be rushed. It so happened that Major David Franks, once an aide to Benedict Arnold, but dispatched by Congress to Europe in the role of diplomatic courier as a mark of confidence in his integrity, had arrived in Spain and was awaiting orders from Jay about his return. Jay made a point of having the Major tell Floridablanca the bad impression caused by the Spaniards when, on the seizure of Pensacola from the British, they allowed the captured garrison to proceed to New York, where they promptly reinforced the redcoat defenders dug in there. "It was ill done," the Spanish Minister confessed. "It won't happen again." True, but the damage had already been done.[79]

In desperation Jay again turned to Montmorin. If Major Franks were to return to America with no other intelligence but a tale of "repeated delays," he warned the French ambassador, he could not vouch for Congress' reaction. Jay followed up this warning by drafting a letter to

Floridablanca, which he submitted to Montmorin for his approval. After reviewing his tedious and frustrating experiences as a negotiator, the American took a high tone. His constituents were "at least entitled," he declared, to the kind of attention that "the most dignified sovereigns usually pay to the friendly propositions of such states as solicit either their aid or alliance in a decent manner." Jay demanded "a candid answer," though he was "sensible" that Spain possessed "a higher degree on the scale of national importance than the United States," and that her friendship was "of more immediate consequence to America" than America's to Spain. Should His Catholic Majesty and his ministers presume to look "beyond the present moment," they might well perceive the advantages of establishing harmony and goodwill between neighbors. "The eyes of America, and indeed of all Europe, are turned towards Spain," Jay concluded. "It is in the power of His Catholic Majesty to increase his friends and humble his enemies." As for Jay himself, he could only hope that history would credit Spain with the kind of support which would contribute to the success of the Revolution, an event whose true importance posterity would most certainly recognize.[80] Anxious as ever to avoid an open break at all costs, Montmorin persuaded Jay to tone down his letter. He addressed to Floridablanca a more pointed and laconic note, with the sting removed. This brought him an immediate appointment.[81]

When the long-sought conference finally materialized at San Ildefonso on September 19th, Floridablanca asked Jay to commit to paper "the outlines of the proposed treaties," advising that these should cover "three great points": the aids requested by America, commercial relations between the two countries, and the treaty of alliance. All this was to be completed by Sunday, less than four days off. Somewhat taken aback by the unwonted precipitancy of the court, Jay nevertheless turned out a set of formal proposals, and submitted them three days later. These included the relinquishment by the United States to Spain of the navigation of the Mississippi south of 31° NL, a Spanish guarantee to the United States of "all their respective territories," and an American guarantee to the Spanish King of "all his dominions in America." Significantly, Jay made the relinquishment of the Mississippi contingent on Spain's acceptance of it. Should Spain put off until a general peace both its acceptance of this offer as well as an alliance, then the United States would cease to consider themselves bound by the offer.[82]

Jay's was indeed a generous offer. The issues of the Mississippi and the boundary of West Florida, which were to plague Spanish-American relations for years to come, could have been clarified to Spain's entire satisfaction at this time. All Spain had to do was to recognize American independence and make an alliance with her. Aranda in Paris had long been urging these two steps upon Floridablanca, but the Spanish Minister preferred to fight the war without the United States as an ally, to postpone the evil day of recognition, and to leave the Mississippi and the Florida boundaries to the future.[83]

Jay had shown more foresight than Congress, which had relinquished the Mississippi without imposing any preconditions. Convinced that a minister plenipotentiary must exercise his discretion when circumstances warranted it, Jay justified his having placed a limited duration on his offer of the Mississippi navigation as being "absolutely necessary to prevent this Court's continuing to delay a treaty to a general peace." He warned Congress that it was the design of the Spanish court "to draw from us all such concessions as our present distress, and the hopes of aid may extort, and by protracting negotiations about the treaty, endeavor to avail themselves of these concessions at a future day, when our inducements to offer them shall have ceased." As such conduct would be "unjust" as well as unfair, Jay was confident that Congress would endorse the limitation he had placed upon the offer. Congress, which soon had second thoughts about its having revised the instructions, in fact endorsed Jay's prudent course with enthusiasm.[84]

With his intense myopia on the American question, Floridablanca signally failed to snatch advantages for Spain while they still could be had for the asking. He disdained personally to negotiate these proposals with Jay, assigning that disagreeable chore to his undersecretary, Campo. While the latter procrastinated, American credit in Spain went from bad to worse.[85] The contemptuous treatment which Floridablanca accorded the proud and touchy American could not help but color the latter's feelings toward the Spanish court. "This government has little money, less wisdom, no credit, nor any right to it," Jay wrote Gouverneur Morris soon after his conference with Spain's Principal Minister. In that same letter he commented on the growing coolness between the Bourbon partners. "This Court and that of France do not draw perfectly well," he observed. "Except a Jew, I can hear nothing so odious to a Spaniard as a Frenchman."[86]

Even after the news of Yorktown, which reached Madrid at the end of November,[87] there was no change in the political climate of Madrid toward America or Americans. William Carmichael found the court lined with attendants undisguised in their anti-American sentiments, and remarked that the Princess of Asturias made a point of treating English visitors "with much condescension and distinction."[88] Once more, in the winter of '82, it was necessary for France, through Franklin's good offices, to come to the financial aid of Jay.[89] To Franklin, Spain's refusal to recognize American independence was not only "disreputable to us," but "hurtful to our affairs elsewhere." If the Spaniards were not so short-sighted, the doctor pointed out to Jay, they would have seized with avidity the chance to secure a neighbor's friendship. "If I were in Congress," Franklin bluntly told Jay, "I should advise your being instructed to thank them for past favors, and take your leave." Not long thereafter he wrote from Passy: "Spain has taken four years to consider whether she should treat with us or not. Give her forty, and let us in the meantime mind our own business."[90] Personally, Jay would have liked nothing better than to follow Franklin's advice and issue an ultimatum to the Spanish court. To do so would have antagonized the Comte de Montmorin, a past master at keeping inconclusive negotiations from sputtering to a halt, as well as his government. "Be patient. Be moderate," the French ambassador counseled. "Keep up the appearance of being well with the Court." Then he added, pityingly, "These various perplexities must keep you constantly in a kind of purgatory."

"If you will say mass for me in good earnest, Monsieur le Comte," the Protestant envoy replied to the Catholic ambassador, "I shall soon be relieved of it."[91]

In the end Jay was reduced to protesting a batch of bills payable on March 14, 1782, for the comparatively trivial amount of £25,000. The French legation tried to dissuade Jay from stating the amount in his pro-test, adding, "It will look as if we had deserted you," but on this Jay refused to back down. "This might save us the Mississippi," he remarked to the embarrassed Montmorin.[92] And it probably did.

With the protests of the bills Jay had written off further Spanish aid or recognition.[93] Spain, Montmorin confided to him, wished "to modify" American independence, and "to keep herself in a situation to mediate" between America and England at "the general peace." Timely succor from Franklin again saved America's credit in Spain,[94] although not before it had been besmirched. If only Jay could have paid the Spaniards off for the little they advanced, it would have been a source of immense personal gratification. "Our pride has been so hurt by the littleness of their conduct," he wrote Franklin, "that I would in that case be for leaving it at the gate of the palace, and quit the country," counsel which Secretary Livingston had already suggested. With the war not officially over, the step was not deemed expedient, but the time would come, Jay predicted, when a "just, a free, and brave people" will have "nothing to fear" from the Spaniards, and nothing "to request of them."[95] In another decade that time did come. Then the United States government, choosing to regard the $150,000 as a loan rather than a subvention, paid it back in full with interest, and wiped the slate clean.[96]

Ever the opportunist, Floridablanca changed his tune when he learned that France had given another subsidy of six millions to America and that Parliament had resolved to cease offensive operations against the rebellious colonies. He dispatched his servant to Jay's residence with an invitation to dine "at his table, every Saturday after the 11th of May next ensuing." The invitation was not addressed to Jay, and his name was carefully omitted therefrom. "Find out if this is a mistake," Jay asked Montmorin. "Yes," Floridablanca admitted, "it must have happened by mistake." He had only intended to ask Jay's orders for Aranjuez. Now the Minister put it up to his King, and Charles III graciously consented to Jay's being invited "as a private gentleman of distinction." As "a Minister or representative of an independent sovereign" Jay felt he could not with propriety accept an invitation which by its own terms impeached his title to that character. Accordingly, he asked Montmorin to decline for him "in the most soft and delicate manner."[97]

A timely call to Paris to take part in the peace negotiations rescued Jay from his intolerable situation. During the previous September Major Franks had delivered to Jay at San Ildefonso Congress' commission to negotiate the peace.[98] On reading its terms, particularly the instruction subordinating the commissioners to the King of France, his reaction was very much like that of John Adams. "There is one among those which accompany the commissions," he complained to Congress, "which occasions sensations I never before experienced, and induces me to wish that my name had been omitted." He recognized that duty required him to exercise his own judgment only in cases referred to his discretion, and otherwise to execute instructions without questioning the policy of them, but he could not forbear remarking that "as an American, I feel an interest in the dignity of my country, which renders it difficult for me to reconcile myself to the idea of the sovereign independent States of America submitting, in the persons of their ministers, to be absolutely governed by the *advice* and *opinion* of the servants of another sovereign, especially in a case of such national importance." Without disputing the gratitude due their French ally, Jay pointed out that "this instruction, besides breathing a degree of complacency not quite republican, puts it out of the power of your Ministers to improve those chances and opportunities which, in the course of human affairs, happen more or less frequently unto all men. Nor is it clear that America, thus casting herself into the arms of the King of France, will advance either her interest or reputation with that or other nations." Thinking it improbable that serious negotiations for peace were likely to begin soon, Jay asked Congress to relieve him from this assignment, one where he "must necessarily receive and obey (under the name of *opinions*) the directions of those on whom I really think no American minister ought to be dependent."[99]

Congress refused to release Jay from his commission. His friend, Robert R. Livingston, the new Secretary for Foreign Affairs, broke the news to him in a letter, the ciphered portions of which have never been published. Livingston reminded Jay that he himself was not in Congress when the instructions were given, but said that he had heard them justified on grounds arising "out of our local politicks." Do not think the instructions imply the "smallest distrust of your zeal and abilities," Livingston reassured Jay. They were voted before the commissioners were designated. Owing to the diversity of interests in Congress it seemed that an agreement on every point involving mutual sacrifices might be attended with "the most dangerous delays." "They then supposed they knew that the peace was absolutely in the power of France, and they thought it more prudent to interest her generosity than give her a plea to do as she chose from our insisting upon what she might deem unreasonable." As further reassurance, he informed Jay that Vergennes had written La Luzerne, declaring that "nothing but the most absolute necessity shall induce him to make the smallest sacrifice of the interest we have entrusted to his care."[100]

Paris now beckoned. "Come hither as soon as possible," Franklin wrote Jay toward the end of April of 1782. Leave Carmichael in charge at Madrid, he advised, lest, as Vergennes put it, "it might not seem as if we abandoned that Court."[101] "A letter from Dr. Franklin calls me to Paris," Jay informed Livingston in May. "I set off in about five days." Prayerfully he added, "I hope my future letters will be less unfortunate than many of my former ones."[102]

When John Jay shook the dust of the Spanish plains from his traveling bags Floridablanca could scarcely conceal his relief. He put it down to pique at the American's lack of success in separating the Spaniards from some of their dollars. "His two chief points," Floridablanca commented to Aranda, were: "Spain, recognize our independence; Spain, give us more money."[103] With this stinging commentary on the Jay mission he paid tribute to an opponent who was not only consistently right, but consistently righteous.

Both Paris and Philadelphia were shocked at the treatment Jay had received in Spain. Lafayette deplored "this failure of health, failure of time, failure of instructions," which had led "to neglecting all the memoirs that have been presented by the American minister," whom he found lacking in neither "good faith" nor "good will."[104] Franklin raised with Livingston the query whether the Spaniards were not planning to "shut us up within the Appalachian Mountains?"[105] Congress went on record approving Jay's course in making the surrender of the navigation of the Mississippi contingent upon an early alliance, and took the occasion to express its astonishment that Spain had not jumped at the offer. Further delays, the resolve declared significantly, would render such a sacrifice on the part of the United States far less exigent.[106]

Above and beyond Congress' resolve there was even talk of striking back. Livingston hinted to Jay that America might well think of ceding the Mississippi lands to some "northern" power in return for important commercial advantages.[107] Livingston's insinuations, according to La Luzerne, cloaked "a bizarre scheme" to offer Russia an establishment in eastern Louisiana in order to win her over to the side of the United States in the forthcoming negotiations, and at the same time to obtain from the Empress a guarantee of America's Western territories. England, too, it should be remembered, had gone beyond talk, and actually offered Russia a bribe to get her on to her side, and some thought was given to encouraging the Russians to seize Spain's Pacific possessions.[108] Everybody, it seems, was trying to seduce Catherine the Great. Fortunately, in America the project never passed beyond the line of meditation.

America's Foreign Secretary had the last word on the Spanish mission. He found it "a little singular" that the Netherlands, "which never gave us the least reason to suppose they were well inclined toward us, should precede Spain in acknowledging our rights." The moral was clear. "We are a plain people," Livingston remarked to Jay. "Courts value themselves upon refinements, which are unknown to us. When a sovereign calls us friends, we are simple enough to expect unequivocal proofs of his friendship."[109]

Such consolation as Jay could derive from his ill-starred mission came from the knowledge that he had not relinquished America's claims to either the Mississippi or the Western lands despite cruel pressure. It would be years yet before the Father of Waters would go unvexed to the sea. Meantime, John Jay had not traded America's birthright for a mess of pottage.

XII

THE BALL AT DR. FRANKLIN'S FOOT

Ⓘ T WAS SOMEHOW FITTING that the most universally esteemed American of the age should be associated with the peacemaking, and that he should be one who had been long identified with humanitarian affairs and particularly with the cause of peace. Edmund Burke addressed Franklin in wartime as "the Philosopher, my friend, and the lover of his Species,"[1] and the doctor managed to live up to his fabulous reputation. "If princes before they went to war were to make an estimate of their expenses," Benjamin Franklin told one British agent, "they would be found to exceed the value of their conquests." "Peace," he reminded his adversary, "could not be too dearly bought."[2] With his customary mental agility, Franklin found no difficulty in reconciling his pacifism with an ardent expansionism[3] and a reverential attachment to the French alliance. Unlike his colleagues, he saw nothing humiliating in the Congressional instructions requiring close consultation with the King of France. While prepared to defer to the wisdom of the French, he was not likely to buy a peace at any price from the British, who, he was convinced, were waging against America a war that was not only "unjust" but even "barbarous." Whigs like Burke, who expected to find Franklin to be still attached to the mother country, did not reckon on his hostility to the war party and the Loyalists.[4]

There was about Benjamin Franklin a certain suppleness and depth that set him apart from his two more unbending and less complicated colleagues in the peacemaking, John Jay and John Adams, neither of whom had his capacity for indolence nor his gift for enjoying the fine art of frivolity. While Franklin was working on weighty diplomatic affairs during the summer of '82 he found the time to draw up a treaty of "eternal peace, friendship, and love" between himself and Madame Brillon de Joüy, his young and very attractive neighbor at Passy. Like a good draftsman

Franklin was careful to preserve his freedom of action, in this case toward other females, while at the same time insisting on his right to behave without inhibitions toward the amiable Madame Brillon.[5] Some months before, Franklin had written:

I often pass before your house. It appears desolate to me. Formerly I broke the Commandment by coveting it along with my neighbor's wife. Now I do not covet it any more, so I am less a sinner. But as to his wife I always find these Commandments inconvenient and I am sorry that they were ever made. If in your travels you happen to see the Holy Father, ask him to repeal them, as things given only to the Jews and too uncomfortable for good Christians.[6]

There was a clandestine side to Benjamin Franklin that his more forthright colleagues could not possibly appreciate. An inveterate literary prankster from his precocious teens until his death, the old doctor perpetrated one literary hoax after another, including the fictitious speech in court of Polly Baker, prosecuted for the fifth time for bearing a bastard child,[7] and his notorious "Advice to a Young Man on the Choice of a Mistress."[8] In the midst of his negotiations with the British he fabricated a hoax about the scalping of Americans by Indians in the pay of the British, and printed it in the guise of a *Supplement to the Boston Independent Chronicle.* This was gruesome propaganda, and he justified his deception by telling John Adams that he believed the number of persons actually scalped "in this murdering war by the Indians to exceed what is mentioned in invoice."[9]

Franklin was the one member of the peace delegation about whom there might be a suspicion of conflict of interest. Throughout the war Franklin remained a secret member of the Vandalia syndicate, a land company with a huge potential stake in the Old Northwest. Because his name was anathema to the law officers of the Crown Franklin on the eve of the Revolution turned in a bogus resignation of his interest in the company, but he had a secret understanding with Thomas Walpole protecting his shares. When he was Minister to France he explained that he retained the share in the English company in the hope that his "Posterity [might] reap the benefit of them".[10] His "posterity," it should be pointed out, stood a much better chance were England to retain the Old Northwest and the Crown validate the Vandalia claim than were title thereto to pass to the new United States. In fairness to the doctor, however, it should be conceded that his speculative interests do not seem to have warped his judgment or diminished his patriotism in the slightest.

Franklin's saltiness, his ribald streak, his long spells of apathy and inattention to official correspondence,[11] his reticence, and his inscrutable ways contrasted sharply with the Roman virtues and explosive frankness of John Adams, but his pessimism about mankind was shared by his Puritan colleague. In June of 1782, at the height of his ticklish negotiations with the archrivals, Shelburne and Fox, the doctor wrote to his scientific friend, Joseph Priestley, that he found men "very badly constructed." They were "more easily provoked than reconciled, more disposed to do mischief to each other than to make reparation, much more easily deceived than un-deceived, and having more pride and even pleasure in killing than in begetting one another. . . . Without blush," the old doctor remarked, "they assemble in great armies at noonday to destroy, and when they have killed as many as they can, they exaggerate the number to augment the fancied glory; but they creep into corners, or cover themselves with the darkness of night, when they mean to beget, as being ashamed of a virtuous action."[12] In his lifetime Franklin had seen many wars and few years of peace. Now, though old and tired, he was determined to write a peace that should last.

Since Franklin was the principal actor among the Americans in the opening phase of the peace talks in the spring of '82, his account of what transpired carries much authority. "Great affairs," he wrote in the "Journal of the Negotiations of the Peace with Great Britain," which he began in May of 1782, "sometimes take their rise from small circumstances." Late that winter Madame Brillon wrote to him from Nice that she had made the acquaintance of an Englishman named Lord Cholmondeley, whose career had hitherto been devoted to dice and dissipation. Cholmondeley, now responding to the shift in the political winds, promised to call on Franklin, and he kept his word.

On March 22nd Cholmondeley dropped in at the Hôtel Valentinois, the handsome headquarters of the American mission in Passy. In the course of conversation the Englishman mentioned Lord Shelburne's "great regard" for Franklin, and confided that "he was sure his lordship would be pleased to hear" from the doctor. Indeed, were Franklin to write a line, "he should have a pleasure in carrying it." So far as Franklin knew, Shelburne was still a member of the Opposition when he took his visitor's hint and wrote the Earl. Assuring Shelburne of "the continuance" of his "ancient respect" for the lord's "talents and virtues," Franklin congratulated him on the new temper in England. "I hope it will tend to produce *a general peace*," the American commented, "which I am sure your Lordship with all good men desires, which I wish to see before I die, and to which I shall with infinite pleasure contribute everything in my power."[13]

When Franklin penned these lines, he had not yet learned that Lord

North had resigned the seals of office two days before, and that Shelburne had come into the Rockingham Ministry as Colonial Secretary. Now affairs moved swiftly. An old friend and former London neighbor of Franklin's named Caleb Whitefoord appeared at Passy and introduced the Scottish merchant, Richard Oswald, bearing letters from both Shelburne and Henry Laurens.[14] And so from this odd chain of circumstances the negotiations for peace began.

Franklin had a wonderful gift for telling stories, but this account leaves out a good deal more than it tells about the momentous months before the British emissaries appeared in Paris and Passy, hat in hand, suing for peace. True, the immediate contacts may well have been sparked by the "casual" meeting Franklin records, but the "great affairs" in which the doctor henceforth played a central role took their rise from Cornwallis' shattering defeat at Yorktown. The reaction of the chief belligerents to Yorktown was understandably antithetical. "I die content," Comte Maurepas was reported to have said on hearing the news on his deathbed.[15] Franklin rejoiced. "The infant Hercules," he declared, "has now strangled his second serpent that attacked him in his cradle."[16] He even had a commemoratory medal struck off utilizing this allegory to which he was so attached.

News of the disaster reached London on November 25, 1781, virtually coinciding with the reports that Comte Maurepas had died four days earlier.[17] Lord George Germain drove immediately from his residence in Pall-Mall to Stormont's home in Portland Place. Together they proceeded to Chancellor Thurlow's on Great Russell Street, Bloomsbury, and, after consulting with him, decided to break the news to Lord North in person. The pair reached Downing Street shortly after noon. North, who had been less than adequate in the crisis of 1780, received the news with great agitation. He took the communication "as he would have taken a ball in his breast," Germain related. Pacing up and down his apartment, he repeated again and again, "O God! It is all over!" At Kew, the King, whose mulish myopia had fended off the evil day for so long, appeared to take it in stride. His note to Germain acknowledging the bad news betrayed no sense of the calamitous turn of events. The only evidence of George III's hidden agitation was discerned by Germain, who remarked that "he has omitted to mark the hour and the minute of his writing with his usual precision." "I trust," the King wrote, "that neither Lord George Germain nor any member of the Cabinet will suppose that it makes the smallest alteration in those principles of my conduct which have directed me in past time and which will always continue to animate me under every event in the prosecution of the present contest."[18]

Unlike their King, the nation's reaction to Yorktown was to demand a quick peace and a change of government, but the King, whose political acumen had saved the North Ministry the previous year, was not one to be pushed. "No essential change of measures is meant," was the Duke of Richmond's sober summation of the situation, "and none of men if it can be avoided." "When I say the Ministry," he reminded the Marquess of Rockingham, "I mean the King; for his servants are the merest servants that ever were."[19] While the North Ministry stalled, Shelburne thundered in the Lords. Edmund Burke, reinforced by a new and eloquent voice, that of the young William Pitt, the Earl of Chatham's second son, denounced in Commons. Fox warned that the Ministry would set to work "their dirty literary engines to place the blame anywhere but in the right place; but in their own weakness, obstinacy, inhumanity, or treason."[20]

Actually nothing but a brilliant military success could have saved the Ministry, despite the King's attachment to it. Victory, however, was not in the cards. The weeks that followed tolled one disaster after another: the fall of St. Eustatius to the French, followed by St. Christopher, Nevis, and Montserrat, the recapture by the French of posts in Dutch Guiana earlier lost to the British, the loss of Minorca to Spain. Thirteen colonies and eight islands had already been lost by the government. Someone had to be the scapegoat. What more natural than to single out Lord George Germain, the man who had been burnt in effigy at the end of the previous war and repudiated then as "a damned chicken-hearted soldier,"[21] and by a strange quirk of fate was directly responsible for the conduct of the American War. Refusing to quit under fire, Germain dared the Commons to impeach him.[22]

To rescue the Ministry from its new embarrassment the King came up with an ingenious plan to edge out Germain painlessly, a project that was pressed relentlessly by Henry Dundas, the Lord Advocate, known for his moderate views on the American War. To replace Sir Henry Clinton George III named Sir Guy Carleton to the post of Commander in Chief in America, well aware that his designee loathed Lord George and would refuse to serve under him. Still breathing fire and brimstone, Germain was privately prepared to be the sacrificial lamb, though at a price. With that touching generosity that monarchs often display toward incompetent placemen, the King elevated his departing Minister to the peerage as Viscount Sackville.[23] To run what was left of the American

War he picked the doddering Welbore Ellis as Germain's successor. The new Colonial Secretary, snorted Horace Walpole, possessed "all the activity of an Aulic counsellor, the circumstantial minuteness of a church-warden, and the vigour of another Methusalem."[24]

Such desperate expedients fended off a censure vote in Parliament by margins increasingly slim. On February 22nd General Conway moved for an address to the King demanding that the American War be halted. It failed by a single vote. Five days later he introduced a similar resolution, which denounced as enemies of King and country all those attempting to carry on "offensive war in America" and granted leave to bring in an Enabling Act authorizing the King to make a peace or truce with "the revolted colonies of North America."[25] It carried by nineteen votes. Now even the die-hard Sandwich was forced to acknowledge that "the rats increase, and I do not know that we can make any further exertions." Despondency gripped the Ministry.[26]

"At last," George III conceded, "the fatal day is come."[27] Thus he reacted to the long and painful interview of March 20th, when North revealed his irrevocable determination to lay down the reins of power. That evening North quieted a turbulent House of Commons with the announcement that "the administration was virtually at an end." Torrents of rain swept the darkening courtyard as North stepped out to ascend his coach, which, having advance notice, was waiting at the head of the line. With a courtly bow to the drenched and hostile members crowding around him, he remarked, "You see, gentlemen, the advantage of being in the *secret*. Good night."[28]

In the closing weeks of the North government several peace moves were made, all reflecting the devious and divided policies of King and Ministry. For some time North had been reconciled to the idea of peace with America. If it could not be obtained on terms of a "Federal Alliance," he was even prepared to accept "a less eligible mode."[29] Contrariwise, the King still refused to be "an instrument" in lowering the prestige of the British Empire among the states of Europe, an eventuality which he felt would result from "a separation from America." He even con-sidered abdicating and returning to the Hanover of his ancestors.[30] By the end of February, 1782, George was prepared to negotiate with America on the basis of the ground possessed, and to treat "with any separate provinces or even districts to detach them from France, even upon any plan of their own, provided they remain separate states."[31] However fanciful his notion of piecemeal negotiations, which the neutral mediators had long advocated, the King's own Ministry leaped at the chance to separate the rebellious colonies from their French ally. Just in case that did not work out, the government also toyed with the notion of a separate peace with France, leaving Britain free to pursue the war against America, as well as a separate peace with Holland to break up the Franco-Dutch combination.

To these ends three different agents—more accurately, three different rogues—were dispatched to the Continent by the North Ministry. A notorious stock speculator, long active in continental espionage work for the British, Paul Wentworth was dispatched to Holland under the guise of arranging a cartel for the exchange of prisoners. To various key people in the United Provinces he put a proposal for a separate peace, providing for the *uti possidetis*, excepting France's retention of the Dutch colonies she had captured from the British, and reaffirming the old Anglo-Dutch Treaty of 1674, with an explanatory article adding naval stores and ship's timbers to the list of contraband.[32] Both the French and the Patriots kept vigilant check on the British agent's activities, the former fearing that the Dutch would jump at the chance of making a secret peace with the British,[33] the latter demanding that Wentworth's visit be terminated.[34] Taking the broad hint, the British agent, his mission a fiasco, returned to England, dashing any hope of Catherine that her emissaries at The Hague could bring about a face-to-face meeting between Wentworth and Adams to settle the American question.[35]

While the North Ministry considered using Goëzmann de Thurne,[36] instead it turned once more to its veteran secret agent, Nathaniel Parker Forth, the high-living, heavy-drinking spy who had once before acted as an intermediary with the Comte de Maurepas. On March 14th Forth spent an hour and a half with Vergennes. His glib proposition boiled down to the *uti possidetis*, universally applied, the suppression of the servitude on Dunkirk, and some concessions in India, possibly also, as Franklin reported, the return of Canada to France. Obviously, the first of this cluster of proposals was detrimental to America, but, with the North Ministry in its deathbed agony, Vergennes was not likely to accept what at one time he might have found a suitable offer. Because of the shady reputation of the emissary,[37] the Comte took pains, both orally and in a written reply approved by the King, to affirm the French position. Louis XVI, he told the British agent, would consider peace only if the court of London was "disposed to treat on equal terms with the allies of France." As news of Forth's visit leaked out, Vergennes was scrupulous about notifying both Madrid and Philadelphia of the latest overture. If the King of England wishes to "throw an apple of discord among the allies, we have prevented him from so doing," he wrote Montmorin.[38] By the time Forth returned to London, the government that dispatched him had dissolved.[39]

A third set of overtures had as their end a separate peace with America short of independence, but the would-be peacemakers of the North Ministry in its dying moments had nothing more inventive to propose for America than the plan devised back in '78, except perhaps for a more liberal trade policy.[40] Franklin, who had been assiduously courted by various well-meaning intermediaries over the years, had time and again rejected such overtures. After Saratoga he had politely turned down propositions made to him by the English Moravian clergyman, James Hutton, as well as by William Pulteney, a member of Parliament and brother of ex-Governor Johnstone[41] He had contemptuously rejected peace feelers carrying implied offers of peerages and substantial pensions for the Patriot leaders.[42] Only recently he had made it clear to the well-meaning David Hartley that America could not consider a separate peace. "Do not dream of dividing us," he had told Hartley. "You will certainly never be able to effect it."[43]

Regularly rebuffed from Passy, the North Ministry had now written off the doctor and turned instead to John Adams, whose well-publicized rift with the French Foreign Office encouraged hopes that he would listen to feelers for a separate peace. As the emissary to Adams, the North Ministry picked the unsavory Thomas Digges, a native of Maryland but a professional spy for the British. Two years before, Digges had transmitted English intelligence to Adams, obviously of a decoy nature inspired by the British government. At that time Adams had made a point of telling his correspondent that any notion of the Whig Opposition that America would enter into a separate peace was "as wrong and as absurd and impracticable as the plans of the ministry." Schemes short of independence he denounced as "visionary and delusive, disingenuous, corrupt and wicked," and the notion that America was on the point of returning to her allegiance to the King of England "as wild as bedlam."[44]

Digges wrapped his visit in mystery. Writing to Adams from the First Bible Hotel in Amsterdam for an appointment, he remarked that he was "totally unknown in the hotel" and requested the reply to be directed "to the gentleman who arrived this night, and lodges in the room number ten." He enclosed a letter from Hartley inquiring whether the American peace commissioners were empowered to "conclude" as well as to "treat." Adams granted Digges an interview, but insisted that anything he had to say must be in the presence of his secretary, Thaxter. Digges first asked if the commissioners had power to treat of a truce. The four commissioners had full power to make peace, Adams replied, and in a stern tone declared, "If the King of England were my father, and I the heir apparent to his throne, I would not advise him ever to think of a truce, because it would be but a real war under a simulated appearance of tranquility, and would end in another open and bloody war, without doing any real good to any of the parties." A responsible emissary, Adams added, would be "treated with great respect," but should he come, Adams would have to consult first with his colleagues and "our allies," and he made clear that America would make no peace but on such terms as would satisfy France.[45]

Except for being allowed to inspect John Adams' peace commission, Digges had accomplished nothing, yet he insisted that there was more than met the eye in his visit with Adams. His written report of the interview carefully avoided mentioning Adams' denunciation of the truce feeler, and even suggested that Adams and his colleagues were prepared to answer "with confidential secrecy" questions which they did not think were necessary to communicate to the French court. Adams himself, Digges reported, gave him his assurance that he was prepared to answer in this mode any questions put to him on ways of opening a parley or entering into a treaty. Nothing in Adams' account of this conversation supports these insinuations, although they cannot be dismissed for that reason alone.

From Amsterdam Digges wrote to Franklin, on the strength of a letter of introduction from Hartley. "I have no confidence in him," Franklin wrote Hartley, "nor in anything he says or may say of his being sent by ministers." Franklin accused Digges of embezzling sums remitted to him for the use of American prisoners. "If Digges was not damned the devil would be useless," the doctor declared, and Horace Walpole perpetuated the remark.[46] Franklin's hostility to Digges ended the latter's usefulness as an intermediary.[47] Three years later Jonathan Williams wrote Franklin from Ireland retailing a morsel that the doctor must have relished. Digges was now in the very prison that had held the American captives whom the rascal had embezzled. "Like all other cunning rogues," this one had "shown himself to be a fool"—a fitting end to an unworthy emissary of the peace.[48]

Franklin summed up the Forth and Digges missions in his own pithy style: "They still seem to flatter themselves with the idea of dividing us." The Enabling Bill in Parliament, he pointed out to Secretary Livingston, avoided naming Congress, but empowered the King to "treat with any *body or bodies of men, or any person or persons, etc.*" While they were trying "to get us to treat separately from France," they were at the very same time "tempting France to treat separately from us, equally without the least chance of success."[49] Truly, the time for deviousness in diplomacy had passed. The North Ministry had had many chances and muffed them all. Its expiring efforts, however fumbling and insincere, proved but the curtain raiser to the great drama of the peacemaking. For the main show a new cast of British actors would now be recruited.

When Thomas Digges returned to London from Amsterdam he discovered that his masters were now out of office. "I found the entire kick-up of the great ones to make much noise and to give universal pleasure," he wrote Adams.[50] "The kick-up of the great ones," as the wily rascal inelegantly phrased the political revolution, took the peacemaking out of the hands of unsavory secret agents and vested it with the formal and public character it merited. The fat man who physically so closely resembled his monarch had quit at last, and North's departure and that of his colleagues had been preceded by hectic days and nights of behind-the-scenes negotiations.[51] For the role of the intermediary between himself and the Opposition the King picked his sharp-tongued Lord Chancellor, whose brow-beating tactics intimidating high and low alike were surpassed only by his intense anti-Americanism. A political opportunist without principles, Thurlow was prepared to make deals under the guise of forming an administration "on a broad bottom."[52] For the King these were indeed troubled days. He heartily disliked Rockingham and loathed Charles James Fox, whose influence over the Prince of Wales he rightly deplored. Both these Whig leaders advocated independence for America. In addition, Rockingham demanded internal reforms.[53]

Still hoping that the ultimate concession of independence could somehow be avoided, the King turned to Shelburne,[54] not because he was a reformer but because he was known to favor a healthy exercise of the royal prerogative and was opposed to the King's acting as "a mere nominal monarch."[55] Furthermore, the Earl was an avowed opponent of American independence in the imperial tradition of Pitt, even though early in the war he had declared the colonies "lost" to Great Britain.[56] He still toyed with the notion that men like Franklin would listen to terms short of independence.[57] In brief, in a choice between evils, Shelburne appeared to the King to be the lesser, a man who might still pull out of his box of tricks one that would spare the King his crowning humiliation. Unfortunately for both the King and the Earl, the latter's tiny strength in Parliament was insufficient to support a ministry while Rockingham commanded the votes. The resulting coalition Cabinet abundantly demonstrated George III's very special talents for spreading dissension. As First Lord of the Treasury Rockingham was the titular Prime Minister in the new govern-

ment, but in the King's mind he shared that office with Shelburne.[58] The
latter accepted the post of Secretary of State for Home, Colonial, and Irish
Affairs. This was the revamped Secretaryship of the Southern Department,
which now included the duties of the abolished American Secretaryship.
The other Secretaryship of State, formerly of the Northern Department,
but now designated for Foreign Affairs, was given to Shelburne's political
rival, Charles James Fox, a man whose great talents were marred by
impetuosity and temperamental instability. As a result, Shelburne was
not only a shadow Prime Minister, competing with Rockingham, but the
holder of a post which brought him into head-on conflict with Fox in
negotiations for the peace.

The titular head of the peace Ministry was an old-fashioned Whig
grandee, unostentatious and accessible, who for reasons never quite clear
acquired a reputation as a daring reformer. What Richmond called "an
ill-placed timidity" was evident in all Rockingham's public actions. Horace
Walpole called him a wet blanket, and the fact is that he seldom mustered
the courage to speak out and exert the party leadership which he claimed.
His previous Ministry had been responsible for the provocative Declaratory Act, which needlessly raised anew the issue of Parliamentary authority
over the colonies. During the Association movement of 1780 he had signally failed to capitalize on the nation's mood of discontent. In addition
to his deficiences of boldness and initiative, Rockingham was a very sick man
when he took over his second administration. A pulmonary condition, ag-
gravated by the wettest weather England had experienced for a half century,
dampened his spirits, sapped his vitality, and deprived his government of
leadership.[59]

The man who was to make the preliminary peace with America is perhaps
the most enigmatic figure of his time and certainly one of the least beloved.
In a later and more dispassionate age Shelburne would be hailed by Disraeli
as "one of the suppressed characters of English history," as "the first great
minister" to comprehend "the rising importance of the middle class," and to
see its potential as a bulwark of the throne against "the Great Revolution
families."

The Earl himself probably would have been in agreement with modern
psychoanalysts who trace so much of the problems of personality to early
childhood and family relations. Upon assuming office he wrote to his King
confessing "my unconquerable aversion to dealing with men."[60] He left to
posterity two different drafts of an "Autobiography"[61] documenting a
wretchedly unhappy childhood. He was born in Dublin in 1737, and spent
his early years in a remote part of southern Ireland under the tyrannical

governance of his aged grandfather, Thomas Fitzmaurice, Earl of Kerry, who ruled his tenants and his family much as the Lords of Kerry had been doing since the time of Henry II. Shelburne's father, the second son of the Earl, was completely under the thumb of his domineering wife. In that household young William Fitzmaurice knew neither love nor books. He was given a feudal upbringing, and had it not been for his aunt, Lady Arabella Denny, who offered him that affection and kindness for which he was starving, he would not even have learned to read. "I loved Lady Arabella Denny," he confessed, "because she loved me." From a narrow-minded Huguenot tutor he acquired facility in the French language, but little else. At the age of sixteen, after spending a wasted year in London, the unlettered lad went off to Christ Church, Oxford, where he had the good fortune to attend Sir William Blackstone's renowned lectures on the common law. Otherwise he thought the college "very low," and when he left it, he still considered himself an uneducated man. "Home detestable," lacking a decent allowance, peace or quiet, he joined the army and served under the dashing James Wolfe, who took a great personal interest in the young man. "He unprejudiced my mind," said Shelburne of the military hero of Quebec. Young Fitzmaurice then served on the Continent, distinguishing himself at the Battle of Minden, where Germain lost his reputation.

Retired with a colonelcy, Fitzmaurice soon became intimate with Lord Bute, the young King's principal adviser, and with Henry Fox, who had fattened on his perquisites as Paymaster of the Forces. On the death of his father, Fitzmaurice, as the new Lord Shelburne, gave up a seat in the Commons for one in the Lords. In the negotiations for peace carried on in secrecy by Lord Bute with the Duc de Choiseul during 1761-63, Shelburne, a strong advocate of ending the war on the Continent, learned a good deal which he would use to advantage twenty years later under similar circumstances.[62]

Shelburne's reputation for deception, for being a "bad bed-fellow under the most favorable circumstances,"[63] stemmed from the unpleasant negotiations he had to carry on with Henry Fox to induce the Paymaster to give up his profitable office in return for a peerage. Fox became Shelburne's implacable foe, and his more famous son carried on the feud. Obsessed by the personal sacrifice the country demanded, the elder Fox accused Shelburne of having betrayed him. Shelburne's conduct was "a pious fraud," Bute was reported by the biased Walpole to have told Fox. "I can see the fraud plainly enough," the retired statesman is said to have retorted, "but where is the piety?"[64] Later a squib writer in the popular press called

Shelburne "a perfect Malagrida," comparing him to the Portuguese Jesuit who some years before had been strangled and burnt for his alleged part in a conspiracy. His reserved, cautious, even secretive nature, his habit of holding his cards close to his waistcoat, his private uncharitable judgments of his patrons, created the public image of the "Jesuit of Berkeley Square," the site of the town home that Shelburne purchased from Lord Bute. Nothing happened during the negotiations of the peace to efface that image.

Shelburne's grasp of American affairs had been demonstrated both as President of the Board of Trade in the Grenville Ministry, and as Colonial Secretary under Chatham. Although he asserted the imperial power in legislative matters as forcefully as did Pitt, he had been opposed to the Stamp Act, viewed the Declaratory Act as an imprudent measure, favored giving the colonial judges tenure for good behavior as in England, and sympathized with colonial pressures for Western settlement.[65]

Shelburne devoted his periods of retirement from politics to the prudent management of his Wiltshire estate at Bowood. Although the big house no longer stands, the Adam Diocletian Wing, the terraces, Keene's courtyards, and the chapel with the Barry clock tower, along with the artificial lake, preserve some of the grandeur that was Bowood's in those days. At Bowood Shelburne collected a great library, and cultivated advanced thinkers like Adam Smith, Richard Price, Benjamin Franklin, and the Abbé Morellet, with whom he carried on a correspondence for many years.[66] His previous experience, reading, and intellectual contacts all shaped his thoroughgoing radical convictions.[67] Shelburne was a prophet rather than a politician. His ideas on free trade were not enacted into law until 1846. In his hostility to primogeniture, the rule of descent of real property to the eldest son, he proved to be a century and a half ahead of his time in England. His advocacy of both Parliamentary and revenue reform stamped him as one of the advanced thinkers of his generation. As he himself would be the first to acknowledge, there was an "immense distance between planning and executing."[68] His nation, perhaps ill-advisedly, was never to permit him to do too much of the latter.

At the start Rockingham proposed to open negotiations with Congress "in manner and form as with an independent state," to evacuate British forces from Charleston, Savannah, and New York, and to enter into a truce of from four to six months.[69] This proposal made no headway owing to the fierce rivalry between Shelburne and Fox. Rumors quickly spread that, as Digges put it to Adams, "Lord Shelburne is the only new minister suspected of not wishing to go the length of declaring American independence."[70] The Earl's recent speeches in Parliament suggested that there was more to this than rumor. By insisting that negotiations with the rebellious Americans fell to his department so long as their independence was not recognized, Shelburne sought to control the American phase of the peace negotiations. Contrariwise, Fox, expecting to direct the negotiations with all the belligerents, openly advocated the unconditional recognition of American independence, not only to assert control over the peacemaking but also in the hope that by concluding quickly with the Americans he could force France to terms. Between the two Secretaries the line of demarcation was continually overstepped. Both pressed tactics of their own to achieve a separate peace with the Americans. Both rushed their own envoys across the Channel,[71] but Shelburne's man, Richard Oswald, arrived first.

The Scottish merchant, who appeared earlier as the author of a plan to win aid for England by allowing Russia a free hand along the Pacific coast of the Americas, had a habit of anticipating the American position and was unusually sympathetic to American propositions. His ideas about the strategy of the peace negotiations are revealed in an undated memorandum to Shelburne written around this time. "I always supposed we must satisfy the Americans," Oswald wrote, "in such manner as to have a chance of soothing them into neutrality." If the colonies could be satisfied by a grant of independence, then Oswald "submitted to better judges whether it ought not to be done without delay as an introductive preliminary to a general peace." Thus the gratitude of the Americans would be "brought to trial." Then it would be seen whether they would stand by their allies or drop out of the war, allowing England to turn all its force against the three remaining belligerents. The first order of business, Oswald advised, was to sound out the American commissioners to find out how they stood on a separate peace.[72]

Oswald crossed the Channel by way of Ostend and conferred with Franklin at Passy on April 12th. He gave it as his "private opinion" that the people of England desired a separate peace with the colonies. Franklin made it clear at once that, while the Americans were prepared to treat for peace, they would do so only in concert with their ally. The old doctor, Oswald reported, showed him "a good deal of civility," but was "sparing of his words." In turn the Scot warned Franklin that England was prepared to fight on rather than accept a humiliating peace. As an indication of her financial readiness to continue war, he mentioned that Parliament was prepared to impose an income tax of 25 percent. Franklin's reaction was characteristic. "Perhaps it should not be the worse for them," he remarked, wasting little sympathy on the new sacrifices ahead for Britain's taxpayers. Since Franklin had reminded Oswald of the obligations under the alliance, the latter sought to find out whether America was bound to guarantee the conquests of France and to feel out Franklin about France's peace objectives.

Franklin's own behavior toward Oswald at this time revealed a curious ambivalence. He confirmed the unity of the allies in war and peace by taking Oswald to Versailles on April 17th. There Vergennes, through Rayneval as interpreter, made it clear that France would not agree to England's making a separate truce or other agreement with the colonies, and that France's treaty with the United States barred such a separate peace. The Comte looked over at Franklin, and the doctor nodded in assent. Only a general peace could conclude the war, Vergennes asserted, and such a peace would have to include all the belligerents. He then reminded Shelburne's emissary of the role the mediators had already played, and while he alluded to St. Petersburg, he seemed to put more emphasis on Vienna. Some talk followed about the site of the peace congress. Vergennes threw out the suggestion of Paris, which Oswald found perfectly agreeable. So far Vergennes would go, but he was not prepared to take up Oswald's suggestion that "the great outlines of such negotiations" be drawn up at that time, so that he might transmit them to his superiors in England. He declined to make any propositions. "They must come from the King of England," Vergennes insisted. George III, he pointed out, had no one else to consult. The King of France, on the other hand, had commitments to various allies, particularly Spain, and could not venture to formulate proposals until Madrid had been consulted. All this would involve a good deal of delay. Again Franklin nodded in assent.

When Oswald went to dine at Franklin's the following day to pick up his passport for Calais, the doctor told him he would like to breakfast with him the next morning before the Scot set out for the return journey. At the leavetaking breakfast the pair spent an hour of "familiar conversation." Franklin took the occasion to turn over to Oswald a confidential paper which he was careful never to reveal to Vergennes. In it he pointed out that the cession of Canada to the United States would solve a number of problems. It would promote a durable reconciliation while at the same time removing a seedbed of animosity. The vacant lands of Canada's vast domain could provide funds both to indemnify Americans for houses burnt by British troops and their Indian allies and to compensate the Loyalists for the confiscation of their estates in America.

Franklin did not press the Canadian proposal as an ultimatum. Indeed, he had no authority to do so. It was merely a suggestion, and he went so far as to imply that it might be more prudent for England to make the offer without even waiting upon a demand from America. For England to give up this territory upon demand might be "humiliating," the doctor conceded. He also admitted, "Perhaps America will not demand it. . . . Some of her political rulers," he added gratuitously, might "consider the fear of such a neighbour as a means of keeping the thirteen States more united among themselves and more attentive to military discipline." A voluntary renunciation, as distinguished from a cession on demand, he argued, would have "an excellent effect" on "the mind of the people in general."

Had Oswald himself been permitted to lay down peace terms Franklin's proposal would have been accepted with alacrity. He might well have felt, as did one correspondent of Shelburne at this time, that the cession of Canada would cause a breach between France and America.[73] Had he been an American, Oswald set down in his Journal under date of May 6th, he would have insisted that all the settled parts of the continent, including Canada, Nova Scotia, Newfoundland, and East Florida, must "be brought under the cover of one and the same political constitution." Believing that the Americans would never become manufacturers, he viewed their prospective expansion into the interior and even to Canada as advantageous to Britain. He was concerned less about the territorial aggrandizement of the Thirteen States than about their naval potential should they remain confederated.[74] Oswald told Franklin that "nothing in his judgment could be clearer, more satisfactory and convincing than the reasonings in the paper," and he assured him that he would do his utmost to convince Lord Shelburne of its merits.[75] So pleased was Franklin with Oswald's reaction that he gave him a letter to Shelburne in which the doctor declared: "I desire no other channel of communication between us than that of Mr. Oswald, whom I think Your Lordship has chosen with much judgment."[76]

The old doctor had some sober second thoughts about the memorandum he had turned over to Oswald. In reporting his conversations with Oswald to John Adams he pointedly omitted the paper on "Notes for Conversation" with the Scot. Franklin records that he "gave the substance" of the "Notes" in his letter to Adams, but that he carefully avoided mentioning the proposal of compensating the Tories for the estates that had been confiscated. "On reflection," the doctor admitted, "I was not pleased with my having hinted a reparation to Tories for their forfeited estates, and I was a little ashamed of my weakness in permitting the paper to go out of my hands."[77] Not knowing of the Loyalist proposal, Adams was enthusiastic about Franklin's ideas about Canada. If there was a real disposition to cede Canada, he wrote Franklin, there should be no difficulty in adjusting "all things between England and America, provided our allies also consented."[78]

All in all, "the old conjurer," as John Adams was wont to call the doctor, had given a curious performance. He had risked his reputation as a man of judgment and honor by entrusting an unofficial agent of an enemy power with an explosive document. It was his good fortune that the trust was not misplaced. At Shelburne's request Oswald left the paper with him for one night. With his customary secretiveness, Shelburne said nothing to the Cabinet, except to his confidant Dunning, and shrewdly avoided giving any answer in writing. For the time being Oswald kept his mouth shut.[79] Neither used the document to create a rift within the American peace delegation. Vergennes never learned about it, nor did Adams ever get the full picture, and he would have suspected the worst. Had Franklin seriously expected to obtain Canada, which was a declared peace objective of the American Congress, he does not seem to have presented a convincing case. Any British statesman who would turn over a vast piece of unconquered territory when he had been reliably informed that the nation with whom he was negotiating peace did not seriously demand it would have been committing political suicide. Franklin's suggestion for compensating the Loyalists found no support in his instructions and ran counter to American public opinion. It was to haunt the whole negotiations. It is inexplicable that the principal proponent of diplomatic unity with the French ally would entrust to an enemy's hands a document revealing that America was prepared to accept territory whose acquisition by the United States France had long opposed, and make such a proposal behind the backs of his good friends in the French Ministry.

In addition to Oswald, Shelburne had another ace up his sleeve, which he decided to play before Fox could show his hand. For over a year one of Congress' peace commissioners had been imprisoned in the Tower of London following his capture on the high seas. When he was seized Henry Laurens had been confident that he would be placed on parole. He had not counted on the vengeful spirit of the North Ministry and its implacable anti-Americanism. At the Tower he suffered a series of petty but persistent persecutions planned for his discomfiture by the Governor of the Tower. By chance Laurens met another inmate, Lord George Gordon, while taking a stroll on the armory pavement. He managed to avoid conversing with the voluble eccentric, but he was punished nonetheless by four days of close confinement.

Laurens' imprisonment aroused Edmund Burke to action on his

behalf, but it was Oswald, a long-time business associate of the South Carolinian, who solicited the Secretaries of State in the North Ministry for the prisoner's release on parole and offered "his whole fortune" as surety for the prisoner's good conduct. Laurens, who had earlier petitioned Parliament for special consideration on account of his long service "to preserve and strengthen the ancient friendship between Great Britain and the colonies,"[80] now informed Oswald that if placed on parole he would "do nothing, directly or indirectly, to the hurt of England," and would either return to America or remain in England as might be demanded. Such a pledge was clearly incompatible with Laurens' freedom of action as a minister plenipotentiary for the peace. Back in Philadelphia Laurens was censured by James Madison and only escaped recall by a sectional vote in Congress.[81] The North Ministry clung to the vain hope of securing Laurens' apostasy. When a shamefaced Oswald found his efforts in that direction fruitless, he then put up an eloquent argument with his old friend for a separate peace, and called America's alliance with France "a choke-pear." Laurens replied, "There is but one way under heaven for effecting a peace: Great Britain must formally or tacitly acknowledge the independence of the United States and withdraw her fleets and armies. Then the United States will treat; but only in terms of that alliance. Your administration forced that pear upon themselves. They must swallow it."[82]

On the very last day of the year 1781 the wretchedly ill Laurens was put into a sedan chair and carried to Searjeant's Inn, where in the presence of the arch-Tory Lord Mansfield, bail was posted for him by Richard Oswald and Oswald's nephew, John Aulem. Then the prisoner was released. From that moment he was courted by the Whigs[83] in the expectation that he might prove an instrument for effecting a separate peace with America. From that moment, too, he was suspect by the French, who had grave doubts about the propriety of a parolee's participation in the peace negotiations and even questioned his loyalty.[84]

Shelburne had several interviews with Laurens on coming into office. The Earl made it clear that he viewed the independence of the United States with regret and that he was confident that the Americans "would not be so happy without, as with the connection with Great Britain."[85] In one of the more amusing interchanges Shelburne let it be known that he feared lest by separating from Great Britain the United States lose the benefit of the Habeas Corpus Act. Considering that his solicitude was expressed to one who had passed an extended period in the Tower of London without enjoying the benefits of that act, Shelburne's concern does seem rather naïve. To Sir William Meredith, who called on Laurens at the Earl's request and presented him with a volume that he had written on the Habeas Corpus Act, Laurens pointedly remarked, "You cannot in England liberate a prisoner with so much facility as we can do in America." Apparently it had not occurred to Shelburne or to his legal adviser that the Thirteen United States were perfectly free to incorporate into their legal system so much of the English law as they might wish to adopt, and that to a large extent this had been done long before independence.

Shelburne did not seem averse to stretching the facts if thereby he might open a breach between America and France. On April 4th he showed Laurens a letter he claimed to have received from Digges at The Hague. Whether it was the actual letter or a doctored version is not clear. Perhaps Laurens was given only a glimpse of it. As the American recalled the letter he had seen, the secret agent of Lord North had therein falsely implied that he had Adams' assurance that he could treat for peace independently of France.[86] Actually Digges, as we know now, never had gone that far in his report. Instead, he had told all and sundry that "he will give his head if a separate peace is made either with Holland or America."[87]

"It is generally a hard matter, my Lord, to prove a negative," Laurens replied on being told of Digges's report. "In the present case I think the business would be difficult."

"If you have doubts," Shelburne rejoined, "I wish you could make it convenient to converse with Mr. Adams yourself."

With Shelburne's guarantee of his personal liberty, Laurens agreed to leave for Holland two days later. The day before he left England Richard Oswald told his old friend in secrecy of his own impending mission to Paris to talk with Franklin. Laurens gave him a letter to the doctor commending Oswald as a man of "the strictest candor and integrity," whom he had known for almost thirty years. Laurens conceded that, while Franklin had a reputation for knowing how to handle a shrewd person, he could be quite frank with an honest one. He also took the occasion to let Franklin know of his own trip to The Hague. "Infirm" as he was, he declared, he was willing "to attempt doing as much good as can be expected from such a prisoner upon parade."[88]

Oswald and Laurens proceeded together to Margate. They talked in public of going to Ostend "for a frolic," hired a packet and, after making the Channel crossing, separated. It was agreed that whoever returned first would wait at Sittingbourne, some forty miles from London, until the other had arrived, and they would exchange information before proceeding to the capital.

Laurens put up in Haarlem at the Golden Lion, and there Adams journeyed to see him. Adams was rather curt. He asked Laurens whether he was at liberty. Laurens replied, as Adams reported it, "No. I am still under parole, but at liberty to say what I please to you." Since Laurens was technically a prisoner, Adams did not feel free to communicate to him even his own instructions, nor even to consult with him as a colleague in the commission for peace. He would merely talk as "one private citizen conversing with another."

Adams gave the lie to everything Shelburne had attributed to Digges. There never could be "a real peace" between England and America, Adams insisted, unless Canada and Nova Scotia were in American hands. At the very least, he urged, there ought to be a stipulation in the peace treaty forbidding England from maintaining a standing army or erecting any forts on the frontiers of either province. His parting words to Laurens were calculated to bolster the latter's resistance to British pressure. America was not especially anxious for peace now, he pointed out, and if England "was not ripe for it upon proper terms," America was prepared to wait her out. In turn, Laurens cautioned Adams that Shelburne still flattered the King "with ideas of conciliation and a separate peace."[89]

Upon returning to England Laurens waited for two days at Sittingbourne until Oswald appeared. The Scot confided that, on the basis of his conversations with Franklin, he would not return to Paris or be employed in any treaty "without authority in his pocket to acknowledge the independence of the United States." The Laurens who conferred with Shelburne upon his return from Holland was a very different man from the American prisoner with whom the Earl had previously conversed. Shelburne found the South Carolinian "*changed*, touchy and conceited, vulgarly so." The Colonial Secretary kept his temper with some difficulty, bearing in mind, as he told the King, that Laurens "must be managed on account of his fundamental aversion to France, and not being devoted to any of his colleagues."[90] Shelburne continued to dangle the imperial connection before Laurens' eyes. He assured the American that "the Constitution of Great Britain is sufficient to pervade the whole world" and expressed the hope that America would be content to stand upon the same footing as Ireland. Laurens tactfully reminded Shelburne that his task was to concentrate on making peace at his back door, not molding a constitution for a people three thousand miles away. When Laurens told Shelburne that Digges had lied and that independence "must be a preliminary and the ultimatum," the Earl replied, "If it must be so, I shall be sorry for it, for your sakes." Later at a time when he had disengaged himself from the peace negotiations, Laurens criticized Shelburne for never having entertained "one forethought of the awkwardness of attempting to wheedle a people after seven years' inefficacious efforts to beat them into compliance." The conviction grew upon him that, although Shelburne had tacitly agreed with him that independence would have to be granted and then even went so far as to instruct Oswald to admit independence as a preliminary, he had no serious intention of acknowledging American independence.[91]

Shelburne's private disinclination to grant America unconditional independence was buttressed by the division of authority over the peacemaking which the Cabinet had authorized. On April 23rd the Cabinet decided to send Richard Oswald back to Paris with authority to name that city as the place for holding the peace negotiations and to set a timetable with Franklin for the start of the negotiations. He was instructed "to represent to him that the principal points in contemplation are the allowance of independence to America, upon Great Britain being restored to the situation she was placed in by the Treaty of 1763." On the other hand, the Cabinet refrained from conferring plenipotentiary powers upon Oswald, and instead authorized Charles James Fox to propose to the King a person who would begin direct negotiations with Vergennes.[92]

The duel between the rivals had now begun in earnest. Shelburne hastened to advise George III that Oswald should be sent back to Paris at once else the King's "interest would suffer severely." Whether to placate the King or because he himself still felt that way, he confessed his chagrin at the terms Oswald would be empowered to propose. Under other circumstances, Shelburne said, he would have sought to avoid responsibility "for a measure which is repugnant to all my passions and all my principle, if necessity did not compel it."[93] The King, who thoroughly agreed with Shelburne on the necessity of having Oswald in Paris as "an useful check on that part of the negotiation that is in other hands," approved the letter the Scot was to take to Franklin. The King even indicated that it would be proper for Shelburne to talk with Fox's emissary to Vergennes.[94] It was clear, then, that from the start of the negotiations by the new Ministry both George III and his Colonial Secretary contemplated Shelburne's exercising paramount authority over the entire negotiations of the peace.

Shelburne showed his hand quite early and in characteristic fashion. He was not prepared to put all his eggs in one basket and trust to the goodwill of the American negotiators in Paris. Notwithstanding the fiasco of the Carlisle Commission to Congress in 1778, he decided to make another direct appeal to Congress and the American people. This overelaboration of method Shelburne's critics would call "duplicity." If any duplicity was practiced on this occasion, it clearly was not toward the King or Cabinet, who were fully apprised of the mission, which Rockingham personally endorsed as contributing to the "safety of our forces at New York."[95] More charitably this devious move might be put down to an excess of caution. Shelburne entrusted this delicate mission to Sir Guy Carleton and Admiral Robert Digby, respectively military and naval commanders in chief in North America, instructing them to inform Congress through General Washington of the change in both administration and policies which had taken place in England and to take all possible steps "to revive old affections or extinguish late jealousies," or, to put it more strongly, "to reconcile and reunite the affections and interests of Great Britain and the colonies," and secure the safety of the Loyalists.[96] As if to emphasize his personal involvement in the fate of this mission, Shelburne dispatched his private secretary, Maurice Morgann, to join Carleton in New York.[97]

The new mission to America was an egregious blunder. Morgann started out with high optimism, buoyed up by the rosy-tinted views held by the Loyalists in New York.[98] The situation soon forced him to make a sober reappraisal and to pass on to his chief in London the stern truth that "the fancy of independence has indeed struck so deep into the minds of the Americans that they must be suffered to run their course, for by arms alone, I am sufficiently persuaded, they cannot be subdued." But he clung to the forlorn hope that public opinion in America might still swing around toward the notion of a "restoration of the empire," to which Shelburne's name was so inescapably attached.[99] Everything went wrong. Washington would not cooperate. Congress not only refused to receive any envoy from Carleton, but adopted a resolution exposing "the insidious steps" of London to break the French alliance, and state after state, beginning with Maryland, reaffirmed the resolve of Congress.[100]

While the Carleton mission pursued its fumbling course in New York, the emissaries of Shelburne and Fox sought to get the Americans and the French to talk peace in Paris. Oswald returned to Paris on May 4th and, to Franklin's surprise, did not carry precise terms of peace.[101] He turned over to the doctor at Passy a letter from Shelburne, which merely confirmed that the Scot was to settle with Franklin "the preliminaries of time and place," and informing the doctor that the Foreign Secretary would soon send over a "proper person" to confer with Vergennes.[102] Oswald also showed Franklin an extract from the Cabinet meeting of April 23rd tying American independence to a restoration of England's position under the Treaty of 1763. Oswald returned to Franklin the "Notes" which the doctor had been so indiscreet as to commit to paper, along with Shelburne's expression of hope that "matters might be settled" to America's satisfaction toward the end of the treaty, but that they "might not be mentioned at the beginning." Franklin took this purposefully ambiguous remark to refer to Canada, whereas Shelburne had carefully avoided making any commitment on that score to Oswald. Though shot through with ambiguity, Shelburne's instructions indicate that he had no intention of yielding Canada and was not ready to consider independence. In his verbal instructions he told Oswald that he would refuse to consider paying reparations to Americans out of Canadian lands, that he had no intention of acknowledging American independence without the Loyalists "being taken care of," and, instead of ceding Canada, expressed a preference that "some more friendly method will be found."

Oswald preferred to stress the constructive rather than the negative side of Shelburne's instructions. Shelburne asked Oswald to propose some kind of federal union, but should the Americans reject it and insist upon independence, he told his emissary, "It will be done roundly and so as to obviate occasion for future wars." More inclined than the Colonial Secretary to meet America better than halfway, Oswald pounced upon this hint to suggest on his own that Britain was prepared to make generous territorial concessions. Did this mean Canada? Shelburne's instructions clearly imply the contrary. He advised Oswald that he was prepared, in accordance with the Cabinet resolve, to evacuate New York, Charleston, and Savannah, but planned to retain British positions in Maine. As the Shelburne memorandum puts it, "Penobscot to be alwise kept." At the time Shelburne was preparing his instructions for Oswald he had before him some memoranda proposing the setting up of a civil government at Penobscot to create a buffer between Nova Scotia and the rebellious colonies and to harass American shipping off the northern New England coast.[103] How seriously Shelburne took these proposals is not known, but it seems obvious that he would hardly have planned to hold on to Maine if he had not not also intended to retain territory farther north.

Shelburne at this time was not prepared to retreat too far. "Lord Shelburne will never give up the Loyalists," reads the memorandum covering his oral instructions to Oswald, which also specified the recognition of all debts owing to British subjects. Oswald was instructed further to insist upon America's terminating her connection with France, and on British ships being allowed free trade to every port in America. The Earl was most tenacious, though, on the score of independence. He told Oswald to make a point of letting Franklin know that "the country at large is no way reconciled to independence," a view substantiated in part by the steady flow of anti-independence letters which continued to be directed to the Earl after his accession to office. His correspondents urged "a constitutional reconciliation," or "reunion," a status for America comparable with that of Ireland, a united Parliament for both England and America, or two American Congresses, one for the North, and another for the South. "Grant America a constitutional freedom, but by no means unconditional independence," one correspondent wrote Shelburne as late as July, 1782, while others retailed gossip indicating that the Americans themselves were leaning toward reunion.[104] Oswald was told to warn Franklin that should negotiations break down those elements opposed to independence would be very likely to take over the government. Hence, it is now or never. Finally, Oswald was advised to tell Franklin in confidence the special way in which Shelburne stood with the King, information calculated to undermine Fox's emissary at Paris.[105] Oswald was shrewd enough to keep to himself most of Shelburne's ill-flavored instructions.

The envoy who next appeared upon the scene was Thomas Grenville, a son of George Grenville, whose ill-conceived Stamp Act touched off the Revolutionary agitation. On May 8th Oswald brought Grenville over to Passy to pay his respects to Franklin. Grenville was Fox's man, and the Foreign Secretary's views on the peace were already rather well publicized. To the Duc de Lauzun Fox had made a pious profession of peace. "Please God that it is near," he wrote.[106] Fox had instructed his envoy to name Paris for the peace talks provided Vienna and Petersburg would not be offended. Grenville was to use his discretion in stating peace terms and was to be prepared to accede to the "complete independency of the Thirteen American states," including the cession of New York, Charleston, and the entire province of Georgia. Otherwise matters were to be restored to the situation as they obtained under the Treaty of Paris of 1763. Grenville was to make a special point of insisting on the acquisition of the island of St. Lucia. In addition, he was told to sound out Franklin on the chances for a separate peace with America should the general negotiations be broken off, as "his countrymen" would then "be engaged in a war" in which they could have "no interest whatever either immediate or remote."[107]

From the first meeting Franklin made it clear to Grenville that America intended to adhere to her two treaties with France, and indicated that France herself would scarcely rest content merely with the independence of America. Probably at Vergennes' prompting, he even put in a word for Spain's claim to Gibraltar, pointing out that, since the British had lost Minorca and had "less commerce to defend," there was little reason to hold on to the Rock.[108] Franklin's first impression of Grenville was of "a sensible, judicious, good-tempered, and well-instructed young man." He so wrote Fox in a note in which he expressed the hope that Grenville's coming might "forward the blessed work of pacification."[109]

Shepherded by Franklin, Grenville paid his court at Versailles the following morning.[110] In the course of two long conversations with Vergennes he saw fit to ignore Franklin's hint and bluntly told the Foreign Minister that, since American independence was the object of the war, once that was conceded, England should recover the conquests France had made of British islands. In turn, she would convey back to the French the little fishing islands of St. Pierre and Miquelon that the English had seized in the course of the war.

The Englishman's notion of *quid pro quo* drew an enigmatic smile from Vergennes. For years the Comte had been talking about the King's desire for "justice" and "dignity." He even used these words in his talks with Grenville. As the war unfolded, however, Vergennes more and more came to yield to the pressures of various interest groups seeking adjustments, particularly in the East and West Indies. In addition, he could not ignore Spain's professed objectives, nor be indifferent to Holland's. As Vergennes expounded his views, "justice" and "dignity" sounded in Grenville's ears like demands of "a most ungovernable extent." Suddenly the veil was dropped from the pious professions of France's disinterested object in going to war. American independence was not "the only cause of the war," Vergennes asserted, for France had found, and not made, American independence. The Treaty of 1763 badly needed revision, he reminded his listener; better arrangements must be made for the fisheries, and hints were thrown out of extensive changes in India. Why could not the British content themselves with Bengal? the Comte asked Grenville. "Truly, your arms are grown too long for your body!" Much the same point was made the next day by the Conde de Aranda, who pointed out to Grenville how Spanish objectives differed from American and who found the British negotiator irresolute and prolix.[111]

Grenville and Oswald at this time seemed to be working in harmonious cooperation. The former confided to the Scot France's views on the need for changes in India and quoted Franklin as having told him that, once the colonies received their independence, "their treaty with France was at an end." To both emissaries it was evident that France and Spain were setting a high price for peace. England's best hope now was to make terms with America, get her out of the war, and then concentrate her fire on her traditional Continental foes. To pass on this advice to the government and in turn secure further instructions it was decided that Oswald should set out at once for London.

On the following day, May 13th, Franklin by chance called upon Oswald at his lodgings and surprised him in the business of packing. As Oswald reported it, in a memorandum from Calais, Franklin assured him that once the American states had gained their objective, "*they desired no more*," and that, when this was attained, he would be "happy" to be of service. If correctly quoted, what did Franklin really mean? The doctor had already made it clear that he felt no need for outside mediators. While Oswald was not quite sure, he was delighted nonetheless that Franklin was less guarded than Vergennes and that the American "spoke the language more of a philosopher" than of one "fettered by the ties of a particular Commission."[112] From Oswald's optimism Shelburne might well have concluded that America could be induced to make a separate peace.

Franklin may have thrown out a few hints, which was his style, but he was certainly not prepared to spell them out any further. To the contrary, he recorded the position he had expressed to the emissaries in quite different language from that which they seemed to have recollected. In a talk with Grenville on May 14th he spoke very much along the lines of his long series of letters to his old friend Hartley. Grenville pressed Franklin. Would America, he asked, once independence had been granted her, feel bound to support demands pressed by her ally if they were unreasonable? Franklin treated his young interrogator to a lecture, making his point in characteristic fashion by considering a homely hypothetical case:

A, a stranger to B, sees him about to be imprisoned for a debt by a merciless creditor; he lends him the sum necessary to preserve his liberty. B then becomes the debtor of A, and, after some time repays the money. Has he then discharged the obligation? No. He has discharged the money debt, but the obligation remains, and he is a debtor for the kindness of A in lending him the sum so seasonably. If B should afterwards find A in the same circumstances that he, B, had been in when A lent the money, he may then discharge this obligation or debt of kindness, *in part,* by lending him an equal sum. *In part,* I said, and not *wholly,* because when A lent B the money there had been no prior benefit received to induce him to it. And therefore if A should a second time need the same assistance, I thought B, if in his power, was in duty bound to afford it to him.

"Isn't this carrying gratitude to some lengths?" Grenville asked. No, Franklin answered. He could find no acceptable arguments for lessening America's obligation to France.[113]

Significantly, Grenville left Franklin's hypothetical case out of his report, in which the talk sounded a different note. "Mr. Franklin's conversation," he told Fox, "has, at different times, appeared to me to glance towards" suggesting that, upon a grant of independence, America might cease supporting the pretensions of France and France's allies. As he related his interview of that very morning, Franklin was quoted as remarking that, once independence was ceded, the treaty with France was terminated, and none remained but that of commerce, "which we too might make if we please."[114]

How much purposeful confusion was concealed in Franklin's talks with the British peace envoys and how much wishful thinking colored their reporting of his remarks is impossible now to determine with precision. Franklin continued to tell Oswald and Grenville that the United States would not make a separate peace, while at the same time he kept throwing out broad hints that, should independence be granted, the influence of the United States might be brought to bear to bring about a general peace settlement.[115] There continued to be a divergence in tone, and to some extent in fact, between the reports by Oswald and Grenville of their conversations with Franklin and the way in which he summed them up in his "Journal." Allowing for the tendency of his auditors to phrase his guarded remarks in their own optimistic language, it would still seem that the old doctor managed to cloak his talks with calculated ambiguity. What he said to the British emissaries, or what he was reported to have said, satisfied both Fox and Shelburne that in the event France persisted in her immoderate course Franklin would, as Shelburne phrased it, "consider himself and his constituents freed from the ties which will appear to have been founded upon no ideas of common interest."[116] On June 1st Franklin deftly evaded the question that Grenville put to him as to how far America's obligations extended to the other belligerents. Once the preliminaries were settled, Franklin answered, then if the other powers pressed "extravagant demands on England" and insisted upon America's continuing in the war until they were complied with, it would "be time enough to consider what our obligations were and how far they extended."[117] In short, for the British emissaries a visit to Franklin at Passy must have been as stimulating to the imagination as a trip by ancient Greek statesmen to the Delphic oracle.

As Fox saw it, Franklin's position was crucial. Since Vergennes' reported views were so "very unfavourable to the expectation of any fair or equitable peace," and a breakdown of the negotiations at Versailles seemed imminent, Fox sought to detach some of France's allies and "to gain some for this country."[118] If that was Fox's game in the spring of '82 his agent in Paris could derive only small crumbs from his talks with Franklin. While much has been written about the rivalry of Shelburne and Fox and the way this power struggle shaped their respective peace tactics, the basic objectives of the otherwise discordant pair seem to have been in essence the same at this time. As Vergennes had shrewdly anticipated,[119] both were more concerned with separating America from France than with ending the war.[120] Both sought the latter's diplomatic isolation.

Grenville's relations with Franklin quickly deteriorated. When he next visited the doctor Fox's envoy informed him that he brought along full powers to treat for peace "with France and her allies." In exchange for this news Franklin let Grenville have a copy of the treaty of alliance between France and America, an item that had been widely publicized long before. The Marquis de Lafayette quickly disabused Franklin as to the extent of Grenville's powers. Lafayette, who at this stage of the negotiations played the rather ambiguous roles of assisting Franklin by direction of Congress and of serving as intermediary between Passy and Versailles,[121] informed the doctor that the full powers received by Grenville related to France only.[122] Vergennes confirmed this when Franklin dined with him on May 28th. "They want to treat with us for you," the Comte told him, "but this the King will not agree to. He thinks it not consistent with the dignity of your state. You will treat for yourselves, and every one of the powers at war with England will make its own treaty. . . . All that is necessary for our common security," the Comte added, "is that the treaties go hand in hand, and are signed all the same day."[123] Two days later Vergennes told Grenville that the issue of independence should be treated by Britain in direct negotiation with the United States rather than with France, which had no authority over the question.[124]

Momentarily it seemed as though Fox's chances were bright of separating America from her ally and obtaining a moderate peace from the other belligerents. On May 23rd the Cabinet authorized him to propose American independence in the first instance rather than to make it a condition of a general treaty,[125] but he failed to have the Cabinet supplant Oswald and concentrate all negotiations in Grenville's hands. Whatever the tentative decision of the Cabinet regarding independence, it is clear that neither Shelburne nor George III accepted it. Instead, Shelburne sent Oswald back to Paris with instructions to proffer peace "either general or separate" as the price of independence, and it was perfectly understood both by the Earl and the King that England was not "bound by the propositions if peace is not the consequence." So serious did the King regard the issue of offering independence *conditionally* rather than outright that he applauded Shelburne's precaution in having a witness in the person of Dunning to his conversations with Oswald.[126]

Around this time British hopes were buoyed up momentarily by the news that on April 12th Rodney had won a smashing naval victory over de Grasse in the West Indies. Neither the new concession nor the good news could be effectively exploited by the Foreign Secretary. Instead of succumbing to appeasement, France took Rodney's victory in stride both on the fighting and diplomatic fronts. "I have lost five ships," Louis XVI was quoted as saying. "I will build fifteen to take their place and one will not find me on this account more tractable at the peace."[127] Vergennes quickly pointed out to Grenville that the latter's full power was insufficient as it did not empower him to treat with the other belligerents, and Franklin again reminded Fox's envoy that America would make no separate peace or truce. The Frenchman and the American repeated their contention that Britain's offer of independence could not be considered as a concession to France.[128]

Grenville now recognized that he was losing ground with Franklin. When he called on the doctor on June 1st, the American pointed out that the discrepancy between the way Grenville had described his powers and the wording of the document itself served only to stir up suspicions at Versailles that England was stalling because of the favorable news from the West Indies. Grenville conceded that "he had no such special power in form" but insisted that his instructions "were full to that purpose." To convince Franklin of his court's sincerity he disclosed that "he was instructed to acknowledge the independence of America, previous to the commencement of the treaty."· Franklin was not to be taken in by words, particularly Grenville's, and the latter sought in vain to get a commitment from him that America would not continue in the war should Spain and Holland demand unreasonable terms. To Fox Grenville reported that his mission seemed headed toward a dead end.[129]

Day by day Grenville's stock was falling. Although Fox's man seemed empowered to offer America more than Oswald did, Franklin had already taken it upon himself to write Shelburne again expressing his hope that he would send Oswald back to Paris, as he prized "his moderation, prudent counsels, and sound judgment." Upon his return to Paris on May 31st, Oswald made no bones about the serious financial plight of England. Speaking with "an air of great simplicity and honesty," he confessed, "Our enemies may now do what they please with us. They have the ball at their foot. We hope they will show moderation and magnanimity." He gave Franklin a copy of a memorandum of Shelburne's, in which the Colonial Secretary indicated his readiness to correspond "more particularly" with the doctor, "if wished." Shelburne informed Franklin that the Enabling Act authorizing peace with America was about to be enacted by Parliament. He then remarked "that an establishment of the loyalists must always be on Mr. Oswald's mind, as it is uppermost in Lord Shelburne's," as well as "a fair restoration or compensation" by the several states for confiscations of Tory property.[130]

To correct the misapprehension that reparations to Tories and debtors were within the jurisdiction of the Confederation, Franklin pointed out that the states, not Congress, had confiscated Tory property, and that the latter had no authority over the matter and could give no power to its commissioners "to treat of a restoration for those people." Neither England nor America should feel under any obligation to them, Franklin contended. England had been drawn into the "miserable war" by the "misrepresentations and bad counsels" of the Tories, while on balance the ravages committed by the Loyalists "all along the coasts of America would more than make up for their sufferings." How about Canada? Franklin asked. Oswald replied that, though Rockingham and Shelburne "spoke reservedly," they did not seem "very averse" to the proposal for ceding Canada, but that Fox "appeared to be startled at the proposition." Still, Oswald was "not without hopes that it would be agreed to."

Franklin continued to find Oswald more conciliatory and sympathetic to America than Grenville, and did not conceal his hope that the former would continue to handle the American negotiations. Early in June the doctor told Oswald that the best way to reach a general peace was to treat separately with each party, and "under distinct commissions to one and the same, or different persons."[131] Shelburne accepted the proposal because it fitted in with his own notions.[132] In pressing separate negotiations, Franklin, it must be remembered, was in no sense defying the French, but merely passing on the proposal of Vergennes, who, as we have seen, had on May 28th told the American that the King approved the idea of separate negotiations and soon thereafter had disclosed this to Grenville. Oswald liked the notion too. He preferred being named to treat solely for America as he did not feel at home in the French language. To Franklin Oswald was "so good and reasonable" that it did seem a pity to have to turn the negotiations over to the twenty-six-year-old Thomas Grenville, possessed of some of the disingenuous traits associated with professional diplomats combined with the kind of ambition which would seek to capitalize on his skill as a negotiator.[133] A peace too unfavorable to England might well spell finis to Grenville's career.

Grenville was in for some unpleasant surprises when, on June 15th, he called on Franklin to let him know that he now possessed powers to treat with France and "with the ministers of any other Princes or States whom it might concern."[134] Instead of proposing American independence on condition of England's being put into the situation she was in at the peace of 1763, he was now ready and authorized, he stated, to *"declare the independence of America previous to the treaty* as a voluntary act, and to propose separately as a basis the treaty of 1763." Franklin did not seem properly responsive. He told Grenville that his powers did not cover America since Parliament had not yet passed the Enabling Act, and the British government had hitherto always regarded the Americans not as a "state" but as "rebellious subjects." When Grenville tried to turn to the broad topic of reconciliation, Franklin cut him off by showing him a copy of the issue of the London *Evening Post* that carried a report attributing to Grenville the disclosure that America had retained the power to treat *"separately* with Great Britain in case her claims or demands were granted."[135] Since his earlier conversations had been misrepresented, would it not be hazardous for us, he asked, to make propositions at present? Grenville pretended to treat the newspaper story lightly, but was plainly taken aback at the unlucky turn.

That same day Grenville had no better luck with Vergennes. He informed the Comte that the King was prepared to recognize the independence of the United States unconditionally, but coupled this announcement with a reminder of Britain's desire that the Treaty of Paris of 1763 serve as a basis for the new peace treaty. "Whenever I hear the reference to the Treaty of Paris it sends shivers up my spine," Vergennes rejoined. "Let us make a just and durable peace," the Frenchman added, "and forget about that treaty and all preceding ones."[136] The French Minister was less inflexible about this than one might have imagined. Whether it was due to a sober reappraisal of the naval defeat in the West Indies[137] or for other reasons equally obscure, the following week he told Grenville that, in addition to the unconditional recognition of the independence of the United States, he would agree to the Treaty of Paris as a basis, insisting nonetheless on new arrangements for the East Indies, Africa, and the Newfoundland fisheries, as well as a commerical arrangement for both nations in Europe. The Conde de Aranda, who joined the conference, requested Grenville to bring a separate power to treat for Spain.[138] Spanish *dignidad* presumably masked Spain's intention to delay negotiations until she could subdue Gibraltar. In the weeks that followed Grenville found the situation "unpromising." Aranda was insistent on Gibraltar. Franklin, who kept reminding him "that the sooner that independence was declared, the less would the business be retarded," let him know that America planned not only to take up "the limits of Canada," but "to have her share in the Newfoundland Fishery." Reading to Grenville a resolution passed by the Maryland Assembly on May 16th against making peace except in concert with France,[139] the doctor warned Grenville that no arrangement "short of compleat and distinct independence in its fullest sense" would be considered in America.[140]

In the widening rift between Grenville and Oswald Franklin played no small part. Capitalizing on the discord in the British Cabinet, the wily doctor gambled that Fox, despite his popularity, would lose, since Shelburne reputedly enjoyed the confidence of the King. He even contemplated writing Shelburne to urge that a commission be vested in Oswald, but then thought better of it. Instead, he wrote a note to the same purpose addressed to Oswald, which the Scot could show to Shelburne.[141] To avoid an open scandal, Shelburne had written Fox on May 20th suggesting full communication between their respective emissaries at Paris, each presumably to be instructed to work in his own sphere, to the end "that it may not be supposed in France there is or can be any difference among us upon the great subjects of Peace and War."[142]

The spark that touched off the powder keg was Franklin's earlier proposal for ceding Canada. Early in June Oswald let drop to Grenville for the first time the revelation of Franklin's confidential paper suggesting the advisability of ceding Canada to America.[143] Still smarting from Franklin's cool reception on June 1st, Grenville rushed to the conclusion that Oswald had told Franklin in his interview with the doctor of the previous day that he was about to be named commissioner for the American peace. The fact is that Oswald did not so inform Franklin until June 3rd. As if to rub salt in the wound, Lafayette had on June 1st laughingly remarked to Grenville that he "had just left Lord Shelburne's ambassador at Passy." His suspicions fully aroused, Grenville wrote a private letter to Fox warning him that Shelburne had all along intended to encroach upon his province. His bitterness spilled over toward Franklin, whom he accused of having encouraged him in the hope of establishing "a partial connection between England and America" while making at the same time such excessive demands upon Oswald. "Having lost thirteen provinces," Grenville could see little reason for England's giving away "a fourteenth." "Once more I tell you," Grenville declared, "I cannot fight a daily battle with Mr. Oswald and *his* secretary." He now asked to be recalled.[144]

Determined to force a showdown with Shelburne, Fox now asked

Grenville for further proofs of "the duplicity of conduct" of the Earl. "I have taken upon me," he wrote, "to show your letter to Lord Rocking-ham and Lord Cavendish, who are as full of indignation at its contents as one might reasonably expect honest men to be." Fox was even prepared to make an issue of the note relating to Canada, of which he had never previously heard, and to block the intended investment of Richard Oswald with full powers. Once the evidence was in his hands he would decide whether to force an open break with Shelburne or merely to secure Oswald's recall. "I own I incline to the more decisive measure," the impul-sive Secretary asserted, "and so, I think, do those with whom I must act in concert."[145] Meantime, while Franklin demurred to Grenville's revised powers and France and Spain stalled, Fox was instructed to make another attempt at conciliating Russia, and to state, that without "formally ad-mitting" the Armed Neutrality, England was prepared to make the prin-ciples of the Russian Declaration of February 25, 1780, the basis of a treaty between the two nations, but on condition that Russia obtain the neutrality of Holland.[146]

Within the Cabinet tension mounted. After the passage of the Enabling Act on June 17,[147] Shelburne pressed for the naming of Oswald as a separate commissioner. Fox sought to block the move, asserting that he had the right of conducting the negotiations himself, and that American independence should be granted even without a treaty of peace. Signifi-cantly, the Cabinet decided against Fox. The majority, while favoring independence in the first instance, felt that it should be incorporated in a treaty. That adverse decision left Fox little reason to stay in the govern-ment.[148]

Meantime, while the Cabinet was rocked by discord its titular head, the Marquess of Rockingham, lay dying of influenza, then sweeping Northern Europe in epidemic proportions. His critical condition was kept even from the King. Were he to die, who would take the helm and how would it affect American independence? George III knew that Shelburne, unlike Fox, was not likely to yield the point of independence "without the price set on it which alone could make this kingdom consent to it." Further-more, as the King saw it, the kind of peace which the Rockingham Cabinet might have agreed to would not have been popular with the country now that Rodney had smashed de Grasse. To ward off an ignominious peace it seemed essential to George that Shelburne succeed Rockingham, not by "being placed" in his shoes, or becoming "the head of a party when in reality he would be the slave of it. He must be the Minister placed on a broad bottom."[149] A few hours after this letter was written Lord Rockingham died.[150] Within days Charles James Fox, unable to block Shelburne's succession, and unwilling, in Burke's words, to act "as a clerk" in the new administration, resigned, leaving Shelburne master of the negotiations with America and the other belligerents.[151]

Shelburne notified Grenville that Fox's resignation would not bring about any changes in the measures of the King's government, particularly in his "ardent desire of peace."[152] Grenville, no longer as an actor but merely as a spectator, would soon see just what Shelburne meant, while the old doctor, who had done as much as anyone to nudge Grenville off the stage, could resume his inscrutable course with Richard Oswald, a negotiator after his own heart. Oswald and Grenville had left the ball at Benjamin Franklin's foot. With one quick kick he advanced it down the field.

XIII

THE LONG CLAY PIPE OF MR. JAY

THE ENDLESSLY WET SUMMER OF 1782 ruined the wine crop and chilled the spirits of the peacemakers. All summer fires burnt morning and evening, but everywhere the dampness clung, fitting the mood of mutual suspicion which settled over the peacemaking.[1] If anything, that mood was fortified by the change in the British Ministry with the consequent shake-up of its team of negotiators, as well as by the arrival of reinforcements to bolster the American side. On June 23rd John Jay and his family had reached Paris from Madrid and installed themselves in an apartment at the Hôtel de la Chine at the Palais Royal. The Jays found France, despite the wretched weather, to be an agreeable change of scene, and confidently looked forward to gayer times than they had enjoyed in Spain. Sally Jay soon became a familiar figure at the Opéra, where her likeness to Marie Antoinette never failed to create a stir upon her entry.[2]

Sally's devoted spouse had observed at close hand the way British agents operated in a foreign capital. What he had already seen in Madrid had only deepened his suspicions of the intentions of the mother country toward her rebellious daughter. Once in Paris, Jay was alerted to the touch-and-go state of the negotiations. The afternoon of his arrival he was cordially received by Franklin at Passy, and in the days immediately following he had talks with all the principals in the negotiations. He chatted with Vergennes, Rayneval, Grenville, and Oswald, and, accompanied by the doctor, paid a social call on the Conde de Aranda.[3]

In his talks with Jay Franklin revealed his troubled state of mind on the score of Britain's sincerity. "I hope our people will not be deceived by fair words," the doctor wrote one correspondent at this time, "but be on their guard, ready against any attempt that our insidious enemies may make upon us."[4] A fortnight earlier he had thrown out the hint to Vergennes that the belligerents prepare to renew the general war should Britain turn upon any one of them after making peace with the others.[5] From Vergennes' undersecretary Franklin and Jay learned that the British government, not content with General Carleton's publicized peace mission, had dispatched "artful emissaries" through the American countryside to stir up public opinion and put pressure on Congress to accept terms "similar to those settling with Ireland."[6] Franklin cautioned Robert R. Livingston that "however willing we might have been at the commencement of this contest to have accepted such conditions, be assured we can have no safety in them at present." He reminded the Secretary for Foreign Affairs that "the King hates us most cordially; and his character for falsehood and dissimulation is so thoroughly known that none even who call themselves his friends have any dependence upon him. . . . Once admitted to any degree of power and government among us, however limited," the doctor warned, George III would soon extend that power "by corruption, artifice, and force, till we are reduced to absolute subjection." In short, "we have no safety but in our own independence."[7]

Coincidentally, two Englishmen at this very moment approached Jay soliciting letters of introduction to persons in America. They struck him as agents to be planted in the States to sow dissension. He, too, warned Livingston that, judging from appearances, the British Ministry sought to get some emissaries into America, "either in an avowed or in a private character," and that it might be the path of prudence to admit no Englishman "in either character within our lines at this very critical juncture."[8] The third peace commissioner, John Adams, then in the course of winding up his taxing negotiations in Holland, shared his colleagues' doubts. The British Ministry was "really to be pitied," he remarked. In fact, as he saw it, "no party in England" seemed to possess enough influence "to dare to make the real advance" toward peace.[9]

The chief British ministers who, in Franklin's opinion, still flattered the King "with the hope of recovering his sovereignty over us in the same terms as we are now making with Ireland" survived the Cabinet shake-up following Rockingham's death. Except for Lord Chancellor Thurlow, the King's man, they were mostly Chatham and Rockingham adherents, who were not likely to contest Shelburne's handling of negotiations with America. Nor was trouble likely to come from the new faces in the Cabinet. The youthful William Pitt became Chancellor of the Exchequer. Replacing Shelburne as Home and Colonial Secretary was Thomas Townshend, afterward Lord Sydney. A stout adherent of Shelburne, he had been conspicuous in Parliament as a facile if superficial critic of the American War. To fill the place of Charles James Fox as Foreign Secretary Shelburne plucked Thomas Robinson, second Baron Grantham, from the retirement of his Yorkshire estate after years of service as minister at Madrid. Neither Townshend nor Grantham was permitted to make an important decision in the peacemaking on his own. Shelburne considered this delicate business as his own private preserve.[10]

Shelburne's elevation was the chief cause of the revived suspicions of the Americans. The Earl's first public move as head of the new government scarcely stamped him as a cordial adherent of American independence. In the hours after midnight on the ninth of July he dashed off a note to the King with the information that Fox planned to bring the question of American independence before the Commons, and to that end was "summoning every person possible to town." Before 8 A.M. that same morning the King reassured the Earl that he was "glad" to hear that Fox was ready to risk a vote on "unconditional independence." To stiffen Shelburne's resistance to such a move, George III reminded him that, in his opinion, "the Nation at large" was not prepared to accept the proposition. Consequently, the party opposing it would stand to win "great credit," and the public would rejoice "at seeing the question decided against the Leaders of Sedition."[11]

How shrewdly the King had gauged public opinion is revealed by newspaper comments and private letters of the period. Fox and his following "are fixed upon the ruin of this country," a Liverpool correspondent wrote the Earl. "Absolute unconditional independence of America would be the absolute unconditional ruin of Great Britain," another correspondent warned, while in Tory New York hopes were kept alive even in July of '82 that the rebellion might still be put down.[12] "Mr. Fox should remember that the rights of this country are not to be sported with," thundered London's *Morning Herald*, "and that the great body of the people differ with him on such a measure." The *Chronicle* accused Fox of striking at "the first jewel of the British Crown."[13]

Shelburne's extreme perturbation was not supported by events. Unwilling to risk a vote on the issue of unconditional independence, Fox took the floor of the Commons on July 9th to reveal that his resignation as Foreign Secretary had been prompted principally by his having been outvoted by the Cabinet on the issue of an unconditional grant of independence to America, a concession which he deemed "necessary to the salvation" of his own country. He had been checkmated by Shelburne, he charged, and the latter had been brought forward to head the Cabinet because he entertained "less friendly ideas" on the subject of American independence "than any of his numerous colleagues in office."[14]

Fox's personal attack left Shelburne no alternative but to answer, especially since, as one observer commented, no one else in the Commons ventured to say that he "thought well of him."[15] Rising in the Lords on the following day, the new First Lord of the Treasury reaffirmed his adherence to the principles of the Earl of Chatham, who had opposed government by party or faction. Shelburne went a step farther. He objected to vesting in the Cabinet the power of filling "all places" and "all vacancies." If this were done, the King, in Shelburne's eyes, "must then resemble the King of the Marratas, who had nothing of sovereignty but the name." In that eventuality, argued the Earl, "the monarchical part of the Constitution would be absorbed by the aristocracy."

Facing the issue of American independence, Shelburne confessed to the Lords that his opinions "were still the same," that he still regarded "the independence of America" to be "a dreadful blow to the greatness of this country." In words identical with those he had used shortly before entering the Rockingham Ministry, he reminded the Lords that, should independence be established, "the sun might be said to have set." To guard England from "so dreadful a disaster" Shelburne claimed that he had employed "every effort in public and private." Alas, circumstances had changed. "The fatal necessity" of granting independence now loomed "in full view." Yes, he might be obliged to yield to necessity, but, he assured his hearers, he would "yield to nothing short of necessity."

Shelburne turned next to the insinuations that the Americans, had they known his views about independence, would have been loath to treat with him. Quite the contrary. During the previous months as Secretary of State he had discovered that "there was no man with whom the Americans would more willingly treat than himself." Shelburne's speech ended on a note of subdued optimism. True, "the sun of England would set with the loss of America," but the speaker himself was resolved "to improve the twilight and to prepare for the rising of England's sun again." Because his words might well have carried an ambiguous ring to his auditors, the Earl, before resuming his seat, reassured his peers that "nothing was farther from his intention than to renew the war in America. The sword was sheathed, never to be drawn again."[16]

Shelburne's speech set off much buzzing on both sides of the Channel. What did it mean? In London the *Morning Herald* carped at the Earl's *double entendre* and confessed that no one who heard his speech could "comprehend what part his Lordship intends to take in respect to a jurisdiction over the Colonies."[17] Within a fortnight that same paper could state categorically that independence was to be granted "not *unconditionally,* as Mr. Fox wished it to be done" and to rejoice "that some regard, at least, is to be paid to the commerce of this country."[18]

Perhaps a clue to the real meaning of Shelburne's strange speech is offered by the King's address the following day at the close of the sessions of Parliament. George III took occasion to mention the "extensive powers" with which he was invested "to treat for reconciliation and amity with the colonies[19] which have taken arms in North America." While indicating his intention to seek "these objects," the King reminded Parliament that, however ardent he might be for peace, he was prepared to continue the war "to obtain fair and reasonable terms of pacification" should he not find his peaceful disposition reciprocated on the part of England's enemies.[20] From his private letters to Shelburne we know now that the King had not abandoned his position, that he still opposed unconditional independence, blamed Fox's precipitancy on that score for the delays in the negotiations, and was prepared to accept independence merely as the price of a general peace. "Common sense tells me," George put it in his inimitable syle, "that if unconditional independence is granted, we cannot ever expect any understanding with America, for then we have given up the whole and have nothing to give for what we want from thence."[21]

Horace Walpole's remark that upon the death of Rockingham the Crown devolved on the King of England[22] may be put down to partisan exaggeration. Nonetheless, it must be conceded that Shelburne was far less likely to ignore the King's wishes than any of Rockingham's followers, and that he appreciated the clever maneuvering that would be involved in getting George III to accept the cruel necessity of unconditional independence. Considerate of the King's feelings and pursuing the line he had marked out in Parliament, Shelburne continued for the better part of the summer to recoil from recognizing the United States by way of preliminaries. "Independence," as the Portuguese ambassador to London observed, was still "difficult to digest."[23]

Despite nagging doubts about Shelburne's intentions Franklin kept the initiative. The old doctor had only recently recovered from a slight bout of influenza, but Jay found him "in perfect good health." To quiet whisperings about Franklin in Congress he reported to Secretary Livingston that he considered Franklin a "valuable Minister and an agreeable companion," and that "his mind appears more vigorous than that of any man of his age I have known."[24] Such differences as were to arise between Franklin and Jay over procedural points in the negotiations never dimmed the cordiality of that relationship or clouded their basic agreement on all the main points at issue in the peacemaking. During the first part of July Jay was laid low with an attack of influenza, then epidemic in Paris, and confined to his apartment for several weeks.[25] Franklin carried on his talks with Oswald alone.

On the morning of July 10th the doctor had a two-hour session with the Scot. Without advance notice to Vergennes, he read to Oswald "a few hints" from a memorandum. Franklin, according to Oswald's account, divided his proposals into *necessary* and *advisable* articles. As regards the latter, Franklin conceded that while "he could not say he had any orders" relating thereto, or that they were "absolutely demanded," he felt nonetheless, as he had at the time of his May proposals, that "it would be advisable to England to offer" them "for the sake of reconciliation and her future interest."

The *necessary* articles included, first, "full and compleat independence to the Thirteen States," with all troops withdrawn; secondly, "a settlement of the boundaries of *their* colonies and the Loyal colonies;" third, confining the boundaries of Canada to what they were before the Quebec Act of 1774, which moved them south to the Ohio River, "if not to a still more contracted state on an ancient footing"; fourth, freedom of fishing on the Banks and elsewhere for both fish and whales. As regards the last point, Franklin did not raise the question of leave to dry fish on shore in Newfoundland, and Oswald did not remind him of the omission. A few days earlier Franklin had intimated to Grenville "for the first time" his views on the Canadian boundary and the fisheries, along with "distinct independence in its fullest sense."[26]

"As a friend" Franklin recommended certain *advisable* articles. These included the indemnification of persons whose homes were destroyed by the British or Indians. The sum involved, Franklin estimated, might run to five or six hundred thousand pounds, but it would not be "ill bestowed, as it would conciliate the resentment of a multitude of poor sufferers," who, lacking other sources of relief, "would keep up a spirit of secret revenge and animosity for a long time to come against Great Britain." He also suggested some sort of acknowledgment by act of Parliament "or otherwise" of Britain's "error" in bringing distress to her former subjects. In addition, Franklin proposed reciprocal shipping privileges in the ports of both Britain and Ireland on the one hand and America on the other. Lastly, he reverted to his favorite theme, "giving up every part of Canada," long an objective of the doctor's diplomacy.[27] He hardly strengthened his case, however, by conceding in advance, and for the second time, that Canada was not demanded by America in the nature of an ultimatum.

With characteristic caution Franklin declined to turn his memorandum over to Oswald. Before preparing more specific terms he would want to confer with Jay, he implied. Were England to settle on these terms, Franklin argued, she would be the beneficiary of substantial trade with America. According to Oswald, he ventured so far as to predict that "at last it might end in a federal union between them." Certainly no man had better qualifications to suggest such a union than the author of the Albany Plan of Union, which both colonies and mother country had rejected almost thirty years earlier. If Franklin did have such a long-range goal in mind it was not the one envisioned by Shelburne or the King, for the doctor hastened to make it clear that England would be "much disappointed" if she expected to retain some sort of sovereignty over the Thirteen States, "for they would yield nothing of that sort." Possibly he had in mind a customs union or an *entente cordiale*. As regards the latter, he made a point of letting Oswald see the "State of Aids" the Americans had received from France, seeking to impress upon him that the debts constituted "the only foundation of the ties France had over" America, "except gratitude." Oswald was not taken in that easily, however, and assumed that the ties between Versailles and Passy were as firm as ever.

Franklin talked about the American business being settled "by a separate commission," and from the tenor of the doctor's remarks Oswald assumed that in such a commission "the power of granting independence would be therein expressly mentioned." "No doubt," Franklin replied. From this remark Oswald jumped to the conclusion that Franklin was not especially sensitive to the distinction between the power of treating to include independence and the power to grant independence separately and then to treat about other matters. He was wrong. Franklin had all along felt that there was a significant difference, although he later was prepared to overlook it out of deference to Vergennes.

Franklin had made it clear to Oswald that it would be impossible to make provision in the treaty for reparations to the Loyalists. Perhaps the states themselves "might do something for them," but as commissioners they could "do nothing." Oswald, perhaps indelicately, reminded Franklin of his April memorandum, wherein he had suggested the possibility of providing reparation "on both sides" out of the "back lands of Canada." Franklin had regretted that slip as soon as he had made it, and he now hastened to correct it. He informed Oswald that the cession of those "back lands" was one of the *necessary* articles "without any stipulation for the loyal sufferers," whereas he still retained as an *advisable* article the indemnification of Patriot sufferers.[28]

A day's reflection only served to confirm Oswald in the view that the British in negotiating for the peace should differentiate between America and the other belligerents. As regards the latter, he advised Shelburne that "the more anxious we appear to be for peace, the more backward the people here will be, or the harder in their terms, which is much the same thing." Toward the American commissioners, on the contrary, the British should adopt a very different style. The Americans had shown a desire to treat and settle "on a separate footing from the other powers," and, Oswald felt obliged to say, "in a more liberal way." He counseled dealing with them "tenderly, and as supposed conciliated friends." Assuming that the Cabinet would not raise objections to Franklin's *necessary* articles, Oswald expressed the hope that so soon as he could get together with John Jay he would advise the Americans to soften the advisable articles or "drop them altogether." Despite his general optimism, Oswald was worried about the Americans. To Shelburne he vouchsafed a fervent wish that "we were done with these people, and as quickly as possible, since we have much to fear from them, in case of their taking the pet, and throwing themselves into more close connection with this Court and our other enemies."[29]

Franklin's informal peace proposals, relayed by Oswald as "Hints," constituted a liberal and sensible interpretation of the various sets of instructions the commissioners had received from Congress. The old doctor showed a lot more backbone than either the Congress or its Secretary for Foreign Affairs. The notorious dispatch of June 15, 1781, which instructed the commissioners to govern themselves by the advice and opinion of the King of France, narrowed down the conditions *sine qua non* to independence "by peace or truce" and the maintenance of the French alliance. "We think it unsafe at this distance to tie you up by absolute and peremptory directions upon any other subject" than these "two essential articles,"[30] Congress conceded, having already manacled the commissioners to the French Foreign Office. Congress had not completely lost sight of its war aims, however, for by its instructions of January 22, 1782, it reminded the commissioners of the importance of both boundaries and fisheries, in the attainment of which objectives the United States optimistically counted upon the backing of the French.[31]

Robert R. Livingston, under unremitting pressure from La Luzerne and Barbé-Marbois, actually surpassed Congress in watering down the original American claims. Only a few weeks before Congress adopted its January, '82, instructions, and entirely on his own, the Secretary for Foreign Affairs wrote Franklin a curious letter, in which he managed to advance and retreat at the same time. He argued that the American title to the territory east of the Mississippi was founded upon justice, but conceded that, should the mediators be disinclined to back this claim, the commissioners might press for an award of the area lying between the Appalachians and the Mississippi "to the nations which inhabit it," such territory to enjoy its independence under the guarantee of France, Spain, Great Britain, and America, and "to be open to the trade of those whose lands border upon them."[32] In a private letter penned only three days later Livingston said that he was prepared to state openly that any claim to the navigation of the Mississippi was inadmissible. "Never was a claim worse founded nor more repugnant to every principle of justice and policy," he declared to Gouverneur Morris.[33] Fortunately Livingston's readiness to coop up the American settlers between the Appalachians and the sea and to perpetuate foreign influence in the West never seems to have been given serious consideration by either Franklin or Jay, and the Secretary himself adopted a less supine course as the tide of battle turned.[34]

The morning following his reading of the "Hints" to Oswald Franklin received a letter from England warning him that, contrary to Grenville's previous assurances, conditions would be attached to American independence, and disclosing that the new administration was less well disposed to the Americans than its predecessor.[35] Franklin knew enough about Shelburne's hopes for imperial reunion and was sufficiently familiar with the Earl's reputation for double-dealing, whether merited or not, as well as with the King's notorious antipathy to the very word "independence" to give some weight to these rumors.

Aside from gossip, buttressed by the reports of Shelburne's frank speech of the tenth of July to the Lords, Thomas Grenville's manner of leaving his post aroused the liveliest suspicions in both Passy and Versailles. It had been Richard Brinsley Sheridan, playwright-politician and town gossip, who had first alerted the British negotiator at Paris to the scheme afoot to undermine him. Sheridan informed him of the split in the Cabinet over the unequivocal acknowledgment of American independence.[36] Grenville chose to believe Fox's confidant and to discount Shelburne's protestations that the change in the Ministry had not altered the King's wish for peace.[37] He let it be known in Paris that Fox's departure would prove "fatal to the present negotiation,"[38] and for a time Vergennes himself was of a mind to believe this.[39]

Rejecting the pleas of his own "dearest brother," Lord Temple, who accepted appointment under Shelburne as Lord Lieutenant of Ireland, Grenville chose to regard his position as untenable. "If I continued at Paris," he wrote his brother, "I should be the meanest and most contemptible wretch that was ever born into the world." "Great God! To what have you exposed me!" Lord Temple replied. Adamantly Thomas Grenville declined to follow his brother into "this den of thieves," as Charles James Fox intemperately characterized the new Ministry, and insisted on quitting his post and joining Fox in opposition.[40] Although Franklin had contributed as much as any man to undermining Grenville with his government, the doctor could not but be troubled at the manner of his leaving. What might it portend for American independence?[41] Late in July Grenville was replaced by Alleyne Fitzherbert, a young career diplomat who had been serving at Brussels.[42]

Franklin's freshly kindled suspicions caused him to scrutinize all correspondence inspired by Lord Shelburne and prompted the latter to open up still another channel of communication with the doctor. This time he chose as his private agent a protégé and confidant named Benjamin Vaughan, an intellectual radical holding opinions quite congenial to the Earl's. Born in Jamaica, Vaughan epitomized the two worlds now at war with each other. His father was a West Indian merchant and planter, his mother a Hallowell of Boston. Only a few months earlier his brother John had consulted John Jay at Madrid about embarking for America and settling in Philadelphia. Jay advised him to put off the taking of an oath of allegiance to the United States until he arrived there, but was impressed by "the sincerity of his professions" and found him an agreeable companion.[43] Benjamin Vaughan was educated at a noncomformist school, studied at Cambridge, and then pursued the law at the Temple and medicine at Edinburgh. Though neither original nor profound, he was a walking encyclopedia on almost all subjects. A familiar of such radicals as Joseph Priestley, Richard Price, Tom Paine, and Horne Tooke, he also became a good friend of Benjamin Franklin, and brought out in 1779, with Franklin's authorization, an edition of the doctor's writings. In addition, Vaughan was related to Henry Laurens by marriage.[44] In short, Shelburne's penchant for picking pro-American agents in dealing with the rebel commissioners at Paris was strikingly exemplified in this instance.

A consistent advocate of conciliation with America, Vaughan had, back in the spring of 1778, urged upon Shelburne a program of reunion with America. "America is only to be regained by systems of liberality shocking to little minds," he then said.[45] Shelburne must have remembered this advice when he came into office, for his liberal proposals to form a Federal Union with America were too advanced for most politicians on either side of the ocean. In March of '82 the thirty-one-year-old Vaughan counseled Shelburne that America, as a new state, could not assume the risks of a separate peace.[46] Yet in the months ahead he was, ironically enough, to be an instrument for achieving that very objective. Convinced that a flourishing America would be "uncontrollably strong" within twenty years, Vaughan pointed out to Shelburne that the Earl stood at one of the turning points of history. "Surely Augustus or Alexander never played a greater hand," he remarked. How could England win back American trade which France had taken over? Since French products had "not quite struck the taste or wants of America," Vaughan's advice was that, with rich trade opportunities at hand, England should soften the "inveteracy" of many Americans "*before* the peace." A friend and disciple of Adam Smith, Vaughan reminded Shelburne that he had formerly argued that "America will *sell* according to interest (in the best markets) but she will *buy* according to whim." The King and Shelburne now had the chance "to fashion that whim either favorably for England, or against England in favor of all Europe."[47] To Shelburne, who conceived Britain's future greatness as resting upon commerce rather than bits of soil scattered throughout the globe, such arguments must have seemed very persuasive.

During the spring of '82 Vaughan had written Franklin about a "proposed dependant state of America" which he thought Oswald would bring up. On July 11th, the day after his important conference with Oswald, the doctor took a fresh look at Vaughan's letter in the light of the current situation. "I have all along understood (perhaps I have understood more than was intended)," he now replied to Vaughan, "that the point of dependance was given up, and that we were to be treated as a free People. I am not sure that Mr. Oswald has explicitly said so, but I know that Mr. Grenville has, and that he was to make that declaration previous to the commencement of the treaty. It is now intimated to me from several quarters," Franklin added, "that Lord Shelburne's plan is to retain sovereignty for the King, giving us otherwise an independent Parliament, and a government similar to that of late intended for Ireland." If that was what was really projected, then, the doctor made clear, negotiations could not go very far. The idea was "impracticable and impossible" as well as "inconsistent with the faith we have pledged, to say nothing of the general disposition of our People." Franklin was prepared to give Shelburne the benefit of a doubt. He conceded that, though he might have held this notion at one time, "he had probably dropt it before he sent Mr. Oswald here." Nevertheless, Vaughan's words "throw a little doubt in my mind," he added, "and have, with the intimations of others, made me less free in communication with his Lordship." Franklin now asked for an *"éclaircissement,"* and Shelburne dispatched Vaughan to Paris to reassure the doctor.[48] Shelburne intended Vaughan to stay for two days,[49] but, except for a celebrated trip to Bowood, he remained for the duration. Looked upon by some as a personal spy of Shelburne's, by others as a stock speculator, Vaughan seemed to have few admirers in British official circles. The King had "but little opinion of his tallents," and Richard Oswald regarded him as an officious busybody. Well-meaning mediator or devious intriguer, Benjamin Vaughan posed more of a problem to the British team of negotiators in Paris than he did to the Americans.[50]

Vaughan was not the only agent to be assigned special tasks. Thomas Walpole, the London banker, whose long-time association with Franklin in Western land speculation had encouraged his aspirations to being named to the post that went to Richard Oswald, was assigned the task of negotiating with the Marquis de Castries concerning the claims of French subjects whose property was seized when the British captured the Dutch island of St. Eustatius.[51] Despite his known aversion to Shelburne, the Earl let him stay on in Paris.[52] In addition, David Hartley was sent back to Paris that summer as a special agent to take up the Loyalist question with the Americans, but on advice from Franklin he declined to serve in that capacity.[53]

The mounting rumors of Shelburne's intentions toward the Americans prompted Franklin on the day following his conversation with Richard Oswald to dispatch a note to the Scot putting a stop to further preliminaries until the Earl's views on independence were clarified and even going so far as to forbid Oswald to revert to the terms he had heard from Franklin's own lips the day before. Oswald remonstrated to Shelburne that he needed clarification just as much as Franklin did, since he himself had stated that the grant of independence was to be absolute.[54] "I shan't be surprised," Oswald added in a postscript to his hastily written note to the Earl, "if the next meeting with the Doctor should turn out more unfavourable than the former." He put it up to Shelburne to take such steps at once as would prevent the negotiations from taking so unfavorable a turn.

The surprisingly onerous French demands which had been revealed to Grenville, in combination with the new coldness on the part of Franklin, made for a gloomy outlook. To Oswald peace now stood on an "unlucky footing." In this mood of despair he called Shelburne's attention to a memorandum he had written a month earlier and which he had entrusted to Mrs. Oswald. He urged Shelburne to peruse it at his leisure when he returned to Bowood, to make sure that it did not get into hands other than his own, particularly as "there are so many Spaniards here."[55] What Shelburne thought about Oswald's daring plan for promoting a Russian expedition to be launched from Siberia against Spain's holdings along the Pacific coast of America[56] he did not perpetuate for posterity. The venerable Oswald may well have been "the wisest merchant" in the King's dominions, but, as Benjamin Vaughan remarked, he could be astonishingly naïve.[57] Despite his negotiator's hare-brained proposal Shelburne clung grimly to Oswald as the peace negotiator with the Americans, however much he discounted his talents as a war planner. Shelburne's determination to keep Oswald did not prevent him from using other instruments to attain his ends without the Scot's knowledge and even behind his back.

For almost a fortnight nothing was heard from either London or Bowood. Was Shelburne still vacillating or had he reached a decision? Two letters penned by the Earl on July 27th for delivery across the Channel offered straws in the wind. To an old acquaintance, the Duc de la Rochefoucauld, he wrote, first, to disabuse the French of the view that, however desirous the King and he were for peace, they would be "ready to accept *any* terms," and, second, to suggest by implication that a direct channel of communication between the Earl and the Comte de Vergennes might be worth opening up.[58] This knowledge the French Minister was soon to exploit. Shelburne wrote another letter that same day. This one was addressed to Richard Oswald and sought to reassure the Americans not to be misled by "the violence and inveteracy occasioned by personal disappointment" on the part of Fox and Grenville, by false assertions or newspaper comment. With the King's approval he sent Oswald a copy of his own secret dispatch to Carleton and Digby of June 5th,[59] and of Fox's dispatch to Russian Ambassador Simolin of June 28th.[60] The former revealed that Grenville had been directed to propose the independence of America "in the first instance instead of making it the condition of a general peace."[61] This seeming generosity, the General and the Admiral were told, was prompted by a desire to persuade America to quit the war rather than fight on for objects of the other belligerents which could be of "no concern" to her and might even be "injurious." The dispatch of Fox to the Russian ambassador indicated that, while Britain was prepared to accept independence as the price of peace, she would insist upon the restitution of all conquests made during the war. Shelburne told Oswald that he was free to communicate to Franklin whatever portions of both dispatches might be sufficient to satisfy the doctor "that there never have been two opinions since you were sent to Paris upon *the most unequivocal ac-*

knowledgment of American Independency to the full extent of the resolutions of the Province of Maryland inclosed to you by Dr. Franklin." To remove all doubts, however, a commission would be forwarded at once to Oswald conferring full power to treat and conclude. Instructions would accompany the commission making "the Independency of the Colonies the basis and preliminary of the treaty now depending." Shelburne expressed the hope that Oswald could persuade Franklin to drop his *advisable* articles, retaining only "as the ground of discussion" the ones he called *"necessary."* If that were done the business might be "speedily concluded."

Finally, Shelburne pointed out that Oswald "very well" knew that the Earl had "long since given up" the hope of reunion "decidedly though reluctantly." Now "the same motives" which made him "perhaps the last to give up all hope of reunion" conspired to render him now "most anxious, if it is given up, that it shall be done *decidedly,* so as to avoid all future risque of enmity, and lay the foundation of a new connection better adapted to the present temper and interests of both countries. . . . My private opinion," he confessed, "would lead me to go a great way for Federal Union, but is either country ripe for it? If not means must be left to advance it. . . . I only desire to add," Shelburne said in conclusion, "that I shall consider myself as pledged to the contents of this letter."[62]

Shelburne's dispatch of July 27th showed the progress his thinking had taken since his speech in the House of Lords earlier that month. The Earl had now committed himself to conceding the Americans their independence, to renouncing British sovereignty over the Old Northwest, and to allowing the Americans to fish off the Banks—Franklin's *necessary* articles. Since the territorial concession north of the Ohio seemed to imply the recognition of America's claims to the south thereof, the major concessions later embodied in the preliminary treaty had already, in Shelburne's mind at least, been made. Nonetheless, in the hard months of bargaining ahead, the British Cabinet, not always taken into Shelburne's confidence, continued to vacillate and to defer a clear-cut decision on the great issue of American independence.[63]

Instead of advancing the cause of peace, the two dispatches Shelburne had forwarded Oswald produced irritation all around. Oswald was flabbergasted to find out that Franklin was already aware of them, and it was necessary for Shelburne to explain rather lamely to the Scot that he had allowed Vaughan to copy certain passages in shorthand "for his private instruction," but that his confidant had handed them over to Franklin. The latter, as was his practice, turned them over to Vergennes,[64] with a comment that the communication to Sir Guy Carleton was "evidently calculated to create division, not only between France and us, but among ourselves"; and the Simolin dispatch was "contradictory respecting a principle point, the Independence."[65] Vergennes, who was constantly being fed intelligence reports from London warning him against Shelburne, that "political sphinx," masquerading as a Whig and a Tory at the same time, affecting attachments to the rights of the people while simultaneously championing the prerogative, needed little substantiating evidence to make him skeptical of Shelburne's peace-loving professions.[66] Shelburne, he observed to Franklin, appeared more interested in "producing a division between the King and the United States" than in promoting "a just and durable peace."[67]

Shelburne's reassurances to the Americans had curiously boomeranged. Had he intended to persuade the Americans that independence would be granted without strings, he should have been more careful in the selection of the documents he entrusted to his agents. Had he proposed to divide the Allies, he overreached himself with these tactics. All Shelburne accomplished was to give his own loyal commissioner in Paris, Richard Oswald, a new sense of insecurity.[68]

When the veil concealing the British Cabinet's intentions was lifted it did little to allay the suspicions of the Americans. On August 6th the advance text of Oswald's still unsigned commission reached Paris.[69] A perusal showed it was deliberately drawn to avoid mentioning by title the United States. Oswald was empowered to treat, agree, and conclude with "any commissioner or commissioners, named or to be named by the said colonies or plantations, or with any body or bodies, corporate or politic, or any assembly or assemblies, or descriptions of men, or person or persons whatsoever, a peace or truce with the said colonies or any of them, or any part or parts thereof."[70] True, the commission referred to "the colonies" rather than "our colonies," but it did not recognize the United States, and even betrayed the Ministry's desire to divide the "colonies" against each other.

The accompanying instructions to Oswald permitted him to treat with the Americans regardless of how they described themselves, and, if necessary, to concede independence to the Thirteen States as "the price" of peace. Oswald was further instructed to secure redress for British creditors, and restitution or indemnification for Loyalist sufferers. For the latter purpose the Ministry was prepared to turn over a portion of the ungranted Crown lands of each province in lieu of what should be restored to the Loyalists. Oswald was to seek for some "political league of union or amity to the exclusion of other European Powers." That failing, he was to make clear that the former colonies could not enter into agreements with any other power "inconsistent with the plan of *Absolute and Universal Independence*, which is the indispensable condition of our acknowledging their Independence of Our Crown and Kingdoms." As a token of reconciliation, Oswald was to propose "an unreserved system of naturalization." Finally, should it prove impossible to enter into a treaty with France or the other belligerent powers, Oswald was to direct his "whole attention" to making a separate peace with the American commissioners in the hope that the concessions he was authorized to make would not only satisfy them but also persuade them that they had no reason to continue in a war which would no longer have any object for them except to advance "French ambition."[71]

Oswald's instructions made three things clear. First, independence would be granted as the price of peace and on condition that the Thirteen States break off their alliance with France. Second, the phraseology betrayed Shelburne's preference for recognizing the Thirteen States on a state-by-state basis rather than as one *united* government. Finally, should no treaty result, the British government would indeed have conceded nothing, for independence was to be acknowledged within the first article of the treaty itself and even then tied to unacceptable conditions.[72]

From this point on Shelburne's commissioner in Paris had to deal with two Americans, not one. While Franklin might have been prepared to waive technicalities, even in the face of his long-avowed position, his instructions from Congress, and his better instincts, John Jay, his legalistically minded colleague, was to prove more tenacious on procedural points. To Shelburne and his associates the former President of the Continental Congress was something of an enigma. He had been by no means precipitate in espousing the cause of revolution, and his conversion to the Patriot side had come as a distinct shock to his Tory acquaintances.[73] In Congress he had resisted the drift toward independence for a time, and in the summer of '75 was a codrafter, with John Dickinson, of the Olive Branch Petition, Congress' final appeal to the King.[74] In view of this background the British might have had ground to hope that Jay would prove more conciliatory than his crafty colleague, Dr. Franklin. One would hardly expect Jay, considering his humiliations at Madrid, to take an extreme stand on behalf of Spanish claims at the peacemaking.[75]

Just how Jay stood toward France was by no means clear. His ancestors had been Hugenot refugees, who had chosen to abandon their country rather than their religion. In his veins ran the blood of martyrs, and he was time and again to remind his own family how, on the revocation of the

Edict of Nantes, dragoons were quartered in his great-grandfather's house before he and his family escaped to England.[76] In childhood Jay had been reared and educated in the Hugenot refugee circle of New Rochelle. Brought up in a household where piety and austerity ruled, Jay was widely known for his suspicion of all things Catholic. His celebrated tract, *The Address to the People of Great Britain,* published in 1774 on the eve of conflict, vigorously denied Parliament's right to establish in Canada "a religion fraught with sanguinary and impious tenets." He had carried his suspicion of Catholicism into the sessions of the state convention which drafted the New York Constitution of 1777. Therein he sought to curb the civil rights of Catholics and was able to persuade his colleagues to require naturalized persons to renounce "all allegiance" to "every foreign king, prince, potentate, and state, in all matters, ecclesiastical as well as civil." In addition, Jay had taken a strong stand against the instructions of Congress, subordinating the peace commissioners to the King of France.

That Jay might have regretted his hot-blooded attachment to the cause of revolution could perhaps be inferred from the ambivalent behavior of his eccentric elder brother, Sir James, who continued to cause his family acute embarrassment. Although he had been knighted for his efforts to obtain funds in England for King's College of New York, he then with-held the funds, and the College had to go into chancery before a compromise settlement was reached.[77] Thenceforward Sir James was known as the "black sheep" of the family flock.[78] To his austere brother John's acute discomfiture James continued to take an opposite stand on most public issues. In the New York Revolutionary legislature, Sir James publicly sided with Arthur Lee's faction against Silas Deane's, and hoped to exploit his support by securing a diplomatic assignment abroad.[79] A blazing Patriot for a time, he rammed through the legislature a harsh bill of attainder and confiscation against prominent Loyalists,[80] which his brother John castigated from Spain as "disgraced by injustice too palpable to admit even of palliation."[81]

"Our Knight of the order of Sisiphus" John called his brother James, and supposed he was "laboring hard to roll some new stone up hill."[82] Others were amused rather than impressed by New York's Don Quixote, and in frustration at his inability to secure recognition from his fellow Patriots, he vented his spleen against them in a series of indiscreet newspaper attacks.[83] By prearrangement Sir James was taken prisoner by the British in New Jersey in April, 1782, and Sir Guy Carleton arranged for him to go to England.[84]

It was Gouverneur Morris who broke the news to John Jay of his brother's apparent disaffection. "Your brother James," he wrote him, "has, I am told, gone to England. If so, his political race like a new market horse has run round in a circle and brought him back to where he started." Morris added: "It is somewhat extraordinary Doctor Franklin's son, your brother, and Mr. Laurens' son are in England."[85] He was herein referring, in addition to Sir James, to Governor William Franklin and Henry Laurens, Jr., the last-named having gone to England on the eve of the Revolution to take up his studies there.

Sir James carefully avoided making his presence known to his more celebrated brother, and the latter reacted to the gossip with a withering blast. "You mention my brother," he wrote to an old friend in England. "If after having made so much bustle in and for America, he has (as I surmised) improperly made his peace with Britain, I shall endeavor to forget that my father had such a son."[86] In June we find Sir James officiously preparing for Shelburne a draft of a bill denying Parliament's jurisdiction over America and authorizing the King to make a peace or truce with America and form a union by incorporating the colonies "into one grand body politic on the solid basis of affection and common interest."[87] In fact, John's surmise was correct. James was something more than a nuisance. Shelburne complained to Townshend that John Jay's brother had refused to give any information concerning America unless he would listen to an "idle story about a naval invention." Perhaps the best way out would be to send Sir James back to Carleton in New York, the Earl remarked, and if he refused, to cut off his stipend.[88] If that was the plan, Sir James eluded it. He managed to make his way to the Continent, and his visit was climaxed by an explosive Paris interview with his brother.

If the loyalty of John Jay's brother was suspect at this time, no one had the slightest doubts about where Benjamin Franklin's natural son stood. Royal Governor of New Jersey when the Revolution broke out, William Franklin was arrested and kept in confinement for a considerable time in Connecticut. Exchanged for a Patriot prisoner, he became the recognized leader of the die-hard Tory faction in America. He had left America under a cloud, charged by both Congress and a British court-martial with responsibility for the hanging of a New Jersey militia officer, Captain Joshua Huddy, under the lawless authority of his Loyalist association.[89] "Nothing has ever hurt me so much, and affected me with such keen sensations, as to find myself deserted in my old age by my only son," Franklin confessed in a letter of reconciliation penned after the peace was made, "and not only deserted, but to find him taking up arms against me in a cause wherein my good fame, fortune, and life were all at stake." The father reminded the son that "there are natural duties which precede political ones," and even in his will Benjamin chided William for "the part he acted against me in the late war."[90] A link between the estranged pair was William Temple Franklin, William's illegitimate son by an unknown woman. Temple, whose patriotism was not in the least suspect, had served in Paris as his grandfather's secretary, and shortly, with Jay's reluctant consent, was to be named secretary to the American commission in Paris.[91] Temple Franklin, who thus owed his elevation to connection rather than ability, intimated to Benjamin Vaughan around this time that he hoped "to see something done for his father, Gov. Franklin, as being the only Governor that gave to his Court plain and wholesome advice before the war." He seems to have had in mind a post in the diplomatic corps.[92] The old doctor seemed utterly unaware of his grandson's impropriety.

The British had little reason to count on these family connections of Jay and Franklin. At this time Franklin stood adamant on the Tories, warning that the negotiations must be broken off should the British persist in demanding reparations for them,[93] while Jay, a man of moderation, was prepared to differentiate between Loyalists who had acted from principle and those inspired by "the most dishonourable of human motives," and who in their conduct had "far outstripped savages in perfidy and cruelty." Against such men, Jay declared, "every American must set his face and steel his heart."[94]

If Jay's family embarrassments hardly disposed him toward conciliation with the mother country, his humiliations at Spanish hands, his well-known aversion to Catholicism, and his conservative temper might well incline him in that direction. From what the British knew of his character and personality, however, they were prepared for a very sticky period of negotiations. A secret service report in the British archives paid grudging tribute to Jay's courage, zeal, and gifts as a speaker and writer, and depicted him as "naturally controversial," "obstinate," "indefatigable," and "dogmatical." He could be more readily persuaded, declared the informant, "by submitting to be confuted by him, than by a direct attempt to convince him." Though spiced with malice, this report of a Tory who had studied with Jay at King's College hit the Achilles' heel in Jay's character—his touchiness and vanity.[95]

At the King's College commencement exercises back in '64 Jay had delivered an oration on "the happiness and advantages arising from a state of peace." Sixteen years later Jay remained a man of peace without being a pacifist,[96] and as such was reconciled to continuing the fight until independence was achieved. "War must make peace for us," he told John Adams, "and we shall always find well-appointed armies to be our ablest negotiators."[97] Still distrustful of Shelburne that first week in August, along with the entire British Ministry, because the Earl continued to talk about acknowledging American independence without actually doing so, Jay was prepared to have the war continue until his grandchildren's generation if America's independence were not conceded.[98] Separated though he was by three thousand miles of ocean from his fellow Patriots on the home front, Jay reflected the thinking of a substantial segment of Americans who were not disposed to lay down their arms until the basic objectives of the war had been secured, whether those objects were broadly defined as setting American nationality upon a solid foundation or more narrowly as guaranteeing the debt owed to the public creditors.[99]

Shelburne's confidants in Paris discovered the two different faces of Mr. Jay—the conciliatory and the obdurate—in their first conferences with the New Yorker. To Benjamin Vaughan Jay appeared "pleasant" and without "unreasonable notions and passions," and he detected leanings toward reconciliation on the part of the man whom he portrayed as being "very bigotted to the English constitution."[100]

Oswald saw a very different side of Mr. Jay. A favorite Spanish proverb of John Jay was "We cannot catch flies with vinegar."[101] In his initial interview with Oswald he seemed bent on proving the proverb wrong. The tough line and even bullying tone adopted by Jay on this occasion convinced the bewildered Scotsman that "we have little to expect from him in the way of indulgence." Oswald had hurried to Passy and shown his commission to Franklin the day after receiving it by courier.[102] "The Doctor seemed to be satisfied," Oswald reported to the Colonial Secretary. Franklin repeated his previous remark. "I hope we shall agree and not be long about it." Oswald then returned to Paris and let Jay have a look at his commission.

A perusal did not satisfy Jay, and he chose to deliver a long lecture to the British commissioner. Why, if Shelburne was sincere in his professions, should he hesitate to concede American independence?[103] Jay's fear of a trap would have been confirmed had he seen the correspondence between Shelburne and George III, clearly emphasizing their sense of the difference between independence at the first instance and as the price of peace. "Independence," Jay insisted, "should not be granted as the price of peace." It should be "no part of a treaty," but ought to have been expressly conceded by act of Parliament. Now that Parliament was prorogued it was too late for that body to act, but the King could do it by royal proclamation, Jay pointed out. More than prestige and technicalities lay behind this insistence upon unequivocal recognition, he said. He was concerned with the military security of the new American nation. He wanted the British garrisons evacuated before the treaty with America was concluded, not after. He feared that otherwise a cease-fire might bring about the disbanding of the American Army, with the war-torn country left at the mercy of the redcoats still snug in their garrison towns.

Jay reminded Oswald of the deep antipathies in America to King and Parliament, animosities which the "younger generation" were likely to harbor and nurture. What he wanted was a "lasting peace."

"Why would not a treaty provide such security?" Oswald asked.

"I would not give a farthing for any parchment security whatsoever," Jay replied. The kind of peace he had in mind, he added, was one that would be settled in such manner "that it should not be the *interest* of either party to violate it." Neither France nor America could be expected to be satisfied merely with the concession of independence for the latter, he pointed out. That would scarcely compensate France for her war expenditures. Nor would it satisfy America, for without adequate indemnification to France the new nation would be placed "under a greater obligation" to her ally "than we incline to," he admitted frankly. Remember, he warned, that the Americans feel themselves obliged to support the demands of France "unless unreasonable," and he even implied that the commissioners from the United States were not prepared to make peace unless Spain and Holland were also included therein. The long and short of Jay's harangue was the implication that the American Congress might expect to act as arbitrator or guarantor of the general peace.

The entire interview, with its climactic note, left Richard Oswald aghast. Nothing he had heard about Jay had prepared him for such imperious terms. "Although he has lived till now as an English subject," Oswald remarked of Jay in reporting this interview, "though he never has been in England, he may be supposed (by anything I could perceive) as much alienated from any particular regard for England as if he had never heard of it in his life." Oswald complained to Townshend that Jay's plan of settlement was "much less liberal" than Franklin's "or at least so much more incumbered with relative connections."

Jay had intimated that treaties had been or were about to be concluded between the Americans and Spain as well as the Dutch. Oswald was too scared to call his bluff. Franklin on the contrary had repeatedly assured the Scot, the latter reported, that once America obtained her independence the treaty with France was at an end. He had only just remarked in his cryptic style that "he hoped we should do well enough and not be long about it." The cheerful prospects that Franklin aroused were now completely "dampt by the said unpleasant reception from Mr. Jay."

Richard Oswald was shrewd enough to realize that Jay's implicit warning that America might act as guarantor of the peace was not capable of immediate implementation. He was concerned about the shape of things to come. Supremely confident of America's rapid growth, the Scot appreciated her vast resources, shipping facilities, and relative security from reprisal. Hence the prospect Jay held out that America might insist on being a guarantor against future wars in Europe posed a formidable threat. It suggested that America planned to assume her station among the big naval powers. As a third force the new nation could be in a position to intermeddle with European concerns and might have to be constantly placated.[104] Much of Oswald's forebodings would some day come to pass, but not for generations would America exert an authority in international affairs commensurate with her strategic power.

In adopting the tough line that Franklin appeared to have followed up to now Jay was confident of the support of one other peace commissioner. John Adams shared Jay's doubts about Shelburne's sincerity and felt that he should not leave for Paris until the English commissioner obtained full power to treat with America as an independent nation. "*I think we ought to take up Fox's idea and insist upon full powers to treat with us in character, before we have a word to say on the subject,*" the New Englander declared. "They are only amusing us."[105] With potent pen Adams continued to hearten Jay in his stand on the point of independence. He was "not the minister of any 'fourth State' at war with Great Britain, nor of any 'American Colonies,'" Adams asserted. "I think we ought not to treat at all until we see a minister authorized to treat with 'the United States of America' or with their ministers," he advised. We must not allow ourselves to be betrayed by "gold and diamonds, and every insidious intrigue and wicked falsehood" into "truces and bad conditions." Conceding that the Americans were "no match for them at this game," Adams added, "we shall have nothing to negotiate with, but integrity, perspicuity and firmness." Insist upon "a sovereignty universally acknowledged by all the world," he declared, adding the caution that "the least oscillation" would "leave us to dispute with the world, and with one another, these fifty years."[106]

Adams felt that Jay's emphasis on explicit recognition was the only correct course, that Franklin's approach to independence was devious, and his views on a truce murky. His temper reached the boiling point when he learned that in the winter of 1781-82 William Alexander, the doctor's Passy neighbor and kinsman by marriage—a Scottish trader who had fled to the Continent to avoid his creditors—had returned to London. Claiming to have Franklin's blessing, he made contacts with the North Ministry and spread word that "America was disposed to enter into a separate treaty with Great Britain" and that "no formal recognition of independence would be required." The idea, as Alexander outlined it to David Hartley, was to provide for the "touchy point" of independence *sub silentio*. When Hartley, in a series of letters, sought to pin Franklin down, the doctor was quick to back away and to insist that America could enter into no treaty without the consent of the King of France. There are no instructions to Alexander on the record. In fact, Alexander left Paris without even talking with the doctor, who merely penned a few words approving Alexander's intention to tell the British that the United States sought only "independence" and that France, were that secured, would be "moderate in other matters." In suggesting tacit independence, Alexander spoke without authorization, for clearly a man as shrewd as Franklin must have recognized the perils of such a course.

Gossip reaching Adams about the Alexander-Hartley talks almost unhinged Franklin's hypercritical colleague. To have entrusted a mission of such delicacy to so indiscreet a double-talker as the bankrupt Alexander convicted the doctor in Adam's mind of ignoring ordinary prudence and discrimination in his choice of agents.[107] Even had Franklin authorized Alexander's peace feelers, it must be remembered that the doctor could not have known that Alexander had previously entered into the secret employment of the British government and had been paid for his services as a mediator with the doctor several years earlier. Still, the Sage of Passy's experience then had been so provoking he was doubtless put on his guard on the second occasion.[108] In retrospect, he would have been more prudent to have simply told Alexander to say nothing whatever about America's peace aims.

Adams, despite his devotion to notions of fair trial, never gave Franklin the benefit of a doubt. He now penned a piping-hot paragraph on the subject of the acknowledgment of independence and embodied it in a draft of a dispatch to Secretary Livingston. Had he been sole commissioner for treating peace, Adams declared, he would have refused to enter into any talks "without full and express powers to treat with the United States of America." He accused Franklin of allowing Alexander to spread the word in England "that no such acknowledgment of our independence would be insisted on." Despairing of putting any checkrein upon the doctor, Adams asked to be relieved of his duties as a peace commissioner. Fortunately for the final conduct of the negotiations, Adams had sober second thoughts about this paragraph. Deeming it "imprudent," he deleted it from his dispatch to America.[109]

Following his startling encounter with John Jay, Oswald hastened to the Hôtel du Parc Royal to fill in Alleyne Fitzherbert on what had transpired. The latter had arrived in Paris on August 2nd to take up his duties as Grenville's replacement.[110] Unlike the Scot, Fitzherbert felt that, in view of the "closest intimacy" prevailing between the two American commissioners, it was unlikely that Franklin did not share Jay's views. Franklin was "extremely disingenuous," he insisted, in holding out a hope of the severance of ties between France and America once independence was acknowledged. Contrariwise, Fitzherbert expected America to extend her ties to include Spain and Holland. In his assumption that the American commissioners were prepared to prolong the war for Spanish objectives, Alleyne Fitzherbert was far off target. Nor was he correct in his second assumption, that John Jay shared Franklin's sense of obligation to the French court or the doctor's deference to the advice of the Comte de Vergennes.[111] Jay was not the man to take dictation from Versailles.

Jay's negotiations with Oswald were being carried on simultaneously with his talks with the Conde de Aranda. The Spaniard had been authorized by Floridablanca to negotiate with the Americans on Western boundaries and trade, but to conclude nothing without referral back to the Spanish court.[112] The mercurial ambassador, who could be as obdurate as he was excitable, lived in a style comparable to his diplomatic colleague from the court of Vienna, the Comte Mercy d'Argenteau. His wine cellars were the talk of Europe. His plate was kept constantly burnished by a silversmith whom he retained in his household for just that purpose. A shrewd man, Aranda sought to counteract Jay's well-known repugnance to the Church of Rome by telling him of his own efforts in Spain to make the trials before the Inquisition public rather than secret affairs and to project himself as a liberal-minded Catholic whose name was anathema in reactionary religious circles at home.[113]

Accompanied by Franklin, John Jay paid a call upon the Conde two days after arriving in Paris, and was received as a private nobleman.[114] Jay liked Aranda on sight. "He appears frank and candid as well as sagacious," he remarked in a letter to the Comte de Montmorin adding, with a back-handed slap at Floridablanca, "but for my part I prefer plain dealing obstinate men to those unstable ones who like the moon change once a fortnight and are mere dispensers of borrowed light."[115]

Jay's siege of influenza held up negotiations for the better part of July. Aranda returned the New Yorker's call, and on August 3rd the pair finally got down to business. Jay turned over to Aranda a copy of his commission and showed him the original.[116] Contrariwise, the Spaniard did not offer to show "any powers of any kind." It was quickly apparent that Aranda's avoidance of any action which might be construed as recognition was dictated by the long-standing policy of the Spanish court, with which Mr. Jay was only too well acquainted.

Since Jay was fluent in neither French nor Spanish, he had to confine himself to the main points and avoid subtleties. Aranda had been prepared to bargain, but his adversary lacked the inclination, the temperament, and the linguistic equipment for haggling. In despair the Conde turned to Vergennes, and the latter arranged to have his English-speaking undersecretary, Joseph-Matthias Gérard de Rayneval, help out in these conferences. Jay soon found that he was obliged to fend off the thrusts of two diplomatic duelists rather than one.[117]

The dialogue carried on during the summer months between Jay and Aranda related to the boundaries claimed by the new United States. Aranda sat down at a table with a French edition of Mitchell's great map of North America before him.[118] "What does the United States expect?" the Conde asked Jay. The American drew his finger along the Mississippi from its then believed source south to 31° NL, the old northern boundary of West Florida from 1763 to 1774. Now Jay's finger moved east along that degree to the Chattahoochee, and then followed the undisputed northern boundary of East Florida to the sea.

A few days later Jay received a map marked by Aranda with a red line, which, as Jay himself described it, ran "from a lake near the confines of Georgia, but east of the Flint River, to the confluence of the Kanawha River with the Ohio, thence round the western shores of Lake Erie and Huron, and thence round Lake Michigan to Lake Superior."[119] His fruitless sessions with the Conde de Floridablanca to obtain for the United States the free navigation of the Mississippi prepared John Jay for what otherwise might have come as a startling proposal. Spain sought to coop up the Americans in a relatively narrow strip of coastal territory almost five hundred miles to the east of the Mississippi. The line, as Jay explained to Livingston, "would leave near as much country between it and the Mississippi as there is between it and the Atlantic Ocean."[120] Save for a segment of Pennsylvania and Virginia lying to the west of the crest of the Appalachians, Aranda's red line bore a striking resemblance to the temporary restraining line that the British had drawn up for the colonies in the Proclamation of 1763. Speaking *"en sus pocas palabras,"* Jay said

"No" to Aranda, who appealed to Rayneval for help in budging the stubborn American.[121]

Two profoundly troubled American commissioners journeyed to Versailles on August 10th on invitation to put their problems to the Comte de Vergennes.[122] Although Franklin was less perturbed than Jay about Shelburne's failure to grant America prior acknowledgment of independence, he shared the latter's indignation at the Spanish boundary proposals. The Americans first took up the text of Oswald's commission. Vergennes revealed his concern that the several peace negotiations be "tied together," though proceeding separately. He now advised accepting the commission as soon as it was authenticated. Why worry about technicalities? Vergennes asked. So long as independence is made an article of the final treaty, the phraseology of the commission is not important. We ourselves, he pointed out to the Americans, have not objected to treating with a British plenipotentiary who presented full powers embodying the traditional phrase denominating the King of England as also King of France. Drawing upon a confidential memorandum recently prepared for him,[123] Vergennes proposed a neat formula to cut the Gordian knot. Enter into a formal exchange of full powers with Oswald, the Minister advised. Once he has received your commissions as plentipotentiaries of the United States of America, he will have in effect committed himself to that form, or as the memorandum put it, "the delivery and acceptance pure and simple by Mr. Oswald of the full powers of Messrs. Jay and Franklin" would fulfill that object.

Confident of approval, he looked inquiringly at the Americans. Franklin, who for months had opposed entering into negotiations without securing explicit recognition in advance, now meekly conceded that it "would do." Contrariwise, Jay let Vergennes know that the formula did not satisfy him and that he deemed it best to proceed cautiously. Vergennes did not choose to take these objections seriously, but considered the business settled.[124] To Lafayette he dictated a formula providing for Great Britain's complete renunciation of sovereignty over America by the first article of the treaty.[125]

Then the Americans turned to the business with Aranda. Vergennes listened to their strong protests and, as Jay reported, was "very cautious and reserved." Not so Rayneval, who happened to be present, and expressed the opinion that "we claimed more than we had a right to." In point of fact, of course, Rayneval voiced Vergennes' views, and the pair had been active over the last fortnight in suggesting to Aranda a compromise proposal that would keep the Americans far from the Mississippi. The French Minister had already taken a stand behind the Americans' backs and was by no means neutral. Two weeks before he had told Aranda that if Jay would not modify his demand for the Mississippi as America's western boundary, there was the alternative of setting up a neutral Indian state, about which Aranda himself was dubious.[126] Soon Rayneval was to draft a compromise line embodying Vergennes' ideas and to buttress his proposal with a lengthy historical memorandum opposing the American claims.

While cautious in expressing himself in the presence of the Americans, the Comte de Vergennes made no secret among his subordinates that he considered the Americans to be extravagant in their boundary claims, not only because of their insistence on the Mississippi as the western boundary, but also for their venturing to assert title to the Northwest Territory, which France hoped England would retain as part of Canada.[127] Confining the Americans within severe limits was no sudden inspiration of the French Foreign Office. It was part of a well-defined policy,[128] but it was now articulated in order to mollify Spain. How much Vergennes was influenced by memoranda submitted to his office that spring and summer would be difficult to evaluate. An unidentified French officer proposed that spring to coop up the Americans between the Appalachians and the Atlantic seacoast, backed the English claims to the Northwest and Canada, and even suggested "arousing" the English to confine the American boundaries.[129] Another proposal advocated strongly fortifying the boundaries hemming in the United States to prevent American expansion, even though the writer conceded that a republic was unlikely ever to embark on a career of conquest.[130] However little weight should be accorded such proposals, it is nonetheless clear that they betrayed a growing concern among Frenchmen over the shape of things emerging in North America.

The August 10th confrontation at Versailles marked a turning point in Franco-American relations. It was clear to Jay, if not to Franklin, that Vergennes and Rayneval had no comprehension of the true nature of the American Revolution, of the twin forces of anticolonialism and nationalism that had been liberated by that conflict. To Jay the evidence of France's motives in backing America had been disclosed. It was apparent that the French Foreign Office had supported the Revolution for reasons of power politics, and that it considered the American War to be no different from other wars which were in the past settled by compromise lines and deals under the table. Vergennes, as Jay saw it, favored independence for America, not out of any attachment to the principles of the Declaration of Independence, but because he regarded such an event to be the heaviest blow he could administer to France's hated rival.[131]

Vergennes seemed to make it painfully evident that he was more interested in trimming the British Empire down to size than in establishing a new nation along new principles and with durable prospects. If the latter were his real aim, would he now be denying America breathing space?

Jay and Franklin, a heavy-hearted pair, rode back in the carriage together from Versailles and stopped off at Passy. In considerable agitation Jay launched into a denunciation of France's current position in the peace-making. Why did Vergennes want to hold off the recognition of independence? he asked, and without waiting for the doctor to reply, he asserted that France's Foreign Minister was slowing up the negotiations to avoid antagonizing Spain.[132] Like a prosecuting attorney summing up his case, he accused France of wanting America to remain under her direction "until not only their and our objects are attained, but also until Spain should be gratified in her demand to exclude everybody from the Gulf and the Mississippi." Franklin conceded that Spain planned "to coop us up within the Allegheny Mountains,"[133] but he was convinced that so far as France was concerned Vergennes was trying to speed up the negotiations, not slow them down.

The secret documents now available to historians prove that Jay was correct in his appraisal of the situation, that since the beginning of July Floridablanca had been pressing Vergennes to defer recognition of the insurgents until a general peace. Otherwise the Americans, once content, he argued, might drop out of the war before Gibraltar was secured. While Vergennes was too cautious to commit to writing a promise to get Britain to delay recognizing America until a general peace, he let the Spaniard know that he was holding up the negotiations with England until the fate of Gibraltar was determined.[134] The French did not wish to make propositions, Fitzherbert was informed, until they had learned the issue of the campaign in the East Indies the previous spring.[135]

Vergennes took no pains to keep the British from learning that the formula he had proposed to Franklin and Jay was drawn for the purpose of deferring recognition until the final peace. Instead, he himself disclosed this to Fitzherbert not long after his conference with the two Americans. Vergennes' amazing indiscretion revealed the split between the allies on a burning issue and confirmed the suspicions of Britain's Foreign Secretary, Lord Grantham, that "the granting Independency to America as a previous measure is a point which the French have by no means at heart, and perhaps are entirely averse from."[136] The British, as one might expect, made sure that Jay was told how Vergennes had crossed him behind his back.[137]

However disturbed Franklin may have been privately about Vergennes' support of Aranda, his loyalty to the French court would not permit him to concede that France was playing the Spanish game. The old doctor snapped back at Jay, "Forget about technicalities. Let us be mindful of the generosity of France to us in the past." Neither Franklin's Journal nor Jay's Diary contains entries covering this heated conversation, but from Jay's letters back home that fall we have a fair notion of what was said. When Franklin cautioned Jay about the instructions of Congress to take the advice of the French court, the New Yorker reminded the doctor: "We have another instruction which sets independence as a pre-condition to entering into a treaty."

"Have we any reason to doubt the good faith of the King of France?" asked Franklin.

"We can depend upon the French," Jay countered, "only to see that we are separated from England, but it is not in their interest that we should become a great and formidable people, and therefore they will not help us to become so."

"If we cannot count upon France, upon whom else may we depend?" Franklin inquired.

"We have no rational dependence except on God and ourselves," Jay replied.

"Would you deliberately break Congress' instructions?" Franklin pressed.

Jay did not hesitate. "Unless we violate these instructions the dignity of Congress will be in the dust," he asserted. "I do not mean to imply that we should deviate in the least from our treaty with France," Jay added. "Our honor and our interests are concerned in inviolably adhering to it, but if we lean on her love of liberty, her affection for Americans, or her interested magnanimity, we shall lean on a broken reed that will sooner or later pierce our hands. If you don't believe that, consider the fates of Geneva and Corsica!"

"Then you are prepared to break our instructions," Franklin pressed, "if you intend to take an independence course now."

Jay had made up his mind. "*If* the instructions conflict with America's honor and dignity I would break them—like this!" Family tradition has it that Jay stood up and hurled his long clay pipe into the fireplace. Strewn among the ashes and embers, the shattered pieces might well have betokened the grand alliance itself. With Jay's impulsive gesture, "independence," for which America had fought long and bitterly, suddenly attained a new meaning and dimension.[138]

XIV

MILORD SHELBURNE PLAYS
THE HOST

As THE COACH bearing the troubled American commissioners from
their August 10th interview with the Comte de Vergennes rattled
across the cobblestoned courtyard of Versailles neither occupant could have
foreseen that the next six weeks would prove climactic equally for American independence and for world peace.

To Lord Shelburne a matchless opportunity now presented itself to
exploit the widening rift between the Americans and the French, or,
more accurately, between John Jay and Vergennes. To whom would he
turn? The answer to that question was in no small measure to shape the
Western world emerging out of a great world war. In mid-August,
however, the Wiltshire nobleman remained inscrutable to friend and foe
alike, his enigmatic posture concealing his own uncertainty about the road
to take. Two visitors to Bowood Park would help Shelburne make up his
mind.

A condition not a theory confronted John Jay. France could no longer
be counted on to support America's revolutionary objectives, aside from
independence. As Jay saw it, America's ambitions were being placed in
jeopardy as much by the actions of her ally as by those of her enemy.
For Jay the sensible course to adopt—and he was above all else a sensible
man—was to pursue a more conciliatory line toward the British adversary
while keeping his distance from his ally.

Each of the American commissioners still advanced propositions unpalatable to the British, but the tone of their conversations with Richard
Oswald now perceptibly moderated. On August 11th the Scot went out
to Passy. There he found Franklin, though noncommittal on the notion

that America intended to act as guarantor of the peace, still by no means reconciled to dropping his "advisable" articles or to providing for the Tories. The latter business, he pointed out to Oswald, fell within the authority of the states, not Congress. Once more Franklin reminded Oswald of Canada. There could be "no dependence on peace and good neighbourhood," he remarked, so long as Canada continued in British hands, "as it touched their States in so great a stretch of frontier."

Oswald's recent session with Jay had prepared him for the worst, even to being compelled to yield "the whole territory,"[1] but Jay appeared in better humor when Oswald next conferred with him, even though he did not budge an inch on the question of treating on the basis of equality. He let Oswald know that he was not content with the latter's instructions of August 3rd, which authorized the acknowledgment of independence in the first article of a treaty irrespective of other articles. The British commissioner may have believed in all sincerity that he had met Jay's conditions, but the New Yorker, as Franklin remarked, thought of "things that did not occur to those who were not lawyers."[2] He did not want to give the adversary that loophole to cut off negotiations which so shrewd an observer of the international scene as Comte Mercy suspected that the British Cabinet was seeking.[3]

Jay and Franklin insisted on clarification of Sir Guy Carleton's role in New York. They had heard that the General had been authorized to make peace proposals directly to Congress.[4] Was this another example of Shelburne's devious tactics? Until they were better informed, they needed to have Oswald's powers clearly delineated. Whether independence could be conceded by King or Parliament constituted a nice legal question. Jay now proposed that, with Parliament prorogued until November, the King should proceed to grant independence by a "patent" or deed under the Great Seal. He made two drafts of such a "patent," but was persuaded by Franklin and Oswald that this procedural move was unnecessary.[5]

Despite this quibbling over the form by which independence was to be given up, John Jay was "much more open and unreserved" with the British than the doctor.[6] The latter, in George III's biased judgment, "only plays with us and has no intention fairly to treat."[7] He was encouraged by the friendly and even optimistic tone of the adversary toward America, and it must have seemed paradoxical to him that Oswald and Vaughan exhibited a sounder understanding of the springs of nationalism and enlightenment in America, of the elements that set the American

Revolution apart from all previous wars, than did Vergennes and Rayneval.

Vaughan and Oswald both pressed Jay for a commitment that, once independence was granted, America would not continue the war to support exorbitant claims advanced by France or Spain. To Vaughan Jay replied cryptically: "Do our business first—as to stirring otherwise, I will not do it." Vaughan was unnerved by this remark. He interpreted it to mean that, while America wanted peace "now and always," she would continue to cultivate France if that nation acted "with ordinary sense" and would proceed "to exterminate the English name in America." Shelburne, as he viewed it, must now see the "good sense" of weighing "the amount of what there is *still to grant them*." Consider the cost of turning them down, Vaughan argued. Consider how little use we ourselves can make of this territory. Consider the probability that "in an age or two and before it can ripen in our hands," the territory will be "torn away by force or fall by neglect." To be generous will prove the profitable course, he urged, since one would not expect passions to be permanent. The Americans, he instructed Shelburne, are planning "to look deeply into the business of education," and it is unlikely that wrong practices will long be followed "in a country where every human being reads and writes."[8]

When Oswald put to Jay the same question that Vaughan had, the New Yorker answered quite candidly and in a manner that disclosed his whole hand. "You have only to cut the knot of Independence," he declared, "to get rid of those apprehensions" that America would support the unreasonable demands of the other belligerents. Jay confessed that he had not proceeded very far with the Spanish treaty. Unless Britain "forced" America into this engagement, he volunteered, "he did not see that the people of America had any business to fetter themselves with them." He went so far, in Oswald's account, as to assure the Scot that he would bring the negotiations with Spain to a halt. With studied casualness Oswald remarked that "when America was independent of England," she "would be so also of all other nations." Jay smiled enigmatically. "We will take care of that," he responded, but his manner did not encourage further explorations of the topic at the time.[9]

Shelburne and Grantham were now being showered with a barrage of missives from Paris to conclude quickly with the Americans. A change of the French Ministry was in the offing, erroneous intelligence advised, and this might provide the British Ministry with an opportunity to capitalize on American uneasiness.[10] Though less partial to the American cause than Oswald or Vaughan, Alleyne Fitzherbert was no less realistic. In his eyes a quick deal with America would give the British an advantage over their European enemies, provided that such an object could be kept "an entire secret" from Vergennes. Even a partial withdrawal of American support from her ally, Fitzherbert pointed out to Shelburne, would force France and Spain to prolong the war.[11] For very different reasons Oswald and Vaughan advised London that it was imperative to win America over at once. Discounting the hold Vergennes still seemed to have over Franklin, they insisted that the American plenipotentiaries were ready for business and filed a prayer that the absent commissioners, the querulous Laurens and the truculent Adams, would not make a sudden appearance in Paris. "Let superiority be given up," Vaughan urged. Then America will behave as a "power," rather than as a "revolter."[12] Vaughan's penchant for retailing gossip calculated to intimidate his correspondent irritated Shelburne no end,[13] but his curiosity always got the better of his inclinations and he kept on opening Vaughan's dispatches. Oswald, who all along had been perturbed about the perilous situation confronting the redcoats and Loyalists remaining in America,[14] now declared that "independence must be absolutely and unconditionally granted," else the negotiations both with the American commissioners and the European enemies would come to a complete breakdown. "Independence," as the Americans envisioned the term and as Oswald chose to define it, embraced significantly "a cession of the whole territory."[15] Day after day the same theme was repeated. American independence must be conceded at once. Though the grounds might vary, the arguments seemed compelling.[16]

Contrariwise, George III kept up from Kew a rear-guard action against premature recognition of his disobedient subjects. As late as August 21st the King told Shelburne that it seemed a "strange view" indeed that England must "decidedly grant independence and restore all troops prior to any treaty." All of this was bad enough, but now George snatched at Jay's intimations that America wanted to be a guarantor of the general peace. "I do not possibly see," the King reminded Shelburne, "how the present Ministry can consent to Independency but as the price of a certain peace." It was by now a familiar chant, for in George III's mind nothing had changed since the spring of '82. Franklin's "Hints," the King contended, had been submitted "only to amuse," and presumably should not be taken seriously. In any event, the King informed his Home Secretary, before you reach a decision, you had better call the Cabinet together within the week.[17]

Jay's growing conviction that the French were in no hurry to have independence conceded to the United States was confirmed by his conversations with Vergennes on August 19th. On that occasion he and Franklin rode out to Versailles to convey the advice proposed by Oswald that Great Britain take immediate steps to concede independence. Vergennes did not seem to see the point upon which the Americans were so insistent, but Jay was as inflexible as ever.[18] Rumors quickly spread, fed by Alleyne Fitzherbert and the English circle in Paris, that the French Foreign Minister "seemed to wear the appearance of being not a little embarrassed by the supposed approach of the acknowledgment of independence" and acted as though he were afraid that, once independence was acknowledged, and New York and Charleston evacuated, the Americans would quit the war and leave the fighting to the others. Vaughan, who managed to spice his up-to-the-minute intelligence from Paris with his "West India vivacity," reported that Vergennes, prior to talking with the Americans, had been prepared to insist that the English make the first moves by stating their propositions. In other words, the French Minister would initiate no moves toward peace until the impending campaign against Gibraltar had reached a decisive stage and the British had shed light on disputed areas like the fisheries, in which France considered the United States to be acting the part of an interloper.[19]

John Jay, now convinced that the policy of the Comte de Vergennes was "to keep America in leading strings," set to work feverishly to extricate his country from this entanglement.[20] One day, while riding in his carriage with Vaughan, he remarked, "Why will not your court cut the cord that ties us to France? Why can they suppose we can be quiet, while the very end of the treaty is independence, till independence is granted?" England should not haggle, Jay advised pointedly. She should concede "this one point," for the best deal she could make with France would be "a good agreement with America." Vaughan quickly caught the implication of Jay's remarks. What Jay was really telling him was that France could make better terms with her enemy if America was tied to her apron strings than otherwise. Abruptly Jay switched from this line of conversation. "If your government does not guarantee independence," he warned, there would be "an end to all confidence."[21]

The wettest August of many summers ended on a bright note, and hopes of peace soared again. Prospects of a quick solution to a thorny problem arose from the suddenly enhanced prestige of John Jay in Paris as well as from the increasingly shaky political position of Lord Shelburne at home. In the third week of August Franklin was suddenly stricken with an acute attack of kidney stone, a painful ailment intensified by the doctor's chronic gout. Rumors spread through the diplomatic corps that he had suffered a paralytic stroke.[22] While his mind was not affected, Franklin remained incapacitated for weeks and confined to his home at Passy. Now a strong note of independence from French direction is sounded in the American camp by the solitary bugler on duty.

For Shelburne time seemed to be running out. His political situation at home was perilous. Without commanding support in Parliament he had to make his moves quickly while Parliament was still in recess. At the same time he had to move with circumspection to avoid affronting a stubborn and touchy monarch. "Don't let the King overshadow you! Be an unshaken Patriot!" one of the Earl's anonymous well-wishers counseled him.[23] Shelburne understood the situation better than his correspondents. He realized the devious course he needed to pursue to win a reluctant King over to accepting a sensible, if humiliating, sacrifice.

To push forward with the peace negotiations at this time involved a military decision. Though barred by Parliament from resuming offensive military action against the Americans, Shelburne was not yet under legal restraints toward the other belligerents. He clearly saw the alternatives. He could make a quick peace with France, thereby avoiding further risky naval and military operations. On the other hand, he could make an immediate settlement with the Americans and continue the war against the European belligerents to strengthen England's diplomatic position.[24] The former course meant cooperating with an ancient foe to keep America a coastal confederacy. The alternative meant treating an errant daughter with generosity, permitting her ample living room, and counting on great commercial advantages from a revivified trade with America. "Act with magnanimity," Shelburne was urged by one correspondent at this time. "Do not act as though America was your enemy and France your friend."[25] By the time this advice reached Shelburne, he had already anticipated it.

No one was quite sure which way Shelburne was leaning, but there was a straw in the wind. On August 23rd his Cabinet decided to send a powerful force under Lord Howe to the relief of Gibraltar, a decision which carried the King's hearty approval.[26] At least so far as the Franco-Spanish combination was concerned, Shelburne seemed determined to negotiate from strength.

Still no action was taken in London to comply with John Jay's demand for immediate and unconditional independence. On that point the British government remained inscrutably silent. Impatiently Oswald awaited the return of a courier authorizing him to yield the point, but Shelburne took a fortnight to reply to his latest letters.[27] Meanwhile Jay was taking no chances. He talked freely with Matthew Ridley, an international man of business, then abroad as agent for Maryland, having only just obtained a loan from an Amsterdam banking firm for that state. Already a warm admirer of the New Yorker, and later to become Jay's brother-in-law, Ridley made a note in his diary that Jay advised him to go ahead and ship the supplies to Maryland that he was ordering. "Make preparations for war down to the very hour of signing the treaty," Jay warned, and with his customary realism remarked further that even after the advent of peace it would still be necessary for America to be armed.[28]

Across the Channel Lord Shelburne, having made the decision to reinforce Gibraltar, seemed determined that the King and Cabinet should yield to the Americans on all essentials. Regardless of the political risks to himself, he recognized the commercial advantages to Britain from such a quick settlement and the opportunity it afforded of weakening the grand alliance against his country. On the twenty-eighth the Cabinet met, only to be deadlocked over the issue. Dunning, a close supporter of Shelburne, who had been elevated that spring to the peerage as Lord Ashburton, was loath to adopt Oswald's recommendation on the score of independence. He was backed in his opposition by the die-hard Lord Chancellor Thurlow. The next day Shelburne, Dunning, and the Chancellor sat down to iron out their differences over the dinner table.[29] The Earl managed to wring a reluctant consent from these holdouts, for at a Cabinet meeting that very evening agreement was reached to offer generous terms to the Americans including a compromise on independence. Should the rebel commissioners still refuse to treat without prior acknowledgment of independence but yet indicate that they were prepared to accept the "Four Articles" sketched out by Franklin in his letter to Oswald of July 10th and grouped therein under the rubric of *necessary*, the Cabinet decided to direct the Scot to hold out the promise of special legislation in Parliament for the absolute and immediate acknowledgment of "the Independence of the Thirteen Colonies."[30] The Cabinet could not bring itself to utter the detested word "States."

What in fact was being offered by the Cabinet? As spelled out in Townshend's instructions to Oswald, the Cabinet was prepared to concede all of Franklin's *necessary* articles, literally construed. The Americans would be admitted to the Newfoundland and Labrador fisheries, but not given liberty to dry fish on the shores since Franklin had neglected to mention that crucial point. British troops would be evacuated from American territory. Canada would be confined to its historic boundaries prior to the notorious Quebec Act of 1774. By restricting Canada's limits to what they were under the Royal Proclamation of 1763, the British government was prepared to renounce not only the Old Northwest but also the southern half of the future Province of Ontario.[31] Oswald's instructions permitted him to waive stipulating by treaty for payment of prewar debts owing British merchants as well as for compensation to the Loyalists. The government counted on world opinion to bring about an equitable settlement of both issues. On the extent of America's Western claims the instructions were silent, for Franklin in his *necessary* articles had neglected to stipulate for the Mississippi as the western boundary.

As regards recognition, Oswald was explicitly instructed by Thomas Townshend not to disclose his full hand until he had attempted to persuade the Americans to accept independence as the first article of the treaty, with Franklin's *necessary* articles as bait. "Only in the very last resort," Oswald was told, would the King agree to recommend to Parliament enabling legislation to acknowledge American independence.[32]

Townshend's instructions of September 1st did not reach Oswald until the fourth, almost a week after the Cabinet's decision of August 30th. Learning from Jay that Franklin was well enough to see him on business, the Scot went out at once to Passy to inform the doctor that the King had authorized him to declare independence in the first article of the treaty. On the following day Oswald, at Jay's request, sent the doctor an extract from Townshend's letter. Significantly, the extract merely expressed the King's intention of "granting to America, full, complete, and unconditional Independence in the most explicit manner, as an *Article of Treaty*." The accompanying note said nothing about terms.[33] Compliant to the views of Versailles, Franklin remarked to Rayneval, "I hope Mr. Jay will agree to this."[34]

A number of new factors conspired to postpone the revelations to the Americans of the crucial portion of the decision reached by the Cabinet at the end of August. First of all, the British were becoming increasingly aware of the views of Vergennes on the American issues. They knew that he was most anxious for England to defer her concession on independence until the treaty itself, fearful that a quick solution of Anglo-American difficulties could seriously compromise the interests of France and Spain. Secondly, they knew too how perturbed Vergennes was about America's fishing claims along the Newfoundland coast. Behind the back of the Americans he was at that very moment asserting French fishing claims, and, as Lord Grantham drily remarked, pressing them "before any American claims may be set forward," and making it almost embarrassingly clear to the British that "there is no doubt of great jealousy between" the French and the Americans "on that score."[35] Moreover, the Comte was becoming increasingly resistant to American expansionist pressures. Convinced that America already had more space than she needed, he pointed out to his envoy in Philadelphia that France could not interfere between Spain and America over the territory east of the Mississippi and around the Ohio. "We are observing the most absolute silence until we are invited to take cognizance of the discussion and to express an opinion."[36] Silent Vergennes certainly had not been, and it is to be remarked that when his undersecretary did talk it was not at Jay's suggestion but in response to Aranda's.

The specter of American defection haunted Vergennes perhaps more than ever, and he required a never-ending stream of reassurances from La Luzerne and Barbé-Marbois in America that the alliance was secure and the anti-French spirit on the decline.[37] He was in fact hearing quite the opposite from his anti-American spy in London. Goëzmann de Thurne was spicing his dispatches with malicious tales of an Anglo-American cabal against Spain's colonies, dire predictions that the Franco-American alliance would not survive a single day after America had gained her independence, and urgent advice to have Vergennes exert pressure to force Carleton and his redcoats to remain in New York "until the pear is ripe for us."[38]

During the critical weeks of late summer when the British still hesitated to concede recognition to America in the first instance, Vergennes abruptly switched roles. From being the chief protractor of the negotiators he now let it be known that he advocated a quick peace with the British. Comte Mercy d'Argenteau attributed the startling *volte-face* to vanity. Vergennes, he wrote Kaunitz, was dazzled by the expectation of settling the peace all by himself and without having to share the glory with the mediators.[39] While ambition may well have played a part, war weariness and the mounting fiscal problems confronting the Bourbon monarchies were indubitably more determining factors in converting Vergennes to appeasement.[40]

Vergennes was encouraged in his hopes for a quick peace by reports of a courtesy call that the Comte de Grasse had paid on the chief of the British Cabinet on August 10th. Victor over Graves and Hood off Yorktown, the Comte was now in England on parole after his defeat and capture by Rodney in the Battle of the Saints that spring. Energetic, enthusiastic, plain-spoken, and unused to the subtleties of diplomacy, the Admiral, a giant of a man, made an incongruous figure besides the obsequious Shelburne, past master of the arts of casuistry. Within the week de Grasse returned to France and passed on to Vergennes terms for a settlement which he attributed to Shelburne. The Earl, according to the Admiral, was prepared to grant America complete and absolute independence, to restore St. Lucia to France, and to arrange for the retrocession of Dominica and St. Vincent. He was willing to abrogate the humiliating terms which France had been obliged to accept concerning British controls in Dunkirk ever since 1713. He was prepared to provide the French with a fishery location on the Grand Bank, and to grant them the right to fortify it, as well as to make arrangements for French trading posts with the African Negroes, and for allowing France to have the commercial establishments in India she had operated between 1748 and 1763. To Spain, according to de Grasse's report, England was ready to cede whatever that country had conquered on the Gulf of Mexico, and to give her a choice of Minorca or Gibraltar, leaving to the British some fort in the Mediterranean for her commerce with the Levant. Holland reputedly was offered the *uti possidetis*, with reciprocal cessions to be negotiated by treaty. Finally, freedom of commerce was to be conceded to all nations according to the principles of the Armed Neutrality.[41] This veritable cornucopia of gifts justified further inspection.[42] Lord Shelburne had dangled some juicy bait before Vergennes, enough to hook his fish.

While these new peace feelers were being explored by the French during the closing weeks of August, Jay was talking with both Oswald and Aranda. Once again the Conde called upon the English-speaking Rayneval to help out. Once again he denied America's right to the Mississippi as her western boundary, an assertion from which Jay never receded a furlong. America was claiming territory which was never a part of the Thirteen Colonies, Aranda protested. He buttressed his arguments by an appeal to history as well as to the facts of recent conquests by the Spaniards, who had recaptured West Florida and gained certain posts on the Mississippi and the Illinois.[43] Aranda completely ignored the temporary occupation of the Northwest by George Rogers Clark. For all the diplomats in Paris seemed to care, the Virginians who had waded the icy waters of the Wabash in their heroic march to Vincennes might just as well have remained by their own firesides.

On August 23rd Aranda appealed once more to Vergennes. True, Jay's claims seemed extraordinary, the Comte conceded, but, he pointed out, there were actual American settlements located far beyond the red line drawn by the Spaniard. The Conde replied that he was not unbudgeable on that line, and asked Vergennes to work out a compromise. "Talk to Rayneval," the French Foreign Minister advised.

The Conde found the undersecretary even more candid in his criticisms of America's territorial claims than his superior. When Louisiana and Canada had been French, Rayneval pointed out to Aranda, the region lying in between, including the Great Lakes, was also considered as belonging to France. The settlement made at the end of the French and Indian War, Rayneval continued, had embraced as part of Canada the territory lying north of the Ohio, and the land to the south of that river was considered as forming a part of the Floridas which the British had taken over.[44] Encouraged by his appreciative auditor, Rayneval agreed to work out a memorandum on the subject. Just before the conference broke up Vergennes came in. When apprised of the discussion, Aranda records in his *Diario*, "he seemed to agree."

Vergennes now decided to push for a settlement of the Spanish-American dispute by securing agreement on a compromise line. When he met Aranda two days later, he proposed that the Conde move his red line farther west to the Wabash River and the western end of Lake Erie. Aranda indicated a willingness to split the difference. For the territory north of the Ohio he was prepared to swing his line forward somewhat to begin not far from the present site of Cincinnati. The Americans would not readily agree to giving up the Wabash, Vergennes pointed out. Accordingly he proposed that river as a boundary line to run south to the Ohio, and below that river suggested the Great Kanawha as a dividing line. This alternative would give the Americans room to exploit their commerce by river courses. For the southern portion of the territory in dispute, Vergennes suggested a line starting from Fort Toulouse on the Alabama. Aranda interrupted to make sure that such a line would include not only the Mobile region of ancient French claims but also the portions of West Florida recently conquered by Spain from Great Britain. At that point Rayneval came in, and promised to draw up a clear statement of the whole question.

Jay made it clear to the Conde at their next conference that a compromise line was unacceptable to the Americans. "We are bound by the Mississippi," he flatly asserted. "I have no authority to cede any territories of it to His Catholic Majesty." "Haven't you been given some discretion?" Aranda asked in rising irritation. "No," Jay replied. "Few ministers plenipotentiary have discretionary power to transfer and cede to others the countries of their sovereigns.

"That territory belongs to free and independent nations of Indians," Aranda rejoined, "and you have no right to it."

"These are points to be discussed and settled between the Indians and ourselves," Jay retorted. "With respect to the Indians we claim the right of pre-emption; with respect to all other nations, we claim the sovereignty over the territory."

Once more Aranda appealed to Versailles to find some way out of the impasse. Vergennes left the Spanish ambassador with Rayneval. Putting their heads together they drew a new red line running from Fort Toulouse on the Alabama to the Tennessee, and then down that river to the Ohio. Aranda objected that at the mouth of the Tennessee the new line almost touched the Mississippi. Obligingly, Rayneval moved the line eastward, so that it left the Tennessee at the confluence of the Pelisipi [Sequatchie], went up the latter to its source, thence to the source of the Cumberland, and followed that river down to the Ohio. Everything north of the Ohio the Frenchman generously awarded to the British, "because it could not be denied to them that this region had been a dependency of Canada and so recognized by France." Aranda was content, and well he might be, for Rayneval's line would keep the Americans "far away" from the Mississippi. Rayneval then read from a memorandum he was preparing on the territorial question, and gave Aranda a copy.[45]

The next step was to put the pressure on the Americans. Obeying a summons from Versailles, Jay conferred with Vergennes and Rayneval on September 5th. Instead of convincing the New Yorker, the French diplomats learned to their chagrin that Jay intended to break off his talks with Aranda because of the latter's lack of powers. The following day Rayneval wrote Jay urging him to continue the talks anyhow. Accompanying the letter was an historical memoir which Rayneval described as his "personal ideas on the way of winding up the boundary discussions with Spain."[46] In a postscript the undersecretary added, perhaps incautiously: "As I shall be absent for some days, I beg you to address your reply to M. Henin, Secretary of the Council of State at Versailles."

Rayneval in this memorandum elaborated upon the historical points he had already made in his talks with Aranda. Before the Treaty of Paris of 1763, he argued, the English never asserted pretensions to lands east of the Mississippi, but confined their claims to the lands located around the source of the Ohio, notably along the Allegheny. Once the cessions had been made under that treaty, England no longer regarded the vast territories lying to the eastward of the Mississippi as forming a part of the Thirteen Colonies. The Proclamation of 1763 indicates, so Rayneval contended, that north of the 31st parallel neither Spain nor the American colonists had any rights.

Having demolished the American case to his own satisfaction, Rayneval then proposed his own line for dividing this territory. He would place the Indians dwelling to the west of that line under Spanish protection, while "those to the eastward should be free, and under the protection of the United States; or rather the Americans may make such arrangements with them as is most convenient to themselves." The navigation of the Mississippi must follow with the property, and belongs "to the nation to whom the two banks belong." Thus, if the treaty gives West Florida back to Spain she alone will be the proprietor of the river from the 31st parallel to the sea. "Whatever may be the case with that part which is beyond this point to the north, the United States of America can have no pretensions to it, not being masters of either border of this river." Rayneval's conclusion, if accepted, would have rendered nugatory a major objective of John Jay's diplomatic mission to Spain.

The next day Rayneval placed in Aranda's hands an even longer memorandum, wherein he denied America's claims to the Northwest on the basis of "the ephemeral raid" made by George Rogers Clark in 1779. He did suggest to Aranda the advisability of conceding to the Americans the privilege of navigating the Mississippi, and of granting them a free port near its mouth in return for an American acknowledgment of the proposed boundary. On the other hand, Rayneval seemed prepared to give Spain absolute control over the territory west of the Cumberland–Tennessee– Appalachicola Bay line without obligating Spain to assume a protectorate over independent Indians to the west of that line. These discrepancies between the two memoranda Jay did not know about. Each seemed rather carefully tailored to make the maximum impact on its designated reader.

Rayneval had more pressing business on his hands than the settlement of the Spanish-American dispute. On September 7th he left for England incognito. Three days later as "Monsieur Castel" he took up lodgings in London. Addressing a letter to Shelburne that very day, he asked permission to call upon him promptly at his country home in Wiltshire in order to give him a letter from Vergennes. Significantly, he signed the note as "Secretary of the Council of State of His Most Christian Majesty."[47] Bowood Park provided the setting for the discussions which began on September 13th and continued for almost a week.[48]

Like so many other well-guarded secrets Rayneval's absence was noted almost at once in Paris and caused a buzz of speculation. Vergennes had shared the secret with Aranda, and even provided the Conde with a copy of his instructions to Rayneval.[49] To cover himself Vergennes also informed the ambassadors of the comediating countries of the mission, but he made a point of not telling his American allies. Word spread quickly, however.

By the ninth, two days after Rayneval had set forth on his trip, Jay had learned of it from Matthew Ridley, who got around in the best circles of Paris, as well as from other sources.[50] Jay's suspicions had already been aroused on learning that on the morning of Rayneval's departure the Conde de Aranda had, "contrary to his usual practice, gone with *post horses* to Versailles," and was two hours in conference with Vergennes and his undersecretary. It seemed only obvious to put two and two together. Assuredly the Spanish ambassador had not taken post horses to turn over to Rayneval a new recipe for *gazpacho*. Jay rushed to Passy. He and Franklin agreed to take no public notice of the journey, but the doctor, unable to contain his curiosity, dashed off a note to Lafayette to find out the purpose of Rayneval's trip.[51]

To Jay the gossip about Rayneval's secret mission sounded an alarm bell in the night. From his own knowledge he had every reason to fear that a quick deal was in the offing between the other belligerents at the expense of the United States. Distorted accounts of Rayneval's visit which leaked out to the British press seemed to support such an interpretation.[52] Apart from rumor, Jay's suspicions seemed confirmed both by the Rayneval memorandum on the West and by a copy of an intercepted cipher dispatch from Barbé-Marbois to Vergennes, which a member of the British mission thoughtfully placed in Jay's hands. The communication, certainly no more indiscreet than countless others from the pens of the Secretary of Legation or the Chevalier de La Luzerne himself, was dated March 13, 1782. Therein Barbé-Marbois referred to the instructions of Congress to the peace commissioners as leaving "the King master of the terms of the treaty of peace, or truce, excepting independence and treaties of alliance." His letter shed further light on the growing breach between the French and Americans over the fisheries. Barbé-Marbois denounced the New England faction in general and Sam Adams in particular for stirring up trouble by insisting on sharing in the fisheries off the Grand Bank. He warned that England might even be tempted to make such a concession just to stir up jealousy between America and France. Such embarrassment might have been avoided had France been so prudent as "to have declared at an early period to the Americans that their pretension is not founded and that his Majesty does not mean to support it." The King, Barbé-Marbois advised now, should express "his surprise that the Newfoundland fisheries have been included in the additional instructions" of Congress and that the United States should have set forth such pretensions "without paying heed to the King's rights." Such a declaration, he urged, should be made before peace came, and, if at all possible, while the redcoats still held New York, Charleston, and Penobscot.[53]

Almost from the moment this interception was placed in John Jay's hands doubts were cast on the letter's authenticity. Vergennes was later to insist that, even if authentic and correctly deciphered, the translation was forced, that Marbois' opinion was "not necessarily that of the King," and, finally, that "the views indicated in the dispatch" had not been followed.[54] Franklin, closely reflecting Vergennes' views, felt that the channel of communication to Jay made the letter suspect, that it could well have been doctored, and that in any event the "forward, mistaken zeal of a secretary of legation should not be imputed to the King."[55] True, doctored and forged interceptions were by no means uncommon in these war years, but Barbé-Marbois' letter does not fall into that category. Its authenticity is today beyond question. Despite the denial of an eminent French diplomatic scholar that no copy of this dispatch was found in the French diplomatic archives, one of the quintuplicate copies did reach France from Philadelphia some time during the summer of '82 and may still be read in the *Correspondance politique, États-Unis* series, at the Quai d'Orsay.[56] The red-faced secretary of legation categorically denied having written the letter,[57] but after the storm abated was reputed on at least two occasions to have admitted authorship.[58]

Massive evidence in the diplomatic archives reveals that the views expressed by Barbé-Marbois on the fisheries and Rayneval on the boundaries were not purely personal to the authors but expressed the deep-seated convictions of their court on both issues. One of the books that John Adams studied abroad with unusual absorption was a French tract published with government approval in 1780, entitled *Observations sur le Traité de la Paix Conclu à Paris.* The author urged that the forthcoming treaty secure for France the unlimited freedom of fishing in North America and advocated the establishment of strongholds in the Gulf of St. Lawrence and Newfoundland for the defense of French fishing ships otherwise exposed to harassment from the British while the New Englanders were finding means of appropriating all the riches of the sea.[59] Repeatedly had Vergennes found it necessary to caution Congress through his envoys at Philadelphia on pressing their claims to the fisheries. From the moment the colonies issued their Declaration of Independence, Vergennes contended, they ceased to share the fisheries. Insisting that France's guarantee bore only on independence, Vergennes wrote La Luzerne as recently as August 12th, "We will not sacrifice our own fisheries and we will not prolong the calamities of war to force England to sacrifice hers."[60]

By early September, when the Marbois dispatch was placed in Jay's hands, the French were deep in discussions with Fitzherbert over the fisheries. They were currently proposing revisions of the Newfoundland fisheries arrangements without any reference whatsoever to the United States, including a demand for a cession giving France *exclusive* possession of that section of Newfoundland where French fishermen were still privileged to dry their fish.[61] Fitzherbert, in a conference with Vergennes and Rayneval toward the end of August, took occasion to remind the Frenchmen that the Americans were likely to advance a claim to participate in the fisheries. "Nothing could be farther from the wishes of this Court," Rayneval replied, "than that such a claim should be admitted." He added gratuitously, "You, too, in your hearts, are not only bound in interest to reject it, but you might do so consistent with the strictest principles of justice on the ground of your being the sole and undoubted proprietor of the Island of Newfoundland, and consequently of the fishery upon its coasts. . . . Of course, I only speak for myself," Rayneval added with his customary caution. Fitzherbert took the disclaimer with a grain of salt. It was "natural to suppose," he reported to Grantham, "that his ideas and language upon this and other political subjects must be nearly the same with those of his principle."[62] This underhand gesture against an ally was one that an adversary was not likely to forget. Retrospectively Fitzherbert commented, "M. de Vergennes never failed to insist on the expediency of a concert of measures between France and England for the purpose of excluding the American states from these fisheries, lest they should become a nursery for seamen."[63]

On the matter of boundaries Vergennes seemed as restrictive as had Rayneval. First of all, he was concerned that the Americans should not acquire Canada. "You know our system with regard to Canada," he wrote La Luzerne. "It is unchanging. Whatever will halt the conquest of this country accords with our views. But you will agree, Monsieur, that this way of thinking ought to be an impenetrable secret from the Americans. It would be a crime that they would never pardon. It is convenient, then, to make an outward show to convince them that we share their views, but to checkmate any steps that would put them into effect in case we are required to cooperate." His interpretation of Canada was so broad as to exclude the Americans from the Great Lakes, which he considered "a part of Canada." As regards the claims to the West put forward by Jay, claims resting on the sea-to-sea provisions of the old charters, Vergennes dismissed them as "foolishness not meriting serious refutation." These ideas are for your ears alone, La Luzerne was again cautioned. Do not reveal this information "because for the present we do not wish to intervene in the discussion between Aranda and Jay."[64]

Without being privy to this correspondence John Jay was convinced that Rayneval's memoir on the boundaries voiced the official French position. At the proper time, he felt, France was prepared to assume the role of arbiter between Spain and America, to contest America's extension to the Mississippi as well as her claim to the free navigation of that river, and most "certainly" to support Britain's claims north of the Ohio. In the event that America would not agree to a division of the West with Spain along Rayneval's lines, then Jay feared that France would favor splitting the territory lying north of the 31st parallel and below the Ohio between Spain and Britain.[65]

With the evidence before him, both direct and circumstantial, Jay now acted swiftly. On September 9th he learned of Rayneval's secret trip. The next day he was handed the intercepted Barbé-Marbois dispatch. Wasting not a moment, he immediately broke off his discussions with Aranda. Like a woman scorned, the Conde fell into a fury. He accused Jay of bad faith and lacking talent for diplomacy, and put the blame for the breakdown on the New Yorker's exalted opinion of his own public character. On one of those rare occasions when the Conde and Spain's first minister saw eye to eye, Floridablanca sent back a consoling note, ridiculing Jay, his pretensions, and his unending cries for recognition and money. In turn, Jay attributed the impasse to Spain's shortsightedness. "There is a tide in human affairs," he wrote the French chargé at Madrid, "which waits for nobody, and political mariners ought to watch it and avail themselves of its advantages."[66]

While the Jay-Aranda negotiations were broken off in Paris, the Rayneval-Shelburne talks were proceeding smoothly. Rayneval's visit was prompted, not by the American issue, despite the apprehensions of the French court about America's pretensions, but by the conviction on Vergennes' part that the Allies should now get out of the war if decent terms were offered them. For a certainty the French Minister was as much concerned about Spain's inflexible position on Gibraltar as he was about prolonging the war to satisfy America's demands. The day Rayneval left for England Vergennes wrote Montmorin at Madrid: "Let us not lose the occasion if it presents itself to end a war honorably, a war promoted less by ambition than to reestablish ourselves in that position of equality becoming to great powers."[67] This was a thinly veiled warning to Spain not to hold out for unreasonable terms.

Rayneval was instructed to ask Shelburne point-blank whether the notions about peace he had discussed with Admiral de Grasse conformed to his present intentions. Should Shelburne disavow them, then Rayneval was to demand his passport and leave England. In other words, he was to feel out Shelburne rather than enter into negotiations, and he was to remind the Earl that it was the King of France's intention of treating only in conjunction with his allies. For that assignment a stay of eight or ten days would suffice, Vergennes figured. The Comte gave Rayneval a personal letter assuring Shelburne that the bearer possessed his "full confidence."[68]

Although Rayneval quickly discovered that Shelburne had no intention of making the generous concessions that de Grasse had attributed to him, and even insisted that he had been misquoted by the Admiral,[69] he did not break off his talks and ask for his passport as instructed. The Frenchman was fascinated by his clever host and seemed captive to the conciliatory mood he sought to arouse. Rayneval's stay at Bowood and a subsequent visit some months later converted him into an ardent admirer of Shelburne. He found the Earl "a minister of noble views" and "winning manners," neither "an intriguer" nor an "equivocator," "whatever persons say who imagine that they know him, but imagine wrongly."[70]

Certain later critics have belabored Jay for his assumption that Rayneval went to England to arrange a deal about the West and the fisheries. In refutation these critics have pointed to Rayneval's formal instructions by which he was told to pursue the conversations begun by de Grasse. These written instructions contained nothing about America's claims, and only passing references to America are found in the contemporary account Rayneval has left us of his conversations with Shelburne. These talks dealt largely with Franco-Spanish grievances, with the West and East Indies, the Newfoundland fisheries, the slave trade, Dunkirk, Gibraltar, and freedom of commerce. Indeed, Jay's detractors have contended that America did not even come up in the conversations.[71]

Jay's sons and grandsons took up the cudgels in his behalf, and were seconded by the articulate progeny of John Adams. With proper allowance for the filiopietistic impulses of Jay's champions, it is now perfectly clear that Jay's critics were unwilling to draw reasonable inferences from the circumstantial evidence at hand and were careless in their reading of Rayneval's own account of his trip. On September 8th Aranda made the significant observation to Floridablanca that regardless of Jay's obduracy the English would be consulted about America's territorial claims and that nothing further could be done with the Americans until Rayneval's return.[72] It was probably no coincidence that a copy of Rayneval's historical memoir found its way into the *Angleterre* section of the *Correspondance politique*, wherein the papers relating to Rayneval's mission are filed. It seems a reasonable inference that the undersecretary took this document with him when he went to see Shelburne.

Rayneval's own report of his conversations belies the assertions that he did not advert to America. The subject of America came up almost at once. Shelburne conceded that he had "always been opposed to independence, that it was the hardest pill to digest, but that he recognized the necessity of swallowing it, and that this object would be decided unconditionally." Later on in the talks independence was again referred to, but taken for granted by both parties.

After luncheon on the first day of their talks the two diplomats took a stroll through the Earl's wooded park, which gently sloped downward to the man-made lake in which Shelburne took special pride. The talks now turned on the fisheries. Without a doubt the Americans would put in some claims here, Shelburne remarked, but he hoped the King would not yield anything to them. Rayneval replied that, while he did not know the views of Congress on the fisheries, he could take it on himself to say that "the King would never support an unjust demand." Thus, while Shelburne was privately repudiating the decision taken by his own Cabinet to concede to the Americans a share in the fisheries, a decision taken hardly more than a week earlier, Rayneval, emboldened by the Earl's apparent accord on this point, declared, *"We do not want the Americans to share in the fisheries."*

After dinner the issue of the mediators came up. Shelburne, in Rayneval's account, "exhibited great coldness for the Court of Vienna," and the two parties readily agreed that peace could be achieved without mediation. "Only three persons should make the peace," Shelburne insisted. By three he included himself, along with Vergennes, and Rayneval as the channel of communication between the two ministers. However flattering Shelburne's posture may have seemed to Rayneval, it was a characteristic sample of Shelburne's penchant for backstage operations, of his readiness to by-pass Alleyne Fitzherbert and Lord Grantham in the Anglo-French negotiations just as he had been prepared to by-pass Thomas Grenville and even the loyal Oswald.[73]

Shelburne continually dangled before the French the prospect that after the peace an Anglo-French *entente* or even a political amalgam of the two might "act as arbiter of the public peace." We could then take a firm stand toward Russia and Prussia, the Earl pointed out, and prevent the kind of partition that had been taking place in Poland. The idea of an *entente* was again reverted to by Shelburne in his closing talk with Rayneval on September 18th. "Let us cease fighting each other," he urged, "and we will lay down the law to the rest of Europe." He reminded Rayneval of the "time when no one dared shoot off a cannon in Europe without the consent of England and France. . . . If we are in accord we can once again assume our former place and we will stop all the revolutions in Europe." Rayneval found the idea of an *entente* a congenial one.

On the second day of their conferences Shelburne and Rayneval agreed that secrecy was necessary to establish the preliminaries of peace. Rayneval pointed out that there were ways of putting the Americans and the Dutch off the track by keeping them in ignorance of the negotiations between England, France, and Spain. The idea seemed to please Shelburne.[74]

At the closing conference on September 18th the talks again reverted to the Americans, whose pretensions were remarked upon during the course of the opening day's talks. Shelburne confided to Rayneval how much trouble the Americans were stirring up over the boundaries and the fisheries, and expressed the hope that the King of France would not support them. Rayneval answered that he had no doubt of the King's intention to do what could be done to "contain the Americans within the bounds of justice and reason."

"What do you think of their pretensions?" Shelburne asked his guest.

"I do not know what they are relative to the fisheries," Rayneval answered, "but whatever they might be, it appears to me that there is a sound principle to uphold in this matter: Recognize that the fisheries in the high seas are *res nullius*, while the fisheries on the coast belong by right to the proprietor of the coast, except where modified by agreement."

Having blasted America's claims to shore rights for drying fish as well as to fishing within coastal waters, Rayneval turned to the boundaries. To sound out Shelburne he expressed his own belief that the Americans would stand on the provisions of their ancient charters. "That would be silly," Shelburne remarked. Rayneval reported that he did not pursue this line of discussion "because I did not wish either to sustain the American pretension or to deny it." He did not switch the subject, however, before pointing out that the British government might find that the negotiations of 1754 relative to the Ohio offered a measuring stick to settle what should be allotted the United States. As Rayneval interpreted it, the rule would have quashed America's claims to the lands lying north of the Ohio. It is scarcely a coincidence that this same emphasis on the 1754 negotiations appears in the memoir Rayneval had put in Jay's hands before departing for England.

Emboldened by the support of the French court implied in Rayneval's remarks as well as by the heartening news to come from Gibraltar, Shelburne was to renege the Cabinet offer of August 30th, and to put up one more desperate stand along the Ohio. Counting on French support in withholding the "back lands" from America, Shelburne instructed Oswald at a later date to learn through Fitzherbert just how Rayneval and his court stood as regards America's territorial claims. According to Shelburne's own acount, Rayneval gave him to understand that, once independence was granted, the French "were disposed to assist us as to the Boundaryes."[75] Indeed, the anti-American overtones of Rayneval's remarks did not pass unnoticed by Shelburne. "He appears rather jealous than partial to America upon other points, as well as that of the Fishery," he reported to George III after his very first conference with the Frenchman.[76] Subsequent talks gave Shelburne no cause to modify his observation. So much, then, for the charge that Jay's superheated imagination magnified an innocuous mission into an anti-American plot.

While Rayneval's conversations with Shelburne provided further confirmation for the British of the widening rift between France and America over terms of peace, they also exposed to view the tightrope on which Shelburne himself was teetering. Regardless of his own convictions about the need for American independence, Shelburne had to pursue a political course demanding acrobatic agility of a high order. He had to deal daily with a King unaccustomed to hearing unpalatable truths and to prepare to face some months off a Parliament and a public still ill-prepared to accept terms of submission. Some of these problems Shelburne mentioned to Rayneval in his closing talk. It was terribly difficult to talk to the King, he told the Frenchman. His ministers had never spoken to him save to refer to his grandeur and his power. They had always elevated him above the greatest monarchs, told him that he commanded infinite resources whereas France was exhausted and without credit. He was informed that by continuing the war he would inevitably smash the French Navy. All these ideas, Shelburne explained, had been drummed into the head of George III in the past. To counteract them was indeed a "delicate and difficult" undertaking, but, he reassured his listener, he had the courage to attempt it and up to a point he flattered himself that he had succeeded. With French assistance, he now hoped he could bring about the King's complete conversion.[77]

The letters passing between Lord Shelburne and George III during these fateful weeks disclose how the former constantly sugar-coated the pill and pursued a zigzag course to overcome the King's suspicions. Thus Shelburne found Rayneval "a well-instructed, inoffensive man of business," who stressed Vergennes' eagerness to "expedite everything which can contribute to an instant and final conclusion" of hostilities. When the conferences started, he told the King, he had been "as clearly of opinion against a peace as I ever was against American independence, till in fact the resolutions of the House of Commons decided the point." Now he reminded the monarch of the state of the army and navy, of the troubles in Ireland, and the temper of the Commons. All these factors pointed to the necessity of a quick peace with France.[78]

Let us not be "too eager to advance the negotiation," the King cautioned his First Lord of the Treasury, and do not be "deceived by the appearance of Monsr. de Rayneval. I owne the art of Monsr. de Vergennes is so well known that I cannot think he would send him if he was an inoffensive man of business; but that he has chosen him from having that appearance whilst well-armed with cunning, which will be the more dangerous if under so specious a garb." Do not rush affairs at the sacrifice of our national interests, he warned a few days later. As for himself, George III could do nothing but pray to heaven for guidance "that posterity may not lay the downfall of this once respectable Empire at my door; and that if ruin should attend the measures that may be adopted, I may not long survive."[79] His deep-dyed suspicions of the French notwithstanding, George III had been cleverly maneuvered into a state of resignation about yielding Gibraltar provided there was equivalent compensation and even to seeing the advantage of pressing the French negotiations to strengthen the hand of the British with the Americans.

John Jay had been quick to perceive the peril to American interests at the peacemaking should France and England arrive at a secret understanding. To divine the nature of the Rayneval-Shelburne conversations was beyond the Americans, who lacked the same kind of intelligence service from inside of Bowood Park that Dr. Edward Bancroft had so obligingly provided the British for years from within Franklin's Passy household.[80] Yet the New Yorker was convinced by a perusal of the Rayneval memoir that France was prepared to frustrate America's major aspirations, aside from independence, and his views were shared by Benjamin Vaughan.[81] Jay conjectured, as he later wrote Secretary Livingston, that Rayneval was sent to England:

1st, To let Lord Shelburne know that the demands of America to be treated as independent previous to a treaty were not approved or countenanced by this Court, and that the offer of Britain to make that acknowledgment in an article of the proposed treaty was in the Count's opinion sufficient.

2dly, To sound Lord Shelburne on the subject of the fishery, and to discover whether Britain would agree to divide it with France to the exclusion of all others.

3dly, To impress Lord Shelburne with the determination of Spain to possess the exclusive navigation of the Gulf of Mexico, and of their desire to keep us from the Mississippi; and also to hint the propriety of such a line as on the one hand would satisfy Spain and on the other leave to Britain all the country north of the Ohio.

4thly, To make such other verbal overtures to Lord Shelburne as it might not be advisable to reduce to writing, and to judge, from the general tenor of his lordship's answers and conversations whether it was probable that a general peace, on terms agreeable to France, could be effected in order that, if that was not the case, an immediate stop might be put to the negotiation.[82]

Convinced that Vergennes would rather "postpone the acknowledgment of our independence by Britain to the conclusion of a general peace than aid us in procuring it at present," Jay took the most audacious step of his career. He dispatched Benjamin Vaughan to England on a mission so secret that neither Vergennes nor Franklin was apprised of it. Vaughan was sent to counteract Rayneval. He was instructed to tell Shelburne that "the manner as well as the matter of the proposed treaty" was important, and that without unconditional acknowledgment of independence "neither confidence nor peace could reasonably be expected." Such acknowledgment Jay labeled "the touchstone of British sincerity." Vaughan was to point out to Shelburne how vain it was to count on France's acting as a moderating influence, for America "never would treat on any but an equal footing," and he was to show how it was in France's interest to postpone such acknowledgment to the very conclusion of the treaty, thereby obliging the Americans, both by the terms of their treaty with France as well as for their own safety, to continue in the war to the end. These considerations, Jay made clear, underscored the "obvious interest of Britain immediately to cut the cords which tied us to France, for that, though we were determined faithfully to fulfill our treaty and engagements with this court, *yet it was a different thing to be guided by their or our construction of it.*"

Adverting to the terms he anticipated Rayneval would be taking up with Shelburne, Jay instructed Vaughan on the fisheries. "We could not make peace," the agent was told, at the expense of England's dividing the fisheries with France and excluding America. He also gave Vaughan instructions on the boundaries and the navigation of the Mississippi. To contest the American claims to either would be "impolitic," he was told. Shelburne was to be enticed into making these concessions by holding out to him "the profits of an extensive and lucrative commerce." Not "the possession of vast tracts of wilderness," but commerce was the true objective of "a commercial European nation," Jay shrewdly reminded Shelburne, the free trader. Dangling the prospects of an immense amount of trade into the interior of the country, Jay now intimated, and without authority either from Congress or his colleagues on the peace commission, that America was prepared to share that interior trade with England, including the free navigation of the Mississippi. England should abandon any idea of retaining any part of the back country or of insisting on extending the bounds of Canada "so as to comprehend the lands in question." Nothing could prevent the Americans from gradually taking possession of the area, Jay prophesied, and to hold on to it would be to sow the seeds of future war. By implication Jay now waived all claims to ancient Canada itself. In short, Vaughan was instructed to impress Shelburne "with the necessity and policy of taking a decided and manly part respecting America."[83]

That Jay should have picked for so delicate a mission a man who was the unavowed agent of the British First Minister may seem astonishing at this day when there is much less tolerance of divided loyalties than in Jay's time. Yet the New Yorker had complete reliance on Benjamin Vaughan's basic friendliness to the American cause, and his trust was not misplaced. Vaughan immediately dashed off a few lines to Shelburne. "In the utmost haste," he informed the Earl that "an affair has occurred which gives much alarm here. M. de Rayneval, Count de Vergennes' principal secretary, will probably soon be with your lordship, as we suspect on deep business. . . . Will your lordship," he asked, "be kind enough to take no sort of measure till one of us comes over, or a courier arrives?"[84]

Jay talked over Vaughan's prospective visit with Richard Oswald, but hid it from Franklin. "It would have relieved me from much anxiety and uneasiness," he confessed to Secretary Livingston, "to have concerted all these steps with Dr. Franklin, but on conversing with him about M. Rayneval's journey, he did not concur with me in sentiment respecting the objects of it." To invite Franklin's opinion on the necessity of the trip would have been to court a possible veto. To have confided in him would have jeopardized the secrecy of the project.[85] Needless to say, Jay did not apprise Vergennes of his plans nor Lafayette. The latter was used by the Comte to pump Jay about the Rayneval mission. On the twenty-first Lafayette remarked casually to Jay that a courier had just come over from England and he wondered what the dispatches were about. "The best way to find out would be to write Mr. de Rayneval in England," Jay replied dryly.

"Why do you believe he is there?" Lafayette asked.

"It's on everybody's lips, and I can't help but suppose it to be true."

"Well, then, why do you think he has gone over?" Lafayette prodded.

"I don't know."

"Well, guess."

"I'd rather not."

Vergennes proved almost as uncommunicative to the Marquis about the Rayneval mission as had Jay. "What did Shelburne say about America?" Lafayette reported that he asked the Comte.

"*Assez convenable,*" was the cryptic reply.[86]

A week before Jay had decided to send Vaughan over to see Shelburne he had finally hit on a satisfactory formula to end the impasse over independence. On September 2nd he informed Oswald that, if Franklin would consent, he was prepared to accept "a constructive denomination of character to be introduced in the preamble of the treaty" which would merely describe their constituents as "the Thirteen United States of America." While Oswald readily agreed, Jay reminded him that he had no authority to treat with the Americans "under that denomination." Jay now narrowed his insistence down to "an explicit authority" to be stated in Oswald's commission.

"How about using the term 'provinces' instead of 'states,' or the expression 'states or provinces'?" Oswald suggested.

"No, neither will answer," Jay replied.

"Then let me have in writing a draft of the alteration you propose."

Jay did so at once, and Oswald forwarded the draft of the new commission to the Home Office. Jay's alteration would have empowered the Scot "to treat of Peace or Truce with the Commissioners and Persons vested with equal powers by and on the part of the Thirteen United States of America."[87] Obligingly, Jay also offered to turn over to Oswald a draft of a letter he might send back "to satisfy His Majesty's Ministers of the propriety of their conduct." The draft again stressed America's insistence on being treated on the basis of equality and restated Jay's objections to having such acknowledgment deferred until the first article of a treaty. To do so would mean, Jay pointed out, "that we are not to be considered in that light until after the conclusion of the treaty, and our acquiescing would be to admit the propriety of our being considered in another light during that interval." Jay presumed that the British court would not wish to press a measure which could not "be reconciled with the received ideas of national honor." Hence he gave his assurances that, had Oswald been commissioned "in the usual manner," the negotiations would have gone forward. The removal of this obstacle, Jay concluded, was a trivial matter to Great Britain, "but so essential and insuperable with respect to us."[88]

Jay showed the draft letter to Franklin, and the pair thrashed the matter out on the evening of the ninth and again the following morning. The doctor, still incapacitated from his severe attack, persuaded Jay not to turn it over to Oswald. The letter was "too positive, and therefore rather imprudent," Franklin argued. Suppose we have to back down? After so peremptory a rejection we would do so with ill grace, he pointed out. Behind his objections, Franklin confessed, lay a deep uneasiness about whether such a move might be considered a violation of the commissioners' instructions which fettered them to the French court. Jay quickly dismissed both objections. He could conceive of no situation, he rejoined, where it would be proper, "and therefore possible," for America "to treat in any other character than that of an independent nation." He reminded the doctor, once again, that as regards the instructions, he "could not believe that Congress intended we should follow any advice which might be repugnant to their dignity and interest."

Leaving Passy without Franklin's signature to the draft letter, Jay returned to Paris, dropping in at Oswald's at noontime. "I can't let you have the letter. You had best phrase it in your own way," Jay informed the British commissioner, who could not conceal his disappointment. Oswald tried now to pin the commissioners down to a definite commitment.

"In your conference with the Doctor this morning," he asked Jay, "did you and he agree that upon my receiving from his Majesty a new commission under the Great Seal such as the last, with an alteration only of my being empowered to treat with you as Commissioners of the Thirteen United States of America, naming the states by their several provincial distinctions, did you both agree in that case to go on with the treaty, and without any other declaration of independence than as standing as an article in that Treaty?"

"Yes," Jay reassured Oswald. "With this we will be satisfied. Immediately upon such commission coming over, we would proceed with the Treaty, and should not be long about it. I might add that perhaps we should not be so hard upon you in the conditions we exact."

Then Oswald turned back to Jay's draft letter. He insisted that he needed it to convince his government of the good faith of the American commissioners. Jay was at length persuaded to turn over to him an unsigned copy of the draft. "With some difficulty I got [it] out of his hands after it had been settled with his Friend that it was not proper to go before any public Board." In transmitting to the Home Secretary Jay's proposed alteration of the commission along with his draft letter, Oswald warned his government that if they rejected Jay's compromise formula "there will be an end to all further confidence and communication with the Americans."[89] "With great difficulty," Oswald wrote Shelburne, "they have yielded to this mode of compromise. . . . I hope His Majesty will grant it. If it is refused, Mr. Fitzherbert as well as me, may go home, and in my opinion it will not be an easy matter for any other to take up the same clue for extracting the Nation out of its difficulties which I think is within our reach." In that same letter Oswald pointed out that the Spaniards apparently wanted a cession from England before the American treaty was ironed out, and that this was the apparent motive behind Rayneval's visit. "If that gentleman goes over," he added, "there can be no difficulty in amusing him."[90]

While these negotiations were going on Vergennes was using Lafayette as an intermediary with the American commissioners to make clear that, although he had no objection to making independence a preliminary, he wanted to be sure that all the preliminaries were signed simultaneously. The Comte still felt that the issue that Jay had raised could be settled if only Oswald would write a letter agreeing to treat with the American commissioners "in their capacity as plenipotentiaries of the United States," with the understanding that George III's renunciation of the territory of the United States would be contained in the first article of the treaty. Jay was not content with such "expedients,"[91] nor with the ambivalent role of Lafayette. Under the character of an American and as aide to Franklin by Congressional designation,[92] the Marquis claimed an insider's role in the British-American negotiations, while as a loyal Frenchman he was constantly leaking confidential information to Vergennes. "This mongrel character of French Patriot and American Patriot," as John Adams uncharitably put it, made Lafayette increasingly suspect in American circles in Paris. "As we have a competent number of commissioners," Jay tactfully advised Secretary Livingston, "it ought not be necessary to trouble the Marquis." Adams put it with his customary bluntness. "There ought to be no Go-between," he declared.[93] What made the situation especially delicate was Jay's conviction that Franklin was passing on to Lafayette a full account of all the moves the New Yorker made, so far as they were known to him. Accordingly, Jay said nothing to his aged colleague about handing over the unsigned draft to Oswald.[94]

Jay's altered proposal gave an urgency to Vaughan's trip. On September 11th Vaughan wrote Shelburne to inform him of his intention of following "a few hours after the present courier," and apprising him of the rumor that Rayneval's journey had for its object an "underhand bargain" between England and Spain. "This is a crisis of the first consequence," Vaughan declared. He urged Shelburne to hold up his negotiations with the Frenchman, but advised him that he should act with "instantaneous despatch" in dealing with the American commissioners and in modifying the form of Oswald's commission to suit Jay's demands. " 'America must have a character,' to use the words of Mr. Adams," Vaughan remarked. Finally, he cautioned Shelburne in language close to that of Oswald's, "If this moment is rudely managed, or slightly passed over, I conceive peace in *consequence* takes its flight." In short, in this crisis the alternatives were "good sense" or "ruin."[95]

That night Vaughan left for London.[96] His arrival in England obliged Shelburne to suspend his zigzag course. A decision to issue a new commission in the form Jay had proposed was not one to be made casually by England's First Minister. Shelburne had, first of all, to consider the King's feelings. Next he had to pay heed to public opinion. During September he continued to receive anonymous letters warning him that "America must be preserved to England," and even threatening him with assassination should he concede independence.[97] So intimate a follower of Shelburne's as Thomas Orde cautioned his chief about the alarm prevailing both in the city and over the countryside as a result of rumors of "the extent of the concessions made by this country." People might digest independence as the price of peace, Orde pointed out, but would with difficulty be reconciled to an unconditional grant so damaging to "our national pride should no concessions be gained thereby." At least there should be an implied agreement on all the issues under discussion *before* the "irretrievable surrender of sovereignty," he pleaded.[98] Another intimate, Lord Ashburton, warned Shelburne that to issue the commission in the form Jay proposed and Vaughan was now urging in person would put "the Executive Government" in a dubious light should peace not be attained, but he did reluctantly agree that the alterations came within the terms of the Enabling Act.[99] Fortuitously for the cause of peace, the Lord Chancellor, who, as might be anticipated, showed no enthusiasm for the new form, was out of town when the Cabinet took action, as was the unpredictable Duke of Richmond. Thurlow, still suspicious of the American commissioners, considered Jay's demands for preliminary independence to be "frivolous," and felt that the British would henceforth be negotiating from weakness, especially in view of their failure to secure advance commitments on the Tories and the debts.[100]

Vaughan's personal appeal, Oswald's threats, and Jay's sober arguments all added up to compelling reasons for complying with the New Yorker's wishes, and overriding the grumblers within the Ministry. A special meeting of "a considerable number" of the Cabinet who happened to be in town was called for the night of September 18th, less than a week after

Vaughan's arrival in England, and on the day of Rayneval's final conference with Shelburne. The Cabinet voted to change the commission and to empower Oswald "to treat, consult, and conclude with any Commissioner or person vested with equal power by and on the part of the Thirteen United States of America," named in geographical order from north to south. Significantly, the Cabinet did not consider the new phraseology to amount to "a final acknowledgment of independence," but merely as providing the American commissioners during the negotiations with "the title they wished to assume." This may have been technically correct, and Shelburne was later to insist on this point in defense of his course before Parliament. Neither Townshend nor Shelburne admitted any such thing to Oswald, however, when on the following day a new commission was sent over to Paris embodying the change that Jay had desired.[101]

How decisive a factor was the Vaughan mission in persuading Shelburne to back down on the issue of independence? The motivations of a figure as inscrutable as Shelburne cannot be pinned down with certitude. The papers of Shelburne and Townshend disclose that it was the "private letters from Paris," presumably brought by Vaughan, which impelled Shelburne to take the forward step. Vaughan himself had no doubts whatsoever about it. Writing many, many years later, he recounted that Shelburne only asked him, "Is the new Commission necessary? and when I answered 'Yes,' it was instantly granted."[102] Shelburne may well have been on the verge, but Vaughan's presence seems to have precipitated the decision to jump. "Mr. Vaughan greatly merits our acknowledgments," Jay reported home.[103]

His business with Shelburne completed, Vaughan returned to Paris on September 27th with word that there was "every disposition in Lord Shelburne for peace." As solid evidence he could point to the new commission for Oswald which the courier had brought and the copy for Mr. Jay. Even Franklin, who had been grumbling about "standing out for the previous acknowledgment of Independency" and been overheard remarking that it was "a pity to keep three or four millions of people in war for the sake of form," was content with the new commission,[104] for which he could scarcely claim credit.[105] Franklin's implied criticism of Jay for stalling the negotiations on a technicality was hardly fair, for, as we now know, it was Townshend who kept Oswald from disclosing his full hand, and it was Jay who speedily devised a compromise formula to end the impasse. Despite some reservations on the part of the doctor about legal quibbling, Jay's solo performance did not lessen Franklin's admiration for him one whit, and the pair henceforth worked together in close harmony.

Had Shelburne finally and irretrievably committed himself to the Americans? The evidence hardly supports so rash an inference. George III, commenting on a report from Vaughan on the progress of the negotiations which Shelburne had passed on to the monarch, remarked significantly:

Lord Shelburne does not, I am clear, admire the style of Mr. Vaughan's letter more than I do. He seems to look alone to our placing implicit trust in the Americans, whilst Lord Shelburne's ideas coincide with mine in thinking it safer to confide in France than in either Spain or America.[106]

Shelburne's colleague, Thomas Townshend, observed to Oswald at the time, "I hope that the frankness with which we deal will meet with a suitable return,"[107] but, considering the reserve which he himself held about the commission, his comment does seem rather disingenuous. Nevertheless the Cabinet had taken a calculated gamble. Lord Shelburne knew full well that in pressing for this modification of the commission he risked his political future, for all he knew his very life. To Oswald he observed: "We have put the greatest confidence, I believe, was ever placed in Men, in the American Commissioners. It is now to be seen, how far they or America are to be depended upon. . . . I have assumed a great risk," he admitted ruefully. "I hope the Publick will be the gainer, else our heads must answer for it, and deservedly."[108]

Despite the mental reservations with which the British granted independence, reservations which the rest of Europe did not share, the Gordian knot had at long last been cut. It was inevitable that there should be loose ends, but, as Jay had predicted, the new commission "would set the whole machine in motion." For Great Britain, American independence was now irretrievable in fact, if not in law; for the world, peace was at last in sight.

XV

SETTING METES AND BOUNDS

ON THE THIRTEENTH of September, 1782, two contrasting scenes of the same drama were being played upon stages almost a thousand miles apart. Bowood Park furnished the setting for the first; Gibraltar, the second. While Gérard de Rayneval seated himself before Lord Shelburne's hearth and took up in conciliatory vein with his host the issues of peace, the Franco-Spanish armada under the Duc de Crillon, conqueror of Minorca, closed in upon a rocky limestone promontory jutting out into the Mediterranean. To soften up the defenses of the great fortress the combined fleet had for several days carried on a tremendous cannonade of the Rock. Then on the morning of the thirteenth a flotilla of ten huge battering ships, designed by the French engineer d'Arçon to be impervious to cannon shot, pulled to within less than a thousand yards of Gibraltar's walls. This was to be the *coup de grâce*. Sir George Elliot, commander of the British defenses, replied with a counterfire of red-hot balls, heated in grates and furnaces hastily constructed within the lines. By evening the battering ships were all afire, destined to blow up or burn to the water's edge. The attackers had suffered cruel punishment. Two thousand of their number were killed or captured. By the light from a lurid night sky the invincible fortress still looked down defiantly on the foe.[1]

"Don't blame Crillon," the influential Duc de Polignac advised Vergennes, merely because he shared the opinion of all the naval people about the "incombustible batteries. . . . As the sailors say, 'when the land commands the sea, everything is screwed up.' " Polignac pointed out that the Spanish Admiral Córdoba was "more than eighty years old, at an age when one is no more fit for war than for love."[2] This boudoir philosophy was small consolation to France's Foreign Minister, who had the unenviable task of persuading the British to yield the Rock to his Bourbon partner.

Everything happened the way John Adams predicted. "They will make a horrid noise with their artillery against the place; but this noise will not terrify Elliot, and Gilbraltar will remain to the English another year, and Lord Howe will return to England, and all Europe will laugh."[3] In this case Adams was blessed with second sight, for Admiral Howe's swifter ships evaded the cumbersome fleets of France and Spain, and succeeded in relieving Gibraltar in October, providing the defenders with all they needed for a prolonged resistance.[4] The Spaniards continued the siege half-heartedly until the following February, but without any constructive effect on the peace negotiation.

But in the waning summer of 1782 all Paris was astir with the news, and the *corps diplomatique* consumed with speculation. The Portuguese ambassador felt that the reports made it quite clear that Spain would not get Gibraltar at the peace, while it was "equally certain" that the English would concede independence to America.[5] The British, whose intelligence service had access to Aranda's dispatches from Madrid, were aware of the humiliating defeat of the combined fleets as soon as the French government.[6] "Not without sorrow," the Abbé Morellet wrote Shelburne on October 3rd to congratulate him on the successful defense of Gibraltar. An avowed pacifist, the Abbé drew consolation in defeat from the glory that would redound to his friend's Ministry.[7]

The humiliation of the armada before Gibraltar stiffened Shelburne's stand both toward his European adversaries and toward America. He has now upped his price, the Portuguese ambassador shrewdly observed.[8] Remarking on the halfhearted efforts of the French to capture the Rock, Benjamin Vaughan made the cynical prediction more than a month before the fiasco of the combined fleets "that at a peace it will not be very important to lose what France so much wishes we would keep."[9] In the wake of Gibraltar war weariness gripped France, most noticeably in the impoverished rural areas. Alleyne Fitzherbert relayed the rising sentiment in Paris that France had been the "dupe of her allies, the Americans and the Spaniards."[10]

London learned the good news from Gibraltar on September 30th,[11] just nine days after the new commission was made out for Oswald impliedly acknowledging the United States. In the light of the private reservations that Shelburne held all along, it is not improper to speculate whether he would have yielded the point of independence to Jay had modern means of instantaneous communication been at his command. Prior to learning the news of Gibraltar the Cabinet had made two major concessions, agreeing to Franklin's *necessary* articles and to Jay's revised commission. Henceforth the British sought to escalate their terms while the Americans fought stubbornly to hold them to their expressed intentions.

Richard Oswald, it must be said, pursued his part in good faith.[12] His counterpart, John Jay, was also ready to iron out the details of the treaty draft. In sending a hasty line to John Adams announcing Oswald's receipt of the commission, Jay added: "I have reasons for wishing that you would say nothing of this till you see me, which I hope and pray may be soon, very soon."[13] With Franklin still in poor physical shape, Jay needed reinforcements for his side badly. Lafayette followed up Jay's letter to Adams with a cautiously optimistic one of his own, in which he predicted that it would be five or six months before the "grand affair of peace" would be concluded. "Many attempts have been made to treat upon an unequal footing, which, by the bye, was a very impertinent proposal, but we stood firm, deaf, and dumb, and as France refused to enter into business until we were made to hear and to speak, at last, with much reluctance and great pains," the British issued the new commission.[14] The Marquis had certainly put the best face he could on France's efforts to thwart preliminary recognition, but Adams was not easily taken in.

He would come as soon as he could clear up business in Holland, Adams assured Jay, but "my health is so far from being robust that it will be impossible for me to ride with as much rapidity as I could formerly, although never remarkable for a quick traveler." He added, significantly, "If anything in the meantime should be in agitation concerning peace, in which there should be any difference of opinion between you and your colleague, you have a right to insist upon informing me by express, or waiting till I come."[15]

To the Americans Richard Oswald must have seemed like a pliant instrument sent from heaven rather than Whitehall. Patient and unruffled under trying circumstances, Oswald proved a good listener. No stickler on etiquette, he treated the commissioners as plenipotentiaries of an acknowledged power.[16] By now he was on the friendliest terms with Jay as well as Franklin, was convinced of the former's essential fairness and deep regard for England, and viewed the not far distant prospect of some "wise association" between England and America generated by common interests. In fact, Franklin now seemed less responsive than did Jay to hints thrown out of a "Federal Union." When Shelburne wrote Oswald to warn that heads would roll if the confidence of the government in the Americans had been misplaced, Oswald rushed to their defense. "Obstinate as they have been," he replied, the commissioners would have held up the negotiations rather than expose the British nation "to the hazard of a change."[17]

Surprisingly enough, no differences did develop between Franklin and Jay after the drafting of the provisional terms. Franklin, as Oswald reported, was still "in but an indifferent state of health."[18] Jay carried on the conversations with Oswald alone, and it is apparent that he dropped certain hints to which Franklin may not have been privy. Before making a provisional draft Jay talked terms over with Oswald. They quickly agreed on the four necessary articles, to which Jay was insistent on adding the "privilege in common" of drying fish on Newfoundland shores as well as on the American coast. This is the way Oswald reported it, but Jay used the much stronger word "right." Jay made it clear that the royal domain remaining ungranted within the states would revert to the States and not to the Loyalists, nor could he offer hope of pardon for Tories remaining at posts which the British might still have to evacuate.

In one controversial aspect of his draft Jay allowed his own perturbation over Spanish objections to the navigation of the Mississippi and to America's Western territorial claims to color his judgment. He was anxious to see West Florida in British rather than Spanish hands. "What are you doing with twenty thousand men?" he asked Oswald. "Why don't you ship the troops from Charleston and New York and seize West Florida?" As bait Jay was prepared to offer England a share in the control of the Mississippi and the freedom of the navigation of that river even beyond prospective British holdings. With Canada and the Floridas in British hands, it is by no means clear that America would have been better off after 1783 than with West Florida under Spanish control. Considering the diplomatic irritations which later could be laid to what turned out to be a gratuitous, unilateral proposition, this proffer, which won endorsement from Jay's fellow commissioners, was too shortsighted to do them credit. It was prompted by a degree of vindictiveness toward Spain which only compounded France's difficulties in maintaining her precarious bundle of alliances. Jay made no bones about his motives. "We will not allow France to saddle us with her engagements to Spain," he assured Oswald. "We shall say to France, 'The agreement we have made with you we shall faithfully perform. But, if you have entered into any separate measures with other people, not included in that agreement; and will load the negotiations with their demands, we shall give ourselves no concern about them.' "

Jay asked Oswald that "it may not be known that he advised it," but the Scot was too modest to take credit for so daring an idea. As a man of business he quickly saw advantages to both the British and the Americans from an English seizure of Florida. The people of Georgia and the

Carolinas, he reported to his government, "would drive their cattle down there in thousands," and sell them to British troop commissaries at forty shillings a head. From New York and Philadelphia, essential supplies of biscuit and flour would flow toward the British encampments. It was Oswald, however, who did propose that the northern boundary of West Florida be moved north three degrees to the 34th parallel. Jay was non-committal, not feeling free to yield territory claimed by any of the states, but confessing that it would be a matter of indifference to the inhabitants involved. Herein was the origin of the secret article attached to the pre-liminary treaty which awarded the British, should they secure Florida at the end of the war, a more advantageous northern boundary line than the Americans were prepared to yield to the Spaniards. The latter would be held to the northern limits that they themselves had set for the territory. So anxious did Jay seem to conclude a treaty that Vaughan quoted him as remarking that "America would not upon such an occasion stand for a few acres."[19] In the case of the Florida boundary, the "few acres" turned out to be a tract ninety odd miles in depth and 382 in length!

Oswald kept prodding the Home Office about the West Florida project, reminding his superiors that the "Americans will never forgive our neglect of this object," because they were determined that the territory should not remain with the Spaniards even "if they should be put to recover it them-selves."[20] Vaughan gave Oswald his complete backing. The acquisition of Florida, he argued, offered three advantages to the British. It would pro-vide business opportunities, a spot for resettling Tories, and offer strategic control of the Gulf of Mexico. Since Jay was offering the British a trade vestibule to the interior of America, Vaughan looked upon Florida as an essential link, along with the Mississippi, the Ohio, the Lakes, and the St. Lawrence. Together, Gulf coast and interior waterways would "form a trad-ing coast at the back of the American Colonies, somewhat as the Atlantic does at the front."[21]

That Franklin found no fault with the startling innovations proposed by Jay suggests that the differences between the two Americans lay in tactics not in objectives. Franklin wanted to avoid affronting the French, but advocated propositions as unpalatable to that court as were Jay's. In their continuing dialogue Franklin sought to persuade Jay of the propriety of keeping Vergennes abreast of the discussions. Jay, on guard against leaks to Versailles ever since his conversation with Lafayette less than a fortnight earlier, insisted that no communication be made to Versailles until the draft of the preliminaries was completed and conditionally signed. "The Comte merits no such confidence," the New Yorker argued. "The Court have communicated none of their secrets to us. I am still ignorant of what Rayneval was sent to England for, and I simply cannot consent to their interfering in our affairs." Franklin, who could be as close-mouthed as Jay when it suited his purpose, agreed to withhold the provisional terms from Versailles,[22] and the American pair managed to conceal most of their moves from the diplomatic corps, including Vergennes' entourage.

It was this fear of France that prompted Franklin to veto Oswald's proposal of a truce at sea, which Jay deemed "noble." Such a truce would be inconsistent with the restraining article in our treaty with France, Franklin pointed out. According to Shelburne's later recollection, Franklin enthusiastically backed Jay's proposal for a British attack on Spanish West Florida, but only wanted to make sure that "the utmost secrecy" was observed. To avoid the appearance of collusion he persuaded Jay to dissuade the British from shipping their troops from New York on such an expedition.[23]

Working around the clock, Jay drew up a provisional treaty draft in his own handwriting which he submitted to Oswald on October 5th on behalf of Franklin and himself. Except for a minor reservation included as an alteration to one article, the British commissioner found the draft entirely acceptable. Accompanying Jay's draft was a covering letter which provided for inserting in the treaty an article holding that the treaty was not to be conclusive until the King of France had accepted the terms of peace with England and was ready to conclude such a treaty.[24]

Jay's provisional draft was fated to undergo much surgery, but it constituted the basis of the preliminary treaty. The draft acknowledged American independence and stipulated for the evacuation of troops and the liberation of prisoners. It set the Mississippi as the western boundary, the 31st parallel as the southern. Following the Treaty of 1763, it divided the United States and Canada by the St. Lawrence and the 45th parallel running to Lake Nipissing; on the northeast, the St. John's River from its source to the Bay of Fundy was to separate Maine from Nova Scotia, but an alteration suggested by Franklin deferred the Nova Scotia boundary to a settlement by a commission "as conveniently may be after the war."

Jay carefully spelled out in his draft "the right to take fish of every kind on the banks of Newfoundland and other places" where the right was exercised before the last war between France and Britain. He was scrupulous to reserve for the Americans the right to dry and cure fish "at the accustomed places," whether in British or American territory. In accordance with his bid to Oswald for quick action Jay included the free navigation of the Mississippi for both parties, as well as providing free access to "all rivers, harbors, lakes, ports and places" belonging to either nation "in any part of the world," saving only to the British chartered companies—notably the Hudson's Bay and East India Companies—the monopolies they then enjoyed.[25] While Jay did not explicitly stipulate for the free navigation of the St. Lawrence by Americans, such a right was the clear implication of his phraseology. While this clause was destined to suffer drastic mutilation,[26] it may truly be said that the St. Lawrence Seaway stands as a monument to his farsighted statesmanship.

For a New Yorker who knew little about fishing or fishermen, John Jay was surprisingly stout in his assertion of the fisheries as a "right." Oswald passed on the word that so far as drying fish was concerned, Jay was not prepared to hold up the treaty for this point, but his reassurance to his government scarcely squares with Jay's careful phraseology covering "drying" or with the latter's pledge to Secretary Livingston: "You shall never see my name to a bad peace, nor to one that does not secure the fishery." At this stage of the negotiations Oswald was prepared to bend far over backward, holding that to grant concessions to the French and deny them to the Americans "would be always attended with a grudge."[27]

Because Jay set aside for the United States in his draft only a small sector of Ontario lying below the 45th parallel, he has been blamed for having "upset the apple cart in which Franklin had been so patiently and so gently trundling Canada."[28] This argument rests on the unproven assumption that Franklin still seriously entertained hope of securing Canada, and that Jay, in his anxiety to secure the West before Spain laid claim to it, yielded to the British a limitless wilderness without a fight. Jay and Oswald had only recently discussed Canada, along with Franklin's other advisable articles, and the Americans were given to understand that Oswald was not permitted to yield an acre north of the Nipissing line. So much the Cabinet had been prepared to concede at the end of August when in its most generous mood, and not an inch more. By the close of September, when the good news from Gibraltar reached London, the British philanthropic mood quickly evaporated. Had Franklin figured there was a real chance of securing Canada, he would have put up a stout battle. All along he had admitted to Oswald that he did not "insist" on Canada or the other *advisable* articles and that he had no "express directions" from Congress on that head. The Scot accordingly construed this proposal as one personal to Franklin which could be safely ignored.[29] That Oswald had made a shrewd guess was revealed when Franklin went along without protest and backed Jay's 45th parallel boundary.

In their anxiety to stake out a claim to the east bank of the Mississippi both Americans were prepared to abandon Canada, which was never more than a very misty prospect in any event. To get a quick decision in their favor regarding the West and the back lands the Americans now tossed in their proffer of the free navigation of the American interior waterways. Later, in dispatching the preliminary articles to Congress, the commissioners defended their relinquishment of Canada in these words: "We knew this Court and Spain to be against our claims to the western country, and having no reason to think that lines more favorable could ever have been obtained, we finally agreed to those described in this article; indeed they appear to leave us little to complain of and not much to desire."[30] Few will argue today with this judicious appraisal.

In affixing his signature to the provisional draft, Oswald hoped that his work was over. He rushed off stout arguments that Jay's draft be finalized and the approval be given "quickly." Oswald knew that the draft he dispatched to England on October 8th, by omitting mention of the Tories and the debts, would not be too palatable to various elements in the government, as well as many members of Parliament. Oswald reasoned that, once the treaty was out of the way, he could persuade the American commissioners to agree to issue some "observations" urging the States to take both objects into consideration in accordance with "justice and humanity." Not wishing to place on the bargain counter the long-range objects of the peace, he did not press for "Federal Union" or "independence of all other nations." As regards the latter, it was his opinion that the States would "grow out of the reach of comparison as to consequence with almost any nation in Europe."

On the evening of October 7th, with the provisional draft out of the way, Jay remarked to Oswald, as the latter reported it, "Once we have signed the treaty, we shall have no more to do but to look on and see what the people here are about. They will not like to find that we are so far advanced, and have for some time appeared anxious and inquisitive as to our plan of settlement. Upon this subject I was lately tried by a certain Marquis, but I gave him no satisfaction and wish that for some time as little may be said about it as possible."

From the tenor of Jay's remarks, Oswald felt assured that the Americans would not permit "unreasonable demands" by the other belligerents to hold up the peace.[31] Realizing that the French court did not wish the American negotiations to outpace their own, the Scot decided not to be a stickler for a few points listed in his instructions, but instead "to rest the issue upon the broad bottom of a mutual disposition to a renewal of former correspondence and friendship." To hold out for "subordinate stipulations" would not only provoke the Americans to make "new demands to ballance those disputed articles," but would seem to betray a lack of confidence in their good will.[32]

In his defense of Jay's provisional draft Oswald was seconded by Benjamin Vaughan, who took the American position on most issues in controversy. He found the back lands "not worth the cavil." Even if we did have the inhabitants to utilize them, which we do not, there is no way whereby we could get to them except through American territory, he reminded Shelburne, an argument which would have remained valid if the 45th parallel had stuck as the northern boundary. To try to defend the undefendable would only sow the seeds of future war. As regards the fisheries, "We might as well think of making game laws for them," he remarked, as attempting to check the New Englanders. In the long run, he prophesied, America will provide the principal market for her own fish, and the fisheries will encourage Americans to turn to seafaring. What will keep those who speak our tongue from passing "for English" and being engaged on our own frigates and privateers? The same thought would occur time and again to captains of royal frigates who were to impress American seamen down to the War of 1812. It was the prospect of reciprocal trade, however, which aroused Vaughan's liveliest enthusiasm. He construed "reciprocal" literally, taking it for granted that the opening of ports to both sides would permit Americans to "carry from our *settlements* to foreign ports and vice versa." Confident that America would enjoy a vast population growth—and the figures he mentioned came uncannily close to what did transpire—Vaughan envisioned the Americans as having their eyes directed for years to come to the "back settlements" rather than Europe, and more likely to turn to the soil than to the sea. Hence, aside from the West Indian trade, he saw little reason to worry about American trade competition, and warned that the imposition of the Navigation Acts against America would force the new nation to turn to others and to levy retaliatory tariffs.[33] In their hostility to trade monopoly Vaughan and Shelburne saw alike, but the latter happened to be a politician who needed the votes for his program. As Shelburne wryly conceded to Rayneval when he left with his visitor a book expounding the prevailing mercantilist system of economics, "nine-tenths of the Publick" were convinced of the virtues of protection and completely unprepared to embrace free trade.[34] Such were the prejudices he would have to surmount.

The sage counsel of Oswald and Vaughan failed to cushion the shock to Shelburne and his Cabinet caused by the arrival of Jay's provisional draft, with the British commissioner's endorsement. Oswald had complied in good faith with the Cabinet decision of August 29th. From the reaction of his government it now seemed that the Cabinet's resolve had been nothing more than a bribe to separate America from her French ally. In the light of France's more conciliatory line as revealed by Rayneval and the good news from Gibraltar, the price Britain had been prepared to pay for peace with America on August 29th seemed very high indeed by the second week of October. Within the Cabinet the malcontents girded for battle. There was Oswald over in Paris handing out big chunks of the British Empire in a mood of unchecked generosity. The man simply had to be stopped. Indeed, unless Shelburne "had some secret view," the Duke of Richmond later complained to the King, it was incomprehensible why he had retained as American negotiator a man whom "every other member of the Cabinet had long seen" as pleading "only the cause of America." Keppel was equally incensed, and, as the King put it to Shelburne, "as I did not think it right to heat the coals at present, I seemed to acquiesce.[35]

With the King's warm approval, a Cabinet meeting was called as soon as Oswald's packet arrived, with its enclosure of the draft treaty.[36] While the discussions of that meeting have not been recorded, it is significant that six days later the Cabinet saw fit to overrule its decision of August 29th. The Cabinet resolve of October 17th reflected what a young delegate to Congress, a fledging lawyer named Alexander Hamilton, called the "many jarring interests that will not be easily adjusted."[37] These "jarring interests" comprehended Canadian fur traders, English fishermen, American Tories, and British and Scottish creditors. To conciliate these very vocal groups the Cabinet directed Townshend to give Oswald a new set of instructions. First of all, he was told to get a better boundary "to the South West of Nova Scotia, vizt., Sagadahock and the Province of Maine [sic]," or else refer the northeast boundary to commissioners. In addition, Oswald was instructed to reassert Britain's claims to the Old Northwest, and "to urge it as a means of providing for the Refugees." From this stand he could recede only upon condition that the United States made "a just provision for the Refugees, or in case other means shall occur in the course of our treaty with France and Spain." He was to deny the right of drying fish on the coasts of Newfoundland "on account of the danger of disputes," and while authorized to agree to the provision for the free navigation of the Mississippi, told that the remainder of the article providing reciprocal free trading privileges "cannot at present be adopted," but was to be deferred to a special treaty of commerce. Lastly, he was called upon to urge the Americans "as strongly as possible" to discharge their prewar debts.[38]

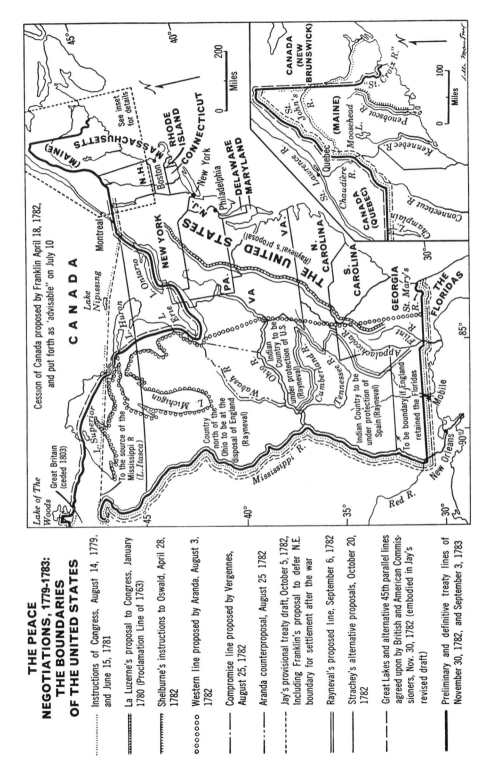

**THE PEACE
NEGOTIATIONS, 1779-1783:
THE BOUNDARIES
OF THE UNITED STATES**

.... Instructions of Congress, August 14, 1779, and June 15, 1781

━━━━ La Luzerne's proposal to Congress, January 1780 (Proclamation Line of 1763)

ᴡᴡᴡᴡ Shelburne's instructions to Oswald, April 28, 1782

ooooooo Western line proposed by Aranda, August 3, 1782

━ ·━ ·━ Compromise line proposed by Vergennes, August 25, 1782

━ ━ ━ Aranda counterproposal, August 25 1782

═══ Jay's provisional treaty draft, October 5, 1782, including Franklin's proposal to defer N.E. boundary for settlement after the war

═══ Rayneval's proposed line, September 6, 1782

━━━ Strachey's alternative proposals, October 20, 1782

━ ━ ━ Great Lakes and alternative 45th parallel lines agreed upon by British and American Commissioners, Nov. 30, 1782 (embodied in Jay's revised draft)

━━━━ Preliminary and definitive treaty lines of November 30, 1782, and September 3, 1783

To stiffen Oswald's backbone the Cabinet dispatched to Paris a "proper and confidential person," who was not unknown to the Americans. Back in September of '76, Henry Strachey had come face to face with the rebel leaders, Benjamin Franklin and John Adams, at a meeting on Staten Island, when he acted as secretary of Lord Howe's ill-fated peace commission. Once more this starched and very proper personage was to confront them, this time as an Undersecretary of State in the Home Office. Before Strachey was sent off to Paris, Shelburne had a Sunday talk with him in the presence of Lord Grantham and Thomas Townshend. Clarifying the written instructions which he was handed, he was told, as had Oswald, to bargain for the boundaries of Canada as fixed by the Quebec Act, which meant securing the whole of the Old Northwest. Then, if turned down, he was to try to obtain a cession of Maine lands to enlarge the territory of Nova Scotia. In neither case, however, Shelburne told him, should he agree to refer the boundary issue to a special commission. Thus Shelburne's oral instruction in this regard ran counter to the new instructions to Oswald and to the Cabinet resolution, but he refrained from putting this caveat down in writing. What Shelburne was seeking was some compensation by way of extra land for the Tory refugees, and he was anxious to have it appear on the record that every effort had been exerted in favor of both the Loyalists and the creditors. Rather than not conclude at all, however, Strachey was instructed to "bring the treaty back in its present form," except in the two inadmissible points of drying fish and reciprocal trade.

Henceforth the Tories, the debts, and the fisheries were the chief points at issue. The boundary concessions served as a club to hold over the heads of the American commissioners if they proved obdurate. Shelburne did not really pant for the "back lands." He merely looked upon them as assets to be thrown into a pool to compensate the Tory refugees "either by direct cession of territory in their favor, or by engaging the half, or some proportion of what the Back Lands may produce" when sold or mortgaged.[39] Maine and West Florida were likewise put on the bargaining counter for the same reason. In fact, Shelburne felt less deeply about conserving the Empire's real estate holdings than he did about the debts. He insisted that "*honest* debts may be *honestly* paid in *honest* money," ruling out "Congress money," doubtless aware, too, of the practice prevalent in Virginia where debts due British merchants were discharged by depreciated local currency paid by debtors to the State Loan Office. He ignored the fact that, while the debts owing the English merchants were payable in sterling, those of the Glasgow businessmen often specified colonial currencies.[40] Fearing unfavorable treatment of British debtors in the local courts, Shelburne wanted some assurance that appeals could be taken to a federal tribunal.[41] Some day John Jay would sit as the first Chief Justice of the United States and uphold the validity of prewar debts guaranteed by the treaty to which his signature was affixed.

To the hard-working and gentle Oswald, Shelburne now sent a stinging rebuke. "I am open to every good impression you give us of Mr. Jay," he wrote, but "I find it difficult if not impossible to enter into the policy of all that you recommend upon the subject both of the fishery and the boundaries, and of the principle which you seem to have adopted of going before the Commissioners in every point of favour or confidence." With obvious sarcasm he instructed Oswald that such a "maxim is not only new in all negotiations, but I consider it as no way adapted to our present circumstances, but as diametrically opposite to our interests in the present moment." As regards the boundaries and the back lands, he again reminded Oswald that these must be considered a *quid pro quo* set off against the Loyalist claims. He now denounced as "nonsense" the claims of the Americans resting upon their old royal charters to "extending as far as the sun sets." For "the good of America," Shelburne urged that a portion of the public lands of the new "provinces" to be carved out of the back lands and running east of the Mississippi—lands which had "always been acknowledged to the King"—be applied to furnish subsistence for the Loyalists.[42]

Townshend took the occasion to add some observations of his own. He turned down the idea of an expedition to West Florida, on the ground that it would place the British fleet to the leeward of all the British islands in the vicinity of Cuba in the event of a not improbable attack. "I have hardly patience when I state the absurdity of such a proposal," he huffed. "It has all possible appearance of a concerted plan between the American Commissioners and the Courts of Versailles and Madrid." On the Loyalists and the debts, Townshend rebuked Oswald for being a "great deal too easy," and appearing to be like putty in the skillful hands of Franklin and Jay.[43] More shocking even than Townshend's lack of faith in the integrity of his own agent was his complete misunderstanding of the motives of John Jay. The notion that Jay was conspiring with the French and the Spanish to trap the British into an unwarranted attack on West Florida was so absurd on its face that even the Home Secretary had second thoughts about it.

To add a cutting edge to their reproofs Shelburne and Townshend each informed Oswald that they were sending Strachey, ostensibly "to explain the boundaries and the authentic documents," and while not empowered to sign, he was to share the responsibility with Oswald, "which is great." Oswald was to call on Fitzherbert, too, if needed. Somewhat lamely Shelburne sought to explain to his commissioner in Paris why he had reversed himself. "You know sufficiently the nature of mankind not to be surprized at hearing that the opinions regarding Independence are not more stable than political opinions generally are with us," he remarked.[44]

After a talk with General Conway, Townshend discovered he had been too rash in disdaining the proposal for an attack on West Florida. Rather lamely he was forced to admit to Strachey that he had expressed himself "with some warmth" on the proposal made by Jay through Oswald. Now he was prepared to eat his words. Sound out Jay, he wrote Strachey a few days later on instructions from the Cabinet, about the evacuation of troops from New York for an eventual attack upon West Florida. While still suspicious of Jay and insecure about Oswald, he now conceded: "If any good can be expected from this scheme of Mr. Jay's, I am sure it is desirable to avail ourselves of it." Was Jay prepared to guarantee the "quiet evacuation" of New York, which Townshend considered "a great object"?[45] West Florida took on for a time even larger importance when, a few days later, a substantial group of merchants and planters argued the importance of its recovery, both for strategic reasons and as an asylum for the Loyalists.[46]

While Shelburne and Townshend had been free in their expressions of lack of confidence in their agent in Paris, the negotiations were at too delicate a stage and time was too pressing to risk the dismissal of Oswald, who accepted his rebukes with a magnanimity rare in the annals of diplomacy. "I am most pleased that Mr. Strachey is coming over," he told the Earl, and promptly arranged quarters for the undersecretary in his own hotel. He did not apologize for his conduct, and he considered that the issue was too big to allow room for personal feelings. Despite the Cabinet's reversal of instructions he could take consolation from the knowledge that what he had done to date had not been rejected out of hand. He admitted that he had made "a great mistake" in minimizing the importance of the fisheries, but warned his superiors that he had been told by the Americans, "If you want more land, by persisting, you may get less." No recriminations, no charges of inconsistency. If his government wished to turn over the tasks of peace to someone else, Oswald made it quite clear by implication that it would have to assume the responsibility for his dismissal.[47]

Shelburne's tortuous course was in no small part plotted by his recognition of the gravity of his position at home, and of the need to settle the issue of peace before Parliament reconvened. "It is our determination," he wrote Fitzherbert, "that it shall be either war or peace before we meet the Parliament; for I need not tell you that we shall by then meet so many opinions and passions, supported by party and different mercantile interests, that no negotiations can advance with credit to those employed or any reasonable prospect for the publick."[48]

Oswald broke the news to Jay on October 24th. He did not enter into particulars, but enough was said to make clear that the cession of the "back lands" was once again being contested by the British, and that despite Oswald's earlier assurances,[49] Jay's draft was not acceptable. Oswald sought to put the blame on Versailles. "I believe this Court have found means to put a spoke in our wheel," he confessed to Jay. The latter felt that it would be unwise to try to keep Strachey's coming a secret. Declare the truth about it, he told Oswald, "that he was coming with books and papers relative to our boundaries."

The French found out soon enough. That same evening Jay dined at Passy. After dinner Rayneval questioned Jay and Franklin about "how matters stood between us and Oswald." The Americans admitted that they could not agree "about all our boundaries," singling out the line marking off Maine from Nova Scotia.

"What do you demand to the north?" Rayneval asked.

"We insist that Canada be reduced to its ancient bound."

Then Rayneval, according to Jay's Diary, "contested our right to those back lands," as well as "the propriety" of the American contention on the fisheries. The latter the Frenchman attributed to "the ambition and restless views of Mr. Adams." America might do well to content itself with the coastal fishery, he counseled.[50]

On his September visit to Bowood Park, Rayneval had made no secret of his discontent with America's boundary claims. Shelburne remembered these remarks, and now took the occasion to remind Thomas Townshend that it was the intention of France to exercise a moderating influence upon the Americans once independence was conceded. Let Oswald and Strachey know this, he instructed, without naming Rayneval directly.[51] Oswald had good reason, then, when he told Jay that Versailles had put a spoke in the wheel.

The name of Rayneval could not be long concealed, for five days later, Strachey, on reaching Paris, proposed to the Americans that "a longitudinal line east of the Mississippi" be drawn to limit America's western extension. Here was the Aranda-Rayneval proposition starkly restated, but now emanating from the British commission. Jay snapped, "If that line is insisted upon, it is needless to talk of peace. We will never yield that point."[52]

The rejection of Jay's provisional draft disabused the Americans on the score of Shelburne's sincerity. "The court and people of England are very changeable," Franklin cautioned Secretary Livingston. "A little turn of fortune in their favor sometimes turns their heads. I shall not think a speedy peace to be depended on till I see the treaties signed."[53]

If the British sent reinforcements for their side, the American line was also bolstered. On October 26th John Adams reached Paris, preceding Strachey by two days. Having successfully negotiated a commercial treaty with the Dutch,[54] the New Englander came in response to Jay's urgent call. Six horses dragged John Adams' carriage through the mire from The Hague to Paris on a trip which consumed ten days. En route he feasted his eyes on Rubens and Rembrandt at Antwerp and chatted with William Lee, already a forgotten man of Revolutionary diplomacy. Upon his arrival in Paris Adams put up at his old haunt, the Hôtel de Valois, on the rue de Richelieu, but moved in a few days to an apartment in the Hôtel du Roi, situated between the Palais Royal and the Quai du Louvre, now the court-yard of the extended Louvre. In this location, as expensive as it was noisy, Adams remained until the final treaty was signed the following year. Almost at once the provident New Englander had to incur other expenses. In obeisance to Paris' dominion in fashion, he had to summon a tailor, a peruke-maker, and shoemaker, to make sure he would be attired in a manner suitable for a diplomat.

On Sunday, the day after his arrival, Adams bathed in the Seine not far from the Pont Royal. Rested and refreshed, he looked up Matthew Ridley, and was put abreast of the negotiations. From Ridley's lips he heard praise of Jay's "firmness and independence" and the New Yorker's refusal to "set his hand to a bad peace." "I wish he was supported," Ridley remarked meaningfully. Adams was chagrined to learn that Franklin's grandson had been appointed secretary of the peace commission with Jay's apparently reluctant consent. The New Englander had favored his own secretary, John Thaxter, for the post. Thaxter, who accompanied Adams to Paris, came of an old New England family, was an English-trained lawyer who had served in the office of Charles Thomson, Secretary of Congress, and as secretary to Henry Laurens, before going to Europe with Adams. In a mean-spirited comment on the appointment of the "young insignificant boy," Arthur Lee, who never forgot and never forgave, remarked, "Thus while Governor Franklin is planning our destruction in London, his father and son are entrusted with all our secrets in Paris."[55]

Though not free of the taint of nepotism himself, Adams resented old Franklin's presumption in this matter, and assumed from Ridley's remarks that there was a good deal more friction between Jay and the doctor than the facts warranted.[56] He fancied himself as mediating differences between his colleagues, arising principally out of the binding character of Congress' instructions, a copy of which, he insisted, had never come into his hands. "Between two as subtle spirits as any in this world," he admitted to his Diary, "the one malicious, the other I think honest, I shall have a delicate, a nice, critical part to act. F's cunning will be to divide us. To this end, he will provoke, he will insinuate, he will intrigue, he will maneuvre. My curiosity will at least be imployed in observing his invention and his artifice."[57]

On Monday the 28th Adams dropped in at the Hôtel d'Orléans on the rue des Petits Augustins, where the Jays were residing. Jay apprised his visitor of the state of the negotiations and offered his own "conjectures as to the views of France and Spain" and of the ties between Franklin and Vergennes. Adams enthusiastically concurred in all the New Yorker had done to date and in the prospective tactics he outlined. "I am pleased, too, that what is, was done before I came or I might have been held to be the cause." So delighted was he with the way that Jay had stood up to the English that he had the presumption to write Abigail, "Jay and I peremptorily refused to speak or hear before we were put on an equal foot."[58] He neglected to tell his devoted spouse that the concession on the point of independence had been made by the British weeks before he arrived in Paris. Writing years later, Adams observed: "It is impossible for any man but Mr. Jay and myself to conceive our mutual feelings upon this sudden discovery, that we had both formed the same opinions of the policy of the Comte de Vergennes and of Dr. Franklin; that we were perfectly agreed in our principles, and our whole system of conduct in the negotiation." In turn, Adams filled Jay's ear with some pretty grim opinions of his own about Franklin. Following dinner the pair continued their animated discussion until well on into the night.[59]

Adams had been in Paris almost four days and still he had not paid his respects to the Sage of Passy. On Tuesday Ridley returned Adams' visit and urged upon him the necessity of paying a courtesy call upon the renowned peace commissioner, senior by years if not by priority of appointment. "After the usage I have received from him, I cannot bear go near him," Adams said. Ridley very sensibly rejoined that this was no time to be touchy. It would be imprudent for Adams to advertise to the world his differences with Franklin. Such gossip could conceivably jeopardize the negotiations. Adams continued to grumble that the doctor should come to see him. "You are always making mischief," the testy Patriot snapped. But Ridley managed to get Adams to put his overcoat on, then struggled with him as he tried to take it off after having some second thoughts, and got him to ride out that evening to Passy. Franklin, sufficiently recovered from "the cruel gout," was prepared to find that his old colleague had not removed the chip from his shoulder. Adams did not disappoint him. He fired a succession of volleys. He approved of Jay's "whole conduct." He endorsed his views on the Comte de Vergennes. He backed him on the boundaries, the fisheries, and the recognition of independence. He strenuously endorsed the New Yorker's resolve to communicate nothing to Vergennes concerning the fisheries and the Western lands. To do so would amount to committing "the lamb to the custody of the wolf," he pointed out to Franklin. Franklin listened politely but said nothing.[60] Adams' monologue was scarcely soothing medicine for a convalescing septuagenarian. The inscrutable Sage had managed to relieve the tension of these weeks by writing a learned letter on the elements that originally composed the earth, and an essay providing information for prospective emigrants to America.[61] He had long appreciated the importance of keeping one's equilibrium come what may. Nevertheless, Adams' frank outburst, coupled with the independent course that Jay had recently been pursuing, were not without effect on Franklin. Realizing the need to present a solid front to the British negotiators, he surprised his two colleagues by declaring, prior to the start of the first conference with the British negotiating team, "I will go with you, and proceed in the conferences without communicating anything to this Court; and the rather, because they communicated nothing to us." Franklin kept his word, much to the chagrin of the Comte and the Marquis.

Talks began on October 29th, when Oswald took Strachey over to meet Jay and Adams, and then to Passy for a chat with the doctor. At eleven o'clock the next morning the first formal conference got under way at Jay's lodgings and continued through dinner. Oswald was accompanied by his fellow Scotsman and secretary, Caleb Whitefoord, wit, littérateur, and connoisseur of the arts, who years before had been Franklin's next-door neighbor in London. Strachey brought along a venerable clerk named Roberts, long with the Board of Trade, who had been sent over with a trunkful of maps and documents to buttress England's efforts to shave down America's boundary claims.[62] Day and night sessions followed, at Oswald's, at the Hôtel Valentinois, Franklin's Passy headquarters, or at Adams' new lodgings. "We lived together in perfect good humour,"

Adams later reminisced. "Had we been merely on our travels, or on a party of pleasure, nothing could have been more agreeable." The gay chatter, along with what Adams called "a surfeit of feasting, fatigue, and ceremony," could not completely eradicate the strain that overhung these sessions, for each participant was fully aware of "the immense responsibility" he himself had to bear.[63]

The speed with which Shelburne had granted the new commission failed to sustain the optimistic outlook of the Americans, quickly dampened by the cold water thrown by the British on arrangements considered settled. In the course of the preliminary visit that Oswald, with Strachey in tow, paid upon Jay and Adams, it was made clear that the parties were at odds on the Loyalists, the debts, and the fisheries, and that the West was again in suspense. The new longitudinal line à la Rayneval bisecting the West, which Strachey had thrown out, was rudely dismissed. Jay referred to that talk as "torrid conversation," and it was an omen of sharp exchanges ahead. The agreeable Oswald took a back seat as Strachey virtually took over. The undersecretary had come to bargain, not to exercise his philanthropic instincts, and he was backed up by Alleyne Fitzherbert. Adams found Strachey "artful and insinuating," pushing and pressing every point "as far as it could possibily go." Benjamin Vaughan, who resented Strachey's coming as diminishing his own importance, discounted his rival's role. Any concessions that the Americans might be prepared to make, he averred, should be attributed to the "friendly and affectionate footing the commissioners are upon with Mr. Oswald" rather than to the efforts of Strachey, who introduced "a style of bargain" in the place of "a style of confidence" and a manner of negotiating not conducive to settling "liberal systems."[64]

Soon after his initiation into these great debates, Adams reflected in his Diary that "the present conduct of England and America resembles that of the eagle and cat. An eagle scaling over a farmer's yard espied a creature that he thought an hair [sic]. He pounced upon him and took him up. In the air the cat seized him by the neck with her teeth and round the body with her fore and hind claws. The eagle finding herself scratched and pressed, bids the cat let go and fall down. 'No,' says the cat, 'I won't let go and fall. You shall stoop and set me down.' "[65] For Adams and his colleagues in Paris the big question now was whether England was really prepared to stoop.

While the negotiations were moving into their most delicate stage Oswald felt it necessary to keep John Jay and Adams fired up against the French. Adams, so Vaughan reported, was "sufficiently well disposed to us at present, but God Almighty defend us from delay!"[66] Just ten days before the preliminaries started, and while Oswald was still awaiting word from home about the fate of Jay's provisional draft, the Scot confided to Jay the Pulteney story with its allegation that Vergennes had that spring made an offer "to divide America with Britain."[67] Of course, the offer could never be substantiated because it had never been made, but after the preliminaries were signed Oswald showed Jay the Mountstuart letter-book, which, as already described, contained detailed if circumstantial revelations connecting Necker with a deal with England in which America would be the sacrificial lamb.[68] Rumors that Vergennes had proposed a partition of America, with Florida and Georgia going to Spain, the Carolinas and Virginia to France, and the rest to England, were spread by the London press. Shelburne was given credit for rejecting the proposition "upon the principle not only that the rice and tobacco colonies were the only valuable ones among the Thirteen," but chiefly because he expected England to recover the trade of all America, notwithstanding independence.[69] The rash of rumors exceeded the bounds of credibility, and fortunately no responsible person gave them heed.

Jay's peace of mind was further unsettled by the uninvited appearance in Paris of his troublesome brother, Sir James. Earlier that month Thomas Townshend had warned Oswald that, after staying in London for several months, James Jay talked of going over to Holland "to negotiate his exchange for Colonel Tarleton, or some other field officer. . . . He is in great disgust with us all," the Home Secretary added, "and I can hardly think for any other reason than because he has not been kept here at a considerable expense to which I am at a loss to know how he is entitled." Sir James, Townshend pointed out, was treated with "common civility, which is all an indifferent man has a right to." Oswald was warned that if John Jay's brother went to Holland he planned "to do ill offices." Be on your guard, the Scot was told.[70] Oswald reassured Townshend that he would do everything within his power to prevent his presence "being attended with any disagreeable consequences," and added, "He is not, as I am told, on the best of terms with his brother here."[71] Only a few days earlier Jay had heard from Philip Van Brugh Livingston, a New Yorker who had come to Paris from Spa. Livingston sought to ease Jay's mind about his brother, whom he had seen in England a month or six weeks earlier, and to remove "the apprehension I had been led to entertain of his having acted improperly," Jay noted in his Diary.[72]

When Sir James later came to Paris John Adams found him "full of projects of burning towns and making fifty gun ships equal to 110 gun ships."[73] Having been turned down by the British, Sir James tried to sell a naval invention to the Marquis de Castries. He also sought a commercial monopoly from Vergennes and expected his brother to assist him in securing it. Aside from his strict sense of propriety, Jay wished nothing less than to be indebted to the Comte at this stage in the negotiations, and he took occasion to warn James of the suspicions to which the latter's conduct had given rise.[74] The confrontation of the two brothers was not recorded, but neither ever forgot the occasion. For the rest of his days John seldom if ever referred to his brother by name.[75] In his twisted way Sir James pursued his own private brand of revenge despite the fact that his brother had interceded with Franklin to obtain his discharge as a prisoner on parole in an exchange with a British officer.[76] James went to the Ministry of Foreign Affairs, where he established contact with Edmond Charles Genêt, the precocious diplomat who had succeeded his father as undersecretary of the Bureau of Interpretation on the latter's death the previous year. According to the latter's recollection, Sir James declared: "John has always been opposed to the independence of the United States. He hated France as much as his ancestors who were Huguenots, and if he could he would procure a reconciliation between England and her old colonies in America and baffle all the expectations of France by an alliance between the two countries" amounting virtually to "reunion."[77] Considering the crooked source whence these malicious remarks emanated, the French Foreign Office may not have been as startled as Sir James had hoped. The diplomats at Versailles had already come to suspect the worst about John Jay.[78]

The independent line that John Jay had been pursuing in Paris was certainly no secret by now from his fellow commissioners. "Our allies don't play fair," he complained to Adams privately. After listening to a long harangue from Jay, in which France was accused of seeking to deprive America of the fisheries, the West, and the navigation of the Mississippi, an amused Adams noted in his Diary: "Mr. Jay likes Frenchmen as little as Mr. Lee and Mr. Izard did. He says they are not a moral people. They know not what it is. He don't like Frenchmen. The Marquis de la Fayette is clever, but he is a Frenchman."[79] Jay's candor with Adams, who relished such talk, did no harm. On the other hand, it was not the shrewdest course for Jay to let the British know how little he trusted the French, and how ready he and his fellow commissioners were to sign a preliminary treaty if France sought to hold up the peace on account of Spain.[80] With the British stiffening their demands a knowledge of America's readiness to sign was not calculated to make Shelburne more yielding. Although Adams for the record refused to express a preference for the English over the

French, the British commissioners found little to choose between the anti-Gallicism of Jay and the New Englander's own private brand. "By Mr. Adams coming over here," Oswald could write Shelburne with satisfaction, "the French interest, I think, seems not to have gained anything." Like Jay, Adams also expressed "a strong desire for a solid and lasting friendship with England."[81] Fortunately for the Americans, events moved too rapidly for the French to muzzle either Jay or Adams, and even Franklin seemed remote.

The negotiations, which continued round the clock from October 30th through November 4th, brought a few concessions to the British. The new American negotiator, John Adams, contrary to predictions, proved no more inflexible than his colleagues, and perhaps surprised both sides by a readiness to make concessions. The first of these seems to have come as an offhand and even impulsive gesture on the part of the New Englander. At his initial informal session with the British commissioners, the issue of debts and Loyalists came up. Adams felt it important to distingush them. "I have no notion of cheating anybody," he asserted. Strachey's face lit up, and his fellow Scotsman, Richard Oswald, wore a broad smile. No doubt Franklin was surprised when Adams informed him that evening of the stand he had taken, without advance consultation with either Jay or the doctor, who for months had been insisting that both the commissioners and Congress lacked the power to deal with the subject. Now that Adams chose to put it on high moral ground, Franklin saw it was useless to protest. Adams persuaded his colleagues to accept a formula whereby Congress would recommend that the states open their courts of justice for the recovery of all just debts. Save for ironing out the phraseology, the British commissioners fell quickly into line. Adams defended his position on the double ground that it would silence "the clamours of all the British creditors against the peace," and prevent them "from making common cause with the refugees."[82] The article agreed upon covered debts contracted by British subjects prior to 1775, but declared those of later date irrecoverable in law on the ground of illegality. It also included a recommendation to the states to correct confiscatory acts respecting lands "belonging to real British subjects." It did not cover debts owing to American Loyalists. This was the very best that could be obtained, Oswald advised his government.[83]

Considering the immensity of the stakes, the struggle over the northern boundary and the "back lands" was over rather quickly. Strachey put up a fight to secure an adequate area in the Old Northwest for the resettlement of Loyalists. "They wanted to bring their boundary down to the

Ohio," reported Franklin, "and to settle their loyalists in the Illinois country. We did not choose such neighbors."[84] No one took very seriously the proposal that Strachey had advanced for a longitudinal line bisecting the West. The Americans attribute this demand to French inspiration, Vaughan hastened to inform Shelburne. He pointed out that the proposal suggested a secret understanding between the courts of France and London, and warned that, if insisted upon, "the treaty will certainly be broke off."[85] This stern warning was hardly necessary since Strachey saw he never had a chance, and quickly settled for much less.

The Americans came to the conference table prepared to offer an alternative northern boundary to Jay's 45th parallel or "Nipissing Line." They now proposed a line through the St. Lawrence and the middle of the Great Lakes.[86] On its face, this also seemed like a concession, as it yielded southern Ontario to the British and made the Great Lakes accessible to Canadians as well as Americans. Again the maps, notably Mitchell's map of 1755, proved deceptive. Under this alternative proposal the line was described as running from the most northwestern point of the Lake of the Woods due west to the Mississippi. No such line would strike that great river, for, as later exploration revealed, the source of the Mississippi lay 151 miles to the south of the Lake of the Woods,[87] a discrepancy that occurred to Benjamin Vaughan. Before the definitive treaty was signed Vaughan alerted Shelburne to this probable defect and suggested substituting in the treaty the words: "and from thence [Lake of the Woods], by a line which shall describe the shortest course for reaching the Mississippi" or "and from thence on a due south course to the Mississippi."[88] The article was not changed in the definitive peace treaty. Without realizing what they had accomplished, the American commissioners by this alternative proposal had enlarged the Old Northwest to include what became the state of Minnesota and reserved for posterity the then unknown Mesabi Iron Range. It should be added that the choice of the Lake of the Woods was to provide a logical ground for later negotiations which extended the boundary westward on the 49th parallel.[89] The alternative line which the Americans proposed was also more advantageous to the Canadian fur traders than the 45th parallel. The latter line, as Vaughan pointed out to Shelburne, would have required them to move their trade goods through a foreign country. The new alternative had another advantage, in Vaughan's eyes. "It waves down into a better climate."[90] When the Canadian traders complained that even this boundary, seemingly modified in their favor, would divert the fur trade away from Quebec and to the American Northwest, Oswald observed that the Indians would trade wherever they were offered the best price. No clause in a treaty could alter the economics of the situation.[91]

Over the Mississippi as the western and the 31st parallel as the southern boundaries there was no dispute. In accordance with the new instructions to Oswald, the Mississippi article was reduced simply to a proposition for free navigation from its source to its mouth. The commercial reciprocity clause in Jay's provisional draft was dropped because it ran afoul of the British Navigation Laws and was simply too radical a proposal to put before Parliament at the moment. Since there was no way of trading down the Mississippi from Canada, and the Ohio was now closed to the British, they sacrificed real for illusory gains by denying reciprocity to America. In fact, it was largely the expectation of securing free access to American markets in the West that had induced Shelburne to yield the Old Northwest to the Americans without putting up a real battle. The parties quickly agreed on awarding Great Britain a more favorable northern boundary for West Florida than either was prepared to allot to Spain.

Shrouded in a thick mist of divergent maps, claims, and counterclaims, the northeastern boundary line remained the one to be most stubbornly contested. Since British troops were still quartered in Maine, Strachey's counterclaim to that province, as least as far south as the Penobscot, caused the Americans some wakeful hours. "A contest over Penobscot would be highly dangerous," Vaughan warned Shelburne, because "Britain is trying the experiments in a very iratible intractible [sic] animal; I mean, a New England government."[92]

Adams came to the conference table with pockets bulging with documents to support the claims of Massachusetts to an expansive Maine frontier extending all the way to the St. John's. He himself would have held out for that river, he later claimed, but his colleagues "thought it would be too hazardous to contend for a river which was not named in the charter of Massachusetts, against a river that was named in it, and I readily acquiesced."[93] The river denominated in the charter to which Adams was referring was called the St. Croix.[94] The commissioners on both sides knew that the location of the St. Croix varied from map to map, but the Americans were no more prepared than Shelburne to submit the precise determination of the line to boundary commissioners. They, too, hoped to forestall later disputes.

This hope proved illusory. Instead of a river St. Croix there turned out to be two more or less parallel streams emptying into Passamaquoddy Bay —the Magaguadavic, the first river west of the St. John's and evidently the river intended by the treaty, and the Schoodiac, nine miles to the west of the former at its mouth. The two streams are not far apart at their outlets, but the distance between lines drawn north from their alleged source amounted to some fifty miles, and involved seven or eight thousand square miles of territory. This became consequential since the treaty provided for a line "drawn due North from the Source of St. Croix River to the High Lands," then down the Connecticut River to 45° NL. Exacerbating the issue was the speed with which the British government granted lands in the disputed area to the Loyalists once the definitive peace was signed.[95] It remained for a mixed boundary commission set up under Jay's Treaty of 1794 to deal with a question which the commissioners had failed to clarify. That commission rendered the dubious finding that the Schoodiac was the original St. Croix.[96]

All in all, the Americans had made substantial concessions in territory, without materially weakening their strategic position. "We have gone the utmost length to favor peace," wrote John Adams. "We have at last agreed to boundaries with the greatest moderation."[97] What they conceded was minor and sensible. What they held on to, the West as spelled out in Jay's provisional draft, converted a string of coastal provinces into a great nation. After the final peace was made Jay passed through England en route to America. Shelburne asked him what the American commissioners would have done had he refused to yield the West. "Would you have continued the war?" he asked. "I believe so, and certainly should have advised it," Jay replied unhesitatingly.[98]

Word quickly got around that the Maine–Nova Scotia boundary was a principal bone of contention. The inquisitive Matthew Ridley, dining at the Lafayettes with Jay and Adams, learned that "the English want to keep us from Penobscot." If Lafayette knew it, so did Vergennes, as John Adams found out when he finally got around to paying a courtesy call upon his old enemy at Versailles. The British want to hold on to Maine for the sake of the masts for the King's Navy, Vergennes remarked. Since the Comte had been prepared to yield Maine to England in the winter of '81 as part of a long-term truce package, the British stand could hardly have come as a shock to him. So well posted were the French on England's counterclaims to Maine and her Loyalist demands that it seemed evident to Adams that Fitzherbert must have been doing some talking to the French. Vergennes and Rayneval both seized the rare opportunity of Adams' presence to put in some words for the Tories. Royal governments simply must take care of their adherents, the undersecretary argued. It is a matter of national honor.

"National honor, bosh!" Adams bluntly replied. He accused the Loyalists of deceiving the British nation and of responsibility for its "almost irretrievable ruin." It did not seem logical to Adams that such a nation was in honor bound to "compensate its dishonorers and destroyers." "Very true," Rayneval admitted. Taking more technical ground, Adams reminded Rayneval, "The confiscation of property is an affair of the states individually."

Adams had been prepared for a reproof, an admonition, "or in plain vulgar English a scolding," when he visited Versailles. On the contrary, he was treated at dinner with every courtesy, and praises for his achievements in Holland were laid on with a trowel. "You have shown in Holland that the Americans understand negotiation as well as war," one guest remarked. Another: *"Monsieur, ma foi, vous avez réussi merveilleusement!"* Still another: *"Monsieur, vous êtes le Washington de la Négotiation!"* Such remarks might well have turned the head of one less prone to vanity than John Adams, and he could not refrain from letting the world know about his reception. "A few of these compliments would kill Franklin if they should come to his ears," Adams confided to his Diary. Nevertheless, he had not been taken in. When he returned to Paris that night Adams remarked to Ridley that neither France nor Spain seemed "ripe for peace" and might well be disposed to needle the British into pressing their demands on behalf of the Loyalists in order to hold up the negotiations with America.[99]

The issues provoking the greatest controversy between the British and American negotiating teams were those in which the French had a strong emotional involvement—the fisheries and the Loyalists. The revised draft to which Oswald now agreed extended the right of fishing to the Gulf of St. Lawrence "and all other places where the inhabitants of both countries used at any time heretofore to fish." Had he not agreed to this concession, the Scot insisted, "there would have been no provisional articles." In a spirit of compromise Newfoundland was omitted from the area where drying of fish was to be permitted.[100]

The parties had reached substantial agreement by November 4th, but it took several days more for Jay to incorporate the modifications into a new set of proposed preliminary articles. These he drafted with meticulous attention to detail. In the new version Jay made the West Florida article a separate provision at the end of the treaty. He also struck out of the treaty an exception the British had sought to include of the islands off Nova Scotia at the mouth of the St. Croix River, later a bone of contention between the United States and Canada. Jay was so precise, Oswald warned Strachey, that he cautioned that "there should not be the least alteration, not a single word different, from those of the draft." Indeed, Oswald was surprised to find Jay "so uncommonly stiff and particular about these matters," and speculated that his rigidity might be the result of some recent news from America.[101]

The Americans had refused to budge on the Loyalist issue, and Oswald and Strachey each made a last appeal for the record. To permit resentment to threaten a solid reconciliation would, Strachey asserted, constitute conduct without "parallel in the history of civilized nations." Strachey chose to forget the grim story of Britain's expulsion of the Acadians or her subjugation of Ireland. The reply of the Americans showed restraint, but hinted that if a request for Loyalist restitution were kept on the agenda the Americans might be prepared to counterclaim for damages to Patriot properties inflicted by Tories, British troops, or their allies. They had previously sought to reassure Strachey that the "less obnoxious Tories might expect to be treated leniently," and that "the bulk of those being besides of low rank" were likely to resume their customary occupations in America and would not have to be transported or maintained. Jay warned, too, that, should the British put off the peace because of this issue, he could not answer for the behavior of the States in the settlement of just debts. Finally, the American commissioners made it clear that they would stick by their guns even though war should be resumed. Strachey felt they were bluffing, though, and that they would accede rather than break off the treaty should the Cabinet make restitution or indemnification a *sine qua non*. "Mr. Oswald is not of my opinion," he added.

On the score of the Tories and the boundaries Vaughan became the American commissioners' strongest advocate. Not only did he support the American position on the Tories, but he volunteered the sage, if unsolicited, counsel to Shelburne not to settle Tories as neighbors to the Americans, "where they will make mischief to *both* of *us*, and to themselves." Subsequent British policy-makers chose to ignore this caution, and bedded down the Tories about as close to the Americans as they could, locating them along the Maine–New Brunswick border and in southern Ontario.[102] Vaughan, who objected to the introduction into the negotiations by Strachey of "a puny, ignoble huckstering spirit," defended the compromises made in the preliminary draft right down the line. On the Maine–Nova Scotia boundary, he observed: "I should be grieved to hear that a little spot of cross frosty land, which an Empress of Russia would give away at breakfast, should spoil a national accommodation." Remember, he urged, the New Englanders will be glad to sell masts, and the only difference will be that the money will go to New Hampshiremen instead of Acadians. Since Shelburne's own philanthropic mood had largely evaporated after Gibraltar, it must have been grating to read his friend's eulogy of the American way of life, of the audacity of American ideas, and of the statesmanlike qualities of the American commissioners.[103]

Jay's new draft treaty prompted Strachey to return home for new instructions. Delayed by contrary winds, he did not reach London until the tenth, but he had written ahead to explain the new terms, the draft of which Oswald had forwarded to him in London. A rough Channel crossing scarcely improved Strachey's mood. On looking over Jay's draft he felt that some polishing of the phraseology was necessary. "Several of the expressions must be tightened," he added, "for these Americans are the greatest quiblers [sic] I ever knew."

If Strachey seemed in an irritable mood, the chiefs of Cabinet found little cause for rejoicing in the terms he had brought back. Richmond and Keppel were openly mutinous and demanded Oswald's recall. Grafton, Camden, and General Conway could not conceal their unhappiness about the concessions Shelburne was prepared to make.[104] Shelburne pushed ahead. He summoned the Cabinet to come to a "provisional agreement" with America. At the same time he took occasion to console his monarch by reflecting that "any evils which may result to Great Britain from so great a dismemberment or to America from the loss of so essential a part of the English Constitution as the Monarch has always proved, do not lye at Your Majesty's door, but at that of others." With a petulance to which his servants were not unaccustomed, George remarked, "I should be miserable indeed if I did not feel that no blame" for the loss of America "can be laid at my door, and did I not also know that knavery seems to be so much the striking feature of its inhabitants that it may not in the end be an evil that they become aliens to this Kingdom."[105]

The Cabinet met on the eleventh of November. After animated discussion it accepted the alternative "line-of-the-Lakes" boundary proposed by the Americans instead of the 45th parallel. Except for minor matters, Jay's preliminary draft served as the basis for a third set of articles Strachey was to take back to Paris, but even the comparatively minor variances spelled trouble ahead. The Cabinet insisted upon an explicit declaration that the prewar debts would be recovered at full value in sterling and by the same legal means as were available to citizens of the United States.[106] The Cabinet wanted "a full and complete amnesty and oblivion" for acts done on either side, but it recognized the expediency of not pressing such amnesty for persons taken in arms.[107] On the more ticklish subjects of Loyalist property, the Cabinet instructed Strachey to return to Paris "to obtain as much satisfaction as possible" on that score. As regards the fisheries article, the Cabinet balked at permitting the Americans to dry fish on the shores of Nova Scotia, but proposed instead that "the unsettled parts of the Magdalene Islands" be made available for that purpose. Lastly, the Cabinet authorized Richard Oswald to sign the treaty whenever he, Fitzherbert, and Strachey should think it "consistent with the spirit of the instructions" which Strachey would bring back to Paris. In effect, Fitzherbert and Strachey were given a veto over Oswald.[108]

To iron out final details the Cabinet met again on the night of the fourteenth and on the following day. With unanimity it settled on a draft of the preliminaries to be submitted to the Americans "to take or leave." Strachey was to be given private instructions stating the different classes of Loyalists, and "which of them are to be finally insisted upon and which only contended for." If the Americans objected to blanket compensation, then the particularly obnoxious Tories might be excepted. If they would still not budge, then Strachey was instructed to try to get compensation for the neutrals. As regards those who bore arms, try to regain for them the price actually paid at the confiscated sales, he was requested. Most significantly, the point was made that the personal security of the Loyalists and provision for payment of the debts were "absolutely indispensable. . . . On them an appeal to France, if necessary, may be hazarded," and Fitzherbert was instructed "to avail himself of France so far as he may judge prudent from circumstances." It was clear, then, that compensation or restitution to the Tories was no longer an ultimatum.[109]

The King accepted the Cabinet's preliminary articles with all the grace of a spoiled child forced to swallow some bitter medicine. Once Parliament to his "astonishment" had granted independence,[110] George contended, he was disabled "from longer defending the just right of this Kingdom." Disclaiming responsibility, he subscribed to the articles out of "necessity not conviction."[111]

Chilled by the gloomy November weather,[112] dispirited by delay, the Americans in Paris continued their talks with Oswald while awaiting word from London. The Scot kept coming back to the Tories. Adams pointed out that the presence of the Loyalists in America might keep up the divisions which had turned a revolution into a civil war. Fearful of the intrusion of European politics into America, he predicted that the Tory presence would create a French and an English party, leaving patriotic Americans no choice but to join the former. For his own part Adams "thought America had been long enough involved in the wars of Europe.

She had been a football between contending nations from the beginning." It was to the interest of England as well as France to involve the new nation in their future wars, but he considered it "our interest" to avoid such involvement "as much as possible, and to be completely independent and have nothing to do but in commerce with either of them."[113] He warned Oswald that the commissioners would be obliged to refer the issue of the Tories back to Congress for lack of powers. It would take from six to nine months to get new instructions, and in the meantime England would be shouldering war costs running each month to a sum larger than was required to compensate the Loyalists for the forfeited estates. This was an argument shrewdly calculated to appeal to a Scotsman. Should the British government reject the terms now before it, Adams warned, the entire negotiation would be broken off, and the French court would "probably be so angry with Mr. Jay and me, that they would do exactly as this Court would have them." From this horrible prospect Oswald recoiled.[114]

Jay was equally tough. The Americans would fight for fifty years rather than "subscribe to such evidence of their own iniquity" as to make "provision for such cutthroats" as the Tories, he declared. In fact, the American commissioners had already been too lenient. They should have insisted on reparation for Patriot losses, and he mentioned the removal of Negro slaves from Southern plantations as a notorious example.[115]

When Oswald learned that his government had rejected Jay's preliminary draft, he turned in discouragement to the New Yorker and urged him to go to England and take up the negotiations in person. To do so would "give rise to jealousies" on the part of the French court, Jay replied. Nevertheless, the need for direct contact with Shelburne seemed exigent. On November 20th Rayneval turned up in London to resume his discussion of the Franco-Spanish peace terms. To Matthew Ridley, as to other Americans in Paris, the French undersecretary's visit seemed "very misterious" and even threatening.[116] Adams even proposed having Rayneval shadowed to see if he was ever in contact with North, Germain, Stormont, Sandwich and Company, and "if the wing clipping system and the support of the Tories should be suggested" by the French court to any member of the former Ministry.[117]

Now thoroughly aroused, Benjamin Vaughan decided to go back to Shelburne and enter one more plea for peace on his own behalf. As a pretext for his journey he mentioned "the critical state of his family, his wife being probably abed." Before leaving on a ten-day trip Vaughan had a long talk with Strachey, who had returned from London. The arguments he recorded were evidently those he marshaled to persuade Shelburne. Jay asked Vaughan to buy him a sword in England. "I had much rather send you an *olive branch*," he replied, "which I trust is more than a summer's plant."[118] Though Vaughan arrived too late to have any impact on the final instructions decided upon by the British Cabinet, he provided Shelburne with ample reasons for conciliating America regardless of the political risks.

From a casual look at the London press Vaughan could not have failed to see that he was out of step with a strong body of British opinion. Diehard sentiment would not down. Writers still argued against the surrender of the Empire, both on Constitutional grounds as well as for reasons of prestige, still expressed the vain hope that something could be salvaged, that America might be partitioned, and that Shelburne might "humour the spirit and wish of the nation at large" by continuing the war for a year or two more. "Let the Tower of London be taken sword in hand before you submit to such a disgraceful ruin as American independence," one extremist exhorted the Earl.[119]

Vaughan took a contrary view. "If we wait longer," he declared to Strachey, and then Shellburne, "I fear the terms cannot grow better, but worse." Congress might well insist upon damages, and the ensuing controversy might "agitate America like a *book of martyrs*, operating against England's politics and trade, and for those of France." Coincidentally, a proposal was then being seriously made to Henry Laurens that coins be struck off for America perpetuating the "cruelties" of the war, "*the deeds of Arnold*," "*New London destroyed*," and other like atrocities.[120] Vaughan conceded that the Americans were not fair in failing to discriminate among categories of Tories, but he himself was encouraged by the commissioners to believe that some exceptions might be made to the general rule of exclusion, and that the Americans might be prepared to set aside a tract of land for the Loyalists. Certainly, one could not expect the Americans to provide for the traitor Arnold, or the hated Tory Ranger Butler, or the notorious clan Hutchinson. As regards the boundaries, Vaughan felt that the Americans could not be budged another inch. Lastly, Vaughan gave a personal vote of confidence to Richard Oswald, whom he styled "a very wise man," one "who judges better of the *proportions* of things than almost any man I ever saw."[121]

Like Vaughan, Gérard de Rayneval did not reach London until the British government had already committed itself on the boundaries and decided to forego compensation to the Loyalists if it could not be won at a last stand.[122] For the Americans in Paris, as well as for the timetable of the peace negotiations, this was indeed fortuitous, for on two of the main points in contention Rayneval had received instructions which could have cruelly thwarted expectations of a quick and satisfactory settlement. Vergennes authorized his undersecretary to defer the issue of the American boundaries to the definitive treaty or to turn the matter over to a special commission. As regards the Loyalists, while Rayneval was instructed to point out the impossibility of reintegrating them in American life and of the adequacy of Britain's resources to compensate them herself, he was also to propose that this issue be deferred to the definitive treaty if it could not be settled.[123] It was the latter article which Rayneval expected would be "the most difficult to work out."[124] Rayneval's instructions belie the report of a British intelligence agent at this time that the French were prepared to insist that Canada be ceded to them, and had made a secret agreement with Congress to that effect. France was to the contrary determined that Canada remain in British hands.[125]

Rayneval must have been surprised when Shelburne told him at their meeting on November 23rd "that there would be little difficulty about boundarys [*sic*]," provided the Americans agreed to a satisfactory article on the Loyalists—a big "if," to be sure. The Earl went on to say that the King wished to avoid future disputes over the fisheries both "upon their account as well as our own." Rayneval in turn made no bones about the coolness which had developed between the American negotiators and himself because of his refusal to support them in what he styled "a variety of unreasonable demands."[126]

On the very day that Rayneval disclosed to Shelburne France's lack of sympathy with certain crucial demands insisted upon by her American ally, the Comte de Vergennes took pen and paper to send a warning to Congress by way of La Luzerne. France, Vergennes now made clear, did not feel herself obliged to prolong the war "to sustain the pretentious ambitions" of the United States as regards both the fisheries and the boundaries. The Americans, he observed with not unaccustomed sarcasm, were not less experienced than the English "in the art of drawing indefinite lines and of claiming title thereto in law." Using language very much like that which he had addressed to John Adams a fortnight before, Vergennes urged upon Congress that the Loyalists be accorded amnesty and restitution of their property, such as was customary in peace treaties. He continued to argue this position even after the preliminaries were signed.[127]

In short, down to the wire the French were in confidential parley with the enemy opposing American claims. The British had already learned from Oswald and Vaughan the substance of what Vergennes told Adams on the latter's visit to Versailles. This information undoubtedly prompted the Cabinet to instruct Strachey to call upon the French as a last resort should the Americans not make any concessions on the Tories.[128] Rayneval had converted gossip into certainty. Commenting on the Frenchman's remarks about the American claims, George III observed to Shelburne, "France, I should hope, will assist us in keeping the American Treaty less liable to be objected to on the score of the Fisheries which certainly in its present shape is too loose and subject to much inconvenience."[129] The very same day that Rayneval made his position clear to Shelburne the latter wrote Richard Oswald that, as regards the Loyalist refugees, "this country is not reduced to terms of *humiliation* and will not suffer them from America."[130]

Shelburne had the choice of holding up the peace until France obtained further concessions for England from the Americans or presenting Parliament with a *fait accompi*. He realized that to expose the secrets of pending negotiations to the thunderous charges of his foes in Lords and Commons would not only jeopardize the peace, but most certainly bring down his own Ministry. With time now the crucial factor, Shelburne persuaded his Cabinet to have Parliament prorogued from November 26th, when it was scheduled to convene, until December 5th.[131] "I am afraid that we shall doubt, delay, decry," Vaughan had remarked to his friend and sponsor some weeks before, "and by the next courier or so, you will hear time is no more."[132]

The last formal round of talks began on November 25th, when the Americans met at Richard Oswald's lodgings to consider the provisional articles formulated by the British Ministry.[133] It was Strachey who broke the bad news, but what he said was scarcely news to the Americans. On the evening of November 21st Jay was visiting at Oswald's when a courier arrived from London. Oswald opened the packet, perused some of the letters, and remarked laconically, "The Tories stick."[134] Fresh from briefings by the Ministry, Strachey pointed out the revisions in Jay's draft upon which his government was insistent. The "grand point," he remarked, was the restoration of Tory property, upon which the Cabinet was unanimous.[135] Article V in the revised draft called for restitution of "all estates, rights and properties which have been confiscated."[136] Strachey warned that should these new terms be rejected the whole business would be thrown into Parliament, "where every man would be for insisting on restitution to the refugees." Strachey himself urged that a few of the "most obnoxious of the refugees" be excepted by name, and the rest be provided for.

While confessing that his government "did not approve" the boundaries, which they thought "too extended, too vast a country," nevertheless "they would not make a difficulty" on that score. Then Strachey turned to the fisheries, expressing ideas which appeared to John Adams "to come piping hot from Versailles." The draft that Strachey brought back from London substituted "liberty" for "right" insofar as *all* fishing and drying privileges were concerned.

For the better part of three days the New Englander by way of rebuttal elucidated the fisheries problem. These were John Adams' great moments at the negotiations. Drawing upon the expert advice of American merchants and mariners who happened to be in either French or Dutch ports at the time,[137] Adams instructed the British on the nature of the fisheries problems. As he saw it, the controversy boiled down to two issues—inshore fishing and the right of drying. As regards the former, he painstakingly explained that the fishery off fogbound Newfoundland had an early and a late fishing season. The first began in February when the cod and haddock went inshore into the bays, harbors, and even the mouths of rivers, seeking the smaller fish. There they stayed until May, when they would move out to somewhat deeper water, settling at last by late spring and early summer on the Grand Bank, a submarine tableland spawning huge quantities of small organisms upon which fish feed. "We have a saying at Boston," Adams remarked, "that when the blossoms fall the haddock begin to crawl." Because of their proximity to the inshore fisheries, the Americans were in a position to pursue the early fishing with the break-up of winter, protected by the shelter of bays and harbors. Contrariwise, the English and French could not get to the fisheries until the later season, when they were joined by the Americans. "The first fare was our only advantage," Adams pointed out. "Neither the English nor the French could have it. It must be lost if we have it not." This was a big advantage, however. It enabled the Americans to sell their fish in the Catholic Mediterranean markets ahead of their European competitors. As a result, the latter not infrequently found their market overstocked by the time they put their fish on sale.

What Townshend and Shelburne were determined to obviate, however, were the future "bickerings of fishermen," which they foresaw if American intrusions were permitted to continue, and, as Fitzherbert was to explain to Adams, they were strengthened in their resolve by the Comte de Vergennes, who was equally determined to set fixed and exclusive bounds between the French and English for fishing.[138] Because the British appeared ready to accommodate the French on the score of the fisheries but seemed ungenerous toward the Americans, Adams warned that the signing of a treaty denying the inshore fishing would be signing a declaration of perpetual war between England and America. In short it was not the "squabbles of fishermen" that alarmed Adams, but the prospect of "altercations between *States*," a prospect that seemed the inevitable consequence of England's assigning her men-of-war to keep the New England fishermen outside the three-league zone.[139]

Adams and his fellow commissioners were chagrined to learn that the British revised draft made the right of drying contingent upon fishing beyond the three-league limit, and only offered the "liberty" of drying on the shores of the Isle of Sables and on the unsettled bays, harbors, and creeks of the Magdalen Islands in the Gulf of St. Lawrence. Again Adams, the pedagogue, was obliged to resume his lesson. The right of drying, he pointed out, was especially important to the New Englanders. While the French, who fished on the banks, cleaned, salted, and packed their catch in brine, and then carried it directly to market, the English and American fishermen, carrying on their operations closer to land, brought the catch ashore, landed it on stages built out over the water, and, after cleaning and salting it, set it in the sun to dry. At the end of the season the catch was loaded in casks or barrels or carried to market in bulk. The Americans, Franklin had already pointed out, required only "a partial drying and salting" in order to prevent the fish from spoiling before the fishermen "went home and delivered them to their wives and children to complete and finish the drying." In Jay's provisional fishing article the Americans, persuaded by Franklin, had agreed to omit Newfoundland from the areas where drying was to be permitted, but the new revisions by the British were far more restrictive.

To the Americans, anxious to conclude their secret preliminaries with the British before their ally could intervene, some scary news was now forthcoming. On the evening of November 25th Dr. Bancroft dropped in on the commissioners with the report that a courier had that day arrived at Versailles from Rayneval, who was back in London conferring on Franco-Spanish issues. After reading the dispatches, Vergennes was reputed to have told the King, "I have the peace in my pocket. I am now master of the peace."[140] Whether or not Vergennes' misjudgment of the state of his undersecretary's parleys with the British had led him to make so incautious a remark, the timing of this piece of gossip from a source now known to have been highly suspect was calculated to put the pressure on the Americans to settle with the English—and quickly.

The next morning, November 26th, Franklin and Adams breakfasted at the Jays, and the Americans agreed upon their strategy toward the Loyalist article. With Franklin's natural son, Governor William Franklin, more royalist than the King and at that very moment bombarding Shelburne with demands for amnesty and compensation for the Tories,[141] the doctor, who might well have considered his son's behavior a blemish on his own patriotism, stood in Adams' words "very staunch against the Tories, more decided a great deal on this point than Mr. Jay or myself."[142] Franklin now proceeded to read his fellow commissioners a letter he had addressed to Richard Oswald. His hearers recognized it, not only as a brilliant propaganda weapon, written, as Jay later remarked, "with a degree of acuteness and spirit seldom to be met with in persons of his age,"[143] but as diplomatic blackmail of the first order. Reminding Oswald that Congress had called upon the States to itemize their claims against the British, the doctor warned that, should the British press the issue of Loyalist compensation, he was prepared to place on the agenda a demand for reparations for damages suffered by Patriots. Franklin's letter cited the burning of Charlestown near Boston, of Falmouth, "just before winter, when the sick, the aged, the women, and children were driven to seek shelter where they could hardly find it," of Norfolk, New London, Fairfield, and Esopus, besides the ravaging of the countryside, and the butchering and scalping of hundreds of farmers, along with their wives and children. The doctor was prepared to propose that both sides exhibit to commissioners hereafter to be appointed accounts of their losses, "and that if a balance appears" in favor of the Loyalists, "it shall be paid by us to you." On the other hand, "if the balance is found due to us, it shall be paid by you."[144] Jay and Adams, not quite so inflexible as Franklin on the score of the Tories, "agreed with him that he should read" the letter "as containing his private sentiments."[145] Even if the British had conquered, it would have been hard to force the Americans to compensate the Tories, Franklin reminded the British when they met that day, "and you will please recollect, that you have *not* conquered us."[146]

The arguments over the Tories and King Cod continued through the next day, the twenty-eighth. Benjamin Vaughan, having returned from London, put in a plea with the Americans for "a large tract of land" for the Tories, "or else amnesty and strong recommendations." He was not arguing on behalf of the refugees generally, but sought consideration for absentees, neutrals, and "persons terrified into submission."[147] Strachey, on the other hand, in the face of an obstinate adversary, appeared to be weakening. He no longer insisted upon a complete restoration of Tory properties, but indicated that his government would find acceptable an arrangement whereby the refugees would be enabled "to purchase in their property at the last sum sold." Something had to be yielded, he pleaded, "to save the King's honor."[148]

Adams, who had devoted the morning to drawing up a revised fishing article, submitted it to the commissioners that same day. Therein he stipulated the right of "subjects of his Britannic Majesty and the people of the United States" to take fish of every kind on the Grand Bank and all the other banks of Newfoundland, as well as the Gulf of St. Lawrence, and in other places where the inhabitants of both countries "used at any time heretofore to fish." As regards the drying of fish, however, he thought it advisable to make a concession to Strachey. He now merely stipulated for the "liberty" of curing and drying fish on the shores of Cape Sable, the unsettled parts of Nova Scotia, or the shores of the Magdalen Islands, and Labrador. The British had urged this modification on the ground that the word "right" would be more "unpleasing" to the people of England than "liberty." He also left out of the new draft the principle of mutuality of fishing rights incorporated in his proposal of November 4th. Adams' article further stipulated that American fisherman be permitted to rent land for terms of years to erect the necessary stages and buildings for curing and drying.

That evening Matthew Ridley called on Adams after dinner. "I have laid down a line," the latter remarked, referring to his draft, "and beyond that I will not go, let who would be ready." These were brave words, and Adams was forced to admit that his article was running into difficulties. He was sure that the obstructions were to be laid at the door of Rayneval and his conversations in England.[149]

Friday, November 29th, the fourth and next to last day of the renewed discussions, proved memorable for two reasons. The preliminary draft was agreed upon, but not before Henry Laurens made a last-minute appearance. Thomas Jefferson, fifth commissioner, never did sail for Europe, and neither participated nor signed. Laurens' coming added a tragic note to the closing sessions. On November 6th Adams had written to Laurens, enclosing a resolution of Congress of September 17th enjoining upon all the commissioners attendance on the negotiations for peace. "Join us as soon as possible," Adams pleaded. That same note bore the melancholy information that Laurens' son John, one of the most brilliant Patriot soldiers produced in the war, had been killed in an obscure action in South Carolina in August, almost a year after Yorktown. "I can say nothing more to you," Adams added, "but that you have much greater reason to say, in this case, as a Duke of Ormond said of an Earl of Ossory,

'I would not exchange my dead son for any living son in the world.' "[150] The grief-stricken Laurens replied: "Thank God, I had a son, who dared to die in defense of his country."[151]

A swarthy, well-knit figure, below middling size, the gout-tortured Laurens now took his seat across the conference table from Richard Oswald, a long-time business associate and perhaps his most intimate friend. Compounding the coincidences, Laurens was indirectly related to Benjamin Vaughan through William Manning, London merchant and Vaughan's father-in-law. Aside from these curious ties to the British on the part of Laurens, the French were understandably cool to the prospect of another descendant of Huguenot refugees joining the American peace delegation. Mr. Jay's prejudices, to their mind, did not need bolstering. In point of fact the anxieties of the French were unwarranted. Laurens, of all the commissioners, seemed the least anxious to sign the preliminary articles without consulting the French. He irritated Adams considerably when he ventured to doubt the authenticity of Barbé-Marbois' letter on the fisheries, and warned against a separate peace. On the score of the Tories he was as deeply uncompromising as Franklin.[152]

The three British and the four American negotiators foregathered at Jay's hotel and spent all of Friday settling the fishing and Tory articles.

"Can you consent to leave out the limitations of three leagues from all shores and the fifteen from those of Louisburg?" Adams asked Oswald.

"Personally, I am for it, but my instructions do not permit me," Oswald replied. The Americans realized that Oswald could not settle either the fishery or Tory articles without the concurrence of Fitzherbert and Strachey. The latter stubbornly insisted on the wording of the draft he brought back from London in which "liberty" of fishing was substituted for "right" as it had been for drying and curing. " 'Right' is an obnoxious expression," Fitzherbert chimed in.

This was John Adams' big moment. Rising to his full five feet seven inches, he exclaimed, "Gentlemen, is there or can there be a clearer right? . . . When God Almighty made the Banks of Newfoundland at three hundred leagues' distance from the people of America and six hundred leagues' distance from those of France and England, did he not give as good a right to the former as to the latter? If Heaven in the Creation gave a right, it is ours at least as much as yours. If occupation, use, and possession give a right, we have at least as much as you. If war and blood and treasure give a right, ours is as good as yours."

"The argument is in your favor," Fitzherbert conceded, but he pointed out that Oswald's instructions did not give them any leeway.

"That is perfectly all right," replied Adams. "We can wait. Send a courier back to London."

"No, no!" exclaimed Fitzherbert, who was horrified at the thought of having "all laid loose before Parliament." That would be "going to sea again."

"Why not leave the fishery article to the definitive treaty?" Strachey and Fitzherbert asked.

"I never could put my hand to any articles without satisfaction about the fishery," Adams rejoined.

"Nor could I," Laurens spoke up. "I will never give my voice to any articles without this."

"It could not be a peace. Without it there would only be an insidious truce," Jay insisted.

Adams recorded all this for history,[153] but what he left out was that he and his colleagues had already agreed to a compromise whereby the Americans settled for a "liberty" to take fish on the "coast" of Newfoundland and the other coasts of British North America, as distinguished from a "right" which was acknowledged to them to fish on the banks and in the Gulf of St. Lawrence. As regards the latter, they were unbudgeable.

Years later Adams remarked, "We did not think it necessary to contend for a word."[154] Nonetheless, his watering down of "right" to "liberty" both as regards coastal fishing and curing and drying was to prove a source of mischievous controversy for the next hundred years.

Until these last revisions peace seemed stalled over some cod and haddock. Franklin chose now to put in his oar by producing a paper from his pocket upon which he had itemized the American claims for reparations. "Remember," he reminded the British, "the first principle of the treaty is equality and reciprocity. You demand payment of us of debt and restitution or compensation to the refugees. If a draper had sold a piece of cloth to a man upon credit and then sent a servant to take it from him by force, and afterward brought his action for the debt, would any court of law or equity give him his demand without obliging him to restore the cloth?" he argued with his homely logic. Citing the carrying off of goods from Boston, Philadelphia, and the Southern states, and the burning of towns, he suggested the propriety of now submitting claims for such damages.[155] Adams chimed in with an account of goods carried off from Boston to Halifax by Gage's soldiers; Franklin remembered the rifling of his own library in Philadelphia; Jay thought of a number of items, and Laurens reminded the negotiators of the plundering of Negroes and plate from the Carolinas. The removal of Negro slaves from Charleston and Savannah had been one of the scandals of the British evacuation, and had already called forth remonstrances to the British from Jay and Adams. "The name of an Englishman is in very bad repute in these Southern Provinces," Vaughan had told Oswald. "God forbid that there should be any foundation" for such charges! Oswald in turn had protested to Strachey.[156]

With the temperature reaching the boiling point, a recess was called. Oswald, Fitzherbert, and Strachey withdrew. Should they refer the issues of the fisheries and the Loyalists back to London? Even had the Americans been agreeable to allowing the issues to remain *in statu quo* during the eight days or so that it would take to get word back from England, there would have been political risks in deferring the settlement until after Parliament convened. However, the Americans expressly reserved the right to introduce "any new articles which they might think expedient." Fearing that Franklin's insistence that reparations be placed on the agenda would open a Pandora's box and "unhinge the whole negotiation," and confronted with the fact that the titular British negotiator, Richard Oswald, was unwilling to put up a fight to whittle down further the concessions on the fisheries, Fitzherbert and Strachey bowed to the inevitable.

On their return to the room Fitzherbert declared that, "upon consulting together and weighing everything as maturely as possible," he and Strachey had advised Oswald "to strike" with the Americans according to the terms the American commissioners had stated as their ultimata on the fishery and the Loyalists. Had we not assented to the fishery article, Strachey stated, there would have been no treaty at all.[157] This concession on the part of the British was no wholesale surrender, however. What the peace commissioners now settled upon was something even more restrictive than Adams' compromise version of November 28th. The changes in the article they agreed to not only watered "right" to "liberty" as regards the coastal fishery, but also involved abandoning the liberty of curing and drying on Cape Sable, as well as the explicit permission to be granted American fishermen to rent land for curing and drying their fish. Instead, the "liberty" of drying and curing was restricted to the period of time that these coastal regions remained "unsettled." Thereafter, it would "not be lawful" for the fishermen to use the land for that purpose "without a previous agreement" with "the inhabitants, proprietors, or possessors of the ground."[158]

The Americans made additional compromises. They now accepted an obligation binding Congress merely to recommend "earnestly" to the legislatures of the states that they provide for the restitution of the property of both "real British subjects" and persons "resident in districts in the possession of His Majesty's arms, and who have not borne arms against the said United States"; and permitting persons "of any other description" to move freely within the United States for twelve months unmolested in their efforts to obtain restitution of such of their properties as may have been confiscated. It was further agreed "that there shall be no future confiscations made, nor any prosecutions commenced against any person or persons, for or by reason of the part which he or they may have taken in the present war." This moral rather than legal obligation left the door open a crack, but the separate states, following a vindictive course, soon proceeded to slam it shut.[159] No provision for indemnification of Patriots was secured, but, of course, the Americans never seriously expected it. In an expansive mood, the Americans agreed to the payment of all debts due to British merchants rather than restricting them to those incurred before 1775, as in Jay's provisional draft.[160]

Despite these concessions, the Americans felt they had put in a good day's work. At dinner that Friday evening Adams was asked if he wanted fish. "No," he laughed, "I have had a pretty good meal of them today." "I am glad to hear it," Ridley rejoined, "as I know that a small quantity would not satisfy you." "Thanks be to God," Adams wrote Elbridge Gerry of Marblehead, "that our Tom Cod are safe in spite of the malice of enemies, the finesse of allies, and the mistakes of Congress," although he was curiously imprecise about letting the folks back home know just what the Americans had won. He could afford to be in an expansive mood. "Doctor Franklin has behaved well and nobly, particularly this day," he declared, an enormous concession for an Adams to make, but he had been agreeably impressed by Franklin's stout stand on the Mississippi and the fisheries, as well as by his willingness to complete the preliminaries without further consultation with the French court.[161]

Toward his colleague from New York Adams was even more generous. He had previously eulogized Jay as a diplomat who achieved results by technical mastery as distinguished from those seeking results from "dresses, horses, balls, or cards." If the French knew as much of Jay's negotiations as they do of mine, he recorded in his Journal, they "would very justly give the title with which they have inconsiderately decorated me, that of *Le Washington de la Négotiation*, a very flattering Compliment indeed, to which I have not a right, but sincerely think it belongs to Mr. Jay." Adams rejoiced at the "entire coincidence of principles and Opinions" which had obtained between Jay and himself, and never failed to pay

tribute to the New Yorker for the central role he played in the transactions.[162]

Signing was set for the next day, Saturday, November 30th. To Caleb
Whitefoord, a fellow Scot of Oswald, the omens seemed propitious, as
it happened to be St. Andrew's Day. The parties foregathered at Oswald's
lodgings at the Grand Hotel Muscovite, on the same street, rue des
Petits Augustins, where the Jays were staying. The principles compared
treaty drafts. The Americans pointed out that Strachey had left out the
twelve-month limitation of time permitted the refugees to reside in
America in order to try to recover their estates. Franklin and Jay looked
surprised, and insisted that the limitation be put back, which was done.[163]
Laurens managed to get a clause inserted forbidding the carrying off of
Negroes or other property of American inhabitants by the evacuating
forces. Oswald agreed.

Just before the signing, according to stories widely circulated at the
time, Franklin stepped out of the room and returned wearing the very
coat that he had worn in January, 1774, on the occasion of his public
humiliation by Solicitor General Wedderburn before a committee of the
Privy Council. Franklin on that occasion had been excoriated for his part
in exposing Massachusetts' Tory Governor, Thomas Hutchinson. For his
role in revealing the Governor's confidential letters Franklin had been
dismissed from his post of Deputy Postmaster General for America. No
one believed that he would ever forget that scorching rebuke. Now, on
the occasion of his triumph, and as an affront both to the King "and the
whole British nation," he allegedly donned the suit of figured blue Manchester velvet that he had worn on that less happy occasion. Although
Franklin had a flair for the dramatic in the matter of costumery, he was
too big a man to let personal spite mar a solemn moment, and this legend
is entirely without substance. The fact is that the doctor never left the
room, never changed his coat, and wore at the signing ceremony a suit
of black cloth in keeping with the period of mourning which had been
decreed by the court of Versailles for the demise of a German prince.
When the story was later called to his attention he indignantly disclaimed
it, as did Caleb Whitefoord, an eyewitness, and Lord Mountstuart, who
reached Paris shortly after the signing. The latter made a point of reporting that "everything passed in the simplest manner with great civility
and decorum on all sides."[164]

The parties affixed their signatures to duplicate originals of both the
preliminary treaty and the separate article. According to protocol, Richard
Oswald, representing the more venerable state, signed first on behalf

of the erstwhile monarch of a now free and independent people, and then the Americans in strict alphabetical order. Whitefoord and William Temple Franklin, as secretaries to their respective commissions, duly attested the signatures. Seals were affixed, and a signed original turned over to each side for transmission to their principals. Curiously enough, the original which went to the Americans has never been found, and we must be content with the single original text in London's Public Record Office.[165]

The signing over, the participants rode out to Passy together to celebrate the event. There they were joined by some French guests, one of whom took occasion to rub salt into the wounds. Turning to the British, he harped on the theme of "the growing greatness of America," and predicted that "the Thirteen United States would form the greatest empire in the world."

"Yes, sir," Caleb Whitefoord replied, "and they will *all* speak English; every one of 'em."[166]

The great moment had passed, and France was not permitted to share therein. The Americans, in accordance with their settled purpose, had concluded the preliminaries without the advice of the French court. However, the evening before the signing Franklin dashed off a note to Vergennes apprising him of the event about to take place, and promising to forward a copy of the articles of peace. This he did almost at once, but without the separate secret article.[167] Rather clumsily Adams disclosed that the agreement covered more than was in Vergennes' copy. On November 5th the Duc de La Vauguyon paid him a call. Adams' own Journal tells what happened: "I showed him our preliminary treaty," he records, "and had some difficulty to prevent his seeing the separate article; but I did prevent him from seeing anything of it but the words "Separate Article."[168] The British were careful not to disclose the secret article to Rayneval in London, but they did hasten to assure him that the fishing rights granted the American did not pose a future conflict in the area that was being set aside for the fishermen of France.[169]

Having deliberately violated the instructions of Congress in pursuing their course apart from the French, the Americans defended their action in a letter to Secretary Livingston and in words penned, appropriately, by John Jay. "As we had reason to imagine that the articles respecting the boundaries, the refugees, and fisheries, did not correspond with the policy of this Court, we did not communicate the preliminaries to the Minister until after they were signed," and not "even then," they admitted, did they inform him of the *separate* article.[170]

Privately Vergennes was shocked at the liberal concessions England had made to her rebellious subjects, thereby stripping him of a heavy club he might have wielded against the adversary to secure Gibraltar, concessions in India, and other demands of the Bourbon partners. After looking over the articles he remarked to Rayneval, "The English buy peace rather than make it," adding, "Their concessions exceed all that I could have thought possible." His undersecretary in reply characterized the treaty with the Americans as a "dream." "I am persuaded," he wrote, "that the English Ministers in making it have the defection of the Americans in view." "The unhappy news" of the signing, he soon pointed out, seriously weakened his position as a negotiator with Lord Shelburne.[171] Vergennes was most upset about the fisheries provisions, as he felt that they violated France's exclusive rights which, by his interpretation, were affirmed by the Treaty of Commerce with America of 1778. Unfortunately, what had been done could not easily be undone. "Our opinion could not influence the negotiations," the Comte later complained to La Luzerne, "since we knew nothing of their details, and because they were completed in the most sudden, unforeseen, and, I might say, extraordinary manner."[172]

When Franklin and Laurens paid their respects to Vergennes some days after the signing, the French Minister remarked that "the abrupt signing of the articles" by the Americans "had little in it which could be agreeable to the King." Although the conversation was amicable, if restrained, Vergennes urged Franklin not to send the provisional treaty on to Congress. Such "an intelligence with England," he argued, "might make the people in America think a peace was consummated, and embarrass Congress, of whose fidelity I had no suspicion."[173] Franklin and his colleagues could not take this plea seriously. Their own responsibilities as commissioners made it incumbent upon them to report to Congress as promptly as possible the course they had taken. On the evening of December 15th Vergennes was disturbed to learn from Franklin that the Americans had received a British passport for protection of an American vessel called the *Washington*, Captain Barney commanding, by which they intended to send dispatches to America, including the transmittal of the preliminary articles. With the presumption that only the doctor among the four commissioners could have ventured to take, Franklin suggested that this vessel offered a safe mode of conveyance for any part of the financial aids that America had lately requested of France, and concluded, "I fear that Congress will be reduced to despair when they find that nothing is yet obtained."

Vergennes felt that the tone of Franklin's letter was "so singular" that it was his duty to reply. "I am at a loss, sir," he remarked, "to explain your conduct and that of your colleagues on this occasion." He pointed out that the Americans had concluded their preliminaries without the communication with the court of France that Congress had prescribed. Worse still, he declared, "You are about to hold out a certain hope of peace to America without even informing yourself on the state of the negotiation on our part."[174]

Franklin proved more than equal to the challenge posed by Vergennes' rebuke. "It was certainly incumbent on us to give Congress as early an account as possible of our proceedings," he replied. What will they think if they hear the news "by other means without a line from us?" He assured Vergennes that nothing had been agreed to in the preliminaries "contrary to the interests of France," and that no peace was to take place between England and America "till you have concluded yours." He conceded that the American commissioners may have been indiscreet in not consulting the Comte before signing the preliminaries, but softened the blow by confessing, "We have been guilty of neglecting a point of *bienséance*." This, he assured the Comte, was not from want of respect to the King, "whom we all love and honor." Now that the "great work" has been "so nearly brought to perfection," Franklin expressed the hope that it would "not be ruined by a single indiscretion of ours. And certainly the whole edifice sinks to the ground immediately if you refuse on that account to give us any further assistance. . . . *The English, I just now learn, flatter themselves they have already divided us*," he deftly added. "I hope this little misunderstanding will therefore be kept secret, and that they will find themselves totally mistaken."[175]

If the English, who learned of this misunderstanding almost at once through their spy Edward Bancroft,[176] had counted on the French terminating their assistance to America, they were to be speedily disillusioned. Despite his private bitterness Vergennes did not think it prudent to insist that Franklin withhold the preliminaries or to refuse the doctor's request for more money.[177] The same ship that set out for Philadelphia with the American peace preliminaries also carried the first installment of the last French loan of six million livres.[178] Not until France and Spain had settled their preliminary terms with England did Vergennes feel it safe to turn off the spigot. Meantime an open breach was avoided. At Versailles a formal declaration was drafted in French to be made by the American commissioners reaffirming their adherence to the French alliance. A preliminary version was drawn up at the start of the year; a final version bore the date January 20, 1783, "done at Passy," and was apparently intended to accompany the Declaration of the Cessation of Hostilities which the Americans issued on the occasion of the signing of the Franco-Spanish preliminaries with England. The circumstances surrounding these drafts are still shrouded in mystery. Whether or not Franklin tried to persuade his colleagues to affix their signatures to the document cannot now be ascertained, as the extant papers of the American commissioners have nothing directly to say on the subject. A fair inference, however, may be drawn from a letter Jay wrote Lafayette from Rouen on January 19th. Expressing surprise that anyone should entertain doubts of "American good faith," he asserted, "America has so often repeated her professions and assurances of regard" for the treaty with France "that I hope she will not impair her dignity by making any more of them." Evidently Jay's colleagues felt the same way, for the unsigned drafts still repose in the archives of the Quai d'Orsay.[179]

Without detracting from Shelburne's astute manipulations which resulted in his driving a wedge between the French and American Allies, albeit at a heavy price,[180] one should not minimize the dexterous performance of the Americans who secured peace while maintaining the semblance of the alliance at the same time. As long as the Americans were in a position to make calls upon their French ally,[181] the British could not hope in the final round of talks to water down the vast concessions they had made America by way of preliminaries.

XVI

THE CONDE SETTLES
AN OLD SCORE

IN THE FALL of '82 the Comte de Vergennes found himself a prisoner of events. The calendar had suddenly become a jailer, allowing him little space for maneuver. Gibraltar's relief, then the signing of the American preliminaries,[1] to be followed shortly by the reconvening of Parliament, left Vergennes little time to come to terms with a conciliatory British Ministry whose days seemed numbered.

While time had shrunken, the stakes of diplomacy now loomed vast and beyond the vision of statesmen when the war began. That war had been undertaken to achieve the liberation of a colonial people. It had now metamorphosed into a world-wide imperial struggle to determine who would control other colonial peoples. It had been waged on Lake Champlain, the Delaware, and the Chesapeake, as well as within sight of the cliffs of Dover. Now it was being fought at Gibraltar, off the Cape of Good Hope, along the Coromandel Coast, and in the Indian Ocean.

Shelburne, though administering the last rites for the old British Empire, paid heed to interests that were determined to lay the basis for a second empire whose center of gravity would be India rather than America. Vergennes stubbornly contested every inch of the ground. The Comte, who had entered the war without thought of territorial gain for France save to buttress that nation's position in the fisheries, was now forced to listen to the expansionist elements within his own court, a faction that made no secret of its conviction that the future of France overseas lay in India and that the larger part of that great subcontinent should be brought under French influence.[2] As a counterweight to the British, Vergennes had no alternative but to support the demands of the Dutch for the total restitution of their dependencies in the East Indies. Thus the Dutch negotiations for peace became inseparable from the French, for, as the British East India Company reminded their Ministry, yielding to the Dutch was tantamount to ceding key points in the Indies to French control.[3]

When one compares the peace objectives of the parties it is clear that the diplomats of the Old World and of the New were pressing in opposite directions. The Americans, in their quest of a durable peace for a new nation under a republican government, were setting the mood of a revolutionary age, while France and Spain, in seeking to retrieve influence and properties they had hitherto been forced to surrender, were casting backward glances toward a time that would never return. In coveting Gibraltar, the Spaniards sought to recover a fortress they had yielded in 1704, while France strained to put the calendar back to the year 1754, when she held supremacy in the Deccan in India and exercised great sway in the Carnatic to the south. France's Indian interests had been under a cloud since the defeat suffered at the hands of Clive at Plassey in 1757. To erase that defeat and strengthen the hand of her diplomats at the peace table, the French court had dispatched to India an expedition under the Comte de Bussy. Although the last detachment had set sail as recently as April, 1782, no word had as yet been received of their situation. Vergennes had not even learned of the naval victories that French Admiral de Suffren had scored against British Admiral Hughes. He did not know that the British had been expelled from the Dutch port of Trincomalee in Ceylon. Until he could confront the British with a *fait accompli*, he could hardly expect Shelburne to defy the formidable East India interest in Parliament and make any significant concessions in the Indies. To appease the French Shelburne would have had to cede territory in the neighborhood of France's old settlements on the Coromandel Coast sufficient to assure her a revenue adequate for defraying the upkeep of all her Indian establishments. In addition, he would be expected to concede to the French the liberty to trade in Bengal, the center of the East India Company's operations.

The French had been very discreet about revealing their war aims, and the British only learned them in piecemeal fashion. Early in September Fitzherbert was apprised of them in broad outline,[4] and Gérard de Rayneval spelled them out in some detail on his first visit to England later that month. Aside from her extravagant pretension to the Newfoundland fisheries and India, France's other demands seemed moderately keyed. She sought to regain Senegal and the Gambia post of Gorée, both lost in the last war. The recovery of these areas would enable the French to develop their own slave trade instead of being compelled to trade through British slavers.[5] Vergennes also sought to annul one of the provisions of the old Treaty of Utrecht that still rankled. This one forbade France to fortify Dunkirk. Rayneval demanded the removal of this prohibition, and Shelburne foresaw little difficulty in obliging the French provided that Dunkirk was not reopened as a port. Toward French demands for reciprocal trade concessions Shelburne manifested genuine cordiality, even though he knew deep down that in the current state of British opinion any such concession would be unrealistic.[6]

The remaining demand related to the Newfoundland fisheries, where the French sought an exclusive right of fishing and drying on parts of the Newfoundland coast to avoid disputes arising between the fishermen of France and England, in addition to full sovereignty over the little islands of St. Pierre and Miquelon.[7] When France, in her anxiety to stake out a claim before the American counterclaim could be filed, pressed these demands early in August, the British hoped to exploit a potential rift over the fisheries between France and her American ally. Indeed, Rayneval made it clear that nothing was farther from the wishes of his court than that the claims of the Americans to the fisheries should be conceded.[8]

Vergennes kept one ear cocked for news from India while the other strained to pick up every report from Gibraltar. The pretensions of France's Bourbon partner to that Pillar of Hercules hung like a dead albatross around the Comte's neck. Before Rayneval had departed for England, the Conde de Aranda had received full powers from his government to conduct negotiations with the British.[9] Three points, Floridablanca instructed him, were to be considered as conditions *sine qua non:* (1) the removal of the English logwood cutters from the Gulfs of Honduras and Campeche, or the placing of the English establishments located there under the supervision of Spain;[10] (2) the exclusion of all foreigners from the Gulf of Mexico; and (3) the cession of Gibraltar and Minorca. In the event that Gibraltar was already conquered at the time the negotiations started, the British would be allowed the free port of Mahon on Minorca for trade only; otherwise they would be offered Oran and its roadstead of Mers-el-Kebir.[11]

Fearing that the imperial mediators might intervene and desirous of directing the negotiations for the Bourbon partners himself, Vergennes sent Rayneval to England in September. Rayneval left with the knowledge and even the approbation of the Spanish court, which recognized the need for sounding out the British Ministry on their war aims.[12] Vergennes' undersecretary was instructed to avoid disclosing these Spanish terms in all their harsh detail, but even so agile a diplomat as Rayneval found it impossible to evade the issue of Gibraltar. When informed by his French visitor that there could be no peace unless the fortress were ceded, Shelburne grimly predicted: "Gibraltar will prove the rock in the negotiations as it was in the sea." It was not the British, however, but the Spaniards who were inflexible on this score. Two years earlier Richard Cumberland's mission had foundered on the Rock of Gibraltar. Now George III, if not Shelburne, was prepared to yield the fortress in exchange for Puerto Rico, Majorca, or some other acceptable equivalent,[13] but in the relatively brief period of time that the cession of Gibraltar remained negotiable the British found unpalatable the few crumbs that the Spaniards were prepared to leave on the banquet table. Rayneval was without power to satisfy the British in either the Mediterranean or the West Indies. He frankly pointed out that Spain did not want the British to be to the windward of the Spanish and French islands, and therefore would not yield Puerto Rico, and at the same time did not want the British to the leeward either, for such a location would threaten Spain's exclusive control of the Gulf of Mexico. Thus Spain was not prepared to offer West Florida and a strip of coast in the vicinity of New Orleans in exchange for Gibraltar, because the British presence would add insuperable obstacles to Spain's efforts to stamp out the contraband trade in the Gulf.[14]

Neither Spanish intransigence over equivalents for Gibraltar nor the extravagant pretension of the French in India prevented Shelburne and Rayneval from coming to a tentative agreement on several outstanding issues before their first series of conferences ended. Shelburne conceded the French the West Indian Islands of St. Lucia and Dominica in return for a restitution to Britain of Granada, St. Vincent, Tobago, St. Kitts, Nevis, and Montserrat. The French sought St. Lucia because of its proximity to Martinique, and Dominica, which lies between her sugar islands of Martinique and Guadeloupe, because it had served as a base for contraband trade while in British hands.[15] The British were also willing to concede to the French the inshore fishery along the northeast and western coasts of Newfoundland, but not to their exclusion, and Rayneval was ready to accept Shelburne's compromise proposal by which France would recover Senegal while Britain would retain her footing on Gambia. Shelburne was even prepared to restore to France a foothold in India as a trader, to restore Pondicherry with a reasonable territorial dependency attached. He was not prepared to recognize France as a political power in India, or to consider restoring to the Dutch *in toto* the territory in Indian waters that the British had seized during the present war.[16]

On his return to Paris Rayneval was exuberant about Shelburne.[17] He was impressed by the latter's flexibility on Gibraltar and his moderate position on the fisheries. As he did not share the views of the expansionist faction at his court he felt that the British and the French were not too far apart on other points.[18] Shelburne had shrewdly appealed to the under-secretary's vanity. Only three persons were necessary to effect peace, the Earl had observed—Vergennes and Shelburne, with Rayneval as the trusted intermediary. "All other persons," he pointedly remarked, "would find in me the greatest reserve." Once more had Shelburne demonstrated his dismaying capacity for by-passing his authorized negotiators. By his indiscreet comment he had reduced Alleyne Fitzherbert from the stature of a plenipotentiary to a mere consultant on points of detail and he had given the French grounds for viewing Lord Grantham, England's Foreign Secretary, as little more than a cipher. On all issues calling for clarification Rayneval was invited to write to Shelburne direct over the heads of both Fitzherbert and Grantham. Shelburne preferred to keep the reins in his own hands even when the coachmen happened to be responsible Cabinet ministers. This was his special style, and he was sufficiently ungenerous to disparage in after years the contributions that Grantham and Town-shend had made to the negotiations and to take all the credit for himself. Shelburne knew the risk he was taking should Rayneval's mission turn out to be purely exploratory. He even told Grantham to burn certain papers in the likely event Parliament demanded to see them. "The game is deep on our part and hazardous," he told his Foreign Secretary, "but infinitely more so in theirs [the French] if they are insincere."[19]

Rayneval's disclosures of English moderation encouraged Vergennes to press the Spanish court to modify its "grandiose pretensions," notably as regards Gibraltar. The Comte had reason for grave concern. French finances were grim, as the Abbé Morellet quite frankly confided to his friend Lord Shelburne. The French Navy had not yet recovered from de Grasse's defeat in the West Indies at Rodney's hands.[20] News from Gibraltar was enough to convert the ever cautious French Minister into an avowed defeatist, who could see little or nothing to be gained by carrying on the war, but much to be risked. Vergennes had nightmares of a new political system emerging in Europe, one that was not under his domination but rather under the joint direction of Joseph of Austria and Catherine of Russia. The latter's aggressive postures against the Turks were disturbing to Versailles.

With all of the worries besetting Vergennes there is little wonder that he sought to scale down the Spanish demands. He dismissed Spanish claims to a share in the Newfoundland fisheries as "chimerical," and did not scruple to let the British know how he felt.[21] Through Montmorin in Madrid he sought futilely to convince Floridablanca that, since the disastrous repulse at Gibraltar had shown that the fortress could not be taken by force, it had to be bargained for, and attractive equivalents offered in exchange. Since Oran and its roadstead of Mers-el-Kebir were not acceptable to England, he suggested as an equivalent for the fortress the two Floridas, New Orleans and its environs, "joined to the vast areas which are situated between the Mississippi, the Lakes, and the Western frontiers of the United States."

Vergennes argued that such an exchange would be advantageous both to England and to Spain. England's First Minister could then yield Gibraltar without sacrificing his political career, and Spain would have a buffer between her own colonies and the bothersome Americans. Jay's arguments over the Florida boundaries had revealed the extent of America's expansionist proclivities. "If the English should recover this province situated between Spain and the United States over the length of the Mississippi, Spain would no longer need to be apprehensive of an invasion by the Americans." Finally, Vergennes dismissed as unfounded Spain's fears that Florida would prove a source of the contraband trade. But at this point the Comte had to break off his communication to Montmorin. A victim of the influenza epidemic which did not discriminate between diplomats of ancient monarchies and plenipotentiaries from infant republics, he referred his ambassador to Rayneval for further details.[22]

Vergennes' unabashed avowal of his willingness to curb the Western pretensions of the Americans to placate his Spanish ally could not fail to be reflected in the Anglo-American negotiations. On August 29th, it must be remembered, the British Cabinet had resolved to yield the entire West to America, and even a fortnight later, when Shelburne conferred with Rayneval, he had no notion of retaining territory along the eastern bank of the Mississippi. Within a short time after he had concluded his first series of conferences with Rayneval Shelburne mustered a batch of arguments for retaining the Old Northwest, and then prompted Strachey to propose a longitudinal line to bisect the West. Perhaps this was coincidental, but in the devious annals of diplomacy coincidences are rare indeed. The American commissioners had stoutly resisted Strachey's new proposal, which amounted to a reversal of the Cabinet's earlier decision, and they secured unexpected help from Floridablanca, who refused to take Vergennes' proposition seriously. The French, as Montmorin saw it, had dropped into the lap of Spain's Foreign Minister "an apple of discord between the English and the Americans which would keep them in a state of almost continual hostility."[23] Floridablanca's concern that England be not restored to a position where she could challenge Spain's trade monopoly on the Gulf led him to drop the apple into the refuse heap.

Spain's refusal to propose an acceptable equivalent for Gibraltar threatened the whole peace structure whose foundations Vergennes had been so laboriously laying. The Comte complained to Montmorin of Aranda's "mournful silence." He reminded his ambassador to Madrid that a basis of negotiations had to be laid down before Parliament reconvened. "If we miss this date," he warned, "the English Ministry will no longer be the master of decision-making, and God knows when the negotiations will be able to be resumed!"[24]

For a time Vergennes had to play the part of spectator watching the chief roles being acted out before his eyes by Aranda and Fitzherbert, but privately he was putting pressure on the Spaniards through Montmorin and Admiral d'Estaing. The latter had been sent to Madrid ostensibly en route to Cádiz to assume command of the combined fleet being readied for an attack on Jamaica. Aranda had seized the initiative upon Rayneval's return from London and opened direct negotiations with Fitzherbert in Paris on October 6th. Although the Conde was shocked by what he considered the "inexplicable" failure of the Allies before Gibraltar, one would never have discerned his perturbed state of mind from the peace terms he outlined. Spain's ambitions were couched in extravagant language. Aranda demanded that Britain cede all territories in the Gulf of Mexico captured by Spain during the war, that English settlers be expelled from the logwood and mahogany-cutting establishments in the Bay of Honduras and Campeche, and that Spain be allowed to participate in the Newfoundland fisheries on the ground that Spaniards had been first on the scene. He further informed Fitzherbert that Cuba and Puerto Rico were the "limbs of Spain" and could not be dismembered to satisfy the British demand for an equivalent to Gibraltar and Minorca. To the British who still clung to Puerto Rico or Cuba as the only tempting equivalents, the Spanish demands were completely unacceptable and Aranda's tactics detestable.[25]

Vergennes was as shocked as the British by Aranda's extravagant claims and made no secret of his views. He let Fitzherbert know that he regarded the Conde's proposals as exorbitant, "going far beyond what that Court is secretly resolved to accept." To his British enemy he denounced the conduct of his Spanish ally, which he disdainfully compared to "that of a petty shopkeeper who thinks that the only way to get a fair price for his goods is to begin by asking ten times more than they are worth." The only way to deal with the Spaniards, he counseled, is for the English to act the part of the "respectable wholesale merchant" and say straight off the terms to which they are resolved in all events to adhere. True, he conceded, inspiration for the proposals had come from Madrid, but they had been put together in Paris by Aranda, "who from the peculiarity of his temper, had given them the most ungracious and inauspicious appearance possible." The British could count on more sympathetic treatment by responding direct to Madrid, he added.[26] Vergennes fancied himself the honest broker who would bring off the big deal despite an immense amount of unseemly haggling between the various principals. To his allies his operations might well have seemed like double-dealing, but fortunately for the peace their worst suspicions were not confirmed.

Bolstered by the knowledge that Vergennes was not prepared to back the Spaniards if they proved intransigent, Fitzherbert denounced the Spanish claims to Aranda's face as "exorbitant." Aranda admitted that he had full powers to conclude and need not write back to his court for fresh instructions. On the other hand, his powers limited him in *"making"* proposals, although he was authorized "to decide absolutely upon such as he should *receive.*" As regards equivalents for Gibraltar, he repeated his refusal to consider Cuba and Puerto Rico, but implied that other possessions of Spain might be put on the trading counter. At that point, he was quite prepared to sacrifice either West Florida or Spanish Santo Domingo. Within a day or two word reached the Conde of Lord Howe's relief of Gibraltar, and with it came a rapid deterioration of his bargaining position.[27]

With Shelburne and King George panting for a rich sugar island as an equivalent for Gibraltar, Spanish Santo Domingo seemed the obvious possibility if Charles III would not part with Cuba or Puerto Rico. The mere possibility set wheels turning within wheels. Floridablanca was perfectly aware of the fact that the cession of Santo Domingo would create a situation thoroughly unacceptable to France, for it would mean that England and France would now hold the joint occupancy of the island, whose western portion, St. Domingue, was the seat of government of the French *Isles sous le Vent*. To obviate that difficulty he proposed a three-way deal. He instructed Aranda to offer Spain's portion of the island to France, leaving it up to his ally to cede to England either Corsica or some French West Indian possessions.

When Aranda put the proposal to the Comte de Vergennes early in November the French Foreign Minister was outraged. St. Domingue was the most valuable of the French Caribbean colonies. Making England a next-door neighbor at St. Domingue would revive the very rivalry the French had been seeking to extinguish, he remonstrated. Besides,

France did not need and did not want the Spanish part of Santo Domingo, he stated brusquely. The French planters were providing all the sugar France needed. The addition of the Spanish part would only result in lowering the value of the French plantations.[28] Yielding Corsica was out of the question, he added. The island was too strategically located for France to consider abandoning it, too essential to safeguarding French commerce in the Mediterranean. Once more Vergennes proposed that Spain cede Florida and New Orleans to the British to give them space to settle the Loyalists. "There is no chance of that," Aranda replied. "The Mississippi is an indelible frontier line." Vergennes' cold fury failed to shake the Conde, who ended his arguments on a threatening note. If the Spanish proposition was not accepted by the time the combined fleet was scheduled to sail from Cádiz for an attack on Jamaica—an expedition that Vergennes viewed with grave misgivings—the proposals would be withdrawn, and Spain would feel free to pursue her own course. France could not make any commitment, Vergennes replied, until she learned whether England was really prepared to yield Gibraltar, and on what terms. For this purpose, the Comte informed Aranda, bringing the stormy interview to a close, the King proposed to send Rayneval back to England.[29]

It was ironic that Gibraltar should now threaten the Bourbon alliance as well as prolong a war that no one wished any longer to fight. Vergennes, like his predecessors in the Foreign Ministry, secretly preferred to see Gibraltar remain in British hands, for a British-held Gibraltar would tighten the bonds of the Family Compact. As the irrepressible Goëzmann de Thurne remarked, "It is in England's interest to return Gibraltar. It is ours to see that she keeps it in order that France will always be necessary to Spain."[30] Yet the Comte was obligated by the alliance to fight on for a fortress that proved impervious to assault.[31] Shelburne and George III were quite prepared to trade it. Gibraltar, "that golden image of English idolatry," at that time possessed little value to Britain's Mediterranean trade and small military importance. Both business interests and military experts downgraded it.[32] Those who opposed ceding the fortress did so for reasons of prestige or plain vanity rather than because they foresaw the immense strategic role Gibraltar would play in safeguarding the trade routes of empire in the century to come.

Vergennes had several crosses to bear. The pride of his Spanish ally was too great to admit that a hated symbol of foreign occupation could not be expunged. The war aims and long-range interests of his American ally seemed absolutely irreconcilable with those of Spain. To cap it all, his Dutch ally, who had proved a total liability as a war partner, stubbornly held out for grandiose objectives which seemed a little ridiculous in the light of her puny naval efforts. He knew that America was not obligated to continue in the war until Gibraltar was captured, and yet he felt that there was less chance of America's defection if she could come to an understanding with Spain.

A year and a half earlier Bernardo de Gálvez had recaptured West Florida from the British. With the Gulf and the Mississippi effectively sealed off to the Americans, Aranda was anxious now to stake out Spain's claims to the Mississippi Valley, at least as far north as the Ohio. With a British-American settlement pending, the Conde's anxiety mounted. Should the British in a moment of misguided generosity grant America the Western domain and the United States in turn come to an understanding with England over the Floridas, Spain's twin objectives in North America would be seriously jeopardized. Since John Jay was then in the very process of shaping such a two-way arrangement Aranda's perturbation was not ill-founded.

On the tenth of September Jay had broken off discussions with the Conde on the ostensible ground that he was not authorized by Congress "to make any cession of any countries belonging to the United States," and that he must await further instructions from Congress. At the same time he did not close the door to further talks leading to treaties of commerce and alliance with a plenipotentiary from Spain "vested with equal powers."[33] The Spaniard, despite this affront and prompted by a reminder from Florida-blanca of Jay's long-lapsed offer to waive the navigation of the Mississippi,[34] reopened talks with the American. They met at Versailles toward the end of September. Jay then insisted on the exchange of certified copies of their respective commissions in accordance with "the usual mode of doing business" by plenipotentiaries. "That could not be expected from us," Aranda remonstrated. "After all, Spain has not yet acknowledged your independence."

"Don't you think it is about time?" Jay retorted. "We declared our independence back in 1776, and since then France, Holland, and even Britain have acknowledged it." Lafayette, who had joined the party, reminded Aranda that "it would not be consistent with the dignity of France for her ally to treat otherwise than as independent." "This remark," Jay reported to Secretary Livingston, "appeared to me to pique the Count d'Aranda not a little."

At this point Vergennes entered the antechamber. Overhearing the conclusion of this heated exchange, he remarked to Jay that, since Spain did not deny America's independence, he could see "no good reason" for Jay's declining to confer with the Spanish ambassador about a treaty. The acknowledgment of America's independence, he argued, "would naturally be the effect of the treaty proposed to be joined." Jay could not see it that way, and insisted that "the dignity of America forbade" him treating "on any other than an *equal footing*."

Privately Vergennes took the occasion to voice to Jay the hope that Spain and America could draw closer together as regards the issue of the lands lying east of the Mississippi. "While these limits remain in contest," Jay was reminded, "a treaty with Spain cannot reasonably be expected."

Jay pointed out that these claims were of recent vintage, and that on his arrival in Spain Floridablanca had merely made an issue of the cession of America's rights to the navigation of the Mississippi, leading the New Yorker to believe that Spain then considered that river to be the western boundary of the United States. "It would be very strange, indeed," Jay said with obvious sarcasm, "that they should insist on our forbearing to navigate a rivers whose waters washed no part of our country, and to which we could not, in consequence, have any pretense of claim."

The Comte rewarded Jay with an enigmatic smile, but declined a direct answer. That same day Rayneval, whom Jay had not seen since his return from England, reminded the New Yorker of the memoir he had left with him, and repeated his arguments on the advantages of having a line bisecting the West, thereby separating the Indians under Spanish protection from those under American.[35] Jay encapsulated his Spanish negotiations in Paris in a letter of October 13th to Livingston. "Count d'Aranda will not or cannot exchange powers with me, and yet wants to treat with me," he remarked. "This Court would have me do it, but I decline it."[36] He might have added that since he was about to get the West from England, he saw no necessity for surrendering America's claim to Spain.

The news of the American preliminaries came as a blow to Aranda. A British intelligence agent, who claimed to have penetrated Aranda's secretariat, reported on the Conde's immense dissatisfaction with the territory Britain conceded to America.[37] Aranda complained bitterly to Floridablanca of the extravagant generosity of the British, and the presumption of both parties in providing reciprocally for the free use of the Mississippi without making Spain a party to the agreement. All this proved the extent of America's alienation from Charles III, he added.[38]

With the Americans going their own way and the Spaniards threatening to do the same, Vergennes realized that he had to act fast to maintain the leadership of the coalition and achieve a peace that would not be insulting to French pride. The British had seemed in a yielding mood when Rayneval had journey to Bowood, but the successful repulse of the Franco-Spanish armada before Gibraltar had encouraged the British to hike their terms toward all the belligerents. In September the British had been prepared to give the French St. Lucia *and* Dominica, but by the latter part of October they withdrew their offer as regards the latter. The British made it clear that they were intent on excluding the French from the important fishing ground on the southern coast of Newfoundland, and therefore no longer planned to return St. Pierre and Miquelon. Instead, they offered the French Belle Isle on the eastern coast.[39] Still the gap between the parties was not too wide, and did not cause Vergennes the distress which he suffered on account of Spain's inflexible stand. It was in fact the Santo Domingo–Corsica proposal of Spanish inspiration which decided Vergennes to send Rayneval back to England to talk with Shelburne. He instructed the undersecretary to sound out the British on equivalents for Gibraltar and told him that France would not put up a fight to support Spain's "impossible" claim to a share in the Newfoundland fisheries. Otherwise Rayneval's instructions differed very little from those he had brought with him to England on the previous trip.[40] Basically, the main reason for Rayneval's visit was Gibraltar, and Aranda agreed to hold up his negotiations with Fitzherbert until the French undersecretary's probing operation in London was completed.[41]

On the afternoon of November 20th Gérard de Rayneval arrived in London. Financial markets responded to his presence by staging a brisk rally on the Exchange.[42] That evening Rayneval sat down with Shelburne at the Earl's stately residence in Berkeley Square. Shelburne faced him across the table with a stronger hand than he had held when they had last confronted each other. The First Minister's bargaining power had been enhanced both by the news from Gibraltar and by the fact that the very day before Rayneval's arrival the preliminary peace terms with the Americans had been provisionally approved by the Cabinet and dispatched to Oswald and Strachey in Paris. Despite intensive French espionage Rayneval had not been apprised of the imminence of the American settlement when he had set out for England, but had been given to understand that the negotiations between the British and the Americans had bogged down over the Loyalist issue.[43] The progress of the American negotiations was the British ace-in-the-hole. Only a week before Rayneval reached London Lord Grantham told Fitzherbert, "I anxiously hope that the state of the treaty with America may be such, as, when known, it may quicken the desire of France to terminate the negotiation by employing her best offices with Spain for this purpose. . . . Surely," he added, "M. de Vergennes will see this in its trew and strongest light."⁴⁴ The imminence of Parliament's convening was the only cloud on Shelburne's horizon.

Rayneval soon found out that Gibraltar was negotiable. Shelburne was prepared to strike a bargain if he could get a profitable sugar island in the Caribbean. Although Vergennes was anxious to settle on the basis of Florida, and possibly New Orleans, and despite the fact that Shelburne had given a qualified approval to the proposals of Jay and Vaughan for the reacquisition of West Florida by Britain, neither Shelburne nor George III was now prepared to consider the undeveloped reaches of Florida as an equivalent for a more immediately lucrative sugar island, like Puerto Rico, Cuba, or Spanish Santo Domingo. Rayneval was well aware of Vergennes' objections to sharing Santo Domingo with England and of Spain's refusal to part with the other two islands, Aranda's "limbs of empire."

If you have nothing to offer in the Leeward group, perhaps you could give us a footing to windward, Shelburne suggested. Rayneval reminded Shelburne that Spain held nothing to windward, that all the islands belonged to France. "Then perhaps your King would be inclined to cede something to us there?" Shelburne replied. He now set his price for Gibraltar. He asked for the territories which Spain had seized during the war, notably Minorca, West Florida, and the Bahamas, and, in addition, he proposed three alternatives: Puerto Rico, Guadeloupe with Dominica, or Martinique with St. Lucia. Rayneval then inquired how France, assuming she were prepared to sacrifice one or two of her islands in such a deal, was to be compensated. By the Spanish part of Santo Domingo, Shelburne answered.

That Shelburne should have put his finger on the most sensitive issue among Britain's enemies was not purely fortuitous. He had learned that day from Benjamin Vaughan, if he had not known from other sources, that Spain was counting on France's making a sacrifice for Gibraltar, and that Corsica was being mentioned in that regard.⁴⁵ Certainly the acquisition of one of the rich sugar islands could be counted on to still the clamor in Parliament over the loss of Gibraltar and to keep the Ministry in being despite some probable defections in the Cabinet. If France were not prepared to make such a sacrifice to provide an attractive equivalent, she would be left with no alternative but to bring pressure upon the court of Spain to drop its demand for Gibraltar.

It was now past midnight, but there was not a moment to lose. Rayneval asked permission to send a courier to Paris at once. Shelburne allowed him, on his own responsibility. The Frenchman accordingly departed for his own lodgings to write his dispatch to Vergennes, and the Earl sat down at once and sent off a report to the King. With his customary promptness George III replied within a few hours of the letter's arrival. "I am ready to avow," he wrote, "that I think the exchange of Gibraltar for either of the three valuable possessions as now proposed is highly advantageous to this Kingdom."[46]

The session with Rayneval the following morning was devoted to drawing up a draft treaty with France, which was submitted to the Cabinet that same afternoon. Richmond and Keppel denounced the proposed cession of Gibraltar, but the majority of the Cabinet was induced to accept the bargain. In addition, Shelburne persuaded the Cabinet to prorogue Parliament from November 26th, when it was due to reconvene, until December 5th, in order to gain extra time needed by Vergennes to settle the Spanish business.

"I have put myself at the mercy of France, and it is for her to pronounce my fate," Shelburne told Rayneval at dinner that evening. He pointedly reminded the French undersecretary that the war spirit in England was on the rise, fanned by recent British victories and the reputed weakness of the French and Spanish navies. He convinced Rayneval that the fall of his Ministry would be a catastrophe for France as well as for domestic reforms in England. Was Gibraltar worth such a price? the French undersecretary asked in his message to his chief. "Without that unhappy fortress," Rayneval added with bitterness, "peace with Spain would be infinitely easy." Yet if we persist in holding up negotiations until we hear from Spain, we shall lose the chance to end the war, he warned. So anxious was Rayneval about the reaction of his own court that he decided to follow his courier to Versailles to expedite the answer.

On the morning of November 24th Rayneval took leave of Shelburne. Before he departed he put out a few feelers about the progress of the American negotiations, concerning which, he frankly admitted, the French court was in the dark. While not authorized to treat of the affairs of the United Provinces or America, Rayneval, if pressed for an opinion, was instructed to uphold the justice of restoring to the Dutch all territory wrenched from them, and to point out that it would be the path of prudence to defer to the definitive treaty the boundary discussions currently pending between the American commissioners and Oswald, along with the issue of compensating the Loyalists. Had England agreed to do so Vergennes could have been in a tactical position to mediate the rival claims of Spain and the United States. The English ignored Rayneval's broad hints. Six days later the American commissioners put their signatures to a preliminary treaty.[47]

Rayneval's report detailing England's three alternatives reached Paris before the undersecretary himself. It elicited a summons to Aranda for a conference at Versailles. The Conde was not prepared to act on the *quid pro quo* for Gibraltar without consulting his court. We too have public opinion to consider, he pointed out to Vergennes, even though the people of France and Spain admittedly do not speak with so loud a voice in the affairs of their governments as do the people of England. Aranda could not conceal his disappointment that Rayneval had quite evidently avoided mentioning Corsica to Shelburne.[48]

Vergennes felt squeezed between the upper and nether millstones. He was pressed by his Bourbon ally to make a deal for Gibraltar, and required by England to return a categorical answer before December 5th. "What shall we do? Therein lies the embarrassment!" the Comte confessed to Montmorin.[49] Realizing that his peace program and his own political future depended now on Shelburne's remaining in office long enough to come to an agreement, Vergennes utilized Rayneval's brief return to apply enormous pressure to Aranda. The de Castries faction in his own Cabinet was prepared to exploit the Comte's failure to press on with the war.[50]

Rayneval arrived back in Paris the morning of the 27th. The following evening he departed for London bringing fresh proposals from Spain and modified terms from France. His thirty-six-hour stay was crowded with conferences and briefing sessions. He was told that while France would continue to insist upon the fishing islands of St. Pierre and Miquelon and the Caribbean isle of Dominica, she was prepared, in the interest of peace, to accept a more modest area around Pondicherry. To elicit fresh proposals from Spain required a seven-hour conference between Vergennes and Rayneval on the one side and the Conde de Aranda on the other. Rayneval spelled out Shelburne's political difficulties, while Vergennes hammered home Spain's weak position. Gibraltar was impregnable, the Conde was told. The British have strongly reinforced Jamaica, and therefore the forthcoming combined operation against that island is extremely hazardous. Remember, he was warned, your provinces in Spanish America are only waiting to "burst their chains." The arguments on both sides were feverish, and Vergennes described Aranda to Montmorin as "a soul in pain." The tortured Conde, manifestly chagrined at the sacrifice Spain was being called upon to make, reluctantly consented to authorize Rayneval to bring back to London a new set of proposals. Spain would cede the Spanish part of Santo Domingo to France, who in turn would yield Guadeloupe and Dominica in exchange for Gibraltar. In turn, Spain would keep Florida up to Cape Canaveral. Vergennes, who persuaded Louis XVI to agree to the cession of Guadeloupe, confessed that he did not know how Aranda's action would be viewed at Madrid. Without it, he argued, war certainly would continue.[51] In fact, Vergennes was so confident that these concessions would lead to a speedy settlement that he sent his son, the Vicomte de Vergennes, to London along with Rayneval on a courtesy visit.[52] "The Count's son," George III shrewdly observed, "I should think would never have been sent had not peace been the intention of that Court."[53]

Peace was both the intention and expectation of the French court, but a rude shock was in store for it. Rayneval and the Vicomte reached London on December 2nd only to find that public opinion was thoroughly aroused over news that had leaked out of the proposal to "barter away Gibraltar."[54] Some spoke now of Puerto Rico as the only decent equivalent. The business interests viewed the proposed cession of Spanish Santo Domingo to France as guaranteeing French dominance of the sugar markets of the world, while the West Indian planters were opposed to Britain's acquiring more sugar islands, fearful that an increase in sugar acreage would lower prices and minimize their profits and property values. Within Shelburne's Cabinet diehards like Richmond and Keppel seemed to be swinging Grafton, Conway, and Camden against surrendering Gibraltar.[55]

Even Shelburne, confronted by a mutinous Cabinet on December 3rd, realized that he could not win enough votes for a deal exchanging Guadeloupe and Dominica for Gibraltar, since Spain now refused to return West Florida. To hold up the peace for West Florida would be "a madness which we can never justify," Shelburne argued privately. That day the Cabinet debated the French and Spanish terms with much acrimony. The obduracy of the Richmond-Keppel faction forced the majority to hike its price for Gibraltar. The Cabinet now resolved that, in addition to the transfer of Guadeloupe, the Bahamas, Trinidad, and Minorca be returned to England.[56] Even these terms did not appease the malcontents. The following day the Duke of Richmond, displaying his customary lack of restraint, denounced to the King's face Shelburne's handling of the negotiations. How could Shelburne, he asked, have the presumption to offer Gibraltar, "the brightest jewel of the Crown," in exchange for so worthless an island as Guadeloupe? Why had we clung to Richard Oswald as a negotiator, when he was really pleading the American cause, not the British? He condemned the fishing rights conceded to the United States, and revealed that "his sole idea" in yielding to the Americans was to strengthen England's stand against France and Spain. This was certainly "the strangest sophistry," George commented later to Shelburne, for "timidity once shown, others will take advantage of it." Keppel pursued the attack, insinuating that both he and Richmond would resign if the Ministry did not cling to Gibraltar. The King, privately concerned that the whole peace effort might collapse, and not anxious to "heat the coals at present," mumbled a few conciliatory words.[57]

It was Lord Grantham who broke the news to Rayneval in a lengthy conference which began at 10 A.M. on the morning of December 4th and continued until ten o'clock that evening. These are the best terms we can persuade our government to accept, Grantham told the French undersecretary. He was reminded of what Shelburne had already told him. Should England be permitted to retain Gibraltar Spain then could keep the Floridas, and the whole unseemly haggling for tiny islands be brought to a close. In dispatch after dispatch Rayneval urged Vergennes to come to an accommodation over the Spanish issue. Describing the present as "a critical moment, when the whole edifice of peace is about to tumble down," Rayneval pressed Shelburne's cause insistently and with eloquence, at the same time denouncing Spain's intransigence as responsible for the "ridiculous" price that Britain was now placing upon Gibraltar.[58]

The Comte de Vergennes received the bad news with somewhat mixed emotions. His shock at the new terms did not prevent him from confessing his admiration of Rayneval for showing enough poise to keep from breaking off the talks at this delicate stage. The impending breakdown of the Franco-Spanish negotiations, he gloomily remarked to Montmorin, would surely have an effect on their American ally. "What line would the Americans take?" Their support could only be retained by further compliance with their demands. There were limits, though, beyond which the King could not go. All the more reason, Vergennes argued, why Spain should show a more accommodating disposition, particularly on the question of the frontiers, now that the Americans, by their agreement with England, have been made "masters of a great hinterland stretching to the Mississippi and from the lakes to the 31st parallel."[59]

Resiliency was one of Vergennes' strongest qualities, and he rebounded magnificently from the new impasse in London. Still determined to remain master of the negotiations, he now notified Rayneval that if the English Ministry would state their terms frankly and in confidence he would engage his country to induce the Spaniards to abandon their demand for Gibraltar. This failing, Rayneval was instructed to renew either the Guadeloupe–Dominica offer, or a Guadeloupe–St. Lucia package. Since in the latter event Martinique would be exposed to interloping trade from Britain and cut off from France in time of war, he was prepared to yield that sugar island too for a proper equivalent in either of the Indies.[60]

The sincerity of these alternatives to the abandonment of Gibraltar could certainly be questioned. The British Cabinet had already turned down Guadeloupe, and Vergennes knew very well that Shelburne would not court the wrath of the East India Company by staging a complete retreat in India, after he had held the French to minimal concessions. Shelburne's mind was made up. Vergennes' first proposal was the only one that was politically acceptable at this time. Get the Spaniards to drop Gibraltar. Offer her the two Floridas and Minorca in return, provided that France added Dominica to the territories she was returning.[61] The King, on the other hand, was quite prepared, as Shelburne put it, "to get back as honourably as we can" to the Guadeloupe proposal. He was now ready and even anxious "to be rid of Gibraltar" in order to acquire "as much possession in the West Indies as possible." Nothing further, though, for France in India. Any additional concessions there he deemed "big with mischief." He did not insist, however, but put it up to Shelburne to do the best he could.[62]

George III stood now almost alone in his kingdom in his desire to abandon Gibraltar. The Cabinet on December 11th unanimously rejected the French equivalents for that fortress, and instead agreed to offer Spain the Floridas and Minorca, to demand the restoration of the Bahamas and to insist upon the right of British subjects to cut logwood in Honduras under regulations. To preserve equality in the West Indies England would insist on the return of Dominica.[63] Rayneval, seated in an adjoining room, anxiously awaited the Cabinet's decision, and at three o'clock he learned it from Grantham.

Rayneval spent a troubled night worrying about the turn in the tide. He and the Vicomte de Vergennes had observed the resurgent belligerency of the Commons at the opening session of Parliament, a frightening scene not soon forgotten. Rayneval's mind was made up. He would have been even more alarmed had he known that Shelburne was prepared to call upon the American commissioners for help in concluding a general peace. The next day he sat down and penned a dispatch to Vergennes. Let us close on this offer, he wrote. Unless we yield, he warned, Shelburne will be thrown out, and that would be "an irreparable loss" for us.[64] In private talks with Shelburne Rayneval made it clear that he regarded the British offer as "not only an honourable but also a fruitful" one. The separation of North America, he said, had been France's "principal object." Everything else she considered "rubbish." While he disdained comment on Britain's generosity toward America as regards both the fisheries and the back lands, he left Shelburne with the distinct impression that the French "seem discontented with the conduct of the Americans but determined to put the best face upon what has passed."[65]

Rayneval had not put up a fight for Gibraltar; Vergennes would not. The French undersecretary's dispatches, along with a note from Grantham, reached Versailles at 3:30 the afternoon of December 15th. Vergennes summoned Aranda to a conference for the following morning. While the Frenchman counted on his ability to persuade the Conde to join him in an appeal to Madrid to accept the terms, he doubted that Aranda had been given plenipotentiary powers to make such a decision on his own. He expected the usual procrastination marking any dealings with the Spanish court.

Vergennes confronted the Conde with the latest terms from England. To the Comte's utter astonishment Aranda was prepared to listen to reason. The morning conference never went beyond midday. The Conde, who had long recognized Gibraltar as the stumbling block of the peace, felt that Spain should concentrate upon goals which were central to the monarchy. High on the list he placed the Spanish empire in America,[66] which, as he saw it, the British counterproposals served to buttress. Accordingly, it did not take him long to decide between Gibraltar and the Floridas.

On his own responsibility Aranda now accepted Grantham's terms and decided to dispatch his Secretary of Legation, Don Ignacio Heredia, to London to clarify a few minor if sticky details involving woodcutting on Honduras and Campeche. Vergennes' reaction to Aranda's decision was one of profound relief. His critics were already heaping him with unpatriotic epithets for his proposal to turn over a French sugar island. "Soon the sweetness of peace" would come, he now wrote Rayneval. He was hopeful that the preliminaries could be signed before the new year.[67]

No single piece of news throughout the humiliating war came as a more painful blow to Floridablanca than the word that his countryman had made peace by yielding the Rock. To obtain Gibraltar, he had already warned Montmorin, Spain would go it alone if necessary. Spain had warred eight hundred years to expel the Moors, and was prepared to carry on for an equally long time to drive the British from Gibraltar, he had shouted dramatically.[68] Communications from the two Spanish diplomats crossed each other. On December 18th Floridablanca explicitly instructed Aranda not to sign the peace preliminaries without obtaining Gibraltar.[69] That same day Aranda took pen in hand and broke the news to Spain's Principal Minister. He marshaled impressive arguments in defense of his course. The opposition in Cabinet and Parliament made it impossible for the British government to cede Gibraltar, he pointed out. For France to have been compelled to sacrifice one of her sugar islands would have deeply offended powerful groups in France and caused an outcry against the government. In the light of present conditions in France, he warned, and his words in retrospect take on the aspect of stark prophecy, "This Kingdom might succumb to revolution and civil conflagration." We must remember, too, he added, the effect of the signing of the American preliminaries by plenipotentiaries who "forget the respect owed to France and the gratitude to which the Court has a right." Their action, he continued, proved that France could not count on America's friendship nor could Great Britain upon the enmity of her former colonies. With the prospect of an Anglo-American combination in North America it was imperative that Spain secure possession of the two Floridas to protect Spanish interests in the Gulf as well as Mexico. For these reasons, Aranda concluded, he had not held out for an equivalent for Gibraltar. He pleaded: *"Una roca, Excelentisimo, quanto turbaba tres Imperios?"** In conceding the Rock he had acted for "our beloved Spain" and to safeguard the nation's primary interest, her American empire.[70] He subsequently pointed out that, in view of Spain's poor showing in the campaign of '82, he had obtained the best possible terms.[71] Arguments along very similar, almost identical lines, were marshaled by Vergennes in support of Aranda's decision. The English, he told Montmorin, had gotten the worst of the bargain in holding on to the "sterile and expensive Rock," while the acquisition of the Floridas would clear the mouth of the Mississippi of the English and shield Mexico from disturbance for a long time to come. As for the Americans, the Comte painted the rosy picture that centuries would pass before they would be strong enough to become "troublesome to their neighbors."[72] Unhappily for Spain, Vergennes' prediction was not borne out by events, but there is no question but that the acquisition of the Floridas, by consolidating Spain's control of both banks of the Mississippi, confirmed her hold on that river's exclusive navigation.[73]

In standing out against King and Ministry the Conde presented an heroic figure. Save for the Americans in Paris who ignored the humiliating instructions of a timid Congress, no such gesture of independence was made on the diplomatic stage throughout the long years of the Revolutionary War. In defying an absolute monarch Aranda ran far greater risk to his person and reputation than did the Americans in disobeying a French-dominated Foreign Secretary and a faction-riddled Congress. "Respect and obedience bound me to blind submission," Aranda conceded, "but the loyalty of a

---

* "How greatly [long], your Excellency, can a rock disturb three empires?"

good subject and an awareness of the real situation compelled me to do what was right."[74]

In making *picadillo* out of Floridablanca's war aims Aranda had paid his rival back in coin of the realm. For a proud man the Conde had for years suffered silently a long series of humiliations and persecutions at the hands of Spain's First Minister. Floridablanca had dispatched him to Paris as a form of exile to remove a political rival and potential troublemaker from the Spanish plains. Aranda had been pointedly ignored, even deceived, in the Hussey-Cumberland affair. His advice about recognizing the United States had been disregarded. He had been on the receiving end of an endless stream of barbed comments from the First Minister. At the time of the de Grasse-Shelburne conversations Aranda had been shocked to learn that Vergennes was informed as to Spain's intentions with the same exactitude as he was.[75] Having encouraged Vergennes and Rayneval to seize the initiative from Aranda, Floridablanca could scarcely complain now about the bitter fruits of their diplomacy.

Aranda's defiance of instructions stunned the Spanish court, and the immediate reaction was that of furious resentment. However, what had been done could not now be undone.[76] Floridablanca managed to calm down the infuriated monarch. It was decided not to recall Aranda, although Floridablanca kept insisting that Gibraltar had to be ceded before the peace preliminaries could be signed. Do not yield Pensacola and Mobile to obtain Gibraltar while there is still a chance to capture the fortress, Aranda was told. Privately Floridablanca seemed ready, after perhaps a two-year truce, to start the war all over again to win back Gibraltar. Meantime Aranda was instructed to obtain a separate agreement from France to see that the Rock was restored to Spain in the event of another war with Britain.[77]

Gibraltar is, as you know, a very touchy subject to the British, Aranda retorted with brutal candor. Spain cannot get it back, nor will the French agree to a separate treaty covering the fortress, he added. The best he could obtain was a promise of a private letter from Louis XVI to the Spanish King offering assurances along that line.[78] Vergennes had put it to Aranda bluntly. The moment when peace is signed is hardly the time to enter into an agreement to renew the war.[79] Charles III let his royal nephew know that he consented to peace *sans* Gibraltar, but not without genuine regret. In reply to *"mon frère et oncle"* Louis XVI politely explained that it had been necessary to abandon what could not be obtained in five years of war.[80]

By exercising a discretion which his superiors did not believe they had granted him the Conde had brought the long war to an end. True, before the preliminaries were signed there were odds and ends to be tidied up. The gap over India was still open though narrow. Shelburne persuaded the powerful East India Company of the wisdom of allowing France a modest concession around Pondicherry and Karikal for prestige, without conceding her a political foothold. This offer was tied to a new proposal to give France the island of Tobago in exchange for Dominica, a swap which could be interpreted as advantageous to both parties. For the French Tobago served as an intermediary point for trade between Guiana and the French islands, whereas Dominica had a proven value as a free port and was considered by Shelburne's naval experts as essential for the preservation of the Antilles.[81]

With misgivings and ill humor Vergennes heard of Shelburne's substitution of Tobago for Dominica. The Comte had to exercise all his persuasive arts to convince Louis XVI that the French were not being short-changed. Nor did Vergennes take kindly to the diminution of the area in India for which France was now expected to settle. He expostulated to Rayneval, "How can you accept terms offering us a miserable revenue of £30,000 when we were asking territory assuring us £500,000?" Rayneval told him that these were the very best terms he could obtain. "If I am to be sacrificed," the undersecretary retorted in dramatic vein, "here is my epitaph: 'Here lies one who preferred peace to renown, and to some villages in Hindustan!' "[82] Subsequent news from India confirmed the prudence of Rayneval's course. Hyder Ali, France's chief Indian ally, had died in the meantime, and even before his death French plans to conquer the Carnatic had collapsed. Meantime Rayneval trembled while awaiting word that Vergennes had agreed to the territorial commitment he had made in India.[83] To add to his anxieties, the courier bringing word of Vergennes' approval was held up for four days at Calais by unfavorable winds.[84]

As though these two hurdles were not sufficient to block the Anglo-French settlement, Vergennes was very balky about the provisions on the fisheries. The English assigned certain coasts in Newfoundland to the French fishermen and returned St. Pierre and Miquelon. Vergennes was insistent on having the French fishing rights recognized as exclusive and on the insertion of a clause protecting French fishermen from the Americans, whose fishing rights in Newfoundland had been, to the Comte's great annoyance, also recognized in their own preliminaries with England. "If we do not have a positive restriction to bar them," Vergennes warned Fitzherbert, "they will crowd in to the areas reserved for us and deprive us of exercising the greatest part of our fishing right." Fitzherbert persuaded the Comte to accept a clause by which Britain undertook to take steps to prevent encroachments on the fisheries "of the subjects of France during the temporary exercise which is accorded them on the coast of the island of Newfoundland." No reference was made to the Americans, as the British assumed that France's fishing rights as against them were covered by her treaty of commerce with the United States of 1778.[85]

Aranda and Heredia had yet to iron out with the British minor details of logwood-cutting in the Gulf of Mexico,[86] but the Dutch still remained to be appeased. Although they were the most badly battered of all the belligerents, likened by one diplomat to "a dead body which must be dragged from behind,"[87] they proved in some respects to be the most obdurate. Their peace negotiations in Paris were conducted by Gerard Brantsen working in collaboration with the Dutch ambassador, Lestevenon de Berkenrode. When John Adams paid a call on Brantsen at the Hôtel de la Chine a few days after the American preliminaries were signed he was told that a British acceptance of the principles of freedom of the seas was regarded by the Dutch as a precondition to entering into any conference. He also learned that the plenipotentiaries from the United Provinces sought the restitution of all the territories in the East and West Indies which the British had captured during the war, along with compensation for damages.

Brantsen found fault with the French court, whose conduct he labeled "*diablement fin.*" The Dutchman charged that they were playing England against Spain, Spain against England, England against America, and "all of you against us and us against all of you, according to their own interests." This was the kind of talk Adams relished, and he entered it all in his Diary.[88]

Adams was much more sanguine about Britain's readiness to agree to the maritime principles of the Armed Neutrality than the facts warranted.[89] Both he and the Dutch plenipotentiaries were rather hard on Vergennes, who in fact was determined to prevent the British from getting possession of the Cape of Good Hope or retaining the port of Trincomalee in the Dutch possession of Ceylon, and thus dominating the ocean approaches to India and the Far East of both Holland and France. The Comte persuaded the English to return Trincomalee to the Dutch in exchange for Negapatam, a minor port south of Madras which had fallen into British hands.[90] The Dutch held out for a long time, and Brantsen was bitter in his recriminations that their preliminaries were not in shape to be signed at the same time as the other belligerents'.[91]

Without advance warning, the Comte de Vergennes notified Franklin to present himself at his office at Versailles along with the other American plenipotentiaries at 10 A.M. on Monday, January 20th. Adams accompanied Franklin, riding out to Versailles in the latter's carriage. Jay was off on a trip to Normandy, and Laurens had gone to Bath to recoup his health. At eleven o'clock the Conde de Aranda and Alleyne Fitzherbert arrived. Then the ministers of the three crowns signed and sealed their preliminaries of peace and an armistice in the presence of the Americans. Franklin and Adams in turn exchanged with Fitzherbert a declaration of an armistice between the Crown of Great Britain and the United States of America.[92] The imperial mediators were apprised of the event though not invited to participate in these preliminaries. Their good offices were politely solicited for the attainment of the definitive treaty.[93] This was small solace to their pride, and in Vienna the news was received as bleakly as though Austria had suffered a defeat. "The impression of our solid advantages from the event is as great as the sorrow is general," Breteuil reported to Vergennes.[94]

While it was natural for all parties concerned to put the best face on the reports under the circumstances, Breteuil's enthusiasm seemed hardly justified, considering the limited extent of France's gains and the immense cost by which they were obtained. As for the Spaniards, Adams regarded the two Floridas and Minorca as "more than a *quantum meruit* for what this power had done,"[95] for by regaining control of the Gulf of Mexico the Spaniards attained an important national objective. Nonetheless, the terms of peace opened grievous wounds to Spanish national pride which it can be said have never healed over.

Among the numerous post-mortems, Rayneval sought to explain Shelburne's apparent duplicity on the score of the equivalents. It was the Americans who were responsible, he charged. The "unhappy news" of the signing of their preliminaries provoked the demand for equivalents for Gibraltar. Shelburne had no alternative but to go along with his Cabinet, else negotiations would have been broken off.[96] Alluding to the cession of the back lands of Canada to America and of Senegal to France, Shelburne remarked to the Abbé Morellet, "You will already have recognized in the treaties of peace, the great principle of free trade, which inspires them from beginning to end. I have no hesitation saying that in my own opinion, a peace is good in the exact proportion that it recognizes that principle."[97]

By that criterion the preliminaries constituted a bad peace, for Shelburne could not sell free trade to his countrymen, and was not permitted to remain in office long enough to bring about the new economic order of which he dreamed. Still, peace, the desperate need of all the belligerents,

XVII

THE FOX AND THE GRAPES

For more than six embattled years, ever since the adoption of the great Declaration, Patriots in America had looked forward to the day when their erstwhile monarch would acknowledge their independence. That day finally came. On the morning of December 5, 1782, George III opened the session of Parliament with a speech from the throne. The event was witnessed by a gathering of foreign notables, including Gérard de Rayneval, and the young Vicomte de Vergennes, along with a cluster of dejected American Loyalists. Among those who managed to squeeze their way into the packed House of Lords and come close to the throne, elbow to elbow with Admiral Lord Howe, was a young New England merchant named Elkanah Watson. He had been employed to carry money and dispatches to Franklin in 1779, had tried his hand at trade in Nantes, and now had come to England with a letter of introduction from the doctor himself to Lord Shelburne.

Watson later recalled that the Parliament buildings were shrouded in a blanket of fog, appropriate to the time of year. The diamond-cut and elevated panes of glass in the House served to increase the gloom within. The spectators looked around at walls hung with dark tapestry depicting the defeat of the Spanish Armada. That event which marked the launching of the First British Empire had transpired three centuries earlier, and now the Lords were gloomily anticipating the formal admission by their King that the Empire which Elizabeth and her royal successors had created with so vast an outpouring of toil and treasure was about to be dismembered.

For two hours Lords and spectators fidgeted while they awaited the King's arrival. At last a roar of artillery announced his approach. Entering by a small door on the left of the throne, George III, clothed in royal robes, seated himself upon the chair of state, his right foot resting upon a stool. His obvious agitation quickly communicated itself to his audience. Drawing from his pocket the scroll containing his speech, the King declared that he had lost no time in giving the necessary orders to prohibit the further prosecution of offensive war upon the North American Continent. All his views and measures, he brashly insisted, had been directed "to an entire and cordial reconciliation" with the colonies. "Finding it indispensable to the attainment of this object, I did not hesitate to go the full length of the powers vested in me, and offer to declare them—"

Here George, visibly shaken and embarrassed, paused. After a moment that must have seemed to him like an eternity he resumed: "and offer to declare them *free and independent States,* by an article to be inserted in the treaty of peace." Sacrificing every consideration of his own to the wishes and opinions of his people, George closed on a note of piety, which Edmund Burke found insufferable. He offered his "humble and ardent prayer to Almighty God" that Great Britain would not "feel the evils which might result from so great a dismemberment of the Empire, and that America may be free from the calamities which have formerly proved, in the mother country, how essential monarchy is to the enjoyment of constitutional liberty." In closing, he could not refrain from expressing the hope that religion, language, interests, and affection would "yet prove a bond of permanent union between the two countries."

The words appeared to have been dragged out of him. "He hesitated, choked, and executed the painful duties with an ill grace which does not belong to him," Watson observed.[1] The Yankee visitor was not the only one to remark the King's embarrassment. "In pronouncing the word 'independence' the King of England did it in a constrained voice," Rayneval reported to his chief.[2]

That evening Watson dined with the talented American-born portrait painter, John Singleton Copley, whose studio was always crowded with royalty and high nobility seeking immortality on canvas. Bostonian by birth, Copley had completed a portrait of his fellow New Englander, and painted in the background a ship bearing to America the news that independence had been acknowledged. The artist had planned a rising sun casting its rays upon the Stars and Stripes streaming from her gaff. Until the King had spoken he had not deemed it prudent to hoist the American flag in his gallery. That evening, as Watson recalled, "with a bold hand, a master's touch, and I believe an American heart," Copley attached to the ship the Stars and Stripes. Watson believed this symbolic flag-hoisting was the first occasion upon which the Stars and Stripes were raised in old

England, for it was a good two months before an American ship entered the Thames estuary.[3]

John Singleton Copley's symbolic gesture notwithstanding, the issue of American independence still seemed by no means foreclosed. For the ensuing confusion blame must fall squarely upon Shelburne's shoulders. His ambivalent public position on the score of independence, together with his failure to make a prompt disclosure of the terms of the preliminary treaty with America, served to light the fires of suspicion that the British people were being asked to make a sacrifice of great enormity.[4]

This time the Earl, who normally paid little attention to men but much to measures, had mobilized his supporters in advance to secure their continued adherence,[5] but he could not shut off the stormy debate which the King's address precipitated in Lords and Commons. In the Lords, Shelburne was baited by that archfoe of American independence, Viscount Stormont. Charging the Ministry with "the most preposterous conduct" and with having fallen into a situation of "the greatest imbecility," Stormont put this rhetorical question to the Lords:

"Does it not say," he asked, "that, without any condition, any qualification, any stipulation whatsoever, America shall be independent whenever France chooses to make peace with us?" In other words, the provisional treaty was "irrevocable," and the government had been so imprudent as to concede unconditional independence without equivalent, forcing "the wretched Loyalists . . . this honest, brave set of men" to be content with "a mere provision for existence, an eleemosynary support?"

Shelburne was on his feet at once. "The noble viscount," he assured the Lords, in his obsequious manner, was "mistaken in his idea of unqualified, unconditional independence being given to America." The offer was not irrevocable, he insisted, arguing that, should France not agree to peace, it could be terminated. Stormont derived a cruel pleasure from reminding Shelburne now that not too long before he had declared in Parliament that the sun of Great Britain would set when American independence was granted. Apparently, the Viscount ironically remarked, the noble lord was now of a different opinion. "That sun is set. There is not a ray of light left. All is darkness."

Shelburne's embarrassments now stemmed from his failure to lay down the line to his supporters in Commons. While Lord North, though privately disturbed by rumors that large territories had been surrendered to the Americans, was unwilling to commit himself until the articles of the provisional treaty were disclosed,[6] the more impulsive Charles James Fox decided to bring the issue to a head. Assuming that unconditional independence was yielded by the first article of the treaty, he endorsed the recognition of America without strings attached, and Burke joined him in insisting that independence had been granted "unconditionally." Sensing the sentiment of the Opposition in Commons, young Pitt, as spokesman for the Ministry, adopted a very different line from that pursued by Shelburne in the Lords. "Unqualified recognition" of American independence, he insisted, was "the clear indisputable meaning of the provisional treaty." General Conway seconded that sentiment, and even Shelburne's man, Tommy Townshend, denied there was any equivocation in the King's speech.[7]

With the Ministry in apparent open division on the question of whether or not the Americans had secured their independence unconditionally, the halls of Parliament continued to buzz, and rumors spread far beyond its walls. He could not go a hundred yards from the House, Fox remarked, without hearing a different interpretation put upon the intention of the King's speech than that of the Ministry.[8] It was only to be expected, then, that when debate on the provisional treaty was resumed on December 13th, the ministers should be lashed for "inconsistency." Driven into a corner, Shelburne took refuge in the need "to keep the secrets of the King." This talk of secrecy only succeeded in making Shelburne's critics even more suspicious. The Earl of Derby demanded "a plain answer to a very plain question: Are the Americans declared to be independent or not?" Shelburne declined to enter into any explanation which in his view might endanger the country. This was not enough to quiet Fox. Five days later he excoriated Shelburne in Commons for his ambiguous course and for hiding behind the cloak of official secrecy. Burke warned the government "to avoid the slippery and unsure ground of proud silence, or of ambiguous communication," and David Hartley, long-time unofficial negotiator with Franklin, reminded Parliament that if Shelburne was consistent with his past record and "a man of honour," he simply had to be against the independence of America. Fox's motion for the production of the provisional articles was, however, rejected 219-46.[9]

Shelburne's hollow victory, one of his last, did not abate the scandal. As Goëzmann de Thurne, the Earl's severe critic, remarked, responsible Cabinet members had declared independence irrevocable in the Commons while Shelburne himself had declared it "equivocal" in the Lords, thus shamefully exploiting these opposing interpretations to win support for the King's address in both houses.[10]

That Pitt had caught Shelburne by surprise in declaring that independence was now irrevocable was clear from the Earl's professions to the King. Pitt went too far, Shelburne complained, and caused "some uneasiness." George III, who found the whole business with the Americans unpalatable, was quick to brand Pitt's interpretation "a mistake, for the Independence is alone to be granted for peace." He continued, "It is no wonder that so young a man should have made a slip," but counseled that it would be "best and wisest if a mistake is made openly to avow it." Stand firm in the Lords, the King ordered his First Minister.[11]

The refusal of Pitt to confess his "mistake," combined with the continuance of Shelburne to talk equivocally on the question of independence provided the foes of the Ministry with additional ammunition to attack its chief. To them the issue over American independence seemed a glaring example of Shelburne's notorious deviousness. William Wyndham Grenville reported that the Earl had postponed a Cabinet meeting rather than risk a direct encounter with his colleagues from the Commons whose public views on American independence did not tally with his own. Indeed, it is true that Shelburne had deferred calling the Cabinet together, fearful, as he confessed, that "a cabinet of communication" might be "converted into a cabinet of discussion." From this Grenville concluded that the Earl was either "the most abandoned and direct liar upon the face of the earth, or he is deceived himself too grossly to be imagined, or the whole world is deceived."[12] Horace Walpole was even less charitable. He commented acidly that Shelburne's "falsehood was so constant and notorious, that it was rather his profession than his instrument. It was like a fictitious violin, which is hung out of a music shop to indicate in what goods the tradesman deals; not to be of service, nor to be depended on for playing a true note."[13] As a principal victim of Shelburne's pruning of the Civil List,[14] Walpole could scarcely be called objective, but biased or no, his vilification of the Jesuit of Berkeley Square attained the standing of a classic.

If nobody in England, least of all Shelburne himself, was quite clear about whether or not America's independence had been unconditionally granted,[15] the American commissioners in Paris were understandably apprehensive as a result of Parliament's reaction to the announcement of the preliminaries. The change in the attitude of the Cabinet "from affirmation to cool reserve," as Benjamin Vaughan put it, and Shelburne's public insistence that the provisional articles would cease to bind should France fail to make peace hardly contributed to the commissioners' collective peace of mind.[16] Something of this disquiet was reflected in Benjamin Vaughan's own correspondence. Writing to his brother in America to deny the rumor that Shelburne was really an enemy of American independence, he conceded that until recently the Earl had believed that America could be recovered. Now he realized that only the American trade could be retrieved. Nonetheless, what Shelburne had done was to make an "offer not unconditionally, not a gift." Vaughan even threw out a dark hint that the tender of independence might be withdrawn should France seek to gain "something for herself, besides independence."[17] So perturbed was Shelburne's confidant about the ambivalent position of the Ministry that he himself asked the Earl that Oswald be instructed to reassure the Americans.

Assurances to the contrary, the Americans acted anything but contented. Franklin seemed to be avoiding Vaughan; the touchy Laurens was ruffled by the manner in which the British had seen fit to publicize his release on parole; Adams was reputedly exposed to the seductions of anti-British circles in Paris; while John Jay, upset by the revelations only now made to him of the Mountstuart letter which seemed to implicate Necker in a nasty piece of double-dealing, acted extremely edgy.[18] Vergennes sought to quiet the fears of the Americans that Parliament would revoke both the commission to negotiate the peace with them as well as recognition. Some of the "hotheads" across the Channel might indeed favor such a course, but he felt confident that the Minister would know how to snuff it out.[19] Almost at the same moment Vaughan was urging Shelburne to end hostilities. "Your lordship probably thinks the same, but the mad English nation—!"[20]

Although anxious about the fate of the preliminaries, the Americans during Shelburne's remaining tenure in office continued to press for incorporation in the definitive treaty of certain basic principles to which hitherto Oswald had not been authorized to accede. Prodded by Secretary Livingston to obtain the right to trade directly with the West Indies, the American commissioners were still hopeful of winning the reciprocal trade concessions that Shelburne had earlier promised.[21] Adams wanted a stipulation of freedom of navigation, along the lines that the Neutral League and the Dutch demanded. He was prepared to enter into a mutual guarantee with the British that "no forts shall be built or garrisons maintained upon any of the frontiers in America, nor upon any of the land boundaries," a path-breaking notion not completely implemented until the later Treaty of Washington of 1871. He further urged that Bermuda be either ceded to the United States or kept unfortified and its use barred to privateers, that Sable Island off Nova Scotia be turned over to America, and that the balance of prisoners' accounts be struck and paid "according to the usages of nations."[22]

Franklin likewise kept up the pressure on the British and advanced some far-reaching proposals to Oswald which the less adventurous Fitzherbert deemed of "an odorous nature."[23] Outwardly the least reconciled to Britain of any of the commissioners, Franklin still argued for compensation by Britain for damages inflicted in America. This was an obvious move to counter any British proposals to ameliorate the treatment accorded the Loyalists, about whom the doctor was still "very sharp."[24] Not wishing "to see a new Barbary rising in America, and our long extended coast occupied by piratical states," the doctor pressed for incorporation into the definitive treaty of a prohibition against privateering.[25] He also sought to guarantee the future safety in time of war of fishermen, farmers, and all unarmed artisans or manufacturers inhabiting unfortified locations.[26] "A good lesson to mankind at least," was Adams' cryptic comment on Franklin's proposed revision of international law.[27] The doctor even talked of a plan for neutralizing the sugar islands of every nation, at the same time showing less than lukewarm interest in a revived proposal of Oswald for Federal Union.[28] With Jay's backing, Franklin also proposed that the treaty of commerce, still to be negotiated between England and America, be signed at the same time as the definitive treaty, but Oswald, appreciating Shelburne's increasingly delicate situation at home, put a stop to what he privately characterized as "this premature and destructive idea." Jay subsequently proposed a three-year moratorium on the collection of debts due British creditors in America, along with the cancellation of interest accrued during the war.[29]

These American demands, some new, some reiterated, above and beyond the preliminary articles, were so disturbing to Fitzherbert that he sounded out the Comte de Vergennes, who was not backward in expressing his disapproval of some of them, venturing his negative reaction even before France had signed her own preliminary articles. To the French court the idea of setting up the rich West Indian islands as neutral independent states, a notion by the way that Franklin shared with the former French Minister Turgot, was plain scandalous. "If urged to it," the British plenipotentiary reported, the French court "would join us in representing to the American Commissioners the monstrous injustice of introducing fresh articles into the treaty."[30]

Shelburne later recalled that Jay and Franklin wanted England to seize the Floridas after the signing of the American preliminaries but before France and Spain had signed their own. The record seems to substantiate him. Well on in January Franklin expressed concern about the fate of West Florida and was quoted as favoring England's reconquest of the territory on the ground that it would bolster the treaty provision for the free navigation of the Mississippi by both the British and the Americans. Vaughan held out hopes that England would get the province back after the peace.[31]

If Shelburne ended the suspense by disclosing the terms of the preliminary treaties his Ministry had made, he only succeeded in causing a new commotion. On January 27th the preliminaries to which France, Spain, and America had acceded were presented to both houses.[32] The treaties were laid upon the table for the inspection of the members, but in deference to rules of secret diplomacy to which all European chancelleries religiously adhered when it suited their purpose, they were neither circularized nor printed. A motion for printing touched off a debate. Fox pointed to the suspicious circumstances attendant upon the preliminaries. Aldermen Wilkes provoked derisive laughter at the Ministry's expense by informing the Commons that the Lords had already ordered the treaties to be printed. The question was quickly carried without a division.

Outside the halls of Parliament the various interest groups affected by the preliminaries now bestirred themselves. The Canadian fur merchants, joined by the Loyalists, laid down a barrage of barbed questions about the cessions in North America. Governor William Franklin asked, "Why were the forts in Indian territories surrendered to the Americans without consulting the Indians?" Oswald riposted neatly. "Your father, Doctor Franklin," he informed him, "insisted on a boundary being drawn. The Doctor ran his finger along the map to indicate the desired boundaries. And what," concluded Oswald, with becoming humility, "could *I* object to a man of Dr. Franklin's influence and authority?"[33] Other critics voiced fears that the northern boundary of the United States would give complete ascendancy in the Ohio Valley to American trade and proposed that portions of the upper valley be given Canada in return for opening the St. Lawrence to free navigation by the Americans. The concessions to France and America in the Newfoundland fisheries were contested by merchants trading to that area as well as by those who feared that if the English fishery declined, the nation would lose its "nursery for seamen."[34] Even Benjamin Vaughan joined the critics of the treaty, privately urging upon Shelburne some modification of the northeastern boundary, which, he correctly contended, was "incompletely, irregularly, and clumsily defined," and drawn without his being consulted.[35]

Other complaints poured in on Whitehall. From the prized West Indies, where even small islands were considered valuable properties not lightly sacrificed, came a deputation of Tobago planters demanding an extension of the time limit given them to sell their plantations, permission to export their sugar to England, and a stipulation assuring them the free exercise of their Protestant faith.[36] West India merchants requested the Ministry to make a pact with Spain covering the restoration of runaway slaves.[37] The logwood merchants, foreshadowing what was to be a long and tedious struggle, asked for a defined and extended settlement area in the Bay of Honduras for the British woodcutters, as well as for Southern Loyalists, who might settle there, and complained that the Mosquito Shore was never a part of Spanish territory.[38] Finally, the East India Company was alert to what it considered the military risks implicit in the concessions to the French in India.[39]

The most piteous cries were raised by the Loyalists, and the preliminaries with America inspired bitter recriminations. "The misery which American independence has brought to individuals is inexpressable," declared one of the victims, "and I assure you that I am one of the most ill-used."[40] Of all the American commissioners, Benjamin Franklin was the least sympathetic to their appeals. In a satirical trifle he wrote soon after the signing of the preliminaries the doctor told how Lion, King of the Forest, influenced by evil counselors, condemned his faithful dogs without a hearing, while a mongrel race, corrupted by royal promises of great rewards, deserted the honest dogs and joined their enemies. Now, with the good dogs victorious, the mongrels, barred from returning, claimed the reward that had been promised them. To settle the question a council of beasts was held. The wolves and foxes sided with the mongrels, but the horse, arguing that the King had been misled by bad ministers "to war unjustly upon his faithful subjects," persuaded the council to reject the mongrels' demand.[41] Franklin never saw fit to revise the fable.[42]

Contrariwise, Benjamin Franklin's natural son William was at that very moment rallying the leading Loyalists in London, who laid siege to Shelburne House and stormed Parliament to secure compensation for their losses.[43] William Franklin contended that the preliminary treaty would not redress their grievances, an argument that was substantially borne out by events. It was in fact to be the British government, not the American states, upon whom the burden was to fall of providing substantial compensation to the Tories.[44] In a somewhat special category were the descendants of William Penn, who were most assiduous in pressing their claims. Ignoring Oswald's advice, Lady Juliana Penn, widow of Thomas, the founder's second son, swooped down on Paris and buttonholed Jay and Franklin, winning their backing for an adjustment of Penn family claims for property which had been confiscated. Skillful diplomacy resulted in escalating the payments for the vacant and unappropriated lands in Pennsylvania formerly belonging to the family, for which the Pennsylvania legislature had already made a settlement.[45]

The issue of confiscation posed certain larger social questions which the revolutionary ferment brought to the fore. As one American correspondent reminded Lady Juliana, any proposals in the peace negotiations to restore Loyalist estates would not apply to the proprietary lands. These were "taken from the Proprietarys," he remarked, "not in a way of confiscation, but upon principle of policy and expedience" that "no subject" should possess an estate of such extent "supposing it dangerous to the public that so much property should rest in the hands of one family."[46] Some people may not have wanted to be reminded that the War for Independence was also a revolution, but the American commissioners never forgot it for a moment.

Emboldened by the hue and cry set off outside Parliament's walls by the printing of the preliminaries, the enemies of the administration launched a full-scale attack, with the opening volley fired off in Parliament on February 17th. The terms confirmed the Opposition's darkest suspicions that the peace negotiations had been mishandled.[47] "The moment America was out of the question," Sir Gilbert Elliot observed, "Samson lost the lock of his strength, and the natural weakness of the Ministry appeared immediately."

The hostile or disaffected Lords, beginning with the Earl of Carlisle, whose own clumsy efforts toward conciliating America had long ago backfired, riddled the American preliminaries. Carlisle, Walsingham, and Lord Townshend found fault with the Canadian boundary, charged that Canada was now insecure, the fur trade sacrificed, and faith broken with the Indians. Viscount Sackville insisted that "the immense district of country which supplied us with masts was gone." Considering these weaknesses, and in addition the lack of reciprocity in the fishing concession, and the threat that the yielding of St. Pierre and Miquelon to the French posed to the English fishery, Townshend found cause to remark that the Americans "had evidently been too cunning for us in the negotiation," and had been an "overmatch for Oswald," of whom Stormont spoke contemptuously as "that extraordinary geographer and politician."

The most punishing blows were dealt by two Cabinet defectors, Richmond and Keppel. The latter had quit the Ministry as soon as the preliminaries were signed while the Duke chose to stay at the Ordnance but withdrew from the Cabinet.[48] Both now argued that the terms Shelburne obtained were unnecessarily humiliating in view of the brightened military prospects of Britain and the comparative inferiority of the French and Spanish fleets.[49]

The bombardment against the battered Ministry continued without letup until the early hours of the eighteenth. That evening Shelburne replied, drawing upon memoranda provided by Lord Grantham and more closely upon an elaborate brief prepared by Benjamin Vaughan, who was now back in London, and apparently acting as the Earl's confidential secretary.[50] Standing on free-trade ground, the Earl defended his sacrifices in America. Missing from the speech was some of the vision of a future reconciliation between England and America that Vaughan had caught in his correspondence with Shelburne, as well as Shelburne's own private notion that the preliminaries foreshadowed changes in imperial relations and trade policy. The House in its black mood would doubtless have rejected such prospects as totally unrealistic. The Earl assured the Loyalists of the generosity of England, while conceding that "a part must be wounded, that the whole of the Empire may not perish." Shelburne chose to make his main stand, however, on the exhausted state of the nation, the tottering of public credit, the deterioration of the navy, its ships unclean, undermanned, its naval stores exhausted, its cordage rotten, and its magazines depleted.[51] Critics then and since have pounced on this argument as a prime specimen of Shelburne's disingenuous line, and have insisted that Shelburne did not paint a credible picture, that this puerile navy bore little resemblance to the magnificent fleet that Howe took into Gibralter or Rodney maneuvered at the Saints.[52] His critics notwithstanding, Shelburne had caught the popular mood of war weariness and the universal desire for a peace, however temporary it might prove. His eloquence won the day for the Address on the Peace, with a majority of thirteen in the Lords.

A very different fate awaited the Shelburne Ministry in Commons. Fox attacked the terms given France in India, Burke assailed the abandonment of the Loyalists and the surrender of the Middle West, and North denounced the cessions as "unfortunate" and "improvident." North's speech provided one hilarious moment. While he was on his feet a dog that had strayed into the House started to bark. Amid shouts of "Hear! hear!" North joined the general laughter. Addressing the chair, he remarked, "Sir, I was interrupted by a new Speaker, but as his argument is concluded, I will resume mine."[53]

Against this strong current Shelburne's lieutenants, Tommy Townshend and young Pitt, made little headway. On the morning of February 18th an amendment proposed by Cavendish to leave out of the Address expressions that might be construed as approving the peace and to substitute a declaration to take it into consideration was carried by a vote of 224 to 208. The edifice was crumbling.[54] How to denounce the peace while still accepting it as a necessary evil now became the chief preoccupation of Shelburne's enemies, aside from jockeying for power. On February 21st they proposed to the Commons a series of resolutions accepting the peace as necessary, approving the grant of independence to the United States as being in conformity with the wishes of Parliament, while condemning the concessions to the enemy as being greater than the comparative strength and actual situation of the belligerents warranted. Another all-night debate ensued, and the vote of censure was carried by the margin of 207-190.[55]

The vote of censure disclosed to the diplomatic observers as well as the rest of the world the preposterous and implausible combination of opposites who had joined forces to bring down their more farsighted, if politically maladroit, rival. His scepter slipping from his grasp, Shelburne had made indirect approaches both to Lord North and to Charles James Fox. The suitor was rudely rebuffed because the objects of his sudden affection were caught up in a heady flirtation of their own. Boreas and Reynard, as Burke nicknamed the pair, united to destroy the Ministry and to set up a successor government in which they expected to divide the spoils. The first appeared easier to achieve than the second.[56] Pitt's desperate effort to defeat the resolutions of censure had failed despite his castigation of "the unnatural coalition." "If this ill-omened marriage is not already solemnized," he warned the Commons, "I know a just and lawful impediment, and, in the name of public safety, I here forbid the banns."[57] In disregard of this solemn interdiction the ill-mated pair entered upon their illicit union.

Two days after the vote of censure Shelburne resigned. "Whence came the idea that the moment a minister loses a question in Parliament he must be displaced?" John Jay inquired in a letter to Benjamin Vaughan.[58] To answer would require a chapter on the rise of the notion of responsible ministries. To the formulation of that Constitutional precept Shelburne himself now made an indispensable contribution. True, young Pitt in similar circumstances followed a different course a year later, but Shelburne's seemingly impulsive action was prompted in no small part by personal pique enkindled by suspicion that he had been double-crossed by the King and let down by his own immediate followers.[59] By no means insensitive to his personal unpopularity, the Earl was shrewd enough to realize that his talk of sweeping reforms, including trade liberalization, had badly frightened the standpatters and that his administrative economies had pinched the pocketbooks of still others. In short, if a scapegoat had to be chosen to bear the onus of a humiliating peace, the retiring First Lord of the Treasury was the ideal target.

Ironic if belated tribute to the skill with which Shelburne had negotiated the peace in his own country's best interest was grudgingly paid by the other belligerents, who proceeded to pick all sorts of flaws in the preliminaries. "The very points which are found fault with here," wrote Grantham plaintively to Sir James Harris, "are those which do not give satisfaction to France."[60] Across the Channel the opposition faction of the Duc de Choiseul marshaled its forces to bring down the Comte de Vergennes, who was particularly excoriated for the paucity of the spoils France retrieved in India.[61] Alarms were sounded that England, having lost America, would now undertake a vast expansion in India. France's course, then, was not to withdraw her troops and ships from that distant area, but to look upon the Indian articles as nothing more than stopgap terms.[62] Vergennes faced additional criticism for ending the war without regaining Canada, and for not having insisted that St. Pierre and Miquelon be fortified, a step which was advised less out of fear of England than from concern over competition and encroachment upon French preserves by American fishermen.[63]

To add to Vergennes' discomfiture, the Dutch blamed him for signing the preliminaries without looking out for their interests. Despite heavy pressure from the French, the obstinate Hollanders continued to insist on Negapatam, offering in its stead lands on the Sumatran coast, and remained adamant about conceding to the English the free navigation of Eastern waters.[64]

The Spaniards were far more affronted by the terms of the preliminaries than the French. Aside from their chagrin over Gibraltar, they were hardly reconciled to the American settlement made without their participation. Three issues between Spain and America still divided the parties: recognition of the United States, conceding America her Western territorial claims, and allowing her the free navigation of the Mississippi. That winter the Marquis de Lafayette was in Spain on a diplomatic mission carrying the endorsement of the American commissioners, who viewed his departure with barely concealed relief. Spain still recoiled from independence, fearful that England and America, as Goëzmann de Thurne astutely remarked, would soon stir up a revolution in her own restless dominions.[65] Indeed, Floridablanca made no secret of his view that the independence of the United States was a "misfortune." Nevertheless, Lafayette managed to persuade that cautious and crusty diplomat to invite Carmichael to a diplomatic dinner, the first overt recognition of the new nation on Spain's part. Lafayette also wrung from Floridablanca an implied conditional recognition of the boundaries as settled between England and America in their preliminaries. "It is his Majesty's intention to abide for the present by the limits established" by the Anglo-American preliminaries, Florida-blanca told the Marquis. "Yet the King intends to inform himself particularly whether it can be in any way inconvenient or prejudicial to settle that affair amicably with the United States."[66]

The Spanish court had opened the door a crack. Once more Aranda took up with Jay the issues in dispute. Whether or not it was temperamentally impossible for the reserved American and the volatile Spaniard ever to see eye to eye, which was Montmorin's opinion, or because the differences were so fundamental, the Spanish government had second thoughts about leaving the negotiations in the Conde's hands. What is more, Spain refused to turn Natchez over to the Americans, despite the fact that this predominantly English-speaking community was located fifty miles north of the 31st parallel. Through Vergennes Spain conducted backstage negotiations with the British to retain it. The restoration by the British of West Florida to Spain knocked the props from under the American case for the free navigation of the Mississippi to its mouth, as little support could be found in international law upholding the right of one power to navigate a river both of whose banks were held by another power. Such a rule would have permitted Spain the unhampered navigation of the Tagus to Lisbon and the subjects of Joseph II the freedom of shipping down the Scheldt to the sea.[67] True, the Americans claimed all the rights that the British had held when West Florida was under their domain, but the French court offered them little or no encouragement. In frustration and annoyance, Jay wisely decided to put off and then to decline an invitation to return to Spain for face-to-face negotiations, and these issues remained unsettled at the peacemaking.[68]

Seeing his negotiations with Jay founder on the rock of rival national interests, Aranda reputedly drew up at this time and submitted to his King a secret memorial pointing out the dangers that the new American nation posed to the Spanish Empire, and proposing as a counterweight to American expansion and annexation that Spain turn over all her colonies except Puerto Rico and Cuba to royal princes, exerting regal powers in their respective domains, while the Spanish King assumed the title of Emperor. The Spanish realms would be united by offensive and defensive alliances and enjoy trade reciprocity, which Aranda was prepared to open to French trade but not to the British.[69] Much has been written about the genuineness of this memoir. It has been suggested that it was concocted years later by Manuel de Godoy, a political enemy of Aranda, in order to discredit the Conde. Incontestably, though, Aranda had already gone on record warning that the United States, though a pygmy in infancy, would some day become the colossus of the West and a formidable menace to Spain's possessions. In 1786, three years after the memoir was allegedly written, Aranda did propose to establish one infante in Spanish America, not three. Despite doubts that will not down on the legitimacy of Aranda's memorial, his sentiments on the effects of American independence were no secret from his government.[70]

The critics of the peacemaking notwithstanding, the major architects of the preliminaries among England's foes took the news of Shelburne's fall badly. Vergennes put it to rancorous party spirit, and kept up a cordial correspondence with the Earl after he left office, as did the Abbé Morellet, much to the succeeding Ministry's annoyance. In fact, distrust of England's intentions about peace were so thick that the Marquis de Moustier, France's ambassador to the Court of St. James's, set up entirely on his own an espionage service in British ports until he was rebuked for his zeal by Vergennes.[71] The Americans were equally uneasy now about the good faith of Parliament toward the preliminaries.[72] Although they never really trusted Shelburne completely, they recognized him as a reformer of their own stripe. They knew that the Earl sought to reform the tax structure, get more work out of civil servants, increase and equalize Parliamentary representation, hold more frequent elections, and extend the suffrage by allowing all landowners to vote, even though he never had the strength to risk a showdown in Parliament.[73] Vaughan was even encouraged to ask Franklin what he thought about extending the suffrage, and the old Revolutionary, though the preliminaries had not yet been signed, had no compunctions about passing on through Shelburne's intermediary the advice that Parliaments should be elected by all the people, and that the only way the lower classes would rise in England would be by elevating them in education and political responsibility.[74]

Now that they had brought about his downfall, Shelburne's enemies, it soon became clear, were putting his peacemaking in jeopardy and scuttling the major part of his reform program, notably the liberal trade policy on which the prospects of long-range peace and prosperity heavily depended. "We have demolished the Earl of Shelburne," Edmund Burke commented following the vote of censure, "but in his fall he has pulled down a large piece of the building." Burke's partisan diagnosis would have placed the onus for the ensuing confusion upon the victim rather than the victors, but he admitted ruefully that he could not tell what direction affairs would take. "For once I confess," he conceded, giving us a glimpse of the later anti-Revolutionary Burke, "I apprehend more from the madness of the people than from any other cause."[75]

An extraordinary interregnum, or more precisely "interministerium," of seven weeks followed Shelburne's fall, during which the peace negotiations were virtually suspended. Grantham clung to the Foreign Office as long as possible, behaving, as Shelburne remarked, like "a sick man who could not get over his illness."[76] George III made desperate efforts to avert a North-Fox Ministry. The previous year he had actually drafted an abdication message and held his royal yacht in readiness for a fortnight.[77] Now, sooner than yield, he would "go to Hanover," he threatened. Rather than accept a coalition including Fox, he would accept North, or Pitt, or Gower, or "Mr. Thomas Pitt or Mr. Thomas anybody."[78] Young Pitt shrewdly declined, regarding the moment unpropitious to head a Ministry. Thurlow, Gower, and others resisted the lures of the Treasury. North refused to break with Fox, and in the end George had to swallow the bitter pill of the coalition, with the Duke of Portland as its titular head, and Charles James Fox as Foreign Secretary.[79]

Aside from his politics, Charles James Fox had long been a thorn in the side of George III. He had deliberately cultivated the spoiled Prince of Wales and encouraged him in his willful and dissolute course. It has been remarked that the Prince had the best possible excuse for being a Whig, "for his father had ruled him exactly as he ruled the Bostonians, and with as little success."[80] Fox, whose financial circumstances had been desperate, had recouped much of his losses at the gaming club of Brooks's. Thence, after rising fashionably late, the disheveled leader would repair with a levee of his hard-drinking, high-playing followers. Their irreverent jests about their monarch, to which the Prince contributed his share, were not confined to the club's walls, and rumor had it that George had vowed that "he would have no peace till his son and Fox were secured in the Tower."[81] Like so many other of his threats George failed to carry this one out. On April 2nd Fox and North kissed hands as Secretaries of State, but the King remained unreconciled, making no secret of his aversion to the new Foreign Secretary in undiplomatic remarks to the French ambassador.[82]

In the new Ministry the Duke of Portland was no more than a cipher, and Lord North interfered not at all in the business of the peacemaking, which Fox henceforth dominated. No greater contrast could be imagined between the temperate, immaculate, and even fawning Shelburne and his undisciplined but charming rival. Having gained office by forcing a vote of censure of Shelburne's preliminaries, Fox was under obligation to make good his charges that Shelburne's peace made one "sicken at its very name," because it was "more calamitous, more dreadful, more ruinous than war could possibly be."[83]

Fox's first move was to make a clean sweep of Shelburne's plenipotentiaries and agents in Paris. David Hartley, member from Hull, long-time correspondent of Franklin, and advocate of Anglo-American reunion, replaced Oswald, although Franklin himself would have been quite "content," as he privately expressed it, "to have finished with Mr. Oswald, whom we always found very reasonable."[84] The Duke of Manchester, the newly appointed ambassador to Paris, replaced a thoroughly disillusioned Fitzherbert as plenipotentiary to conclude peace with Holland and make definitive treaties with France and Spain, and Vergennes found the replacement "as cunning as he is weak and callous."[85] The King was doubtless happy to see the end of Vaughan's solicitous activities in Paris, for he considered Shelburne's confidant "so void of judgment that it is fortunate he has had no business, and the sooner he returns to his family the better; indeed the fewer engines the better, and those of the most discreet kind."[86]

Aside from bringing in new faces, Fox found the peacemaking heavy going. He was sticky, negative, obstructive, but unable to obtain radical revisions in the preliminary terms. While he conceded that public faith required that the preliminaries be ratified,[87] he made no bones in talks with foreign diplomats of his discontent with Shelburne's achievements. To Comte d'Adhémar, who succeeded Moustier as French ambassador to London, he damned "those devils" who had made the preliminaries, denouncing Shelburne and Grantham as "pusillanimous ministers without any shred of character." Peace had been bought dearly, he complained because "those villainous persons have tied my hands in every conceivable manner."[88] Fox held out stubbornly against giving the French exclusive fishing rights in Newfoundland, and secured from Vergennes the acceptance of the word "concurrent" instead of "exclusive." He also won such trivial concessions as the freedom of Protestants on Tobago to exercise their religion "privately."[89] A few declarations and counterdeclarations as to commerce and India completed the settlement with the French.

Fox soon locked horns with the Spaniards over the status and geographical limits of the logwood settlements in Honduras. The logwood cutters were concerned about obtaining a large and permanent foundation for the mahogany trade and retaining all the logwood rivers formerly possessed as well as opening up fresh channels of supply. Manchester finally obtained a minor adjustment of the northern and western boundaries, but he was forced to accept Grantham's stipulation that the British abandon their settlements on the Mosquito Shore.[90] Nothing whatever came of Fox's notion of securing some lands in northern Florida for the Georgia Loyalists to form a buffer between the Spanish and American dominions.[91]

Against the Dutch Fox held more trumps in his hand than against the other belligerents. Nevertheless his tenacity came as a surprise to Netherlanders, who had assumed that the "man of the people" would do everything he could to support the Patriot faction in Holland, which he had earlier held in such high esteem.[92] Turning his back on his long professed sentiments, Fox felt that he could drive a harder bargain than did Shelburne since the Dutch were in a tight corner. First of all, though, he had to get free of a trap of his own making. In the spring of 1782 he had proposed as Foreign Secretary the acceptance of Russia's offer to mediate between Great Britain and the Dutch on the basis of the Anglo-Dutch Treaty of 1674, and he had secured the Cabinet's endorsement of a proposal to recognize the principles of the Armed Neutrality. With a general peace imminent, Shelburne saw no necessity for making so lavish a concession, nor for having Russia mediate with the Netherlands.

The Dutch clung to three demands without being in a military posture to secure a single one of them. They insisted that all their captured colonies be returned, that Great Britain acknowledge the principles of the Armed Neutrality, and that the British pay damages for all captures made during the war in violation of neutral rights. They were particularly insistent on the restitution of Negapatam and on opposing the opening of the Eastern seas to the free navigation of the British. The latter concession the East India Company deemed essential if the British were to trade freely with the Spice Islands and the Moluccas. Fox appeared willing to bargain over Negapatam, proposing half jokingly that the French yield Tobago in return for the Indian post, or that the Dutch turn over Demerara in Dutch Guiana or the southern portion of Sumatra, though the last proposal was in effect vetoed by the East India Company directors. Even John Adams, staunch friend of the Dutch Patriot faction, intervened through Hartley to persuade the British to show some moderation.[93]

Talk about equivalents dragged on. The Dutch envoys pointed out that the constitution of their republic would not permit them to conclude a definitive treaty without first gaining the approval of the various provinces. Finally, Vergennes notified the Dutch that France was about to sign a definitive peace. Bereft of the backing of their ally, the Dutch had no course but to capitulate. The concessions England gained proved of considerable value for the future of the Empire. Negapatam gave a *point d'appui* for the British smuggling trade to the island of Ceylon, and the Dutch concession of the right to trade and navigate freely in Eastern waters opened a path for Britain's penetration in Malaysia.[94] In substance, however, Fox did not improve upon the terms that Shelburne and Vergennes had previously agreed upon for the Dutch.

In no aspect of the peacemaking was Fox's meddling more inept and its consequences more mischievous than in his negotiations with the Americans. A leading critic of the American War from the moment news had come of the shots fired on Lexington green, Fox had earned the antipathy of the King and the North Ministry by the fervor of his advocacy of American independence. So far as the American settlement was concerned, he might have been expected to rise above personal and party rancor and to recognize that Shelburne's liberal inclinations looking toward *rapprochement* deserved hearty endorsement and implementation. Quite the contrary proved the case. Although he never challenged the grant of American independence and in any event could not take back what had already been given up, he would not budge another inch.

After the preliminaries the major outstanding issue between the Americans and the British concerned the trade settlement. Shelburne had maintained that his treaties proved that "we prefer trade to dominion," and that a peace was good "in the exact proportion that it recognizes" the principle of free trade.[95] True, his own Cabinet had rejected the article drafted by John Jay providing for complete reciprocity between England and America on the ground that the executive had no authority to alter the operation of the Navigation Laws. It was understood, however, that such matters would be covered by a treaty of commerce,[96] and the preamble to the provisional articles declared the intention of putting the principle of reciprocity into effect between the two nations.

Supported by some British merchants, a small coterie of Americans in London, including Elkanah Watson and the apostate Silas Deane, whom the American commissioners shunned as a moral leper,[97] sought to drum up sentiment for liberalizing commerce with the former colonies.[98] Shelburne's adviser on trade, John Pownall, counseled that special legislation would be needed to carry out this principle.[99] A bill was accordingly drafted permitting American produce for the time being to enter British ports on the same footing as though British-owned, while treating American ships carrying such produce as those of other foreign states. During this interim period the bill would have permitted American ships to carry American goods to British colonies and islands in America and to export any goods whatsoever from such British possessions. Duties and charges would in both cases be the same as for British-owned merchandise, transported by British ships and crews.

By the time the bill was introduced Shelburne was already out of office, and Pitt, still holding on as Chancellor of the Exchequer, assumed responsibility for steering the measure through the House. When the bill came up to the House on March 7th, Pitt proved a lukewarm advocate, while its opponents were thoroughly aroused. Fox advocated caution. He deemed the bill to infringe upon England's commercial treaty with Russia, which accorded that power most-favored-nation treatment. Burke compared the proposed legislation to a one-sided courtship. "Great Britain was extremely fond in her wooing, and in her love-fit was ready to give largely; whereas, to his knowledge, America had nothing to give in return."

It was William Eden, offended by Shelburne's obvious disregard, who proceeded to demolish the proposal. His arguments reflected a careful reading of a tract just published, entitled *Observations on the Commerce of the American States*. Its author, Lord Sheffield, marshaling an imposing array of statistics, argued that Americans must be treated as foreigners and not permitted to enjoy those branches of the carrying trade with the Empire in which they had previously participated, notably the trade in foodstuffs and timber with the British West Indies. Hewing to the Sheffield line, Eden attacked the bill as introducing "a total revolution in our commercial system," and warned that the Americans would monopolize the supply of provisions to the West Indies to the ruin of the provision trade of Ireland and the disadvantage of the sugar refiners of England. He painted a disturbing picture of American ships returning from British ports, their holds stuffed with tools and emigrant artificers, and he appealed to the patriotism of his listeners, arguing that by this concession England would lose her great nursery of seamen, would languish in peace and be helpless in war.[100] The bill was sent to committee, where it was altered beyond recognition.

With the Shelburne project moribund, the Fox-North coalition, from its inception in April, was confronted with the need to set guidelines for reopening trade with America. According to Henry Laurens, who had returned to England for his health, Fox showed "a disposition to proceed to business with us with liberality and effect," and rumors spread that not only trade reciprocity but dual citizenship was in contemplation.[101] The coalition had accepted Eden's amendment to the Shelburne bill, vesting discretionary power in the King in Council to regulate all such matters for a limited period,[102] in effect giving the new Ministry a free hand to work out a trade program *ad interim*. The Ministry then had no one else to blame but itself for making a shambles of its own negotiations in Paris.

When, toward the end of April, the American commissioners sat down with the bespectacled David Hartley in the latter's apartment at the Hôtel d'York they were confronted with a well-meaning liberal of unsullied probity, whom Adams in an uncharitable mood found "talkative and disputatious and not always intelligible,"[103] a negotiator apparently oblivious to the rising tide in England against trade concessions to America. The emasculation of Shelburne's trade bill notwithstanding, both sides went through the motions. The Americans carefully prepared propositions which they submitted to Hartley, and he in turn advanced counterproposals. These American propositions Hartley described as professing "one simple and invariable principle for the basis of their negotiations, viz., reciprocity; reciprocity upon any terms whatsoever, from the narrowest limits to the utmost extent of mutual intercourse and participation."

In deference to instructions from Congress to secure, if possible, the direct trade with the British West Indies[104] the American commissioners proposed to Hartley on April 29th that the rivers, harbors, and ports of both countries, including areas under the dominion of Great Britain, be opened to the citizens of the other.[105] Hartley "approved of it greatly," the American commissioners later reported, but he earned a stinging rebuke from his chief for his generosity. Fox insisted that Hartley had not attended to his instructions, and that only American ships laden with *American produce* be admitted to British ports. To compound Hartley's mortification, the Foreign Minister enclosed a copy of an Order in Council issued the previous day, May 14th, permitting *unmanufactured* goods of American production to be imported into England in British or American ships, but saying nothing about manufactures from the States.[106] A shamefaced Hartley passed on this Order in Council to the Americans. As might be expected, they proceeded to denounce as discriminatory this denial on the part of Britain of the admission of American manufactures into England in American ships.[107] In retrospect John Adams castigated the proclamation as "the first link in that great chain of Orders in Council which have been since stretched and extended, till it has shackled the commerce of the globe."[108]

Hartley defended his position with dignity, and warned Fox that it was his "firm conviction the American principle of equal reciprocity and the restrictive principle of the British Acts of Navigation must come to issue."[109] To reconcile the Ministry's point of view with that of the Americans he made a counterproposal on May 21st, suggesting, as a temporary expedient, that both parties return to the conditions of trade regulation existing at law before the start of the American Revolution. He would have allowed American trade with the West Indies, but confined American exports therefrom to the produce of the islands.[110]

"Can you sign in case we agree?" the Americans asked. Hartley admitted he could not. "Then we think it improper to proceed to consider it until after you obtain the consent of your Court."[111] Hartley argued eloquently with Fox for some affirmative action on the part of the Ministry. "As surely as the rights of mankind have been established by the American War, so surely will all the Acts of Navigation of the world perish and be buried amongst occult qualities. . . . Throw out a loose and liberal line," he urged. With Anglo-American friendship as his longer-range objective, Hartley predicted that the American States would "be the foundations of great events in the new page of life."[112]

Fox, the fiery revolutionary, now sought to chill Hartley's liberal fervor with the reminder that "literall reciprocity is impossible as much from their engagements as from our system of navigation." The best he could do would be to permit trade between the United States and the West Indies, but he was not prepared to admit West Indian commodities brought to Great Britain in American vessels.[113]

Hartley came up with still another compromise, one that would permit Americans to trade between the islands and Canada, a proposition which the Americans quickly accepted.[114] Fox let the proposal lie on his desk unanswered. Nothing came of this proposal, nor of John Jay's propositions that British subjects be barred from exporting slaves into America, "it being the intention of the said States entirely to prohibit the importation thereof," and that trade between America and Ireland be liberated from prewar restrictions.[115]

Virtually ignored henceforth by the Ministry, Hartley, whose "zeal exceeded his authority," as the commissioners later attested, was forced to concede that "prejudices" in England were so strong that a relaxation of the Navigation Laws could never be undertaken without a full Parliamentary inquiry.[116] Vergennes put the matter aptly when he remarked to Adams that Fox "was startled at every clamour of a few merchants."[117] The final rebuff came on July 2nd, when an Order in Council was issued barring American ships from the West Indian trade. Its author, William Knox, a long-time public official and die-hard Tory, claimed that the order, which he had first drafted as a bill, entitled him to have engraved upon his tombstone a tribute for " having *saved the navigation of England*."[118] The appearance of this order "convulsed the negotiation in Paris," Hartley reported in despair.[119] "Mr. Hartley," John Adams remarked, "is probably kept here if he was not sent at first merely to amuse us, and to keep him out of the way of embarrassing the coalition."[120] In his chargin Adams struck out wildly, with the French court and American apostates in England his special targets.[121] True, the Comte de Vergennes was by no means displeased by the breakdown of the British-American trade negotiations, for he and his aides at that very moment were engaged in consultations with John Jay's contrary brother, Sir James, to promote Franco-American trade relations at Britain's expense. With quite adverse inclinations, John Jay reputedly was hostile to encouraging imports into the United States of luxury products from France.[122] It was neither the Comte nor Sir James Jay, however, who blocked a trade agreement with England. Rather must credit go to the forces mobilized by Sheffield & Company, a combination too awesome to be defied by their government.

If Adams was correct and the coalition had been formed at the gaming tables and conducted itself "upon no other than gambling principles,"[123] it had shown a timidity in the face of odds which one normally does not associate with gamblers. By its behavior the coalition had opened up a grievous and festering wound in Anglo-American relations. The Orders in Council, along with the demise of the Hartley negotiations, disclosed that the shooting war was to be succeeded by one of intense commercial rivalry between the belligerents.[124] All sorts of interest groups had been marshaled to oppose Shelburne's program of trade liberalization,[125] and although British shipping and manufacturing interests would reap a short-term harvest, the British West Indian planters, now forced to pay exorbitant prices for salt, fish, and timber from Canada and Honduras, with the cheaper supplies from New England cut off, would suffer mortal injury by this impairment of their competitive position.[126] Fox still mumbled about a separate trade treaty with America, not "under the eye of France,"[127] but his heart was no longer in the business, if it ever really had been, and time was running out for him. The following year, when the irrespressible Hartley was in Paris to exchange ratifications of the peace treaty, he once more put out feelers to the Americans for a commercial convention. Pitt's youthful Foreign Secretary, the Marquess of Carmarthen, peremptorily ordered him home.[128] In turning his back upon Shelburne's liberal trade principles, Pitt, the Earl's protégé, also chose to swim with the tide, and to uphold rivalry and exclusion in the place of cooperation and the prospect of federal union.

Aside from the issues of trade, all the belligerents, even the reluctant Dutch, had virtually come to terms. On August 8th the plenipotentiaries of the belligerent powers, excepting the United States, whose envoys expressed no desire to be present, assembled at the home of Mercy d'Argenteau to learn the proposed final terms of peace.[129] To the chargin of the titular mediators a trivial if dignified role had been assigned them by Vergennes. The Comte had made no secret to the other belligerents of his wish that the treaties be settled by the parties themselves, a wish that Fox fully shared. The latter's fears that the mediators might try to introduce the new maritime code into the body of the definitive treaties[130] seemed well founded, for the mediators made motions to that end. Vergennes stopped them in their tracks. Despite his lip-service dedication to the cause of neutral rights, he now made it clear that he did not want to embarrass England when the moment of reconciliation between the two nations seemed at hand. Fox hastened to make a parallel response to the mediators.[131] As for the American treaty, the British made it known that they did not wish the mediators to interfere in their private concerns,[132] while the Americans, having lost none of their suspicions of the mediators, told Hartley that they preferred to conclude without them, a preference implicitly endorsed by Vergennes himself.[133]

On August 16th Franklin reported to Vergennes that the British Ministry, not agreeing to any propositions made "either by us or by their Minister here," had instead sent over a plan for a definitive treaty, which consisted merely of the preliminaries formerly signed, along with short introductory and concluding. paragraphs, confirming and putting into effect the preliminary articles. "My colleagues seem inclined to sign this with Mr. Hartley, and so to finish the affair," he added.[134]

As the great moment drew near the British plenipotentiaries asked for instructions on the presents to be made to the ministers of the different nations participating in the signing in accordance with custom. Fox asked the King, and George, with little enthusiasm, replied, "Give whatever the French do." "This will do very well with regard to the mediators," Fox informed Manchester, "but what are we to do with the four Americans?" It was customary to give diamond-encased portraits of the monarch in whose name the present was made, but Fox thought that the Americans would prefer money to pictures. He was hardly so rash as to presume that they would be flattered with a jeweled portrait of George III, whose rule they had foresworn. Perhaps a thousand pounds apiece, he suggested, would be "thought a great deal," an amount which Manchester and Hartley deemed "very handsome and satisfactory." Hartley made a point

THE FOX AND THE GRAPES

of mentioning this to Franklin,[135] but neither the doctor nor his colleagues made an entry of any such transaction. Since it was the season for gifts, the Abbé Morellet was rewarded by Vergennes at Shelburne's prompting with a handsome pension, a beneficence which did not sit well with Fox.[136] One other conciliatory gesture was made toward the Americans, this time by their implacable adversary, Charles III of Spain. Ten days before the final signings Carmichael was presented to the King and royal family at San Ildefonso in his capacity of chargé d'affaires of the United States.

Almost until the moment of signing, as delay followed delay, mutual suspicions festered.[137] Then an element of tragic mystery intruded itself into the final preparations. In an especially peevish mood, George III let it be known that he was discontented with the pace which the Duke of Manchester had set in Paris and took special exception to the Duke's secretary, Maddison.[138] On the eve of the signing, Maddison was taken violently ill and died of poisoning within two days. Whether the secretary had taken his own life in a mood of despondency or was the victim of foul play, his death added a macabre note to the closing rites that ended the war.[139]

The date for those closing rites was finally set. Word came to Franklin from Vergennes on August 29th. The Comte, so Rayneval informed the doctor, "has directed me to say that nothing ought to prevent your signing at Paris on Wednesday next, the day proposed for the signature of the other treaties." Rayneval requested that the signing with Hartley take place at nine o'clock in the morning so as to give time for a courier to be dispatched to Versailles with word of the event, as the Comte was "desirous of being informed of the completion of your labors at the same time with his own."[140]

On the morning of September 3rd, after some last-minute consultations in anticipation of another hitch,[141] the Americans at Hartley's invitation repaired to the British commissioner's lodgings at the Hôtel d'York. That edifice, standing in one of the most crowded streets in the Quartier Latin, close by the venerable Hôpital de la Charité (since demolished to make way for a big white medical school building), no longer serves as a residential hotel, but houses the publishing firm of Firmin Didot. It would be another six years before Louis Jacques Daguerre would make his bow on the world stage, and in the absence of on-the-spot photography we must accept a witness secondhand to the event, Benjamin West's celebrated painting of the signing. This renowned canvas perpetuates an historical image which is incorrect in two particulars. It includes Henry Laurens among the American signers, along with Jay, Franklin, Adams, and the secretary to the American delegation, William Temple Franklin. Laurens was actually in England at the time,[142] and Franklin's grandson was not accorded the honor of attesting the final signings. The artist had in fact sketched in the cast of characters who participated in the preliminaries, hoping that his commemorative painting would not need to be altered, but he left a large blank space on the right-hand side of the canvas to paint in either Richard Oswald and Caleb Whitefoord, or, if he had chosen to update it, David Hartley. Blind of one eye and conscious of his rather repelling physiognomy, Oswald was notoriously shy about sitting for any portraits, and declined on this occasion. For West to have painted in David Hartley instead would have involved re-doing the left side of the canvas. The bespectacled Hartley did pose, however, for Romney, who painted him seated before a copy of the treaty.[143] Indeed, it was perhaps fitting that West's painting was never finished, because, for the Americans, the definitive signing was anticlimactic.

That same afternoon the Duke of Manchester signed the treaties with France and Spain at Versailles. Separate declarations certifying the role of the mediators were affixed to both the French and Spanish treaties and signed by Comte Mercy for Joseph II, and by Bariatinski and Markov for Catherine. Everything was done with dispatch. The last signature was affixed by three that afternoon. The previous day in Paris Manchester had signed the preliminaries with the Dutch, who begged off signing definitively.[144]

On the very evening of the signing of the definitive treaties a company of Americans, including Matthew Ridley and Thomas Barclay, a Philadelphia merchant and American Consul General in France, sat down to dinner with Lafayette and the Marquis de Castries at Versailles. Conversation turned on future trade relations between the two countries. The Americans were shocked to hear the Minister of Marine remark, apropos of the French West Indies, "Our colonies are our slaves, the greater part of which would have to be destroyed."[145] To the court circle at Versailles the official ending of this world war brought not even a glimmer of the new era in the relations of colonies and metropolis which the War of the American Revolution had inaugurated.

To the delays which had put off the signing and to the event itself George III, who had lost an empire, professed equal indifference.[146] Contrariwise, the Comte de Vergennes did not conceal his relief and gratification. His strength sapped by the protracted negotiations, his nerves strained by Cabinet intrigues behind his back by traditional foes joined by the Queen herself, he avowed to Montmorin, "The end was for so long a time the unique object of my solicitude."[147]

But this was not the end of it. Despite the signings, the insistent question remained unanswered: Would there be peace? Idealists like David Hartley envisioned "the fairest prospects," "reciprocal advantage," and a joining of hearts and hands by Britons and Americans "in one common cause for the reunion of all our ancient affections and common interests."[148] More realistic statesmen, thinking of the shorter term, were for less confident, for both in the Old World and the New there was ground for concern about the shape of things to come.

XVIII

BLESSED ARE THE PEACEMAKERS

Nations are notoriously prone to apotheosize their war heroes and forget their peacemakers. America is no exception, and furnishes some glaring examples. From the point of view of national interest the two most advantageous treaties ever negotiated for the United States were drawn up by envoys who defied orders but were too remote from the seat of government to be effectively repudiated. These were the treaties made at Paris in 1782 and at Guadalupe Hidalgo in 1848. The latter, an unauthorized treaty by a disavowed agent, was signed by Nicholas P. Trist, the chief clerk in the State Department, after his commission had been annulled. For his exercise of good judgment on the spot Trist was condemned to wait for twenty-two years before being reimbursed for his salary and expenses for the period following his recall.

The four American commissioners at Paris some sixty-six years earlier, having deliberately defied their government's instructions, had few illusions about what was in store for them. Even before the preliminaries had been consummated, Franklin discounted Henry Laurens' prediction that the doctor for his part in "the great work" would be "called blessed by all the grateful of the present generation." "I have never yet known of a peace," Franklin replied, "that did not occasion a great deal of popular discontent, clamour, and censure on both sides." Franklin attributed this reaction to "the usual management" of the statesmen of the warring powers. To maintain national morale, they would paint conditions in brighter hues than the facts warranted, and arouse expectations of better terms than could be obtained. He cited the examples of the Peaces of Utrecht and of Aix-la-Chapelle, in both cases attributed in England to French gold and in France to English guineas, and the last Peace of Paris which brought down upon its maker, Lord Bute, a torrent of abuse almost without precedent in its savagery. "The blessing promised to peacemakers, I fancy, relates to the next world," Franklin reminded Laurens, "for in this they seem to have a greater chance of being cursed."[1]

After signing the preliminaries Laurens and Adams exchanged half-hearted jests about the possible hanging that awaited them at home. "John Adams & Co. may be hanged, but no damage will arise to the United States," Laurens remarked, in a comment elicited by Shelburne's reputed boast about how he had managed to separate the Allies. "I cannot think our country will hang her ministers merely for their simplicity in being cheated into independence, the fisheries, and half the Great Lakes," Adams rejoined. "Our countrymen love buckskins, beaverskins, tom-cod, and pine trees too well to hang their ministers for accepting them, or even for purchasing them by a little too much 'reciprocity' to the tories."[2]

The American peacemakers capitalized on the factors of time and distance to act on their own initiative, to the annoyance of Congress and its Secretary for Foreign Affairs. More than once Robert R. Livingston rebuked his commissioners for failing to keep him posted. "The ignorance in which we are kept," he pointed out, "renders it impossible for the sovereign to instruct their servant, and of course forms them into an independent privy council for the direction of their affairs, without their advice and concurrence."[3] With characteristic patience and courtesy Franklin in reply cited the difficulties confronting the commissioners in their efforts to keep up a regular and punctual correspondence with Philadelphia. Letters sent through the regular mails were opened up in the post office; no systematic schedule of ship sailings existed; before a reply to a letter was received some five to six months on an average had elapsed. European diplomats, by contrast, could send an express from Paris to their respective courts in under a fortnight. If he and his colleagues had acted as a "privy council," it was not from choice but from necessity, he added, for American ministers in Europe, by their very remoteness from their own capital, had to be allowed ampler discretionary powers than European courts were accustomed to grant their plenipotentiaries.[4]

One is entitled to speculate on the extent to which the debates and resolves of Congress would have hampered the American commissioners had they been apprised of them in time, or, to put it Livingston's way, had they acted as agents rather than as "an independent privy council." Of course, they did not work entirely in the dark. When they affixed their signatures to the preliminaries they were aware that Congress, under the twin impact of military reverses and French pressure, had withdrawn all its peace ultimata except independence and the injunction to follow the advice of the King of France. It was no secret to the commissioners that the pro-French party in Congress had been mobilized and cajoled by the affable Chevalier de La Luzerne and his alert, presumptuous, and intriguing Secretary of Legation, Barbé-Marbois.[5] The anti-Gallicans derived malicious satisfaction from passing on such gossip to John Adams and Francis Dana, along with stories about the way in which the French mission in Philadelphia had reputedly undercut the American war effort when it was not directed to coincide with the peace aims of France.[6]

The anti-Gallicans were no less shortsighted than their opponents. Having no knowledge of the independent course being pursued by Jay in Paris, they moved in Congress to reconsider both the commissions and the instructions. The bilious Arthur Lee and his cohorts would have excluded Franklin and Jay from the peacemaking and withdrawn the others from the direction of France. Considering the delicate stage at which the negotiations with Richard Oswald then stood, one could hardly have managed timing more inept or potentially mischievous. Fortunately young James Madison thwarted the move.[7] Lee and Izard continued to spread the word that Franklin could not be trusted to fight for the West because of his connections with a speculative group that opposed Virginia's Western land claims,[8] and they still considered Jay suspect because of his alleged ties with the French faction when he had been President of Congress back in 1779.

The delusion about Jay was dispelled just in time. On August 2, 1782, a letter from the New Yorker was read to the Congress recounting his frustrations in Spain and, in Madison's view, adding "fresh leaven to the antigallic ferment."[9] Once more Lee moved to revoke the crucial instruction, but after a long and torrid debate Madison prevailed with a new motion authorizing a committee to draw up certain facts and observations to be submitted both to La Luzerne and to the commissioners with a view to persuading the King of France of the validity and importance of the American claims.[10] On October 3rd Congress adopted a report of Madison's committee which avowed the territorial claims of the states, the fisheries, and the free navigation of the Mississippi, "not only as their indubitable rights, but as essential to their prosperity."[11] To mollify an infuriated La Luzerne, who all along had contended against holding out for such objectives, Congress reiterated its timeworn assurances not to "enter into the discussion of any overtures for pacification, but in confidence and in concert with his Most Christian Majesty."[12]

Unbeknown to Congress, the commissioners defied their principals and went on to sign their preliminaries without consulting the French. It was months before that news reached Philadelphia. Meantime, on the eve of Christmas a communication from Jay, enclosing a copy of the intercepted letter of Barbé-Marbois, was laid before Congress. Once more passions mounted. The anti-Gallicans moved to revise the instructions to free the American plenipotentiaries from the obligation to conform to the advice of France. Once more the arguments for and against the notorious instructions were trotted out. Once more James Madison, opposing repeal on the ground that the instruction was at worst nothing more than a "sacrifice of our pride to our interest," mustered enough votes to postpone action on the resolution and keep all trace of it out of the Journals.[13]

Suspenseful days followed until, on March 12th, Captain Joshua Barney and his packet *Washington* reached Philadelphia bearing dispatches from the commissioners along with the provisional treaty. Grumble though they would over the articles on the Loyalists and the debts, the delegates had little ground to cavil about most of the terms, which, as Madison put it, "appeared to Congress on the whole extremely liberal."

Two aspects of the preliminaries came in for sharp criticism, nonetheless. Pointed barbs were directed at the "separate and secret manner" in which the commissioners had conducted their negotiations. This criticism was not entirely spontaneous. La Luzerne showed Livingston a letter from his chief remonstrating on the conduct of the American commissioners. He even took his complaint directly to President Elias Boudinot. What the delegates did not know was that Vergennes had countermanded his instructions to La Luzerne by a subsequent dispatch. Therein the Comte professed that Franklin's explanations had been found acceptable. When one Congressman in some perturbation asked Barbé-Marbois whether the court of France meant to complain to Congress about the commissioners, he replied, "Great powers never *complained*, but they *felt* and *remembered*."[14]

What caused a real rumpus was the separate and secret article on West Florida. An indignant Livingston told the delegates that they were reduced to the alternatives either of dishonoring themselves by becoming a party to the concealment or of wounding the feelings and destroying the influence of their ministers by disclosing the article to the French court. He proposed that he be authorized to show the article to La Luzerne and to instruct the commissioners that whichever nation might be given West Florida in the final treaty be allowed the boundaries set forth in the separate article. He also proposed that Congress go on record as expressing its understanding that the preliminary articles should not take effect until peace had been signed between England and France.[15]

In Madison's eyes, the separate article impaled Congress on the horns of a dilemma. "If they abet the proceedings of their ministers, all confidence with France is at an end," he wrote Edmund Randolph. "If they disavow the conduct of their ministers by their usual frankness of communication, the most serious inconveniences also present themselves."[16] "The torment of this dilemma" provoked some of the most uncharitable comments on the peace commissioners' conduct that had ever been voiced inside the halls of Congress. Congress debated the issue, according to La Luzerne, gripped by "wild and unfounded rumors." Arthur Lee, Oliver Wolcott, and John Rutledge spoke up for the commissioners, while their conduct was excoriated by John Francis Mercer of Virginia as "a mixture of follies which had no example." It was "a tragedy to America," he contended, "and a comedy to all the world besides." That fledging legislator, Alexander Hamilton of New York, harped on Shelburne's "insincerity and duplicity," and tartly observed that, although John Jay "was a man of profound sagacity and pure integrity, yet he was of a suspicious temper," a trait which "might explain the extraordinary jealousies which he professed." With Madison's backing, Hamilton proposed a compromise resolution which, while commending the commissioners, would authorize Livingston to communicate the separate article to the French.[17] Fortunately as events turned out, Hamilton's motion was rejected, and a committee resolution of like purport, whose passage would have amounted to a vote of no confidence in the commissioners, was held up.[18]

The next day was the Sabbath. Darkness had already come when shouts of "Peace! Peace!" resounded through the streets of Philadelphia. An express rider galloping up from the Delaware brought word from Commander Duquesne of the cutter *Triomphe,* thirty-seven days out of Cádiz, that the preliminaries of France and Spain, as well as of America, had been signed, and that hostilities in America were to cease on March 20th, already three days past. "Happy may it be indeed called," wrote Madison, "whether we consider the immediate blessings which it confers, or the cruel embarrassments from which it saves us."[19] The "cruel embarrassments" to which Madison referred stemmed from the restless state of the army and the financial instability of the nation.

Despite the joyful tidings the pro-French party in Congress was still determined to rebuke the four audacious men in Paris. Even though the preliminaries between Spain and Britain transferring West Florida to the former rendered the separate article completely nugatory and the issue obsolete, debate continued. Arguing with more heat than light, neither side could carry the day, and Congress adjourned without going on record one way or the other.[20]

Congress's nonaction did not deter Robert Livingston from performing what he considered to be his duty. On the very day Congress adjourned, and without even consulting that body, the Secretary proceeded to take pen in hand and administer to the commissioners a severe dressing down. Grudgingly, he conceded that the articles met with the "warmest approbation," that the commissioners' steadfastness in refusing to proceed without an acknowledgment of American independence was not only "approved," but that it was not denied that it "accelerated that declaration"—an explicit endorsement of Jay's course. Nor did Livingston have ground for complaint on the score of the boundaries and the fisheries, nor register any serious objections to the articles on the debts and the Loyalists. While not finding fault with the results of the treaty, the Secretary expressed "no little pain at the distrust" in its management. Why had they not communicated with the court of Versailles until after the signing? he asked. Why did they conceal the separate article from that court? Such concealment was, in his opinion, not only "absolutely unnecessary," but the secret article itself carried "the seeds of enmity to the court of Spain."[21]

The sullen temper of Congress, save for a few generous spirits,[22] and the surly response of Secretary Livingston seemed shabby recompense to the architects of the peace for their valiant performance. As Vaughan observed to Shelburne, the preliminaries were calculated to "disgust in America those who are to pay debts, those who are to restore estates, those who are to make money by war, those who are suspicious of England, and those whom the money, politics, or conduct of France have corrupted or deceived."[23] Considering Congress' low standing with its own army at the time and its inability to put its financial house in order, it did seem transparently unfair for responsible delegates to criticize agents so far removed from their direction who had managed to achieve so much. As the irrespressible Baron von Steuben observed, while "this glorious peace" had effected an "extraordinary turn" in his spirits, he was still concerned that Congress and the people act promptly to restore the nation's credit. If they would not heed sound advice, he for one was prepared to tell the people just what they could do with their independence.[24]

The commissioners took Livingston's strictures in stride, although neither Adams nor Jay quickly forgave their critics in Congress. While Jay was later to collaborate with two of his critics, James Madison and Alexander Hamilton, in writing *The Federalist* letters, he was not one to forget the key role that the young Virginian had played in supporting the "unwarrantable philippic of censure" which La Luzerne's partisans had futilely sought to ram through Congress.[25] The commissioners were buoyed up by private congratulatory messages, even by one to Jay from Hamilton, who had so roundly denounced him on the floor of Congress. "The peace, which exceeds in the goodness of its terms the expectations of the most sanguine," wrote the Janus-faced delegate from New York, "does the highest honour to those who made it."[26] With his pessimistic view of human nature, Jay was "not surprised that men of certain characters should censure the terms of peace," but consoled himself with the assurance that the majority of the people were content.[27] Considering the complications and perils of the peacemaking and how "all these difficulties were dissipated by one decided step of the British and American minister," John Adams felt only "too strongly" a sense of gratitude to heaven for having been conducted safely through the storms and could not be "very solicitous whether we have the approbation of mortals or not."[28]

Nevertheless, Livingston's letter carried a sting, and the crusty Adams, who was considerably out of sorts, grumbled in reply that "your late dispatches, sir, are not well adapted to give spirits to a melancholy man or to cure one sick of the fever." With uncommon patience he explained that, had the Americans communicated their terms before they signed, Vergennes would have insisted, "You must not sign till we sign." As the Duc de La Vauguyon advised Adams, a Franco-Spanish expedition under d'Estaing would then have sailed from Cádiz, in which case "nobody would have signed to this day." Indeed, had not the commissioners acted contrary to the sentiment of Congress, Adams concluded, "our country would have lost advantages beyond computation."

Jay drafted a joint answer on behalf of all three commissioners then in Paris. Defending the secret article on the ground of expediency and national interest, the Commissioners stoutly declared: "Since we have assumed a place in the political system, let us move like a primary and not like a secondary planet." Out of deference to Franklin's objection, Jay forebore including in the public letter any "justification" of the signing of the preliminaries. The doctor was unable to restrain his younger colleague, however. The very next day Jay came right to the point in a private letter to "Dear Robert." He showed how on every important British concession—independence, boundaries, fisheries, and the Loyalists—the French had advanced views that were "far from being such as America would have preferred." He even went further than Adams and insisted that a postponement of the signing at the likely insistence of Vergennes might, "and probably would," have allowed the British to take advantage of the delay and repudiate Richard Oswald. Such action would have allowed Vergennes more time to press the Americans to moderate demands which, in Jay's judgment, were "too inconsistent with the claims of Spain to meet with his concurrence." In short, "it was a risk of too great importance to run."[29]

In defending their actions the Americans in Paris failed to present a united front. Franklin temporized. France had little ground for complaint, he insisted, since "nothing was stipulated to their prejudice, and none of the stipulations were to have force, but by a subsequent act of their own. . . . We did what appeared to all of us best at the time," he added, "and if we have done wrong, the Congress will do right, after hearing us, to censure us." Had the doctor stopped there he might have allayed criticism of his course, but he went on to qualify his defense of the American commissioners with the gratuitous observation that personally he did not feel that either the controversial letter attributed to Barbé-Marbois or the talks he and Jay had had with French diplomats on the issues of the peace constituted conclusive evidence that "this Court wished to restrain us in obtaining any degree of advantage we could prevail on our enemies to accord. . . . One of my colleagues," he conceded, and he meant Adams, "is of a very different opinion." As John Quincy Adams scathingly remarked many years later, Franklin had a language official and a language confidential. Officially he stood by his colleagues, but privately he let both Vergennes and the delegates in Congress know that the separate preliminaries were not his doing.[30]

Franklin's halfhearted defense, coupled with a previous disclosure by Laurens that he did not fully share his colleagues' suspicions of the French court,[31] provided confirmation, if such were needed, of the lack of unanimity in the councils of the peacemakers. For months partisans of Adams and Franklin had been spreading malicious gossip about the role of one or the other. Almost immediately after the definitive treaty had been signed Franklin felt obliged to call upon Jay and Adams to vindicate his course. Jay's response was fair-minded and generous; Adams', more grudging.[32] Their partisans would not let the matter rest. Years later, and long after Franklin's death, the charge was revived that he had worked secretly against the treaty. Right after the signing of the preliminaries, according to these allegations, the doctor had written James Moylan, the agent of the United States at L'Orient, along with his kinsman Jonathan Williams, that the treaty had been negotiated "without his privity," and would not be confirmed by Congress. Accordingly, he was reputed to have advised them both to continue their commercial speculations, and both were ruined by following this tip. Jasper Moylan, James's brother, told the story to Timothy Pickering, the High Federalist critic of all things French. John Jay was shocked by the story. He still insisted that "Dr. Franklin cooperated with me fairly in obtaining the best terms that we could for our country," and told Pickering that such "strong" accusations needed substantiation. Such substantiating evidence is not found among the extant Franklin papers. On the contrary, by 1782 Franklin had become cautious about entrusting government business to relatives.[33] What is significant is not that Franklin was in fact guilty as charged but rather that the suspicion of conflict of interest would not down despite disclaimers by the doctor, and that in his case the ghost still haunts the peacemaking.

The dispatches from Paris, though varying in intensity, shook up the delegates in Congress, even those most complacent about the French connection. A note of nationalism and even isolationism was quickly sounded. Congress proceeded not only to reject American membership in the Armed Neutrality, but in June unanimously adopted a resolution of Madison's that "the true interest of these states requires that they should be as little as possible entangled in the politics and controversies of European nations."[34]

This resolution merely echoed the sentiments of Jay and Adams. Both had seen enough of the Old World to want to keep the new nation clear of its involvements. "I have but few attachments in Europe much stronger than those we sometimes feel for an accidental fellow traveller, or for a good inn and a civil landlord," Jay confessed to Gouverneur Morris. Like Hamilton back home, he recognized the compelling need for the United States to act "like one nation" if it wished to obtain trade concessions from Great Britain and conserve its diplomatic gains. Having for so long "been a foot-ball between contending nations," Adams remarked to both Whitefoord and Oswald that "it ought to be our rule not to meddle" in European affairs. Later, in a conversation with Markov, the Russian plenipotentiary at Paris, he reputedly declared that America did not plan to have "intimate relations" with any European power.[35] Dr. Franklin meantime continued his quiet negotiations with various European nations to obtain treaties of commerce and amity.

Livingston's unauthorized rebuke stood on the record as the Confederation government's last word on the subject, save to proclaim the end of hostilities on April 12th. Congress grumbled, but ratified the preliminaries nevertheless without including the separate article. Then it proceeded to order the discharge of prisoners-of-war without taking the elementary precaution of obtaining guarantees that the Western posts would be evacuated by the British.[36]

Men talked peace, but there was no peace, merely an armistice pending an exchange of ratifications of the definitive treaty. On November 22, 1783, John Thaxter, Jr., Adams' private secretary abroad, reached Philadelphia with an official copy of the definitive treaty, which he delivered to Thomas Mifflin, only just chosen as President of the Congress. Noting that ratifications were required to be exchanged within six months from the day of signing, Mifflin promptly wrote the governors of the Thirteen States impressing upon them the necessity of having their delegates repair to Congress at once to acquit this last remaining task of the Revolutionary War.

Considering the urgencies of peace one might have expected the delegates to take flight to Annapolis, the nation's temporary capital, on the wings of the dove. Instead, they dragged their heels. New York held off even after the British on November 25th evacuated its principal city. By mid-December delegates from only seven states had made their appearance at Annapolis' State House. For several days they earnestly debated whether a ratification by a bare majority of the Thirteen States would be valid. Thomas Jefferson, now a delegate from Virginia, pointed out to his colleagues that under the Articles of Confederation Congress required the assent of nine states to make a treaty. The situation seemed so desperate that Congress even considered going to Philadelphia and descending upon the sickroom of Richard Beresford, a delegate from South Carolina, in order to secure that state's representation. In despair Jefferson himself backed down, and now proposed that the treaty be ratified by seven states and transmitted to the commissioners, with the instruction that they obtain an extension of time for a proper exchange of ratifications. Should such an extension not be obtainable, they were to offer a partial ratification, accompanied by a pledge that full ratification by nine states would be dispatched just as soon as that number could be assembled. Then, on January 13, 1784, two delegates from Connecticut managed to weather the wintry blasts and put in an appearance. On the following day the convalescing Beresford, the true hero of the ratification, arrived in Annapolis. At last the necessary nine states were represented, and Congress proceeded to vote unanimous ratification at once.[37]

The vote failed to allay the suspense, however, since the delegates realized that a bare six weeks remained to transmit the ratification to Paris in compliance with the terms of the treaty. A race began in earnest.

Three different agents were entrusted with copies of the ratification, and ordered to take passage on the first ship available. Colonel Josiah Harmar dashed to New York to catch a French packet. His ship sailed on January 21st, but ran aground, and he was obliged to return to port. Colonel David Franks was also stranded for weeks on a British packet until the harbor was clear of ice. Both finally got under sail the same day, February 17th, over a month after departing from Annapolis. A third set of ratifications was transmitted to the agent of Marine to be forwarded "by any good opportunity." Harmar reached Paris first, arriving the very end of March, and just ahead of Franks, who reached London the next day. Technically, the ratifications had come too late, but the British Ministry was not disposed to higgle over the delay. On the twelfth of May Franklin and Jay for the United States and Hartley for Great Britain amicably exchanged ratifications in Paris.

The debates in Congress over ratification and the irresponsibility of many of its delegates constitute one of the less creditable episodes in the history of that central agency of the Confederation whose prestige had declined almost to the vanishing point. Well might Charles Thomson, Congress' perennial secretary, remark in a letter to Jay, "There has been a scene for six months past over which I would wish to draw a veil."[38]

At long last the time had come for Americans to celebrate. Even before Congress had ratified the definitive treaty the Pennsylvania Assembly appropriated a sum not to exceed £600 for the erection of a triumphal arch at the upper end of Philadelphia's Market Street. The design and construction were entrusted to the "ingenious" Charles Willson Peale, who was experienced in the use of "transparent paintings" for display. Peale put up a triumphal arch in the style of the Romans, forty feet in height and fifty in width, which he adorned with paintings and inscriptions suitable to the occasion. Among the paintings affixed to the framework of the scaffolding forming the arch was one of George Washington, for which the General sat during a week-long visit to Philadelphia in December, 1783.

Setting a feverish pace, Peale had all in readiness on the night of January 22, 1784, the date fixed for the celebration. As dusk fell some eleven hundred lamps were in place. Peale was perched atop the arch, engaged in fixing the uppermost lamp, when a rocket was set off prematurely, igniting the paper and canvas covering the frame. The arch burst into flames. His clothing afire, Peale dropped twenty feet to the ground, breaking two of his ribs in the descent. A number of spectators were burned and a sergeant of artillery killed in the disaster.[39]

Almost immediately a move was under way to raise the necessary funds to do the paintings all over again. On an impulse Peale offered to make up the difference between the sums raised from the public and the actual cost of the new paintings, a philanthropic gesture which left him considerably out of pocket. Finally, on the evening of May 10th, almost coincidentally to the day when ratifications were to be exchanged in Paris, the triumphal arch, "a marriage of classic Rome and modern Peale," was displayed. This time there were no fireworks, with less spectacular if more successful results.

What the good people of Philadelphia saw fit to commemorate is perhaps worth noting. Over the center arch there appeared in Latin and English this inscription: *"A great and new Order of Ages commences."* A bust of Louis XVI adorned the south side of the balustrade; a pyramidal cenotaph in memory of those who had died for their country appeared on the opposite side. The three lilies, the arms of France, stood conspicuous on the south side of the frieze, in company on their left with the coat-of-arms of Pennsylvania—plow, sheaves of wheat, and a ship under sail. The sun, emblematic of France, and the thirteen stars, for the United States, were represented still further along the frieze, the two emblems bound together by the motto: *"Caelo Sociato"*—"Allied in the Heavens." Other ornamentation commemorated peace and commerce, the fidelity of the army, the Christianizing of the Indians, and the arts and sciences, which were symbolized by a library building. The next pedestal was decorated with a large tree bearing thirteen principal and distinct branches laden with fruit (*"By the Strength of the Body will these ripen"*), along with a large figure of Cincinnatus crowned with laurel returning to his plow, the countenance of the Roman patriot bearing a striking resemblance to General Washington. To underscore the Roman motif Peale inscribed on the spandrels of the center arch the letters *"S.P.Q.P."* (The Senate and People of Pennsylvania).[40] Everything and everybody, it would seem, even the mutinous militia, were duly commemorated, save the persons responsible for the occasion—the peacemakers themselves.

Peale's artistic oversight by no manner of means reflected the vast reservoir of goodwill that the rank-and-file of the American people were storing up for the peacemakers. Quickly forgotten were the years of partisan wrangling and backbiting in Congress when the negotiators came home. Jay and Laurens were the first to return, both in the summer of 1784. The former was given the freedom of his native city,[41] and learned on his arrival that he had been elected Secretary for Foreign Affairs, a post that Livingston had relinquished. Jay conducted the foreign relations of the nation until he became the first Chief Justice of the United States, and ended his public career as a two-term Governor of New York. Choosing retirement in preference to another term as Chief Justice, he was fated to outlive all those connected with the peacemaking in Paris save Benjamin Vaughan and Alleyne Fitzherbert.

Prematurely aged by imprisonment, grief, and illness, Laurens returned to South Carolina to find his plantations ravaged, his Charleston town house a virtual shambles. Painstakingly he set to work to rebuild his estate, preferring to end his days in rural retreat rather than to accept the variety of political offices a grateful state showered upon him. In death the contentious peacemaker was as unconventional as in life. Laurens' will directed that he be cremated, and upon his death in 1792 in his sixty-ninth year a funeral pyre was built atop a hill looking down upon his mansion. Save for some aboriginal Americans, Laurens is the first person known to have been cremated in America. Appropriately his ashes were buried beside the grave of his son, Colonel John Laurens, Revolutionary War hero, who had shared his father's advanced and nonconforming views espousing the emancipation of Negro slaves.[42]

Perhaps the least concerned of all the commissioners as to how the peace was received, Benjamin Franklin had expressed to a scientific colleague in England the fervent wish that peace would be "lasting, and that mankind will at length, as they call themselves reasonable creatures, have reason and sense enough to settle their differences without cutting throats; for, in my opinion, *there never was a good war or a bad peace.*"[43] No unpleasantness marred the doctor's homecoming in 1785, and he was agreeably surprised at the warmth of the reception his fellow Philadelphians accorded him. Although his long vigil abroad had spanned thirty years, during which he had scant time for private affairs, the doctor found that his estate had more than trebled in value since the Revolution as a result of the rise in real property.[44] In his eightieth year the grand old man of the Revolution was chosen to serve as president of the Executive Council of Pennsylvania. "They have eaten my flesh," he remarked humorously of his countrymen, "and seem resolved now to pick my bones."[45] At the age of eighty-two he took his seat in the Constitutional Convention. Fittingly, his last public act was to affix his signature to a memorial to Congress for the abolition of slavery. His death in 1790 proved to be as sorrowful an occasion to the French people as it was to his fellow Americans. The National Assembly decreed three days of mourning.[46] He who had restrained "alike thunderbolts and tyrants," as his friend Mirabeau remarked on that occasion, had been a devoted friend of France and had seen that friendship put to the severest tests.

Last of the four American peacemakers to return to his native shore was that unreconstructed New England Puritan, John Adams. Before coming home Adams served a stint as Minister to the Court of St. James's. As a Tory refugee friend of old, Jonathan Sewall, remarked, he lacked the personality and peculiar talents for diplomacy as the art was then practiced. "He can't dance, drink, game, flatter, promise, dress, swear with gentlemen, and small talk and flirt with the ladies—in short, he has none of the essential *arts* or *ornaments* which make a courtier—there are thousands who with a tenth part of his understanding, and without a spark of his honesty, would distance him infinitely in any court in Europe."[47] Considering his intemperate style and prickly manner, Adams had done much better than many of his contemporaries were prepared to concede. On his homecoming in 1788 he was greeted by a volley from the fort in Boston, and escorted to Braintree by a squadron of light cavalry. Even before his arrival he had been elected a delegate to the Congress, but much greater honors were in store, the Vice Presidency under Washington and the Presidency.

The other peacemakers had more reason to be concerned about their respective fates than had the Americans. The British had surrendered an empire and were not allowed to forget it. Well might it have been written in ancient times, "Blessed are the peacemakers," remarked Caleb Whitefoord, whose signature, along with that of William Temple Franklin, adorned the preliminary treaty as a witness, "but in those of modern date *on a changé tout cela,* and changed too with a vengeance."[48] "Are we to be hanged or applauded for thus rescuing you from the American War?" Strachey asked an associate back home. He confessed the night before the signing that he was "half dead with perpetual anxiety, and shall not be at ease until I see how the Great Men receive me." "God forbid I should ever have a hand in another peace," he declared the following night.[49] Benjamin Vaughan could have added a loud "Amen," for, as he later recalled, Oswald and himself "healed wounds as fast as Mr. Strachey made them."[50]

Lord Shelburne remembered well the fate of Lord Bute, whose protégé he had been. He was reconciled to being vilified, but at least wanted to be certain that he could not be properly charged with exploiting his inside knowledge of the moment the war would end by making a killing on the Exchange. Accordingly, about a week in advance, he notified the Director of the Bank of England and the Lord Mayor of

London that the negotiations had reached a concluding point. In revenge the speculators and Opposition party hacks accused the Earl, without a shadow of proof of course, of taking advantage of his official position to speculate. One of the most celebrated of Gillray's caricatures depicts the Earl, with a booted and spurred French courier on his left just arrived from Paris bearing news that the preliminaries had been signed, and on his right a group of Jewish moneylenders waiting to receive payment of sums allegedly advanced on the security of Shelburne House, and about to be paid off with the fruits of stock manipulation. On the wall before the Minister were hung the portraits of Ignatius Loyola, Malagrida, and Calvin. It was no coincidence that the same charges had been leveled against Lord Bute, the former owner of Shelburne House, at the time of the Peace of 1763. That they could again be raised proved an evil omen of what might be in store for so dedicated and forward-looking a public servant as the Earl of Shelburne.[51] Blame was attached to him not only for the preliminaries but also for the definitive peace, which was the responsibility of his successors. These final treaties were denounced by the English press as a "Sun-Set peace," an ill-humored allusion to Shelburne's unfortunate phrase. Somehow and in some unfathomable way, the nation felt betrayed.

Though elevated in rank and title as the Marquess of Lansdowne, Shelburne never served in His Majesty's government again. Pitt, cold and remorseless for all his twenty-four years, took a firm hold on the reins of power shortly after the definitive treaties had been signed. Although he had been Shelburne's protégé he saw to it that the Jesuit of Berkeley Square was frozen out. His personal following gone, his few supporters either dead of incapacitated, Shelburne confessed to the Abbé Morellet in 1786 that he was "growing very insignificant, very fast in the political world."[52] In his sylvan retreat at Bowood Lansdowne played host to a dazzling array of British and Continental intellectuals. A Tory radical, he was untouched by the conservative contagion which swept England in the wake of the French Revolution. That cataclysm, oddly enough, brought him much closer to his ancient enemy, Charles James Fox, than had the exigencies of the peace back in 1782. Time mellowed the judgments of Americans about Shelburne's role if it did little to temper the strictures of his compatriots. Back in 1782 John Adams could denounce the Earl as "a palaverer beyond all description," while he was later to concede that Shelburne was "a better friend to America" than either Fox or Burke.[53] So far as the peacemaking is concerned few if any would now presume to challenge Adams' retrospective evaluation, for the peace that was concluded by Shelburne's successors fell considerably short of his idea of reconciliation "on the noblest terms and by the noblest means."[54]

Boreas and Reynard did not long survive the definitive peace. The coalition's downfall was less the consequence of its role in the making of an unpopular peace than of its proposals to shake up the government of India. The King, who had been biding his time, instructed his followers to give the detested Ministry the *coup de grâce,* and in the crisis Fox's loyal follower, the Prince of Wales, failed him. North like Shelburne retired from active competition, but Fox's cumulative blunders obliged him to sit for more than twenty-two years on the Opposition benches.

Richard Oswald, the old-time slave trader whom tough-minded British politicians regarded as a simple merchant and a political innocent, went down to Dover in 1784 to bid farewell to John and Sally Jay when they set out for New York. He died not long thereafter. Franklin commented on his death: "It is unlucky, I think in the affairs of this world, that the wise and good, be as mortal as common people, and that they often die before others are found fit to supply their places.[55] Caleb Whitefoord, the diligent and companionable secretary to the British commission, whom Burke dismissed as a mere *diseur des bons mots,* was neglected by his government, and only after repeated representations and a delay of seven years did he receive some compensation for his services and outlays in Paris, to which was later added a modest pension.[56]

When Franklin sailed for home he bade a touching farewell to his "dear friend Mr. Hartley." "We were long fellow labourers in the best of all works, the work of peace," he wrote. "I leave you still in the field, but having finished my day's task, I am going home to *go to bed!* Wish me a good night's rest, as I do you a pleasant evening. Adieu!"[57] For Hartley, the year of his last mission in Paris, to which he returned to exchange ratifications of the peace treaty, also saw his final defeat at the polls. He spent the remaining three decades of his life in retirement, continuing to correspond with Franklin, Jay, and Jefferson on American affairs, to act the courageous and outspoken liberal during the frenzy of the French Revolution, and his last days found him peacefully absorbed in studies in political philosophy.

Like Hartley, Benjamin Vaughan was convinced of the grandeur of America's future. He toyed with the notion of going to the States on Jay's advice almost immediately after the conclusion of the peace, but put off his emigration for over a decade, during which he devoted himself to political matters and free trade. An enthusiast for the French Revolution, he abruptly terminated his career in Parliament by fleeing to France when his government pressed an investigation of English radicals. In Paris he was imprisoned in a Carmelite monastery, only to be released through the good offices of Robespierre. In 1796 he followed his family to America, settling at Hallowell, Maine, on family estates. In that more peaceful world to which he had made his own very peculiar contribution he found it possible to pursue literary and scientific studies over the many years still in store for him.

As for the monarch who had so stubbornly held off the concession of independence, thereby delaying the peace for years, George III was sadly dispirited by the terms of that peace to which he had at last consented with such ill grace, but he was to be even more provoked by the antagonistic behavior of the Prince of Wales and his younger brother Prince Frederick. Cunning in political strategy and shrewd in appraising public opinion, George suffered intermittent spells of insanity. King in name for almost forty years after the peace, George was adjudged no longer fit to rule during the last nine years of his reign when his detested son and rival, the Prince of Wales, acted as regent.[58]

Charles Gravier, the Comte de Vergennes, who for years had been juggling a half dozen balls without managing to drop any, found that the coming of peace called for a new set of parlor tricks. Indefatigable and shrewd, rather than brilliant or original, he knew how to put the best possible face on adversity and to create the illusion that everything was working according to plan. This was a considerable talent, but it was less than genius. A realist, the Comte privately did not delude himself about what he had accomplished. When an English correspondent sent him a eulogy, including the assertion that "the United States of America are bound in gratitude to erect a monument to his memory," he requested his admirer to refrain from publishing his remarks in the English papers.[59] He knew that in actuality if not in law the Franco-American alliance was at an end. "We have never based our policy toward the United States upon their gratitude," he wrote La Luzerne even before he had heard of the Congressional resolution against entanglement in European affairs. "That sentiment is infinitely rare between sovereigns, and republics know it not."[60]

Gratitude or no, Vergennes merits recognition as the chief architect of the Franco-American alliance. That alliance, observed Benjamin Vaughan in retrospect, was not "the vile speculation" that Vergennes' French critics called it during the French Revolution. Neither was it "a pure act of philanthropy." Its primary aim was to strengthen France at England's expense.[61] It was an expression of Vergennes' mechanistic conception of countervailing power, of his desire to right the balance so disarranged by the previous war. Vergennes fought what he thought was a war for limited gains, one which, by fixing the American satellite to France's orbit, would enhance French prestige and diminish Britain's to the same extent. Total victory was never within his purview. Such a prospect, as he saw it, would have only served to unite an alarmed Europe against France. Trapped by superannuated formulas, the Comte never seems to have realized that he had involved his own nation in a new kind of war without the least commitment on his part to spreading revolutionary ideas which he in fact abhorred. Having exposed his own people to the contagion of liberty, he might have expected them to break out with some of its more disturbing symptoms.

Measuring Vergennes by his own yardstick, the enhancement of France's national interest, one can only conclude that his gains were meager and short-lived. America proved a restless satellite. She had already begun to pull out of France's diplomatic orbit, and had never been firmly fixed in the French economic orbit. The new republic failed to return to France the solid dividends Vergennes had anticipated when he made the commercial treaty with the United States in 1778, a pact whose liberal trade features were confirmed by Order in Council of August 30, 1784. Once the war was over, the United States exploited its advantage of being able to export raw materials to the French Islands, and, with the proceeds, to import in large quantities manufactured goods from England rather than France. Similarly, a liberalized trade treaty which Vergennes made with England inundated France with British manufactures, and contributed to her growing economic crisis.[62]

On the European Continent the ties that Vergennes had formed were soon loosened, as France's other and equally difficult allies proved extremely restive under the Comte's magisterial eye. Although the King of Spain made the gesture of conferring upon him the Order of Charles III,[63] there was little satisfaction in the Spanish camp with the results of Vergennes' war. France's other ally, the Dutch, accused Vergennes of having let them down in the peacemaking, an accusation by no means ill-founded. The Dutch had additional reason to be unhappy about the role France played in the quarrel which subsequently broke out between Joseph II and the United Provinces over the opening of the Scheldt. Vergennes' ambassador to Holland, the Marquis de Vérac, was outmaneuvered and outclassed by Britain's audacious Minister to the Hague, Sir James Harris. Almost singlehanded the latter managed to reassert Britain's paramount influence in the Dutch Republic and nullify Vergennes' influence.[64]

Perhaps the greatest blow to the power structure that the Comte de Vergennes had so painstakingly rebuilt came out of the East. "I do not feel tranquil in spirit," he wrote the Comte de Montmorin on the day the definitive peace treaties were signed, "seeing that the affairs of the Levant will replace those of America."[65] Vergennes was alluding to the moves that Catherine II had already disclosed as part of her long-range plans to reorganize European Turkey. Seizing upon a flimsy pretext, the Empress had unilaterally proclaimed the annexation of the Crimea. Vergennes might protest, but without the help of England he could not curb the Russian bear, and Charles James Fox was in no mood for further broils.[66] The most that the Comte could accomplish was to keep Joseph II from sharing in the spoils and detaching Moldavia and Walachia from the Turkish Empire. Joseph's hesitancy, however, failed to deter Catherine from moving unilaterally. "When the cake is ready, everyone will develop an appetite," she told Potëmkin.[67] With Poland already weakened by partition, the seizure of the Crimea in open scorn of the Sublime Porte attested to the degree of disintegration taking place in the satellite system Vergennes had so tirelessly cultivated.[68]

"Nothing but death could remove the Comte," Rayneval told Hartley on the eve of the signing of the definitive peace.[69] Rayneval proved an accurate prophet, for despite a formidable combination of enemies in the persons of Castries, Breteuil, and Marie Antoinette herself, Vergennes held the reins of powers until his death in 1787. He died before national bankruptcy, in no small part the result of France's participation in his American War, set off a great conflagration. Before it had consumed itself all Europe was scorched from end to end, Vergennes' royal master and mistress had sacrificed their heads, and his diplomatic triumphs had been reduced to ashes.

Of Vergennes' aides identified in one way or another with American affairs and the peacemaking, Rayneval was destined to spend the greater part of the French Revolutionary years in forced retirement, and to devote himself thereafter to writing tracts in international law. His brother, Conrad Alexandre Gérard, abandoned diplomacy upon his return from America for a career as a magistrate in Strasbourg. With the start of the French Revolution he resigned his post and died the following year. Gérard's successor, the Chevalier de La Luzerne, stayed long enough in America to be intrigued by the spirit of equality he found there, fascinated by the abundant life which the people of the lower orders shared with their betters, and impressed by the familiarity of the American people with the mechanisms of self-government. Perhaps more than his master, he recognized the foresight of the American peacemakers in fixing national boundaries with a seemingly limitless potential for Western expansion.[70] The

Chevalier faced the revolution in America with a greater degree of equanimity than he did the subsequent one in France. His own brother, Caesar-Henri, was forced out of office as Minister of Marine in 1790, and the following year, while serving as ambassador to England, the Chevalier died of a paralytic complaint. Arrangements were made to have him interred in the family estate at Beuzenville in Lower Normandy, but the Chevalier was not allowed to rest in peace. His remains were disinterred and thrown into the River Orne by revolutionary die-hards.[71]

The years following the Peace of 1783 would also prove turbulent ones for the Chevalier's Secretary of Legation, Barbé-Marbois. Seized and deported to French Guiana in 1797 (his exile contributing to his American wife's mental breakdown), he returned to France at the accession of Bonaparte. He filled, among other posts, that of Minister of Finance, in which capacity, ironically, he negotiated with his long-time friend, Robert R. Livingston, the sale of Louisiana. By an unprecedented stroke of generosity, at Napoleon's prompting, he thus more than made up for his earlier assiduous efforts to trim America's territorial aspirations down to size.[72]

For Vergennes' spy, Louis-Valentin Goëzmann, a grim fate was in store. On July 25, 1794, he was guillotined at Paris as an enemy of the people.[73] The dread Committee of Public Safety had finally caught up with a secret agent of the peacemaking, and few will argue that he did not at last get his just deserts.

In a lengthy defense of his foreign policy, the Conde de Floridablanca pointed with pride to the reacquisition of the Floridas at the peace and the settlements over Honduras and Campeche, and argued that, by sealing off the Gulf of Mexico to foreign penetration, he had achieved a major objective of Spanish diplomacy. His was an arid pride and his gains of the short-run variety. Ultimately the free navigation of the Mississippi had to be yielded to the Americans, Louisiana was to be turned back to France, and by the latter to America, and the Floridas lost. By putting off recognition of the United States and making aid dependent upon concessions the Americans could not afford to make, the Conde signally sacrificed an opportunity to win the new nation's friendship and gratitude. With Spain it was a case of too little and too late.[74]

In his latter days Floridablanca was haunted by the specter of that other revolution, which threatened to spill across the Pyrenees and engulf the Spanish monarchy. In 1790, while walking alone in the royal palace at Aranjuez, he was stabbed in the back by a man who cried out, "*Muera este pícaro!*"* The would-be assassin, an unbalanced Frenchman, was executed

* "Death to the scoundrel!"

in Madrid,[75] and although Floridablanca, now a thoroughgoing counter-revolutionary, survived the stabbing, it was only to be dismissed by his King and supplanted by his archrival, the Conde de Aranda. The latter took no chances, but arrested Floridablanca and confined him in the fortress of Pamplona.

Unlike Floridablanca, Aranda had accepted the results of the American Revolution with considerable good humor, while not deceiving himself about the threat that the new American republic posed to the Spanish Empire in America. In the late spring of '83, he remarked to John Adams, as the latter recorded it, "*Tout, en ce monde, a été Révolution.*" Adams replied didactically, "History is but a string of them." As for himself, Adams confessed, "One revolution is quite enough for the life of a man." He hoped he never would "have to do with another." Aranda laughed heartily, and declared, "I do believe you."[76]

Sensitive to the revolutionary climate of the age, the Conde sought to reverse his predecessor's policies and for a time, until the arrest of the French royal family, to relax the official attitudes toward the French Revolution. Replaced as First Secretary by Manuel de Godoy, Aranda was dismissed from the Council and banished from Madrid. The aged statesman never returned to the Spanish capital.

Within days after the signing of the definitive treaties the brothers Montgolfier, French inventors, demonstrated a successful balloon ascension in Paris. By the late fall of '83 flights as long as twenty-five minutes had been made across the Seine, and to an altitude of almost ten thousand feet. People chose to forget the long war that had just ended and to ignore the new war clouds then darkening the eastern sky. In Paris the talk was of nothing but balloons. "Don't you begin to think of taking your passage in one next spring?" Sally Jay wrote to John, who had gone on a trip to England. Caught up in the fad, seamstresses planned balloon petticoats to permit air travel, and serious thinkers argued that balloons upset the new balance of power and would give France military supremacy.[77]

Air travel and air domination may have seemed like flights of fancy in the year 1783, but the revolutionary age which the American War for Independence heralded proved a reality that few European statesmen grasped. Neither of the Bourbon partners had much to fear from America, a French Foreign Office memorandum pointed out to the Spaniards by way of consolation. The new nation could be expected to share the lethargy of other republics, compounded by sectional rivalries.[78] In downgrading the durable character of the American republic Vergennes by no means stood alone among the statesmen of Europe. Baron von der Goltz, the Prussian ambassador at Paris, saw in America "only a people poor, exhausted, and afflicted with the vices of corrupt nations." His monarch, the great Frederick, predicted that "little by little, colony by colony, province by province," the Americans would "rejoin England and their former footing."[79]

Men of little vision and less faith could not discern the shape of things to come. It was this prescience with which the American commissioners were endowed which rendered their diplomacy at once so effectual and by the same token so distasteful to their European counterparts, save for visionaries like Oswald and Hartley. Franklin, Jay and Company were instruments of a new revolutionary society. They were principals in a great confrontation of the Old Order and the New. The Old Order, in which even adversaries were bound together by ties of blood and caste, was unaccustomed to treating as equals men of lesser social rank. With its balance-of-power politics, its pseudo-Machiavellian ethics, and its objectives of limited gains, the Old Order could not comprehend revolutionary ends, which, in the rhetoric of the day so faithfully reported from America by Barbé-Marbois, could accept "no middle ground" between "slavery and liberty."[80]

True, the Peace of Paris and Versailles of 1783 was no *diktat* forced upon a conquered people, but rather a negotiated peace with an adversary who had managed, aside from North America, to avoid humiliating defeat. Such a peace involved concessions on both sides. What was so remarkable about the achievements of the American commissioners was that where they compromised it was on inessentials and where they conceded it was to yield the trivial. From beginning to end they remained unswerving on the score of obtaining both absolute independence and a continental domain for thirteen littoral states. On the main objectives of national survival they proved uncompromising.[81] Because the American commissioners resolutely contended for the right of a sovereign people to choose their own form of government and because they secured grudging recognition of that right from the Old Order, a free people is eternally in their debt.

Years later in Paris Bonaparte was to tell Robert R. Livingston, "You have come to a very corrupt world."[82] Jay and Adams had discovered that for themselves long before. The peacemaking began as an encounter between innocence and guile, but the Americans rapidly acquired a measure of sophistication sufficient for the task at hand. Neophytes in the arts of secret diplomacy at the start, they were the peers of their Old World counterparts at the finish. "Undisciplined marines as we were," Adams commented, "we were better tacticians than was imagined."[83]

The Definitive Treaty of Peace

Signed at Paris, September 3, 1783[1]

In the Name of the most Holy & undivided Trinity.

It having pleased the divine Providence to dispose the Hearts of the most Serene and most Potent Prince George the third, by the Grace of God, King of Great Britain, France & Ireland, Defender of the Faith, Duke of Brunswick and Lunebourg, Arch Treasurer, and Prince Elector of the Holy Roman Empire &c[a] and of the United States of America, to forget all past Misunderstandings and Differences that have unhappily interrupted the good Correspondence and Friendship which they mutually wish to restore; and to establish such a beneficial and satisfactory Intercourse between the two Countries upon the Ground of reciprocal Advantages and mutual Convenience as may promote and secure to both perpetual Peace & Harmony,[2] and having for this desirable End already laid the Foundation of Peace & Reconciliation by the Provisional Articles signed at Paris on the 30th of Nov[r] 1782. by the Commissioners empower'd on each Part, which Articles were agreed to be inserted in and to constitute the Treaty of Peace proposed to be concluded between the Crown of Great Britain and the said United States, but which Treaty was not to be concluded until Terms of Peace should be agreed upon between Great Britain & France, And his Britannic Majesty should be ready to conclude such Treaty accordingly: and the Treaty between Great Britain & France having since been concluded, His Britannic Majesty & the United States of America, in Order to carry into full Effect the Provisional Articles abovementioned, according to the Tenor thereof, have constituted & appointed, that is to say His Britannic Majesty on his Part, David Hartley Esq[r], Member of the Parliament of Great Britain; and the said United States on their Part, John Adams Esq[r], late a Commissioner of the United States of America at the Court of Versailles, late Delegate in Congress from the State of Massachusetts and Chief Justice of the said State, and Minister Plenipotentiary of the said United States to their High Mightinesses the States General of the United Netherlands; Benjamin Franklin Esq[re] late Delegate in Congress from the State of Pennsylvania, President of the Convention of the s[d] State, and Minister Plenipotentiary from the United States of America at the Court of Versailles; John Jay Esq[re] late President of Congress, and Chief Justice of the State of New-York & Minister Plenipotentiary from the said United States at the Court of Madrid; to be the Plenipotentiaries for the concluding and signing the Present Definitive Treaty; who after having reciprocally communicated their respective full Powers have agreed upon and confirmed the following Articles.

ARTICLE 1st

His Britannic Majesty acknowledges the s^d United States, viz. New-Hampshire Massachusetts Bay, Rhode-Island & Providence Plantations, Connecticut, New York, New Jersey, Pennsylvania, Delaware, Maryland, Virginia, North Carolina, South Carolina & Georgia, to be free sovereign & Independent States; that he treats with them as such, and for himself his Heirs & Successors, relinquishes all Claims to the Government Propriety & Territorial Rights of the same & every Part thereof.

ARTICLE 2^d.

And that all Disputes which might arise in future on the Subject of the Boundaries of the said United States, may be prevented, it is hereby agreed and declared, that the following are and shall be their Boundaries, Viz. From the North West Angle of Nova Scotia, viz. That Angle which is formed by a Line drawn due North from the Source of Saint Croix River to the Highlands along the said Highlands which divide those Rivers that empty themselves into the River St Lawrence, from those which fall into the Atlantic Ocean, to the Northwestern-most Head of Connecticut River: Thence down along the middle of that River to the forty fifth Degree of North Latitude; From thence by a Line due West on said Latitude until it strikes the River Iroquois or Cataraquy; Thence along the middle of said River into Lake Ontario; through the Middle of said Lake until it strikes the Communication by Water between that Lake & Lake Erie; Thence along the middle of said Communication into Lake Erie; through the middle of said Lake, until it arrives at the Water Communication between that Lake & Lake Huron; Thence along the middle of said Water-Communication into the Lake Huron, thence through the middle of said Lake to the Water Communication between that Lake and Lake Superior, thence through Lake Superior Northward of the Isles Royal & Phelipeaux to the Long Lake; Thence through the Middle of said Long-Lake, and the Water Communication between it & the Lake of the Woods, to the said Lake of the Woods; Thence through the said Lake to the most Northwestern Point thereof, and from thence on a due West Course to the River Mississippi, Thence by a Line to be drawn along the Middle of the said River Mississippi until it shall intersect the Northernmost Part of the thirty first Degree of North Latitude. South, by a Line to be drawn due East from the Determination of the Line last mentioned, in the Latitude of thirty one Degrees North of the Equator to the middle of the River Apalachicola or Catahouche. Thence along the middle thereof to its Junction with the Flint River; Thence strait to the Head of St Mary's River, and thence down along the middle of St Mary's River to the Atlantic Ocean. East, by a Line to be drawn along the Middle of the River St Croix, from its Mouth in the Bay of Fundy to its Source; and from its Source directly North to the aforesaid Highlands, which divide the Rivers that fall into the Atlantic Ocean, from those which fall into the River St Lawrence; comprehending all Islands within twenty Leagues of any Part of the Shores of the United States, & lying between Lines to be drawn due East from

the Points where the aforesaid Boundaries between Nova Scotia on the one Part and
East Florida on the other, shall respectively touch the Bay of Fundy and the Atlantic
Ocean, excepting such Islands as now are or heretofore have been within the Limits of
the said Province of Nova Scotia.

ARTICLE 3ᵈ.

It is agreed that the People of the United States shall continue to enjoy unmolested the Right to take Fish of every kind on the Grand Bank and on all the
other Banks of New-foundland, also in the Gulph of St Lawrence, and at all other
Places in the Sea where the Inhabitants of both Countries used at any time heretofore
to fish. And also that the Inhabitants of the United States shall have Liberty to take
Fish of every Kind on such Part of the Coast of New-foundland as British Fishermen
shall use, (but not to dry or cure the same on that Island) And also on the Coasts Bays
& Creeks of all other of his Britannic Majesty's Dominions in America, and that the
American Fishermen shall have Liberty to dry and cure Fish in any of the unsettled
Bays Harbours and Creeks of Nova Scotia, Magdalen Islands, and Labrador, so long
as the same shall remain unsettled but so soon as the same or either of them shall be
settled, it shall not be lawful for the said Fishermen to dry or cure Fish at such Settlement, without a previous Agreement for that purpose with the Inhabitants, Proprietors
or Possessors of the Ground.

ARTICLE 4ᵗʰ

It is agreed that Creditors on either Side shall meet with no lawful Impediment to
the Recovery of the full Value in Sterling Money of all bona fide Debts heretofore
contracted.

ARTICLE 5ᵗʰ

It is agreed that the Congress shall earnestly recommend it to the Legislatures of the
respective States to provide for the Restitution of all Estates, Rights and Properties
which have been confiscated belonging to real British Subjects; and also of the Estates
Rights and Properties of Persons resident in Districts in the Possession of his Majesty's
Arms, and who have not borne Arms against the said United States. And that Persons
of any other Description shall have free Liberty to go to any Part or Parts of any of
the thirteen United States and therein to remain twelve Months unmolested in their
Endeavours to obtain the Restitution of such of their Estates Rights & Properties as
may have been confiscated. And that Congress shall also earnestly recommend to the
several States, a Reconsideration and Revision of all Acts or Laws regarding the
Premises, so as to render the said Laws or Acts perfectly consistent, not only with
Justice and Equity, but with that Spirit of Conciliation, which, on the Return of the
Blessings of Peace should universally prevail. And that Congress shall also earnestly
recommend to the several States, that the Estates, Rights and Properties of such last
mentioned Persons shall be restored to them, they refunding to any Persons who
may be now in Possession, the Bonâ fide Price (where any has been given) which such

Persons may have paid on purchasing any of the said Lands, Rights or Properties, since the Confiscation.

And it is agreed that all Persons who have any Interest in confiscated Lands, either by Debts, Marriage Settlements, or otherwise, shall meet with no lawful Impediment in the Prosecution of their just Rights.

ARTICLE 6.th

That there shall be no future Confiscations made nor any Prosecutions commenc'd against any Person or Persons for or by Reason of the Part, which he or they may have taken in the present War, and that no Person shall on that Account suffer any future Loss or Damage, either in his Person Liberty or Property; and that those who may be in Confinement on such Charges at the Time of the Ratification of the Treaty in America shall be immediately set at Liberty, and the Prosecutions so commenced be discontinued.

ARTICLE 7.th

There shall be a firm and perpetual Peace between his Britannic Majesty and the said States and between the Subjects of the one, and the Citizens of the other, wherefore all Hostilities both by Sea and Land shall from henceforth cease: All Prisoners on both Sides shall be set at Liberty, and his Britannic Majesty shall with all convenient speed, and without causing any Destruction, or carrying away any Negroes or other Property of the American Inhabitants, withdraw all his Armies, Garrisons & Fleets from the said United States, and from every Port, Place and Harbour within the same; leaving in all Fortifications the American Artillery that may be therein: And shall also Order & cause all Archives, Records, Deeds & Papers belonging to any of the said States, or their Citizens, which in the Course of the War may have fallen into the Hands of his Officers, to be forthwith restored and deliver'd to the proper States and Persons to whom they belong.

ARTICLE 8.th

The Navigation of the River Mississippi, from its source to the Ocean shall for ever remain free and open to the Subjects of Great Britain and the Citizens of the United States.

ARTICLE 9.th

In Case it should so happen that any Place or Territory belonging to great Britain or to the United States should have been conquer'd by the Arms of either from the other before the Arrival of the said Provisional Articles in America it is agreed that the same shall be restored without Difficulty and without requiring any Compensation.

ARTICLE 10.th

The solemn Ratifications of the present Treaty expedited in good & due Form shall be exchanged between the contracting Parties in the Space of Six Months or sooner if possible to be computed from the Day of the Signature of the present Treaty. In Witness whereof we the undersigned their Ministers Plenipotentiary have in their Name and in Virtue of our Full Powers signed with our Hands the present Definitive Treaty, and caused the Seals of our Arms to be affix'd thereto.[3]

Done at Paris, this third Day of September, In the Year of our Lord one thousand seven hundred & eighty three.

D HARTLEY   JOHN ADAMS.   B FRANKLIN   JOHN JAY[4]

[Seal]   [Seal]   [Seal]   [Seal]

Notes

A   Conde de Aranda
AF   Alleyne Fitzherbert (Baron St. Helens)
BF   Benjamin Franklin
BV   Benjamin Vaughan
CG   Conrad Alexandre Gérard
DH   David Hartley
F   Conde de Floridablanca
G   George III
H   Earl of Hillsborough
HL   Henry Laurens
JA   John Adams
JH   Sir James Harris (1st Earl of Malmesbury)
JJ   John Jay
K   Prince Wenzel Anton Kaunitz-Rietberg
L   Chevalier Anne César de La Luzerne
LV   Duc de La Vauguyon
M   Comte de Montmorin
MA   Marie Antoinette
MDA   Comte Mercy d'Argenteau
MT   Maria Theresa
O   Richard Oswald
R   Joseph Matthias Gérard de Rayneval
RRL   Robert R. Livingston
S   William Petty, 2nd Earl of Shelburne (1st Marquess of Lansdowne)
ST   David Murray, Lord Stormont
TG   Thomas Robinson (2nd Baron Grantham)
TT   Thomas Townshend (Baron Sydney)
V   Charles Gravier, Comte de Vergennes
W   Thomas Thynne (3rd Viscount Weymouth)

Adm.   Admiralty Papers (Public Record Office, London)
A.G.   Archives du Ministère de la Guerre (Château de Vincennes)

AGI   Archivo General de Indias (Seville)
AHN, E Archivo Histórico Nacional, Estado series (Madrid)
A.M.   Archives de la Marine (Archives Nationales, Paris)
AMON   Archives ou Correspondance Inédite de la Maison d'Orange-Nassau, 5th ser., ed. by F. J. L. Kramer (Leyden, 1915)
AN   Archives Nationales (Paris)
AP   Adams Family Papers (Massachusetts Historical Society)
ARH   Algemeen Rijksarchief, The Hague
BFAW   Benjamin Franklin's Autobiographical Writings, ed. by Carl Van Doren (New York, 1945)
BFB   John Bigelow, ed., The Complete Works of Benjamin Franklin (10 vols., New York, 1887-88)
BFS   Albert H. Smyth, ed., The Writings of Benjamin Franklin (10 vols., New York, 1905-07)
BM   British Museum
BN   Bibliothèque Nationale
CG   Correspondence of King George the Third (1760-1783), ed. by Sir John Fortescue (6 vols., London, 1928)
CL   William L. Clements Library, University of Michigan
CO   Colonial Office Papers (Public Record Office, London)
CP   Correspondance politique, Ministère des Affaires Étrangères (Paris)
            CP A   Correspondance politique, Angleterre
            CP Aut Correspondance politique, Autriche
            CP E   Correspondance politique, Espagne
            CP EU   Correspondance politique, États-Unis
            CP H   Correspondance politique, Hollande
            CP R   Correspondance politique, Russie
D   Henri Doniol, Histoire de la Participation de la France à l'établissement des États-Unis d'Amérique (5 vols., Paris, 1886-92)
DC   Manuel Danvila y Collado, Reinado de Carlos III (5 vols., Madrid, 1893-94)
Diary   Diary and Autobiography of John Adams, ed. by L. H. Butterfield (4 vols., Cambridge, Mass., 1961)
FC   Memorials and Correspondence of Charles James Fox, ed. by Lord John Russell (3 vols., London, 1853)
FO   Foreign Office Papers (Public Record Office, London)
FP   Papers of Benjamin Franklin (Yale University Library)
FS   Lord Edmond Fitzmaurice, Life of William, Earl of Shelburne (3 vols., London, 1876)
GP   Grantham Papers (Bedfordshire Rolls Office)
HLP   Henry Laurens Papers (South Carolina Historical Society)
HMC, R Royal Commission on Historical Manuscripts, Reports (London, 1874——)
HP   Sir Lewis Namier and John Brooke, The History of Parliament: The House of Commons, 1754-1790 (3 vols., New York, 1964)
JAW   Works of John Adams, ed. by Charles Francis Adams (10 vols., Boston, 1850-56)
JCC   Journals of the Continental Congress, ed. by W. C. Ford and Gaillard Hunt (34 vols., Washington, 1904-37)
JP   Papers of John Jay (Special Collections, Columbia University Libraries)
JPJ   Correspondence and Public Papers of John Jay, ed. by H. P. Johnston (4 vols., New York, 1890-93)
KBGS   Königlich Bayerisches Geheimes Staatsarchiv (Munich—microfilm LC)
LC   Library of Congress

LMCC *Letters of Members of the Continental Congress,* comp. by E. C. Burnett (8 vols., Washington, 1921-36)
LP Shelburne (Marquess of Lansdowne) Papers (William L. Clements Library)
LPB Shelburne (Marquess of Lansdowne) Papers, Bowood, Calnes, Wiltshire
NA National Archives
PCC Papers of the Continental Congress (National Archives)
PCFG *Politische Correspondenz Friedrich's des Grossen,* ed. by G. B. Volz (45 vols., Berlin, 1918-37)
PH *Parliamentary History*
PR *Parliamentary Register*
R Rockingham Papers, Wentworth Woodhouse Collection, Sheffield Public Libraries
RDC *The Revolutionary Diplomatic Correspondence of the United States,* ed. by Francis Wharton (6 vols., Washington, 1889)
SF B. F. Stevens, *Facsimiles of Manuscripts in European Archives Relating to America, 1773-83* (25 vols., London, 1889-98)
SGH Archief Staten Generaal (Algemeen Rijksarchief, The Hague)
SKD Staatskanzlei, Diplomatische Korrespondenz (Haus-, Hof-, und Staatsarchiv, Vienna)
SP State Papers (Public Record Office, London)
Sparks *Diplomatic Correspondence of the American Revolution,* ed. by Jared Sparks (12 vols., Boston, 1829-30)
SRIO *Sbornik imperatorskago russkago istorichesgkago obshchestva* (St. Petersburg, 1867-1916)
WO War Office Papers (Public Record Office, London)
YU Juan F. Yela Utrilla, *España ante la Independencia de los Estados Unidos* (2d ed., 2 vols., Lérida, 1925)

CHAPTER I. THREE VOYAGERS IN SEARCH OF PEACE

1. JJ to RRL; to Governor George Clinton, both dated Aug. 18, 1779. JP.
2. Robert Morris to JJ, Philadelphia, Oct. 18; RRL to JJ, Kingston, Oct. 6; Philadelphia, Dec. 22; George Washington to Sarah Livingston Jay, West Point, Oct. 7; William Livingston to Sarah Jay, Trenton, Oct. 7; William Livingston, Jr. to Sarah Jay, Oct. 16, 1779. JP. Miralles notified José de Gálvez of JJ's departure (Oct. 21, 1779), AGI Santo Domingo 2598.
3. JJ to RRL, Oct. 25, 1779. JP. JJ soon scrapped this cipher on the ground that it had become "useless." JJ to RRL, Martinique, Dec. 24, 1779. JP.
4. William Carmichael to Samuel Huntington, Oct. 25, 1779. *RDC,* III, 393.
5. The time of the accident was later fixed at 5:30 A.M. Council of Commissioned Officers of the *Confederacy,* Nov. 23, 1779. JP.
6. Council of Commissioned Officers of the *Confederacy,* Nov. 23, 1779. JP.
7. Harding to JJ, Fort Royal, Dec. 27 (letterbook copy); JJ to Harding, St. Pierre, Dec. 27, 1779 (draft). JP. Unfortunately the *Confederacy* did not prove a very good sailor with her new rigging. Henceforth, Harding was, if anything, overcautious about pushing her to the utmost, and he was forced to strike her colors to the British in an encounter off the Delaware Capes in April, 1781. A hard-luck captain, Harding was captured twice during the war. "Private Journal on Board the *Confederacy* Frigate Kept by Captain Joseph Hardy, in Command of Marines," in James L. Howard, *Seth Harding, Mariner* (New Haven, 1930), pp. 213-277.
8. The accounts of JJ's voyage and his stay at Martinique are found in JP, notably in his letters to Samuel Huntington, President of Congress, Dec. 25, 1779, Jan. 27, 1780; in letters of Sarah Jay to Susannah French Livingston, Dec. 12, 14, 15, 18,

26, 1779; to Peter Jay, Jan. 9, 1780; to Catherine W. Livingston, Cádiz, March 4, 1780; and in her letterbook, pp. 8-10; in Henry B. Livingston to Susannah French Livingston, Oct. 25, JP; in CG to V, Dec. 20, 1779. CP EU 10: 352; and in JJ to RRL, Feb. 19, 1780. R. R. Livingston Coll., N.Y. Hist. Soc.

9. Edmund Pendleton to JJ, Oct. 11, 1779. JP.

10. This correspondence in CP EU 3-12, and CP EU Sup. 1, 3, has been conveniently assembled by J. J. Meng, *Despatches and Instructions of Conrad Alexandre Gérard, 1778-1780* (Baltimore, 1939).

11. Morris to Deane, June 29, 1777, N.Y. Hist. Soc., *Colls.*, XX, 77-84. For the proposal that delegates be barred from "any post of profit or honor that lies in the appointment of Congress," see William Lee to HL, Dec. 24, 1782. HLP.

12. *SF*, no. 1413; *BFS*, X, 310-313.

13. Deane's speculative involvements are spelled out in *SF*, nos. 300, 301, 489, 1413; and in Julian P. Boyd, "Silas Deane, Death by a Kindly Teacher of Treason?," *William and Mary Quarterly*, ser. III, XVI (1959), 334n.; T. P. Abernethy, "Commercial Activities of Silas Deane in France," *Amer. Hist. Rev.*, XXXIX (1934), 477-485; and *Western Lands in the American Revolution* (New York, 1937), pp. 183-185.

14. See S. F. Bemis, "The British Secret Service and the Franco-American Alliance," *Amer. Hist. Rev.*, XIX (1924), 474-494; Boyd, *loc. cit.*, XVI (1959), 165-187, 319-342, 515, 550. For a note of caution about Bancroft's alleged espionage role, see Richard W. Van Alstyne, "Great Britain, the War for Independence, and the 'Gathering Storm' in Europe, 1775-1778," *Huntington Library Quarterly*, XXVII (1964), 311-346.

15. *JCC*, XIII, 75. To soften the blow CG, so he asserted, took Paine on as a paid propagandist for the French cause in America. CG to V, Jan. 17, 1779, Meng, *Despatches*, p. 480.

16. *JCC*, XII, 1203-1206; HL to Rawlins Lowndes, Dec. 16, 1788, *LMCC*, III, 537-539.

17. JJ must have been seriously embarrassed to learn that his eccentric and uncontrollable brother, Sir James, had entered the lists against Deane. RRL to JJ, March 4, 1779. JP.

18. Since Deane left his papers in Europe they could not be audited. When Secretary for Foreign Affairs, JJ urged Jefferson to acquire the accounts, and a portion of them were purchased abroad. Nobody either then or since has been able to disentangle his public from his private business and to spell out with precision the extent of his private speculations and traffic with the enemy. For the mystery surrounding Deane's trunk full of papers, see Boyd, *loc. cit.* (1959), pp. 515-528. The Deane papers have been published in N.Y. Hist. Soc., *Colls.*, XIX-XXIII, wherein the controversy is documented, as well as in *RDC*, III, and *LMCC*, III, IV.

19. PCC, 193, 194; C. O. Paullin, *Out-Letters of the Continental Marine Committee*, II, 260-262; Richard B. Morris, "The Revolution's Caine Mutiny," *American Heritage*, XI (April, 1960), 10 *et seq.*

20. See W. C. Ford, ed., *Letters of William Lee* (New York, 1891), I, 284-286, 300, 341-343, 368-370; *JCC*, XIII, 368. For Lee's scandalous tactics to evade a lawsuit by George Mason, see *LMCC*, IV, 445n.

21. Richard Henry Lee to Patrick Henry, May 26, 1777, and to George Wythe, Oct. 19, 1777, in James C. Ballagh, ed., *The Letters of Richard Henry Lee* (New York, 1911-14), I, 298-301, 336-337.

22. Richard Henry Lee to George Mason, June 9, 1779. *LMCC*, IV, 255.

23. *JCC*, XIII, 94.

24. *JCC*, XIII, 364. The motion to recall Franklin was defeated on April 22, 1779. *Ibid.*, p. 500.

25. *JCC,* XIII, 366.
26. The remark appeared in V to CG, Oct. 26, 1778, Meng, *Despatches,* p. 358. See also James Lovell to JA, June 13, 1779. *LMCC,* IV, 262; *JCC,* XIV, 536.
27. HL, Notes of Proceedings, *LMCC,* IV, 438 (Sept. 25, 1779).
28. HL puts the voting on September 25th; the official Journal on the 27th. *JCC,* XV, 1113.
29. Massachusetts and Connecticut voted for JJ, who carried eight states in all, three not voting, and New Hampshire for Lee.
30. Lovell to JA; to Richard Henry Lee, Sept. 27, 1779. *LMCC,* IV, 443, 447.
31. HL to William Whipple, Sept. 28, 1779. *LMCC,* IV, 453.
32. Sept. 28, 1779, *LMCC,* IV, 450.
33. CG to V, Sept. 27, 1779. Meng, *Despatches,* p. 897.
34. Miralles to José de Gálvez, Sept. 26, 27, 1779, Oct. 17, 1779. AGI, Santo Domingo 2598.
35. For the close relationship between Miralles and CG, see Miralles to Diego Josef Navarro, Feb. 15, 1779. AGI, Cuba 1281.
36. V to A, April 26, 1777. CP E 584, no. 40; Marcel Trudel, *Louis XVI, le Congrès Américain et le Canada* (Quebec, 1949), pp. 110-141.
37. For R's views, see *SF,* XIII, 310; *D,* I, 244; for V's, *D,* I, 381 *et seq.;* II, 213 *et seq.;* III, 33. See also "Considerations upon the Necessity of France declaring at once for the American Colonies, even without the Concurrence of Spain," unsigned documents containing statements from earlier papers of V, in Edward S. Corwin, *French Policy and the American Alliance of 1778* (Princeton, 1916), pp. 398-403. See also D. D. Irvine, "The Newfoundland Fishery," *Canadian Hist. Rev.,* XIII (1932), 268-284.
38. Only the last was explicitly listed therein. R. H. Lee, *Life of Arthur Lee* (Boston, 1829), I, 378-379, 383.
39. *DC,* V, 39.
40. CG to V, Mar. 6, 1779. Meng, *Despatches,* p. 561.
41. When the Spaniards originally proposed the truce, V laid down as an indispensable condition that Great Britain evacuate all territory forming a part of the Confederation. V to M, Dec. 24, 1778. CP E 591: 409. Later he was to temporize on this point.
42. M to V, March 29, 1779. *D,* III, 749.
43. *D,* III, 850, 851.
44. *D,* III, 767-768, 770, 801-803.
45. *DC,* V, 55-56. See also W to TG, May 4; CP E 594: 27-28; Almodóvar to V, May 4, 1779, *ibid.,* p. 29; Reflections on Spanish Truce Proposals, May 1779, CP E 594: 189-194.
46. *D,* III, 803-810.
47. See John Jay, *The Fisheries Dispute* (New York 1887), p. 24.
48. *D,* III, 806.
49. Count von Belgiojoso to K, London, Jan. 1, 1779, SKD, England, 163; M to V, May 17, 1779, CP E 594: 72-74. Anglophiles like the Marquise du Deffand, the indefatigable French correspondent of Horace Walpole, felt the same way about helping the rebels. See her letter to Walpole of June 20, 1779. *Lettres de la Marquise du Deffand à Horace Walpole,* ed. by Mrs. Paget Toynbee (London, 1912), p. 533.
50. See R. Konetzke, *"Die Politik des Grafen Aranda"* in *Historische Studien,* CLXXXI (Berlin, 1929), 144-151.
51. See Arthur S. Aiton, "Spain and the Family Compact, 1770-1773," in A. Curtis Wilgus, ed., *Hispanic American Essays* (Chapel Hill, N.C., 1942), pp. 135-149; Julius Goebel, Jr., *The Struggle for the Falkland Islands* (New Haven, 1927);

Vera Lee Brown, "Studies in the History of Spain in the Second Half of the 18th Century," *Smith College Studies in History* (Northampton, Mass., 1929), p. 30. See also *DC*, 432-444; Francis Renaut, *Le Pacte de Famille et l'Amérique* (Paris, 1922); Louis Blart, *Les Rapports de la France et de l'Espagne après le Pacte de Famille* (Paris, 1915).

52. See Corwin, *op. cit.*, p. 205, and S. F. Bemis, *The Diplomacy of the American Revolution* (Bloomington, Ind., 1957), pp. 84-86. For the view that the Treaty of Aranjuez did not tie America to the Spanish kite, see *RDC*, I, 359; *D*, III, 762n.-764n.; Paul C. Phillips, *The West in the Diplomacy of the American Revolution* (Urbana, Ill., 1913), p. 107.

53. For Spain's separate military objectives in North America, see Gálvez to Navarro, Aug. 29, 1779, in Laurence Kinnaird, ed., "Spain in the Mississippi Valley, 1765-1794," American Historical Association, *Annual Report*, 1945, II, 355-357, 364-366.

54. *D*, III, 771.

55. V to M, April 3, 1778. CP E 589: 27.

56. CG to JJ, Jan. 10, 1779. PCC 94: 83; *RDC*, III, 17.

57. *RDC*, III, 23: *JCC*, XIII, 63 (Jan. 14, 1779).

58. *RDC*, III, 39-40: Memorandum of William Henry Drayton, *LMCC*, IV, 69, 70.

59. Miralles to José de Gálvez, Dec. 28, 1778. AGI, Ind. Gen. 1606.

60. V to CG, Oct. 28, 1778. CP EU 5: 119; Meng, *Despatches*, p. 359.

61. See CG to V, Oct. 20, 1778. CP EU 5: 68-84; Meng, *Despatches*, pp. 344-345.

62. JJ inserted the words quoted.

63. *JCC*, XIII, 239-244; PCC 25: I, 71.

64. CG to V, Feb. 15, Mar. 1, Mar. 3, 1779. CP EU 7: 215, 290, 319; Meng, *Despatches*, pp. 521-524, 545-548, 552.

65. Letter partly in cipher decoded by E. C. Burnett (Mar. 1, 1779). *LMCC*, IV, 84. For a critical appraisal of CG's role, see Phillips, *op. cit.*, pp. 108-130.

66. *JCC*, XIII, 339-341.

67. Lovell to JA, Sept. 27, 1779. *RDC*, III, 339.

68. *JCC*, XIII, 348-352; *RDC*, III, 95.

69. *JCC*, XIII, 372, 373; *RDC*, III, 97, CG to V, April 4, 1779; Meng, *Despatches*, pp. 594, 595.

70. CG to JJ, May 22, 1779. *RDC*, III, 175-178.

71. *RDC*, III, 194 (May 27, 1779). For Miralles' observations on the fisheries dispute, see his dispatches of May 18, June 15, 23, AGI, Ind. Gen. 1606.

72. *RDC*, III, 202-205.

73. *JCC*, XIV, 749; *RDC*, III, 225-228.

74. *JCC*, XIV, 834 (July 12, 1779), CG to V, July 14, CP EU: 79-96; Meng, *Despatches*, 777-785; Miralles to José de Gálvez, July 13, AGI, Ind. Gen. 1606.

75. John Dickinson authored this compromise. Dickinson to HL, July 22, 1779, with "Propositions for a Treaty of Peace." HLP. See also *JCC*, XIV, 896, 897; CG to V, July 31, 1779; Meng, *Despatches*, 815, 816.

76. *JCC*, XIV, 960 (Aug. 14, 1779).

77. CG to V, Mar. 10, 1779. CP EU 7:367; Meng, *Despatches*, p. 574. Earlier Miralles had hopes that a compromise settlement might be worked out with Congress. Miralles to Diego Josef Navarro, Feb. 14, 1779, AGI, Cuba 1281.

78. *JCC*, XIII, 369.

79. *JCC*, XIV, 924-926.

80. *RDC*, III, 310, 311 (Sept. 9, 1779); CG to V, Sept. 10, 1779; Meng, *Despatches*, pp. 884, 885.

81. *Ibid.*, p. 312; *JCC*, XV, 1045-1047.
82. *JCC*, XV, 1080-1084; *RDC*, III, 324-326. JJ himself voted against this instruction, which passed by seven states to three. See also CG to V, Sept. 17, 25, 1779; Meng, *Despatches*, pp. 889, 890, 894.
83. *JCC*, XV, 1074; *RDC*, III, 343-345, 352-353; Sparks, VII, 169. Minor stipulations were added to the original instructions. For the factional division over the election of ministers and the drafting of peace instructions, see Herbert J. Henderson, "Political Faction in the Continental Congress, 1774-1783," Ph.D. dissertation, 1962, Columbia University. For draft letter to BF concerning the JJ mission, Oct. 16, 1779, see PCC 25: I, 32.
84. *RDC*, III, 137 (April 27, 1779).
85. *Diary*, IV, 175, 176. Dickinson had cast his vote for BF, but since BF had not even been nominated, the vote of eleven states was considered unanimous for JA. *JCC*, XV, 1103-1113.
86. *Ibid.*, p. 177 (Nov. 4, 1779).
87. *Ibid.*, p. 191. JA had sailed abroad in February, 1778, and returned from France in August, 1779.
88. V to M, Jan. 29, 1780, CP E 597: 222-223.
89. The JA trip is recounted in *Diary*, pp. 175-240.
90. *Ibid.*, pp. 181-183.
91. *Ibid.*, p. 196 (Dec. 11, 1779).
92. V to JA, Feb. 15, 1780, *ibid.*, pp. 245-247.
93. HL to Committee of Foreign Affairs, Feb. 14, 1780. *RDC*, III, 494.
94. See Francis P. Renaut, *La Politique de Propagande des Américains pendant la Guerre d'Indépendance*, II (Paris, 1925), 139-146.
95. "A Narrative of the Capture of Laurens," S.C. Hist. Soc., *Coll.*, I (1857), 18-68; Henry Laurens, MS. Brief Journal, in N.Y. Pub. Lib.; D. D. Wallace, *Life of Henry Laurens* (New York, 1915).

CHAPTER II. ARMADA AGAINST ENGLAND

1. Only "vague" reports via the West Indies of a battle in the Channel had reached Philadelphia at the end of November. RRL to George Clinton, Nov. 30, 1779. *LMCC*, IV, 530.
2. CP E 595: 350-352.
3. Valonges, June 23, 1779, in C. Hippeau, *Le Gouvernement de Normandie au XVIIe et au XVIIIe Siècle* (Caen, 1863), II, 12.
4. June 10, Aug. 17, 1779; CP EU, sup. I, 311-313; *SF*, no. 1614; Lafayette to Washington, Oct. 7, 1779, *Mémoires, correspondance et manuscrits du Général Lafayette* (Paris, 1837-38), I, 324. See also Louis Gottschalk, *Lafayette and the Close of the American Revolution* (Chicago, 1942), pp. 1-55.
5. See original instruction of M. de La Rozière, with approval in the hand of Louis XV, July 26, 1763; La Rozière to Broglie, Dec. 16, 1763. A.M., S/Ser. B4 297.
6. Comte de Broglie, Plan de guerre contre l'Angleterre, 1763-66, 1778. Bib. de l'Arsenal; also A.M., S/Ser. B4 297-299. The general invasion plan was put to Spain by V in a letter of Feb. 12, 1779, V to M. CP E 592: 32-40. For the advocacy of the Portsmouth–Isle of Wight objective, see A.G. Ang. 1414:16; Hippeau, II, 147-154; WO 30/72:253-268; F to V, Feb. 26, 1779. CP E 592: 76-80. On the basis of an intelligence report of the defenses of the Portsmouth area, the French Ministry at a conference held at the home of the Comte de Maurepas, June 21, 1779, ordered the main attacking force to the Isle of Wight area, but also authorized another landing under the protection of the Armada

at some other point as far west as Bristol. A.M., B4 159:259. See also A, Diario, June 25, 1779. AHN, E, 4116:2. For Plymouth as an objective, see M to V, May 14; V to M, May 28, 1782. CP E 594: 67-69, 175-176. Accounts of the invasion based on French sources are found in A.G. 3726-3732; also G. Lacour-Gayet, *La Marine militaire de la France sous la règne de Louis XVI* (Paris, 1905); R. Castex, *Les idées militaire de la marine au dix-huitième siècle* (Paris, 1911); J. Tramont, *Manual d'histoire maritime de la France* (Paris, 1927); and, more recently, in Paul del Perugia, *La tentative d'invasion de l'Angleterre de 1779* (Paris, 1939), A. T. Patterson, *The Other Armada* (Manchester, 1960), and Piers Mackesy, *The War for America, 1775-1783* (Cambridge, Mass., 1964), pp. 279-300. The French and English investigators have not exploited the Spanish sources for the invasion project. See also report of Francesco Pesaro, Sept. 28, 1779. Archivio di Stato, 180:164, Venice.

7. ST to W, Aug. 27, 1777. *SF*, no. 1662 (4-5).
8. See *Mémoires de M. Le Prince de Montbarrey* (Paris, 1826), II, 274-279, 344-347; also Comtesse de Coislin to the Duc d'Harcourt, July 9, 1779. Hippeau, II, 22, 182; Comte de Mirabeau, Notebooks, Bib. de l'Arsenal.
9. *Mémoires de Montbarrey*, II, 267, 268, 288, 293-295; Baron de Besenval, *Mémoires* (Paris, 1805), II, 264-267.
10. See F to A, Aug. 21, Sept. 12, 1779; A to F, July 29, Oct. 29. AHN, E, 4116:2; 4614. Cf. also M to V, May 5, 1779. CP E 593:589.
11. F to A, July 31, 1779, AHN, E, 4116, apt. 1, doc. 29. A, Diario, June 24— July 29, 1779, *loc. cit.*, apt. 2.
12. V to M, July 23, 1779. CP E 594: 461-464.
13. Hippeau, I, 442. The epidemic first hit the French fleet and then spread to the Spaniards. F to A, Oct. 27; A to F, Oct. 29, 1779. AHN, E, 4116:9 (5).
14. V to M, Sept. 11, 1779, CP E 595: 302.
15. *The Letters of Horace Walpole*, ed. by Mrs. Paget Toynbee (Oxford, 1904), XI, 16. For a critique of Walpole as a reporter of events, see *HP*, III, 596, 597.
16. G to North, Aug. 5, 1779. *CG*, IV, 403, 407.
17. G to North, Sept. 1, 1779. *CG*, IV, 418. For other companies raised by the nobility and gentry, April 16—July 30, 1779, see WO 1/616.
18. To Sir Horace Mann, June 30, 1779. *Letters*, X, 432.
19. WO 34/115; 34/154.
20. The King did not think those convicted of capital offenses were "proper objects to enlist." WO 1/682. See also WO 4/106.
21. *PH*, XIII (1779), 471, 515.
22. *PH*, XIV (1778-79), 570.
23. R 1-1858; *Annual Register*, 1779, p. 230; *Letters of Horace Walpole*, X, 375, 376; J. W. Fortescue, *A History of the British Army* (London, 1911), 297, 298.
24. June 13, July 2, 1779, *passim*. WO 1/682.
25. *PH*, XIII (1779), 495, 506.
26. *PH*, XIII, 553 *et. seq.* This proposal was calculated to meet BF's earlier criticism of the truce proposals made by the North Ministry under the conciliation bill of 1778. BF had then pointed out to DH that the commissioners might proclaim a truce and then revoke their proclamations as soon as the militia had gone home. *BFS*, VII, 107-109. For DH's previous motions on the American war, see *HP*, II, 592, 593.
27. *Annual Register*, 1779, p. 168.
28. *PH*, XIII (1779), p. 564; XIV (1778-79), p. 541.
29. *Annual Register*, 1779, p. 167.
30. *Letters*, X, 392.

31. Richmond's motion to that effect of June 17, 1779. *PH*, XIV (1778-79), 501.
32. *CG*, IV, 364-377, *passim*; *PH*, XIII (1779), 509-513.
33. *PH*, XIV (1778-79), 530-536, 559; XIII (1779), 513, 525.
34. *CG*, IV, 392, 393, 430; *Hist. Brit. Army*, III, 296.
35. *CG*, IV, 416.
36. To Sir Horace Mann, Sept. 5, 1779, *Works*, XI, 18.
37. *PH*, XIV (1778-79), 539, 540, 550, 553.
38. See, e.g., Patterson, *op. cit.*, pp. 85-87, and George Martelli, *Jemmy Twicher* (London, 1962), p. 205; but cf. Mackesy, *op. cit.*, p. 515, for a recent hostile verdict.
39. See Rockingham's notes and correspondence on the court-martial. R 1-1812, 1814. See also *HP*, III, 9, 10.
40. *The Last Journal of Horace Walpole*, ed. by A. F. Steuart (London, 1910), 232-233; *Letters of Horace Walpole*, X, 378; G. R. Barnes and J. H. Owen, eds., *The Private Papers of John, Earl of Sandwich, 1771-1782* (London, 1932-38), II, 249, 255-256; *Annual Register, 1779*, pp. 153-160.
41. *PH*, XIV (1778-79), 507, 517. See also Keppel to Rockingham, July 18, 1779, and miscellaneous papers of Rockingham on the "Ignorance and Mismanagement in the Conduct of the Naval Department," 1779-80. R 1—1837; 17—7-10.
42. *FS*, III, 48-50; LP B. See also *HP*, II, 50-53.
43. A.M., B4 297:234 *et seq.*, where the project of setting up Ireland as a republic under the protection of France and Spain was proposed.
44. Lafayette to V, May 23, 1779, CP EU, sup. I, no. 172 bis.
45. This was the ostensible reason for organizing these military groups. *PH*, XV (1779-80), p. 29. See also Matthew Ridley, Diary, Mar. 24, 1782, Mass. Hist. Soc.
46. P. L. Ford, ed., "Benjamin Franklin, 'An Address to the Good People of Ireland on Behalf of America, Oct. 4, 1778,'" *Winnowings in American History* (Brooklyn, N.Y., 1891).
47. Lafayette, *Mémoires et Corr.*, I, 293; *D*, IV, 233n.; CP E 594: 320-322.
48. *CG*, IV, 402, 403; E. W. Harcourt, ed., *The Harcourt Papers* (Oxford, 1880), IX, 303, 366; X, 90, 196-197, 271. For intelligence report of May 24, 1779, see R 17-9-2, 3b; for the double agent Thomas Hussey's advice to the British of "an immediate descent" on the Irish coast, see William Wardlaw to [Richard Cumberland?], Aug. 9, 1779. HMC, *R*, IX, pt. 3, p. 120.
49. *CG*, IV, 414. See also Keppel to Rockingham, Aug. 20 (14), 20, 1779, and unsigned letter, Aug. 20, 1779. R 1—1845, 1846, 1847.
50. Paul Jones's cutter *Cerf* found this out to its sorrow when, in October, it landed at Ballinskellip Bay and was promptly captured by the King's Rangers. John Paul Jones, Letterbook, 1779, NA.
51. See Lord Sandwich's Thoughts upon Naval Measures to be taken, Sept. 14, 1779, *CG*, IV, 441.
52. *Sandwich Papers*, III, 61.
53. Horace Walpole to Sir Horace Mann, *Letters*, XI, 14.
54. Lieutenant General Sir David Lindsay to the Secretary of State, Aug. 31., 1779. SP Dom, 1779; also WO 34/116:85.
55. The Ministry vetoed the proposal for the boom on the ground that it would prevent access to the harbor by British naval vessels. *Sandwich Papers*, III, 65-78.
56. *PH*, XV (1778-79), 55-58, 65, 71; *Annual Register, 1780*, p. 35.
57. *Sandwich Papers*, III, 77, 78, 81, 82; R-1877.
58. V to M, May 29, 1779, CP E 594: 258-259. But by July 30 V had reports of troops close by Plymouth. CP E 594: 342-345.

59. *Sandwich Papers*, III, 63, 64.

60. July 23, 1779. CP E 594: 336-340.

61. A, Diario, July 27, 1779. AHN, E, 4116: apt. 2. V to M, July 30, 1779. CP E 594: 342-345.

62. V to M, August 12, 1779. CP E 595: 11.

63. M to V, Aug. 21, 1779. CP E 595: 23-25. See also F to A, Aug. 21, 1779. AHN, E, 4116: 1, pt. 3, no. 1.

64. Duc d'Harcourt to Comte de Vaux, Sept. 12, 1779. Hippeau, II, 87. Falmouth's defenses had already been further depleted by the transfer of a company of militia from that port to Penzance. July 31, 1779. WO 1/616. For the Cornwall operation as a commerce-raiding project, see V to M, Aug. 12, 1779. CP E 595: 101.

65. *CG*, IV, 386.

66. *Sandwich Papers*, III, 89.

67. Kempenfeldt to Middleton, Aug. 6 (1779), in "Letters and Papers of Charles, Lord Barham, Vol. 1," *Naval Records Society Publications*, XXXII, 293.

68. *CG*, IV, 404.

69. *Sandwich Papers*, III, 94, 95.

70. *CG*, IV, 410-411.

71. Countess Cornwallis to William Cornwallis, Oct. 7, 1779. HMC, *R*, VI, 321.

72. *Sandwich Papers*, III, 92.

73. His sick list was kept down to 824, and most of the illness was attributed by Sandwich to "pressed men and people from jails." *CG*, IV, 423.

74. Walpole, *Letters*, XI, 9, 20.

75. *CG*, IV, 419.

76. Mulgrave to Sandwich, Sept. 3, 1779. *Sandwich Papers*, III, 92.

77. *Sandwich Papers*, III, 95-98. For Richmond's attack in Parliament in November on the "humiliation and disgrace" attendant upon Hardy's flight, see *PH*, XV (1779-80), p. 53.

78. *CG*, IV, 432 (Sept. 13, 1779).

79. Frederick to Queen Mother of Denmark, Mar. 24, 1780. *PCFG*, XLIV, 152.

80. Horace Walpole to the Rev. William Mann, Nov. 16, 1779, *Works*, XI, 56.

81. G. A. R. Callendar, "With the British Fleet in 1780," *The Mariner's Mirror*, IX (1923), 258, 259.

82. CP E 595: 441-442.

83. For V's outspoken criticism of Sartine, see A to F, Dec. 22, 1779. AHN, E, 4116. See also A to F, Sept. 5, 12, 1779. AHN, E, 4116, apt. 1, pt. 2, 3.

84. A to F, Sept. 21, 1779. AHN, E, 4116, apt. 2.

85. F to A, Oct. 11, 1779. AHN, E, 4116, apt. 1, pt. 4, no. 1.

86. Lacour-Gayet, *La Marine Militaire sous Louis XVI*, pp. 275-276.

87. Sept. 12, 1779. CP E 595: 79-80.

88. Comtesse de Coislin to Duc d'Harcourt, Aug. 17, 1779, Hippeau, II, 54, 55.

89. Duc du Châtelet to Duc d'Harcourt, Aug. 28, 1779, Hippeau, II, 67.

90. Duc d'Harcourt to Comte de Vaux, Sept. 18, 1779, Hippeau, II, 92; A to F, Oct. 29, 1779, AHN, E, 4116.

91. Comte de Vaux to Prince de Montbarrey, Oct. 5, 1779. A.M., B4 159:/760.

92. For English intelligence about the invasion effort, see Duc d'Harcourt to Prince de Montbarrey, Sept. 15, 1779, Hippeau, II, 90.

93. Duc du Châtelet to Duc d'Harcourt, Sept. 23, 1779, Hippeau, II, 96; see also Lafayette to V, Sept. 11, 1779. *D*, IV, 244.

94. Hippeau, II, 81, 87, 93, 96, 101. For an appraisal of du Chaffault, see A to F, Sept. 5, 1779. AHN, E, 4116, apt. 2.

95. Comte de Vaux to Prince de Montbarrey, Oct. 5, 1779. A.M., B4 159: 760. Nevertheless, as late as December 17 V wrote to M that the proposal of an agent of Sartine to attack the town and fortress of Plymouth was either a piece of foolishness or a trick. CP E 596: 203-206. For post-Armada invasion proposals of the Marquis de Jaucourt and the renegade Robert Mitchell Hamilton, see Patterson, *Other Armada*, pp. 226, 227.

96. MA to MT, Oct. 14. Alfred d'Arneth and M. A. Geoffroy, eds., *Correspondance secrète entre Marie-Thérèse et le Comte de Mercy-Argenteau* (Paris, 1875), III, 357, 358; V to M, Oct. 15, 1779. CP E, 596; 125-140.

97. On October 20 the Joint Chiefs in Brest granted the Spanish fleet permission to sail for Spain. AHN, E, 4201. See also MA to MT, Nov. 16, 1779, *Corr. Marie-Thérèse et Mercy*, III, 365; A to Gaston, Dec. 31, 1779. AHN, E, 4143.

98. A to Gaston, AHN, E, 4145, 1599, encl. E.

99. A to F, Sept. 21, 1779. AHN, E, 4116, apt. 2.

100. Cf. Jones to Bancroft, Oct. 26, 1779. J. P. Jones MSS., Jones to Lafayette, Oct. 29, 1779, *ibid.*, LC; Rockingham correspondence on the defense of Hull, Sept. 23, 25, 28, Oct. 1, Nov. 3, 1779. R 1-1849-1852-1864; *Burke Corr.*, IV, 128, 129; *PH*, XV, (1779-80), p. 12.

101. A to F, AHN, E, 4210; F to Charles III, Aug. 20, 1780. AHN, E, 4202:3, no. 23.

CHAPTER III. PRIEST AND PLAYWRIGHT AT THE PARDO

1. JJ to George Clinton, Feb. 1, 1780. JP.

2. JJ to Philip Schuyler, Feb. 19, 1780. Schuyler Mansion Docs., no. 8. JP.

3. JJ to Dr. O'Kelly, Madrid, July 6, 1780; JJ to President of Congress, Madrid, May 26, 1780, JP. Cf. also report of Francesco Pesaro, Madrid, Dec. 7, 1779. Archivio di Stato, 180, no. 174—Venice. The dispirited temper of the people reflected the dissatisfaction of high officials with the progress of the war. See F to A, Jan. 10, 1780. AHN, E, 4143. As a minimum effort, F felt that the limited invasion project proposed the previous August against Falmouth or Bristol should be revived.

4. *D*, II, 196, 197.

5. See Juan de Miralles to José de Gálvez, Oct. 17, 1779. AGI, Santo Domingo 2598 (draft).

6. JJ to Carmichael, Jan. 27, Feb. 25, 1780. PCC 110: I; *YU*, II, 469-472; *RDC*, III, 472-474; JJ to Gálvez, Jan. 27, 1780, *ibid.*, pp. 476-478. See also rough draft of instructions for Carmichael, Jan. 27, 1780, JP; and Carmichael to JJ, Feb. 15, 21, 1780. JJ Letterbook.

7. Frederick to Baron Goltz, Feb. 28, 1780. *PCFG*, XLIV, 102.

8. K to MDA, Dec. 2, 1779. SKD, Frankreich, 234.

9. M to V, Jan. 10, 1780. CP E 597: 83-84.

10. M to V, Mar. 29, 1780. CP E 598: 319-322.

11. V to M, Jan. 29, Feb. 22, 1780. CP E 597: 219-223, 361-365.

12. M to V, Feb. 14, Mar. 13, 18, 1780; V to M, Mar. 2, 13, 1780. CP E 597: 293-294, 304-306; 598: 13, 18, 121-124.

13. M to V, Feb. 22, 1780. CP E 597: 346-351.

14. F to JJ, Pardo, Feb. 24, 1780; JJ Letterbook, JP; CP E 597: 393-395.

15. JJ to Samuel Huntington, Mar. 3, 1780; to F, Mar. 6, 1780, JJ Letterbook, JP; PCC 110: I; M to V, Mar. 13, 1780. CP E 598: 115-120.

16. Sarah Jay to Susan Van Brugh Livingston, May 13, 1780, Sarah Jay Letterbook. JP.

17. See JJ to Peter Jay, May 23, 1780; Sarah Jay to Catherine W. Livingston, May 14, Dec. 1, 1780; to William Livingston, May 14, 1781. JP.

18. Harold Acton, *The Bourbons of Naples* (London, 1956), pp. 180-192.

19. See Vicente Rodríguez Casado, *Política interior de Carlos III* (Valladolid, 1950), pp. 25-29, and, *per contra* on the mutiny of 1766, P. Eguia, *Los Jesuítas y el Motín de Esquilache* (Madrid, 1947). See also François Rousseau, *Règne de Charles III d'Espagne, 1759-88* (Paris, 1907), I, 176-417; Richard Herr, *The Eighteenth Century Revolution in Spain* (Princeton, 1958), pp. 11-22.

20. For critical estimates of F, see M to V, Feb. 21, 22, 1780. CP E 597: 337, 346-351.

21. Juan Antonio Llorente, *Historia Crítica de la Inquisición de España* (Madrid, 1870), I, 557, 558, 559, 561-564. DC, IV, 54-55.

22. Jacobo de la Pezuela, "El Conde de Aranda," *Revista de España*, XXV (1872), 36, 43-44, 359-361.

23. YU, I, 183-193; F to A, Mar. 5, 1777. AHN, E, 4072.

24. F to JJ, Mar. 9, 1780; JJ to F, April 25, 1780. *JPJ*, I, 277-302.

25. Committee of Foreign Affairs to JJ, Dec. 11, 1779. JP.

26. JJ to Robert Morris, April 25, 1782. Windsor Castle Archives; copy, JP. Cf. also JJ to Mrs. (Samuel) Meredith, Aranjuez, May 12, 1780, copy N.Y. Hist. Soc.

27. Sarah Jay to Catherine W. Livingston, May 14, 1780, Sarah Jay Letterbook. JP.

28. Brockholst Livingston to William Livingston, Madrid, July 12, 1780, *Magazine of American History*, III (1879), 512.

29. Carmichael to JJ, Aranjuez, June 13, 1780. JP. That morning the Cumberlands also reached Aranjuez, Carmichael reported.

30. See Almodóvar to F, London, June 11, 1779. AGI, E, 7005; 198. On October 20, 1779, Hussey was ordered to communicate regularly with A in Paris, sending his résumés by regular mail, unsigned, and addressed to Romberg et Cie. at Ostend. AHN, E, 4116: 1571, enc. 1 (A to Hussey). For one job Hussey was paid £444. A to F, AHN, E, 4116: 1571 (Nov. 25, 1779). AHN, E, 4115: 1, pt. 7. On the Spanish spy ring in London, see also Pedro Voltes Bou, "Thomas Hussey y Sus Servicios a la Política de Floridablanca," *Hispania*, XIX (1959), 92-141.

31. Wardlaw to Germain, Aug. 9, 1779. Germain Papers, 65, CL. Cf. also Hussey to Almodóvar and to A, undated, AHN, E, 4116: 1571, enc. 3, 4; Wardlaw to [Richard Cumberland?], Aug. 9, 1779. HMC, R, IX, p. 3, p. 120.

32. Richard Cumberland, *Character of the Late Lord Viscount Sackville* (London, 1785). See also M. Bishop, *Recollections of Table-Talk of Samuel Rogers* (London, 1952), p. 96.

33. Samuel F. Bemis implies this in his masterly treatment, *The Hussey-Cumberland Mission and American Independence* (Princeton, 1931), pp. 17, 18.

34. Cumberland to Germain, Nov. 19, 20, 1779. Germain Papers, 67-70. CL.

35. Germain to Hussey, Nov. 29, 1779. Germain Papers, 72-74. Hussey promised Germain to do his best (Dec. 1, 1779), *ibid.*, pp. 75-77. CL. Hussey turned over Germain's letter to F. AHN, E, 4220, exp. 2, doc. 60, p. 3.

36. AHN, E, 4220, exp. 2, doc. 61.

37. F, memorandum for Hussey, Jan. 20, 1781; draft in F's own hand. AHN, E, 4220, exp. no. 2, doc. 72, p. 4; doc. 74, p. 3 is a copy in Hussey's hand. Cf. Bemis, *op. cit.*, appendix no. 1, pp. 135-136.

38. Hussey to Germain, Jan. 31, 1780. AHN, E, 4220: 2, doc. 79, p. 4.

39. Hussey to Germain, Feb. 3, 1780. Germain Papers, pp. 81-82, CL; AHN, E, 4220: 2, doc. 80, p. 2.

40. Hussey to F, London, Feb. 16, 1780 (in cipher). AHN, E, 4220: 2, doc. 81, p. 2; doc. 82, p. 3.

41. Sparks MSS., CII; Corwin, *French Policy*, p. 109.
42. Cumberland, "Narrative of Secret Negotiations with Spain, 1780-81." Add. MSS. 28851, BM.
43. AHN, E, 4220: 2, docs. 13-16; printed in Bemis, *op. cit.*, pp. 139-144.
44. F to Hussey, AHN, E, 4220: 2, doc. 99, p. 2.
45. F to Hussey, Mar. 2, 1780. SP 44/209, 1-2, 5-6; AHN, E, 4220: 2, doc. 94, p. 4; Bemis, *op. cit.*, pp. 149-150.
46. F memorandum (*c.* March 1780), AHN, E, 4220: 2, doc. 98, p. 22; Bemis, *op. cit.*, pp. 153-159. The letter of March 5, 1780, is in the hand of Bernardo del Campo, F's secretary. AHN, E, 4220: 2, doc. 101, p. 4; Bemis, *op. cit.*, pp. 150-152. In lieu of the fishing rights in the Newfoundland area, which Spain desired to share, she would accept "that part of Florida that looks into the Gulf of Mexico leaving to the English the eastern part." For the British mission to America of 1778, see *Annual Register, 1778*, pp. 327-329; H.M.C., *R.*, VI, 356-357; Auckland Papers, Add. MSS. 34, 414, pp. 441-447; 34, 415, pp. 398-399; 34, 416, pp. 33-34, BM; *SF*, nos. 446-447, 496, 500, 519, 529, 1104, 1107, 1110, 1116, 1119, 1144, 1213; also Weldon A. Brown, *Empire or Independence, a Study in the Failure of Reconciliation, 1774-83* (University of Louisiana, 1941).
47. Project of preliminary articles (April ?, 1780), SP 94/209, 25-42; 94/254, 279-284.
48. George Gordon to Rockingham, (*c.* Dec., 1778—Jan., 1779), R 1-1805. See also *HP*, II, 684, 685.
49. Cantofer to F, Nov. 30, 1779, AHN, E, 4220: 2, doc. 3, p. 4; Johnstone to Fernan Nuñez; Nuñez to F (*c.* Feb. 24, 1780), AHN, E, 4220: 2, docs. 11, 19 (also doc. 95 with notes, p. 2); Bemis, *op. cit.*, pp. 145-146.
50. Hussey to Germain, Feb. 3, 1780. AHN, E, 4220: 2, doc. 80, p. 2.
51. F to Hussey, Mar. 2, 1780. AHN, E, 4220: 2, doc. 20, p. 3.
52. F to A, Dec. 13, 1779. AHN, E, 4220: 2, doc. 6, p. 2. However, the Spanish Minister did not inform the French of his instructions to Fernan Nuñez, the Spanish ambassador to Portugal and an intermediary with Johnstone. See also *D*, IV, 448, 475. Spain also notified other courts of the Johnstone proposals, including Petersburg. CP E 597: 231 (Jan. 29, 1780).
53. F to Fernan Nuñez, Dec. 10, 1779. AHN, E, 4220: 2, doc. 4, pp. 3, 27-29, 32, 34, 35.
54. Hussey to F (Feb. 16, 1780), AHN, E, 4220: 2, doc. 82.
55. HMC, *R*, Stopford-Sackville MSS., II, 103-104 (*c.* March, 1778).
56. *RDC*, III, 727-731; JJ to M, April 11, 1780, PCC, Item 110:I; M to JJ, April 13, 1780. JP; JJ to JA, April 26, 1780. JP; AP, pt. IV, 350; M to V, April 22, 1780. CP E 598: 492, 493. It was clear to M that Dalrymple was without power to treat. F to A: "One does not take these overtures seriously." Aug. 7, 1780. CP E 600: 72.
57. M to V, April 22; V to M, April 27, May 8, 1780. CP E 598: 454-455, 492, 493; 599: 44. See also "Project of Lord Rocheford," *ibid.*, 133-142.
58. H to F (copy) (April 17, 1780). Cumberland Papers, 58-60. BM.
59. Instructions from H to Cumberland (April 17, 1780). Cumberland Papers, 49-57. BM.
60. Cumberland to Germain, April 21, 1780. Germain Papers, 83-84. BM.
61. Hussey to H, April 26, May 18, 1780. SP 94/209, 49-50. Cumberland to H, May 19, 1780. SP 94/209, 53-54, 65, 66; *Memoirs*, p. 222. Cumberland to Germain, May 25-26, 1780, Germain Papers, 85-88. Daugnac to V, CP Portugal 111 (May 30, 1780).

62. Hussey to H and Cumberland, May 31, 1780, and memorandum. SP 94/209, 108-110. Hussey sent along a detailed itinerary for the trip to Aranjuez, a list of what the Cumberlands needed to take along, and the necessary passports to enter the country. Memorandum, May 31, 1780. SP 94/209, 69.

63. Cumberland to H, May 19, 1780. SP 94/209, 55-60.

64. Cumberland to Hussey, June 6, 1780. SP 94/209, 69-70.

65. Cumberland to H, June 6, 7, 1780. SP 94/209, 67-68, 103-107. Walpole to H, June 8, 1780. SP 94/209, 112-113. While Cumberland took his family with him to give color to the pretext that he was traveling through Spain to Italy for his health, he also let it be known that he was on a mission to arrange for an exchange of prisoners. Daugnac to V, CP Portugal 111 (June 13, 1780).

66. Cumberland to H, Aranjuez, June 26, 1780. SP 94/209, 73-74.

67. Cumberland to F, June 24, 1780. SP 94/209, 87-90.

68. *Gazeta de Madrid*, June 23, 1780. Cumberland to F, June 25, 1780. SP 94/209, 85-86.

69. F to H, June 26, 1780. SP 94/209, 71, 93-94.

70. On July 11 Walpole wrote Cumberland that the riots had been quashed. SP 94/209, 139-140.

71. A to F, Aug. 29, 1780. AHN, E, 4202: 1.

72. Cumberland to H, June 26, 1780. SP 94/209, 71-80.

73. See dispatch of Ambassador Francesco Pesaro, Aranjuez, June 27, Sept. 5, 1780, Archivio di Stato, letters 203, 213, Venice. The Papal Nuncio Colonna was reported to have advised the Russian ambassador that F intended to make a separate peace. Cumberland to H, SP 94/209, 81-84. See also Haslang to Vieregg, London, June 27, July 4, Oct. 10, 1780. KBGS 502/4: 79-80, 83-84, 294-297; Van Rechteren to T.H.M., Madrid, July 10, 1780. SGH 6857; Graf von Kaunitz to K, Sept. 7, 1780, SKD, Spanien 142, sect. 3; K to MDA, Oct. 1, 1780, SKD, Frankreich, 234; Count von Belgiojoso to K, London, July 28, Oct. 17, 1780, SKD, Spanien, 164.

74. (June 24, 1780) SP 94/209: 87-89; Spanish text in Hussey's hand, entitled "Cumberland's Discourses and Reflexions on the Way of Establishing Peace without the Intervention of France," is in AHN, E, 4220: 2, doc. 165, dated June 25, 1780.

75. Germain to Cumberland, July 29, 1780, *Stopford-Sackville* MSS., I, 334; H to Cumberland, Aug. 4, 22, 1780. SP 94/209, 158-163, 179-182.

76. Cumberland to H, July 14, 1780. SP 94/209, 114-120.

77. Cumberland to H, July 21, 1780. SP 94/209, 114-120. Bernardo del Campo to Cumberland, July 22, 1780. SP 94/209, 143-144.

78. Campo to F, memorandum, July 23 or 24, 1780. AHN, E, 4220: 2, docs. 168-172.

79. Cumberland to H, July 21, 1780. SP 94/209, 123-130.

80. Cumberland to Hussey, Aug., 1780. SP 94/209, 175-176.

81. Cumberland to H, Aug. 24, 1780. SP 94/209, 185-188.

82. Hussey to Cumberland, Sept. 10, 1780. AHN, E, 4220: 2, doc. 125, 126.

83. Bessière to V, Aug. 3, 1780. CP E 600: 58.

84. Cumberland, "Narrative of Secret Negotiations with Spain, 1780-81," Add. MSS., 28851, BM.

85. Panin was quoted as telling Normande, the Spanish chargé at Petersburg, that Cumberland's mission was doomed to fail. Vérac to V, Sept. 8, 1780. CP R 105: 77.

86. JA to President of Congress, Amsterdam, Aug. 23, 1780, extract. CL; *RDC*, IV, 41.

87. F to A, Oct. 11, Nov. 25, 1779, AHN, 4116: 1, pt. 4, no. 6; F to H, Nov. 4, 1780. SP 94/209, 236-238. For Hussey's activities in England, see Hussey to H, Nov. 30, 1780. SP 94/209, 242; H to F, Dec. 9, 1780. SP 94/209, 247-248.

88. AHN, E, 4220: 2, doc. 105; Mr. Hussey's Account (Oct. 27, 1780), SP 94/209, 220-221. For the rumor that Hussey was to receive a pension from the Spanish court, see Graf von Kaunitz to K, Oct. 16, 1780. SKD, Spanien, 142, sect. 3.

89. "Paper delivered by His Excellency confidentially to Don Thomas Hussey," Sept. 21, 1780. AHN, E, 4220: 2, docs. 128-130.

90. Warwick Castle, Oct. 7, 1780 (French translation copied by V). CP A 533: 231. For a similar account, see Hussey to F, Lisbon, Dec. 28, 1780. AHN, E, 4220: 2, doc. 131.

91. CG, V, 142.

92. Hussey to F, Lisbon, Dec. 28, 1780; F to Hussey, Pardo, Jan. 20, 1781. AHN, E, 4220: 2, doc. 131, 134.

93. F's ultimatum (Jan. 20, 1781). Cumberland Papers, 91-95. BM; SP 94/209, 273-278.

94. Cumberland to H, Jan. 31, 1781. SP 94/209, 261-264.

95. H to Cumberland, Feb. 14, 1781. SP 94/209, 279-280.

96. Cumberland to Germain, Dec. 13, 1780. Germain Papers, 107-112. CL.

97. Cumberland, Memoirs, pp. 250-259.

98. Ibid., p. 255. "Narrative of Secret Negotiations." Add. MSS. 28851, BM.

99. See Memorial of Cumberland to Lord North (n.d., 1781?), Cumberland Papers, 123-127, BM.

100. Memoirs, pp. 274-293.

101. See "Particulars of the Secret Negotiation between England and Spain carried on at Madrid in 1780 and 1781" (n.d., 1781?), Cumberland Papers, 95-102, BM.

102. Memoirs, p. 265.

103. Richard Cumberland, Posthumous Dramatic Works (2 vols., London, 1813), I, 71-154.

104. Memoirs, p. 300. Hussey to Campo, Bologna, June 22, 1782. AHN, E, 4220: 2, doc. 147.

105. See Louis I. Newman, Richard Cumberland, Critic and Friend of the Jews (New York, 1919); Stanley T. Williams, Richard Cumberland, His Life and Dramatic Works (2 vols., New Haven, 1917).

106. AHN, E, 4220: 2, docs. 140, 141.

107. AHN, E, 4220: 2, docs. 143-145.

108. Mountstuart to Hussey, June 22, Aug. 2, Nov. 20, 1782, urging the latter to send on to London any intelligence about Gibraltar, Letter Books of Viscount Mountstuart, XI, 322, 341, 364. Add. MSS. 36, 804, BM.

109. JA to President of Congress, April 18, 1780, RDC, III, 623.

110. JA to Gênet, May 17, 1780, ibid., p. 687.

111. JA to BF, Aug. 17, 1780, ibid., IV, 35.

112. JA to JJ, Paris, May 13, 1780. JP.

113. JJ to BF, Sept. 8, 1780. JP.

114. JJ to BF, Oct. 25, 1780. FP; JP.

115. See MDA to K, Aug. 16, 1780. SKD, Frankreich, 235.

116. V's attitude toward the Hussey-Cumberland negotiations is reflected in his correspondence with M. See, especially, CP E 598: 125, 160-162, 288-295, 342, 400-402, 405-414; 601: 445-448.

CHAPTER IV. EIGHT DAYS IN JUNE (JUNE 2—9, 1780)

1. For foreign reaction to rising English discontent, see, e.g., Frederick to Goltz, Mar. 20, 1780, *PCFG*, XLIV, 145; A to F, Jan. 7, 1780, AHN, E, 4202, 1; Haslang to Vieregg, KBGS 502/4: 232-236, 265-266, 286-288, 314-316; von Belgiojoso to K, Feb., 1780, SKD, England, 164:I.
2. See, e.g., *PR*, XVI, 18.
3. See Jenkinson to G, Oct. 18, 1779. *CG*. IV, 465, 466; also *HP*, III, 209-210.
4. For the suggestion that the Bedford faction were behind "some plott," see Jenkinson to G, Dec. 23, 1779. *CG*, IV, 532.
5. *Ibid.*, pp. 471, 486; *HP*, III, 620.
6. Reginald Lucas, *Lord North* (London, 1913), II, 98.
7. North to G, Nov. ?, 1779. *CG*, IV, 493, 494.
8. Jenkinson to G, Nov. 28, 1779, *ibid.*, p. 500.
9. Add. MSS. 38, 312, pp. 79-82, BM.
10. G to Thurlow, Dec. 11, 1779. *CG*, IV, 517.
11. G to Thurlow, draft endorsed by G, delivered Nov. 12, 1779, and then reissued Dec. 3. *CG*, IV, 507, 508. See also G to Thurlow, Dec. 11, 1779, *ibid.*, pp. 517, 518.
12. *Ibid.*, p. 503.
13. G to Thurlow, Dec. 16, 1779, *ibid.*, pp. 520-523. At this time, however, S and Rockingham did not seem far apart on the American issue. While overtly favoring American independence, Rockingham privately expressed the hope that, once passions had subsided, America would judiciously weigh whether "in good policy for herself, as an *independent state*, the annihilation of England as a great power was advisable." Rockingham to Admiral Keppel (Nov., 1779), Earl of Albemarle, *Memoirs of the Marquess of Rockingham* (London, 1852), II, 388.
14. *CG*, IV, 522.
15. G to North, Dec. 20 (?), 1779, *ibid.*, pp. 525, 526.
16. Add. MSS. 38, 212, pp. 225-232, BM; H. Butterfield, *George III, Lord North, and the People* (London, 1949), pp. 117-177; *HP*, III, 365.
17. *CG*, IV, 509; see also draft of resolutions, Dec. 8, 1779, *ibid.*, pp. 511, 512.
18. *PR*, XV, 53-60, 65, 66, 71-73.
19. *Ibid.*, pp. 38-43, 81-87, 92; XVI, 33-35. Other critics of the administration's handling of the Irish question included General Conway. *Ibid.*, XVI, 65, 66.
20. *PR*, XVI, 188-194.
21. John Almon, *The Remembrancer; or Impartial Repository of Public Events* (17 vols., London, 1775-84), I, 165-166.
22. *PR*, XV, 11, 37-46, 49-51; XVI, 14, 29, 31-33, 66, 67, 74, 90, 92, 96, 98, 99, 103, 108, 110, 124, 125, 131, 157, 160-162.
23. *PR*, XVI, 187.
24. Butterfield, *op. cit.*, pp. 176, 177.
25. Papers concerning county meetings, 1779-1780, R 136-138, and correspondence in Dec., 1779, relating to the calling of the Yorkshire meeting. R 1-1867-1873, 1875. See also C. Wyvill, *Political Papers, chiefly respecting the attempt of the County of York and other Considerable Districts . . . to effect a reformation of the Parliament of Great Britain* (6 vols., London, 1794-1808); I. R. Christie, *Wilkes, Wyvill, and Reform* (London, 1962), pp. 68-77; Caroline Robbins, *The Eighteenth-Century Commonwealthman* (Cambridge, 1959), pp. 370-373; S. Maccoby, *English Radicalism, 1762-1785* (London, 1955), pp. 287-304, 312; Eugene C. Black, *The Association* (Cambridge, Mass., 1963), pp. 31-82.

26. *PR*, XVII (1780), 72-75.
27. For Rockingham's views that the time was not ripe for such "crude" or "speculative" propositions, see R-1881, 1882, 1892, 1896, 1955; Albemarle, *Memoirs of Rockingham*, II, 396-400, 402-405, 408-409; for his concern about the "security of property," see Rockingham to Rev. Henry Zouch, Mar. 23, 1780. R 1-1883. As the Duke of Portland saw it, "Very many well-meaning men were running wild." *Ibid.*, pp. 410-415. "Decision and correctness" had not prevailed at York. Rockingham to S, April 2, 1780. LPB.
28. *LP*, 165; 167-173.
29. Memorandum agreed to by the Marquis of Rockingham, S, and the Duke of Richmond, March 19, 1780. Shelburne Political Notes, LPB; Rockingham to Burke, Mar. 31, 1780. Burke, *Corr.*, IV, 216, 217. For S's opposition to annual elections and "a total change of the representation," see Wyvill, *Political Papers*, IV, 131-136. But cf. Burke, *Corr.*, IV, 193.
30. *PR*, XVII, 79.
31. *Ibid.*, pp. 93-116; Edmund Burke, *Works* (Boston, 1865-67), II, 267-364; *Annual Register, 1780*, pp. 94-100.
32. *Ibid.*, pp. 127, 128, 130-131, 136.
33. *PR*, XVII, 239-240. See also *HP*, III, 354-360.
34. *Ibid.*, pp. 243, 277.
35. *Ibid.*, p. 278.
36. Charles William Wentworth Fitzwilliam, Earl, ed., *Correspondence of the Right Honorable Edmund Burke; between the year 1774, and the period of his decease in 1797* (London, 1884), II, 339; also Burke to Richard Champion, May 24, 1780, Burke, *Corr.*, IV, 240.
37. Rockingham to S, April 5, 1780. LPB. See also *FS*, II, 318; *HP*, II, 368.
38. Barré to S, April 7, 1780. LPB.
39. *Letters*, XI, 149. See also *Journals*, II, 294-298.
40. *CG*, V, 39-40.
41. *FS*, III, 81.
42. Wyvill, *Political Papers*, III, 194 (May 14, 1780).
43. For the endorsement by Fox and the Westminster Committee of S's stand in the Lords, see Fox to S, Feb. 19, 1780, with enclosure, LPB.
44. Wyvill, *Political Papers*, III, 228 et seq.
45. *PR*, XVI, 121, 122; *HP*, II, 8, 9: Sir George O. Trevelyan, *George the Third and Charles Fox* (London, 1915), II, 238-242; Christopher Hobhouse, *Fox* (London, 1947), p. 89.
46. Charles Jenkinson to James Robinson, July 21, 1780. HMC, *R*, X, app. pt. V, pp. 31-32.
47. For the Duke's radical program, see Walter King to Burke, Nov. 5, 1779. Burke, *Corr.*, IV, 165-168.
48. Walpole, *Last Journals*, II, 272, 273.
49. Richmond's peerage was registered in the Parlement on July 1, 1777, oddly enough not many months before France entered the war. Richmond visited France in 1776 and again the following year. Mrs. Paget Toynbee, ed., *Lettres de la Marquise du Deffand à Horace Walpole* (London, 1912), III, 244-257 *passim*; 330-352 *passim*. See also A. G. Olson, *The Radical Duke* (London, 1961).
50. *Annual Register, 1780*, p. 209.
51. *PR*, XVII, 374; *PH*, XXI, 218, 459; Walpole, *Journals*, II, 301, 302. Both Fullarton and Stormont implied that BF was the Paris correspondent of S. Walpole, *Letters*, XI, 144, 153, 154; *Journals*, II, 289-291; *FS*, III, 75-77; Trevelyan, *op. cit.*, II, 235-237.

52. Fox to S (undated, 1780). LPB. See also Richmond to S, Mar. 24, 1780, *loc cit.*; Morellet to S, June 7, 1780. Morellet, *Lettres à Shelburne*, p. 180.
53. Walpole, *Last Journals*, pp. 288-291, 340; *PR*, XVII, 407; *HP*, II, 475.
54. *Letters*, XI, 16, 125.
55. *PR*, XVII, 116.
56. Gordon receives sympathetic treatment at the hands of Robert Watson, *The Life of George Gordon* (London, 1795). More critical treatments are found in Percy Colson, *The Strange History of Lord George Gordon* (London, 1937), Christopher Hibbert, *King Mob* (Cleveland and New York, 1958), pp. 15-29, and *HP*, II, 513-515. Dickens' *Barnaby Rudge* provides an unforgettable account of the riots, but the leadership is an almost unrecognizable caricature. For the broader issue of the role of the "crowd" as distinguished from the "mob" see George Rudé, *The Crowd in History, 1730-1848* (New York, 1964).
57. 18 George III, c. 60.
58. W. Forbes, *Memories of Scottish Catholics during the 17th and 18th Centuries* (Leith, 1909), II, 375; *Lettres de la Marquise du Deffand*, III, 496.
59. For Haslang's account, see Haslang to Vieregg, June 6, 9, 13, 23, July 4, 14, 18, 21, Aug. 25, 29, 1780; Vieregg to Haslang, June 22, 29, 1780; Stormont to Haslang, July 18, 1780. KBGS 502/4; 21-25, 35-36, 42-44, 73-78, 86-91, 102-122, 250, 251. See also Abbé MacDermott to V, June 15, 1780. CP A 533: 159; Walpole, *Journals, II*, 307; *Letters*, XI, 196. Stormont personally apologized to the diplomats involved, and compensation was later awarded their governments by Great Britain.
60. See J. Paul de Castro, *The Gordon Riots* (London, 1926), pp. 73, 101.
61. *Horace Walpole's Correspondence*, ed. W. S. Lewis (New Haven, 1937), II, 224.
62. *Letters*, XI, 202.
63. Frederick to Goltz, Aug. 14, 1780. *PCFG*, XLIV, 415.
64. William Bodham Donne, *The Correspondence of King George the Third with Lord North from 1768 to 1783* (London, 1867), II, 322, 333.
65. Walpole, *Journals*, II, 312.
66. *History of the Criminal Law* (London, 1883), II, 274.
67. For Gordon's last days, see Colson, *Strange History*, pp. 166-277; *HP*, II, 514, 515.
68. *Letters*, XI, 241, 261.
69. Burke, *Corr.*, IV, 255-257; Colson, *op. cit.*, p. 103n.; De Castro, *op. cit.*, p. 236.
70. *Fanaticism and Treason; or, a Dispassionate History of the Rise, Progress, and Suppression of the Rebellious Insurrections in June 1780 by a Real Friend to Religion and to Britain* (London, Printed for G. Kearsly, No. 46, Fleet Street, 1780), p. 85; Hibbert, *op. cit.*, p. 144.
71. *Fanaticism and Treason*, p. 29; Walpole, *Letters*, XI, 226; Donne, *op. cit.*, II, 323n.; Hibbert, *op. cit.*, p. 122. See also SP 37/20, 172-173, 278-279, 280-281; Mr. Batte to James Harris, June 8, 1780, Earl of Malmesbury, *A Series of Letters of the First Earl of Malmesbury, His Family and Friends from 1745 to 1820* (London, 1870), I, 465; Sir Joseph Yorke to JH, June 24, July 8, 1780. Hardwicke Papers, Add. MSS., 35434, BM.
72. MacDermott to V, written from Hôtel du parlement d' Angleterre, rue Coqueran, June 15, 1780. CP A 553: 159.
73. George F. Rudé, "The Gordon Riots: A Study of the Rioters and Their Victims," Royal Historical Society, *Transactions*, 5th ser., VI (1956), 93-114.
74. MacDermott to V, June 21, 1780; V to MacDermott, June 30, 1780. CP A 553: 166, 171.
75. *Gazeta de Madrid*, June 23, 1780. SP 94/209, 95-100.
76. *Annual Register*, 1777, pp. 28-31, 246-247.

77. James Smith to JJ, Brussels, Sept. 12, 1780. JP.
78. *BFB*, VII, 87.
79. Lord Mountstuart to Charles Stuart, June 3, 1780, John Stuart Bute, *A Prime Minister and His Son* (New York, 1925), p. 193; Walpole, *Letters*, XI, 231, 232.
80. Walpole, *Letters*, XI, 241.
81. S to Richard Price, Sept. 5, 1779. LPB.
82. *PH*, XX, 650.
83. Sir Nathaniel William Wraxall, *Historical Memoirs of My Own Time* (Philadelphia, 1837), p. 142.
84. *PH*, XXI, 671.
85. *Ibid.*, p. 682.
86. *Fanaticism and Treason*, p. 50; but cf. *FS*, III, 84-89.
87. Frederick Reynolds, *Life and Times, written by himself* (London, 1826), I, 130. Hibbert, *op. cit.*, pp. 122-123.
88. Albemarle, *Memoirs of Rockingham*, II, 403, 408.
89. *PR*, XVII, 277.
90. CP A 533 (March 14, 1780). For views of foreign diplomats on the Gordon Riots, see, e.g., CP Aut 341: 221; SKD England, 164, pt. 1 (June 20, July 11, 18), SKD Spanien, 235 (June 18, 1780); AHN, E, 4622, p. 79; 4202, apt. 1, letter 1712, pp. 153-160. See also S. Hardy, "Mes Loisirs, ou Journal des événements tels qu'ils parviennent à ma connaissance." MSS. Français, nos. 6680-87, IV, 303, BN.
91. To the Rev. William Mason, June 29, 1780, *Letters*, XI, 232.
92. *Annual Register, 1780*, p. 200; cf. also Conway to Keith, Aug. 30, 1780, Keith, *Memoirs*, II, 169. For S's innuendoes against the government, see *Fanaticism and Treason*, p. 38.
93. *CG*, V, 71, 73.
94. See I. R. Christie, "The Marquis of Rockingham and Lord North's offer of a coalition, June-July 1780," *English Historical Review*, LXIX (1954), 394-401.
95. Rockingham to Portland, Sept. 1, 1780. Portland MSS., cited by I. R. Christie, *The End of North's Ministry, 1780-1782* (London, 1958), p. 45.
96. For his role, see W. T. Laprade, ed., *Parliamentary Papers of John Robinson, 1774-1784* (London, 1922), pp. 31-48; and Christie, *op. cit.*, pp. 33-45. The government disbursed some £103,000 in that campaign. *HP*, I, 80-87.
97. Christie, *op. cit.*, p. 159.
98. Walpole, *Journals*, II, 319; Sir Joseph Yorke to JH, June 24, July 8, 1780. Hardwicke Papers, Add. MSS. 35, 434, BM. See also William Eden to Germain, June 18, 1780. HMC, *R*, IX, 101.
99. *PR*, XVII, 751, 753.

CHAPTER V. JACQUES NECKER'S PRIVATE PEACE FEELERS

1. See BF to Carmichael, Passy, June 17, 1780, *RDC*, III, 799; also Gaspard M. Leblond, *Mémoires pour servir a l'histoire de la révolution opérée dans la musique par M. le Chevalier Gluck* (Naples and Paris, 1781); J.-G. Prod'Homme, *Gluck* (Paris, 1948), p. 338.
2. *The Life and Writings of Turgot, Comptroller-General of France, 1774-6*, ed. William Walker Stephens (London and New York, 1895), pp. 295-296, 321-324.
3. *D*, I, 522-524, 617.
4. See Baron Jehan de Witte, ed., *Journal de l'Abbé de Véri* (2 vols., Paris, 1928-30), II, 344, 345.
5. Deane to the Committee of Secret Correspondence, Paris, Aug. 18, 1776. *RDC*, II, 123.

6. JJ to the President of Congress, Madrid, Nov. 6, 1780. *RDC*, IV, 123.
7. See, e.g., BF to Dumas, Paris, July 26, 1780; JJ to De Neufville and Son, Madrid, July 29, 1780. *RDC*, IV, 11, 12, 15, 16.
8. L to V, May 28, 1780. CP EU 12: 148-156.
9. Véri, *Journal*, II, 320 (July 6, 1780).
10. *RDC*, III, 848, 870, 871.
11. *RDC*, III, 605, 806, 808-816, 827-829, 844; IV, 3-11, 13, 16-18.
12. JA to V, July 17, 1780; V to JA, July 25, 1780, *RDC*, III, 861-863, 882-883. JA's rejoinder, July 26, 1780, *ibid.*, IV, 4-11.
13. Véri, *Journal*, II, 357.
14. JA to BF, Amsterdam, Aug. 17, 1780, *RDC*, IV, 34, 35; Véri, *Journal*, II, 344, 345 (Aug. 23, 1780).
15. See, e.g., Breteuil to V, Vienna, July 29, Aug. 20, 30, 1780; V to Breteuil, Sept. 9, 1780. CP Aut 341: 232, 233, 235, 260, 279, 283; Marie-Daniel Bourrée, Chevalier de Corberon, *Journal Intime: Un diplomat français à la cour de Catherine II, 1775-1780* (Paris, 1901), pp. 2, 231 *et seq.*; Vérac to V, July 13, 1780, CP R, 104.
16. MT to MDA, Mar. 4, July 31, 1775, *Corr. Marie-Thérèse et Mercy*, II, 302, 360; André Castellot, *Marie Antoinette d'après les documents inédits* (2nd ed., Paris, 1953), p. 135.
17. MA to MT, *Corr. Marie-Thérèse et Mercy*, III, 474; Véri, *Journal*, II, 315.
18. *Corr. Marie-Thérèse et Mercy*, III, 448, 449, 467, 479, 488; M. Alphonse Jobêz, *La France sous Louis XVI* (Paris, 1881), II, 299, 300; Castellot, *Marie Antoinette*, p. 140.
19. See Necker to Maurepas (n.d.), Cartons des Rois, Louis XVI, K 163, AN; Montbarrey, *Mémoires*, II, 374, 375, for a hostile portrait.
20. For an analysis of Necker's financial program and the intrigues against him, see Mirabeau, Notebook, Bib. de l'Arsenal; see also Necker's wartime letter to Edmund Burke, May 5, 1780, expressing his appreciation for the latter's extravagant praise in Parliament (Burke, *Corr.*, IV, 233), and for his assistance to Burke's family, Necker to Burke, July 21, 1780. Fitzwilliam MSS. See also Frederick to Goltz, Mar. 30, 1780. *PCFG*, XLIV, 165. See also *Corr. Marie-Thérèse et Mercy*, III, 405, 406, 414, 422, 433, 435; Morellet to S, July 13, 1780. *Lettres à Shelburne*, pp. 184-185.
21. Véri, *Journal*, II, 352, 353.
22. See Paul Wentworth to Suffolk, *c.* May 15, July 17; to Eden, Dec. 22, 1777. *SF*, nos. 182, 233, 694; MT to K, Oct. 17, 1779. A. Arneth and J. Flammermont, *Correspondance Secrète du Comte de Mercy-Argenteau avec l'Empereur Joseph II et le Prince de Kaunitz* (Paris, 1890), II, 542; also Edouard Chapuisat, *Necker, 1732-1804* (Paris, [1938]), pp. 98, 99.
23. Beaumarchais to V, Jan. 22, 1778. *SF*, no. 1845.
24. Beaumarchais to V, Mar. 16, 1778. *SF*, no. 1897.
25. For the secret funds of the Department of Foreign Affairs, as well as of the royal family, see France Weiss, *Acquits et ordonnances de comptant; histoire des fonds secrets sous l'ancien régime* (Paris, 1939), pp. 134 *et seq.*
26. Necker to Maurepas (1780, n.d.), Cartons des Rois, K163, No. 13^{12}, AN.
27. See Cartons des Rois, Louis XVI, K163, no. 13, 21$^{1-3}$ (Oct. 8, 1780).
28. Véri, *Journal*, II, 323.
29. V to the King, Sept. 27, 1780. Cartons des Rois, Louis XVI, K164, no. 3, AN.
30. CP E 601, nos. 16, 17, 18, 25; *D*, IV, 489, 493.
31. Véri, *Journal*, II, 377 *et seq.*
32. For Forth's role on the eve of France's entry into the war, see *D*, II, 526, 537,

538, 591, 596, 597, 774, 807, 808; A to F, Mar. 7, 1778, AHN, E, 3884, p. 906; YU, II, 226-243; R to BF, April 12, 1782, RDC, V, 298-299. See also R. W. Van Alstyne, *Huntington Lib. Qly.*, XXVII (1964), 323, 324. For Maurepas' later checking up on Forth's standing and integrity, see Baudouin to V, Sept. 26, 27, 1781. CP A 534: 104, 105.

33. *CG*, V, 103, 104.
34. Mr. Hobart to S, May 6, 1782, with enclosure, "A Proposed Sketch in 1779 between the Powers at War," LP.
35. Lewis Dutens to H, Turin, Aug. 2, 30, 1780. SP 92/83.
36. Corberon, *Journal Intime*, pp. 250, 251 (July 13, 1780).
37. Notes by Thomas Walpole, July 31, Aug. 8, 28, Sept. 2, 4, 5, 1780. Thomas Walpole Papers AB/1 (courtesy of David Holland, Esq.); *HP*, III, 600-601.
38. North to G; G to North, both Sept. 18, 1780. *CG*, V, 122, 123.
39. Véri, *Journal*, II, 386, 398. For Véri's admiration of Turgot, see Morellet, *Mémoires*, I, 224.
40. Walpole to North, Oct. 2, 14, Nov. 12 (copies); North to Walpole, Oct. 31; Necker to Walpole, Nov. 11. T. Walpole Papers AB/1; G to North, Oct. 30, 31; North to G, Oct. 31 (?) 1780. *CG*, V, 144, 45.
41. Sir Joseph Yorke to William Eden, April 6, 1779. *SF*, no. 1281; Véri, *Journal*, II, 381, 386; Philip Sagnac, *La fin de l'Ancien Régime et la révolution Américaine, 1763-1789* (Paris, 1952).
42. For the combined operations of Necker and the Queen's favorites to bring down Sartine and Montbarrey, see Baron de Besenval, *Mémoires* (Paris, 1805), II.
43. Véri, *Journal*, II, 394.
44. Carmichael Papers, PCC 88; *RDC*, IV, 51-52; also Carmichael to Comm. of For. Affairs, Sept. 25, 1780. *Ibid.*, p. 71.
45. M to V, Sept. 10, 1780. CP E 600: 398-403.
46. Carmichael to Comm. of For. Affairs, Nov. 28, 1780, Carmichael Papers, PCC 88; *RDC*, IV, 164, 165.
47. L to V, Mar. 25, April 1, 18, 1781. CP EU 16: 48, 116, 128, 191.
48. See *FS*, I, 137; *The North Briton* (collected ed., London, 1763), July 3, 1762, No. 5; *PH*, XVII, 763-785 (Jan., 1770), where the bribery charge was pronounced to be "in the highest degree frivolous and unworthy of credit." See also Walter L. Dorn, "Frederick the Great and Lord Bute," *Journal of Modern History*, I (1929), 557-558. For a refutation of the gossip about a liaison between the Princess Dowager and Bute, see Romney Sedgwick, *Letters from George III to Lord Bute, 1756-1766* (London, 1939), p. lvi. As recently as Nov., 1778, Mountstuart felt obliged to reassure the public that his father had no intention of returning to office. Walpole, *Last Journals*, p. 201.
49. H to William Deane Poyntz, Aug. 6, 13; Mountstuart to H, Oct. 5, Dec. 15, 1779; draft of instructions to Mountstuart, Oct. 13, 1779; SP 92/82. Count von Belgiojoso to K, SKD, England 163.
50. Mountstuart to H, Mar. 25, 1780; H to Mountstuart, April 14, 1780.
51. Poyntz to W, Oct. 27, 1779. SP 92/82.
52. H to Mountstuart, June 13, 1780; Mountstuart to H, July 3, 1780. SP 92/83.
53. Mountstuart to H, June 5, July 10, 1780. SP 92/83.
54. Choiseul to V, Turin, July 19, Aug. 23, 1780; V to Choiseul, Aug. 11, 1780. CP Turin 262: 203, 228, 239. For Geneva as a sphere of French influence and intervention, see Letters and Papers of Mountstuart and Dutens to the Secretary of State and Drafts to Them, Jan. 12—Dec. 29, 1781. FO 67/1.
55. In 1781 Mountstuart's help was sought by a prominent member of the counterrevolutionary Negatifs to ascertain the intentions of the coguarantors, France and

Sardinia, toward Geneva. Mallet to Mountstuart, Jan. 10, 1782. Add. MSS. 38, 744, pp. 137-139, BM. For the intrigues of England and France in the internal affairs of Geneva, see J. L. Soulevie, *Historical and Political Memoirs of the Reign of Louis XVI* (London, 1802), V, 188-251.

56. Frank Brady and Frederick A. Pottle, eds., *James Boswell, on the Grand Tour: Italy, Corsica and France, 1765-1766* (New York, 1955), pp. 9-20, 87, 88, 95, 103, 116, 129; *Boswell, in Search of a Wife, 1766-1769* (New York, 1956), pp. 14, 30n.; *Boswell for the Defense, 1769-1774* (New York, 1959), pp. 58, 62, 80, 130, 214; *Letters of James Boswell to the Rev. W. J. Temple*, ed. by Thomas Seccombe (London, 1908), pp. 147-150, 159-160.

57. J. C. L. de Sismondi, *De la vie et des écrits de Paul Henri Mallet* (Geneva, 1807); Hélène Stadler, *Paul-Henri Mallet* (Lausanne, 1924).

58. In the spring of 1780 Mountstuart was writing home condemning the "weakness and indecision" of the government in prosecuting "an unlucky and unsuccessful war" and foresaw "a civil war at perhaps no great distance." Mountstuart to Sir William Musgrave, Turin, April 28, May 17, 1780. Bute Papers, Mount Stuart.

59. Mountstuart to Sir William Musgrave, Turin, July 3, 1780. Bute Papers, Mount Stuart.

60. "Most secret," Mountstuart to H, Geneva, Sept. 18, 1780. SP 92/83. The letter was received by H on October 14th "by a private hand."

61. Mountstuart to H, Turin, Oct. 18, 1780. SP 92/83.

62. Mallet's letters are found in "Letters to Lord Mountstuart, 1779-1783," Add. MSS. 38, 774, pp. 31, 32, 35, 36-39, 42-49, BM. Copies of Mountstuart's replies of Oct. 18 and Nov. 15, 1780, are in "Letterbook of Viscount Mountstuart," Add. MSS. 36, 803: 56-57, BM.

63. "Letters of the Secretary of State to Mountstuart, 1779-83," H to Mountstuart, St. James's, Nov. 21, Dec. 5, 1780, Add. MSS. 36, 801, pp. 126-130, 135, BM; copies in SP 92/83. The Dec. 5th dispatch in reply to Mountstuart's letter of Nov. 15 reaffirmed H's of Nov. 21.

64. Mountstuart to H, "Secret and private," in cipher, 1780. SP 92/83.

65. MDA to K, Nov. 18, 1780. SKD, Frankreich, 235.

66. Lord Mahon, *History of England* (London, 1858), VII, Appendix, pp. xiii-xv.

67. *CG*, V, 102, 103.

68. *CG*, V, 163.

69. Marquis of Abergavenny Papers, HMC, *R*, X, App. VI, pp. 39-40, No. 336, Dec. 19, 1780. "A letter of importance has been safely delivered with the seals unbroken, but not quite as was, perhaps, expected, from accidents not material to mention." (Endorsed by J[ohn] R[obinson]) "Secret. Lord North's note to Mr. Necker. Copied in a feigned Italian hand, and sent the same night to Mr. Todd at the Post Office, directed 'À Monsieur Neckar, à Paris'—with a most secret letter to Mr. Todd, entrusting it to his care, and to be forwarded this night by the mail to Ostend, unperceived and unobserved by anyone."

70. Pierre Joly, *Necker* (Paris, 1951), p. 191.

71. G. Bancroft, *Histoire de l'action commune de la France et de l'Amérique pour l'independence des États-Unis*, translated by A. de Circourt (Paris, 1876), III, 153.

72. Joly, *Necker*, p. 202.

73. MDA to K, Jan. 21, 1781. Bancroft-Austria, NYPL.

74. MDA to K, Feb. 7, 1781. Bancroft-Austria, NYPL.

75. For foreign reaction to the *Compte rendu*, see Giuseppi Doria Pamphili to Pallavicini, Feb. 19, 1781, Nunzio Francia, Vatican Archives; La Vauguyon to V, Mar. 8, 27, 1781, CP H 543: 395, 495; Grimm to Catharine II, Feb. 27/Mar. 10, 1781; Catharine to Grimm, Mar. 19/30, 1781, *SRIO*, XXXIII, 117-119, 197.

76. See Necker to the King, April 9, 1787; to Calonne, Jan. 29, Feb. 7, 1787. Cartons des Rois, Louis XVI, no. 163, no. 13, AN.

77. See Jacques Necker, *Compte rendu au roi* (Paris: Imprimerie Royale, 1781), pp. 9, 10, 16, 105, 190.

78. J. M. Augeard, *Mémoires secrets* (Paris, 1866), pp. 98 *et seq.*; MDA to K, June 23, 1781, *Corr. secrete Mercy avec Joseph II et Kaunitz*, I, 46 (letter 28). Necker's removal was appraised by Mountstuart as "worth two victories or rather the most brilliant campaign." Mountstuart to Sir William Musgrave, Turin, Feb. 16, 1781. Bute Papers, Mount Stuart. See also Grimm to Catharine II, June 6/17, 1781. *SRIO*, XXXIII, 194-196.

79. Letters of intelligence, Paris, May 19, 20, 22, 1781. *CG*, V, 237-239; M. Alphonse Jobez, *La France sous Louis XVI* (Paris, 1881), II, 441.

80. Mountstuart had personally written S on Jan. 24 and Mar 12, 1783, to be appointed to one of the embassies arising from the peace preliminaries. LPB.

81. Mallet to Mountstuart, Nov. 7, 1781, Jan. 10?, n.d., and May 25?, 1782, "Letters to Lord Mountstuart, 1779-1783," Add. MSS. 38, 774: 72, 73, 137, 138, 140; Mountstuart to Mallet, June 26, 1782, Add. MSS. 36, 803: 202; Mountstuart to Charles James Fox, April 17, May 9, June 12, 26, FO 67/2; copies in Add. MSS. 36, 802: 224-227. BM.

82. Mountstuart to Fox, Turin, June 26, 1782. FO 67/2; copy in Add. MSS. 36, 802: 228-229.

83. Mountstuart to Hussey, Turin, Aug. 2, 1782, *ibid.*, pp. 212, 213.

84. Mountstuart explained to Hussey that he had no wish to remain an idle spectator "of what is going forward," and promised to keep him posted if anything happened "relative to the business we have so often conversed on." Mountstuart to Hussey, Nov. 20, 1782, *ibid.*, pp. 226, 227.

85. Mountstuart to Liston, Paris, Dec. 20, 21, 24, 1782. "Letter book of Mountstuart," Add. MSS. 36, 804: 17-27, BM.

86. For Pulteney's relations with BF, see Frederick B. Tolles, "Franklin and the Pulteney Mission: An Episode in the Secret History of the American Revolution," *Huntington Library Quarterly*, XVII (1953-54), 37-58: *HP*, III, 342, 343.

87. *Diary*, III, 47 (Nov. 5, 1780). No documents bearing out this story are found among the Pulteney Papers, Huntington Library.

88. For JJ's entries, see Frank Monaghan, ed., *Diary of John Jay During the Peace Negotiations of 1782* (New Haven, 1934); *Diary*, II, 98.

89. Genêt Papers, LC. See also Frederic Masson, *Le Départment des Affaires Etrangères pendant la Révolution* (Paris, 1877), p. 42.; Meade Minnegerode, *Jefferson, Friend of France: The Career of Edmond Charles Genêt* (New York, 1928), pp. 64, 65.

CHAPTER VI. THE LION, THE FOX, AND THE ASS

1. See Besenval, *Mémoires*, II, 221, 222; Louis Bonneville de Marsangy, *Le Chevalier de Vergennes, son Ambassade à Constantinople* (2 vols., Paris, 1894), I, 339-365; *Le Comte de Vergennes: Son ambassade en Suède, 1771-1774* (Paris, 1898), pp. 46-48; E. and J. de Goncourt, *La Femme au dix-huitieme siècle* (Paris, 1903), p. 223. When Louis XV died, Marie Antoinette only permitted Mme. de Vergennes to be presented at court when the Austrian Chancellor, K, approved. *Ibid.*, p. 430n.

2. V to M, Dec. 13, 1777, CP E 587, no. 103; D, II, 644.

3. LV to V, June 16, 1780, CP H 541: 191-192; to BF introducing "M. Dumont," June 17, 1780, FP, 1st ser. 3, Legation Letter Books, 1779-1780, p. 55, LC.

4. For a sympathetic estimate of LV's role, see P. Coquelle, *L'Alliance Franco-Hollandaise contre L'Angleterre* (Paris, 1902), pp. 211-289. V to LV, June 17, 1780. FP, 1st ser. 3, Legation Letter Books, 1779-1780, pp. 191-192.
5. A to V, June 22, 1780, CP E 599: 326-327.
6. V to A, June 22, 1780, CP H 541: 193.
7. V to M, June 22, 1780. CP E 599: 328; BF to R, June 24, 1780. *BFS*, VII, 108-109.
8. A to F, enclosing copies of correspondence with V, June 26, 1780, AHN, E, 4143, no. 1724.
9. Résumé of the Conversation with M. Montagu (June, 1780), Mém. et Docs., EU 56: 301.
10. "Notes sur la proposition du Sieur Montagu" (June, 1780), Mém. et Docs., EU 56: 296-298.
11. V to LV, June 25, 1780. CP H 541: 210.
12. V to M, June 26, 1780. CP E 599: 360.
13. Heredia to A, July 3, 1780, AHN, E, 4202, apt. 1, no. 1731, p. 177.
14. Written in English in a disguised hand, July 18, 1780, AHN, E, 4211, apt. 5, doc. 5, p. 3.
15. Aug. 14, 1782, CP H 541: 451-452.
16. CP H 542: 16-17 (Oct. 2, 1780).
17. Aug. 12, 1780, CP H 541: 439. Copy of another document, dated July 21, 1780, and signed by Richmond, S, Sir George Savile, and Charles Fox, named as agents to make contact with the French ambassador at The Hague: George Bertie, William Montague, John Lutterell, and Sir R. W. Bottle. Mém. et Docs., EU 56, 303, 304.
18. A to Fox, Aug. 19, 1780, AHN, E, 4143, no. 1763.
19. V to M, Aug. 18, 1780, CP E 600: 181.
20. M to V, Aug. 28, 1780, *ibid.*, p. 307.
21. LV to V, Aug. 2, 1780, CP H 541: 497-506.
22. Sebastian de Llano to F, Sept. 6, 1780, AHN, E, 4202, apt. 6, no. 100, pp. 1146-1153; A to F, *ibid.*, 4143, no. 1788.
23. LV to V, Sept. 2, 1780, CP H 542: 7-8.
24. De Llano to F, Sept. 6, 1780, AHN, E, 4202, apt. 6, no. 100, pp. 1146-1153.
25. Mém. et Docs., EU 56: 302.
26. See Wyvill to Lord Mahon, Sept. 29, 1780, *Wyvill Papers*, III, 264.
27. F to A, Sept. 5, 1780, AHN, E, 4143.
28. A to Sanafé, Sept. 10, 1780, AHN, E, 4202, apt. 6, no. 101, pp. 1154-1156.
29. M to V, Sept. 11; V to M, Sept. 28, 1780, CP E 600: 445-448; 601: 302-309.
30. See comment on ST letter by V to M, Nov. 27, 1780, CP E 601: 364-366.
31. LV to V, Oct. 2, 1780, CP H 542: 116-118.
32. M to V, Oct. 30, 1780, CP E 601: 234-237.
33. A to V, Oct. 17, 1780, CP A 533: 229.
34. LV to V, Feb. 2, 1781, CP H 543: 212.
35. CP A 534: 12.
36. LV to V, Mar. 1, 8, 1781, CP H 543: 363-364, 395.
37. V to LV, Mar. 7, 1781, CP H 543: 387-388.
38. Contemporary authentic signatures of S indicate that the angle of his signature differed considerably from that in the document Fox turned over, that the "r" and final "e" were made differently, while other characters are clearly labored simulations of the original.
39. The ornate "R" of the Fox document is not characteristic of Richmond; the "c" and "h" are customarily joined to letters which follow them, whereas herein they are separated; nor did the final "d" correspond with the Duke's usage.

40. Olson, *The Radical Duke*, p. 56.
41. Richmond to S, Jan. 16, April 9, June 16, 1780, LPB.
42. *FC*, I, 252, 253.
43. July 21, 22, 1780, HMC, *R*, X, App. VI, 31, 32.
44. Almon, *Remembrancer, 1780*, pt. II, p. 376. For the proposed visit of James Bowdoin's son-in-law, John Temple, to Spa to see Richmond and Camden the previous year, see Bowdoin-Temple Papers, Mass. Hist. Soc., *Proceedings*, 6th ser., IX (1897), 432-434 (May 7, 1779).
45. [Delauney], *Histoire d'un pou françois; ou l'espion d'une nouvelle espèce tant en France qu'en Angleterre* (Impr. royale, 1781).
46. A to F, Mar 3, 1781, AHN, E, 4211, apt. 3, no. 1895, p. 15.
47. MDA to K, Mar. 18, 1781. Bancroft-Austria, NYPL.
48. See correspondence in Admiraliteits Colleges, April 13-16, 1781, XXXVII, 485 (microfilm LC); Joachim Rendorp, *Memorien dienende tot opheldering, van het gebeurde, geduurende den laatsten Engelschen oorlog* (Amsterdam, 1792), I, 136; LV to V, April 21, 1781; V to LV, May 6, 1781, CP H 544: 105-106, 164.
49. LV to V, May 5, 1781, CP H 544: 156-160. See also Mém. et Docs., EU 56: 300 (May 19, 1781).
50. LV to V, July 6, 1781, CP H 545: 29.
51. V to LV, July 8, 1781, CP H 545: 48; LV to V, July 12, 1781, *ibid.*, pp. 69, 70.
52. V to LV, July 12, 1781, *ibid.*, p. 72.
53. Rendorp, *op. cit.*, pp. 136 *et seq*.
54. LV to V, Aug. 7, 1781, CP H 545: 285-294.
55. CP H 546: 288 (Oct. 31, 1781).
56. LV to V, July 24, 1781, CP H 545: 175-182.
57. Receveur to V, Aug. 10, 1781, CP H 545: 310, 311.
58. See HMC, *R*, X, App. VI, pp. 42, 43. LV to V, Aug. 7, 9, 1781, CP H 545: 285-299.
59. V to LV, Aug. 16, 1781, CP H 545: 325; Chevalier de Nadaillac, Commandant at Givet, to V, Aug. 23, 1781, *ibid.*, p. 377.
60. V to LV, Aug. 26, 1781, *ibid.*, p. 392.
61. Chevalier de Cologne to V, Jan. 8, 20; V to Cologne, Feb. 3, 1782, CP A 536: 22, 40, 57.
62. See Francis P. Renaut, *Le Secret Service de l'Amirauté Britannique, 1776-1783* (Paris, 1936). For Marguerite Wolters' itemized expenses for her secret correspondence (Dec. 31, 1782), see FO 27/3.
63. V to M, Jan. 22, 1781, CP E 602: 31-34.
64. Francis P. Renaut has treated aspects of Fox's intrigue in a series of brief connected monographs, which largely ignore the Spanish sources, thereby missing the full significance of the agent's operations. See *L'Affaire Montagu Fox ou l'évadé de la Tour de Londres* (Paris, 1937); *Le Traître de l'Amirauté* (Paris, 1937); *Un Dossier de Faux* (Paris, 1937). The affair is superficially treated in Coquelle, *L'Alliance Franco-Hollandaise*, pp. 248, 249. For the ST-S contretemps, see Walpole, *Last Journals*, pp. 301, 302.
65. Francis Bickley, ed., *Diaries of Sylvester Douglas, Lord Glenbervie* (Boston, 1928), I, 248, 249: Alan Valentine, *Lord George Germain* (London, 1961), p. 474. For the revival of the gossip about Thompson's espionage activities, see Memorandum Book entry of Rufus King of September 25, 1801, in C. R. King, ed., *Life and Correspondence of Rufus King* (New York, 1896), III, 518-519. See also Allen French, *General Gage's Informers* (Boston, 1932), pp. 144-146. For Thompson's mischief-making propensities while serving as a technical expert with Hardy's fleet in '79, see Patterson, *Other Armada*, pp. 173-175, 198.

66. See M to V, July 20, 1780, CP E 499: 494-501.
67. V to M, Mar. 15, 1781, CP E 602: 99-100.
68. M to R, April 24, 1781, CP E 603: 136; M to V, April 25, 1781, *ibid.*, pp. 138-140; V to M, May 14, 1781, *ibid.*, pp. 145-147.
69. *AMON*, 5th ser., II, 240-242, 244, 245.
70. *Diary*, II, 438.
71. *JAW*, VII, 404. For criticism of JA's headstrong course by LV and Bérenger, secretary of the French embassy, see CP H 544, *passim* (1781).

CHAPTER VII. ON THE TRAIL OF THE APPEASERS

1. *Annual Register, 1781*, pp. 161, 162, 184, 239. Further documents relating to Lutterloh and the La Motte trial are in SP 37/15, 44/95: 150. See also Lutterloh to the Secretary of State, Jan. 17, 1782, SP 37/15, where he offered his services to the British government. For the identification of "B," "D," and "Soyez" as La Motte, see CP A 531: 74-75; Intercepted Letters of French Agents, Soyez to Bowers, July 28, 1780, signed "de La Motte," SP 78/25. See also Donovan Papers, Special Collections, Columbia Univ. Lib., for a number of leads.
2. His application dated back to January, 1779, and was transmitted through the diplomatic pouch of the Spanish legation in London. "J.B." to V, Jan. 22, 1779, CP A 531: 26-27; also Jan. 29, April 9, *ibid.*, pp. 37-38, 124-126.
3. £8,000 plus £2,000 on account of future services. Baxon to V, May 30, 1781 (2 letters), CP A 534: 80-85; Baudouin to V, June 4, 1781, *ibid.*, p. 92.
4. V to Baudouin, June 8, 17, 1781; Baudouin to V, June 13, 1781, *ibid.*, pp. 93, 94, 101, 103.
5. Baxon to [Baudouin], July 14, 1781, *ibid.*, pp. 126-134; Baxon to V, Aug. 17, 1781, *ibid.*, pp. 176-177.
6. CP A 534: 104, 105.
7. Baudouin to V, Sept. 23, 1781, *ibid.*, pp. 207-208.
8. Thus Thurne reported the appearance of a brochure under the title of *Uni Bono*, in the form of letters addressed to M. Necker, in which the former director general was urged to hire out his brains for the service of England. Thurne to V, Dec. 25, 1781. CP A 534: 381.
9. Précis pour le Sieur Götsmann de Thurn, CP A 544: 217-220; Paul Huot, *Goetzmann et sa famille (1649-1794)* (Colmar, 1863); Hoefer, *Nouv. Biog. Gén.*, XXI, 69-70.
10. For the prodigious literature on the *affaire Goëzmann*, see Henri Cordier, *Bibliographie des Oeuvres de Beaumarchais* (Paris, 1883), pp. 85-93; M. Sainte-Beuve, *Mémoires de Beaumarchais dans l'Affaire Goëzman* (new ed., Paris, 1873); Mme. Goëzmann's name appears as author of three tracts published in Paris in 1773: *Pièces du Mémoire; Observations;* and *Mémoire*, Louis-Valentin Goëzmann publisher. *Addition au Mémoire de Mme. de Goezmann*, and *Note, . . . à MM. ses Confrères*, both in 1773. See also *Lettres, Mme. Du Deffand à Walpole*, II, 583-596, *passim*.
11. The view that the libel came from the pen of Beaumarchais is denied by E. Lintilhac, *Beaumarchais et ses oeuvres* (Paris, 1889). See also Loménie, *op. cit.*, I, 388-404.
12. See *Pièces relatives aux déméles entre Mademoiselle d'Eon de Beaumont et le Sieur Caron de Beaumarchais* (1778); *Très-humble réponse à très-haut, très-puissant seigneur . . .* par Charlotte-Geneviève-Louise-Auguste-Andrée-Timothée d'Eon de Beaumont (London, n.d.); Frédéric Gaillardet, *Mémoires sur la Chevalière d'Eon* (Paris, n.d.).

13. Louis de Loménie, *Beaumarchais et son temps* (Paris, 1856), II, 84-112; *D*, I, 130-137.

14. Certified copy of original undated letter of Sartine to V, made Aug. 25, 1783, CP A 544: 83, 84; Thurne to V, Sept. 6, 1783, *ibid.*, pp. 207-211. Sartine felt that 2,000 livres a year would be sufficient for the agent's maintenance, as well as that of his son, an officer in the French Army.

15. Goëzmann to Maurepas, Aug. 10, 1781, CP A 534: 158-161; Goëzmann to the King, *ibid.*, pp. 162-164; Goëzmann to V, Sept. 6, 1783, *ibid.*, 544: 207-211. For the expenses of his trip to London the King authorized a payment of 1,200 livres to be paid out of the secret funds of the Ministry of Foreign Affairs. Décision du Roi (copy), Dec. 5, 1781, *ibid.*, 534: 355.

16. Lerchenberg, Memoir of observation of correspondence (May, 1782). CP A 537: 108.

17. In addition, code names were provided for Bute, Germain, North, Mansfield, Sandwich, and ST. Thurne to V, Aug. 15, 1781, CP A 534: 172-173; Mémoire d'Observations pour ma correspondance, May, 1782, CP A 537: 108-110.

18. Thurne to V, Dec. 25, 1781. CP A 534: 381.

19. Thurne to V, Dec. 28, 1781. *Ibid.*, 390.

20. Thurne to V, May 24, 1782. CP A 537: 76.

21. Baudouin to V, with enclosure, London, April 12, 1782. CP A 537: 340.

22. *Annual Register, 1782*, pp. 216, 217. Tyrie's service in French intelligence went back at least to 1774. Garnier to V, Nov. 19, 1774, Feb. 10, 1775. CP A 507: 17; 508: 241-250.

23. Thurne to V, Nov. 8, 1781. CP A 534: 299.

24. Baudouin to V, Nov. 20, 1781. CP A 534: 306.

25. Baudouin to V, Jan. 1782, with enclosure of Dec. 4, 1781. CP A 536: 21-22.

26. G. Smith to Mrs. Smith, Jan. 2, 1782. *Ibid.*, 15.

27. Baudouin to V, Jan. 14, 1782. *Ibid.*, 35.

28. V to Baudouin, Jan. 15, 1782. *Ibid.*, 37.

29. Baudouin to V, Feb. 23, Mar. 9, 1782. *Ibid.*, 127, 208.

30. Baudouin to V, reporting the arrival of the "telescope" and the "case of instruments," without the accompanying letter, and noting that he had written Smith to this effect on June 10 and July 24. CP A 540: 57-60.

31. Baudouin to V, Jan. 7, 1783. *Ibid.*, 94.

32. London, Jan. 21, 1783. *Ibid.*, 243-245; Baudouin to V, Jan. 28, 1783. *Ibid.*, 279.

33. Baudouin to Smith, Jan. 30, 1783. *Ibid.*, 295-296.

34. Smith to Baudouin, April 16, 1783. CP A 542: 134.

35. Baudouin to V, April 27, 1783. *Ibid.*, 153.

36. V to Baudouin, Mar. 8, 1782. CP A 536: 208.

37. Mémoire of Thurne (*c.* Dec., 1782). CP A 539: 388-389.

38. Le Noir [William Lee?] to V; Baudouin to V, Feb. 24; V to Le Noir, Feb. 25, 1783; Baudouin to V, Feb. 25, Mar. 7, 1783; Thurne to Baudouin, Mar. 7, 1783. CP A 541: 50, 59, 61, 132, 133, 134.

39. Thurne to Baudouin, Mar. 12, 1783; Baudouin to Maréchal de Camp, Mar. 12, 1783. *Ibid.*, 168-170; also *ibid.*, 586: 340.

40. V to Moustier, Mar. 25, 1783. CP A. 541: 257-258.

41. Moustier to V, Mar. 16, 31, 1783, *ibid.*, pp. 196-199, 309-310; Thomas Evans to Moustier, April 7, 1783, CP A 542: 37-46; of Thomas Evans, *ibid.*, 47-49; Moustier to V, April 21, May 6, 1783, *ibid.*, pp. 79, 80, 201-202. For the bill, see *ibid.*, pp. 81-86.

42. Moustier to V, Mar. 19, 1783. CP A 541: 207.

43. Moustier to V, Mar. 23, 31, 1783, *ibid.*, 234-237, 305-306.

44. Moustier to V, Mar. 23, 1783, *ibid.*, 239-240. In addition, Moustier believed that some of the libels were authorized by Brissot de Warville and Lafite de Pellepore. Moustier to V, April 21, 1783. CP A 542: 81. Both V and Le Noir gave Brissot a clean bill of health, the latter reporting that, so far as he knew, he was in England to make a serious study of the British Constitution. V to Moustier, April 15, 1783; Le Noir to V, May 4, 1783, *ibid.*, 542: 115, 187, 188. For negotiations with Pellepore to obtain copies of *Les Passe-Temps d'Antoinette*, the libel of greatest concern to the court, see V to Moustier, April 24, 1783, *ibid.*, 102-104; Baudouin to V, Mar. 20, 1783; Thurne to Baudouin, April 1, 4, 1783; Thurne to V, April 4, 1783, *ibid.*, 211, 316-317, 344; Le Noir *to* V, April 4, 1783, *ibid.*, 351.
45. *Ibid.*, 378 (London, April 7, 1783).
46. CP A 542: 105.
47. Thurne to V, May 2, 13, 16, 1783. *Ibid.*, 177, 178, 236, 237, 256, 257.
48. Mme. Goëzmann to V, Paris, May 20, 1783; *ibid.*, 266; also Thurne to V, London, May 21, 1783; Le Noir to V, May 24, 1783; V to Le Noir, May 24, 1783. *Ibid.*, 266, 271, 272, 291, 292, 295.
49. V to d'Adhémar, May 21; d'Adhémar to V, May 27; Receveur to Le Noir, May 22, V to d'Adhémar, May 29, 1783. *Ibid.*, 282, 310, 313-317, 320.
50. Thurne to V, May 30, June 30; Receveur to V, June 4, 1783. *Ibid.*, 352-354, 358; d'Adhémar to V, June 12, 19, 1783. *Ibid.*, 373-375, 383, 384.
51. Receveur's report on the Libelists, May 22, 1783. *Ibid.*, 285-289.
52. Thurne to V, June 24, July 22, 1783. CP A 543: 101, 102, 271-273.
53. V to d'Adhémar, June 25, 1783; d'Adhémar to V, July 29, 1783; Mme. Goëzmann to V, July 30, 1783. *Ibid.*, 108, 109, 318-320.
54. Thurne to V, Versailles, Aug. 28, 1783, with enclosure from John Kent to Thurne, Aug. 19, 1783, and Thurne's comment. CP A 544: 54-55, 60, 108, 109. In addition to serving as ambassador to Turin, Lord Mountstuart held the sinecure office of Auditor of the Impost from 1781 until its abolition the following year. He was compensated for its loss with a grant of £7,000 a year for life.
55. For Franklin's comment on *Le Mariage de Figaro*, see *BFS*, IX, 305.

CHAPTER VIII. THE GORDIAN KNOT

1. F. B. Dexter, *The Literary Diary of Ezra Stiles* (3 vols., New Haven, 1901), II, 21.
2. Barthélemy to V (code), Oct., 6, 1781, CP Aut 343: 170. The Emperor's assertion may have been based upon advice received from London that the Carlisle Commission, according to H, had exceeded their instructions and were only authorized to accept the colonies' submission. Belgiojoso to K, June 8, 1781, Bancroft-Austria, NYPL.
3. *Annual Register, 1778*, pp. 327-329; HMC, *R, XV*, Appendix VI (1897), pp. 322-333; *Stopford-Sackville Papers*, II, 105-106; *SF*, nos. 1104, 1144; *LMCC*, III, 298-299; *JCC*, XI, 615; Joseph Reed, *Remarks on Governor Johnstone's Speech in Parliament* (Philadelphia, 1778), pp. 16-22.
4. Worthington C. Ford, ed., *Letters of William Lee, 1766-1783* (3 vols., Brooklyn, N.Y., 1891), II, 690n. (June 25, 1779).
5. Thus the baseless rumors that a separate peace was about to be made with the Southern provinces. Belgiojoso to K, Jan. 7, 1780, SKD, England 164, pt. I.
6. Liverpool Papers, Add. MSS. 38, 383, pp. 2-3, BM.
7. This time the rumor had it that Georgia was to be independent, with a truce for the rest of America. Marie Daniel Bourré, Baron de Corberon, *Un diplomate*

français à la cour de Catherine II, 1775-1780, journal intime (Paris, 1901), II, 250, 251. Corberon's source appears to have been a Comte de Martinengo, recently arrived at St. Petersburg from Turin, and rumored to be bearing peace proposals, with King Victor-Amedée III of Sardinia as intermediary.

8. JA to President of Congress, May 9, 1780, Sparks, V, 84-86.
9. *Lee Letters*, III, 779-781, 783.
10. V to CG, Dec. 25, 1778. CP EU 5: 368; Meng, p. 451; CP E 593: 360-368.
11. DH to BF, April 22, 1779; BF to DH, May 4, 1779, *RDC*, III, 127-131, 154-156. As usual, BF kept V fully apprised of these proposals. *D*, III, 770, 771. See also V to M, Aug. 6, 1779. CP E 595: 51-53.
12. *PR*, XIII, 557, 558, 564.
13. *D*, III, 850-851. W to TG; V to Almodóvar, May 4, 1779, CP E 594: 27-29; also Haslang to Vieregg, Feb. 9, 1779, KBGS, reel 502/3, pp. 273-275.
14. V to M, May 14, 17, 1779, CP E 594: 67, 75-76; Reflections on Spanish truce proposal, May 1779, *ibid.*, pp. 189-194.
15. BF to Arthur Lee, Mar. 21, 1777. *RDC*, III, 296-298.
16. See William Lee to Francis Lightfoot Lee, *Lee Letters*, II, 632-633.
17. *Lee Letters*, I, 345, 356 (Jan. 22, 1778).
18. *Ibid.*, pp. 346 *et seq.*
19. *Ibid.*, p. 430 (May 10, 1778). For William Lee's role in the French espionage service as "Le Noir," see Minnegerode, *Jefferson*, pp. 33, 45 *et seq.*
20. Mrs. Gillespie Smyth, ed., *Memoirs and Correspondence of Sir Robert Murray Keith* (London, 1849), II, 76, 82-84.
21. Breteuil to V, May 27, 31, June 10, 27, July 29, 1778. CP Aut 336: 117-119, 125-129, 170-172, 206-209, 231-234, 382-389.
22. *Lee Letters*, II, 455. For the view that the treatment of Lee was really a snub to France, see also Barthélemy to V, Feb. 25, 1780. CP Aut 351: 51. Cf. also Hanns Schlitter, *Die Beziehungen Österreichs zu den Vereinigten Staaten von Amerika* (Innsbruck, 1885), I.
23. MT expressed herself with equal warmth. William Coxe, *History of the House of Austria*, 3rd ed. (London, 1847), III, 472, 473.
24. Despite his pro-French bias Frederick, after having denied G permission to move German recruits for America across his territories earlier in the war, later granted such consent (Nov. 20, 21, 26, 1780). *PCFG*, XLV, 47, 54, 64. For Frederick's reaffirmation of "perfect neutrality," see Frederick to von Schulenburg, Jan. 9, 1781. *Ibid.*, p. 169.
25. Lee to Committee of Foreign Affairs, Sept. 28, 1779, *Lee Letters*, II, 739-745.
26. Frederick to Goltz, Feb. 14, May 4, 22, July 20, 1780; to Goertz, Jan. 28, 1780. *PCFG*, XLIV, 52, 53, 79, 80, 238, 260, 364.
27. MT to Louis XVI, May 15, 1779, CP Aut 340: 179; M to V, June 3, 1779, CP E 594: 203-210. Four days later K also proposed to the British that Austria mediate. Keith to W, May 19, 1779, SP 80/221. The British government kept the door ajar. W–Keith dispatches, July 16, 31, 1779. *Ibid.*
28. See Barthélemy to V, Mar. 15, 1780, CP Aut 341: 83 *et seq.*; MT to MA, June 30, July 13, 1779, *Corr. Marie-Thérèse et Mercy*, III, 444, 445; Frederick to Goltz, June 8, 1780, *PCFG*, XLIV, 289.
29. *Corr. Mercy avec Joseph II et Kaunitz*, II, 562, 563. For the French subsidy to K, see J. W. Thompson and Saul Padover, *Secret Diplomacy* (New York, 1963), p. 114.
30. See, e.g., K to MDA, Mar. 4, 1780, *ibid.*, 551 *et seq.*
31. Frederick to Goltz, Dec. 18, 1780, *PCFG*, XLV, 118.
32. *Corr. Mercy avec Joseph II et Kaunitz*, I, ii-viii, xxix.

33. For Teschen, see CP Aut 340 *passim;* G. F. de Martens, *Receuil des traités,* 2nd ed. (Göttingen, 1817), pp. 485-487. For the flattering exchange between Frederick II and Catherine over Teschen, see *SRIO,* XX, 383-386. See also Harold W. V. Temperley, *Frederick the Great and Kaiser Joseph* (London, 1915); Adolph Unzer, *Der Friede von Teschen* (Kiel, 1903); P. Oursel, *La diplomatie de la France sous Louis XVI: succession de Bavière et paix de Teschen* (Paris, 1921).

34. See MT to MDA, June 30, July 30, 1779; MA to MT, Dec. 1, 1779, *Corr. entre Marie-Thérèse et Mercy,* III, 324, 334, 376; V to Vérac, May 6, 1780, *Receuil des Instructions,* IX, 352-371; Barthélemy to V, May 7, 1780, CP Aut 341: 159 *et seq.* For a more pessimistic view, see Frederick to Riedesel, Feb. 16, Mar. 1, 1780; to Goltz, May 8, 1780, *PCFG,* XLIV, 81-82, 106-107, 241. Austria's annoyance with France over Teschen is underscored in Keith's dispatches, Jan.-June, 1779. SP 80/221.

35. Louis XVI to MT, May 27, 1779, CP Aut 340: 222-223; Charles III to MT, June [7], 1779, CP E 594: 225-226.

36. V to Breteuil, June 9, 17, 1779; Breteuil to V, July 12, 1779; Barthélemy to V, Sept. 29, Dec. 24, 1779; V to Barthélemy, Feb. 12, 1780. CP Aut 340: 237, 238, 241, 302, 306 *et seq.,* 345 *et seq.,* 434, 439, 444; 341: 28.

37. Breteuil to V, June 22, Oct. 9, Dec. 14, 17, 1779. CP Aut 340: 261, 280, 368, 431, 433.

38. MT to MA, July 1, Aug. 4, 1779; MA to MT, Aug. 16, 1779, Jan. 1, Feb. 1, 1780, *Corr. entre Marie-Thérèse et Mercy,* III, 327, 338, 339, 385, 386, 396. For reputed efforts of MT to put pressure on Charles III through the royal courts of Tuscany and Naples, see Breteuil to V, Aug. 13, 1779. CP Aut 340: 328-330.

39. K to MDA, Aug. 3, Sept. 1, 1779; MDA to K, Nov. 16, 1779, *Corr. Mercy avec Joseph II et Kaunitz,* II, 540-543.

40. F to Count Kaunitz, Aug. 30, 1779; *DC,* V, 336-337.

41. MDA to K, Jan. 17, 1780. SKD, Frankreich, 235. Keith had previously pressed for instructions on the issue of mediating independence or permitting American representation at the mediation. Keith to W, July 31, Aug. 7, 1779. On Dec. 31 ST informed him that a precondition to peace was the relinquishment by France and Spain (!) of their engagements with the Americans. SP 80/221. For ST's response to Belgiojoso, see ST to Keith, April 28, 1780. SP 80/222.

42. Sir Joseph Yorke to JH, The Hague, Sept. 18, 1779, Hardwicke Add. MSS. 35, 434, BM.

43. Goltz to Frederick, April 17, 1780. *PCFG,* XLIV, 228.

44. M to V, April 20, 1780. CP E 598: 445-447.

45. Corberon to V, April 14, 1780. CP R 104: 202.

46. Breteuil to V, June 24, 1780(2), CP Aut 341: 198 *et seq.,* 206, 210.

47. A to F, AHN, E, 4143, no. 1761; M to V, CP E 601: 379-382.

48. Breteuil to V, Oct. 5, 1780. CP Aut 341: 310 *et seq.*

49. Belgiojoso to K, Oct. 27, 1780. SKD, England, 164, pt. i.

50. See *Russki Arkhiv* (1875), II, 114.

51. Grimm to Catherine, Paris, Oct. 28, 1782. *SRIO,* XLIV, 287; also XX, 223-224; XXXIII, 1-2. See also Dimitri S. von Mohrenschildt, *Russia in the Intellectual Life of Eighteenth-Century France* (New York, 1936), p. 134; Peter Gay, *Voltaire's Politics: The Poet as Realist* (Princeton, N.J., 1959), p. 148.

52. Despite her admiration for Voltaire his *Semiramis* was one play the Empress did not enjoy. Corberon, *Journal intime,* II, 261.

53. A. G. Bruckner, *Istoria Ekateriny II* (St. Petersburg, 1885), III, 278. For

shrewd, if not always accurate, appraisals of Catherine and her major aides, see V to Vérac, May 6, 1780, *Receuil des Instructions*, IX, 352-371.

54. See, e.g., JH to W, May 23/June 3, 1779. SP 91/103, no. 31.

55. G. P. Gooch, *Catherine the Great and Other Studies* (London, 1954), pp. 37-97.

56. *SRIO*, XIX, 463-464, 489, 509; V to Juigné, Oct. 18, 1776, CP R 99: 449-450.

57. *SRIO*, XXIII, 444; XXVII, 28; Juigné to V, Oct. 15, 1776, CP R 99: 444-446. See also F. A. Golder, "Catherine II and the American Revolution," *Amer. Hist. Rev.*, XXI, 92.

58. JH to ST, Aug. 31/Sept. 11, 1781. FO 65/4; Catherine II to Grimm, June 8, 1778. *SRIO*, XXIII, 98; also Sept. 23, 1780, *ibid.*, p. 192. See also Joseph to MT, July 2, 1780. A. von Arneth, *Maria Theresia und Joseph II: Ihre Correspondenz* (Vienna, 1867), III, 268.

59. JH to W, Sept. 9/20, 1779. SP 91/103, no. 56, incorrectly quoted in *Diaries and Correspondence of James Harris, First Earl of Malmesbury* (London, 1844), I, 252.

60. Grimm to Catherine, Sept. 6/17, 1780; *SRIO*, XXIII, 66-68, 133-135; XLIV, 112.

61. See, e.g., Breteuil to V, Dec. 21, 1780. Bancroft-Austria, NYPL.

62. Catherine to Grimm, May 8, 1784. *SRIO*, XXXIII, 304.

63. Dispatch of Prince Bariatinski, Feb. 24/March 7, 1779. Bancroft-Russia, NYPL.

64. Frederick to Goertz, Jan. 11, 1780. *PCFG*, XLIV, 18.

65. *Lee Letters*, I, 648 (June 6, 1778); Malmesbury, *Diaries*, I, 242, 255.

66. ST to Elliot, May 9, 1780. Bancroft-Great Britain, NYPL.

67. *Russki Arkhiv* (1875), II, 117; Vérac to V, Oct. 19, 1780, CP R 105: 266. JH himself portrayed Potëmkin's desire for wealth and power as "insatiable." JH to Suffolk, Dec. 20/31, 1778, SP 91/102, no. 107; also JH to W, Jan. 18/29, 1779, SP 91/103, no. 4.

68. Sir Joseph Yorke to JH, Nov. 12, 1779, Hardwicke Papers, Add. MSS. 35, 434; JH to ST, Dec. 29/Jan. 9, 1780/81, FO 65/1, no. 170. ST considered JH's expenditures for intelligence as "moderate." Jan. 19, 1781, FO 65/1, no. 10.

69. Le Comte de Ségur, *Mémoires ou souvenirs et anecdotes* (Paris, 1826), II, 281-282. See also George Soloveytchik, *Potemkin* (London, 1938); Gooch, *Catherine the Great*, pp. 42-55.

70. Marsangy, *Vergennes: Son Ambassade à Constantinople; Son Ambassade en Suède*.

71. Frederick II, "Considérations sur l'état présent du corps politique de l'Europe," *Oeuvres posthumes de Frédéric II, roi de Prusse* (Berlin, 1788), VI, pp. 2-52.

72. E. V. Tarle, *Chesmenskŭ boĭ* (Moscow, 1945), p. 100.

73. Instructions to Juigné (1775), *Receuil des Instructions*, IX, 309-323.

74. V to Durand (received by Juigné), Sept. 3, 1775, *ibid.*, IX, 326-327.

75. S. M. Soloviev, *Istoria Rosii s drevneyshikh vremen* (2nd ed., 29 vols., St. Petersburg, 1894-95), XXIX, 1113.

76. Corberon to Vérac, Feb. 5, 1779. *D*, III, 739-740. However, for the effect of Franco-Russian mediation in the Bavarian dispute on promoting French sympathies at St. Petersburg, see JH to Suffolk, Dec. 20/31, 1778, Dec. 28, 1778/Jan. 8, 1779, SP 91/102, no. 106; 91/103, no. 111.

77. Catherine to Grimm, July 18, 1779; Jan. 12, 1780. *SRIO*, XXIII, 154, 169-171. See also V to Vérac, May 6, 1780, *Receuil des Instructions*, IX, 352-371.

78. JH to Suffolk, Dec. 20/31, 1778, SP 91/102, no. 105; Feb. 8/19, 15/26, 1779, SP 91/103, nos. 10, 12; JH to W, April 16/27, 1779, SP 91/103, no. 25.

79. V to Corberon, June 13, 1779, P. Fauchille, *La diplomatie française et la ligue des Neutres de 1780* (Paris, 1893), p. 277. JH to W, May 23/June 3, 1779, SP 91/103, no. 30.

80. W to JH, July 2, 1779, SP 91/103, no. 18.
81. JH to W, July 5/16, 1779, SP 91/103, no. 41; JH to ST, Feb. 15/26, 1780, SP 91/104, referring to a conversation in the summer of '79.
82. *Arkhiv Knyaza Vorontsova* (Moscow, 1888), XXXIV, 388-401.
83. William Lee to Ralph Izard, Aug. 31, 1779; to T. Digges, Oct. 7, 1779. *Lee Letters*, III, 728, 757-758.
84. V. N. Aliksandrenko, *Russkiye diplomaticheskije agenty v Londone v XVIII v* (Warsaw, 1897), II, 195; Soloviev, *op. cit.*
85. Malmesbury, *Diaries*, I, 137, 166, 169, 242; JH to W, Sept. 9/20, 1779, SP 91/103, no. 56.
86. JH to ST, Feb. 15/26, 1780, SP 91/104; Goertz to Frederick, Dec. 3/14, 1779, Bancroft-Circourt, *Histoire*, III, 229; Frederick to Goltz, Jan. 3, 1780, *PCFG*, XLIV, 6-7.
87. JH to ST, Feb. 15/26, 1780, SP 91/104, no. 13.
88. See Isabel de Madariaga, *Britain, Russia, and the Armed Neutrality of 1780* (New Haven, 1962), pp. 59-68. For British seizures of Dutch ships at that time, see Adm. Coll., XXXVII, no. 484 (microfilm, LC).
89. See, e.g., Vérac to V, Jan. 7, July 29, 1777, CP Danemark 161: 8, 149; Goertz to Frederick, May 16, 1780, *PCFG*, XLIV, 276.
90. Sacken to Panin, Sept. 18, 29, 1778. *Morskoÿ Sbornik*, XLIII, 44.
91. Carlton Savage, *Policy of the United States toward Maritime Commerce in War, 1776-1914* (Washington, 1934), I, 2. For Congress' resolution to conform to the principles of the Armed Neutrality, see Vérac to V, Feb. 5, 1781. CP R 106: 106-111.
92. Fauchille, *op. cit.*, pp. 3, 29. See also Bancroft-Circourt, *Histoire*, III, 223-225.
93. V to Corberon, Dec. 27, 1778, CP R 101: no. 30; Fauchille, *op. cit.*, p. 228.
94. Madariaga, *op. cit.*, pp. 71-77. For British seizure of Swedish ships trading with the rebels, see *British Diplomatic Instructions, 1689-1789*, V (Sweden) (London, 1928), 236-237.
95. Madariaga, *op. cit.*, pp. 83-90; Corberon to V, Mar. 9, 1779, CP R 102: no. 10; Fauchille, *op. cit.*, p. 269.
96. Catherine to Panin, Feb. 25, 1780. *Morskoÿ Sbornik* (St. Petersburg, 1859), XLIII, 89; Alexander Brückner, *Istoria Ekateriny Vtoroi* (5 vols., St. Petersburg, 1885), III, 472; Goertz to Frederick, July 28, 1780, *PCFG*, XLIV, 411. For the Declaration, see CP R 104: 123-124; London *Evening Courant*, May 13, 1780.
97. V to M, April 3, 1780. CP E 598: 367-370. See also *JCC*, XVIII, 864, 866, 899, 905 *passim*.
98. Dispatch of Pesaro, Archivio di Stato, letter 198, Venice.
99. For correspondence of Dutch officials with the Spanish government over ship seizures, Jan. 24—Dec. 18, 1780, see SGH 6857. See also dispatch of Pesaro, Jan. 11, 18, 25, 1780, Archivio di Stato, letters 179-181, Venice; M to V, Jan. 26, 1780, CP E 597: 187; V to M, Mar. 27, 1780; M to V, Mar. 29, 1780, *ibid.*, 598: 277-278, 302-306; also *ibid.*, pp. 371-374. See also CP R 104: 60, 67, 76, 85, 95-98, 120, 128, 134-319. See also CP E 598: 12-15; AHN, E, 4202, apt. 5, no. 50, pp. 885-890; *Morskoÿ Sbornik*, XLIII, 83; Malmesbury, *Diaries*, I, 270, 278, 279; Goertz to Frederick, Feb. 29, 1780; Queen Mother of Denmark to Frederick, April 1, 1780, *PCFG*, XLIV, 180, 181; Madariaga, *op. cit.*, pp. 157-159.
100. M to V, April 15, 24, 1780, CP E 598: 425-427; V to M, April 21, 1780, *ibid.*, pp. 463-464, 499; Dispatch of Pesaro, May 2, June 6, 1780, Archivio di Stato, letter 195, 200, Venice; King of Spain to court of Copenhagen, Aug. 7; to court of Stockholm, Aug. 13, 1780, SGH 6857.

101. James Brown Scott, ed., *The Armed Neutralities of 1780 and 1800* (New York, 1918), pp. 273, 274.
102. F to the Minister of Russia, Nov. 25, 1780. SP 94/209, 249-260.
103. Fauchille, *op. cit.*, p. 445; but cf. Madariaga, *op. cit.*, p. 233n.
104. Panin to Catherine, May 23/June 4, 1780, *Morskoÿ Shornik*, XLIII, 378.
105. Sainte Croix to V, April 6, 1780. CP R 104: 187, 192; cf. also ST to Sir Thomas Wroughton, Feb.-June, 1781. *British Diplomatic Instructions: V* (Sweden), 250-253.
106. Yorke to JH, Aug. 19, 1780. Hardwicke Papers, Add. MSS., 35, 434.
107. Madariaga, *op. cit.*, pp. 173-193; V to Vérac, July 19, 1780. Bancroft-France, NYPL.
108. Vérac to V, July 25, Aug. 15, Sept. 1, 12, 1780; LV to Vérac, Aug. 8, 1780, CP R 104: 186; 105: 37, 49, 62, 96; JH to ST, Sept. 1/12, 1780. SP 91/106, no. 103.
109. *AMON*, II, 341; V, 290 *et seq.*; ST to JH, Nov. 14, 1780, SP 91/106, no. 66; Yorke to JH, Nov. 10, 1780, Hardwicke Papers, Add. MSS., 35, 434; Scott, *op. cit.*, pp. 346 *et seq.*
110. JH to ST, June 12/23, 1780. SP 91/105; Malmesbury, *Diaries*, I, 318. For impressive exports from Russia to Britain of naval stores and iron in the year 1780, see JH to ST, Jan. 26/Feb. 6, 1781. FO 65/1.
111. JH to ST, May 15/26, 1780. SP 91/105, no. 49. For the view that the Armed Neutrality was not consequential, see W. E. Hall, William Manning, in Scott, *Armed Neutralities*, pp. 109, 155; *per contra*, Jean de Boeck, Carlos Calvo, Dmitri Katchenovsky, Ernest Nys, *ibid.*, pp. 33, 72, 116.
112. Corberon, *Journal Intime*, II, 231, *et seq.*; Vérac to V, July 13, 1780, CP R 104: no. 2; JH to ST, July 14/25, 1780, SP 91/105, no. 82. See also Catherine II to Grimm, Sept. 7, 1780, *SRIO*, XXIII, 190-191. Goertz at Petersburg advised Frederick to counter Joseph's move by sending the Prince of Prussia on a visit to the Russian court. Partly because of the Prince's defects of personality, partly because of Catherine's sudden pro-Austrian orientation, the visit was a failure. Goertz to Frederick, Mar. 3, 1780, *PCFG*, XLIV, 134-135; Corberon to V, Oct. 6, 1780; V to Vérac, Nov. 12, 1780; CP R 105: 222-228, 330. For Frederick's uneasiness about Mogilev, see *PCFG*, XLIV, *passim*.
113. Madariaga, "The Secret Austro-Russian Treaty of 1781," *Slavonic and East European Review*, XXXVIII (1959), 114-145. An understanding between Russia and Austria to carve up Turkish territory was forecast by Breteuil as early as July, '79. Breteuil to V, July 12, 1779; V to Breteuil, June 17, Aug. 4, 1779. CP Aut 340: 286 *et seq.* 307, 313. As late as November, 1780, V outlined a variety of reasons why the Empress would not make such an alliance with Austria. V to Breteuil, Nov. 18, 1780. CP Aut 341: 339.
114. V to M, Jan. 13, 1780. CP E 597: 100-103; AHN, E, 4143; M to V, March 28, 1780. CP E 598: 288-295, V to Corberon, March 12, April 22, 25, 1780. CP R 104: 158, 232, 238.
115. F to A, Jan. 13, 29, 1780, AHN, E, 4202: 1, letter 1606, pp. 32-37; 4143: 1, with enclosure to Normande, Jan. 28, 1780. See also Corberon, *Journal Intime*, II, 350-351.
116. M to V, Jan. 26, Mar. 28, 1780. CP E 597: 192; 598: 298. For A's reservations about Russian mediation, see A to F, March 3, 1780. AHN, E, 4143, no. 1633.
117. JH to ST, March 13/24, 1780. SP 91/104.
118. Joseph to MT, June 8, 1780. *Corr. Maria Theresia und Joseph II*, III, 250, 255; Bancroft-Great Britain, NYPL.
119. JH to ST, March 24/April 4, 1780. SP 91/104, no. 27.

120. ST to JH, April 25, 1780. SP 91/104, no. 28.
121. Corberon to V, May 23, 1780; V to Corberon, June 25, 1780. CP R 104: 239-245, 303-306.
122. Corberon to V, June 23, 1780. CP R 104: 367-374. The obligation of "complete, unlimited recognition of independence" is "inviolate." Corberon to Panin (copy), June 24, 1780. *Ibid.*, p. 381.
123. Normande to F (in Spanish and French), June 13/24, 1780; M to V, July 24, Sept. 11, 1780; F to A, Aug. 7, 1780 (translation); CP E 599: 357-358; 600: 17-22, 72-76, 348-385, 445-448; Corberon, *Journal Intime*, II, 320-321.
124. JH to ST, June 12/23, 1780. SP 91/105, no. 72; M to V, Sept. 1, 1780. D, IV, 408-409; Bemis, *Hussey-Cumberland Mission*, p. 113n.; ST to JH, Aug. 15, 22, 1780; JH to ST, Sept. 4/15, 11/22, 1780. SP 91/105, nos. 46, 47; SP 91/106, nos. 106, 110.
125. *DC*, V, 159n.; *D*, V, 464.
126. V to M (enclosed memorandum), Aug. 18, 1780. CP E 600: 172-175.
127. Vérac to V, Sept. 1, 1780. CP R 105: 96, 337-346.
128. *Arkhiv Knyaza Vorontsova*, XXXIV, 388; R. G. Albion, *Forests and Sea Powers* (Cambridge, 1926), pp. 40 *et seq.*
129. V to Vérac, two letters, Oct. 8, 1780; again in a dispatch of Oct. 12, 1780. CP R 105: 241, 243, 368, 369.
130. V to L (intercepted dispatch, deciphered), Sept. 4, 1780. LP 35.
131. V to L (intercepted and deciphered), Oct. 23, 1780. LP 35.
132. V to Vérac, Oct. 12, 1780. CP R 105: 245-248.
133. Vérac to V, Nov. 14, 1780. *Ibid.*, 324-331.
134. Corberon, *Journal Intime*, II, 370; *PCFG*, XLV, *passim.*
135. ST to JH, Oct. 20, 1780; JH to ST, Dec. 13/24, 1780. SP 91/106, nos. 61, 158.
136. Malmesbury, *Diaries*, I, 357; *Russkaia Starina*, CXXXV (1908), 457-458.
137. ST to Simolin, Dec. 16, 1780. Bancroft-Austria, NYPL.
138. Breteuil to V, Nov. 29, 1780; V to Breteuil, Dec. 7, 1780. CP Aut 341: 357, 363, 367. At the same time the British ambassador detected a new pro-French tone in the Emperor. Keith to ST, Nov. 18, 1780, FO 7/3.
139. *BFS*, X, 339, 340.

CHAPTER IX. THE PLOT TO PARTITION AMERICA

1. For an account of the last rites of MT, see Doria Pamphili to Pallavicini, Jan. 1, 1781. Nunz. Francia, Vatican Archives.
2. ST to Simolin, SP 91/106—draft reply of verbal answer sent to JH, Dec. 26, 1780; ST to Keith, Dec. 26, 1780, SP 80/223, no. 67.
3. Keith to ST, Jan. 10, 1781, FO 7/1, no. 8.
4. Keith to ST, Dec. 10, 1780, SP 80/223, no. 112; K to MDA, Jan. 10, 1781, SKD, Frankreich 237; Bancroft-Austria, NYPL; Joseph to MDA, Jan. 10, 1781, Arneth and Flammermont, *Corr. Jos. II avec Mercy*, II, 13; K to Cobenzl, Jan. 10, 1781, A. Beer and J. R. Fiedler, eds., *Joseph II und Graf Ludwig Cobenzl: Ihr Briefwechsel—Fontes Rerum Austriacarum* (Vienna, 1901), I, 108.
5. Keith, *Memoirs*, II, 118-119; Belgiojoso to K, Jan. 22, 1781, Bancroft-Austria, NYPL.
6. Goltz to Frederick, June 2, 1780, *PCFG*, XLIV, 297; V to M, Aug. 18, 1780, CP E 600: 217-226; ST to Keith, Feb. 13, 1781, Hardwicke Papers, Add. MSS. 35, 521 BM.
7. M to V, Aug. 7, 1780, CP E 600: 81-83.

8. Bezborodko to Rumyantsov, Jan. 25/Feb. 5, 1781; Mar. 15/26, 1781, *Starina i Novizna*, III, 233, 235; Keith to ST, Jan. 10, 17, Feb. 3, 1781, FO 7/1, nos. 9, 12, 19; ST to Keith, Jan. 20, 1781, FO 7/1, no. 7; JH to Keith, Jan. 18/29, 1781, Hardwicke Papers, Add. MSS. 35, 521; JH to ST, Jan. 19/30, 1781, FO 65/2, no. 12; Breteuil to V, Feb. 18, 1781, CP Aut 342: 81; Breteuil to Vérac, Feb. 25, 1781, CP R 106: 132-133; Vérac to V, Feb. 18/Mar. 1, 1781, CP R 106: 156-163; Cobenzl to Joseph, Feb. 5, 19, 1781, Beer and Fiedler, *Joseph II und Graf Cobenzl*, I, 111, 120.

9. Breteuil to V, Jan. 13, Mar. 10, May 21, 1781. CP Aut 342: 19, 35, 366; V to Vérac, Jan. 30, 1781, CP R 106: 66-70; K to MDA, Feb. 8, 1781, Bancroft-Austria, NYPL.

10. V to Breteuil, Feb. 16, 1781, CP Aut 342: 76, and copy with favorable comments on Joseph II and K underlined by Breteuil to show to them, *ibid.*, p. 115; V to Vérac, Feb. 16, 1781, CP R 106: 113-115; Bancroft-Austria, NYPL.

11. MDA to K, Feb. 21, 1781, SKD, Frankreich 238; Bancroft-Austria, NYPL; V to Breteuil, Mar. 4, 1781, CP Aut 342: 92; F to La Torre, Mar. 1781, AHN, E, 4200, apt. 1, p. 446.

12. K to Joseph, Jan. 9, 1781, Bancroft-Austria, NYPL; A. Beer, *Joseph II, Leopold II, und Kaunitz* (Vienna, 1873), p. 29; Vérac to V, Jan. 19/30, 1781, CP R 106: 58; Vérac to V, Jan. 15/26, 1781, CP R 106: 46-52.

13. V to Vérac, Jan. 30, 1781, CP R 106: 61-65; Goltz to Frederick, Mar. 30, 1781, *PCFG*, XLV, 369; MDA to K, Jan. 21, 1781, Arneth and Flammermont, *Mercy avec Joseph II*, I, 18; K to Joseph II, Feb. 6, 1781, Beer, *Jos. II*, pp. 35-37; K to MDA, Feb. 8, 1781, Bancroft-Austria, NYPL; F to Normande, Dec. 23, 1780; to A, Feb. 6, 1781; to K, Feb. 3, 1781, *DC*, V, 346, 347, 543; to Aguilar, Jan. 1781, AHN, E, 4200, pt. 1; to La Torre, Mar. 23, 1781, *loc cit.*; V to Breteuil, Mar. 29, 1781, CP Aut 342: 159; K to MDA, Mar. 31, 1781, SKD, Frankreich 237; ST to JH, Jan. 11, 1781, FO/65, no. 11; Aguilar to F, April 14, 1781, AHN, E, 4200, apt. 1.

14. K to Joseph, Jan. 9, 1781, Beer, *Jos. II, Leopold II und Kaunitz*, p. 29; K to Keith, réponse verbale, Jan. 9, 1781, FO 7/1; Simolin to ST, Mar. 11, 1781, FO 65/2; ST to JH, Mar. 13, 1781, FO 65/2, no. 21; ST to G, Mar. 13, 1781, *CG*, V, 203; ST to Keith, Mar. 16, 1781, FO 7/1, no. 25.

15. Yorke to JH, Mar. 21, 1780, Hardwicke Papers, Add. MSS. 34, 434.

16. ST to Keith, Feb. 27, 1781, FO 7/1, no. 19; Hardwicke Papers, Add. MSS. 35, 521.

17. ST to Keith, Jan. 9, 1781, Jan. 20 (private), Feb. 4, 27, FO 7/1, unnumbered and no. 10; Hardwicke Papers, Add. MSS. 35, 521. ST also suggested that Joseph extend toleration to Protestants in Flanders.

18. Keith to ST, Feb. 7, 1781, FO 7/1, no. 22; ST to Keith, Feb. 27, 1781, no. 17; Hardwicke Papers, Add. MSS. 35, 521.

19. Graf von Kaunitz to K, Aug. 9, 10, 1781, SKD, Spanien 143; ST-JH dispatches, July-Aug., 1781, FO 7/3.

20. W. Coxe, *Memoirs of the Kings of Spain of the House of Bourbon* (London, 1813), III, 448.

21. See JH to ST, Nov. 24/Dec. 5, 1780, SP 91/106, no. 150; Malmesbury, *Diaries*, I, 345; *Sandwich Papers*, IV, 23-29; *CG*, V, 178, 181, 182, 185, 186.

22. ST to JH, Jan. 19, 1781, FO 65/1, nos. 4 (with a note for the Empress enclosed), 5; Malmesbury, *Diaries*, I, 374. Should the Empress decide to dispose of Minorca, preference should be given to Great Britain. FO 65/1, no. 6.

23. Vérac to V, Jan. 29/Feb. 9, 1781, CP R 106, no. 8; note of Simolin's "*représentation verbale*," Mar. 5, 1781, FO 65/1.

24. A Tereshchenko, *Opyt obozveniia zhizn sanovnikov upravliavshikh inostranymi delami v Rossii* (St. Petersburg, 1837), pt. ii, 139-140; JH to ST, Feb. 5/16, Mar. 5/16, Mar. 13/24, 1781, FO 65/2, nos. 20, 35, 37, 38; JH to ST, July 14/25, 1781, FO/3, no. 104. See also, Madariaga, *op. cit.*, pp. 297, 298. For the Empress' reluctance to get involved in America without compensatory guarantees against the Turks and Tartars, see Catherine to Simolin, Oct. 27, 1781. *Russkaia Starina*, CXXI (1905), 430.

25. JH to Mrs. Robinson, Mar. 13/24, 1781, Harris Papers, Merton College, Oxford.

26. For earlier memoranda on the state of America and the war, see *SF*, nos. 2031, 2037, and memorandum of Aug. 9, 1779, Oswald Papers, CL.

27. Oswald Papers, CL; HMC, *R*, XIV, 477-478. See also R. A. Humphreys, "Richard Oswald's Plan for an English and Russian Attack on Spanish America, 1781-1782," *Hispanic American Review*, XVIII (1938), 95-101.

28. *BFS*, VIII, 486.

29. O to S, July 12, 1782, *FC*, IV, 256; LP 72: 121-189.

30. Vérac to V, Jan. 22/Feb. 2, 1781, CP R 106: 74-77.

31. Vérac to V, Feb. 18/Mar. 1, 1781, CP R 106: 156-163.

32. *"Comme elle étoit"* in the French of that day.

33. Breteuil to V, Feb. 11, 1781, CP Aut 342: 56.

34. V to Breteuil, Mar. 4, 1781, CP Aut 342: 92.

35. CP EU 15: 50, 170-178 (Jan. 31, 1781), for the original imprint and translation sent at the request of the Georgia delegates.

36. K to MDA, Feb. 8, 1781, SKD, Frankreich 237.

37. L to V, Feb. 2, 1781, CP EU 15: 205-208.

38. See John Calef to Lord George Germain, Mar. 2, 1781, LP 66: 444-445.

39. "Memoir (of V, minuted in part by Rayneval) on the separation of North America from its former mother country and the cause and object of the present war." Feb., 1781, CP EU 15: 269-278. For a compromise suggestion of an eight-to-ten-year truce, see Frederick to Lusi, Oct. 29, 1781, *PCFG*, XLVI, 236.

40. See Bemis, *Dip. Hist. of the Amer. Revol.*, pp. 181, 182.

41. L to V, Mar. 31, 1781, CP EU 16: 86, 89.

42. L to V, April 9, 1781, CP EU 16: 146.

43. L to V, April 19, May 4, 1781, CP EU 16: 202, 240-247.

44. L to V, May 12, 1781, CP EU 16: 259; Aug. 20, 1781, CP EU 18: 110, 114.

45. V to L, June 30, 1781, CP EU 17: 234.

46. La Torre to F, April 13, 1781, AHN, E, 4200, apt. 1.

47. Breteuil to V, Mar. 5, 1781, CP Aut 342: 127.

48. V to Breteuil, Mar. 19, 1781, CP Aut 342: 142; V to Vérac, April 2, 1781, CP R 106: 214(2).

49. V to Vérac, Mar. 11, 1781, CP R 106: 177-179.

50. He also warned of Austrian schemes to by-pass Catherine's insistence on freedom of the seas. V to Vérac, April 7, 1781, CP R 106: 229-232. For complaints by the Spaniards that Galitzin was under K's control and could not be influenced in favor of Spain, see La Torre to Normande, April 13, 1781; Aguilar to F, April 14, 1781, AHN, E, 4200, apt. 1.

51. Breteuil to V, April 19, 1781, CP Aut 342: 237.

52. V to Breteuil, May 7, 1781, CP Aut 342: 300.

53. Keith to ST, Feb. 28, 1781, FO 7/1, no. 30; ST to Keith, Mar. 23, 1781, Hardwicke Papers, Add. MSS. 35, 522.

54. ST to Keith, Mar. 16, 1781, Hardwicke Papers, Add. MSS. 35, 522.

55. ST to Keith, Mar. 16, 1781 FO 7/1, no. 25; Hardwicke Papers, Add. MSS. 35, 522 ("separate and confidential"); Keith to ST, Mar. 31, April 7, 8, 1781 ("very

private"), FO 7/1, nos. 44, 50; Hardwicke Papers, Add. MSS. 35, 522; ST to Keith, April 20, 1781, FO 7/2, no. 38; Hardwicke Papers, Add. MSS. 35, 522; K to MDA, Mar. 31 (extract); Breteuil to V, April 1, CP Aut 342: 162, 224; Belgiojoso to K, April 27, 1781. Bancroft-Austria, NYPL.

56. ST to Keith, Feb. 27, 1781; Keith to Yorke, May 21, 1781, Hardwicke Papers, Add. MSS. 35, 522.

57. Note accompanying copies of instructions sent to ambassadors of the imperial courts in Paris, Madrid, and London, May 23, 1781. SKD, Frankreich 237: 0126-0130; FO 7/2; RDC, IV, 860-863; CP Aut 342: 381, 390; Bancroft-Austria, NYPL. For Panin's possible role in drawing up these proposals, see Madariaga, op. cit., pp. 325, 326n.

58. K to Joseph, Sept. 5, 1781, Bancroft-Austria, NYPL; K to MDA, Sept. 8, 1781, Oct. 7, 1781, SKD, Frankreich 237, pt. ii; Frederick to Finckenstein, Feb. 8, July 24, Aug. 6, Sept. 26, 1781; to Goltz, April 12, 23, May 24, July 23, 26, 1781; to Riedesel, May 6, July 12, 25, 1781; to Goertz, Aug. 20, 1781, PCFG, XLV, 233-234, 376, 407-408, 483, 440; XLVI, 55, 60-61.

59. Belgiojoso to K, June 8, July 6, 1781, SKD, England 164, pt. II; Bancroft-Austria, NYPL; ST to G, June 1, 1781, CG, V, 240; to JH, June 12, 1781, FO 65/3, no. 43; to Keith, June 12, 1781, FO 7/2, nos. 48-50; Hardwicke Papers, Add. MSS. 35, 522; to Belgiojoso, June 14, 1781; to Simolin, June 15, 1781, FO 65/3; K to Cobenzl, June 29, 1781, SKD, Frankreich, 237.

60. RDC, IV, 863, 864. Cf. also "Propositions and reasoning submitted to Lord George Germain," July 25, 1781, wherein direct negotiation with the European belligerents was favored over mediation. LP 72: 29-37.

61. RDC, IV, 864, 865.

62. Keith to ST, July 1, 7, Aug. 20, 1781, FO 7/2, nos. 81, 83, separate and secret.

63. Keith to ST, Aug. 29, Sept. 8, Dec. 1; ST to Keith, Dec. 6, 1781, FO 7/3, nos. 83, 113, 114, 118, private and confidential, 149. Much more important than Ostermann in policy-making following Panin's fall was the astute A. A. Bezborodko, the Empress' former private secretary, an expansionist like Potëmkin, and Pyotr Bakunin, formerly Panin's right-hand man.

64. JH to ST, June 4/15, July 14/25, 1781, FO 65/3.

65. "Preliminary observation on the articles to serve as a basis of negotiation for the establishment of a general peace," minute in the hand of Rayneval, July 6, 1781, CP Aut 343: 49.

66. MDA to K, June 1, 1781, Arneth and Flammermont, Corr., I, 37n; Bancroft-Austria, NYPL; V to M, Mar. 26, May 31, 1781, D, V, 8, 11. See also "Observations verbales," accompanying K's letter of May 21, 1781, CP Aut 342: 385, 393; V to Vérac, Aug. 16, 1781, CP R 106: 73-75; D, V, 24; RDC, IV, 860-863; Aguilar to K, Aug. 23, 1781, Barthélemy to K, Aug. 23, 1781, Vienna, SKD, Frankreich 237.

67. Note by Spanish Minister regarding mediation propositions, June 15, 1781, AHN, E, 4200, apt. 1; CP Aut 343: 13. See also Aguilar to F, May 24, 1781; M to F, June 14, 1781, AHN, E, 4200, apt. 1. See also memorandum of Aug. 7, 1781, and the Spanish acceptance of the French reply (F to A, Aug. 7, 1781), loc. cit.

68. La Torre to F (privately transmitted), Aug. 30, 1781, AHN, E, 4200, apt. 1; Barthélemy to V, Sept. 1, 1781, CP Aut 343: 115, 116.

69. Breteuil to V, May 3, 1781, CP Aut 342: 280.

70. Keith to ST, July 11, 1781; Oct. 19, 1782, FO 7/2, no. 87; FO 7/5, no. 76; Barthélemy to V, Sept. 15, 1781, CP Aut 343: 133.

71. The principal source of the Dana mission is the Dana Family Letterbooks, Mass. Hist. Soc., including Vérac to Dana, Aug. 22/Sept. 2, Sept. 1/12, 1781; Dana

to JA, Jan. 11/22, Sept. 8/19, Oct. 4/15, 1782; JA to Dana, Mar. 4/15, 1782, May 24, 1783; RRL to Dana, Mar. 2/13, 1782; Arthur Lee to Dana, June 25/July 6, 1782; Dana to Vérac, Feb. 24/Mar. 7, 1783; conversation between Dana and Bezborodko's secretary, Feb. 22/Mar. 5, 1783; Bakunin to Dana, Feb. 23/Mar. 6, 1783. In addition: Précis sur les relations de la Cour Impériale de Russie avec les États Unis de l'Amérique sous le règne de l'Impératrice Catherine II (Microfilm, LC, from Russian Archives); cf. also ST to JH, April 3, 1781; JH to ST, April 16/27, 1781, FO 65/2, nos. 27, 60; Breteuil to V, July 10, 27; V to Breteuil, July 23, 1782, CP Aut 345: 262, 303-306, 312; F. P. Renaut, *Les Relations Diplomatiques entre la Russie et les États-Unis: La Mission Dana* (Paris, 1923); W. P. Cresson, *Francis Dana: A Puritan Diplomat at the Court of Catherine the Great* (New York, 1930).

72. K to MDA, July 13, 1781, SKD, Frankreich 237, pt. ii.
73. Keith to ST, May 23, 1781, FO 7/2, no. 65.
74. Vérac to V, Jan. 4, 1782, CP R 108: 3-7.
75. V to L, July 27, 1781, CP EU 17: 455.
76. Marbois to M, July 5, 1781, CP E 604: 15-20; L to V, July 22, 1781, CP EU 17: 448, 452; Aug. 4, Aug. 7, 1781, CP EU 18: 59, 67, 68.
77. V to L, Sept. 7, 1781, CP EU 18: 212.
78. L to V, Sept. 27, 1781, CP EU 18: 338.
79. L to V, Oct. 3, 1781, CP EU 18: 433.
80. F to Goertz, Dec. 1, 1781; to Finckenstein, Dec. 1, 1781, *PCFG*, XLVI, 309-311.
81. F to A, Jan. 14; to Aguilar, Jan. 15, 1782, AHN, E, 4079, 4200, apt. 1; K to MDA, Jan. 15, Feb. 18, 1782; MDA to K, Jan. 28, 1782, SKD, Frankreich 239: 0028-0030; 240: 0020-0027; V to Breteuil, Jan. 28, 1782, CP Aut 345: 30-39; V to Vérac, Jan. 29, 1782, CP R 108: 66-78.
82. F to La Torre, Feb. 16, 1782; La Torre to F, Mar. 30, April 29, 1782, AHN, E, 4200, apt. 1; also in French translation in CP Aut 345: 129-131.
83. K to MDA, Feb. 18, 1782, SKD, Frankreich 239; Vérac to V, Mar. 1, 1782, CP R 108: 132-135.
84. MDA to K, May 24, June 12, 1782, SKD, Frankreich 240: 0163-0204, 0214-0238.
85. Memorandum from O to S, May 18, 1782, FO 95/511.
86. MDA to K, May 5, 1782, SKD, Frankreich 240: 0136-0160; Belgiojoso to K, May 7, 1782, SKD, England 165; F to A, May 17, 1782, AHN, E, 4079; A to F, June 1, 1782, AHN, E, 4200, apt. 1; Carmichael to JJ, July 23, 1782, JP.
87. K to MDA, May 18, Aug. 19, Sept. 23, Dec. 7; MDA to K, July 5, Aug. 10, 1782, Bancroft-Austria, NYPL; Arneth and Flammermont, *Corr. Mercy avec Joseph II et Kaunitz*, I, 123-125, letter 76; SKD, Frankreich 239: 0013-0016; 240: 0239-0279, 0284-0307.
88. MDA to K, Aug. 10, 1782; Joseph to MDA, Aug. 18; MDA to Joseph, Sept. 8, 1782, SKD, Frankreich 240: 0308-0312; Arneth and Flammermont, *op. cit.*, I, 123, 126-127.
89. Breteuil to V, Jan. 6, 1783, CP Aut 346: 7-10.
90. MDA to K, Sept. 8, 1782, SKD, Frankreich 240: 0324-0356; V to Breteuil, Sept. 10, 1782, CP Aut 345: 351.

CHAPTER X. MYNHEER ADAMS PUTS A SPOKE IN THE WHEEL

1. *Correspondence to the Boston Patriot*, p. 101.
2. See the comment of his colleague Prince de Montbarrey, *Mémoires*, II, 114.
3. *JAW*, III, 137.

4. JA to Warren, Mar. 16, 1780, *Warren-Adams Letters* (Boston, 1917-25), II, 129-130.
5. *JAW*, I, 659 *et seq.*
6. JA to V, May 9, 12, 1780, *RDC*, III, 665; *JAW*, VII, 165; JA to President of Congress, June 2, 1780, *ibid.*, p. 756; to M. Genêt, May 17, 1780, *ibid.*, p. 172-176.
7. *Diary*, III, 328, 329.
8. Meng *Despatches*, pp. 451, 643, 794.
9. L to V, Oct. 8, 1779. CP EU 10: 197.
10. JA to Thomas Digges, May 13, 1780, *RDC*, III, 676, 677; addressed to "W. S. Church" and signed "F. R. S.," suggested by Fernando Raymon San, JA's guide in Spain.
11. JA to V, Feb. 12, 1780; V to JA, Feb. 15, 1780. *Diary*, IV, 243, 245 ("Instructions" underscored by JA).
12. "Autobiography," in *Diary*, IV, 245-247.
13. *JCC*, XIV, 960-962.
14. *RDC*, III, 518.
15. JA to President of Congress, Mar. 30, 1780. *RDC*, III, 581.
16. JA to Lovell, Mar. 16, 1780. *RDC*, III, 551.
17. JA to Abigail Adams, n.d., 1780, *Familiar Letters of John Adams and his Wife Abigail Adams during the Revolution*, ed., C. F. Adams (Boston, 1876), p. 380.
18. JA to V, June 20, 1780; V to JA, June 21, 1780. *JAW*, VII, 188-192.
19. JA to Samuel Adams, Mar. 4, 1780. *RDC*, III, 532.
20. JA to V, June 22, July 1, 13, 1780; V to JA, June 30, 1780; JA to President of Congress, June 26, 1780; V to BF, June 30, 1780; BF to V, July 10, 1780. *RDC*, III, 805-816, 818, 819, 827-829, 844.
21. JA to V, July 17, 1780. *RDC*, III, 861-863.
22. V to JA, July 20, 1780. *RDC*, III, 870, 871.
23. V to JA, July 25, 1780, *RDC*, III, 883; *JAW*, VII, 235-241; V to L, Aug. 7, 1780. CP EU 13: 252.
24. JA to V, July 27, 1780; V to JA, July 29, 1780. *JAW*, VII, 241-243; *RDC*, IV, 16-17.
25. Lee to JA, July 8, 1780; JA to Lee, July 20, 1780. *JAW*, VII, 217, 232.
26. DH to JA, Aug. 14; JA to DH, Sept. 12, 1780. *JAW*, VII, 246, 247, 253.
27. V to L, Oct. 22, 1780, Feb. 19, 1781. CP EU 14: 157; 15: 258; also William E. O'Donnell, *The Chevalier de la Luzerne* (Bruges and Louvain, 1938), pp. 124-137.
28. President of Congress to JA, Jan. 10, 1781. *JAW*, VII, 353. See also C. F. Adams' comments in *ibid.*, I, 314-316.
29. *BFS*, VIII, 128; *D*, IV, 425-463.
30. BF to JA, Oct. 2, 1780. *BFS*, VII, 262, 263.
31. June 20, 1780, *JCC*, XVII, 535-537; *RDC*, III, 847; JA to the President of Congress, Aug. 14, Sept. 19, 1780, *JAW*, VII, 244-246, 258-260. JA received his commission on Sept. 16.
32. JA to Cushing, Dec. 15, 1780, *RDC*, IV, 193 (intercepted letter); Nov. 18, 1782, *Diary*, III, 60; L to V, Mar. 4, 1781, CP EU 16: 69.
33. Oct. 5, 1780. *RDC*, IV, 80, 81.
34. Mar. 8, 1781. *RDC*, IV, 274, 275, 276.
35. JA to Searle, Feb. 4, 1781; JA to President of Congress, Feb. 7, 1781. AP.
36. Leo Gershoy, *From Despotism to Revolution* (New York, 1944), p. 44.
37. JA to JJ, Mar. 28, 1781. JP.
38. John Quincy Adams, Diary, Aug. 14, 1780. AP.

39. H. T. Colenbrander, *De Patriottentijd* (2 vols., 1897-99), I, 78, 79; LV to V, Jan. 2, 1781. CP H 543: 5.
40. JA to President of Congress, Sept. 25, 1780. *RDC*, IV, 67-69.
41. JA to President of Congress, Aug. 14, 1780. *JAW*, VII, 245.
42. JA to BF, Aug. 15, 1780. AP.
43. JA to Jean Luzac, Sept. 1, 1780. AP.
44. *JAW*, VII, 266-312; published several times after the Revolution, and included in *Correspondence of the Late President Adams* (Boston, 1809), pp. 195-250, at p. 229.
45. *Boston Patriot*, p. 104.
46. See P. J. van Winter, *Het aandeel van den Amsterdamschen handel aan den opbouw van het Amerikaansche gemeenebest* (The Hague, 1927-33); JA to BF, Nov. 24; to President of Congress, Nov. 25, 1780, *JAW*, VII, 333; *RDC*, IV, 160-161. For JJ's intercession with the de Neufvilles on JA's behalf, see JJ to JA, Feb. 24, 1781, JP; AP, pt. IV, 354.
47. JA to President of Congress, Dec. 25, 1780, Mar. 19, 1781; *Boston Patriot*, letter XL; *RDC*, IV, 313-315.
48. Yorke to ST, Nov. 7; to JH, Dec. 9, 1780. Hardwicke Papers, Add. MSS., 35, 434, BM.
49. See *AMON*, II, 290-338 *passim*, 403-408; Admiraliteits Colleges, XXXI, no. 253; XXXVII, no. 485, ARH; also Sanafé to F, Dec. 5, 25, 1780, AGI: 6373, 133-136, p. 3; 153-157, p. 4; A to F, Dec. 27, 1780. AHN, E, 4211, apt. 1, let. no. 1855, p. 10.
50. Walpole to Countess of Ossory, Jan. 2, 1781, *Letters*, IX, 354-357. For Opposition attacks on the Dutch war, see R 1-1942, 1946a, 1947, 1949, 1953.
51. JA to Jenings, Dec. 6, 1780; to Lovell, Dec. 7, 1780; to William Temple Franklin, AP; JA to President of Congress, Dec. 31, 1780. *RDC*, IV, 219.
52. JA to Jenings, Dec. 18, 1780. AP.
53. JA to Congress, Jan. 4, 1781, Jan. 14, 1781, AP; LV to V, Jan. 5, 1781. CP H 543: 23.
54. See correspondence of LV with V, April 21—May 17, 1781, CP H 544; *AMON*, ser. 5, II, 468, 469, 478-481; *JAW*, VII, 404-406; *Boston Patriot*, pp. 430-439; cf. also Sanafé to F, April 24, 1781, AGI: 6374, 109-111, p. 2.
55. F. P. Renaut, *Les Provinces-Unies et la guerre d'Amérique* (Paris, 1924-25), V, 37; Dumas Collection, ARH; also *RDC*, IV, 370-376; *Correspondence in the Boston Patriot*, pp. 439-448; *Diary*, III, 457n.
56. JA to BF, May 23, 1781. FP, Amer. Philos. Soc.
57. JA to President of Congress, Mar. 19, 1781. *RDC*, IV, 313-315.
58. Prince of Orange to Counsellor-Pensionary, May 2, 1781, *AMON*, II, 454, 455; to Hartsink, May 4, 1781, Adm. Coll. XXXVII, no. 485. For regulations regarding American privateers entering the United Provinces and shipments to America before formal recognition of the United States, see Adm. Coll. XXXVII, no. 485 (May 7, June 12, 1781).
59. JA to President of Congress, June 26, 1781. *RDC*, VI, 517-519.
60. BF to President of Congress, Mar. 12, 1781, JP; V to Bérenger, May 31, June 17, 1781, CP H 544: 260, 382; Bérenger to JA, June 5, 1781, AP; *JAW*, VII, 423-424.
61. JA to Dumas, Oct. 4, 1780, *JAW*, VII, 262, 263; *RDC*, IV, 77, 78.
62. JA to President of Congress, May 16, 1781, Adams Letterbooks.
63. *Boston Patriot*, pp. 108, 110.
64. JA to President of Congress, June 23, 1781. *RDC*, IV, 515.

65. JA to President of Congress, July 11, 1781. Adams Letterbooks; *RDC*, IV, 560; *Boston Patriot*, letter XXII, pp. 111-112.
66. JA to V, July 13, 1781. CP EU 17: 380-388; Adams Letterbooks; *RDC*, IV, 571-573.
67. JA to President of Congress, July 15, 1781. *RDC*, IV, 575-576.
68. JA to V, July 18, 1781. Adams Letterbooks; CP EU 17: 408-412; *RDC*, IV, 576.
69. V to JA, July 18, 1781. Adams Letterbooks; CP EU 17: 426; a somewhat different translation in *RDC*, IV, 589.
70. *Boston Patriot*, p. 123.
71. JA to V, July 18, 1781. CP EU 17: 424-425; Adams Letterbooks; *RDC*, IV, 589-590.
72. JA to V, July 19, 1781. CP EU 17: 427-428.
73. Vérac to Dana, Aug. 22/Sept. 2, Sept. 12/23, 1781. Adams Letterbooks; *Boston Patriot*, pp. 133-138.
74. JA to V, July 21, 1781. CP EU 17: 441; Adams Letterbooks; *RDC*, IV, 595-596.
75. *Boston Patriot*, p. 130.
76. *Boston Patriot*, p. 133; *JAW*, VII, 452n.
77. See, e.g., V to L, Feb. 19, April 19, 1781. CP EU 15: 253-260; 16: 197.
78. L to V, May 13, 1781. CP EU 16: 265-274; *D*, IV, 608n.; O'Donnell, *La Luzerne*, pp. 64, 65n.; citing La Luzerne Private Archives.
79. See Arthur Lee to Samuel Adams, April 21, 1782. Samuel Adams MSS., NYPL.
80. Washington to BF, Jan. 15, 1781. CP EU 15: 82.
81. BF to V, Feb. 13, 1781, *RDC*, IV, 254; V to L, Mar. 11, 1781; Memoirs of John Laurens to V, Mar. 18, April 18, 1781, CP EU 15: 341, 413; 16: 194.
82. Barbé-Marbois to V, July 11, 1781, CP EU 17: 316, 317; L to V, Oct, 12, 1781, CP EU 19: 15-52.
83. L to V, Feb. 2, Mar. 20, 1781. CP EU 15: 205-208; 16: 3.
84. *Continental Journal and Weekly Advertiser*, April 13, 1780; *Observations upon the Effects of Certain Late Political Suggestions*, by the Delegates of Georgia (Philadelphia: R. Aitken, bookseller, 1781); CP EU 15:50, 170-178.
85. V to L, Mar. 9, 1781, CP EU 15: 345. At the same time V asked BF to write Congress for instructions for dealing with the mediation proposal. BF to President of Congress, Mar. 12, 1781. JP; *RDC*, IV, 281.
86. V to L, May 11, 1781. CP EU 16: 252.
87. V to L., April 19, June 30, 1781. CP EU 16: 197; 17: 264.
88. L to Rochambeau, May 19, 1781, A.G. A¹ 3736: 150; L to V, June 1, 1781, CP EU 17: 30.
89. See Joseph Jones to George Washington, May 31, 1781. *LMCC*, VI, 106.
90. For a change in the phraseology of this last clause from an affirmative to a negative instruction, see draft in *JCC*, XX, 605, 606.
91. *Diary*, IV, 253.
92. L to V, June 8, 1781. CP EU 17: 91.
93. *Ibid.*
94. *JCC*, XX, 612-615.
95. *RDC*, IV, 471-477; *JCC*, XX, 615-618.
96. L to V, June 11, 1781. CP EU 17: 123-136; *JCC*, XX, 625-627 (June 11, 1781).
97. *RDC*, IV, 505; *JCC*, XX, 651, 652 (June 15, 1781).
98. L to V, CP EU 17: 125-139; *RDC*, IV, 478-481; PCC, 25: I.
99. Diary (July ?, 1781), *LMCC*, VI, 144.
100. L to V, June 14, Aug. 11, 1781. CP EU 17: 182-183; 18: 78.

101. *RDC*, IV, 507-511.
102. L to V, May 18, 1781. CP EU 16: 308-309.
103. L secured the appointment of one of RRL's secretaries, Pierre S. Duponceau, L to V, Aug. 11, Nov. 1, 1781, CP EU 18: 78-82; 19: 172-173; Arthur Lee to Samuel Adams, Aug. 13, 1781, Samuel Adams Papers, NYPL.
104. L to V, Aug. 11, 1781. CP EU 18: 78. See also RRL to Barbé-Marbois, Aug. 24, 1781, RRL MSS., N.Y. Hist. Soc.; George Dangerfield, *Chancellor Robert R. Livingston of New York* (New York, 1960), pp. 140, 142-144.
105. See Page Smith, *John Adams* (New York, 1962), I, 470-471.
106. James Lovell to JA, June 21; to Abigail Adams, June 26, 1781. *LMCC*, VI, 125, 129.
107. *Boston Patriot*, p. 387.
108. JA to Dana, Feb. 23, 1783, Dana Family Papers, Mass. Hist. Soc.

CHAPTER XI. JACOB'S BARGAIN

1. See Arthur S. Aiton, "The Diplomacy of the Louisiana Cession," *Amer. Hist. Rev.*, XXXVI (1931), 701-720; E. Wilson Lyon, *Louisiana in French Diplomacy* (Norman, Okla., 1934), pp. 13-35; F. P. Renaut, *Le Pacte de Famille*, pp. 50-52.
2. Henry to Bernardo de Gálvez, Jan. 4, 1778. AGI, Cuba, 2370.
3. CG to V, Oct. 20, Dec. 22, 1778. Meng, *Despatches*, pp. 344, 345, 433, 434.
4. *JCC*, XII, 1083 (Oct. 31, 1778); John W. Caughey, *Bernardo de Gálvez in Louisiana, 1776-1783* (Berkeley, Calif., 1934), pp. 85-101; James A. James, *Oliver Pollock* (New York, 1937).
5. M to V, Oct. 15, 1778. CP E 591: no. 22; *D*, III, 556, 557.
6. V to M, Oct. 23, 30, 1778. *D*, III, 561, 563n. In his instructions to CG, V advised that, should the Americans conquer Florida, it would be desirable to have Pensacola and the surrounding area ceded to Spain. *RDC*, I, 436; *D*, III, 569-570.
7. M to V, Nov. 12, 1778, CP E 591: 169; V to M, Nov. 27, 1778, *D*, III, 581.
8. CG to V, July 16, 25, Aug. 29, 1778. Meng, *Despatches*, pp. 156-160, 186, 239; *D*, III, 393-394, 395; Miralles to José de Gálvez, Dec. 28, 1778, *YU*, I, 390.
9. CG to V, Oct. 20, 1778. Meng, *Despatches*, pp. 345, 346; *D*, III, 72-73.
10. V to CG, Oct. 26, 1778. *D*, III, 569-570; Meng, p. 359.
11. CG to V, Dec. 22, Jan. 28, 1779. Meng, pp. 433, 434, 493-495.
12 CG to V, Feb. 17, Mar. 10, 1779. Meng, pp. 529, 579.
13. V to L, July 18, 1779. CP EU 9: no. 1; John Jay, *The Peace Negotiations of 1782 and 1783* (New York, 1884), pp. 147, 148.
14. *JPJ*, I, 248-250, and above chap. II.
15. Gálvez to Navarro, Aug. 29, 1779; Navarro to Nayorga, Dec. 23, 1779. Lawrence Kinnaird, *Spain in the Mississippi Valley* (Washington, D.C., 1949), II, 355, 364.
16. The term "new enemies" is used by Martin Navarro, intendant of New Orleans, in a dispatch dated September 24, 1780, although some historians believe that it was in fact written some years later. See Caughey, *Gálvez*, p. 249n.
17. William Jay, *Life of John Jay* (New York, 1833), I, 99-101.
18. Instructions for Carmichael, Jan. 27, 1780, JP; *JPJ*, I, 266-267; Sparks, VII, 205.
19. F to JJ, Feb. 28, 1780; JJ to President of Congress, March 3, 1780, JJ Letterbook, JP; PCC 110: 1; *JPJ*, I, 273-275.

20. Fr. Pesaro dispatch, April 11, 1780. Archivio di Stato, Spanish dispatches, letter 192, Venice.
21. JJ to Committee of Foreign Affairs, May 27, 1780, JJ Letterbook, JP; PCC 110: 1.
22. JJ to F, April 29, 1780. English draft, JP; French translation, CP E 599: 21-22; Spanish excerpt in YU, II, 302, 303; JPJ, I, 311-314.
23. JJ's Notes on Conference with F, May 11, 1780. JPJ, I, 317-324; RDC, III, 722-725.
24. Carmichael to President of Congress, May 28, 1780. Carmichael Letters, PCC 116: 1.
25. JJ to President of Congress, May 26, 1780. RDC, III, 725.
26. JJ to President of Congress, Nov. 6, 1780. JP; PCC 110: 1; Sparks, VII, 309-310.
27. JJ to JA, June 4, 1780. Draft in JP. See also AP; JPJ, I, 343-345.
28. F to JJ, June 7, 1780. PCC 110: 1; JJ Letterbook, JP; YU, II, 305-306; JPJ, I, 345-347; Sparks, VII, 310-314.
29. JJ to F, June 9, 1780. JJ Letterbook, JP; PCC 110: 1; YU, II, 303-313; Sparks, VII, 314-321.
30. JJ to F, June 19, 1780; to President of Congress, Nov. 6, 1780; F to JJ, June 20, 1780. JJ Letterbook, JP; Sparks, VII, 322-323.
31. F to JJ, June 20, 1780. PCC 110: 1; JJ Letterbook, JP.
32. JJ to F, June 22, 1780. PCC 110: 1, JJ Letterbook, JP; JPJ, I, 358-362; YU, II, 314-318; Sparks, VII, 323-327.
33. He followed up with a request for more information about bills which the mercantile house of Messrs. Joyce of Bilbao had presented to JJ amounting to some $10,000. JJ to F, June 28, July 4, 1780; F to JJ, June 29, July 3, 1780; PCC 110: 1; JJ Letterbook, JP; YU, II, 320, 321; Sparks, VII, 328-331. Some $15,000 in bills were accepted for payment by Spain at this time. Carmichael to President of Congress, July 17, 1780. Carmichael Papers, PCC 116: 1.
34. JJ to President of Congress, Nov. 6, 1780. PCC 110: 1; JJ Letterbook, JP; Sparks, VII, 331; JJ to JA, July 17, 1780. AP.
35. JJ to President of Congress, Nov. 6, 1780. PCC 110: 1; JJ Letterbook, JP; Sparks, VII, 331-336; cf. George Washington to Diego José de Navarro, Governor of Havana, April 30, 1780. Washington Papers, LC.
36. JJ to President of Congress, May 26, 1780; April 25, 1781; John de Neufville & Zoon to JJ, c. May, June 1, 8, July 25, 28, 1780; JJ to de Neufville & Son, June 18, 28, July 29, Aug. 16, 1780; Le Couteulx & Co. to JJ, July 4, Oct. 3, 1780; JJ to Le Couteulx & Co., Oct. 15, 1780; Robert Morris to JJ, July 9, 1781; JJ to Messrs. Gardoqui & Sons, Nov. 5, 1781. JJ Letterbook, JP.
37. JJ to James Lovell, Oct. 27, 1780. Sparks, VII, 304-305.
38. BF to JJ, July 31, 1780. JP.
39. JJ to Robert Morris, April 28, 1782 (draft). JP.
40. JJ to F, Aug. 11; F to JJ, July 29, Aug. 12, 1780. JJ Letterbook, JP; Sparks,
42. For M, see Masson, Le Département des Affaires Étrangères, pp. 56-59. For M's VII, 338, 339.
41. JJ to F, Aug. 16, 18, 25, 1780; YU, II, 322-324; JP. account of this interview, see M to V, Sept. 11, 1780. CP E 601: 445-448; for JJ's, JJ to Congress, Nov. 6, 1780. JJ Letterbook, JP; Sparks, VII, 347-357.
43. Cumberland to H, July 21, 1780. SP 94: 209/124-125.
44. DC, V, 110.
45. H to F, Aug. 3 (4), 1780. AHN, E, 4220, exp. 2, doc. 177; SP 94: 209/154.

46. Hussey to Cumberland, Sept. 10, 1780. AHN, E, 4220, exp. 2, doc. 125; Cumberland to H, Sept. 24, 1780. SP 94: 209/211.
47. JJ to V, Sept. 22, 1780. JJ Letterbook, JP; Sparks, VII, 366, 367.
48. Carmichael to President of Congress, Aug. 22, Sept. 6, 1780. PCC 116: 1.
49. JJ to Committee of Foreign Affairs, Nov. 30, 1780; to Lovell, Oct. 27, 1780; to J. Johnson, Jan. 21, 1781. JP; Sparks, VII, 304, 305, 401-403.
50. Carmichael to President of Congress, Sept. 9, 1780. PCC 116: 1; also ch. V above.
51. JJ to F, Sept. 14, 1780. JJ Letterbook, JP; YU, II, 324, 325; Sparks, VII, 361, 362.
52. F to Campo, Sept. 15, 1780; Gardoqui to JJ, Sept. 15, 1780; to Campo, Oct. 4, 1780. YU, II, 325-326; JPJ, I, 400-401; Sparks, VII, 362-364.
53. JJ to V, Sept. 22, 1780; to BF, Sept. 22, 1780. PCC 110: 1; JJ Letterbook, JP; RDC, IV, 63-66; Sparks, VII 364-370.
54. JJ to President of Congress, Nov. 6, 1780. PCC 110: 1; JPJ, I, 415-428 RDC, IV, 112-150; Sparks, VII, 306-389. Some of the conversation reported in JJ's lengthy dispatch has been put into direct discourse, but the text has been rigidly adhered to. Words italicized were underscored by JJ. The paragraph in cipher appears in deciphered form, along with the complete dispatch, in JJ Letterbook, Huntington Lib.
55. See Carmichael to President of Congress, Sept. 25, 1780, Jan. 29, 1781. PCC 116: 1.
56. Sarah Livingston Jay to Susannah French Livingston, Aug. 28, 1780; to Susannah Livingston [Symmes], Aug. 28, 1780; to Mary White Morris, Sept. 1, 1780. JP.
57. Carmichael's more optimistic view toward Spanish policy can be found in Carmichael to JA, April 22; to Comm. of For. Aff., May 28, July 17, Aug. 22, Sept. 9, 25, Dec. 19, 1780; Jan. 29, Mar. 11, Sept. 28, 1781. RDC, III, 624, 625, 737-739, 865-866; IV, 39-40, 53, 71, 198-243, 279, 732.
58. For Arthur Lee's characterization, see Deane Papers, IV, 99. For Carmichael's relations with Bancroft, see William to Arthur Lee, Mar. 24, 1780. Letters of William Lee, III, 793-795; BFS, X, 310-313. For Carmichael's suspicious relations with Hynson, a fellow Marylander and acknowledged traitor, and his contacts with British secret agents, see SF, nos. 250, 670, 675, 810; Sarah Jay to William Livingston, June 24, 1781, JP.
59. Sarah Jay to William Livingston, June 24, 1781; William Livingston to JJ, Jan. 8, 1783. JP. Sir Guy Carleton to Washington; to William Livingston, May 7, 1782. British Headquarters Papers (photostat), NYPL.
60. The JJ-Littlepage correspondence is in JP. See also JJ's lengthy pamphlet, Letters, Being the Whole of the Correspondence between the Hon. John Jay, Esquire, and Mr. Lewis Littlepage (New York, 1786); Curtis C. Davis, The King's Chevalier: A Biography of Lewis Littlepage (Indianapolis, 1961), pp. 32-126.
61. See JJ to M, Oct. 17, 1780 (draft); to BF, Dec. 25, 1780. JJ Letterbook, JP.
62. JJ to BF, Jan. 11, Mar. 28, 1781; to Carmichael, Mar. 8, 1781, JP; to RRL, April 25, 1781, Livingston Papers, N.Y. Hist. Soc. For financial dealings with Cabarrus, Gardoqui, and Yranda in this period, see, e.g., Carmichael to JJ, Jan. 3, 13, 26, Feb. 1, 7, 14, 22, Mar. 7, 19, 31, April 2, 6-8, 15, 17, May 16, 1781; JJ to Carmichael, April 1, 7, 14, 16, June 27, 1781, JP. Carmichael to President of Congress, Jan. 4, 1781. PCC 116: 1.
63. This grandiose promotion never materialized, and CG's claim to some 300,000

acres, pressed by his brother R on his death, was ultimately disallowed. Meng, pp. 914-918.

64. L to V, June 11, 1780. CP EU 12: 74.

65. *RDC*, III, 78, 79.

66. JJ to President of Congress, Oct. 3, 1781. *RDC*, IV, 738.

67. *JCC*, XVIII, 908; W. T. Hutchinson and W. M. E. Rachal, eds., *The Papers of James Madison* (Chicago, 1962), II, 114-117, 127-136; Kathryn Sullivan, *Maryland and France, 1774-1789* (Philadelphia, 1936), pp. 88-90; Elijah W. Lyon, *The Man Who Sold Louisiana: The Career of François Barbé-Marbois* (Norman, Okla., 1942), p. 25; O'Donnell, *La Luzerne*, p. 110. For a misleading report on Congress' new instruction, see Barbé-Marbois to V, Oct. 21, 1780. CP EU 14: 139-147.

68. JJ to President of Congress, April 25, 1781. *RDC*, IV, 384; PCC 110: 1. JP. See also JJ to Gouverneur Morris, Sept. 28, 1781. JP.

69. *JCC*, XVIII, 1070-1072, 1121.

70. *Va. Mag. of Hist. and Biog.*, XLIII (1935), 43.

71. Bland to Jefferson, Nov. 22, 1780. *Madison Papers*, II, 194-196.

72. *Ibid.*, p. 302 (Feb. 1, 1781); *JCC*, XVIII, 1070-1071; XIX, 151-154.

73. *Ibid.*, pp. 151-154; *RDC*, IV, 257; *JPJ*, I, 460-461; Sparks, VII, 403, 404; JP. Only Massachusetts, Connecticut, and North Carolina voted against the motion.

74. Lovell to JJ, Feb. 20, 1781. *RDC*, IV, 261; *LMCC*, V, 595.

75. JJ to President of Congress, Oct. 3, 1781. PCC 110: 1; JP; Sparks, VII, 454-470; *RDC*, IV, 743, 744.

76. JJ to F; to M, July 2, 1781. PCC 110: 1; *YU*, II, 340, 341; JJ Letterbook, JP.

77. Samuel Huntington to JJ, May 28, 1781. JP; *RDC*, IV, 451-453; cf. also Report of Committee of Congress, May 2, 1781. PCC 32: 25, I.

78. JJ to President of Congress, Oct. 3, 1781. PCC 110: 1; *RDC*, IV, 748, 749; JP.

79. For the threat posed by these released British troops, see RRL to JJ, July 6, 1782. Livingston Papers, N.Y. Hist. Soc.; William Bingham to JJ, July 13, 1781; JP. For Gálvez's refusal to carry out a similar pact concerning prisoners taken at the Mississippi and Mobile, see Bernardo de Gálvez to Sir Henry Clinton, British Headquarters Papers, CL.

80. JJ to M, Sept. 16, 17, 1781, JJ Letterbook, JP; PCC 110: 1; *JPJ*, II, 108-109.

81. JJ to F, Sept. 17, 1781; F to JJ, Sept. 19, 1781. JJ Letterbook, JP; PCC 110: 1; *JPJ*, II, 114; Sparks, VII, 489.

82. JJ to F, Sept. 22, 1781. PCC 110: 1; *YU*, II, 341-350; CP E 605: 418-425; JJ Letterbook, JP; *JPJ*, II, 121-128; Sparks, VII, 495-501. For F's note on JJ's propositions, Sept. 22, 1781, see *YU*, II, 350-351.

83. See S. F. Bemis, *Pinckney's Treaty* (New Haven, 1960), pp. 28, 29.

84. JJ to President of Congress, Oct. 3, 1781. PCC 110: 1; JJ Letterbook, JP; *RDC*, IV, 738-765; *JPJ*, II, 75-132; Sparks, VII, 454-506; RRL to JJ, April 16, 1782, JP; *JPJ*, II, 187-190.

85. Robert Morris to JJ, July 4, 1781; Mar. 5, 8, 1782. JP; *RDC*, IV, 531-539; *JPJ*, II, 40; Sparks, VII, 421-435.

86. JJ to Gouverneur Morris, Sept. 28, 1781. JP.

87. See Carmichael to JJ, Dec. 1, 1781, JP; report of Dutch Minister, Dec. 10, 1781, SGH, no. 6857.

88. Carmichael to President of Congress, Nov. 17, 1781. Carmichael Papers, PCC 116: 1.
89. See JJ to JA, Dec. 15, 1781. AP, pt. IV, 355.
90. BF to JJ, Jan. 19, April 22, 1782. JP; Sparks, VIII, 57-59; JJ to President of Congress, Feb. 6, 1782. PCC 110: 1; JJ Letterbook, JP. Some of the more significant items in JJ's financial correspondence include: BF to JJ, Sept. 29, 1781, Jan. 15, 1782, enclosing a letter from V of Dec. 31, 1781; JJ to BF, Oct. 3, 29, Nov. 21, 1781; JJ to F, Nov. 16, 1781; JJ to Campo, Feb. 1, Mar. 2, 1782; Campo to JJ, Feb. 3, 1782; Cabarrus to JJ, Feb. 25, 1782; Carmichael to Congress, Dec. 24, 1781. PCC 116: 1; Grand to R, Mar. 10, 1782; M to V, Mar. 18, 1782; JJ to Bourgoing, April 5, 1782. CP E 607: 277, 324-325, 405.
91. JJ to RRL, April 28, 1782, JP: *JPJ*, II, 245.
92. JJ to F, Mar. 14, 1782. *YU*, II, 353, 354; M to JJ, Mar. 15, 1782; Carmichael to President of Congress, April 14, 1782. PCC 116: 1.
93. JJ to RRL, Mar. 14, 1782. JP.
94. BF to JJ, Mar. 16, 1782. JP; Sparks, VIII, 88.
95. RRL to JJ, Nov. 28, 1781; JJ to BF, Mar. 18, 1782. JJ crossed out "My" in his draft and substituted "Our." JP.
96. Bemis, *Pinckney's Treaty*, pp. 325-334; *American State Papers: Financial*, I, 672.
97. F to JJ, undated (received Mar. 30, 1782); JJ to M, April 27, 1782. JP draft letter has significant variance from *RDC*, V, 376.
98. *RDC*, IV, 503-504; also FO 27/2; 95/511; Hartley Papers, III, CL.
99. JJ to President of Congress, Sept. 20, 1781. PCC 110: 1; JJ Letterbook, JP; *JPJ*, II, 69-73; Sparks, VII, 451-453; *RDC*, IV, 716-718. For a comment on JJ's "servile situation," see Gouverneur Morris to JJ, June 17, 1781. JP.
100. RRL to JJ, Dec. 13, 1781, JP. Again on May 9, 1782, RRL wrote to inform JJ that Congress had declined to give him the leave of absence he requested.
101. BF to JJ (2 letters), April 23, 1782. JP.
102. JJ to RRL, May 11, 14, 1782. JP.
103. F to A, Sept. 20, 1782. AHN, E, 4062; *YU*, II, 364, 365.
104. Lafayette to V, Mar. 20, 1782. CP EU 20: 438-440.
105. BF to RRL, April 12, 1782. *BFB*, IX, 192. Cf. also JJ to RRL, April 26, 1782. PCC 125; JP; RRL to JJ, April 28, 1782, JP; Livingston Papers, N.Y. Hist. Soc.; *RDC*, V, 377.
106. Resolution of Congress, April 30, 1782. JP; CP EU 21: 121-122.
107. RRL to JJ, April 16, 1782. JP.
108. L to V, May 10, 1782. CP EU 21: 154-157.
109. RRL to JJ, June 23, 1782. JP; Sparks, VIII, 112. Neutral intelligence proved overly optimistic about Spanish recognition of the United States. See de Hauteville (for Victor Amadeus III of Sardinia) to Cordon. LP 35: 16.

CHAPTER XII. THE BALL AT DR. FRANKLIN'S FOOT

1. Burke to BF, Aug. 15, 1781. Burke, *Corr.*, IV, 362-365.
2. O to S, June 12, 1782, LP 71.
3. Gerald Stourzh, *Benjamin Franklin and American Foreign Policy* (Chicago, 1954), pp. 186-213.
4. See Burke to BF, Feb. 28, 1782. Burke *Corr.*, IV, 418, 419; BF to DH, April 5, 1782. *RDC*, V, 293-295; CP EU 21: 16-18.
5. In French in *BFS*, X, 432-436; in English in *BFAW*, pp. 584-586; dated

"Passy, July 27," presumably 1782, and in answer to Madame Brillon's complaint, drawn up in legal form, charging BF with neglecting her while she was at Nice while he paid court to ladies nearer at hand.

6. BF to Madame Brillon, Dec. 25, 1781. French original in *BFS*, VIII, 349-351; translation in *BFAW*, pp. 511, 512.

7. Max Hall, *Benjamin Franklin and Polly Baker; The History of a Literary Deception* (Chapel Hill, N.C., 1960).

8. Carl Van Doren, *Benjamin Franklin* (New York, 1941), pp. 150-154.

9. *BFS*, VIII, 437-447; Van Doren, *Franklin*, p. 673.

10. BF to Thomas Walpole, Jan. 12, 1774, with attached memoranda, July 14, 1778, NYPL; Jack M. Sosin, *Whitehall and the Wilderness* (Lincoln, Neb., 1961), p. 210.

11. See V to L, Feb. 19, 1781, CP EU 15: 253-260; L to V, Feb. 27, 1782, LP 35: 70.

12. BF to Priestley, June 7, 1782. *BFS*, VIII, 451-452.

13. BF to S, *FS*, III, 175; to V, April 15, 1782. CP EU 21: 53-55; *CG*, V, 431; on S's treatment of Cholmondeley, see Walpole, *Last Journals*, II, 441.

14. *BFS*, VIII, 459-462. In his Diary, O writes of having met BF during a visit to Paris, but BF, in his "Journal" seems to have had no recollection of the meeting. Edward E. Hale and Edward E. Hale, Jr., *Franklin in France* (Boston, 1888), II, 50n.

15. Hale, *op. cit.*, II, 10.

16. BF to JJ, Jan. 19, 1782. JP.

17. For the reaction of neutral observers to the news, see Doria Pamphili to Pallavicini, Nov. 19, 26, 1781. Nunz. Francia, Vatican; MDA to Joseph, Nov. 20, 1781. SKD, Frankreich 238.

18. H. B. Wheatley, ed., *The Historical and Posthumous Memoirs of Sir Nathaniel William Wraxall, 1772-1782* (5 vols., New York, 1884), II, 137-142.

19. Richmond to Rockingham, Dec. 12, 1781. R 1-1970; Duke of Buckingham and Chandos, *Memoirs of the Court and Cabinets of George the Third* (2 vols., London, 1853), I, 23.

20. *PH*, XXII, 700 (Nov. 27, 1781).

21. Alan Valentine, *Lord George Germain* (Oxford, 1962), p. 58.

22. *PH*, XXII, 829 (Dec. 12, 1781).

23. G to ST, Dec. 23, 1781; to North, Dec. 26, 1781. *CG*, V, 319, 362. For the Marquess of Carmarthen's motion of condemnation and Burke's reaction, see *PH*, XXII, 999 *et seq.*; Burke, *Corr.*, IV, 404, 405.

24. Walpole to the Countess of Upper Ossory, Feb. 9, 1782. *Letters*, XII, 160-62.

25. *PH*, XII, 1087-1101 (Mar. 4, 1782), 1103-1109 (Mar. 5, 1782); North to G, Mar. 4, 5, 1782. *CG*, V, 376, 377; *Annual Register, 1782*, pp. 171, 172; Burke to BF, Feb. 28, 1782. Burke, *Corr.*, IV, 418, 419. For the five critical divisions of Feb. 20, 22, 27, and Mar. 8 and 15, see Christie, *End of North's Ministry*, pp. 376-405.

26. Sandwich to John Robinson, Mar. 15, 17, 19, 22, 1782. Marquess of Abergavenny MSS., HMC, *R*, X, *App.*, pt. vi, pp. 50-52; also XV, pt. 5, 158; pt. 6, pp. 560-562, 574-576.

27. G to North, Mar. 27, 1782, *CG*, V, 421.

28. *FC*, I, 296; cf. also Wraxall, *Hist. and Post. Mem.*, pp. 282-284. North's decision was a well-advertised secret, as rumor had it that a few days before he had remarked to several persons that "the game is up." Temple to Rockingham, Mar. 18, 1782. R 1-1999.

29. North to G, Jan. 2, 1782. *CG*, V, 337.

30. See G to North, Jan. 21, 1782; to Thurlow, Mar. 17, 1782. *CG*, V, 391, 392.
31. G to North, Feb. 28, 1782. *CG*, V, 375, 376.
32. *AMON*, II, 559; III, 1, 3-9, 19, 23. See also Madariaga, *Armed Neutrality*, pp. 348-360.
33. See LV to V, July 3, 6, 13, Nov. 18, Dec. 7, 1781, Feb. 26, Mar. 1, 1782; Bérenger to V, Dec. 28, 1781, Jan. 11, 1782; V to Bérenger, Jan. 3, Feb. 10, 1782. CP H 546: 16, 17, 39-44, 76, 363, 451, 530-535; 547: 11, 41, 219-220, 366; 548: 3.
34. Bérenger to V, Feb. 1, 1782; LV to V, Mar. 5, 15, 22, 1782. CP H 547: 151; 548: 21, 87-96; *AMON*, III, 30-35, 37.
35. LV to V, Mar. 19, 1782. CP H 548: 109-122; also Dumas to JA, Mar. 16, 20, 1782. *JAW*, VII, 547, 549. Galitzin to Markov, Feb. 21, 1782. Bancroft Transcripts, NYPL.
36. Thurne to Baudouin, Mar. 5, 1782. CP A 536: 194.
37. See warning of Abbé Mary to V, Mar. 16, 1782. CP A 536: 244.
38. V to M, Mar. 22, 1782, CP E 606: 185; V to L, Mar. 23, 1782. CP EU 20: 143; *D*, V, 40. For the Spanish reaction, see A to F, Mar. 16; F to A, Mar. 30, 1782, AHN, E, 4079. Another approach by the North Ministry had been previously made through the Chevalier de Cologne, ostensibly seeking a Franco-British alliance. Chevalier de Cologne to V, Jan. 8, 1782, CP A 536: 22. For the rumor of Forth's visit to Versailles, see Du Pont to V, Mar. 14, 1782, CP A 536: 233; Matthew Ridley's Diary, Mar. 19, 1782, Mass. Hist. Soc. See also *Revue d'histoire diplomatique*, XIV, 161 *et seq.*; *RDC*, V, 298, 299, 303-305; *JCC*, XXII, 302-303. Thurne's dispatch to Baudouin, Mar. 5, 1782, also suggests that the restoration of Canada may have been in the minds of some members of the Ministry. CP A 536: 194.
39. A Paris correspondent informed Rockingham of the Forth mission shortly after the Marquess assumed office. Henry Seymour to Rockingham, April 7, 1782. R 1-2032.
40. See Thurne to Larcher [Baudouin], Mar. 5, 1782. CP A 536: 192.
41. See James Hutton, "Some Account of James Hutton's Visit to Franklin in France, in December of 1777," *Pa. Mag. of Hist. and Biog.*, XXXII (1908), 223-232. Hutton made contacts with influential French figures in 1781-82, but his notions were extremely vague. Du Pont to V. CP A 534: 95, 102, 254, 270, 289, 367, 395-400; 536: 62, 95, 292. On Pulteney's early efforts see *CG*, IV, 101; for his change of name, see *HP*, III, 341.
42. BF to "Charles de Weissenstein," *SF*, nos. 835-837; VII, 166-172; *JAW*, III, 178. For the notion that Patriot leaders could be bought, see Sir George Rodney to Germain, Dec. 1780. HMC, *Stopford-Sackville MSS.*, II, 192-194.
43. See chap. VII above, and BF to DH, Dec. 15, 1781, Jan. 15, 1782. *RDC*, V, 61, 80-85, 113-114; CP EU 20: 21-31, 86-88. See also opinion of William Alexander, translated and sent on to R by BF on Mar. 22, 1782. *Ibid.*, p. 145; *D*, V, 76-77; DH to BF, Jan. 24, 1782. *RDC*, V, 127, CP EU 20: 146-150. See also DH to BF, Feb. 1, 1782. *RDC*, V, 144; CP EU 20: 243; also DH's Breviate, Feb. 7, 1782. *RDC*, V, 390-392; BF to DH, Feb. 16, 1782. *BFB*, VI, 391; *RDC*, V, 169, 170; CP EU 20: 309-311. For the conciliatory letter to BF from DH's half-brother, Col. Winchcombe Henry Hartley, Feb. 28, 1782, see CP EU 20: 360-361.
44. Digges to JA, May 2, 1780; JA to Digges, May 13, 1780. *JAW*, VII, 158, 167, 168.
45. Digges to JA, with enclosure from DH, "Wednesday night 10 o'clock"; JA to Digges, Mar. 21, 1782; to BF, Mar. 26, 1782. *JAW*, VII, 549-551, 554-555.

See also Ridley, Diary, May 20, 1782, for JA's close recollection of his conversation. JA kept the French and BF informed of the conversations, and, in turn, V revealed to him the gist of the Forth proposals. See LV to V, Mar. 22, 27, April 19, 1782; V to LV, Mar. 28, April 4, 1782. CP H 548: 147-151, 181-184, 185-188, 255, 336; V to L, June 8, 1782. CP EU 21: 293.

46. *Last Journals*, II, 422.

47. G to S, Mar. 13, 1782, enclosing a copy in G's hand of Digges's "Account of what passed between him and Mr. Adams"; S to G, April 5, 1782. LP 72: 13-15; *CG*, V, 431-433, 442, 443. See Rockingham to S, Mar. 29, 1782, LPB.

48. DH to BF, Mar. 11, 12, 1782; Digges to BF, Mar. 22, 1782; BF to DH, April 5, 1782. *RDC*, V, 236, 237, 269, 270, 293; CP EU 20: 402-403; S to O, June 20, 1782; Jonathan Williams to BF, June 17, 1785. Hale, *op. cit.*, II, 45n.-47n.

49. BF to RRL, Mar. 30, 1782. *RDC*, V, 277. For a similar reaction in America to the Forth and Digges missions, see William Few to James Jackson, June 2, 1782; James Madison to Edmund Randolph, June 11, 1782. *LMCC*, VI, 362, 370.

50. Digges to JA, April 2, 1782. See also JA to LV, April 10, 1782. *JAW*, VII, 562, 567.

51. For these negotiations, see *FC*, II, 289-98; Rockingham's account, R 1-1124; G to Thurlow, Mar. 15, 18, 1782. *CG*, V, 391-398; Albemarle, *Memoirs of Rockingham*, II, 457-460.

52. See Rockingham's minutes of his conversations with Thurlow, Mar. 11-14, 1782. R 1992, 1993. See also Albemarle, *Rockingham*, II, 447-453, 458-462. Thurlow was not overly frank in revealing Rockingham's unpalatable terms to G. See *ibid.*, p. 456. Cf. also *HP*, III, 529-531.

53. Rockingham's statement to Thurlow, Mar. 11, 1782. Albemarle, *Rockingham*, II, 452, 458-467, *passim*. See also Rockingham to S (?), Mar. 26, 1782. R 1-2009; Papers relating to economical reform, 1782, R 18.

54. In the fall of '81 S had proposed uniting his and Rockingham's factions, but at that time could not get the Marquess to agree on a reform platform. Notes of S's Negotiations with Lord Rockingham, Nov., 1781. LPB.

55. See S's Memorandum, Nov., 1781, LPB.

56. S to Barré, Oct. 13, 1775. LPB.

57. See Richard Jackson to S, *c.* 1782. LP 72: 9-10.

58. In fact G was at pains to tell Rockingham and S that he would receive their advice "separately with great attention." Memorandum of G to Rockingham and S, April 7, 1782. *CG*, V, 447. S from the start refused to consider himself "an ordinary Secretary of State." S to G, *ibid.*, pp. 502, 503.

59. In his brief time in office he was largely preoccupied with Irish and domestic issues. See Rockingham to S, Mar. 20, May 2, 1782. LPB. See also R 1-2059, 2074, 2094. For a sympathetic portrait, see Albemarle, *Rockingham*, II, 359.

60. S to G, April 29, 1782, *CG*, V, 502.

61. Both drafts are in LPB, and an attempt was made to combine them by Lord Edmond Fitzmaurice in *FS*, I, 1-95.

62. Memorandum on the events of 1762. LPB.

63. G. O. Trevelyan, *Charles James Fox*, p. 142.

64. *Memoirs*, I, 258; *FS*, I, 149-150, 156-166 *passim*.

65. See S to Barré, Feb., 1765, LPB; S to the Lords of Trade, April 9, 1767; Moore to S, Feb. 21, 1767. *FS*, II, 30, 31.

66. See especially the Morellet correspondence in LPB; published in part in *Lettres de l'Abbé Morellet à Lord Shelburne, 1772-1803* (Paris, 1898).

Morellet kept in close touch with BF during the peace negotiations. See Morellet to S, April 22, 1782. LPB.

67. See Bentham, *Works*, X, 92, 99, 103, 116.

68. S, "Autobiography," LPB.

69. Compare propositions concerning the opening of peace negotiations with America (*c.* Mar. 30, 1782), R 1-1217-25, 2022; with *CG*, V, 435, 436.

70. Digges to JA, April 2, 1782. *JAW*, VII, 563.

71. S to BF, April 6, 1782. FO 95/511.

72. Memorandum of O to S, *c.* April 6, 1782. LP.

73. James Buran to S, April 5, 1782. LP 87: 12a.

74. O's Journal, May 6, 1782. FO 95/511, No. 7.

75. O's Journal, April 18, 1782. FO 95/511.

76. BF to S, April 18, 1782. *BFAW*, pp. 519-523; copy sent by BF to V on May 4, 1782, CP EU 21: 23, 57 (with V's observations). For British intelligence reports on the Oswald visit, see report of Captain Taylor (?), April 29, 1782. LPB.

77. BF, "Journal of the Negotiations of the Peace with Great Britain," in *BFAW*, p. 523; BF to JA, April 20, 1782, *ibid.*, p. 524. Bemis is incorrect when he states that JA was not informed by BF of his proposal for the cession of Canada. *The Diplomacy of the American Revolution*, p. 201n.

78. JA to BF, May 2, 1782. *JAW*, VII, 580.

79. *FS*, III, 183.

80. *Annual Register, 1781*, p. 322.

81. David W. Wallace, *The Life of Henry Laurens* (New York, 1915).

82. "A Narrative of the Capture of Henry Laurens, of his Confinement in the Tower, 1780, 1781, 1782," S.C. Hist. Soc., *Coll.*, I (1857), 53, 54. For the documents relating to HL's imprisonment, see *ibid.*, pp. 69-83; for Edmund Burke's activities in connection with the proposed HL-Burgoyne exchange, see Burke, *Corr.*, IV, 303-315, 387 *et seq.* On the exchange of HL for Cornwallis, see LP 72; FO 95/511; HL to BF, April 30; BF to HL, July 2, 1782. HLP.

83. See Burke to BF, Feb. 28; to HL, Mar. 27, 1782. Burke, *Corr.*, IV, 418, 419, 428.

84. Thurne to Baudouin, Jan. 8, Mar. 8, 1782. CP A 536: 16, 206; L to V, Feb. 27, 1782. CP EU 20: 340-355; LP 35: 70; Marbois to V, April 12, 1782. CP EU 21: 45.

85. "Narrative," p. 61.

86. "Narrative," p. 63.

87. BV to S, April 10, 1782. LP.

88. HL to BF, April 7, 1782, "Narrative," pp. 67, 68; CP EU 21: 31 (copy in French).

89. JA to BF, April 16, 1782. *BFAW*, pp. 526, 527.

90. S to G, April 24, 1782. *CG*, V, 486, 487. Another intermediary with HL at this time found him both garrulous and peevish, hardly the ideal combination of traits for a diplomat. BV to S, April 2, 22, June 17, 1782. LP 72; LPB. For an undated draft letter of HL to BF (*c.* May 3, 1782) reporting on his talks, see HLP.

91. HL to James Bourdieu, Aug. 10, 1782. Extract in LP 35: 55. The conversation to which HL refers evidently took place in April on his return from his visit to JA in Holland. See also HL "Narrative," p. 66. For later contacts with S, see HL to S, April 27, 1782, LPB; May, 1782, sold with Lacarta Papers by Sotheby, April,

1934. For criticisms of HL's behavior for not joining his colleagues, see Bemis, *op. cit.*, p. 203, *BFAW*, pp. 530, 531, 545, 546, 565-571. For the embarrassment that HL caused BF by arranging without authorization for his own exchange with Cornwallis as a prisoner of war, see Conversation between HL and Cornwallis, April 29, 1782, relative to their exchange. LP 72; S to O, May 10, 1782, May 10, 1782 (copy, CL); also FO 95/511. As to whether or not Cornwallis was given a conditional or unconditional discharge from his parole, see BF to O; O to S, June 11, 1782. LP 71.

92. Minute of Cabinet in S's hand. *CG*, V, 488 (erroneously placed by the editor at April 25, but actually April 23, 1782). FO 95/511; *FS*, III, 183, 184.

93. S to G, April 27, 1782. *CG*, V, 492.

94. G to S, April 27, 1782. *Ibid.*, p. 494.

95. Rockingham to S, May 14, 1782. LPB.

96. S to Carleton, April 4, 1782. British Headquarters Papers, NYPL (photocopy).

97. Instructions to Carleton and Digby, April 4, 1782. Jared Sparks, ed., *Writings of Washington* (Boston, 1835), VIII, 297 *et seq.*; S to Carleton and Digby, June 5, 1782, "Secret and Confidential," CO 5/178: 437-471.

98. Morgann to S, May 10, 1782. LP 68: 369.

99. Morgann to S, June 12, 1782. LP 68: 373. For a more optimistic view, see enclosure in anonymous note to S, July 26, 1782. LP 69: 113.

100. For examples of Carleton's conciliatory moves, see Carleton to Washington; to Governor William Livingston, May 7, 1782. British Headquarters Papers, NYPL (photocopies). For the refusal of Washington to allow Morgann to go to Philadelphia, see Washington, *Writings* (Fitzpatrick, ed.), XXIV, 241-242, 270; L to V, May 18, 1782. CP EU 21: 185; also p. 264. For state resolves, see CP EU 21: 180, 183-184, 237, 242, 256, 322, 381, 393, 439-449; 22: 238-242, 365.

101. *BFAW*, pp. 532-534; BF to JA, May 8, 1782. *Ibid.*, pp. 534, 535.

102. S to BF, April 28, 1782. *BFAW*, pp. 530, 531. The letter also disclosed that HL was not discharged from the engagements he had entered into when admitted to bail.

103. John Caleb to [Germain]. March, 1782; John Nutting to S, April 22, 1782. LP 66: 445-448, 469-481.

104. Amor Patriae to S, May 10, 1782, LPB; Plan of operations recommended for America and the West Indies sent to Col. Isaac Barré (*c.* 1782), LP 72: 211-219; A True Briton to S (July, 1782), *ibid.*, p. 306; C.W.J. to S (*c.* 1782); Proposal for Taxes Due (*c.* 1782), LP 87: 161, 343; cf. also John Trevor to Charles James Fox, April 16, 1782. LP 34.

105. Memorandum of instructions to O in conversation, April 28, 1782. Further memorandum, April 28, 1782; the latter document headed "Private—to be burnt. No part to be communicated to Dr. F but in the greatest confidence. And not to be mentioned to the French Minister or any other person." LP 71: 21, 25; Political Notes, LPB (copy); see also *FS*, III, 188, 189.

106. Fox to Duc de Lauzun, April 4, 1782. CP A 536: 286.

107. Fox to BF; to V, April 30, 1782. FO 27/2; Fox to Grenville, April 30, 1782 (draft), FO 27/2: 42-47; *FC*, IV, 174-179; O to S, May 10, 1782. FO 95/511: 557-558; BF to Fox, May 10, 1782, FO 97/157, FO 95/511; FO 27/2; *BFB*, III, 104.

108. For other occasions when BF pressed Spain's claim to Gibraltar, see O to S, June 21, 1782, LP 71; Minutes of O, June 26, 1782. LP 72.

109. BF to Fox, May 10, 1782, FO 97/157, FO 95/511, FO 27/2; *BFB*, III, 104; *FC*, IV, 186.

110. Grenville bore a letter of introduction from the Duke of Richmond to V, April 30, 1782 (CP A 536: 338), signed "Richmond, Lenox and Aubigny," stressing the Duke's dual nationality.
111. Conference with Grenville, May 9, 1782. CP A 537: 27-29; Grenville to Fox, May 10, 1782. FO 27/2: 58-63; FC, I 347; IV, 180-184; cf. also V to Grenville, V to Fox, V to Richmond, May 11, 1782. CP A 537: 38-41; BF to S, May 10, 1782; O to S, May 10, 1782. FO 95/511; A to F, AHN, E 4215: apt. 1.
112. O to S, May 10, 1782. FO 95/511.
113. BFAW, pp. 541, 542.
114. Grenville to Fox, May 14, 1782. FO 95/511; FO 27/2; FC, IV, 188-191. See also S to Carleton and Digby, June 5, 1782. CO 5/178; Minutes of the Meeting of Commissioners, June, 1782, Strachey Papers transcripts, Bancroft—America, France, and England, NYPL; S to Thurlow, May 15, 1782, distinguishing between BF's and V's attitudes. LPB.
115. See J.N. to Philip Wray, June 17, 1782. LP 35, 52.
116. S to O, May 21, 1782. FC, IV, 201, 202; LP 70: 2-5, FO 27/2: 207 (drafts).
117. BFAW, p. 557.
118. Fox to G, May 18, 1782. FC, I, 351, 352. For Fox's efforts to form a Quadruple Alliance with Russia, Prussia, and Denmark at this time, see Count Lusi to Frederick, May 9, June 11, 1782, LP 35: 33 (extract); Fox to Lusi, June 16, 1782, LP 34: 57, 58; Frederick to Lusi, June 17, 1782, LP 35: 34; Fox to Lusi, June 28, 1782, LP 34: 357-368.
119. V to L, Mar. 23, 1782. CP EU 20: 463-470.
120. See Fox to G, May 18, 1782, FC, I, 351, 352; S to O, May 21, 1782. FO 97/157; 95/511; 27/2; LP 70; FC, IV, 200, 202.
121. BFAW, p. 548.
122. For Grenville's powers, see FO 95/511.
123. BFAW, p. 553.
124. Fourth Peace Conference, May 30, 1782. CP A 537: 101-104.
125. Recommendation of the Ministry, May 23, 1782. FO 95/511; Fox to Grenville, May 26, 1782, FO 27/2; 95/511; FC, IV, 206-209.
126. S to G; G to S, May 25, 1782. CG, VI, 44, 45.
127. Grenville to Fox, May 30, 1782, FO 27/2; See de Hauteville (for Victor Amadeus III of Sardinia) to de Cordon, June 8, 1782. LP 35: 16. For Beaumarchais' efforts to raise subscriptions for new ships to make up the loss suffered by de Grasse, May 27, 28, 1782, see CP A 537: 88, 97-98.
128. For French account of third conference with Grenville, May 26, 1782, see CP A 537: 82-84; D, V, 112-118; Grenville to Fox, May 30, June 3, 1782. Add. MSS. 47, 562, BM; FO 27/2; FC, IV, 209-215.
129. BFAW, pp. 555-558; BF to JA, June 2, ibid., pp. 558-560; Grenville to Fox, June 4, 1782. FO 95/511; RDC, V, 474.
130. BF to S, May 13, 1782. FC, IV, 187; S's memorandum to O, FS, III, 201-202. In a deleted part of his answer, S expressed the hope that he would soon welcome BF at his home, confident that BF was a friend of his as well as of England. S to BF (draft), Sydney Papers, I, CL; cf. also FO 27/2; LP 70.
131. O to S, June 9, 1782. FO 97/157; FO 95/511; FO 27/2; FC, IV, 216, 217.
132. S to O, June 30, 1780. FC, IV, 224.
133. BFAW, pp. 560-564.
134. "With any other of the enemies of Great Britain" is the way Fox phrased it. Fox to Grenville, June 10, 1782. FO 95/511; FO 27/2; FC, IV, 218, RDC, V, 496. See also BFAW, pp. 572, 573.

135. *BFAW*, p. 566, 572, 573, citing the *Evening Post*, May 30, 1782. O quoted Grenville as having told him that BF on May 11th had indicated his general agreement with the statement attributed to HL, that when independence was obtained the treaty with France was at an end. O to S, July 8, 1782. *FC*, IV, 231.

136. Fifth Peace Conference, June 15, 1782. CP A 537: 171-172; *D*, V, 116, 117.

137. For V's memoir on the occasion of de Grasse's defeat, May 27, 1782, see AN, K 164, no. 3; *D*, V, 118-120.

138. Conference of June 21, 1782. CP A 547: 192-200; incomplete in *D*, V, 116, 117; S to Carleton and Digby, July 8, 1782. CO 5/178; Grenville to Fox, June 21, 1782, FO 27/2, *FC*, IV, 222.

139. Extract from *Maryland Gazette* in FO 95/511; FO 97/157; LP 72.

140. Grenville to S, July 9, 1782. FO 27/2; Seventh Peace Conference, July 9, 1782. CP A 537: 324; *D*, V, 118.

141. BF to S, June 27, 1782. *FC*, IV, 234, 235; O to S, July 8, 1782, *ibid.*, pp. 228-234; *BFAW*, pp. 572-576.

142. S to Fox, May 20, 1782. LPB. For instruction to O to cooperate with Grenville, with a clear implication of the division of authority between the two envoys, see S to O, May 21, 1782, LP 71: 29-34; *FC*, IV, 200-202.

143. Grenville to Fox (private), June 4, 8, 1782; to Sheridan, June 8, 1782, Add. MSS. 47,562, BM; *FC*, I, 359-366.

144. Grenville to Fox (private), June 4, 24, 1782. *FC*, I, 359-366. Add. MSS. 47,562, BM.

145. Fox to Grenville, June 10, 1782. Add. MSS. 47,562, BM.

146. *FC*, I, 331.

147. On June 19 the bill received royal assent. *Journals of House of Commons*, XXXVIII, 1028; *Journals of House of Lords*, XXXVI, 529, 535.

148. *FS*, III, 204 *et seq.*

149. G to S, July 1, 1782. *CG*, VI, 70.

150. Albemarle, *Rockingham*, II, 483; S to G, July 1, 1782. *CG*, VI, 70, 71.

151. Burke had advised Fox "to put the whole issue sturdily and violently in the house of commons." Burke to Fox, July 2, 3, 1782. Wentworth Woodhouse Papers. For Fox's effort to induce S to have G name Portland as Rockingham's successor, see Fox to Portland, July 6, 1782, Add. MSS. 47, 560, BM; Buckingham, *Memoirs*, I, 50.

152. S to Grenville, July 5, 1782. *FC*, IV, 226, 227.

CHAPTER XIII. THE LONG CLAY PIPE OF MR. JAY

1. There had been eighty-seven days of rain before June 11. London *Public Advertiser*, July 8, 1782. In France the rain continued until early fall. Sarah Jay to Catherine Livingston, Aug. 14, 1782; JJ to Mrs. Margaret Livingston, Aug. 26, 1782. JP.

2. William Temple Franklin to JJ, June 5, 1782; JJ to RRL, June 14, 25, 1782; JJ to M, June 26, 1782; JJ to Carmichael, Aug. 3, 1782; Sarah Jay to Susannah French Livingston, Aug. 28, 1782. JP.

3. *The Diary of John Jay during the Peace Negotiations of 1782*, with introd. by Frank Monaghan (New Haven, 1934), June 23-26, 1782; *BFAW*, p. 576.

4. June 25, 1782. *BFAW*, p. 579.

5. BF, Journal, June 11, 1782. *BFAW*, p. 570; *RDC*, V, 577.

6. *BFAW*, pp. 580, 581. The French Foreign Office fed the mediators a similar story. MDA to K, July 5, 1782. SKD, Frankreich 240: 0239-0279.

7. *BFAW*, pp. 582, 583.

8. *Diary*, June 27, 1782; JJ to RRL, June 28, 1782. JP; *RDC*, V, 527, 528; cf. James Parton, *Life and Times of Benjamin Franklin* (New York, 1844), II, 481. V relayed this news to L, June 28, 1782. CP EU 21: 346-347.

9. JA to JJ, July 8, 1782. JP; *JPJ*, II, 322, 323.

10. For S's own admission of this, see Abbé Morellet, MS. on Lord Shelburne's administration, 1782-83. LPB. On TT, see *HP*, III, 554-556.

11. S to G, G to S, July 9, 1782. *CG*, VI, 77, 79.

12. "True Briton" to "William Pitt" via S (July, 1782), LP 72; "R.M." to S, July 7, 1782; LPB; Kenneth Mackenzie to S, July 12, 1782, LP 72; Wrixton (?) to S, July 24, 1782, LP 87; Lt. Col. William Martin to Sir Guy Carleton, July 26, 1782. British Headquarters Papers (photocopy), NYPL.

13. London *Morning Herald*, July 5, 1782; London *Morning Chronicle*, July 24, 1782; cf. also *ibid.*, July 8, 1782. For proindependence arguments in the press at this time, see Eunice Wead, "British Public Opinion of the Peace with America, 1782," *Amer. Hist. Rev.*, XXXIV (1938-39), 515, 516.

14. *PH*, XXIII, 168-178; *Annual Register, 1782*, pp. 183, 184.

15. See Sir Gilbert Elliot to Lady Elliot, July 10, 1782. Countess of Minto, ed., *Life and Letters of Sir Gilbert Elliot* (London, 1784), I, 81, 82.

16. *PH*, XXIII, 191-194; *Annual Register, 1782*, p. 187. For a running commentary on the ambiguous position of S at this time, see Thurne's dispatches, July 5, 12, 23, 1782. CP A 537: 293-294, 324, 357-358.

17. London *Morning Herald*, July 13, 1782.

18. *Ibid.*, July 27, 1782.

19. The word "colonies" was inserted in the draft of the speech by S. S to G, July 11, 1782. *CG*, VI, 80.

20. *PH*, XXIII, 202, 203.

21. G to S, July 11, 1782. *CG*, VI, 81, 100. Indeed, G and S were prepared to go to extreme lengths, even to stoop to scandalmongering to destroy the reputation of Fox, now the symbol of "unconditional independence." See G to S, July 13, 16, 1782; S to G, July 16, 1782. *Ibid.*, pp. 85, 88.

22. Countess of Minto, *Elliot*, p. 255.

23. D. Vincente de Sousa Coutinho to Ayres de Sá e Mello, A. N. da Torre do Tombo (Lisbon), MNE (France), no. 1136, Cauxa 13, doc. 181, p. 3.

24. JJ to RRL, June 25, 1782. PCC 110: 2; JP; *RDC*, V, 516-517; *JPJ*, II, 314.

25. BF to O, July 12, 1782, *FC*, IV, 258; JJ to JA, Aug. 2, 1782. AP; JJ to Carmichael, Aug. 3, 1782. JP. For an estimate of 100,000 people in Paris stricken by the influenza epidemic, see Sarah Jay to Catherine Livingston, Aug. 14, 1782. JP.

26. Grenville to S, July 9, 1782. FC, *IV*, 237, 238.

27. See Stourzh, *Franklin and American Foreign Policy*, pp. 208-211.

28. O to S, July 10, 1782. LP 70; FO 27/2; FO 95/511; FO 97/157; *FC*, IV, 239-244.

29. O to S, July 11, 1782; LP 70; 27/2; FO 95/511; *FC*, IV 247-249.

30. *JCC*, XX, 651-652.

31. *Ibid.*, XXII, 44-45.

32. RRL to BF, Jan. 7, 1782. *RDC*, V, 87-94. For a critical view of this letter from the French point of view, see *D*, V, 64-65.

33. RRL to Gouverneur Morris, Jan. 10, 1781. Livingston Papers, N.Y. Hist. Soc.

34. RRL to JJ, April 28, authorized a more positive position toward lands east of the Mississippi, but his second draft and final letter did not go so far as the first draft, which would have permitted JJ to cite this as "in the ultimata of Congress." Also, cf. RRL to JJ, Aug. 8; to BF, Aug. 9, 1782. Livingston Papers, N.Y. Hist. Soc.; JP.

35. O to S, July 11, 1782. LP 70; FO 95/511; 27/2.
36. See R. B. Sheridan to Thomas Grenville, May 21, 26, July 4, 1782. Buckingham, *Memoirs*, III, 28, 30, 54.
37. S to Grenville, July 6, 1782. FO 27/21; LP 71.
38. BF to O; O to S, July 12, 1782. FO 95/511; 97/157; 27/2; *RDC*, V, 608. See also Francès to [V], June 28, July 2, 1782. CP A 537: 218-219, 245-246. The disunity between the British negotiators in Paris was common gossip. Belgiojoso to K, July 16, 1782. Bancroft-Austria, NYPL; SKD, England, 165.
39. V to M, July 13, 1782. CP E 608: 48-49.
40. T. Grenville to Lord Temple, July 9, 1782; Lord Temple to T. Grenville, July 12, 1782; Fox to Grenville, July 13, 1782. Buckingham, *Memoirs*, III, 57, 60, 63, 64; Grenville to S, July 9, 12, 1782. FO 27/2; *FC*, IV, 238, 252-253; S to Grenville, July 13, 1782. FO 27/2; *FC, IV*, 259-260; LP 71.
41. For BF's concern, see S to O, July 13, 1782. FO 95/511; 97/157.
42. S to TG (July). GP LO 30/14 307; TG to AF, July 23, 1782. FO 95/511; 97/157.
43. See JJ to del Campo, Nov. 3, 1781; to Robert Morris, Feb. 5, 1782; to BF, May 31, 1782. As regards the problem of attaining citizenship in all the states instead of just one, see JJ to John Vaughan, Feb. 5, 1782. JP; John Vaughan to JJ, Mar. 5, 1782. Amer. Philos. Soc.
44. BV's father-in-law was William Manning, a prominent London merchant, and at the time of his mission BV was in trade. See R. H. Gardiner, "Memoir of Benjamin Vaughan," Maine Hist. Soc., *Coll.*, ser. 1, VI, 85-92.
45. BV to S, April 14, 1778 (copy). CL.
46. BV to S, Mar. 3, 1782. LPB.
47. BV to S, Aug. 6, 1782. Vaughan Papers, Amer. Philos. Soc.
48. *FS*, III, 242, 243; MDA to K, Aug. 10, 1782. SKD, Frankreich, 240.
49. S to O, Sept. 3, 1782. LP 71.
50. See William Hodgson to BF, July 19, 1782. FP, III, Misc. 33; Pa. Hist Soc.; BV to S, Aug. 4, 1782. Vaughan Papers, Amer. Philos. Soc.; G to S, Aug. 12, 1782. *CG*, VI, 100; O to S, Jan. 8, 1783. *FS*, III, 321.
51. See Fox to Walpole, May 1, 1782. FO 27/2. Walpole's negotiations with Castries are covered in FO 27/2. See especially, July 1, 1782. CP A 537: 244. Fox had privately authorized Walpole to sound out all parties on a "general peace," but when O and Grenville were dispatched to Paris both Fox and S felt obliged to make polite explanations. Fox to Walpole, April 18, May 1; S to O, May 21, 1782. T. Walpole Papers, A1, pp. 62-66.
52. See unsigned intelligence from Paris, Aug. 22, 1782; TG to S, Sept. 13, 1782, with a comment on the magnitude of the French claims. LPB.
53. See S to TT, July 24(?), 26, 1782 (transcript), LP 71; *RDC*, V, 615: S to O, Sept. 3, 1782. LP 71.
54. He had always avoided "unconditional," holding that such a qualification was "unnecessary." O to S, July 12, 1782. LP 70; *FC*, IV, 253-255; BF to O, July 12, 1782. *Ibid.*, p. 258.
55. O to S, July 12, 1782 (2), LP 71; *FC*, IV, 256, 257.
56. See above, ch. VIII.
57. See BV to S, Aug. 18, 1782 (copy), CL.
58. S to the Duc de la Rochefoucauld, July 27, 1782. LPB.
59. S to Carleton and Digby, June 5, 1782. LP 87; erroneously dated June 25, 1782, in *RDC*, VI, 15, 16.
60. Fox to Simolin, June 28, 1782. FO 65/7; CP EU 21: 348.

61. "General treaty" instead of "general peace" was the term Carleton and Digby used in their communication to Congress of August 2. In publicizing that communication, Congress affirmed its intention of negotiating the peace in Paris, declared that it found the letter "inexplicit as to the nature and extent of the independency proposed" by the British plenipotentiaries, and urged the states "not to remit of their exertion for carrying on the war with vigor." *JCC*, XXIII, 463, 464 (Aug. 12, 1782); cf. FO 97/157.

62. S to O, July 27, 1782. LP 71; words in italics are underscored by S in the original letter, printed only in part in *FS*, III, 246-249. On July 25 the Cabinet had agreed to give O full powers to treat with BF, "and to consent to treat with him under whatever title he should claim." For a significantly variant wording in TG's hand, see *CG*, VI, 91.

63. S does not seem to have confided to his Cabinet the contents of his letter to O, to which the Earl considered himself "pledged." Apparently he made his pledge to O before securing the unanimous approval of his Cabinet, several of whose members, including the Attorney General, were out of town. See TT to S, July 27 (2), 28, 1782, LPB. Vincent T. Harlow, *The Founding of the Second British Empire* (London, 1952), I, 273, places the date of the Cabinet meeting when unanimous approval was secured earlier than the documents indicate.

64. BF to V, July 24, 1782. CP EU 21: 460. V in turn sent them to M, July 28, 1782. CP E 608: 79.

65. BF to V, July 24, 1782. CP EU 21: 460-461.

66. See, e.g., Lerchenberg to Nancy, May 28, July 30, 1782. CP A 537: 99, 100, 376-378; Thurne to Nancy, Nov. 9, 1782. *Ibid.*, 538: 416-418.

67. V to BF, July 28, 1782. CP EU 21: 489-491; *RDC*, V, 616, 617.

68. See S to O, Sept. 3, 1782 (Private), LP 71.

69. O to TT, Aug. 6, 1782. LP 70; cf. also CP A 538: 16, 20.

70. G's warrant for O's first commission was dated July 25, 1782. FO 27/2. The formal commission was delayed by the absence in the country of the Attorney General and Lord Chancellor. TT to G, Aug. 2, 1782. Sydney Papers, I, CL. TT to O, Aug. 3, 1782. FO 27/2; 95/511; 97/157. The commission is reprinted in *RDC*, V, 613, 614; *FC*, IV, 262-265.

71. Instructions to O, July 31, 1782. FO 27/2; *FC*, IV, 267-273; TT to O, Aug. 3, 1782. A preliminary draft, in LP 70: 91-101, refers to "the limits and boundaries assigned them under our Proclamation of 1763." That clause was omitted in the final instructions.

72. Cf. Vincent T. Harlow, *The Founding of the Second British Empire*, I, 272-274; Bemis, *Dip. Amer. Revol.*, pp. 209, 210.

73. See W. Laight to John Vardill, Mar. 27, 1775. AO 13/105. For a malicious comment by a turncoat on JJ's neutral course, see William Smith, Diary, April 8, 25, 1777. NYPL.

74. For a draft of that petition in JJ's handwriting, see JP.

75. O to S, May 18, 1782. FO 95/511.

76. See unfinished "Memoir," in William Jay, *Life*, I, 1-7.

77. James Jay's published letters (1771, 1774) on this affair are in Columbia University Libraries' Columbiana. See also Thomas Jones, *History of New York during the Revolutionary War* (New York, 1879), II, 223-224, 475-480.

78. Frederick Jay to JJ, Mar. 6, 1776. JP.

79. *New York Senate Journal*, Mar. 1, 1779; Richard Henry Lee to HL, May 27, 1779. *LMCC*, II, 225.

80. Jones, *op. cit.*, II, 225, 226, 530-538.

81. JJ to George Clinton, May 6, 1780. JP.

82. JJ to Frederick Jay, Mar. 15, 1781. JP.
83. Thomas Bee to John Laurens, Mar. 28, 1781. Emmet Coll., NYPL; RRL to JJ, July 22, 1781; Frederick Jay to JJ, Nov. 8, 1781. JP.
84. William Smith, "Memoirs," VII, Mar. 11, April 15, May 6-11, 15, 1782. NYPL; New York *Royal Gazette*, April 17, 1782.
85. Gouverneur Morris to JJ, Aug. 6, 1782. JP.
86. JJ to Peter Van Schaick, Sept. 17, 1782. JP; omitted from *JPJ*, II, 343-345. See also JJ to Egbert Benson, Aug. 26, 1782; to RRL, Sept. 4, 1782. JP. For James' defense of his loyalty to America, see James Jay to JA, Nov. 21, 1782. AP, reel no. 359.
87. James Jay to S, June ?, 1782. LP 72.
88. S to TT, n.d., Additional Sydney Papers, III, 17. CL.
89. The British court-martial's verdict so infuriated Governor Franklin that TT was tempted almost jokingly to send him over to Paris to talk with his father. TT to S, Sept. 24, 1782. LPB.
90. BF to William Franklin, Aug. 16, 1782. *BFS*, X, 403-406; copy in LPB.
91. Commission by BF and JJ, Oct. 1, 1782. *RDC*, V, 789.
92. BV to S, July 31, 1782. Mass. Hist. Soc., *Proceedings*, 2nd ser., XVII (1903), 414n.; *JAW*, I, 373n.
93. BV to S, Aug. 6, 1782 (later copy). LP.
94. JJ to Peter Van Schaick, Sept. 17, 1782. JP; *JPJ*, II, 343-345.
95. John Vardill to William Eden, April 11, 1778. *SF*, no. 438. The writer was a spy who was to be disappointed in his desire to return in triumph to New York as Regius Professor of Theology at King's College.
96. See JJ to Eleazar Lord, Feb. 7, 1817, JP, wherein he asserted that there "have been just and lawfull wars," and that neither war nor capital punishment had been forbidden by the moral law.
97. JJ to JA, Aug. 2, 1782. AP; *JPJ*, II, 324, 325; *RDC*, V, 638-639.
98. BV to S, Aug. 24, 1782. Vaughan Papers. Amer. Philos. Soc.
99. Rush to Nathanael Greene, April 15, 1782. *Letters of Benjamin Rush*, ed., L. H. Butterfield I (Princeton, 1951), 268, 269. See also extract of a letter from Maryland to Matthew Ridley, Mar. 28, 1782. CP EU 20: 488, 489. CF. William Bingham to JJ, Aug. 14, 1782. JP.
100. BV to S, July 31, Aug. 6, 1782. Vaughan Papers, Amer. Philos. Soc.
101. Jay, *Life*, I, 445.
102. BF duly reported the visit to V, Aug. 8, 1782. CP EU 22: 18.
103. For a retrospective account, see JJ to BV, Mar. 28, 1783. JP; Jay, *Life*, II, 116.
104. Minutes of Conversation with the American Commissioners, Aug. 7, 9, 1782. O to TT, FO 95/511; LP 70.
105. JA to JJ, Aug. 10, 1782. JP.
106. JA to JJ, Aug. 13, 1782. Royal Archives, Windsor Castle; JP; *RDC*, V, 660-661; *JAW*, VII, 10; *JPJ*, II, 327-329. JJ was in complete agreement. JJ to JA, Sept. 1, 1782. JP. See also JA to JJ, Aug. 17, 1782, JP, reporting the receipt of a letter from Boston, dated June 17, relating that the states were giving strong instructions to their delegates in Congress that no peace should be considered short of independence and without the consent of France.
107. Alexander's role is brought out in William Alexander to BF, Dec. 15; BF to Alexander, Dec. 15, 1781, and in the DH-BF correspondence. FP. BF apparently turned over copies of his correspondence on this subject to the French Ministry, and it appears in CP EU. The translation differs from the English version in some significant places. See also JA to JJ, Aug. 13, 1782. JP; Ridley Diary, July 7, 1783, Mass. Hist. Soc.; JA to RRL, Aug. 18, 1782. Princton Univ. Lib.

108. *SF* no. 1946; F. B. Tolles, "Franklin and the Pulteney Mission," *Huntington Library Quarterly*, XVII, 37-58.

109. JA to RRL, Aug. 18, 1782. Princeton Univ. Lib.; suppressed portion not included either in *RDC* or *JAW*. It was an enclosure in JA to John Trumbull, Jan. 23, 1795.

110. AF to V, Aug. 2, 1782. CP A 538: 9. For a report (Aug. 11, 1782) of the O-AF meeting, see CPA 538: 20.

111. AF to TT (private), Aug. 8, 1782. LP 87: 185. See also AF to TT, Aug. 17, 1782. LP 87: 190, wherein V's hold over BF, and to a lesser degree over JJ, is again stressed.

112. F to A, May 17, 1782. AHN, E, 4079.

113. Jay, *Life*, I, 140, 141.

114. JJ to A, June 25, 29, 1782. JP; *JPJ*, II, 386-387; *RDC*, VI, 21; A to JJ, June 27, 1782. JP; to F, July 6, 1782. AHN, E, 6609. See also JJ, *Diary*, June 25, 28, July 25.

115. JJ to M, June 26, 1782. JP.

116. A to F, Aug. 10, 1782. AHN, E, 6609.

117. A, Diario, July 23, 1782. AHN, E, 3885, exp. 1.

118. For the Mitchell map, see J. Winsor, *Narrative and Critical History of America*, VII (Boston, 1888), 171-184; John Bassett Moore, *History and Digest of the International Arbitrations to Which the United States Has Been a Party* (Washington, 1898), I, 152-161; Bemis, *Dip. Amer. Revol.*, p. 216n. See also A, Diario, July 21, 1782. AHN, E, 3885, exp. 1.

119. JJ to RRL, Nov. 17, 1782. *RDC*, VI, 23. A's more detailed description is found in his Diario, Aug. 3, 1782. AHN, E, 3885, exp. 1; *YU*, II, 355-357.

120. JJ to RRL, Aug. 13, 1782. Livingston Papers, N.Y. Hist. Soc.; Jay, *Life*, II, 101-102.

121. A, Diario, July 26, 30, 1782. AHN, E, 3885, exp. I.

122. V to BF, Aug. 8, 1782. *RDC*, V, 652.

123. "Réflexions sur l'acte du 25 juillet 1782" (on the advance text of O's commission). CP EU 21: 473-476.

124. V to L, Aug. 12, 1782. CP EU 22: 46-51; Hale, *Franklin in France*, II, 155.

125. BF Papers, no. 2594, LC.

126. A, Diario, July 25, 1782. AHN, E, 3885, exp. 1.

127. V to L, Oct. 14, 1782. CP EU 22: 368-373; this portion of the dispatch was omitted by *D*.

128. For L's concern about the progress of George Rogers Clark in his advance in 1779 into the Northwest, see L to V, May 12, 1781. CP EU 16: 259. For his assumption that Canada would be retained by England, including possibly some portions of Vermont, see L to V, Aug. 20, 1781. *Ibid.*, 18: 110, 114.

129. "Mémoire sur les principaux objets dont on doit s'occuper dans la négociation pour la paix" (May, 1782). CP A 537: 111-131.

130. B. Bruny, "Réflexions sur la paix à faire," July 2, 1782. CP A 537: 253-291.

131. "The most fatal" blow was how one French Foreign Office memorandum phrased it. Memorandum on peace objectives, May, 1782. CP A 537: 111-137.

132. This notion was supported by the Bruny memorandum, "Réflexions sur la paix," July 2, 1782. CP A 537: 253-284.

133. BF to RRL, Aug. 12, 1782. *RDC*, V, 657.

134. M to V, July 8, 12; V to M, Aug. 10, 1782. CP E 608: 15, 113, 119; JJ to RRL, Nov. 17, 1782. *RDC*, VI, 17.

135. AF to TG, July 31, 1782. FO 27/3. An extract from an intercepted dispatch of

Sir Edward Hughes (July 15, 1782) reporting an inconclusive naval engagement with Suffren is in CP A 537: 336.

136. AF to TG, Aug. 20, Sept. 11, 1782. FO 558/166, 257. See also Bemis, *Dip. Amer. Revol.*, pp. 210, 211.

137. See JJ to Gouverneur Morris, Oct. 13, 1782. Gouverneur Morris Papers, Col. Univ.

138. This reconstructed conversation is based on JJ to Gouverneur Morris, Oct. 13; JJ to RRL, Sept. 18, Nov. 17, 1782. JP; *RDC*, V, 740; VI, 45-49. The family tradition of the pipe-breaking has been preserved in Monaghan, *Jay*, p. 197.

Chapter XIV. Milord Shelburne Plays the Host

1. O to TT, Aug. 10, 11, 1782. FO 95/511; LP 70.
2. Observations of O, Aug. 15, 17, 1782; O to TT, Aug. 10, 11, 1782. FO 95/511; O to S, Aug. 16, 1782. *BFB*, VIII, 150; *RDC*, VI, 16.
3. MDA to K, Aug. 10, 1782. SKD, Frankreich, 240: 0284-0307.
4. Cf. L to V, April 27, 1782. CP EU 21: 82-104. For BF's uncertainty, see BF to HL, July 2, 1782, HLP.
5. Drafts proposed by JJ, Aug. 10, 16, 1782. FO 27/2; 95/511; LP 34, 70; BF to JJ, Aug. 16, 1782. Bancroft-America, III, 299, NYPL.
6. AF to TG, Aug. 17, 1782. FO 27/3.
7. G to S, Aug. 12, 1782. *CG*, VI, 100.
8. BV to S, Aug. 18, 1782 (copy), CL.
9. O to TT, Aug. 15, 17, 1782. FO 95/511; AF to TT, Aug. 17, 1782. LP 87: 190.
10. Secret report to S, Aug. 25, 1782 (in French). LPB.
11. AF to TG, Aug. 17, 1782; AF to S, Aug. 17, 1782. LP 71.
12. BV to S, Aug. 17, 18, 1782. BV Papers; Amer. Philos. Soc.; copy, CL.
13. See S to O, Sept. 3, 1782. LP 71.
14. See O to TT, Aug. 10, 1782. FO 95/511.
15. O to TT, Aug. 17, 18, 1782. FO 95/511; 97/157; 27/2; LP 70. O therein reports that JJ was prepared to accept absolute and unconditional independence in a first article of the treaty separately ratified and to drop his previous insistence on a grant by patent under the Great Seal.
16. For a similar stand taken earlier, see [DH] to George Savile, July 8, 1782. LP 87.
17. G to S (draft), Aug. 21, 1782. *CG*, VI, 110, 111. Cf. letter penned a few hours earlier. *Ibid.*, pp. 109, 110. G to TT, Aug. 21, 1782. TT Papers, Huntington Lib.
18. Matthew Ridley, Diary, Aug. 28, 1782.
19. BV to S, Aug. 25, 1782. Amer. Philos. Soc. (copy); [Edward Bancroft] to S, Aug. 29, 1782. LPB. For a similar view that V wanted to hold up negotiations until October to await news from Gibraltar, see MDA to K, Aug. 10, 1782. SKD, Frankreich, 240: 0284-0307.
20. Ridley, Diary, Aug. 28, 1782.
21. BV to S, Aug. 24, 1782. LP, copy.
22. See BV to S, Aug. 24, 1782. Amer. Philos. Soc.; Ridley, Diary, Aug. 28, 1782; also O's note on reverse of DH to BF, July 26, 1782, LP 71; not printed with DH's letter in *RDC*, V, 615; and O to TT, Aug. 27, 1782. FO 95/511; 97/157; LP 70. For the reports of the Tuscan chargé d'affaires, F. F. Favi (Sept. 2), and Daniel Dolfin, the Venetian ambassador, see Antonio Pace, *Benjamin Franklin in Italy* (Philadelphia, 1958), p. 118.

23. Anon. letter (1782). LPB.

24. The Cabinet even considered the possibility of employing Hessian troops outside America, and reviewed the various German treaties relating to troop-hiring. TG to S, undated and *c.* Sept. 13, 1782, LPB.

25. Edward Bridgen to S, Aug. 26, 1782, forwarding a letter believed to have been written by Edmund Jenings from Brussels. LP 87: 87. Jenings was a place-hunting American and pamphleteer, who resided during the American Revolution in several European countries.

26. *CG*, VI, 113-114; also S to G, Aug. 11, 20, 1782; G to S, Aug. 20, 1782. *Ibid.*, pp. 99-100, 105-106.

27. S to O, Sept. 2, 1782, replying to O's dispatches of Aug. 18 and 21. LP. See also Ridley, Diary, Aug. 28, 1782.

28. Ridley, Diary, Aug. 31, 1782.

29. Ashburton to S, Aug. 29, 1782. LPB.

30. Cabinet minute in TT's handwriting. *CG*, VI, 118; another copy in Additional Sydney Papers, CL, wherein the point is also made "that we will enter freely in the adjustment of the other Articles mentioned by Dr. Franklin as advisable." It is clear from TG's notes of the Cabinet discussions that O under his commission had not been empowered to offer independence. GP L 29/665. Such an offer was embodied in the original memorandum for the Cabinet, but was deleted. TT Papers, Huntington Lib.

31. The Proclamation defined the government of Quebec as "bounded on the Labrador coast by the river St. John, and from thence by a line drawn from the head of that river, through the lake St. John, to the south end of the lake Nipissim; from whence the said line, crossing the river St. Lawrence and the lake Champlain in 45 degrees of north latitude, passes along the high lands which divide the rivers that empty themselves into the said river St. Lawrence from those which fall into the sea." *Annual Register, 1763*, pp. 208-213.

32. TT to O, Sept. 1, 1782, with enclosed memorandum. LP 70; with drafts in FO 95/511; also FO 27/2; 97/157. Deleted from the draft of the instructions: "You are again to remonstrate *(as already instructed) that there are no existing Powers for concluding a Treaty upon that footing*" (i.e., irrevocable acknowledgment "without reference to the final settlement of the rest of the Treaty").

33. O to BF, Sept. 5, 1782. LP 70: FO 95/157. The extract is not included in *RDC*, V, 699.

34. BF to R, Sept. 4, 1782. CP EU 22: 186.

35. TG to AF, Sept. 3, 1782 (draft) FO 27/3; dispatch of same date including dossier on Franco-British discussions in 1775-76 concerning the fisheries. FO 27/3. This Anglo-French rivalry was also noted by G. G to TG, Aug. 25, 1782. *CG*, VI, 117.

36. V to L, Aug. 12, 1782. CP EU 22: 52-57.

37. D'Ammours to Castries, June 12, 1782. French Consular Papers (Baltimore), I, 18-19. See also L's letters to V, in Aug., 1782, in CP EU 22: 19-27, 59-65, 163.

38. Lerchenberg to Baudouin, April 2, 12, May 7, 22, 27, July 12, Sept. 6, 20, 1782. CP A 536: 307; 537: 23-24, 76-78, 354; 538: 119-120, 207-208. For the admission that the Americans were more anxious to see Carleton quit New York than were the French, see L to V, Sept. 12, 1782. CP EU 22: 226-232.

39. MDA to K, Aug. 10, 1782. SKD, Frankreich, 240: 0284-0307.

40. See fiscal proposals in unsigned memorandum (Aug., 1782), CP A 538: 94-99; also Lerchenberg to Baudouin, Aug. 9, 1782. *Ibid.*, pp. 212-222. For Spain's financial straits, see "Copy of Intelligence from a Person of Credit upon the Present State of Finance in Spain, 1782," LP 168; Carmichael to RRL, Sept.

29, 1782, *RDC*, V, 750-752. On the scarcity of specie in France, see TG to S, Aug. 18, enclosing an extract of a letter of Lord Torrington, Aug. 16, 1782. LPB.

41. For de Grasse in England, see Belgiojoso to K, Aug. 9, 1782. SKD, England, 165; de Grasse to S, Aug. 10, 1782. LP 71; S to G, *CG*, VI, 99; for his communications with V, and the latter's outline of S's reputed proposals, see de Grasse to V, Aug. 17, 18, 1782. CP A 538: 56, 58; Outlines of Preliminaries, Aug. 17, 1782. CP A 538: 54-55; *D*, V, 104. See also de Grasse to S, Aug. 18, Sept. 2, 1782. LP 71; S to de Grasse, Sept. 3, 1782. LP 71; CP A 538: 116.

42. A to F, Aug. 18, 1782. AHN, E, 4215, apt. 2: 233-238, p. 5; O to TT, Aug. 21; to S, Aug. 21, 1782. FO 95/511; 97/157; 27/2; LP 70. Cf. also AF to TG, Aug. 21, 1782. FO 27/2.

43. L to V, Aug. 9, 1782. CP EU 19-27.

44. A, Diario, Aug. 23, 25, 1782. AHN, E, 3885, exp. 1; *YU*, II, 358-359.

45. A, Diario, Aug. 30, 1782; A to F, Sept. 1, 1782. AHN, E, 6609.

46. R to JJ, Sept. 4, 6, 1782. CP EU 22: 197, 198; CP A 537: 385-399; PCC 110: 2; translation in JJ Letterbook, JP; *JPJ*, II, 391-398; A to F, Sept. 7, 1782. AHN E, 6609. The CP EU copy is in R's handwriting. It bears an endorsement in another hand indicating a date of July, 1782. However, it is placed in that liber at the very end of September. Bemis dates the original copy between Aug. 23 and 30, 1782; the CP A copy *c.* Aug. 30 and Sept. 6; and the A copy, made from the latter, before Sept. 8. See S. F. Bemis, "The Rayneval Memoranda of 1782 on Western Boundaries and Some Comments on the French Historian Doniol," Amer. Antiq. Soc., *Proceedings* (April, 1937), pp. 3-80.

47. See V to R, Sept. 6, 1782. CP A 538: 117-118; to S, Sept. 6, 1782. LP 71; S to G, Sept. 13, 1782. *CG*, VI, 123-125.

48. CP A 538, passim.

49. A to F, Sept. 8, 1782. AHN, E, 4215, apt. 2, no. 2294, p. 32.

50. Matthew Ridley to JJ, n.d. [Sept. 13, 1782]. Mass. Hist. Soc.; Ridley, Diary, Sept. 13, 1782; [Edward Bancroft] to O, Sept. 9, relayed to S in dispatch of Sept. 11, 1782. LPB; JJ to RRL, Nov. 17, 1782. *RDC*, VI, 29.

51. Ridley, Diary, Sept. 21, 1782.

52. Thurne forwarded to Baudouin a clipping from a London paper, September 17, 1782, asserting that France's purpose in sending R was "to treat for a separate peace, and to totally renounce their connections with America." CP A 538: 200-201.

53. The decoding and translation with minor variations appear in *RDC*, V, 238-241, and Jay, *Life*, I, 490-494.

54. V to L, Sept. 7, 1783. *D*, V, 296-297.

55. BF to Samuel Cooper, Dec. 26, 1782. CP EU 22: 588-589; *BFS*, VIII, 649.

56. CP EU 20: 407-417. There is a copy in CO 5/40. The copy that JJ forwarded to RRL with his letter of Sept. 18, 1782, is in PCC 110: 2. See also AP, IV, 358. Cf. *RDC*, V, 241n., 242n.

57. Madison, *Writings* (Hunt ed.), I, 463-464n.

58. Boston *Patriot*, Aug. 24, 1811. In a conversation with William Beach Laurence, editor of Wheaton's *International Law*, mentioned by Jay, "The Peace Negotiations of 1782-83," in Justin Winsor, ed., *Narrative and Critical History of America* (Boston, 1888), VII, 120.

59. Zoltan Haraszti, "More Books from the Adams Library," *Boston Public Library Quarterly*, III, no. 2 (April, 1951), 109-126; Boston *Patriot*, Aug. 21, 1811.

60. V to L, Sept. 1779; Oct. 7, 1781; June 28, Aug. 12, 1782. Jay, *Peace Neg.*, pp. 149-152; CP EU 19: 41-46; incomplete in *D*, IV, 679n.; CP EU 21: 336-

345; incomplete in *D*, V, 92; CP EU 22: 52-57; L to V, Jan. 1, 9, 11, 18, 25, 28, 1782. CP EU 20: 3-20, 43 *et seq.*, 74, 106-110, 152-163, 208-213.

61. See Memoirs on Newfoundland Fisheries, Aug. 15, 20, 1782. CP A 538: 36-49, 59; AF to TG, Aug. 17, 1782. FO 27/3.

62. AF to TG, Aug. 29, 1782. FO 27/3. For S's reaction to the Barbé-Marbois interception, see S to TG [Aug. 26, 1782], GP L 30/14.

63. Quoted by John McVickar, in the *New York Review* (Oct., 1841); Jay, *Peace Neg.*, p. 206.

64. V to L, Oct. 14, 1782. CP EU 22: 368-373. This portion of the letter was omitted from *D*.

65. R to James Monroe, Nov. 14, 1795. William C. Rives, *History of the Life and Times of James Madison* (Boston, 1873), I, 655-660.

66. F to A, Sept. 2, 1782; A to F, Sept. 1, 8, 15, 1782. AHN, E, 3885, exp. 1; JJ to Bourgoing, Sept. 26, 1782 (extract), Bancroft-America, IV, 171, NYPL.

67. V to M, Sept. 7, 1782. CP E 608: 315-318.

68. See "Ouvertures de M. le Comte de Grasse et propositions de L'Espagne alors remises à M. le Comte de Vergennes," Sept. 4, 1782 (in A's hand), AHN, E, 4203, apt. 1, p. 35; V to R, S, and TG, all dated Sept. 6, 1782. CP A 538: 117-118, 121-124; LP 71; *D*, V, 105.

69. S to G, Sept. 13; G to S, Sept. 14, 1782. *CG*, VI, 123-125; R to V, Sept. 15, 1782. CP A 538: 193-194.

70. R to V, Sept. 13, Dec. 25, 1782. CP A 538: 146-162; 539: 314-317; R to S, Sept. 28; S to V, Sept. 21, 1782. LP 71.

71. Sparks, III, 208-212; *North American Rev.*, LXVI (Jan., 1830), 15; James Brown Scott, "Historical Introduction," in *The American Secretaries of State and Their Diplomacy* (New York, 1927), I, 73, 74.

72. A to F, Sept. 8, 1782. AHN, E, 3885, exp. 1.

73. Conferences between R and S, Sept. 13, 16, 18, 1782. CP A 538: 146-162, 172-192, 197-198.

74. Conference between R and S, Sept. 14, 1782. *Ibid.*, pp. 163-170.

75. S to TT, *c.* Oct. 28, 1782 (incorrectly dated *c.* Sept. 15, 1782). FO 95/511.

76. S to G, Sept. 13, 1782. *CG*, VI, 125.

77. Conference between S and R, Sept. 18, 1782. CP A 538: 172-192.

78. S to G, Sept. 13, 1782. *CG*, VI, 125.

79. G to S, Sept. 14, 16, 23, 27, 1782. *CG*, VI, 125, 129, 135, 137.

80. S was promptly posted on the status of the V-JJ controversy, and told by an insider that America would take it amiss should Britain cede the back country to Spain. [Edward Bancroft] to S, Sept. 9, 1782. LPB.

81. BV to James Monroe, Sept. 18, 1795. Monroe Papers, VIII, 964. LC.

82. JJ to RRL, Nov. 17, 1782. JP; *RDC*, VI, 29.

83. For a sharp criticism of JJ's offer to share the navigation of the Mississippi with the British, see George Bancroft, *History of the United States of America* (New York, 1897), V, 568.

84. BV to S, Sept. 9, 1782. BV Papers, Amer. Philos. Soc.

85. JJ to RRL, Nov. 11, 1782. JP; *RDC*, VI, 32.

86. Ridley, Diary, Sept. 21, 1782.

87. Proposed alteration by JJ, dated by O, Sept. 10, 1782. FP, XII, 341-342; LP 70; FO 95/511. See also BF to O, Sept. 8, 1782, with O's comment. FO 97/157.

88. Draft by JJ (undated) turned over to O on Sept. 10th and forwarded by him to S the next day. LP 71; Jay, *Life*, II, 466, 467.

89. Endorsement on draft forwarded by O to S, Sept. 11, 1782. LP 71: 15. JJ to

RRL, Nov. 17, 1782. *RDC*, VI, 18-21. O to TT, Sept. 10, 1782. FO 95/511; 97/157; 27/2. "Sketch of an alteration proposed by Mr. Jay to be made in His Majesty's Commission," Sept. 10, 1782. FO 95/511; LP 70; FO 97/157.

90. O to S, Sept. 11, 1782. LP 71. TT referred O's "two large packets" dealing with the change in form of the commission to G, and indicated to S the likelihood that G would want a Cabinet opinion. TT to S, Sept. 14, 1782. LPB.

91. JJ to RRL, Sept. 18, Nov. 17, 1782. *JPJ*, II, 348, 385-386. Lafayette to BF (*ante* Sept. 18, 1782), FP, no. 2594. LC.

92. *JCC*, XXI, 1134-1136.

93. JJ to RRL, Oct. 13, 1782; *JPJ*, II, 349; JA to Warren, April 16, 1783, *Warren-Adams Letters*, II, 214, 215.

94. Ridley, Diary, Sept. 14, 21, 1782. Ridley was in error in asserting that JJ did not let O know that BF opposed sending on the draft letter. *Ibid.*, Sept. 26, 1782.

95. BV to S, Sept. 11, 1782. Amer. Philos. Soc.

96. Ridley, Diary, Sept. 11, 1782.

97. See anonymous letters to S of Sept. 5, 23, 1782. LPB.

98. T. Orde to S, Sept. 26, 1782. LPB.

99. TT to TG, Sept. 15, 1782. GP L 30/14; Ashburton to S, Sept. 16, 18, 1782. Add. Sydney Papers, 3: 11. CL; LPB.

100. Thurlow to TT, Sept. 18, 22, 1782. TT Papers, Huntington Lib.

101. Minutes of Cabinet Meeting, Sept. 19, 1782, in TT's hand forwarded by S to G. *CG*, VI, 131. TT to Thurlow, Sept. 20, 1782 (draft); to Richmond, Sept. 23, 1782; Add. Sydney Papers, 3: 13, 14; Thurlow to S, *c.* Sept. 23, 1782. LPB; TT to O, Sept. 19; to S, Sept. 24, 1782. LP 70; LPB; FO 27/2; 95/511; 97/157; PCC 106; CP EU 22: 248-252 (in French and English); Hartley Papers, III, CL.

102. Hale, *Franklin in France*, II, 146, 147.

103. JJ to RRL, Sept. 28, 1782. JJ Letterbook, JP; PCC 110: 2. The commission, dated Sept. 21, reached Paris on the same day as BV, Sept. 27. *RDC*, V, 779; *JPJ*, II, 348; Sparks, VIII, 128.

104. BF to RRL, Sept. 26, 1782. *BFS*, VIII, 602; BV to S, Oct. 3, 1782, Amer. Philos. Soc. James Parton, *Life of Franklin* (New York, 1864), II, ch. XV, speaks of the doctor "during the month wasted upon *this nonsense.*"

105. Ridley, Diary, Sept. 21, 1782.

106. G to S, Nov. 3 (error for Oct. 3, 1782), *CG*, VI, 138, 139.

107. TT to O, Sept. 24, 1782. FO 95/511; 97/157; 27/2.

108. S to O, Sept. 23, 1782. LP 71.

CHAPTER XV. SETTING METES AND BOUNDS

1. The news of the British victory was not known in England during the five days of R's talks at Bowood. Contrariwise, a report was circulated, but not credited, that the Hanoverian troops had mutinied and that Sir George Elliot was dead. TG to S, Sept. 13, 1782; TT to S, Sept. 14, 1782. LPB. Carmichael forwarded to Congress an eyewitness account of a Spanish officer. Carmichael to RRL, Sept. 29, 1782. PCC 88; *RDC*, V, 783-785. Lewis Littlepage, who participated in the siege in defiance of JJ's advice, kept a journal of the siege and sent JJ a copy. Lewis Littlepage to JJ, Oct. 29, Nov. 18, Dec. 29, 1782, JP. Gibraltar loomed large in the correspondence of the diplomats. See, e.g., Graf von Kaunitz to K, Aug. 29, Sept. 2, 1782. SKD, Spanien 144; MDA to K, Sept. 25, 28, 1782. SKD, Frankreich 240: 0361-0372; Doria Pamphili to Pallavicini, Sept. 23, Oct.

7, 1782. Nunz. Francia, Vatican. For a contemporary English account, see John Drinkwater, *A History of the Late Siege of Gibraltar* (London, 1783). Spanish accounts are found in *DC*, V, 219-332; C. Bernandez Duro, *Armada española* (Madrid, 1901), VII, 319, 331.

2. Polignac to V, Oct. 23, 1782. CP E 609: 128-129. Polignac overstated the Admiral's age by five years.

3. JA to RRL, Sept. 23, 1782. *RDC*, V, 750-752.

4. Intelligence from Capt. Taylor, Oct. 24. FO 95/2; Sir John Hort to S, Nov. 10, 23, 1782. LP 34: 303-307; 317-320.

5. D. Vicente de Sousa Coutinho to Ayres de Sá e Mello, Sept. 23, 1782. A. N. da Torre do Tombo, MNE (France), no. 1152, p. 1.

6. The British intelligence service claimed to have expanded £138/15 for the period July 9-Sept. 20, 1782, in examining A's dispatches. Intelligence from Captain Taylor, Sept. 18, 21, 26, 1782. FO 95/2; LPB; AF to TG, Sept. 26, 1782. FO 27/2. See also secret intelligence from Madrid, Sept. 30, 1782. FO 72/4.

7. Morellet to S, Oct. 3, 27, 1782. *Lettres à Shelburne*, p. 198; LPB.

8. D. Vicente de Sousa Coutinho to Ayres de Sá e Mello, Nov. 11, 1782. A. N. da Torre do Tombo, MNE (France), no. 1155, Caixa 13, doc. 202, p. 2.

9. BV to S, Aug. 7, 1782. BV Papers (copy), CL.

10. AF to TG, Oct. 3, 1782. FO 27/3.

11. TG to G, Sept. 30, 1782. *CG*, VI, 138.

12. See comment of HL to O, Sept. 12, 1782; from Nantes; forwarded to S, Sept. 19. LP 71.

13. JJ to JA, Sept. 28, 1782. JP; AP; *RDC*, V, 778. BF did not forward a copy of the commission to the French court until Oct. 13, and then at R's specific request. BF to R, Oct. 13, 1782. CP EU 22: 367.

14. Lafayette to JA, Oct. 6, 1782. *JAW*, VII, 644; *RDC*, V, 800.

15. JA to JJ, Oct. 7, 1782. *RDC*, V, 803.

16. See O to TT, Oct. 3, 1782. LP 70: FO 27/2; 95/511; 97/157; BV to James Monroe, Sept. 18, 1795. AP, Microfilm No. 256.

17. O to S, Oct. 3, 1782. LP 71; BV to S, Oct. 3, 1782; Amer. Philos. Soc.; Mass. Hist. Soc., *Proc.*, 2nd ser., XVII (1903), 410.

18. See also BF to JJ, Oct. 9, 1782. JP.

19. O to TT, Oct. 2, 5, 1782. LP 70; FO 95/511; 27/2; 97/157; BV to S, Oct. 3, 1782. Amer. Philos. Soc.; Mass Hist. Soc., *Proc.*, 2nd ser., XVII (1903), 410.

20. O to Strachey, Oct. 2, 1782. LP 70; O to TT, Oct. 5, 1782. FO 95/511; 27/2; 97/157; LP 70.

21. BV to S, Oct. 3, 1782. Mass. Hist. Soc., *Proc.*, 2nd ser., XVII, 410-413. Herein he pointed out the advantages of using the Isthmus of Panama for the passage of troops and stores to the Pacific. See also copy of article agreed to by O on the navigation of the Mississippi. AP Microfilm No. 359; BV's Minutes on Porto Rico, West Florida, and Trinidad (Sept., 1782). AP Microfilm No. 488.

22. [Edward Bancroft] to S, Oct. 2, 1782. LPB; Ridley, Diary, Oct. 2, 5, 1782. See also Doria Pamphili to Pallavicini, Oct. 7, 1782. Nunz. Francia, Vatican.

23. Memoranda, "Louisiana," Mar. 26, 1802, in Rufus King, Memorandum Book, N.Y. Hist. Soc.; C. R. King, ed., *Life and Corr. of Rufus King*, IV, 93, 94.

24. Articles of treaty proposed and agreed upon Oct. 5; transmitted by O, Oct. 7, 1782. JP (copy by O); CO 5/8; LP 71; *RDC*, V, 805-808.

25. For a sympathetic analysis of the article, see Baring's remarks (1782), LP 72: 431-434.

26. See G. W. Brown, "The St. Lawrence in the Boundary Settlement of 1783," *Canadian Hist. Rev.*, IX (1928), 223-238.
27. JJ to RRL, Oct. 13, 1782. JJ Letterbook, JP; PCC 110: 2; *RDC*, V, 809; *JPJ*, II, 348-349; Sparks, VIII, 128-129; O to TT, Oct. 11, 1782. FO 95/511; 27/2; 97/157; LP 70.
28. Bemis, *Dip. Amer. Revol.*, p. 230.
29. O to TT, and Abstract, Sept. 11, 1782. FO 97/157; 95/511.
30. *RDC*, VI, 132. Cf. also S. F. Bemis, *Dip. Amer. Revol.*, pp. 230, 231.
31. O to TT, Oct. 8, 1782. LP 70; FO 97/157; 27/2.
32. JJ allegedly promised to give thought to the possibility that individual states might enter into compacts with France or Spain, although the articles would seem to have foreclosed such arrangements. O to TT, Oct. 11, 1782, including "Minutes of Sundry Articles recommended in my instructions not included in the treaty." FO 95/511; 27/2; 97/157; LP 70.
33. BV to S, Oct. 11, 1782. Amer. Philos. Soc.; Mass. Hist. Soc., *Proc.*, 2nd ser., XVII (1903), 414-418.
34. S to G, Sept. 26, 1782. *CG*, VI, 136.
35. G to S, Dec. 5, 1782. *CG*, VI, 171-172.
36. TT to O, Oct. 11, 1782; to G, Oct. 14, 1782; FO 97/157; 95/511; 27/2; LP 70; Sydney Papers, I, CL; *CG*, VI, 143.
37. Alexander Hamilton to George Clinton, Dec. 27, 1782. Mitchell Kennerly Coll., copy, CL.
38. Cabinet resolution, Oct. 17, 1782. Strachey Papers, Bancroft transcript, NYPL. Slight variance in *CG*, VI, 143, 144.
39. The idea may have been suggested to him in Connolly to S, Sept., 1782. LP 72.
40. Memorial of George Dempster to S, April 22, 1782. LP 72.
41. Minutes of S's conversation with Strachey at TG's. Oct. 20, 1782. LP 87: 209; S's instructions to Strachey, Oct. 20, 1782. LP 87: 194; *FS*, III, 282-287. See also I. S. Harrell, *Loyalism in Virginia* (Philadelphia, 1926).
42. S to O, Oct. 21, 1782. LP 71.
43. TT's instructions to Strachey, Oct. 21, 1782. Strachey Papers, Bancroft transcripts, NYPL.
44. S to O, Oct. 23, 1782. TT wrote O similarly, Oct. 23, 1782. He also informed BF that Strachey was going to Paris "with some particulars for Mr. Oswald which were not to be easily explained in writing." TT to BF, Oct. 23, 1782. FO 95/511; 97/157; 27/2; LP 70; *RDC*, V, 828.
45. TT to Strachey, Oct. 23, 26, 1782. Lamson-Strachey MSS., LC; photostat, CL; FO 95/511. Similarly TT wrote to O, referring to "a proposal of Mr. Jay's which seems to have been frequently and eagerly urged by him." Oct. 26, 1782. FO 95/511; 97/157. In return for assistance in evacuating troops from New York for the attack on West Florida, the Cabinet was prepared "to engage not to attack any French islands this season." Cabinet Minute, Oct. 25. GP L29/670; TT Papers, Huntington Lib.
46. Memoir of London merchants to S, Oct. 31, 1782. LP 66: 771-774.
47. O to S, Oct. 24, 1782. LP 71.
48. S to AF, Oct. 21, 1782. LP 71; variant version in *FS*, III, 287.
49. JJ, *Diary*, Oct. 24, 1782.
50. *Ibid.*
51. S to TT (Oct. 28 or Nov. 4, 1782). FO 95/511.
52. JJ, *Diary*, Oct. 29, 1782.
53. BF to RRL, Oct. 14, 1782. *BFB*, X, 17.
54. JA to RRL, Oct. 8, 1782. *RDC*, V, 803-805; Hartley Papers, II, 29, CL.

55. *Warren-Adams Letters*, II, 186. Arthur Lee to JA, Dec. 12, 1782.

56. Ultimately, and to avoid any appearance of division on the question, all the American commissioners went on record endorsing the selection of William Temple Franklin. See Boston *Patriot*, Aug. 7, 10, 1811.

57. See *Diary*, III, 29-39, Oct. 17-27, 1782; Boston *Patriot*, July 24, 1811; Ridley, Diary, Oct. 27, 28, 1782.

58. Ridley, Diary, Nov. 6, 1782; JA to Abigail Adams, Nov. 8, 1782. AP Microfilm No. 359.

59. JJ, *Diary*, Oct. 28, 1782; Boston *Patriot*, July 27, 1811.

60. Ridley, Diary, Oct. 28, 1782; *Diary*, III, 39; Boston *Patriot*, July 27, Aug. 24, 1811.

61. BF to Abbé Soulavie, Sept. 22, 1782. *BFB*, X, 5-11; "Information to those who would wish to remain in America," *BFS*, VIII, 603-614.

62. Strachey to TT, Oct. 29; O to S, Oct. 29; to TT, Oct. 29, 1782. LP 71; FO 97/157; 95/511; 27/2. BV and Ridley were also present at the first dinner. Ridley, Diary, Oct. 30, 1782. *Diary*, III, 39-40.

63. Boston *Patriot*, July 24, 31, 1811.

64. BV to S, Nov. 1, Dec. 4, 1782. Amer. Philos. Soc.; CL; Vaughan Papers; Mass. Hist. Soc., *Proc.*, 2nd ser., XVII, 423. See also *Diary*, III, 46.

65. *Diary*, III, 45 (Nov. 3, 1782); for JA's letter putting the fable in a different context and his attribution of it to BF, see *Corr. in the Boston Patriot*, pp. 45-46.

66. BV to S, Oct. 29, 1782. Mass. Hist. Soc., *Proc.*, XVII, 420.

67. JJ, *Diary*, Oct. 21, 1782.

68. See *ante*, chap. V.

69. London, *Chronicle*, Dec. 10-12, 1782. As late as Dec. 30, a British spy in Paris assured his superiors that France intended to retain Rhode Island, Long Island, New York, and the Chesapeake, along with a substantial part of the tobacco trade. Intelligence from Capt. Taylor, Dec. 30, 1782. FO 95/2.

70. TT to O, Oct. 11, 1782. FO 27/2; FO 97/157; 95/511; LP 70, CL.

71. O to TT, Oct. 23, 1782. FO 27/2; 97/157; 95/511; LP 70.

72. JJ, *Diary*, Oct. 28, 1782.

73. *Diary* (Dec. 26, 1782), III, 100.

74. James Jay to JA, Nov. 21, 1782. AP Microfilm No. 359.

75. One of the last occasions was in a letter to Frederick Jay, Dec. 7, 1782. JP.

76. BF's discharge of Captain Dundas on parole. Nov. 25, 1782. FO 97/157.

77. Genêt Papers, Memoirs, LC; also James Jay to Edmond Charles Genêt (*c.* Oct.–Nov., 1782), Genêt Papers, XIX.

78. See also JJ to Kitty Livingston, July 1, 1783. Mass. Hist. Soc.

79. *Diary* (Nov. 6, 1782), III, 46, 47; Boston *Patriot*, Aug. 31, 1811.

80. TG to S, Nov. 3, 1782. LPB; TG to G, Nov. 3, 1782. *CG*, VI, 150, where he attributes such sentiments to all the American commissioners.

81. O to S, Nov. 5, 1782. LP 71.

82. *Diary*, III, 43, 44 (Nov. 3, 1782).

83. Strachey to TT, Nov. 8, 1782. LP 70. Project of an article in JJ's handwriting (Nov., 1782), AP Microfilm No. 359; O to S, Nov. 5, 1782. LP 71; *FS*, II, 293. O hoped that the States would take action to protect Loyalist creditors. [O], Observations on the American Treaty, LP 87: 215.

84. BF to RRL, Dec. 5, 1782. *RDC*, VI, 113.

85. BV to S, Oct. 29, 1782. Mass Hist. Soc., *Proc.*, 2nd ser., XVII, 418-420.

86. *Diary*, III, 41 (Nov. 2, 1782).

87. See S. F. Bemis, "Jay's Treaty and the Northwest Boundary Gap," *Amer. Hist. Rev.*, XXVII (April, 1922), 465-484.

88. BV to S, Feb. 21, 1783. Vaughan Papers (photostat), CL.
89. The 49th had been considered the southernmost limit of the Hudson Bay Company. See A. J. Hill, "How the Mississippi River and the Lake of the Woods Became Instrumental in the Establishment of the Northwestern Boundary of the United States," Minn. Hist. Soc., *Coll.*, VII (1893), 305-352; C. O. Paullin, "The Early Choice of the Forty-Ninth Parallel as a Boundary Line," *Canadian Hist. Rev.*, IV (1923), 127-131.
90. BV to S, Nov. 1, 1782 (Postscript, Nov. 2). CL.
91. [O], "Observations on the American treaty," Feb. 6, 1783. LP 87: 215. See also Peter Thoppison to S (*c.* 1782), LP 72.
92. BV to S, Nov. 4, 1782. John Quincy Adams Papers, Microfilm No. 488.
93. Boston *Patriot*, July 31, Sept. 7, 1811. See also JA, Peace Journal, Nov. 2, 1782. One copy was sent to RRL. PCC 84; RDC, IV, 242-296. For the lost copy sent to Abigail Adams and presumably turned over to Jonathan Jackson, a delegate from Massachusetts, see the learned note in *Diary*, III, 41n.-43n.
94. See Massachusetts' claim to the territory of Maine (*c.* 1782). LP 72: 451-452.
95. For an early proposal to settle Loyalists in Nova Scotia or Canada at British expense, see Joshua Upham to Col. [Thomas] Carleton, Nov. 12, 1782. LP 69. For a contrary proposal to settle the Loyalists on the wastelands of England, see David Barclay to S, Dec. 12, 1782. LP 87: 141.
96. Strachey to TT, Nov. 8, 1782. LP 70, CL. See also J. B. Moore, ed., *History and Digest of International Arbitrations* (Washington, 1898), I, 19 (deposition of President John Adams, Aug. 15, 1797); BF to Jefferson, April 8, 1790, *ibid.*, p. 22. Years later JJ insisted that "respectable opinions in America at that time considered the St. John's as the proper eastern limit of the United States." *Ibid.*, p. 21. See also Winsor, *Narr. and Crit. Hist.*, VII, 173-174n.
97. JA to RRL, Nov. 6, 1782. *RDC*, V, 156.
98. Brissot de Warville, "Notes in America in 1788," *Mag. of Amer. Hist.* (Mar., 1884), p. 246.
99. *Diary*, III, 43n, 48-51. When this portion of JA's Journal was read in Congress the friends of the New Englander were much embarrassed. It was one count in Alexander Hamilton's curious indictment, *Letter from Alexander Hamilton, concerning the Public Conduct and Character of John Adams, Esq., President of the United States* (New York, 1800), pp. 7-8. For JA's reply, see Boston *Patriot*, Aug. 31, Sept. 4, 7, 1811. See also Ridley, Diary, Nov. 4, 10, 1782.
100. O to Strachey, "Observations respecting the Article of the fishery," Nov. 8, 1782. FO 95/511; Strachey to TT, Nov. 8, 1782. RDC, V, 868, 869. See also R. G. Lounsbury, *The British Fishery at Newfoundland, 1634-1763* (New Haven, 1934), p. 56.
101. O to Strachey, Nov. 8, 1782. FO 95/157; 27/2; *RDC*, V, 851-853. See also "Observations respecting the article of the fishery," in O to Strachey, Nov. 8, 1782 (4), FO 95/511.
102. O to American commissioners, Nov. 4; BF to TT, Nov. 4; JA to O, Nov. 5; Strachey to American commissioners, Nov. 5; American commissioners to Strachey, Nov. 6; to O, Nov. 7; BV to S, Nov. 5, 1782. Strachey Papers, HMC, *R*, VI, pt. I, 403-404; Bancroft Coll., NYPL; AP Microfilm No. 359; FO 95/511; 27/2; 97/157; LP 70: 349, 369, 372; *RDC*, V, 848, 850; Sparks, X, 98-101; Vaughan Papers, CL.
103. BV to S, Nov. 1, 1782. Amer. Philos. Soc.; Vaughan Papers, CL.
104. Sir William R. Anson, ed., *Autobiography and Political Correspondence of Augustus Henry, third duke of Grafton* (London, 1898), pp. 345, 346.

105. S to G; G to S, Nov. 10, 1782. *CG*, VI, 153, 154; S to TT, Nov. 17, 18, 1782. FO 95/511; LPB.
106. S had been afraid that JJ's phraseology assuring "no lawful impediment" to the recovery of debts might "admit of a quibble," but the phrase was retained on the advice of Lord Ashburton. S to TT, Nov. 9, 17, 1782. FO 95/511; Orde to Thurlow, Nov. 18, 1782. FO 95/511.
107. This embodied the sense of S's memorandum of Nov. 8, 1782. FO 95/511.
108. Rough Cabinet Minutes, Nov. 11, 1782, in TT's hand; TT Papers, Huntington Lib., *CG*, VI, 155 (incomplete report).
109. Memorandum from S, Nov. 15, 1782. LP 87; Cabinet Minutes on the Preliminaries with America, Nov. 15, 1782. LP 72; Substance of proposed instructions, Nov. 16, 1782. Sydney Papers, I; Notes attributed to TT, *c.* Nov. 15, 1782; Thomas Orde, Draft of proposed instructions, deletions, and insertions in the treaty, *c.* Nov. 15-20, 1782. TT Papers, pt. I, CL. Some proposed changes in the treaty draft (*c.* Nov. 18, 1782), in TT's hand. Sydney Papers, I; Thurlow's memoranda, Nov. 18, 1782. FO 95/511; Orde to Thurlow, Nov. 18, 1792. FO 95/511. S's Private Notes, *c.* Nov. 19, 1782. LP 87: 203; TT to O (draft), Nov. 19, 1782. FO 95/511; 97/157; Memorandum of Henry Strachey on the refugees and the debts, *c.* Nov. 18, 1782. TT Papers, pt. I.
110. "Independence" was written above "a Separation," which was crossed out.
111. G to TT, Nov. 19, 1782. TT Papers, Huntington Lib.; variance in *CG*, VI, 157.
112. JA to Abigail Adams, Nov. 19, 1782. AP Microfilm No. 259.
113. *Diary*, III, 51, 52 (Nov. 11, 1782).
114. *Diary*, III, 55, 56, 59-61 (Nov. 17, 18, 1782).
115. O to S, Nov. 16, 1782. Oswald Papers, CL.
116. Ridley, Diary, Nov. 19, 20, 1782; London *Public Advertiser*, Nov. 25, 27, 1782.
117. *Diary*, III, 66 (Nov. 20, 1782).
118. BV to JJ, Calais, Nov. 18, 1782. Bancroft-America, IV, NYPL; JP.
119. See London *Morning Herald*, Oct. 11, 29; *Morning Chronicle*, Nov. 20, 30, 1782.
120. "An Independent Citizen of the World" to HL, Oct., 1782. JP.
121. BV to Strachey, Nov. 18 (Calais); to S, 21, 27, 1782, Lamson-Strachey MSS., LC; Emmons Transcripts, CL; also *Diary*, III, 57, 58; Ridley, Diary, Nov. 23, 27, 1782. A similar view of the necessity of accepting the American peace terms was expressed by Richard Jackson to [TT], Nov. 12, 1782. FO 95/511.
122. TT to G, Nov. 19, 1782; S to G, Nov. 20, 1782. *CG*, VI, 156-158.
123. Instructions for R, Nov. 15, 1782. CP A 538: 395-399.
124. R to V, Nov. 18, 1782. CP A 538: 411-412.
125. Intelligence reports of Capt. Taylor, Nov. 10, 22, 1782. FO 95/2.
126. S to G, Nov. 24, 1782. *CG*, VI, 161.
127. V to L, Nov. 23, Dec. 20, 1782. CP EU 22: 490-493, 576-580; *D*, VI, 176-179.
128. O to TT [Nov., 1782], Nov. 15, 1782. FO 97/157; 95/511; 72/2; CO 5/8-3; BV to S, Nov. 15, 1782. Vaughan Papers, Lansdowne Transcripts, CL; LP 87: 352; TT to S, Nov. 19, 1782. FO 97/157; 95/511; CO 5/8-3.
129. G to S, Nov. 25, 1782. *CG*, VI, 163.
130. S to O, Nov. 23, 1782. LP 71; CO 5/8-3.
131. Cabinet Minute (Nov. 21, 1782). *CG*, VI, 159.
132. BV to S, Nov. 1, 1782. Amer. Philos. Soc.
133. For copies of the articles, see AP, Microfilm No. 109; *RDC*, VI, 74-77; part of a rough copy sent to Strachey (Nov., 1782), FO 95/511.
134. *Diary*, III, 69, 70.

135. Strachey to American commissioners, Nov. 25, 1782. Bancroft-Strachey, NYPL.
136. The Cabinet did not go to the lengths the Lord Chancellor proposed. His draft of Article V declared all forfeitures in the United States rescinded and annulled, and provided that persons should be enabled to sue to recover their estates in the same manner as citizens of the United States. Article V proposed by Chancellor Thurlow (TT's hand), c. Nov. 18, 1781. TT Papers, I, CL.
137. See Alexander Coffin to JA, Nov. 12; Ingraham Bromfield to JA, Nov. 14, 1782. AP, Microfilm No. 359. See also *Diary*, III, 75-81.
138. TT to O, Nov. 22; S to O, Nov. 23, 1782. FO 27/2; 97/157; CO 5/8-3; LP 71; *Diary*, III, 75-77.
139. O to Strachey, Jan. 8, 1782 (copy). AP Microfilm No. 256.
140. *Diary*, III, 75.
141. TT to G, Sept. 24, 1782. *CG*, VI, 135; G to TT, Sept. 25, 1782. TT Papers, Huntington Lib.; William Franklin to S, Nov. 12, 1782, with enclosure. FO 95/511.
142. *Diary*, III, 77; BV to S, Dec. 10, 1782. AP Microfilm No. 488.
143. JJ to RRL, Dec. 12, 1782. PCC 110: 2; JP; *RDC*, VI, 130.
144. BF to O, Nov. 26, 1782. *BFB*, X, 23-31; *RDC*, VI, 77-80; CP A 539: 45-50.
145. *Diary*, III, 75.
146. W. A. S. Hewins, ed., *Whitefoord Papers* (Oxford, 1898), p. 188.
147. BV to S, Nov. 27, 1782; April 7, 1782; Vaughan Papers, Lansdowne Transcripts, CL; AP, Microfilm No. 488; *Diary*, III, 77, 78.
148. Ridley, Diary, Nov. 27, 1782.
149. Ridley, Diary, Nov. 28, 1782.
150. *JAW*, VII, 658. See also RRL to HL, Sept. 17, 1782. HLP.
151. HL to JA, Nov. 12, 1782, AP, Microfilm No. 359; *Diary*, III, 68; HLP.
152. HL to Delegates from South Carolina in Congress, Dec. 16, 1782; to William Manning, Dec. 24, 1782; HL memoranda, Dec. 19, 1782. Wallace, *op. cit.*, pp. 405-407; HL to Bridgen and Waller, Aug. 10, 1782. LP 35.
153. *Diary*, III, 79-81.
154. See JA to William Thomas, Aug. 10, 1822. *JAW*, X, 404; John Jay, *The Fisheries Dispute* (New York, 1887).
155. BF's counterproposal, "An Article proposed and read to the Commissioners before signing the preliminary articles, with a state of facts." *BFS*, VIII, 632n.; copy in AP, Microfilm No. 359.
156. BV to O, Nov. 14; O to Strachey, Nov. 15; to TT, Nov. 15; John Barry to TT, Nov. 27, 1782. FO 95/511; 27/2; 97/157. According to S's later recollection, O had told him that BF threatened to sell the German prisoners unless the Negroes were restored or paid for. Rufus King, *Life and Corr.*, IV, 94.
157. BF to RRL, Dec. 5; *BFS*, VIII, 632-634; AF to TG, Nov. [17] 29; Manchester Papers 1220, No. 1, CL; to S, Dec. 4, LP 71; to Strachey, Dec. 19, 1782. Lamson-Strachey MSS., LC.
158. Three "projects" of the fisheries article are in AP, Microfilm No. 359. The first is a version of JA's Nov. 4th proposal; the second, in JA's hand, is, except for the omission of the words "agreed that," the final version contained in the Nov. 30th treaty; the third, save for an inversion in the last sentence, is the same as JA's draft of Nov. 28th. O confessed that by mistake he had thrown "the fishing minutes" into the fire along with a batch of unimportant papers. O to Strachey, Dec. 18, 1782. LP 70.
159. Later Caleb Whitefoord insisted that the Americans "did admit" the British

claim for indemnification of the Loyalist but did not insist upon indemnification for their own people. *Whitefoord Papers*, p. 202. For loose papers summarizing the arguments of the Americans on the refugees, see AP, Microfilm No. 488.

160. O to TT, Nov. 30, 1782. FO 95/511; 97/157; LP 70: 416.
161. Ridley, Diary, Nov. 29, 1782; *Diary*, III, 64; JA to Elbridge Gerry, Dec. 14, 1782. AP.
162. JA to Arthur Lee, Oct. 10, 1782; *Diary*, III, 82, 85; Benjamin Rush, *Autobiography* (Princeton, 1948), p. 215 (1792).
163. O to TT, Nov. 30, 1782. CO 5/8-3.
164. *Whitefoord Papers*, pp. 200, 201n.; Mountstuart to Liston, Dec. 20, 1782. Mountstuart Letter Book, Add. MSS. 36, 804, BM.
165. Draft of alterations proposed in JP; copies of preliminaries in JP; FP; AP, Microfilm No. 103; CO 5/8-3; PCC 106; 135: 1 (minus separate article); LP 34; 70: 405; *RDC*, VI, 96-100; Hunter Miller, ed., *Treaties and Other International Acts of the United States of America, 1776-1863* (8 vols., Washington, 1931-48), II, 96-107.
166. *Whitefoord Papers*, p. 187.
167. See CP EU 22: 502-507; BF to JA, Dec. 3, 1782. AP; E. Edwards [Bancroft] to Strachey, Dec. 4, 1782. FO 97/157. At V's request BF marked "with a strong red line" the boundaries of the United States settled by the preliminaries. BF to V, Dec. 6, 1782. CP A 539: 168.
168. *Diary*, III, 90.
169. R to V, Dec. 4, 1782. CP A 539: 155-156.
170. Commissioners to RRL, Dec. 14, 1782. *JAW*, VIII, 18-20. Although the original draft is in the handwriting of JA, the paragraph touching their action toward the French court is in JJ's hand. For HL's private dissent from this paragraph, see Ridley, Diary, July, 1783.
171. V to R, Dec. 4; R to V, Dec. 12, 25, 1782. CP A 539: 158-159, 220-222, 314-317.
172. V to L, July 21, 1783. CP EU 25: 67-68; cf. also Jan. 22, April 12, 1783. CP EU 23: 72; 24: 33.
173. V to L, Dec. 19, 1782; *RDC*, VI, 151. V's displeasure was no secret from other diplomats. MDA to K, Dec. 6, 1782. SKD, Frankreich, 0412-0428.
174. BF to V, Dec. 15; V to BF, Dec. 15, 1782. *RDC*, VI, 137-138, 140.
175. BF to V, Dec. 17, 1782. *RDC*, VI, 143, 144.
176. AF to TG, Dec. 18, 1782, FO 27/3, wherein BF's position toward the alliance is contrasted with JJ's more critical attitude.
177. This latter point he also made to R, Dec. 30, 1782. CP A 539: 374-375, 380-381. See also, V to L, Dec. 19, 24, 1782. CP EU 22: 562-563, 586-587; D, V, 192-194, 198-199.
178. Ridley, Diary, Dec. 30, 1782.
179. See Declaration of American Commissioners. Jan. 2 (draft) (also Jan. 20), 1783 (unsigned) (both in French). CP EU 23: 14-15, 70-71. See also JJ to Stephen Sayre, Dec. 15, 1782. JP; to Lafayette, Jan. 19, 1783. *JPJ*, III, 25.
180. See Harlow, *Founding of Second British Empire*, I; Clarence W. Alvord, *Lord Shelburne and the Founding of British-American Goodwill* (London, 1925), p. 18; R. W. Van Alstyne, *The Rising American Empire* (New York, 1960), p. 68.
181. See Contract between King of France and the United States, Feb. 25, 1783. Treaty ser. no. 83 1/2, NA; PCC 145: 323-327.

CHAPTER XVI. THE CONDE SETTLES AN OLD SCORE

1. See V to L, Dec. 24, 1782. CP EU 22: 586-587; to R, Dec. 30, 1782. CP A 539: 380-381. For the view attributed to some people in France that American independence went against France's national interest, see intelligence from Mr. Oakes (Nov., 1782), FO 27/2.

2. Numerous memoranda stressing the importance of India and the need for France's securing "a less precarious" hold in the Far East were submitted to V in the course of 1782, including Du Pont to V, Jan. 4; De Lessart to V, June 12; La Toul to V, Aug. 29; M. Bruny, "Mémoire sur la paix prochaine," July 2; "Observations sur les Indes orientales par rapport aux conditions du traité de paix," Sept.; "Memorandum on French Conflict with the British East India Co. in Bengal," Baudouin to V, Oct. 19; Moracin to V, Nov. 15; "New plan for administration of possessions of British India Co.," Nov., 1782; Memoranda on the East Indies, Nov., 1782. CP A 536: 13; 537: 234-239, 285; 538: 76, 81, 244-257, 298, 391-394; 539: 79-83.

3. See Secret Committee of the East India Co. to TG, Oct. 23; TG to Secret Committee, Oct. 24, 1782. LP 72. For an illuminating analysis of the issues over the East Indies, see Harlow, *Second British Empire*, I, 337, 341 *et seq.*

4. Preliminary proposal to the English. Sept. 6, 1782. CP A 538: 123-133.

5. For the relatively minimal value of the British gum and slave trades with Senegal and Gambia, see Memoranda to S, Sept. 18, Oct., 1782. LP 72, 87. The government asked O to provide further light on the African trade. TG to AF, Sept. 23, 1782. Manchester Papers, 1221. CL. See also Le Boucher to V, June 25, 1782. CP A 537: 209; Lawrence H. Gipson, *The British Empire Before the American Revolution*, VIII (New York, 1954), 174-177.

6. Conference between R and S, Sept. 14, 1782. CP A 538: 163-170; S to G, Sept. 26, 1782. *CG*, VI, 136-137.

7. For the destruction wrought by the British on those islands in 1778, see Memorial, Nov., 1782. CP A 539: 109-110; also *ibid.*, pp. 92-108.

8. AF to TG, Aug. 7, 17, 21, 29, 1782; TG to AF, Sept. 3, 1782. FO 27/2; 27/3; S, Observations, Sept. 3, 1782. LP 86: 88.

9. Charles III to A, Aug. 26, 1782. AHN, E, 4215, apt. 2, p. 4.

10. See William Dalrymple to S, May 24, 1782, for a proposed invasion of the Bay of Honduras. LP 79: 41-63.

11. F to A, Aug. 29, 1782. AHN; E, 4203, apt. 3. A's instructions were communicated in confidence to V, and in turn to R. M to V, Aug. 25, Sept. 20. CP E 608: 282, 283, 437-438; V to R, Sept. 6, 1782. CP A 538: 123-133. The Oran proposal was revealed by M to V on July 8. CP E 608: 21-27.

12. V to M, Aug. 22; M to V, Aug. 22, 25, 1782. CP E 608: 235-237, 239-242, 265-267, 336-337.

13. G to S, Sept. 14, 1782. *CG*, VI, 125-126. That same day S insisted to R "on the impossibility of *ever* ceding" Gibraltar. S to TG, Sept. 14. GP LO 30/14.

14. R, Précis of Conferences, submitted to A, Sept. 30, 1782. CP A 538: 217-227. For a sympathetic analysis by a Frenchman of Spain's need for exclusive control of the Gulf, written evidently before the Treaty of Paris was signed in 1763, but dug up to guide the negotiations of '82, see "Observations on Spain's interest in American possessions," CP E 609: 466-477.

15. For the importance of St. Lucia to the French, see Le Boucher to V, June 25, 1782; Kerquelen to V, Sept. 16, 1782; Bertrand to V, Oct. 10, 1782; Le Mory,

Memoir, Dec. 15, 1782, CP A 537: 209; 538: 199, 274-276; 539: 236-242. For Dominica, see Dorothy B. Goebel, "The 'New England Trade' and the French West Indies, 1763-1774: A Study in Trade Policies," *William and Mary Quarterly*, 3rd ser., XX (1963), 331-372.

16. The British did not wish to see the Cape of Good Hope pass from Dutch into French hands, because, as Sir Francis Baring pointed out, the Cape was "a much greater key" to India than Gibraltar was to the Mediterranean. Baring to S, Sept. 24, 27, 1782. LP 72. Cf. also M. Moracin to V, Oct. 28, 1782. CP A 538: 352, 353.

17. AF to S, Oct. 3, 1782. LP 71: 257.

18. So V revealed to MDA. MDA to K, Oct. 9, 1782. SKD, Frankreich 240: 0378-0384.

19. S to TG, *c*. Sept. 21, 27, Dec. 28, 1782. GP L30/14; Abbé Morellet, "Lord Shelburne's Administration, 1782-83," LPB. For a later warning to S against bringing still another intermediary into the negotiations, see TG to S, Dec. 22, 1782. LPB.

20. Morellet to S, Nov. 6, 1782. *Lettres à Shelburne*, pp. 199-200. See "Memorandum on the West Indies," June 26, 1782. CP A 539: 330-339. D'Estaing relayed this gloomy picture to the Spanish court. CP E 509: 342-345.

21. AF to TG, Oct. 24, 1782. FO 27/3 (referring to previous conversations with V).

22. V to M, Oct. 6, 13. CP E 609: 47-54, 83-84. See also V to M, Sept. 28, Oct. 8 (2); M to V, Sept. 20, 1782. *Ibid*. 608: 481-483, 490; 609: 55-66.

23. M to V, Oct. 17, 24, 1782. CP E 609: 103-105, 135-136.

24. V to M, Oct. 8, 1782. CP E 610: 63-66; TG to AF, Oct. 21, 1782. FO 27/3.

25. A to F, Oct. 4, 6, 1782. AHN, E, 4215: 2, nos. 2313, 2316; Propositions of Spain to England communicated by A to AF, Oct. 6. CP A 538: 260-269; AF to TG, Oct. 7. FO 27/3; *CG*, VI, 144-145; TG to AF, Oct. 13, 21, Nov. 9, 15. *British Diplomatic Instructions*, VII, 192-199; FO 27/3; TG to A, Oct. 9, Nov. 9. CP A 538: 272-273, 379-380; FO 27/3; S to AF, Oct. 21. LP 71; "Réponse aux propositions de l'Espagne, Nov. 9, 1782," CP A 538: 379-380; FO 27/3 (draft); S to R (secret), Nov. 13, 1782. LP 71.

26. AF to TG, Oct. 24, 1782. FO 27/3.

27. AF to TG, Oct. 28, Nov. 15, 1782. FO 27/3; TG to S, Nov. 3, 1782. LPB; GP L30/14; Richard Konetzke, *Die Politik des Grafen Aranda (Historische Studien*, vol. 182, Berlin, 1929), pp. 163-164; *DC*, V, 375.

28. This was clearly the point of view of the French sugar interests. See Le Mory, Memoirs on St. Domingue, Dec. 15, 1782. CP A 537: 231-233.

29. *DC*, V, 375-376; A to V, V to A, Nov. 7. AHN, E, 4203: 1; A to F, Nov. 14. *Ibid.*, 4215: 2, no. 2333; V to M, Nov. 12, 14, 1782. CP E 609: 84, 85, 102, 171-178, 207-216, 227-228; V, "Observations on Spanish Proposal," Nov. 12, 1782. *Ibid.*, pp. 181-187.

30. Lerchenberg to Larcher [Baudouin], Jan. 3, 1783. CP A 540: 47-48. See also Stetson Conn, *Gibraltar in British Diplomacy in the Eighteenth Century* (New Haven, 1942), p. 214.

31. R to S, Nov. 3, 1782. LPB.

32. See Roger Curtis to Evan Nepean, Feb. 2, 1783. LP 72: 515-522. [Sir Francis Baring], Memorandum on Gibraltar, stated that British interests could be handled better through the Jewish merchants at Leghorn. LP 83: 19a-f; Lt. Gen. George P. Towry to S, Dec. 14, 1782; John Motteux to S, Dec. 14, 1782. LP 82: 15a-d; 83: 14a-h.

33. JJ to A; A to JJ, Sept. 10. JJ Letterbook, JP; *JPJ*, II, 400, 401; A to F, Sept. 15, Oct. 4, 1782. AHN, E, 6609; *YU*, II, 355-364.